INDIANA PRACTICE SERIES™

Volume 29

WORKER'S COMPENSATION LAW AND PRACTICE

2016-2017 EDITION
Issued in December 2016

By
RANDAL M. KLEZMER
Indianapolis, Indiana
NATHAN B. MAUDLIN
Evansville, Indiana

THOMSON REUTERS®

For Customer Assistance Call 1-800-328-4880

Mat #41746154

ISBN 978-0-314-84094-3

INTRODUCTION TO 2016–2017 EDITION

This 2016-2017 Edition of *Worker's Compensation Law and Practice* provides a detailed and comprehensive overview of the issues pertaining to the administration and practice of worker's compensation law in Indiana.

New features and recent developments in this 2016-2017 Edition include:

• Discussion of recent Court of Appeals of Indiana cases *Bush v. Robinson Engineering and Oil Co.*, *Gordon v. Toyota Motor Manufacturing* and*Hall v. Hollman Constructions, LLC*.

• Updated forms

DEDICATION

The authors would like to thank Steve Bola for his great assistance in preparing this book.

ABOUT THE AUTHORS

Randal M. Klezmer has practiced worker's compensation law before the Indiana Worker's Compensation Board since 1992. He has handled thousands of worker's compensation cases throughout Indiana and has spoken at dozens of seminars. Mr. Klezmer is a member of the Indiana Trial Lawyers Association, the Indiana State Bar Association, and the American Bar Association. You may find his websites at www.klezmermaudlin.com and www.workerscompindiana.com.

Nathan B. Maudlin joined Klezmer & Associates (now Klezmer Maudlin P.C.) in July 2003. He focuses his practice on representing workers in claims arising out of work-related injuries including worker's compensation claims, wrongful or retaliatory discharge claims, and violations of the Americans with Disabilities Act. Before joining Mr. Klezmer, Mr. Maudlin represented employers in similar claims for over seven years. A native of Logansport, Indiana, Mr. Maudlin graduated cum laude from the Indiana University School of Law—Indianapolis in 1995, and was admitted to the Indiana Bar later that same year.

PREFACE

The Worker's Compensation Act in Indiana is a set of laws, often referred to as a statutory scheme. A worker's rights, remedies, and lack of rights are governed by the Indiana Worker's Compensation Act.

As worker's compensation practitioners, we have been both pleased and frustrated by the assistance the Act provides in handling worker's compensation claims. Oftentimes, common sense mirrors the language contained in the Act. Unfortunately, fairness and common sense do not always prevail in representing injured workers. Usually, when common sense and fairness do not mirror the laws in the Act, a single hearing member, before the Indiana Worker's Compensation Board, might be called upon to protect the interest of the injured worker. We have found in handling thousands of cases before the board that the single hearing members strive to protect the injured worker and to protect principles of fairness.

We hope you enjoy reading this book. It is an attempt to summarize the case law that stems from the Indiana Worker's Compensation Act. The book also contains the complete text of the Act. Many new cases are decided every month by the Indiana Court of Appeals and the Indiana Supreme Court. These new cases will be addressed in supplements to the book. If questions arise that are not addressed in the book, please feel free to contact our law firm.

Randal M. Klezmer
Nathan B. Maudlin

October 2016

RELATED PRODUCTS

STATUTES AND COURT RULES

West's Annotated Indiana Code

West's Indiana Administrative Code

Indiana Rules of Court, Federal, State and Local

United States Code Annotated

CASE LAW, REPORTERS, DIGESTS, ATTORNEY GENERAL OPINIONS

Indiana Cases

Indiana Digest, 2d

North Eastern Reporter, 2d

GENERAL INDIANA LEGAL REFERENCES

Indiana Law Finder

Indiana Law Encyclopedia

INDIANA DATABASES ON WESTLAW

Cases, General & Topical

Statutes and Index

Legislative Service & Bill Tracking

Administrative & Executive

Court Rules

Insurance, Securities & Tax Materials

Indiana Practice Series

Legislative History

CD-ROM

Indiana Practice, Premise® CD-ROM

West's Annotated Indiana Code

United States Code Annotated

West's Supreme Court Reporter

Federal Reporter, 1st, 2d, and 3d Series

Federal Supplement

Federal Rules Decisions

Wright & Miller, Federal Practice and Procedure

Topical CD-ROM Libraries

PRACTICE AND PROCEDURE

Arthur, Civil Trial Rule Handbook

Arthur, Civil Trial Practice

Smith, Trial Handbook for Indiana Lawyers

Harvey and Arthur, Rules of Procedure Annotated

VanWinkle, Rules on Alternative Dispute
Resolution Annotated

Arthur, Procedural Forms with Practice Commentary

Patton, Appellate Procedure

Finley and McGuire, Indiana Motions in Limine

Essential Forms

CRIMINAL LAW AND PRACTICE

Kerr, Criminal Procedure

Finley and McGuire, Indiana Motions in Limine

DOMESTIC RELATIONS

Smithburn, Nash, and Polando, Family Law

Smithburn, Nash, and Polando, Family Law—Children in Need of Services

PERSONAL INJURY

Fisher and Miller, Personal Injury Law and Practice

PROBATE AND JUVENILE LAW

Kennedy, Anderson's Probate Forms

Kennedy, Anderson's Wills, Trusts and Estate Planning

Smithburn, Nash, and Polando, Family Law

Smithburn, Nash, and Polando, Family Law—Children in Need of Services

BUSINESS ORGANIZATIONS

Woods, Uniform Commercial Code Forms Annotated

Galanti, Business Organizations

EVIDENCE

Miller, Jr., Indiana Evidence

Miller, Jr., Courtroom Handbook on Indiana Evidence

APPELLATE PRACTICE

Patton, Appellate Procedure

REAL ESTATE

Real Property Code Annotated

LABOR LAW

Klezmer et al., Worker's Compensation Law and Practice

FORMS

Essential Forms

West's Legal Forms

Thomson Reuters® thanks you for subscribing to this product. Should you have any questions regarding this product please contact Customer Service at 1-800-328-4880 or by fax at 1-800-340-9378. If you would like to inquire about related publications or place an order, please contact us at 1-800-344-5009.

 **THOMSON REUTERS**   Thomson Reuters
610 Opperman Drive
Eagan, MN 55123

legalsolutions.thomsonreuters.com

Summary of Contents

Table of Contents

CHAPTER 4. CLAIMS AND BENEFITS

CHAPTER 5. ADMINISTRATION OF THE INDIANA WORKER'S COMPENSATION ACT

CHAPTER 6. WORKER'S COMPENSATION INSURANCE POLICIES

CHAPTER 7. THE INDIANA OCCUPATIONAL DISEASES ACT

CHAPTER 8. LEGAL REPRESENTATION

CHAPTER 9. THE RESIDUAL ASBESTOS INJURY FUND

CHAPTER 10. VOCATIONAL REHABILITATION

CHAPTER 11. THE EMPLOYERS' LIABILITY ACT OF 1911

CHAPTER 12. FORMS

APPENDIX

Chapter 1

The Indiana Worker's Compensation Act

§ 1:1   Worker's Compensation Act—Purpose
§ 1:2   —Characteristics

> **KeyCite®:** Cases and other legal materials listed in KeyCite Scope can be researched through the KeyCite service on Westlaw®. Use KeyCite to check citations for form, parallel references, prior and later history, and comprehensive citator information, including citations to other decisions and secondary materials.

§ 1:1   Worker's Compensation Act—Purpose

The Indiana Legislature had in mind a number of goals when it formulated a system for worker's compensation for the state. It sought to create new rights and remedies, unknown to the common law, and specifically provide a mechanism for the presentation and enforcement of those rights and remedies.[1]

Generally, the purpose of the Indiana Worker's Compensation Act is to protect employees engaged in industry.[2] It establishes a method for compensation for injured employees regardless of whether the employee or the employer was at fault for causing the injury complained of.[3]

The theory underlying the Act is that economic losses arising from industrial accidents and injuries are to be borne by the industries employing workers, or by consumers of their products or services, and not by workers themselves.[4] The Act recognizes a fixed and permanent duty of the employer to compensate the injured employee or surviving dependants and the fixed and per-

---

[Section 1:1]

[1]Fogle v. Pullman Standard Car Mfg. Co., 133 Ind. App. 95, 173 N.E.2d 668 (1961).

[2]Frampton v. Central Indiana Gas Co., 260 Ind. 249, 297, 297 N.E.2d 425, 63 A.L.R.3d 973 (1973).

[3]Waldridge v. Futurex Industries, Inc., 714 N.E.2d 783 (Ind. Ct. App. 1999).

[4]Mann v. Schnarr, 228 Ind. 654, 95 N.E.2d 138 (1950); In re Duncan, 73 Ind. App. 270, 127 N.E. 289 (1920).

1

manent right of the employee or dependants to receive such compensation.[5]

The Act seeks to eliminate the need for litigation between an injured worker and his or her employer.[6] Instead of litigation, the Act contemplates that an employee's claim (and his or her employer's liability) will be determined and resolved expeditiously, keeping delay to a minimum.[7] Jury verdicts thus are unnecessary, and businesses are able to more adequately predict the costs associated with employees' injuries.[8]

With the advent of the Act came a recognition that a greater social purpose would be served by shifting the burden for the consequences of workers' injuries from the individual to the business employing him or her. It has been stated that:

> [T]he compensation plan is based upon a realization of the obligation which industry owes to its workers. It is social legislation designed to provide a means by which a workman or his dependants can obtain necessary economic assistance when wage earning capacity is limited or extinguished . . . . [T]he Act was not designed to narrow the rights of an injured workman as they existed in common law, but instead, to protect employees and their families with an expeditious remedy for personal injury or death.[9]

§ 1:2 Worker's Compensation Act—Characteristics

It is the contractual nature of the employment relationship which forms the basis for the application of the Indiana Worker's Compensation Act.[1] In order for an injured worker to enjoy the protections and benefits afforded by the Act, the worker must first come within the purview of the Act.[2] As long as there is a valid, binding contract of employment, the provisions of the Act are binding.[3]

It has been stated that:

> [T]he rights and duties provided for in the Workmen's Compensation Act are contractual; that is to say, that these rights and duties

---

[5]Indiana State Highway Commission v. White, 259 Ind. 690, 291 N.E.2d 550 (1973).

[6]Bedwell v. Dixie Bee Coal Corp., 99 Ind. App. 336, 192 N.E. 723 (1934).

[7]Hibler v. Globe Am. Corp., 128 Ind. App. 156, 147 N.E.2d 19 (1958).

[8]Evans v. Yankeetown Dock Corp., 491 N.E.2d 969 (Ind. 1986).

[9]Fogle v. Pullman Standard Car Mfg. Co., 133 Ind. App. 95, 101, 173 N.E.2d 668 (1961).

[Section 1:2]

[1]Calkins v. Service Spring Co., 103 Ind. App. 257, 7 N.E.2d 54 (1937).

[2]Mid-Continent Petroleum Corp. v. Vicars, 221 Ind. 387, 47 N.E.2d 972 (1943).

[3]Elkhart Sawmill Co. v. Skinner, 111 Ind. App. 695, 42 N.E.2d 412 (1942).

adhere to and must of necessity spring out of contract. It would therefore seem to follow that these rights and duties would, in so far as our Compensation Act is concerned, attach only to an Indiana contract or to a contract made in contemplation of performance, or at least part performance in Indiana.[4]

There is, in Indiana law, a presumption that, without proof to the contrary, the parties to an Indiana employment contract have agreed to accept and be bound by the provisions of the Act, and that their respective rights, duties, and obligations are exclusively governed by the Act.[5]

With its enactment of the Indiana Worker's Compensation Act, the General Assembly sought to substitute the provisions thereof for the rights and remedies available at common law. Since the Act was framed as remedial in nature, the appellate courts of Indiana have consistently found that its sections should be given a liberal construction to accomplish the humane purposes for which it was enacted.[6] In providing some historical perspective to this issue, the Appellate Court of Indiana, in its opinion in the matter of *Homan v. Belleville Lumber & Supply Co.*,[7] stated:

The function of the Worker's Compensation Law can only adequately be had when it is suited to the life of the people. With this radical change comes also the imperative demand that this creature of statute shall be interpreted to satisfy the needs which such change has created. Since the legislature has created a new administrative agency we should not formulate legal doctrines suited to such situations except by examining the product of the legislative body, namely, the act itself, and to discern from that the objects it sought.

We believe that it should be the concern of the court to interpret the act in such manner as to help the legislature accomplish the end that it intended and that the act should be used as a starting point from which judicial reasoning should begin with a view to the correction of the evils and an accomplishment of the ends sought. We do not believe there is any need to restrict activities which the legislature intended such administrative bodies should perform and we think the objects sought to be gained by such legislation should be given every help in that direction by our interpretation.

. . . .

Early in the interpretation of this administrative act this court

---

[4]Elkhart Sawmill Co. v. Skinner, 111 Ind. App. 695, 42 N.E.2d 412, 414 (1942), quoting Calkins v. Service Spring Co., 103 Ind. App. 257, 7 N.E.2d 54 (1937).

[5]Hagenback v. Leppert, 66 Ind. App. 261, 117 N.E. 531 (1917); Hickman v. Western Heating & Air Conditioning Co., 207 F. Supp. 832 (N.D. Ind. 1962).

[6]McQuade v. Draw Tite, Inc., 659 N.E.2d 1016 (Ind. 1995); Cox v. Worker's Compensation Bd. of Indiana, 675 N.E.2d 1053 (Ind. 1996).

[7]Homan v. Belleville Lumber & Supply Co., 104 Ind. App. 96, 8 N.E.2d 127 (1937).

recognized that the legislature was seeking to correct the prior evils and abuses by introducing this new legislation for the "advancement of the public welfare" and said that it was remedial in character and should be construed with regard to the former laws which it supplemented and the defects or evils which it sought to correct and concluded that it should be liberally construed so that the purpose of the legislature should be promoted . . . .[8]

With respect to substantive rights and liabilities under the Act, the statutory provisions in force and effect at the time of the occurrence of the injury complained of govern.[9] However, with respect to purely procedural matters, provisions or amendments to the Act may be given a retroactive effect, especially if there is no infringement of a previously vested right or violation of some constitutional guaranty.[10] In *Brenon v. First Advantage Corp.*,[11] Brenon, the claimant, was a resident of Wisconsin who was hired to perform investigative services in Indiana. He suffered a serious injury while in the course of his employment. He filed a worker's compensation claim against the employer in Wisconsin. In Wisconsin the employer argued that he was not in the scope of his employment at the time of the accident and Wisconsin did not have jurisdiction over his worker's compensation claim. Brenon reached an agreement with the employer and its Wisconsin carrier, Zurich North America Insurance Co., to settle the Wisconsin worker's compensation claim. That agreement specifically stated that claims in other jurisdictions with other insurance carriers for the employer would remain open. Brenon did file a claim in Indiana and the Indiana insurance carrier filed a motion to dismiss claiming collateral estoppel. The Board granted the motion to dismiss. The Court of Appeals, in reversing the Board's dismissal, pointed to evidence that the Wisconsin settlement agreement excluded claims in other jurisdictions (such as Indiana) and that collateral estoppel is not available because matters were not litigated and the parties are different. The Court also held that plaintiff may pursue his Indiana claim; however, the Indiana insurance carrier will be entitled to take a credit for amounts already paid.

---

[8]Homan v. Belleville Lumber & Supply Co., 104 Ind. App. 96, 8 N.E.2d 127, 132 (1937).

[9]Indiana Steel Products Co. v. Leonard, 126 Ind. App. 669, 131 N.E.2d 162 (1956).

[10]In re Smith, 115 Ind. App. 494, 60 N.E.2d 147 (1945); Standard Acc. Ins. Co. v. Miller, 170 F.2d 495 (7th Cir. 1948).

[11]Brenon v. First Advantage Corp., 2012 WL 3055860 (Ind. Ct. App. 2012).

Chapter 2

The Indiana Worker's Compensation Board

> **KeyCite®:** Cases and other legal materials listed in KeyCite Scope can be researched through the KeyCite service on Westlaw®. Use KeyCite to check citations for form, parallel references, prior and later history, and comprehensive citator information, including citations to other decisions and secondary materials.

---

§ 2:1   Worker's Compensation Board—Generally

The Worker's Compensation Board of Indiana was created in 1915 by an act of the Indiana General Assembly.[1] The Worker's Compensation Board was formerly known as the Indiana Industrial Board. It presently consists of seven members, one of whom serves as chairman. Each member of the board is appointed by the governor. The chairman must be an attorney.

For purposes of administration of the Act, the State of Indiana is divided into six geographical districts. Each district is represented by a member of the board. The chairman of the board conducts his or her activities from the general offices of the board located in Indianapolis, Indiana.

Each board member holds office for four years, and must continue in office until his or her successor is appointed by the governor and qualified.[2] A board member may pursue an employment in addition to his or her work for the board, but the member is prohibited from engaging in any occupation or business which would interfere with or be inconsistent with the discharge of his or her duties for the board.[3]

[Section 2:1]
> [1] IC 22-3-1-1.
> [2] IC 22-3-1-1(b).
> [3] IC 22-3-1-1(e).

The members of the board serve at the pleasure of the governor and, therefore, any member may be removed at any time, but only for incompetence, neglect of duty, misconduct in office, or other good cause which must be stated in writing in the governor's order of removal.[4] It is the board who has the power to appoint and remove an executive secretary, and such secretary, in addition to his or her other duties, has the authority to administer oaths and issue subpoenas to further the administration of the Act.[5] The board may also employ and fix the salaries of such other clerical and administrative assistants as it deems necessary; however, with respect to these employees, the board must secure the approval of the governor.[6]

All salaries and expenses of the board are to be audited and paid out of the state treasury. The members of the board and their assistants are entitled to receive their actual and necessary expenses while traveling on the business of the board, and the chairman of the board is charged with the responsibility of approving those expenses prior to the time payment is made.[7]

It has been held that the members of the board are appointed officials of the state, and that they constitute the appointing authority for those employed by the board. However, employees appointed by the board are merit employees under the State Personnel Act, as it applies to employees within the Department of Labor.[8]

§ 2:2   Worker's Compensation Board—Duties

It is the duty of the board to administer the provisions of the Indiana Worker's Compensation Act.[1]

§ 2:3   Worker's Compensation Board—Rules

The board has the authority to adopt rules to effectuate the provisions of the Act.[1] It has been deemed:

apparent that the statutory authorization given to the Board to adopt rules has for its purpose the enabling of the Board to provide

---

[4]IC 22-3-1-1(d).

[5]IC 22-3-1-1(f).

[6]IC 22-3-1-1(g).

[7]IC 22-3-1-1(h) and (i).

[8]1972 Ind. Op. Atty. Gen. No. 18, p. 53.

[Section 2:2]

[1]IC 22-3-1-2.

[Section 2:3]

[1]IC 22-3-1-3(a).

by needed or necessary rules for the prompt and efficient handling and carrying out of its functions and duties in the administration of the provisions of the Workmen's Compensation Act, including the hearing, determination, and review by the full board of all claims for compensation under said act and the Workmen's Occupational Disease Act.[2]

It has consistently been held that the board is an administrative agency, not a court of law, and, pursuant to the statute creating it, has the authority to promulgate rules of procedure applicable to hearings and other proceedings before it.[3] Those rules must be construed in such a way that the underlying purposes of the Act are accomplished.[4]

§ 2:4 Worker's Compensation Board—Powers

The General Assembly has given the board certain powers to further the purposes of the Act.[1] It is authorized to hear, determine, and review all claims for compensation under the Act.[2] It can require that medical services be provided for injured employees.[3] It has the power to approve claims for medical services, including those charges submitted by nurses and hospitals, and attorney fees.[4] The approval of agreements is within its authority.[5] It may modify or change awards.[6] It can make conclusions of facts and rulings of law.[7] It may certify questions of law for determination by the court of appeals.[8] It has the authority to approve deductions in compensation payments made by employers if it appears that amounts were paid in excess of the amount required by law.[9] It may approve agreements between employers and employees, including his or her dependents, for lump sum cash payments of compensation or, in the case of a person under

---

[2]U.S. Steel Corp. v. Douglas, 125 Ind. App. 212, 217, 123 N.E.2d 899 (1955) (citations omitted).

[3]Rhoden v. Smith & Decker Electric Co., 107 Ind. App. 152, 23 N.E.2d 306 (1939); Wilson v. Betz Corp., 130 Ind. App. 83, 159 N.E.2d 402 (1959).

[4]Sissom v. Commodore Corp., 169 Ind. App. 547, 349 N.E.2d 724 (1976).

[Section 2:4]

[1]IC 22-3-1-3(b).

[2]IC 22-3-1-3(b)(1).

[3]IC 22-3-1-3(b)(2).

[4]IC 22-3-1-3(b)(3).

[5]IC 22-3-1-3(b)(4).

[6]IC 22-3-1-3(b)(5).

[7]IC 22-3-1-3(b)(6).

[8]IC 22-3-1-3(b)(7).

[9]IC 22-3-1-3(b)(8).

18, to order cash payments.[10] The board is authorized to establish and maintain a list of independent medical examiners and to order physical examinations.[11] The board may subpoena witnesses[12] and administer oaths.[13] It may, also, apply to the circuit or superior courts to force the attendance and testimony of witnesses and the production and examination of books and documents.[14] The board may create and undertake a program designed to educate and provide assistance to employees and employers alike regarding their respective rights and remedies under the Act and, furthermore, the board has the authority to provide for the informal resolution of disputes.[15] Either upon its own initiative, or upon application by a party, the board may assess and collect penalties provided for in the Act.[16] Finally, the board has the right to exercise all other powers and duties conferred upon it by law.[17]

While the powers given the board appear broad and far-reaching, it has consistently been held by the appellate courts of Indiana that it only has the authority to do those things which the General Assembly has expressly, or by necessary implication, authorized it to do. It may not resort to the common law or any other source for additional authority to act.[18]

IC 22-3-1-4 establishes a schedule of attorney fees for those who represent a claimant before the board when the claim for compensation results in a recovery. The attorney is entitled to receive: (1) a minimum of $200; (2) 20% of the first $50,000 of recovery; (3) 15% of the recovery in excess of $50,000; and (4) 10% of the value of unpaid medical expenses, out-of-pocket medical expenses, or future medical expenses. The board maintains continuing jurisdiction over all attorney fees in cases before it, and has the authority to order a different attorney fee or allowance in any particular case.

------

[10]IC 22-3-1-3(b)(9).

[11]IC 22-3-1-3(b)(10).

[12]IC 22-3-1-3(b)(11).

[13]IC 22-3-1-3(b)(12).

[14]IC 22-3-1-3(b)(13).

[15]IC 22-3-1-3(b)(14).

[16]IC 22-3-1-3(b)(15).

[17]IC 22-3-1-3(b)(16).

[18]Smith v. Thompson Const. Co., 224 Ind. 565, 69 N.E.2d 16 (1946); In re Moore, 79 Ind. App. 470, 138 N.E. 783 (1923).

Chapter 3

Defining the Eligibility of Workers and Injuries and Determining Liability

> KeyCite®: Cases and other legal materials listed in KeyCite Scope can be researched through the KeyCite service on Westlaw®. Use KeyCite to check citations for form, parallel references, prior and later history, and comprehensive citator information, including citations to other decisions and secondary materials.

§ 3:1 Basis for inclusion within Act

Generally, every employer and every employee, respectively, shall comply with and be bound by the provisions of the Indiana Worker's Compensation Act to pay and accept compensation for personal injury or death by accident arising out of and in the course of the employment.[1]

§ 3:2 Basis for inclusion within Act—Employee defined

The Act defines an "employee" as "every person, including a minor, in the service of another, under any contract of hire or apprenticeship, written or implied, except one whose employment is both casual and not in the usual course of the trade, business, occupation, or profession of the employer." The term includes within its scope an executive officer of a corporation (other than a municipal corporation, governmental subdivision, or a charitable, religious, educational, or other nonprofit corporation, unless such person is specifically brought within the coverage of the corporation's insurance contract),[1] and the dependents of a deceased employee.[2] It has been stated that the term includes all employees in industrial pursuits not expressly excepted therein.[3] It has long been held by the appellate courts of Indiana that:

> A measure of liberality is indulged in construing the legislative definition of "employee," to the end that in doubtful cases an injured workman or his dependents may not be deprived of the benefits of the humane provisions of the compensation plan; and doubt as to whether the claimant was an employee or an independent contractor is resolved in favor of the former status.[4]

[Section 3:1]

[1]IC 22-3-2-2(a).

[Section 3:2]

[1]IC 22-3-6-1(b). An officer of a corporation who is an employee of the corporation under IC 22-3-2 through IC 22-3-6 may elect not to be an employee of the corporation under IC 22-3-2 through IC 22-3-6.

[2]IC 22-3-6-1(b).

[3]In re Boyer, 65 Ind. App. 408, 117 N.E. 507 (1917).

[4]Meek v. Julian, 219 Ind. 83, 85, 36 N.E.2d 854 (1941); Schraner v. State Dept. of Correction, 135 Ind. App. 504, 189 N.E.2d 119 (1963); Kunkler v. Mauck, 108 Ind. App. 98, 27 N.E.2d 97 (1940).

In Frontz v. Middletown Enters., Inc.,[5] Frontz was an employee of Wimmer Temporaries, Inc., a professional employment agency that provides temporary workers to other businesses. Wimmer assigned Frontz to Middletown. Frontz was performing duties in Middletown's Sinclair Glass factory at which he was subjected to extreme heat. As a result of this exposure Frontz was diagnosed with severe heat stroke resulting in multiple organ failure and permanent injuries. Frontz pursued both workers' compensation benefits and filed a civil suit against both Wimmer and Middleton. Wimmer and Middleton both moved for summary judgement in the civil suit pursuant to the exclusivity provisions of Indiana's Workers' Compensation Act. Frontz dismissed his civil action against Wimmer and the trial court granted Middletown's motion for summary judgement. The Court of Appeals cited IC 22-3-3-31 as contemplating that an employee might be injured while in the joint service of two or more employers with both employers being liable for workers' compensation benefits. Further, IC 22-3-6-1(a) provides that "Both a lessor and a lessee of employees shall be considered joint employers of the employees provided by the lessor to the lessee for purposes of" the Act. The Court of Appeals noted that the reference to lessor and lessee was not intended as a term of art excluding temporary employees. The trial court's grant of Middletown's motion for summary judgment was affirmed.

§ 3:3   Basis for inclusion within Act—Employer defined

The term "employer" includes:

the state and any political subdivision, any municipal corporation within the state, any individual or the legal representative of a deceased individual, firm, association, limited liability company, or corporation or the receiver or trustee of the same, using the services of another for pay. A parent corporation and its subsidiaries shall each be considered joint employers of the corporation's, the parent's, or the subsidiaries' employees . . . . Both a lessor and a lessee of employees shall each be considered joint employers of the employees provided by the lessor to the lessee . . . . If the employer is insured, the term includes the employer's insurer so far as applicable. However, the inclusion of an employer's insurer within this definition does not allow an employer's insurer to avoid payment for services rendered to an employee with the approval of the employer. The term also includes an employer that provides on-the-

---

[5]Frontz v. Middletown Enterprises, Inc., 15 N.E.3d 666 (Ind. Ct. App. 2014), transfer denied, 26 N.E.3d 614 (Ind. 2015).

job training under the federal School to Work Opportunities Act (20 U.S.C. 6101 et seq.) to the extent set forth in IC 22-3-2-2.5.[1]

One case involving the definition of "employer" was *Taylor v. Ford Motor Co.*[2] At the time of his injury, James Taylor was employed by Visteon Corporation and leased to work at Automotive Components Holdings, LLC (ACH, a subsidiary of Ford). Visteon Corporation and ACH had entered into an hourly employee lease agreement which provided in pertinent part: "employer definition. Visteon shall be the employer of the leased employees and ACH shall not be considered the employer." Taylor was seriously injured at the ACH plant when Adams, a Ford employee, struck him with a forklift. Taylor did receive worker's compensation benefits from Visteon Corporation and filed suit against Adams, ACH and Ford for negligence. The defendants, Taylor and his wife, moved to dismiss, arguing that since IC 22-3-6-1(a) defines "employer" as including both the lessor and lessee of employees and that a parent and its subsidiaries shall also be considered joint employers for purposes of worker's compensation, the exclusive remedy for James is worker's compensation that was paid by Visteon. Taylor argued the definition of employer as provided in the agreement between Visteon and ACH applies, and that the definitions found in the Act only apply as a default position. The Court of Appeals, in affirming the trial court's grant of defendants' motion to dismiss, held the statutory language defining the term "employer" is mandatory, and since ACH was the lessee and Ford was the parent of ACH, Taylor's exclusive remedy was worker's compensation.

In Hall v. Hollman Constructions, LLC, and AT&T Services, Inc.,[3] the worker was employed by Ameritech and fell over the snow covered legs of a construction sign in a walkway at the AT&T building in downtown Indianapolis. She received worker's compensation payments from Ameritech. She filed a suit against the construction company and later against AT&T Services. AT&T Services filed its first motion for summary judgment alleging that AT&T Services and Ameritech are joint employers. The trial court agreed and granted the motion. However, the court of appeals reversed holding that a factual issue of whether AT&T and Ameritech were in fact joint employers existed.[3.50] In its second Motion for Summary Judgment AT&T Services produced

---

[Section 3:3]

[1]IC 22-3-6-1(a).

[2]Taylor v. Ford Motor Co., 944 N.E.2d 78 (Ind. Ct. App. 2011), transfer denied, 962 N.E.2d 639 (Ind. 2011).

[3]Hall v. Dallman Contractors, LLC, 51 N.E.3d 261 (Ind. Ct. App. 2016).

[3.50]See Hall v. Dallman Contractors, LLC, 994 N.E.2d 1220 (Ind. Ct. App.

evidence establishing that Ameritech and AT&T Services are both subsidiaries of AT&T Inc. and therefore joint employers of Hall. Accordingly, IC 22-3-6-1(a) which provides that the employer includes a parent or subsidiary, AT&T Services claimed it was protected by he exclusive remedy provision. The trial court again granted AT&T Services motion for summary judgment. The court of appeals, in affirming the trial court, looked to the Indiana Business Corporation Law's definition of subsidiary to determine that AT&T Services was in fact a subsidiary of the same parent as Ameritech and that it would be considered joint employers pursuant to the Worker's Compensation Act's definition of employer.

§ 3:4   Basis for inclusion within Act—Necessity of employment relationship

The right of a person to receive and the corresponding duty of a person to pay compensation under the Act depends, in the first instance, upon the existence of an employer-employee relationship. The relationship is contractual in nature and must be created by contract, either express or implied.[1] But often it is difficult to determine whether or not an employment relationship exists. Such was the case in the matter of *GKN Co. v. Magness*,[2] There Magness, a truck driver, sued his general contractor for injuries he sustained while working on a highway construction project. GKN filed a motion to dismiss for lack of subject matter jurisdiction, contending that Magness was its employee and, therefore, his exclusive remedy rested with the Indiana Worker's Compensation Act. The trial court denied GKN's motion. Following a series of appeals, the Indiana Supreme Court affirmed the trial court's judgment. In doing so, it stated:

> Here, Magness contends that he is entitled to recover against GKN because he was not employed by GKN at the time he was injured. Rather, according to Magness, Starnes Trucking employed him. GKN does not dispute that Starnes Trucking employed Magness. It contends, however, that Magness was a "dual employee" of both GKN and Starnes Trucking.
>
> The Act contemplates that one worker may simultaneously have two employers . . . . Determining whether an employer-employee relationship exists ultimately is a question of fact. *Detrick v. Midwest Pipe & Steel, Inc.*, 598 N.E.2d 1074, 1077 (Ind. Ct. App. 1992). In making this determination, the fact-finder must weigh a

---

2013) (*Hall I*).

[Section 3:4]

[1]In re Moore, 97 Ind. App. 492, 187 N.E. 219 (1933); Taylor v. Brainard, 111 Ind. App. 265, 37 N.E.2d 714 (1941).

[2]GKN Co. v. Magness, 744 N.E.2d 397 (Ind. 2001).

number of factors, none of which is dispositive. This Court has identified the most important of those as: (1) right to discharge; (2) mode of payment; (3) supplying tools or equipment; (4) belief of the parties in the existence of an employer-employee relationship; (5) control over the means used in the results reached; (6) length of employment; and, (7) establishment of the work boundaries. *Hale v. Kemp*, 579 N.E.2d 63, 67 (Ind. 1991). A number of cases suggest that if a majority of the seven *Hale* factors is present, then an employer-employee relationship exists. However, consistent with *Hale*, we now reaffirm that the factors must be weighed against each other as a part of a balancing test as opposed to a mathematical formula where the majority wins. As explained in greater detail below, when applying this balancing test, the trial court should give the greatest weight to the right of the employer to exercise control over the employee.

. . . .

Our research does reveal that the intent or belief of the parties may be an important factor but only to the extent that it indicates an assumption of control by one party and submission to control by the other party . . . . [A] determination concerning control is more objective. Among other things, it suggests a certain economic interdependency and implicates the employer's right to establish work boundaries, set working hours, assign duties, and create job security. We conclude therefore, that although not dispositive, the right to control the manner and means by which the work is to be accomplished is the single most important factor in determining the existence of an employer-employee relationship.[3]

The Court went on to find that since GKN was the party challenging the trial court's jurisdiction, it had the burden to establish that the trial court lacked subject matter jurisdiction to hear and decide the matter. The Court further found that GKN failed in its burden of proof. In part, it relied upon the evidence presented in the form of the GKN-Starnes Trucking contract which stated quite clearly that an independent contractor status existed between the parties. Pursuant to the contract, Starnes had "sole control over the means and methods by which his work is to be done, including all requirements for doing the work safely, and [GKN] is not in charge of the construction, means and methods, or of the safety of [Starnes's] work."[4]

The Court noted that there were a few facts which indicated that GKN may have exerted some control over Magness, but that it did not do so concerning the means used in the results reached.

---

[3]GKN Co. v. Magness, 744 N.E.2d 397, 402–03 (Ind. 2001) (citations omitted) (footnotes omitted).

[4]GKN Co. v. Magness, 744 N.E.2d 397, 406 (Ind. 2001).

In that regard, the Court concluded that Magness's relationship with GKN was typical of that of an independent contractor.[5]

In the final analysis, the Court decided that, having balanced the *Hale* factors, and having given considerable weight to the element of control, there was sufficient evidence before the trial court to show that Magness was not an employee of GKN. Therefore, the Court found that the trial court properly denied GKN's motion to dismiss for lack of subject matter jurisdiction, and affirmed the judgment of the trial court.[6]

§ 3:5 Basis for inclusion within Act—Compliance; binding effect

In the absence of proof to the contrary, it is presumed conclusively that the parties accept the application of the Act and agree to be bound thereby.[1] Every provision of the Act becomes a part of the contract of service and, therefore, the beneficent, humane purposes of the Act are encouraged and furthered.[2]

§ 3:6 Act inapplicable to certain individuals—Railroad employees

It is specifically stated that the provisions of the Indiana Worker's Compensation Act do not apply to railroad employees, i.e., those engaged in train service as engineers, firemen, conductors, brakemen, flagmen, baggage men, foremen in charge of yard engines, and their helpers.[1] In order for the Act to be inapplicable, it must be shown that the individual is both a railroad employee *and* "engaged in train service." What constitutes "train service" within the meaning of the Act was presented to the Appellate Court of Indiana in the matter of *Squibb v. Elgin, J. & E. Ry. Co.*[2] There, the evidence established that Squibb was injured while employed by the defendant as a switchman at its switchyard in Gary, Indiana. At the time of his injury, Squibb was participating in the switching movement of several railcars which needed to be weighed within the confines of the switchyard. His applica-

---

[5]GKN Co. v. Magness, 744 N.E.2d 397, 406 (Ind. 2001).

[6]GKN Co. v. Magness, 744 N.E.2d 397, 407 (Ind. 2001).

[Section 3:5]

[1]Hagenback v. Leppert, 66 Ind. App. 261, 117 N.E. 531 (1917); Hickman v. Western Heating & Air Conditioning Co., 207 F. Supp. 832 (N.D. Ind. 1962); Pearson v. Rogers Galvanizing Co., 115 Ind. App. 426, 59 N.E.2d 364 (1945).

[2]Hagenback v. Leppert, 66 Ind. App. 261, 117 N.E. 531, 533 (1917).

[Section 3:6]

[1]IC 22-3-2-2(b)(1) to (7).

[2]Squibb v. Elgin, J. & E. Ry. Co., 99 Ind. App. 136, 190 N.E. 879 (1934).

tion for compensation was dismissed by the board for want of jurisdiction. In its opinion reversing the decision of the board, the appellate court stated:

> It is apparent that appellant was not engaged in train service within the meaning of section 2 of the Workmen's Compensation Act of 1929. The evidence conclusively shows that he was engaged exclusively in switching cars from one part of the local yard to another, and at no time was he engaged in train service within the common acceptance and meaning of the term. We think that this statute should be construed to include railway employees who are actually engaged in the movement of trains, which means a connected line of cars or carriages on a railroad being transported from one terminal to another, and does not mean a mere movement of cars in a switchyard either for the purpose of making up trains, or placing them in one part of the yard from another. It would be a stretch of imagination to hold that appellant, in the act of switching at the time of his injury, while performing his duties as a switchman, should be held to be engaged in "train service," and thus to exclude him from the provisions of the Workmen's Compensation Act.
>
> . . . There is no substantial similarity between the ordinary train service of a railroad company and switching operations in its yards; at least no such similarity as to justify the conclusion as a matter of law that they are the same.
>
> We hold that appellant, being a switchman employed in a switchyard, and in the business of switching cars, was not engaged in train service, and, as far as section 2 of the Workmen's Compensation Act is concerned, he is within the meaning of the act and entitled to compensation.[3]

Although the Court's opinion is somewhat confusing and lacking in substance, it appears that, in order for an employee to be excluded from the Act's coverage, more is needed than simply being a railroad employee. He or she must also at the time of injury, be engaged in work associated with notions of everyday rail service; in other words, something more than the mere movement of railcars within a local switchyard. It is unclear from the court's opinion what all is needed for an individual activity or series of activities to rise to the level of "train service." Does it matter whether the movement by rail is of people or freight? Does the distance from terminal to terminal have a bearing upon the definition? Are certain "services" contemplated by the Act while others are not? Are the occupations now specifically enumerated in IC 22-3-2-2(b)(1) to (7) the only railroad employees for whom the Act has no application? The courts will need to further define the parameters for "railroad employees engaged in train services" under this section of the Act.

---

[3]Squibb v. Elgin, J. & E. Ry. Co., 99 Ind. App. 136, 190 N.E. 879, 881 (1934) (citation omitted).

§ 3:7 Act inapplicable to certain individuals— Firefighters and police officers

The Act, furthermore, does not apply to employees of municipal corporations in Indiana who are members of a municipality's fire or police department *and* a firefighters' or a police officers' pension fund.[1] It has been held that this exclusion does not apply to county police officers[2] and, therefore, they fall within the coverage of the Act. The appellate court in *Artz v. Board of Com'rs of Vigo County*[3] opined that the General Assembly, when it enacted subsection IC 22-3-2-2(c)(1) in 1943, could not have intended to exclude county police officers from coverage since, at that time, county police officers, as such, did not exist. Their predecessors, deputy sheriffs, were not covered by a pension plan until 1961, and it was not until 1981 that each county in Indiana had a county police force. Finally, the General Assembly's reference to common councils (which only cities have) in subsections (c), (e), and (f), and its reference to the city in subsections (e) and (f), in IC 22-3-2-2, evidence an intent to limit the exclusion of cities, according to the court. (Note: The wording of these provisions has been slightly changed since the court's opinion in *Artz*).

The General Assembly has, however, provided for limited coverage under the Act if a city's common council has elected to purchase worker's compensation insurance to insure fire and police employees with respect to medical benefits. In such case, the medical provisions of IC 22-3-2 to IC 22-3-6 apply to members of the fire or police department who are also members of a firefighters' or police officers' pension fund.[4] But those members of a fire or police department so covered are limited to a recovery of medical and surgical care, medicines, laboratory, curative and palliative agents and means, x-ray, and diagnostic and therapeutic services and then only to the extent that such services are provided for in the worker's compensation policy procured by the city.[5] If a firefighter or police officer for whom a worker's compensation insurance policy has been purchased elects to recover medical benefits pursuant to the policy, he or she may not also recover, in

---

[Section 3:7]

[1]IC 22-3-2-2(c)(1) and (2).

[2]Artz v. Board of Com'rs of Vigo County, 566 N.E.2d 1105 (Ind. Ct. App. 1991). Indiana State Police officers are not excluded from coverage under the Act pursuant to IC 22-3-2-2(c). See Indiana State Police Dept. v. Carich, 680 N.E.2d 4 (Ind. Ct. App. 1997).

[3]Artz v. Board of Com'rs of Vigo County, 566 N.E.2d 1105 (Ind. Ct. App. 1991).

[4]IC 22-3-2-2 (c).

[5]IC 22-3-2-2(f).

addition to that policy, those same benefits provided in IC 36-8-4.[6] It appears that the benefits recoverable pursuant to IC 36-8-4 may be more extensive than those recoverable under the Act.

Depending upon the coverage afforded by a policy procured by a municipality, a situation may arise where the medical benefits provided by the policy terminate before the injured firefighter or police officer is fully recovered. In such case, the city must continue to provide all necessary medical benefits until the injured firefighter or police officer is no longer in need or medical care or treatment.[7]

In City of Mitchell v. Phelix,[8] Phelix was employed as a police officer for the City. During his employment he dismantled methamphetamine labs. Phelix was diagnosed with diabetes, peripheral neuropathy, systolic hypertension and renal disease. Phelix notified his employer and requested disability benefits from the Public Employees' Retirement Fund ("PERF"). Phelix asked the city to pay his medical benefits pursuant to IC 36-8-4-5 and filed a claim for workers' compensation benefits. His claim for workers' compensation benefits was denied on the grounds that his condition did not arise out of his employment. Phelix did not challenge the denial of workers' compensation benefits by filing an application with Indiana's Workers' Compensation Board. Phelix continued to request medical benefits be paid by the City pursuant to IC 36-8-4-5.

The Court of Appeals found that once the City elected to utilize workers' compensation under IC 22-3-2-2, Phelix was obligated to seek the payment of his medical expenses under the Act. The Court found he had initiated the process but failed to follow through once the workers' compensation carrier denied his claim. As such, Phelix failed to exhaust his remedies under the Act. PERF found Phelix's condition at least in part was a result of his employment, but the workers' compensation carrier determined his medical condition was not related to his employment. "[T]hat inconsistency would have been better addressed by Phelix

---

[6]IC 22-3-2-2(f). IC 36-8-4-5(a) provides:

A city shall pay for the care of a police officer or firefighter who suffers injury while performing the person's duty or contracts illness caused by the person's duty, including an injury or illness that results in a disability or death presumed incurred in the line of duty under I.C. 5-10-13. This care includes (1) medical and surgical care; (2) medicines and laboratory, curative and palliative agents and means; (3) x-ray, diagnostic, and therapeutic service, including during the recovery period; and (4) hospital and special nursing care if the physicians or surgeon in charge considers it necessary for proper recovery.

[7]IC 22-3-2-2(g).

[8]City of Mitchell v. Phelix, 17 N.E.3d 971 (Ind. Ct. App. 2014), transfer denied, 26 N.E.3d 981 (Ind. 2015).

exhausting his administrative remedies in the worker's compensation proceedings." Finding the trial court erred in awarding Phelix payment of his medical bills under I.C. § 36-8-4-5 (which requires payment once workers' compensation benefits have been terminated) despite the denial of workers' compensation benefits, the award was reversed.

§ 3:8   Act inapplicable to certain individuals—Independent contractors

The Indiana Worker's Compensation Act does not apply to either a person who enters into an independent contractor agreement to perform youth coaching services on a part-time basis with a tax-exempt nonprofit corporation or to the tax-exempt nonprofit corporation itself.[1] This particular section of the Act, IC 22-3-2-2(d), appears to be rather limited in scope, but the larger consideration of whether one is an employee or an independent contractor has been the subject of abundant litigation.

Generally, an independent contractor is not an employee within the meaning of the Act and, therefore, the Act does not apply to an individual found to be an independent contractor.[2] The determination of independent contractor status is quite fact-sensitive, however, and each case will necessarily turn upon the particular facts applicable to it. The Court of Appeals of Indiana has devised a test to aid litigants and the Worker's Compensation Board in making the determination.[3]

In *Howard v. U.S. Signcrafters*,[4] the facts disclosed that Howard operated a sign business known as Custom Signs. U.S. Signcrafters engaged Howard to remove some gas station signs. While removing one sign, Howard was seriously injured when it came in contact with power lines. The full board concluded that Howard was not the employee of U.S. Signcrafters, that his injury was not compensable, and therefore denied his claim for worker's compensation benefits. In affirming the board's decision, the court stated:

> To determine employee versus independent contractor status in the context of worker's compensation, we apply the ten-factor test from the Restatement (Second) of Agency. *Id* at 30. These factors are:

[Section 3:8]

[1]IC 22-3-2-2(d).

[2]Clark v. Hughey, 233 Ind. 134, 117 N.E.2d 360 (1954); Tromley v. Padgett & Blue, Inc., 125 Ind. App. 688, 125 N.E.2d 808 (1955); Downham v. Wagner, 408 N.E.2d 606 (Ind. Ct. App. 1980).

[3]Howard v. U.S. Signcrafters, 811 N.E.2d 479 (Ind. Ct. App. 2004); Expressway Dodge, Inc. v. McFarland, 766 N.E.2d 26 (Ind. Ct. App. 2002).

[4]Howard v. U.S. Signcrafters, 811 N.E.2d 479 (Ind. Ct. App. 2004).

(a) the extent of control which, by the agreement, the master may exercise over the details of the work;

(b) whether or not the one employed is engaged in a distinct occupation or business;

(c) the kind of occupation, with reference to whether, in the locality, the work is usually done under the direction of the employer or by a specialist without supervision;

(d) the skill required in the particular occupation;

(e) whether the employer or the workman supplies the instrumentalities, tools, and the place of work for the person doing the work;

(f) the length of time for which the person is employed;

(g) the method of payment, whether by the time or by the job;

(h) whether or not the work is part of the regular business of the employer;

(i) whether or not the parties believe they are creating the relation of master and servant; and

(j) whether the principal is or is not in business.

We consider all factors, and no single factor is dispositive.[5]

It should be noted that the ten-factor test set forth in the court's decision in *Howard* differs from the seven factors considered by the Indiana Supreme Court in *GKN Co. v. Magness*.[6] *Howard* involved a determination of employee versus independent contractor. The issue in *GKN* was whether a person (Magness) was an employee of two separate employers (GKN and Starnes Trucking). The appellate court has ruled that, when the issue is employee-independent contractor, the ten-factor Restatement test is the one which the court will use to make the determination.[7]

§ 3:9   Act inapplicable to certain individuals—Casual employees

A worker whose employment is *both* casual and not in the usual course of the trade, business, occupation, or profession of the employer is excluded from the coverage of the Act.[1] Work is "casual" when not permanent or periodically regular, but occasional. If the work performed is incidental and temporary in character, then it is generally deemed to be casual. It is the kind of work done and not the duration of service which is the determining

---

[5]Howard v. U.S. Signcrafters, 811 N.E.2d 479, 482 (Ind. Ct. App. 2004) (citations omitted).

[6]GKN Co. v. Magness, 744 N.E.2d 397 (Ind. 2001). See § 3:4, Basis for inclusion within Act—Necessity of employment relationship.

[7]Howard v. U.S. Signcrafters, 811 N.E.2d 479 (Ind. Ct. App. 2004); Expressway Dodge, Inc. v. McFarland, 766 N.E.2d 26 (Ind. Ct. App. 2002).

[Section 3:9]

[1]IC 22-3-6-1 (b).

factor.[2] Again, this issue is fact-sensitive, and each case must be decided upon the facts peculiar to it. For example, it has been held that the performance of odd jobs on an irregular basis is casual employment.[3] Employment in the repair of a building has also been found to be casual.[4]

The question of whether or not work is performed in the "usual course of the trade, business, occupation or profession of the employer" is also fact-sensitive and, as one would expect, the appellate courts of Indiana have found certain work to be within the employer's usual business[5] and also work which was not.[6] Instructive on this issue is the opinion of the court of appeals in the matter of *Scott v. Rhoads*.[7] There, the decedent was working on Scott's oil well at the time he received injuries from which he eventually died. Although he admitted that he owned and operated the oil well, Scott contended that he was a farmer; consequently, the work performed by the decedent on Scott's oil well was not performed in the usual course of Scott's business. In affirming an award by the board in favor of the decedent's dependents, the court wrote:

> Appellant earnestly contends that because his principal occupation was farming, the employment of decedent was not in the usual course of his trade, business, etc. It will be noted the provision of the Workmen's Compensation Act here under consideration does not provide that the employment must be in the usual course of the "principal" trade, business, etc. of the employer, but only that the employment must be in the course of the trade, business, etc. of such employer. We are of the opinion that an employer may be engaged in various separate and independent kinds of businesses or occupations, and that his employees in the usual course of each of said businesses or occupations are entitled to the benefits of the Workmen's Compensation Act. Any other construction of the provision of the statute herein involved would tend to nullify the humane purposes which the Workmen's Compensation Act seeks to accomplish.[8]

---

[2]Crabill v. Livengood, 142 Ind. App. 624, 231 N.E.2d 854 (1967); Mason v. Wampler, 89 Ind. App. 483, 166 N.E. 885 (1929).

[3]Bailey v. Humrickhouse, 83 Ind. App. 497, 148 N.E. 428 (1925).

[4]Herthoge v. Barnes, 94 Ind. App. 225, 180 N.E. 489 (1932).

[5]Scott v. Rhoads, 114 Ind. App. 150, 51 N.E.2d 89 (1943); Heffner v. White, 113 Ind. App. 296, 45 N.E.2d 342 (1942); J. P. O. Sandwich Shop v. Papadopoulos, 105 Ind. App. 165, 13 N.E.2d 869 (1938).

[6]Coffin v. Hook, 112 Ind. App. 549, 45 N.E.2d 369 (1942); Mason v. Wampler, 89 Ind. App. 483, 166 N.E. 885 (1929); Hale v. Kemp, 579 N.E.2d 63 (Ind. 1991).

[7]Scott v. Rhoads, 114 Ind. App. 150, 51 N.E.2d 89 (1943).

[8]Scott v. Rhoads, 114 Ind. App. 150, 51 N.E.2d 89, 91 (1943).

§ 3:10   Act inapplicable to certain individuals—Farm or agricultural employees

The Indiana Worker's Compensation Act does not apply to farm or agricultural employees[1] and, as a result, they may not avail themselves of the benefits of the Act. In each case, a factual analysis is required in order to determine whether or not a worker is a farm or agricultural employee. For purposes of the Act, the terms are essentially synonymous.[2]

If there is any difference, the latter expression which necessarily includes the former has a broader meaning. The term "agriculture" is defined as "the science or art of cultivating the soil, producing crops, and raising livestock and in varying degrees the preparation of these products for man's use and their disposal (as by marketing)." Webster's Ninth New Collegiate Dictionary.[3]

It has consistently been held that, in order to make a determination regarding the worker's status at the time of injury, the entirety of the character of the work which he or she is required to perform is paramount, and not simply the nature and scope of the general occupation or business of the employer.[4] Persons employed for the purposes of detasseling corn, picking cucumber pickles, transporting tomatoes from a farm to a canning factory, performing general farm labor, planting and cultivating crops and cutting weeds, and feeding and caring for poultry, have been found to be farm or agricultural employees under the Act.[5]

In the matter of *In re Boyer*,[6] the Indiana Court of Appeals decided that an individual employed by one other than a farmer as a separator hand on a wheat threshing machine was not a farm or agricultural employee within the meaning of the Act, and, therefore, sustained an award of worker's compensation benefits. When placed in its historical context, the court's deci-

---

[Section 3:10]

[1]IC 22-3-2-9(a)(2).

[2]Fleckles v. Hille, 83 Ind. App. 715, 149 N.E. 915 (1925).

[3]Rieheman v. Cornerstone Seeds, Inc., 671 N.E.2d 489, 492 (Ind. Ct. App. 1996).

[4]Smart v. Hardesty, 238 Ind. 218, 149 N.E.2d 547 (1958); Dowery v. State, 84 Ind. App. 37, 149 N.E. 922 (1925); Evansville Veneer & Lumber Co. v. Mullen, 116 Ind. App. 616, 65 N.E.2d 742 (1946); H. J. Heinz Co. v. Chavez, 236 Ind. 400, 140 N.E.2d 500 (1957).

[5]Rieheman v. Cornerstone Seeds, Inc., 671 N.E.2d 489, 492 (Ind. Ct. App. 1996); H. J. Heinz Co. v. Chavez, 236 Ind. 400, 140 N.E.2d 500 (1957); Smart v. Hardesty, 238 Ind. 218, 149 N.E.2d 547 (1958); Dowery v. State, 84 Ind. App. 37, 149 N.E. 922 (1925); Evansville Veneer & Lumber Co. v. Mullen, 116 Ind. App. 616, 65 N.E.2d 742 (1946); Fleckles v. Hille, 83 Ind. App. 715, 149 N.E. 915 (1925).

[6]In re Boyer, 65 Ind. App. 408, 117 N.E. 507 (1917).

sion appears logical and correct. In 1917, farmers rarely, if ever, threshed their own wheat. They did not have the machinery necessary to do the work. Consequently, they hired other workers to perform the work. The court noted that wheat threshing was a business or industrial pursuit unto itself, entirely separate from and independent of farming operations.[7]

In *Rocky River Farms Inc. v. Porter*,[8] the appellate court upheld the determination that the employee of an equestrian facility was not subject to the agricultural exemption. The court found that the employee's primary duty was to train trail horses that were used recreationally at an equestrian center and this was too long of a stretch to classify the recreational use of horses as farming activities simply because a farm animal is involved.[9]

In *Hahn v. Grimm*,[10] the appellate court found that Hahn was not a farm or agricultural employee of Grimm even though he was hired, in part, to operate a corn-shredding machine and keep it in good operating condition. The court based its decision on the following analysis:

> The mere fact that appellee's chief occupation was farming, and that he intended to shred his own corn on the day appellant was injured, or that the shredding of corn may be properly considered as the doing of agricultural labor, is not controlling. As heretofore stated, there is no evidence that appellant had, prior to his injury, been employed to perform general farm work, but, to the contrary, the evidence conclusively proves that he was employed as a corn-shredder hand, his employment requiring of him that he go from farm to farm during the time his employer was engaged in the corn shredding business, and to feed and keep in working condition the machine used by his employer in the transaction of such business. . . . One may be doing labor on a farm that has become necessary to be done because of farming operations, and yet not be a farm or agricultural employee within the meaning of that phrase as used in our Compensation Law.[11]

The Court noted that Grimm actually pursued a number of business ventures. He was a farmer, but he also owned a threshing machine, a sawmill, and a corn-shredder. Each season, he used his shredder to shred corn for others for hire.

---

[7]In re Boyer, 65 Ind. App. 408, 117 N.E. 507, 508 (1917).

[8]Rocky River Farms, Inc. v. Porter, 925 N.E.2d 496 (Ind. Ct. App. 2010), transfer denied, 940 N.E.2d 821 (Ind. 2010).

[9]Rocky River Farms, Inc. v. Porter, 925 N.E.2d 496, 499 (Ind. Ct. App. 2010), transfer denied, 940 N.E.2d 821 (Ind. 2010).

[10]Hahn v. Grimm, 101 Ind. App. 74, 198 N.E. 93 (1935).

[11]Hahn v. Grimm, 101 Ind. App. 74, 198 N.E. 93, 94 (1935).

In *Strickler v. Sloan*,[12] the appellate court once again found that an employee working on a farm at the direction of his employer was *not* a farm or agricultural employee who would be denied benefits under the Act. The court noted that an "employee of a partnership in the farm implement and farming businesses employed to travel from farm to farm harvesting crops is not a farm or agricultural employee excluded from the Compensation Act."[13] The court cited with approval the following language from the court's opinion in *Makeever v. Marlin*:[14]

> "A workman is not a farm laborer simply because at the moment he is doing work on a farm; nor because the task on which he is engaged happens to be what is ordinarily considered farm labor. The employee of an implement dealer does not become a farm laborer while engaged in correcting the behavior of a self-binder in the grain field of the owner, a farmer and customer of the dealer.
>
> . . . Neither the pending task nor the place where it is being performed is the test. The whole character of the employment must be looked to determine whether he is a farm laborer."[15]

The common thread tying each of these cases together is the operation of a hazardous piece of machinery by the employee. In each case, the employee was found not to be a farm or agricultural employee within the meaning of the Act. In commenting upon the court's opinion in *In re Boyer*, the court in *Dowery v. State*[16] stated:

> It may be that, within the letter of our Compensation Act, the man employed to assist in the threshing of wheat is doing agricultural labor, but in construing and administering the law we must not lose sight of its scope and purpose. It is apparent that farm laborers, like domestic employees, were excluded from the operation of the act because such labor is less hazardous; being less hazardous, there is less need of protection. To be sure, the farm laborer may have some days each year of hazardous employment, but they are the exception and not the rule. With the employee engaged as a threshing machine hand, and going from farm to farm, it is different. His work is constantly of the most hazardous nature, much more hazardous than the work of the average factory employee. It is not reasonable to suppose that the law makers would intentionally exclude from the benefits of the Compensation Act those who were regularly employed as machine men in the threshing of grain. The Compensation Act is remedial in character, and, as was well stated in *In re Duncan* (1919) 73 Ind. App. 270, 127 N.E. 289:

---

[12]Strickler v. Sloan, 127 Ind. App. 370, 141 N.E.2d 863 (1957).

[13]Strickler v. Sloan, 127 Ind. App. 370, 378, 141 N.E.2d 863 (1957).

[14]Makeever v. Marlin, 92 Ind. App. 158, 174 N.E. 517, 518 (1931).

[15]Strickler v. Sloan, 127 Ind. App. 370, 379–80, 141 N.E.2d 863, 867 (1957).

[16]Dowery v. State, 84 Ind. App. 37, 149 N.E. 922 (1925).

"It should be liberally construed to the end that the purpose of the Legislature, by suppressing the mischiefs and advancing the remedy, be promoted, even to the inclusion of cases within the reason, although outside the letter, of the statute."[17]

Whether or not the court's rationale is viable today is debatable, especially under those circumstances where the employee operating the machinery is an employee of a farmer.

§3:11 Act inapplicable to certain individuals—Household employees

The Act does not apply to household employees.[1] These individuals were designated as "domestic servants" prior to the Act's amendment in 1997. Case law interpretations of this provision of the Act are virtually nonexistent, but an issue could arise in the appropriate case depending upon the nature and scope of the employee's duties. For instance, is a person whose job it is to care for the sick or elderly in their own homes excluded from coverage under the Act? What about a nanny hired to care for or home-school children? What if a small amount of time each day is spent cleaning the home, preparing meals, or doing laundry? Which domestic or household chores, the performance of which, would exempt a worker from coverage under the Act?

§3:12 Act inapplicable to certain individuals— Employees and employers in interstate or foreign commerce

The Act does not apply to employees and employers engaged in interstate or foreign commerce wherein the laws of the United States provide for compensation or for liability for injury or death by accident to such employees.[1] The issue, under IC 22-3-2-19, is whether or not the employee's duties further or affect interstate or foreign commerce. The employee bears the burden of proving that they do not, if he or she wishes to enjoy the benefits of the Act and forego remedies provided by federal law.[2]

In *Prader v. Pennsylvania R. Co.*,[3] the court of appeals discussed the interrelationship between the predecessor to the

---

[17]Dowery v. State, 84 Ind. App. 37, 149 N.E. 922, 923 (1925).

[Section 3:11]

[1]IC 22-3-2-9(a)(3).

[Section 3:12]

[1]IC 22-3-2-19.

[2]Chicago, M. & St. P. Ry. Co. v. Turpin, 82 Ind. App. 78, 145 N.E. 316 (1924).

[3]Prader v. Pennsylvania R. Co., 113 Ind. App. 518, 49 N.E.2d 387 (1943).

current section of the Act and the 1939 amendment of the Federal
Employers' Liability Act of 1908. It stated:

> On August 11, 1939, Congress amended the Federal Employers'
> Liability Act of 1908, and as it is upon this amendment that the ap-
> pellee rests its defense we quote the same in full: "Any employee of
> a carrier, any part of whose duties as such employee shall be the
> furtherance of interstate or foreign commerce; or shall, in any way
> directly or closely and substantially, affect such commerce as above
> set forth shall, for the purposes of this chapter, be considered as be-
> ing employed by such carrier in such commerce and shall be
> considered as entitled to the benefits of this chapter . . . ."

> One of the main purposes of this amendment was to eliminate
> the necessity of establishing that at the moment of his injury the
> employee was actually engaged in the movement of interstate
> traffic. Its effect was to broaden the field in which the federal rem-
> edy is applicable and include therein all of a carrier's employees,
> any part of whose duties were in the furtherance of interstate
> commerce.

> While it is true, in the instant case, that the appellant was not
> engaged in interstate commerce at the time he was injured, yet a
> part of his duties as an employee of the appellee was the mainte-
> nance and repair of tracks used for the transportation of interstate
> trains. That such work constitutes employment in interstate com-
> merce is no longer open to controversy. Thus it would seem that the
> appellant is squarely within the scope of the Federal Employers' Li-
> ability Act as amended in 1939, and the Industrial Board was cor-
> rect in denying jurisdiction.[4]

§ 3:13 Act inapplicable to certain individuals—Real estate professionals

The Act is inapplicable to real estate professionals if they are
licensed real estate agents, have written agreements with real
estate brokers stating that they are not to be treated as employees for tax purposes, and derive substantially all of their remuneration from sales volume as opposed to the number of hours
worked.[1] The relevant section, IC 22-3-6-1(b)(6), seems to be in
harmony with other provisions of the Act. A real estate agent
who has in effect a written contract with his or her broker stating that he or she is not an employee for tax purposes and, thus,
is presumably an independent contractor, should not be entitled
to the benefits provided by the Act. In addition, one whose earnings may not bear a reasonable relationship to his or her work
and the time actually spent working should be excluded from the

---

[4]Prader v. Pennsylvania R. Co., 113 Ind. App. 518, 49 N.E.2d 387, 390
(1943) (citations omitted).

[Section 3:13]

[1]IC 22-3-6-1(b)(6).

Act's coverage. The compensation provisions of the Act require, in part, computations based upon the individual's average weekly wage. Usually, calculating an average weekly wage is relatively simple. The process becomes more complex, however, when "earnings" depend upon "sales volume" instead of payment for work on a fairly defined basis.

The nature of the real estate business is such that an agent may in any given week work as much or as little as he or she wishes. The agent may work full-time or only on a part-time basis. A listed property may be bought or sold with a minimum amount of work having been performed by the agent or, conversely, with an amount of time and effort far exceeding the commission eventually obtained. A piece of real estate may sell rather quickly or take months or even years to sell. Consequently, the agent's "average weekly wage" may be incapable of accurate computation, since the commission eventually paid to the agent may not be received within the time frame envisioned by the Act.

§ 3:14 Those to whom Act specifically applies

There are certain classifications of individuals to whom the Act specifically applies. For instance, members of the Indiana General Assembly and field examiners employed by the State Board of Accounts are included within the coverage of the Act.[1] Volunteer workers and students participating in on-the-job training pursuant to the federal School-to-Work Opportunities Act are provided limited coverage under the Act, assuming certain criteria are met.[2] Employees of the state, political divisions thereof, and all municipal corporations within the state are extended coverage (with the exception of municipal firefighters and police officers, as discussed in § 3:7, Act inapplicable to certain individuals—Firefighters and police officers).[3] Those engaged in mining coal are subject to the provisions of the Act.[4]

§ 3:15 Those to whom Act specifically applies— Volunteers

The General Assembly has determined that certain individuals performing volunteer work for local government entities may be covered by the medical treatment provisions of the Act only. In order to obtain medical benefits, the individual must be a

---

[Section 3:14]

[1]IC 22-3-2-2(h)(1) and (2).

[2]IC 22-3-2-2.1, IC 22-3-2-2.3, IC 22-3-2-2.5.

[3]IC 22-3-2-18.

[4]IC 22-3-2-18.

"rostered volunteer," i.e., one whose name has been listed on a roster for a volunteer program operated by a township, a municipality, or a county. The person must have been approved by the proper authorities of the governmental unit to perform volunteer services. This section of the Act, IC 22-3-2-2.1, extending coverage to rostered volunteers does *not* include volunteer firefighters or inmates assigned to correctional facilities operated by the state or a local unit of government.

In addition, according to IC 22-3-2-2.3, a "volunteer worker" performing services of any nature for certain state institutions will qualify to receive medical benefits under the Act, provided that the individual is not compensated in any manner for his or her work and has been approved and accepted as a volunteer worker by the director of either the division of disability and rehabilitative services or the division of mental health and addiction. The institutions encompassed by this section of the Act are those owned or operated by the state, under the administrative control of a division of state government, and concerned with the observation, care, treatment, or detention of an individual. Seven specific state hospitals or treatment centers are now included within the term "state institution" for purposes of this section.[1]

In *Community Action Program of Evansville v. Veeck*,[2] the Court of Appeals of Indiana was called upon to decide whether or not a participant in a federally funded program administered by an eligible local organization was entitled to receive the medical benefits extended to volunteers by IC 22-3-2-2.3. Veeck was a volunteer foster grandmother helping special-needs children at the Evansville Psychiatric Children Center through the Foster Grandparents Program administered by Community Action Program of Evansville (CAPE). She worked 20 hours per week. Veeck did not receive a salary for her services, but she did receive a stipend of $2.45 per hour for each hour she worked. While working at the center one day, she tripped, fell, and broke her hip. Surgery was required to treat her injury, and a five-month period of follow-up care and the inability to work ensued.

The board found that Veeck was not entitled to worker's compensation benefits since she was not an employee, but that

---

[Section 3:15]

[1]IC 22-3-2-2.3, IC 12-7-2-184(a). Subsection (b) of the latter provides: "The term ['state institution'] includes the following: (1) Evansville State Hospital. (2) Evansville State Psychiatric Treatment Center for Children. (3) Larue D. Carter Memorial Hospital. (4) Logansport State Hospital. (5) Madison State Hospital. (6) Richmond State Hospital."

[2]Community Action Program of Evansville v. Veeck, 756 N.E.2d 1079 (Ind. Ct. App. 2001).

she was entitled to the payment of her medical expenses as a volunteer worker at a state institution. CAPE appealed, arguing that the stipend Veeck received for her services was compensation and, therefore, she was not a volunteer worker as defined by the Act. In affirming the board's award, the court noted the intent of Congress in enacting the Foster Grandparents Program, and the explanation of the program contained in the Code of Federal Regulations.[3] It was clearly stated therein that any payment for supportive services or reimbursement of out-of-pocket expenses made to participants in the program was not to be treated as wages or compensation for purposes of worker's compensation. The court concluded that the hourly stipend Veeck received was simply a reimbursement of her expenses and, therefore, as an uncompensated volunteer at a state-owned psychiatric hospital, she was entitled to the medical expense coverage provided by IC 22-3-2-2.3.[4]

In *Einhorn v. Johnson*,[5] the Court of Appeals addressed, in part, an issue regarding the exclusivity provision of the Workers' Compensation Act as to a claim against Purdue University Board of Trustees. Einhorn was an unpaid volunteer at the 4-H Fair when he sustained serious injuries after being trampled by a horse which had been spooked. After the accident Einhorn, who had not applied for workers' compensation benefits, was notified that he was eligible for medical benefits under Purdue's workers' compensation policy under which he received almost $80,000 in medical benefits. Einhorn filed a negligence action against multiple defendants including Purdue. Purdue was dismissed by the trial court which agreed with its argument that since Einhorn accepted workers' compensation benefits from them the exclusivity provision of the Act was triggered. Einhorn argued he was not a Purdue employee and therefore was not precluded from pursuing a civil action. Purdue did not argue Einhorn was an employee. It argued that his acceptance of medical payments through Purdue's workers' compensation carrier bound Einhorn to the exclusivity provisions under the Act. The evidence showed Einhorn was an unpaid volunteer. Einhorn did not apply for medical benefits nor did he agree to be bound by the exclusivity provisions of the Act by accepting such benefits. The Court of Appeals held that Einhorn's acceptance of medical payments from Purdue's workers' compensation carrier did not change his status from a volunteer to an employee and he was not bound by the exclusivity provisions of the Act.

---

[3]45 C.F.R. § 1208.3-5 (now 45 C.F.R. § 2552). See also 42 U.S.C.A. § 5058.

[4]Community Action Program of Evansville v. Veeck, 756 N.E.2d 1079 (Ind. Ct. App. 2001).

[5]Einhorn v. Johnson, 996 N.E.2d 823 (Ind. Ct. App. 2013), transfer denied, 9 N.E.3d 170 (Ind. 2014).

§ 3:16 Those to whom Act specifically applies—School-to-work students

A student participating in on-the-job training pursuant to the federal School-to-Work Opportunities Act[1] is entitled to medical benefits and certain compensation payments under the Act.[2] The student may receive a lump sum payment for permanent partial impairment upon agreement or a final award.[3] If death results from the injury, the student's dependents or, if the student has no dependants, his or her parents may receive a death benefit of $175,000 payable upon agreement or a final award.[4] Burial expenses, not to exceed $7,500, are also provided.[5] The student is *not*, however, entitled to receive temporary total disability or temporary partial disability compensation.[6]

Except for those remedies available under the Compensation for Victims of Violent Crimes Act,[7] a recovery of medical benefits or compensation under IC 22-3-2-2.5(e) is the exclusive right and remedy for a school-to-work student and his or her personal representatives, dependents, or next of kin on account of personal injury or death by accident arising out of and in the course of school-to-work employment.

§ 3:17 Those to whom Act specifically applies— Governmental employees

The Act applies to the state, to all its political divisions, to all municipal corporations within the state, and to the employees thereof (with the exception of certain municipal fire and police department employees, as discussed in § 3:7, Act inapplicable to certain individuals—Firefighters and police officers).[1] There is no doubt that, under the Act, public employees are extended coverage and entitled to the benefits provided by the Act. The question, however, is who is and who is not a public employee. A distinction has arisen under Indiana law between public officers or officials and public employees. It has been held that a public officer or official is not an employee within the meaning of the

---

[Section 3:16]

    [1]20 U.S.C.A. §§ 6101 et seq.

    [2]IC 22-3-2-2.5.

    [3]IC 22-3-2-2.5(b).

    [4]IC 22-3-2-2.5(b)(3).

    [5]IC 22-3-2-2.5(b)(3).

    [6]IC 22-3-2-2.5(d).

    [7]IC 5-2-6.1 et seq.

[Section 3:17]

    [1]IC 22-3-2-18, IC 22-3-2-2(c).

Act and is not entitled to the benefits granted by the Act. The case of *Union Tp. of Montgomery County v. Hays*[2] is illustrative. There, William Hays, a deputy township assessor, received fatal injuries when he fell on the courthouse steps while on his way to measure some real estate improvements in Crawfordsville, Indiana. His widow filed her claim for compensation which was granted by the board. In reversing the award, the appellate court stated:

> The primary issue in this appeal is whether or not decedent was an "employee" under the Indiana Workmen's Compensation Act, thus entitling his surviving widow to benefits thereunder . . . .
>
> It is well settled in this State that a public officer is not an "employee" under the Workmen's Compensation Act.
>
> A public officer is "a position to which a portion of the sovereignty of the state attaches for the time being, and which is exercised for the benefit of the public. The most important characteristic which may be said to distinguish an office from an employment is that the duties of the incumbent of an office must involve an exercise of some portion of the sovereign power."
>
> "However, it must be noted that while a state and its subdivisions may be bound as employers under the Act, they can be bound only to the extent that persons working for them can be called employees. If a particular position is of such a character that it can be called a public office, where the holder is invested with some portion of the state's sovereignty and is responsible to the public at large, no employment in the true sense can be found. Any claim against the state or any of its subdivisions must therefore be scrutinized carefully to determine whether the workman was an employee of the state, or whether he was a public officer." Small, *Workmen's Compensation Law of Indiana*, Ch. III, Sec. 3.2, p.41.
> . . . .
>
> In *County of St. Joseph v. Claeys* (1937), 103 Ind. App. 192, at page 195, 5 N.E.2d 1008, at page 1009, quoting from 46 C.J. Sec. 22, p. 930, it is said:
>
> "Generally speaking, one of the requisites of an office is that it must be created by a constitutional provision, or it must be a authorized by some statute, and an important distinction between the status of an officer and that of an employee rests on the fact that an office is based on some provision of law, and does not arise out of contract, whereas an employment usually arises out of a contract between the government and the employee. . . ."
>
> A deputy township assessor, by virtue of his office, exercises a portion of the State's sovereign power to assess and tax its citizens. He is required to take the oath of his principal . . . .
>
> In *Brinson v. Board of Commissioners, supra*, 97 Ind. App. 354, at pages 356–357, 186 N.E. 891, at page 892 . . . it is said:
>
> "When an individual has been appointed or elected, in a manner

---

[2]Union Tp. of Montgomery County v. Hays, 138 Ind. App. 280, 207 N.E.2d 223 (1965).

required by law, has a designation or title given him by law, and exercises functions concerning the public assigned to him by law, he must be regarded as a 'public officer.' "[3]

The Court found that, at the time he sustained his injury, Hays was performing the duties of his office as deputy township assessor and, therefore, was not an employee as that term is defined by the Act.[4]

§ 3:18 Those to whom Act specifically applies—Persons engaged in mining coal

Employees of persons, partnerships, limited liability companies, and corporations engaged in mining coal are extended coverage under the Act.[1]

Constitutional challenges to this provision of the Act were made early on and dismissed, with the U.S. Supreme Court finding that the Indiana Worker's Compensation Act did not violate either the federal Constitution or the Indiana Bill of Rights, even though the provisions of the Act were made compulsory upon coal mining companies and all of their employees, while as to all other private businesses within the state (except railroad employees engaged in train service) it was purely optional.[2]

An interesting factual situation was presented to the Indiana appellate court in the matter of *Hanna v. Warren*.[3] For many years, Hanna owned and operated a farm in Greene County, Indiana, upon which his brother lived. He resided there practically all of his life, and never engaged in any occupation or business other than farming. In 1920, Roy Price offered to buy from the Hannas whatever coal they could obtain from an outcropping on the farm. They agreed, and hired Warren and others to do the work. The coal appeared on the surface of the farm, and no mining or other operation was necessary, except to blast it, load it into wagons, haul it to a switchyard, and shovel it into railcars. The Hannas did not invest in any machinery or mining tools or equipment of any kind, and those performing the work used only farm teams, wagons, scrapers, and shovels in loading and transporting the coal. The Hannas and their employees performed

---

[3]Union Tp. of Montgomery County v. Hays, 138 Ind. App. 280, 282–84, 207 N.E.2d 223 (1965) (citations omitted).

[4]Union Tp. of Montgomery County v. Hays, 138 Ind. App. 280, 207 N.E.2d 223 (1965).

[Section 3:18]

[1]IC 22-3-2-18.

[2]Lower Vein Coal Co. v. Industrial Bd. of Indiana, 255 U.S. 144, 41 S. Ct. 252, 65 L. Ed. 555 (1921).

[3]Hanna v. Warren, 77 Ind. App. 1, 133 N.E. 9 (1921).

this work pursuant to their contract with Price for only four weeks, then, when it no longer was profitable for them to continue, they quit. It was during that four-week period, however, that Warren was injured. He sought compensation under the Act, and the Hannas responded that they were farmers and not subject to the requirements of the Act. The court found that, while their employees were engaged in the work covered by their contract with Price, the Hannas were not farmers, but, instead, engaged in the coal mining business and, thus, subject to the provisions of the Act.[4]

§ 3:19 Employer's duty to pay and employee's duty to accept compensation

Every employer to whom the Act applies is bound to pay, and every employee entitled to the benefits of the Act is bound to accept, compensation for work-related injuries or death, provided the compensability of the claim is established.[1] With few exceptions, every such employer is required to insure and keep insured the liability to pay compensation to its employees and their dependents, or furnish the board satisfactory proof of its financial ability to pay directly the compensation in the amount and manner and when due. With respect to the latter, the employer must procure from the board a certificate authorizing the employer to carry such risk without insurance, and may be required to post a security, indemnity, or bond, acceptable to the board, to secure the payment of compensation liabilities as they are incurred.[2] The following entities need not insure the payment of compensation: the state, counties, townships, cities, towns, school cities, school towns, school townships, other municipal corporations, state institutions, state boards, state commissions, banks, trust companies, and building and loan associations.[3]

The state, however, is prohibited from purchasing worker's compensation insurance. Instead, it may establish a program of self-insurance to cover its liability under the Act, and may administer the program itself or contract out the administration of the program.[4]

---

[4]Hanna v. Warren, 77 Ind. App. 1, 133 N.E. 9, 10 (1921).

[Section 3:19]

[1]IC 22-3-2-2(a), IC 22-3-2-5(a).

[2]IC 22-3-2-5(a).

[3]IC 22-3-5-1.

[4]IC 22-3-2-5(b).

Hickman v. Western Heating & Air Conditioning Co.,[5] was a case wherein decedent's employer both failed to insure its worker's compensation liability and prove to the board its financial ability to pay claims. There was no allegation by decedent's administratrix that the employer specifically rejected the provisions of the Act or chose to be exempt from its application. The administratrix argued that, by virtue of the employer's failures, she could elect to proceed with her lawsuit and was not confined to a claim for compensation under the Act. In dismissing her wrongful death action, the court held that:

> The Workmen's Compensation Act provides that an employer bound by the Act shall be liable to any employee and his dependents for personal injury or death by accident arising out of, and in the course of, employment only to the extent and manner specified in the Act . . . .
>
> . . . .
>
> [F]ailure to comply with financial proof requirements under (the current section's predecessor) is not tantamount to exemption and rejection of coverage by the Act.[6]

Furthermore, the General Assembly has provided that all rights of compensation granted to an employee shall have the same preference or priority against the employer's assets as is allowed by law for any unpaid wages for labor.[7]

§ 3:20   Employer's duty to pay and employee's duty to accept compensation—Exclusivity of remedy

The rights and remedies granted to an employee subject to the Act on account of personal injury or death by accident shall exclude all other rights and remedies available to such employee and his or her personal representatives, dependents, or next of kin at common law or otherwise, except for those remedies available under the Compensation for Victims of Violent Crimes Act, IC 5-2-6.1 et seq.[1] Once the jurisdictional prerequisites of an employee's claim have been met, the employee must seek recovery under the Act and before the Worker's Compensation Board.[2] It has been held that "the Legislature intended the Board's jurisdic-

---

[5]Hickman v. Western Heating & Air Conditioning Co., 207 F. Supp. 832 (N.D. Ind. 1962).

[6]Hickman v. Western Heating & Air Conditioning Co., 207 F. Supp. 832, 833–34 (N.D. Ind. 1962) (citations omitted). See Landers v. Pickering, 427 N.E.2d 716 (Ind. Ct. App. 1981).

[7]IC 22-3-2-16.

[Section 3:20]

[1]IC 22-3-2-6.

[2]Fleischmann v. Wausau Business Ins. Co., 671 N.E.2d 473 (Ind. Ct. App.

tion in such cases to be original and exclusive, and resort may not be had to the courts until the administrative process has been completely exhausted."[3] The purposes underlying the rule have frequently been stated as follows:

> The Act initially developed because of the obstacles and delays that hindered the working person's ability to recover against an employer for industrial related accidents. With the enactment of the worker's compensation system, "workers who were previously precluded from recovery under common law theories are [now] guaranteed compensation." Under the Act:
>
> > [e]mployers must "provide limited compensation to workers whose injuries arise out of and in the course of [their] employment, regardless of fault." "In return for the employer's payment of benefits, the employer is given immunity from civil litigation with his employee." "The scheme is . . . social legislation designed to aid workers and their dependents and 'shift the economic burden for employment related injuries from the employee to the employer and consumers of its products [and services].' "
>
> Thus, worker's compensation was designed as a quid pro quo exchange between the employee and the employer. The employer assumed the cost of paying regular and relatively quantifiable amounts under the worker's compensation system in exchange for obviating the threat of large and unexpected awards. In return, the employee gave up his right to pursue a common law remedy for injuries sustained in work-place accidents in exchange for a certain, although possibly smaller, remedy without litigation.[4]

The General Assembly has determined that compensation awards under the Act are subject to the enforcement of a child support order. The maximum amount that may be withheld is one-half of the compensation award. With that single exception, no claims for compensation under the Act are assignable, and all compensation and claims therefore are exempt from all claims of creditors.[5]

In the case of *Estate of Smith v. Stutzman*,[6] Smith suffered an injury while working for Stutsman. A settlement agreement was

---

1996) (disapproved of by, GKN Co. v. Magness, 744 N.E.2d 397 (Ind. 2001)); DePuy, Inc. v. Farmer, 847 N.E.2d 160 (Ind. 2006); Wolf Corp. v. Thompson, 609 N.E.2d 1170 (Ind. Ct. App. 1993); Consolidated Products, Inc. v. Lawrence, 521 N.E.2d 1327 (Ind. Ct. App. 1988).

[3]Rassbach v. Alcala, 775 N.E.2d 353, 356 (Ind. Ct. App. 2002).

[4]Rassbach v. Alcala, 775 N.E.2d 353, 358 (Ind. Ct. App. 2002) (quoting Spangler, Jennings & Dougherty P.C. v. Indiana Ins. Co., 729 N.E.2d 117, 120 (Ind. 2000)); Ross v. Schubert, 180 Ind. App. 402, 388 N.E.2d 623 (1979); Wine-Settergren v. Lamey, 716 N.E.2d 381 (Ind. 1999); Larson, Workmen's Compensation Law, § 1.03 (2002). See also: Williams v. Delta Steel Corp., 695 N.E.2d 633 (Ind. Ct. App. 1998); DePuy, Inc. v. Farmer, 847 N.E.2d 160 (Ind. 2006); Clem v. Steveco, Inc., 450 N.E.2d 550 (Ind. Ct. App. 1983).

[5]IC 22-3-2-17.

[6]Estate of Smith v. Stutzman, 964 N.E.2d 904 (Ind. Ct. App. 2012).

entered into by the decedent's sole presumptive dependent, his widow, the employer and the employer's insurance carrier for settlement of a worker's compensation claim for payment of $100,000. A few months after the Board approved the settlement agreement, the estate filed a complaint against Stutsman alleging that decedent was working as an independent contractor when he fell to his death, and that Stutsman was negligent in maintaining a safe work place. The estate argued that merely entering into the worker's compensation settlement agreement was not a concession that the decedent was an employee at the time of death. The trial court found the Worker's Compensation Board has exclusive jurisdiction in this matter and ordered the case be dismissed. In affirming the trial court's decision, the Court of Appeals restated that the general rule that where an employee accepts compensation under the Act, the employee concedes the injury arises out of and in the course of employment, and the exclusive remedy is worker's compensation. As such, the trial court did not have subject matter jurisdiction over this matter.

In *Johnson v. Poindexter Transport, Inc. and Crane Service*,[7] the Court of Appeals considered the claim of Donavon Johnson, an employee of general contractor R.L. Turner ("Turner"). Turner contracted with Poindexter Transport, Inc., and Crane Service ("Poindexter") to provide for crane operations who assigned David Creel as crane operator. Creel worked at the direction of Turner employees. Turner directed Creel on what materials to move and when and where to move them. Turner provided rigging and straps for the project. Turner approved Creel's hours and then turned the timesheet over to Poindexter who paid Creel. As Creel was lowering a wooden form used for the construction of concrete walls, one form came apart and Johnson was struck by a piece of the falling form. Johnson and his wife sued Poindexter for negligence. Poindexter filed a Motion to Dismiss, arguing that Creel was a borrowed employee of Turner and therefore the Creel and Johnson were co-employees. As such, Poindexter argued the trial court would lack jurisdiction to hear the claim and Johnson's exclusive remedy was to pursue Workers' Compensation benefits. The trial Court dismissed the complaint and the Johnsons appealed to the Court of Appeals. The Court of Appeals applied the *Hale* 7-factor test to the facts of the case to determine if an employer-employee relationship existed between Creel and Turner.[8] Balancing the *Hale* factors, giving considerable weight to the element of control, the Court affirmed the trial court's dis-

---

[7]Johnson v. Poindexter Transport, Inc. and Crane Service, 994 N.E.2d 1206 (Ind. Ct. App. 2013).

[8]Hale v. Kemp, 579 N.E.2d 63 (Ind. 1991).

missal of the Johnson's complaint and concluded that Creel was a borrowed employee of Turner therefore the Johnson's exclusive remedy was to pursue a claim for benefits under the Workers' Compensation Act.

In *Musgrave v. Aluminum Company of America, Inc.*,[9] the Court of Appeals addressed the question of whether a party in a joint venture is considered an employer for the purposes of the exclusivity provisions of the Workers' Compensation Act. In January 2006, Bil Musgrave filed suit against Aluminum Company of America ("Alcoa") and it's wholly owned subsidiary, Alcoa Fuels, alleging he had been exposed to Alcoa's toxic chemicals both in the course of his employment on land owned by Alcoa Fuels and his recreational use of that land. This exposure allegedly caused Bil to develop a rare form of cancer. Before trial, the trial court dismissed Musgrave's work-related claims pursuant to the exclusivity provisions of the Workers' Compensation Act. Following trial on Bil's recreational use claims, the jury returned a general verdict in favor of Alcoa and Alcoa Fuels based on a statute of limitations defense. The Musgraves appealed.

Alcoa had entered into a "Joint Venture" with Peabody Coal Company. The Joint venture was called Squaw Creek Coal Company ("SCCC"). Bil worked for SCCC from 1977 through 2000. Bil was diagnosed with a rare form of cancer in September of 2000. Within one month of his diagnosis Bil self reported to his doctors that he may have suffered an "occupational hazard." There was additional evidence in the case that the Musgraves suspected Bil had been exposed to a cancer causing agent on the lands where he had played as a child and where he later worked for the joint venture SCCC. The Court of Appeals looked at whether Alcoa and Peabody were engaged in a joint venture and answered that question in the affirmative. Then the Court addressed whether the Act grants the members of a joint venture immunity as a matter of law. In so considering, the Court noted that the definition of an employer included an "association" and that the definition of a joint venture as an "association of two or more persons formed to carry out a single business enterprise for profit." The Court concluded that an "association" under the definition of employer included a joint venture. Further, the Court found it well-established Indiana law that an employee of a joint venture is the employee of each member of the joint venture. Since SCCC was a joint venture of Alcoa and Peabody, Alcoa was the employer of any joint venture employee. Therefore, since there was objective evidence to support the conclusion that Bil was the employee of the joint venture SCCC, Alcoa as a member

---

[9]Musgrave v. Aluminum Co. of America, Inc., 995 N.E.2d 621 (Ind. Ct. App. 2013).

of the joint venture was entitled to immunity from Bil's work-related tort claim. Finally, the Court affirmed the dismissal of Bil's recreational claim based on the statute of limitations.

In *Hall v Dallman Contractors, LLC*,[10] the Court of Appeals considered whether Hall's negligence claim was barred by the exclusivity provisions of the Workers' Compensation Act. Hall was an employee of AT&T. In the winter of 2007 Hall tripped on the snow covered leg of a construction sign placed on the sidewalk near the AT&T building in downtown Indianapolis injuring her arm. Hall was provided workers' compensation benefits and at the conclusion of her claim she entered into a settlement agreement, in which she stipulated she was an employee of "AT&T f/k/a Ameritech Home Services." The workers' compensation board approved the agreement and thereby awarded compensation to Hall from "AT&T f/k/a Ameritech Home Services."

In 2008, Hall filed her negligence claim against defendants including "American Telephone & Telegraph Company f/k/a AT&T Property Management" alleging they had failed in their duty to keep the sidewalks and adjacent areas of the AT&T building free from snow, ice and debris. AT&T Property Management moved to substitute AT&T Services as the real party in interest. After which, AT&T Services moved for summary judgment arguing that they were Hall's joint employer and therefore her complaint should be dismissed because of the Act's exclusivity provisions. Hall argued AT&T Services was not a joint employer with "Ameritech Home Services, Inc." AT&T Services argued Hall was an employee of AT&T which included AT&T Services and "AT&T f/k/a Ameritech Home Services." After reviewing "inartful drafted" affidavits the Appeals Court found the designated evidence did NOT support that conclusion that AT&T Services was Hall's employer. AT&T Services did not establish that because Hall was employed by an AT&T entity and recovered workers' compensation benefits from an AT&T entity, the exclusive remedy provisions of the Act barred Hall's negligence claim against AT&T Services.

AT&T Services also argued it was a "joint employer" under the Act and as such Hall was limited to her workers' compensation claim against them. At issue was the definition of a subsidiary. The Court noted that the Act does not define "subsidiary." The Court borrowed the definition from the Indiana Business Corporation Law and concluded the evidence did not support the conclusion that Hall's employer and AT&T Services were joint employers. The Court noted it would not be sufficient to show both AT&T Services and Ameritech Home Services were in the

---

[10]Hall v. Dallman Contractors, LLC, 994 N.E.2d 1220 (Ind. Ct. App. 2013).

same corporate structure. The Court concluded there were material issues of fact regarding whether AT&T Services was Hall's employer or joint employer therefore the dismissal of her complaint was improper.

In City of Mitchell v. Phelix,[11] Phelix was employed as a police officer for the City. During his employment he dismantled methamphetamine labs. Phelix was diagnosed with diabetes, peripheral neuropathy, systolic hypertension and renal disease. Phelix notified his employer and requested disability benefits from the Public Employees' Retirement Fund ("PERF"). Phelix asked the city to pay his medical benefits pursuant to IC 36-8-4-5 and filed a claim for workers' compensation benefits. His claim for workers' compensation benefits was denied on the grounds that his condition did not arise out of his employment. Phelix did not challenge the denial of workers' compensation benefits by filing an application with Indiana's Workers' Compensation Board. Phelix continued to request medical benefits be paid by the City pursuant to IC 36-8-4-5.

The Court of Appeals found that once the City elected to utilize workers' compensation under IC 22-3-2-2, Phelix was obligated to seek the payment of his medical expenses under the Act. The Court found he had initiated the process but failed to follow through once the workers' compensation carrier denied his claim. As such, Phelix failed to exhaust his remedies under the Act. PERF found Phelix's condition at least in part was a result of his employment, but the workers' compensation carrier determined his medical condition was not related to his employment. "[T]hat inconsistency would have been better addressed by Phelix exhausting his administrative remedies in the worker's compensation proceedings." Finding the trial court erred in awarding Phelix payment of his medical bills under I.C. § 36-8-4-5 (which requires payment once workers' compensation benefits have been terminated) despite the denial of workers' compensation benefits, the award was reversed.

§ 3:21 Personal injury or death

Employees are entitled to recover compensation under the Act for personal injuries or death, provided the other essential elements of a claim for compensation are established.[1] It is not always necessary for the employee to prove a physical, bodily injury in order to prevail. It has consistently been held that "a

---

[11]City of Mitchell v. Phelix, 17 N.E.3d 971 (Ind. Ct. App. 2014), transfer denied, 26 N.E.3d 981 (Ind. 2015).

[Section 3:21]

[1]IC 22-3-2-2.

personal injury, as that term is used in the Workmen's Compensation Act, has reference not to some break in some part of the body or some wound thereon, or the like, but rather to the consequences or disability that results therefrom."[2]

In its opinion in the matter of *Eastham v. Whirlpool Corp.*,[3] the Court of Appeals of Indiana stated:

> Mental conditions may be compensable under the Indiana Workmen's Compensation Act if the condition is a result of a primary injury compensable under the act, *Sears Roebuck & Co., supra,* at 830 (where the primary injury arises out of the employment, every consequence which flows from it likewise arises out of the employment), or, in the absence of a physical injury, if the disorder itself is the primary injury arising out of and in the course of employment. *Hansen v. Von Duprin* (1987), Ind., 507 N.E.2d 573, 576.

As the Indiana Supreme Court stated in *Hansen v. Von Duprin, Inc.*,[4] "Whether the injury is mental or physical, the determinative standard should be the same. The issue is *not* whether the injury resulted from the *ordinary* events of employment. Rather, it is simply whether the injury arose out of and in the course of employment."

The indications are clear that mental, as well as physical, injuries are compensable, as long as there is a causal connection between the injury and the employment.[5] However, before recovery will be allowed for purely mental or emotional injuries, there also must be evidence of some degree of disability or impairment resulting therefrom. The opinion of the Indiana Supreme

---

[2]Indian Creek Coal & Mining Co. v. Calvert, 68 Ind. App. 474, 119 N.E. 519, 525 (1918). In Kingan & Co. v. Ossam, 75 Ind. App. 548, 121 N.E. 289, 292 (1918), the Court held:

> The fact that appellee was suffering from a mental or nervous condition resulting from a physical injury, rather from the physical injury itself, cannot have the effect of relieving appellant from liability. This court is committed to the doctrine that a "personal injury," as that term is used in the Workmen's Compensation Act, has reference not merely to some break in some part of the body, or some wound thereon or the like, but also to the consequences or disability that results therefrom. It is apparent that certain mental and nervous conditions may be as effective in producing disability as a physical wound or the loss of a member. Such conditions, therefore, afford a basis for compensation. (citations omitted).

See also Burton-Shields Co. v. Steele, 119 Ind. App. 216, 83 N.E.2d 623 (1949); Bethlehem Steel Corp. v. Cummings, 160 Ind. App. 160, 310 N.E.2d 565 (1974).

[3]Eastham v. Whirlpool Corp., 524 N.E.2d 23, 28 (Ind. Ct. App. 1988).

[4]Hansen v. Von Duprin, Inc., 507 N.E.2d 573, 576 (Ind. 1987).

[5]Rayford v. Lumbermens Mut. Cas. Co., 44 F.3d 546 (7th Cir. 1995) (psychological problems stemming from a work-related leg injury); Crowe v. Blum, 9 F.3d 32 (7th Cir. 1993) (assault and intentional infliction of emotional distress resulting from an employee's admonishment by her superior).

Court in the matter of *Perry v. Stitzer Buick GMC, Inc.*,[6] is illustrative. With regard to Perry's injury claim, the Court stated:

Although we have not had occasion to give formal definition to the term "personal injury," case law makes clear that its scope includes both physical injury and the somewhat different notions of "disability" and "impairment." "Impairment" is a term of art for purposes of workers compensation that denotes an injured employee's loss of physical functions. "Disability" refers to an injured employee's inability to work. The extent of a disability is determined by a worker's physical and mental fitness for various employment opportunities.

In the instant case, Perry alleges he has been injured by various affronts and slanderous racial slurs. He asserts that he has suffered embarrassment, humiliation, stress, and paranoia, and that his character and reputation have been damaged. Both parties concede, however, that he has not sustained any physical injury or loss of physical function. Likewise, the evidence indicates that, but for his termination, Perry was both able and willing to continue to perform his duties at Stitzer. In sum, the injuries at the heart of Perry's complaint were not physical, nor was there any impairment or disability as those terms are comprehended by the act. Accordingly, we hold that Perry's claims are not barred by the exclusive remedy clause of the Worker's Compensation Act because, alone, they present no injuries covered by the act.[7]

§ 3:22 Accidents

The injury for which benefits are claimed under the Act must

---

[6]Perry v. Stitzer Buick GMC, Inc., 637 N.E.2d 1282 (Ind. 1994).

[7]Perry v. Stitzer Buick GMC, Inc., 637 N.E.2d 1282, 1288–89 (Ind. 1994) (citations omitted). See also Dietz v. Finlay Fine Jewelry Corp., 754 N.E.2d 958, 965 (Ind. Ct. App. 2001) ("Here, as in *Perry*, Dietz does not claim to have suffered physical injury or loss of physical function. Rather, she alleges loss of sleep, anxiety tension, depression, humiliation, extreme emotional distress, and injury to her reputation, injuries that are not physical in nature. Dietz also seeks economic damages for loss of wages, benefits, and detriment in seeking other employment, damages unrelated to any impairment or disability. Because the injuries at the heart of Dietz's complaint do not involve personal injury as defined by the Act, her claims may be pursued in court."); Terrell v. Rowsey, 647 N.E.2d 662 (Ind. Ct. App. 1995) (claims for defamation, embarrassment, and loss of quiet enjoyment of property do not concern physical injuries are not covered by the Act, and are not foreclosed by the Act's exclusivity provision); Landis v. Landis, 664 N.E.2d 754 (Ind. Ct. App. 1996) (trial court and the Worker's Compensation Board, had jurisdiction to award an employee damages for assault and battery, intentional interference with business relationship, and intentional infliction of emotional distress after she disclaimed recovery for physical injuries, medical expense, or any impairment or disability defined by the Act); Branham v. Celadon Trucking Services, Inc., 744 N.E.2d 514 (Ind. Ct. App. 2001) (employee's claims of embarrassment, humiliation, injury to reputation, and extreme emotional distress, having no disabling qualities associated therewith, were not "personal injuries" within the context of the Act).

be "by accident."[1] As will be discussed later, this does not mean that an injury must be caused by "an accident," since, under certain circumstances, intentional or even willful misconduct may give rise to a compensable claim.

As used in the Indiana Worker's Compensation Act, the term "injury or death by accident" means unexpected injury or death.[2] As stated by the Court of Appeals of Indiana in its opinion in the matter of *Inland Steel Co. v. Almodovar*:[3]

> Perhaps it is a mistake to attempt to define "accident" when what we are concerned with is not the definition of the word standing alone but the concept expressed in the phrase: "injury by accident." If we accept, which we do, the concept expressed in Indian Creek then "injury by accident" is the equivalent of "accidental injury." Which is to say that "injury by accident" is not the equivalent of "injury caused by an accident" or "injury resulting from an accident." "[T]he test as to whether an injury is unexpected and so if received on a single occasion occurs 'by accident' is that the sufferer did not intend or expect that injury would on that particular occasion result from what he was doing."[4]

Whether the injury itself was unexpected is the question which must be answered to settle this inquiry, not whether the injury resulted from an unusual, unexpected, or untoward event.[5] In *Fields v. Cummins Employees Federal Credit Union*,[6] a credit union employee claimed that she was subjected to repeated incidents of sexual harassment by her supervisor. She initiated a common law tort action against her employer and supervisor, but the trial court granted summary judgment in favor of the defendants. On appeal, she claimed that her alleged injuries were not "by accident," and, therefore, the remedies available under the Act were not her exclusive remedies. She further claimed that, while the initial episode of sexual harassment may have been unexpected, the repeated episodes thereof lost their

---

[Section 3:22]

[1]IC 22-3-2-2 (a).

[2]Evans v. Yankeetown Dock Corp., 491 N.E.2d 969, 975 (Ind. 1986) ("To the extent this clarification is inconsistent with prior holdings, they are overruled.").

[3]Inland Steel Co. v. Almodovar, 172 Ind. App. 556, 361 N.E.2d 181 (1977).

[4]Inland Steel Co. v. Almodovar, 172 Ind. App. 556, 361 N.E.2d 181, 186–87 (1977); West v. LTV Steel Co., 839 F. Supp. 559 (N.D. Ind. 1993); Bailor v. Salvation Army, 854 F. Supp. 1341 (N.D. Ind. 1994), judgment aff'd, 51 F.3d 678 (7th Cir. 1995).

[5]Bertoch v. NBD Corp, 813 N.E.2d 1159 (Ind. 2004); Savich v. Blaw-Knox Foundry & Mill Machinery, Inc., 501 N.E.2d 464 (Ind. Ct. App. 1986).

[6]Fields v. Cummins Employees Federal Credit Union, 540 N.E.2d 631 (Ind. Ct. App. 1989) (disapproved of by, Wine-Settergren v. Lamey, 716 N.E.2d 381 (Ind. 1999)).

unexpected characteristic and ceased to be accidental. The court ruled that an injury need not result from a single occurrence in order to be considered accidental, and therefore concluded that her injuries were "by accident" within the meaning of the Act.[7]

In *Gordon v. Chrysler Motor Corp.*,[8] an assembly line worker was struck in the face by his foreman while at work and sustained serious injuries and subsequent permanent disabilities. Thereafter, he filed both a claim for worker's compensation benefits and a tort action against his foreman and employer. The trial court granted Chrysler's motion for summary judgment, and the court of appeals affirmed. The facts, as set forth in the court's opinion, and Gordon's arguments, are somewhat unique. The court wrote:

> Gordon argues that because he "expected" Harris's verbal and physical outburst, a finding that the event occurred "by accident" is precluded. Gordon claims he anticipated the impending assault after he learned of the reason for the meeting due to Harris's "violent reputation for a pattern of abuse and profanity . . . among Chrysler employees that Foreman Harris supervised." Thus, Gordon asserts he anticipated the beating because his "previous knowledge formed his state of mind."
>
> In *Yankeetown* our supreme court concluded the statutory phrase "by accident" should be construed literally and not be reinterpreted to mean "by *an* accident." The court then explained that an injury by accident under the worker's compensation laws in an *unexpected* injury, i.e., an injury that the sufferer did not expect to occur. Thus, the supreme court refers to the unexpectedness of the injury, not the unexpectedness of the behavior causing or resulting in the injury. Accordingly, an unexpected injury need not occur on a single occasion . . . .
>
> Thus, an injured worker's state of mind is generally irrelevant except when establishing a bar to compensation, e.g., an employee who intentionally self-inflicts a wound (or encourages another to wound him or her) in an illegal attempt to obtain monetary compensation that he or she is not entitled to under the confines of the Act . . . .
>
> . . . Gordon's claim he anticipated the beating as a result of his "previous knowledge" (established from rumors of Harris's abusive reputation) cannot, as a matter of law, eradicate the "unexpectedness" of Gordon's injury. The altercation between Gordon and his foreman is an "expected" incident because fist fights are an expected occurrence among co-workers. *See, e.g., Skinner v. Martin* (1983), Ind. App., 455 N.E.2d 1168. Assuming Gordon's "anticipation" reasonably may have caused him to expect a confrontation, perhaps resulting in being struck and suffering a red face or being knocked

---

[7]Fields v. Cummins Employees Federal Credit Union, 540 N.E.2d 631, 634, (Ind. Ct. App. 1989) (disapproved of by, Wine-Settergren v. Lamey, 716 N.E.2d 381 (Ind. 1999)).

[8]Gordon v. Chrysler Motor Corp., 585 N.E.2d 1362 (Ind. Ct. App. 1992) (rejected by, Baker v. Westinghouse Elec. Corp., 637 N.E.2d 1271 (Ind. 1994)).

to the floor, no reasonable employee would expect injuries resulting in his disability.

The trial court did not err in determining that as a matter of law Gordon's injury occurred "by accident," thus satisfying the first requirement for leaving a compensatory relief claim solely under the auspices of the Act.[9]

The Indiana Supreme Court went one step further and approached this issue from a different perspective in its opinion in the matter of *Tippmann v. Hensler*.[10] There, Hensler sustained a severe and permanent injury to his eye while at work when he was struck by a paintball fired by his co-employee, Tippmann, when the two of them were in a room where paintball guns were serviced. Hensler filed a worker's compensation claim against his employer and reached a settlement with the company. He then filed a lawsuit against Tippmann. Tippmann moved for summary judgment arguing that the exclusivity provision of the Act barred Hensler's action against him. The trial court denied Tippmann's motion, an interlocutory appeal ensued, and, ultimately, the Supreme Court granted transfer. The Court was called upon to decide what legal effect a co-worker's intent to harm had within the context of a defense made by him that the employee whom he injured sustained his injury "by accident." After noting that the exclusivity provision of the Act extends immunity not only to the employer, but also to those "in the same employ" as the injured employee, the Court stated:

> In *Baker v. Westinghouse Elec. Corp.*, 637 N.E.2d 1271 (Ind. 1994), we reaffirmed the *Evans* interpretation of "by accident" as meaning an unexpected injury, rather than an unexpected or unusual event. We noted, however, that *Evans'* victim-focused "by accident" test left out another important consideration for determining when an employee's injury, if caused by his employer, was accidental: the *employer's* intentions and expectations. *Id.* at 1273. Thus, we stated, "Because we believe an injury occurs 'by accident' only when it is intended by neither the employee nor the employer, the intentional torts of an employer are necessarily beyond the pale of the act."
>
> . . . .
>
> . . . We think that the same considerations which prevent an employer who has intentionally injured its employee from claiming that the injury was "by accident" also prevent a co-employee who has intentionally injured a fellow employee from asserting the injury was "by accident." Therefore, following the logical progression from *Evans* to *Baker* to the case at hand, we hold that a party to a worker's compensation suit cannot claim that the injury at is-

---

[9]Gordon v. Chrysler Motor Corp., 585 N.E.2d 1362, 1363–64 (Ind. Ct. App. 1992) (rejected by, Baker v. Westinghouse Elec. Corp., 637 N.E.2d 1271 (Ind. 1994)) (citations and footnote omitted).

[10]Tippmann v. Hensler, 716 N.E.2d 372 (Ind. 1999).

sue occurred "by accident," and thereby receive compensation or immunity under the Act, when that party intended harm to arise from the acts which resulted in the injury. Therefore, the appropriate test for determining whether the injury was accidentally caused is the question, "Did the party who is advocating the applicability of the Act intend for harm to result from the actions that party undertook?" If so, then the injury did not occur "by accident" for that particular litigant.[11]

The Court was not unmindful of the fact that its holding could create some uncertainty and confusion for future litigants since the element of an individual's intentions was now being interjected into the definition of the term "by accident." The Court analyzed and decided the issue:

> Because this test focuses more on the intentions of the party alleging "accidental" injury than on the injury itself, one might notice that the same injury can be both "by accident" and not "by accident," depending on who is alleging the applicability of the Act. Such a circumstance, however, is not unusual. According to the North Carolina Court of Appeals, "[t]he mere fact . . . that an injury is termed 'accidental' from the injured employee's viewpoint, requiring the employer to pay compensation under the Act, does not mean that the injury is accidental from the viewpoint of the intentional assailant." *Andrews v. Peters*, 55 N.C. App. 124, 284 S.E.2d 748, 750 (1981). For instance, an employee who is repeatedly stabbed by a fellow employee during an argument at work could file a claim for and receive worker's compensation on the premise that the injury she suffered was "by accident." In this instance, neither the employee nor the employer intended or expected the injury; therefore, to those parties it was unexpected and accidental.
>
> When the same employee, however, then brings suit against the co-employee for the intentional tort, it is the co-employee tortfeasor, and not plaintiff who, in order to receive immunity, must allege that the stabbing injury he inflicted was "by accident," something he is unable to do. As Professor Larson states, "The legal reason for permitting the common-law suit for direct assault by the employer or co-employee . . . is that the same person cannot commit an intentional assault and then allege it was accidental." 6 Arthur Larson, *Larson's Worker's Compensation Law*, § 68.21(b), at 13-123 (1997). He further states, "There is nothing inconsistent in this result, curious as it may seem on the surface, since it is quite proper to analyze the incident in each type of action from the standpoint of the person having the burden of establishing his case or defense." *Id.* § 68.12 at 13-12.[12]

The Court then recognized that its rationale might seem at odds with those prior decisions of the appellate courts finding that a co-employee's intentional torts were deemed to produce

---

[11]Tippmann v. Hensler, 716 N.E.2d 372, 375–76 (Ind. 1999) (citations and footnote omitted).

[12]Tippmann v. Hensler, 716 N.E.2d 372, 376–77 (Ind. 1999).

injuries "by accident" for purposes of coverage under the Act. The
Court noted:

> There is one important distinction, however, between these many
> cases and the case at bar. These cases involved either an injured
> employee's attempt to sue her employer for an injury intentionally
> caused her by a co-employee, *see e.g., Foshee v. Shoney's, Inc.*, 637
> N.E.2d 1277 (Ind. 1994); *Evans v. Yankeetown Dock Corp.*, 491
> N.E.2d 969 (Ind. 1986); *Gordon v. Chrysler Motor Corp.*, 585 N.E.2d
> 1362 (Ind. App. 1992); *Fields v. Cummins Emp. Fed. Credit Union*,
> 540 N.E.2d 631 (Ind. App. 4 Dist. 1989); *Shelby v. Truck & Bus
> Group Div. of GMC*, 533 N.E.2d 1296 (Ind. App. 1989); or an
> employer's attempt to overturn an award of compensation to an em-
> ployee who was intentionally injured by a co-employee, *see e.g.,
> Inland Steel Co. v. Flannery*, 88 Ind. App. 163 N.E. 841 (1928);
> *Furst Kerber Cut Stone Co. v. Mayo*, 82 Ind. App. 363, 144 N.E. 857
> (1924); *Payne v. Wall*, 76 Ind. App. 634, 132 N.E. 707 (1921); *Muel-
> ler v. Klingman*, 73 Ind. App. 136, 125 N.E. 464 (1919). None of
> these cases involved the applicability of the Worker's Compensation
> Act to an intentional tort action between fellow employees. This is
> an important distinction, because in all these cases the party alleg-
> ing that the injury was "by accident" was not the party that had
> intentionally caused the harm. Thus, from the standpoint of the one
> alleging accidental injury in each case, the injury was not intended
> or expected, and was, to him or her, "accidental."[13]

In a footnote, the Court stated:

> Our review of Indiana cases produces only one that clearly finds
> a intentional tort action against a fellow employee barred by the
> Worker's Compensation Act, and another that involves what might
> be construed as an intentional tort but is never discussed as such.
> The former is *Skinner v. Martin*, 455 N.E.2d 1168 (Ind. Ct. App.
> 1983), in which an employee who was assaulted by his co-employee
> brought an action against that co-employee for the resulting
> injuries. The court found that action barred by the Worker's
> Compensation Act, but its analysis focused entirely upon the "aris-
> ing out of and in the course of" requirements, implicitly finding the
> "by accident" requirement met by stating "Such employment-related
> assaults are not uncommon, . . . and the Act should be liberally
> construed to include them as compensable . . . . The other case is
> *Nelson v. Denkins*, 598 N.E.2d 558 (Ind. Ct. App. 1992), in which
> . . . [t]he Court of Appeals, citing *Evans*, considered only the
> *victim's expectations* when deciding the injury was "by accident." *Id.*
> The outcome would remain the same, however, even if the court
> had also reviewed the intentions of the tortfeasor in its "by ac-
> cident" determination: nowhere does the opinion indicate that
> Nelson alleged an intent to harm on the part of Denkins, nor does a

---

[13]Tippmann v. Hensler, 716 N.E.2d 372, 377 (Ind. 1999) (footnote omitted).

shove on the shoulder, accompanied by the command to "get back to work," generally carry with it an intent to cause injury.[14]

The Court found three specific justifications for excluding intentional tortfeasors from immunity, pursuant to the Act, when they are defending an intentional tort claim. First, the common understanding of an injury which is accidental in nature does not encompass one inflicted by the intent, design, or obvious motivation of the one causing the injury. Second, those intentionally causing injuries should be deterred from doing so and should be exposed to regular civil damages. It would be counterproductive and serve no social purpose to allow one guilty of intentional misconduct to shield itself from liability through the use of the exclusivity provision of the Act. Third, Indiana generally denies the ability to insure against or waive liability for intentional torts, and, therefore, the public policy of this state would not be served by a back-handed attempt to do so.[15]

The Court's opinion in *Tippmann* is well reasoned, consistent with prior decisions on the subject matter, and instructive of the manner in which future litigants, the board, and the courts should address the issues raised therein.

Although dissimilar factually, cases involving repetitive motion or cumulative trauma injuries have presented like arguments since by nature, those types of injuries do not arise from a single, well-defined occurrence, and the employee does not anticipate that disability will result therefrom. For example, in *Four Star Fabricators, Inc. v. Barrett*,[16] the claimant sought compensation for an injury to his back. His job required him to repeatedly maneuver and lift heavy steel plates. On one occasion, a plate struck him in the back, he sought medical treatment for the pain he experienced, missed three days work, and then returned to his job. Four years later, the demands of his job increased substantially. He once again began to experience back pain while working and the pain continued. At home one day, he stooped over to pick up his child and felt a sharp pain and something "pop" in his back. He was diagnosed with a herniated disc and did not return to work for seven months after this incident. He was later laid off, and thereafter applied for and was granted worker's compensation benefits for his back condition. On appeal, his employer argued that there was no relationship between Barrett's injury and his employment at Four Star. In affirming the board's award in favor of Barrett, the court of appeals stated:

---

[14]Tippmann v. Hensler, 716 N.E.2d 372, 377 n.6 (Ind. 1999).

[15]Tippmann v. Hensler, 716 N.E.2d 372, 379–80 (Ind. 1999).

[16]Four Star Fabricators, Inc. v. Barrett, 638 N.E.2d 792 (Ind. Ct. App. 1994).

Four Star places undue emphasis on the fact that Barrett's diagnosis with a herniated disc and resulting worker's compensation claim arose only after he suffered an episode of acute back pain in the home. We cannot agree that the place of this one episode of back pain determines whether Barrett's injury occurred in the course of his employment at Four Star. In *Evans v. Yankeetown Dock Corp.* (1986), Ind., 491 N.E.2d 969, our supreme court clarified the requirement of an accidental injury under the Worker's Compensation Act and held that an injury is accidental "when it is the unexpected consequence of the usual exertion or exposure to the particular employee's job." *Id.* at 974. The *Evans* decision represents a shift under the Worker's Compensation Act from an inquiry into whether an injury is the result of *an* accident as a discrete event to whether the injury is *accidental* or unexpected. *See id.*

In *Union City Body Co. v. Lambdin* (1991), Ind. App., 569 N.E.2d 373, this court interpreted *Evans* and noted that an injury may be compensable under the Act if it "happens day after day on the job and the combination of all the days produce [sic] the injurious result." *Id.* at 374. Accordingly, when a disabling condition is produced by repeatedly performing the same job function over several years, the claimant is not required to show the resultant injury and damage "was due to one particular blow which produced the particular injury." *Lovely v. Cooper Indus. Prod., Inc.* (1981), Ind. App., 429 N.E.2d 274, 278–79. An employee may have a compensable worker's compensation claim when his condition gradually develops from the cumulative effect of his work activities. *See Duvall v. ICI Americas, Inc.* (1993), Ind. App., 621 N.E.2d 1122, 1126.

Thus, our courts have recognized that the definition of an "accidental injury" under the Worker's Compensation Act includes those injuries which occur incrementally over time. In other words, the repetitive motions required by the employee's job functions may give rise to a compensable injury, even though the injury is not attributable to any discrete and identifiable date, time or event. *See Duvall,* 621 N.E.2d at 1126 (carpal tunnel syndrome resulting from repetitive, day-to-day motions required at job); *Lambdin,* 569 N.E.2d at 373–74 (employee's day after day bending, twisting, stooping and lifting while working combined to produce injurious result); *American Maize Prod. Co. v. Nichiporchik* (1940), 108 Ind. App. 502, 511, 29 N.E.2d 801, 805 (traumatic concussions delivered to employee's hands by air hammer over long period of time produced Dupuytren's contraction).

In determining whether an employee's "cumulative trauma" injury arose "in the course of" employment, the focus is not merely on the place where the injury manifested itself. *Cf. Holland-St. Louis Sugar Co. v. Shraluka* (1917), 64 Ind. App. 545, 550, 116 N.E. 330, 331 (accident or injury may arise out of or in the course of employment even when employee is not actually working at time of accident or injury). Rather, where the evidence demonstrates that a cumulative trauma injury developed during the performance of the employee's job functions, the injury occurs "in the course of" employment, whether it first manifests itself in or out of the workplace. This conclusion is consistent with both our supreme court's interpretation of the accidental injury requirement in *Evans* and the humane purpose of the Worker's Compensation Act which requires a broad and liberal construction of the phrase "in the course of the employment." *See Goldstone v. Kozma* (1971), 149 Ind. App. 626, 631–32, 274 N.E.2d 304, 307.

. . . .

Accordingly, the evidence demonstrated that Barrett's herniated disc injury was produced at least in part by the cumulative effect that his work functions had on his back, despite the fact that the injury first manifested itself outside the workplace. Thus, Barrett's injury, arising from the cumulative effect of workplace trauma to his back, was an injury which arose out of and in the course of his employment at Four Star just as though the trauma had occurred as a discrete event in the workplace. *See Duvall,* 621 N.E.2d at 1126 . . . . [T]he medical evidence established that Barrett's herniated disc was the result of a degenerative condition produced in part by his bending and lifting at Four Star. There is no conflicting medical evidence that Barrett's ordinary act of bending to pick up his child was the sole cause of his herniated disk condition. Barrett's incident at home was merely one bending motion which followed countless, damaging others in the workplace.[17]

§ 3:23   Injuries arising out of employment

In order for an injury to be compensable under the Indiana Worker's Compensation Act, it must "arise out of" the injured employee's employment.[1] Whether the injury did or did not arise out of the worker's employment is an issue which must necessarily be determined by the facts unique to his or her case.[2] Needless to say, there has been an abundance of opinions written on this subject, and certain principals of law have become apparent:

"Out of" portends some probe into causation and the relationship of a particular accident and a particular harm to the employment sought to be charged. The primary inquiry is directed toward the question of whether the accidental injury or death was the

---

[17]Four Star Fabricators, Inc. v. Barrett, 638 N.E.2d 792, 795–96 (Ind. Ct. App. 1994) (emphasis in original). See also discussion of Duvall v. ICI Americas, Inc., 621 N.E.2d 1122 (Ind. Ct. App. 1993), in § 7:12, Occupational diseases— Essential elements to claim for compensation (court of appeals holding that carpal tunnel syndrome is not an occupational disease), and Inland Steel Co. v. Pavlinac, 865 N.E.2d 690 (Ind. Ct. App. 2007).

[Section 3:23]

[1]IC 22-3-2-2(a).

[2]Tapia v. Heavner, 648 N.E.2d 1202 (Ind. Ct. App. 1995); Burke v. Wilfong, 638 N.E.2d 865 (Ind. Ct. App. 1994); Sanchez v. Hamara, 534 N.E.2d 756 (Ind. Ct. App. 1989); L. W. Edison, Inc. v. Teagarden, 423 N.E.2d 709 (Ind. Ct. App. 1981).

outgrowth of the employment, whether it was due to the employment, whether it was work-induced.[3]

It has been stated that "an injury arises out of the employment when there exists a causal connection between it and the employment, or, expressing the same idea in different form, when the employment is in some way responsible for the injury. It is upon this principle of industrial responsibility that the compensation acts find their theoretical and constitutional basis."[4] In its opinion in *Construction Management and Design, Inc. v. Vanderweele*,[5] the court of appeals stated:

> The phrase "arising out of the employment" refers to the origin and cause of the injury, and has been defined as follows:
>
> "For an accident to arise out of employment, there must be a causal relationship between the employment and the injury. However, such a connection is established when the accident arises out of a risk which a reasonably prudent person might comprehend as incidental to the work." *Thiellen, supra*, 530 N.E.2d at 767 (quoting *Blaw-Knox Foundry & Mill Machinery, Inc. v. Dacus* (1987), Ind. App., 505 N.E.2d 101, 102, *trans. denied*).
>
> Generally, the causal connection between the work and the accident must be such that a reasonably prudent person would comprehend the injury as incidental to the work undertaken. *See Crowe v. Blum* (7th Cir. 1993), 9 F.3d 32 (decided under Indiana law). The causal connection is evaluated by considering the type of accident that caused the injury in relation to the nature of the employment.[6]

In *Price v. R. & A. Sales*,[7] the court of appeals further defined the issue:

> An injury arises "out of employment" when a causal nexus exists between the injury sustained and the duties or services performed by the injured employee. *Weldy*, 616 N.E.2d at 404. This causal relationship is established when a reasonably prudent person considers a risk to be incidental to the employment at the time of entering into it or when the facts indicate a connection between the conditions under which the employee works and the injury. *Id.*[8]

Perhaps the most expansive definition of "arising out of employ-

---

[3]B. Small, *Workmen's Compensation Law in Indiana*, § 6.1 (1950).

[4]Burroughs Adding Mach. Co. v. Dehn, 110 Ind. App. 483, 39 N.E.2d 499, 502 (1942); Broderick Co. v. Flemming, 116 Ind. App. 668, 65 N.E.2d 257 (1946).

[5]Construction Management and Design, Inc. v. Vanderweele, 660 N.E.2d 1046 (Ind. Ct. App. 1996).

[6]Construction Management and Design, Inc. v. Vanderweele, 660 N.E.2d 1046, 1051 (Ind. Ct. App. 1996).

[7]Price v. R & A Sales, 773 N.E.2d 873 (Ind. Ct. App. 2002).

[8]Price v. R & A Sales, 773 N.E.2d 873, 875 (Ind. Ct. App. 2002); Weldy v. Kline, 616 N.E.2d 398 (Ind. Ct. App. 1993); Suburban Ready Mix Concrete, (Div.

ment" is contained in the opinion of the Indiana Supreme Court in the matter of *Wine-Settergren v. Lamey.*[9] There, Wine-Settergren and Lamey were co-employees at a radio station. Lamey, in an attempt to apologize for shouting at another employee and to console Wine-Settergren, who had been startled by his conduct, embraced her in a strong hug. Wine-Settergren had recently returned to work after having surgery on her nose. Lamey's hug was too forceful and, as a result thereof, Wine-Settergren's nose was injured further. Even though her worker's compensation insurance carrier paid for nearly all of her medical bills, Wine-Settergren never filed a worker's compensation claim for additional benefits under the Act. Instead, she sued Lamey to recover damages in tort. In affirming the trial court's dismissal of her action based upon the exclusivity provision of the worker's compensation act, the Supreme Court stated the following:

> An accidental injury "arises out of employment" when a causal nexus exists between the action causing the injury and the employee's employment. *Gordon v. Chrysler Motor Corp.,* 585 N.E.2d 1362, 1365 (Ind. Ct. App. 1992). This nexus is established when a reasonably prudent person considers the injury to be born out of a risk incidental to the employment, or when the facts indicate a connection between the injury and the circumstances under which the employment occurs. *Id.* "Employment" here means more than merely performing services directly related to the job for which the employee was hired. It includes activities reasonably incidental to one's employment, such as recreation at an employer-sponsored off-site business meeting or after-hours party, *e.g., Noble v. Zimmerman,* 237 Ind. 556, 146 N.E.2d 828 (1957); *Ski World, Inc. v. Fife,* 489 N.E.2d 72 (Ind. Ct. App. (1986), driving to or exiting from work, *e.g., Thiellen,* 530 N.E.2d 765; *O'Dell,* 173 Ind. App. 106, 362 N.E.2d 862, and personal acts reasonably necessary to the life, comfort, and convenience of an employee even though they are not technically act of service to the employer, *Evans,* 491 N.E.2d at 976; *Vendome Hotel, Inc. v. Gibson,* 122 Ind. App. 604, 608, 105 N.E.2d 906, 908–09 (1952); *Holland-St. Louis Sugar Co. v. Shraluka,* 64 Ind. App. 545, 549–50, 116 N.E. 330, 331 (1917). "For example, where an employee is washing up after work, satisfying his thirst, seeking fresh air, answering telephone calls, eating lunch, or going to the toilet, such personal acts have been held to be in the pursuit of personal comfort or convenience and thus incidental to employment." *Indiana & Michigan Elec. Co.,* 494 N.E.2d at 993 (citing 30 I.L.E. *Workmen's Compensation* § 125 (1960); B. Small, *Workmen's Compensation Law* § 6.15 (1950).

> Maintaining a congenial work environment where employees get along with one another is desired by both the employer and the employees. For the employer, such an environment increases employee productivity and teamwork and decreases employee turnover.

---

of Terre Haute Concrete) v. Zion by Zion, 443 N.E.2d 1241 (Ind. Ct. App. 1983).

[9]Wine-Settergren v. Lamey, 716 N.E.2d 381 (Ind. 1999).

For the employees, it increases the amount of enjoyment they have while at their place of business . . . . While embracing another employee in an apologetic and conciliatory hug may not be found in Lamey's job description, such actions are ones that could be reasonably expected between co-employees. Counsel for Lamey articulated this sentiment well:

> "A wide variety of interaction occurs among employees in a work place. Hands are shaken, backs are patted, hugs are given all as part of the natural and habitual activities of employees working together. This kind of activity is as much a part of the employment as the machinery used in the workplace."

Even among co-employees who are not the closest of friends, such actions could be reasonably expected. As Judge DeBruler noted in *Moran v. State,* 644 N.E.2d 536, 541 (Ind. 1994), "[I]nhabitants of this state have always valued neighborliness, hospitality, and concern for others, even those who may be strangers." Because no evidence was presented to show that [the employer] had prohibited such actions, or had previously reprimanded employees for similar activities in the past to the common knowledge of all the employees, the accidental injury caused by Lamey's actions arose out of his employment.[10]

The Indiana Supreme Court, in *Depuy, Inc. v. Farmer,*[11] explained a "risk incidental to employment" in the following language:

> Whether a risk or injury is incidental to employment is determined by the activity in which the employee was engaged when injured and its relationship to: 1) "his duties;" 2) "the reasonableness of employee's acts in relation to the sum total of conditions and circumstances constituting the work setting at the time of the injury;" and 3) "the knowledge and acquiescence of the employer in situations where acts incidental to employment are being done in violation of company rules." *March,* 813 N.E.2d at 1169 (citing *Segally v. Ancerys,* 486 N.E.2d 578, 581 (Ind. Ct. App. 1985).
>
> . . . Farmer's injuries were incurred while he was performing services for Depuy (i.e., walking towards the time clock to end his shift), and Swindel's loss of control and unprovoked attack does not change that. Accordingly, the incident was within the scope of employment as ordinary courtesies to a fellow employee, and Farmer's injuries "arose out of" his employment.[12]

While this may seem simple enough, it isn't; woven within the fabric of these principles is the analysis which the appellate courts have undertaken, since 1981, on the "increased risk" and "positional risk" doctrines.

The "increased risk" doctrine, generally, requires an employee

---

[10]Wine-Settergren v. Lamey, 716 N.E.2d 381, 389–90 (Ind. 1999) (footnotes omitted).

[11]DePuy, Inc. v. Farmer, 847 N.E.2d 160 (Ind. 2006).

[12]DePuy, Inc. v. Farmer, 847 N.E.2d 160, 164–65 (Ind. 2006).

to show that the accident and the employee's resulting injuries occurred because of an increased risk created by the employment. If the employee can demonstrate that, because of the requirements of the job, he or she was exposed to a quantitatively greater degree of risk, or a risk more frequently, or exposed to risk for a longer period of time than the general public, then the employee will be permitted to recover. The doctrine, however, is fraught with difficulties, as Professor Small has noted:

"An increased risk might be said by some to be a risk greater than that to which the public generally is subjected. Others might say it is a risk greater than that to which others in the same locality are subjected. Others might say it is a risk greater than that to which other fellow-employees are subjected. And others might say it is a risk greater than that to which the particular workman is normally exposed. There are precedents in the Indiana cases to support any of these propositions; and there are precedents which support none of them."[13]

An "increased risk" analysis was made by the Court of Appeals of Indiana in the matter of *Kovatch v. A.M. General*.[14] The case involved a fall at work resulting in death. The specific cause of the employee's fall was unclear, but there was evidence presented by the employer that Kovatch did suffer from a condition which may have caused him to fall in the past. The court stated:

Workplace falls can result from either an employment, personal, or neutral risk, or from a combination thereof. Some falls clearly result from risks personal to the employee; that is, they are caused by a pre-existing illness or condition unrelated to employment. *See* 1 Arthur Larson, *The Law of Worker's Compensation*, § 12.00 at 3-416 (1996). As a general matter, these "idiopathic" falls are not compensable. *Id.* § 12.11 at 3-423. In contrast, some falls are 'unexplained' in that there is no indication of causation. *Id.* § 1031(a) at 3-104. Most jurisdictions compensate such falls, classifying them as neutral risks. *Id.*

A more difficult analytical situation arises when the employment itself increases or contributes to the harm or risk suffered by an employee in an idiopathic fall. Larson states:

"When an employee, solely because of a nonoccupational heart attack, epileptic fit, or fainting spell, falls and sustains a skull fracture or other injury, the question arises whether the skull fracture (as distinguished from the internal effects of the heart attack or disease, which of course are not compensable) is an injury arising out of the employment.

---

[13]B. Small, *Workmen's Compensation Law in Indiana* § 6.2, pages 50–51 (1976 supp.), as quoted in Olinger Const. Co. v. Mosbey, 427 N.E.2d 910, 913 (Ind. Ct. App. 1981). See also E. I. Du Pont De Nemours Co. v. Lilly, 226 Ind. 267, 79 N.E.2d 387 (1948), wherein the Indiana Supreme Court noted the lack of consistency in prior opinions, and the "despair" encountered by lower courts in resolving disputes through application of the doctrine.

[14]Kovatch v. A.M. General, 679 N.E.2d 940 (Ind. Ct. App. 1997).

The basic rule, on which there is now general agreement, is that the effects of such a fall are compensable if the employment places the employee in a position increasing the dangerous effects of such a fall, such as on a height, near machinery or sharp corners, or in a moving vehicle. The currently controversial question is whether the effects of an idiopathic fall to the level ground or bare floor should be deemed to arise out of the employment."

Id. § 12.11 at 3-416 to 3-423. Our supreme court has decided that question in *Pollock v. Studebaker Corp.* 230 Ind. 622, 623–24, 105 N.E.2d 513, 513–14 (1952). In *Pollock*, the court affirmed the Board's denial of compensation to an employee for injuries that he sustained as result of an idiopathic fall onto a concrete floor. *Id.*

In the present case, the Board found that the conditions existing in the area where Kovatch fell did not increase his risk of falling and that Kovatch had several pre-existing conditions which caused his fall. The Board therefore denied Kovatch death benefits under the Act. Given our deferential standard of review, we cannot disturb the Board's conclusion that Kovatch's fall was idiopathic and, therefore, noncompensable.[15]

In *Conway ex rel. Conway v. School City of East Chicago*,[16] a school bus driver had completed his duties for the day and was headed home in his own personal vehicle. Before he exited the lot where he was required to park his school bus, he was shot and killed by an employee of the lot. There was some evidence in the case of a personal dispute that existed between the decedent and his assailant prior to the shooting. In affirming a denial of worker's compensation benefits, the court stated:

Under an increased risk analysis there is *per se* no causal nexus when an injury arises from a personal conflict unrelated to work. . . . [T]he Board in the case at bar determined that Curt's death was a result of prior animosity by Harris. No evidence was presented to the Board nor does the record reveal that Harris's animosity toward Curt may have been work related. This personal risk, which Curt was subjected to, was not incidental to his employment because the public at large is also subjected to that same risk of being attacked for personal reasons on a daily basis, regardless of where they are employed. As such, we find that Curt was not subjected to an increased risk of Harris harming him by working for the City. Therefore, Curt's death did not arise out of his employment with the City.[17]

The "positional risk" doctrine states, essentially, that an ac-

---

[15]Kovatch v. A.M. General, 679 N.E.2d 940, 943–44 (Ind. Ct. App. 1997) (footnotes omitted); Conway ex rel. Conway v. School City of East Chicago, 734 N.E.2d 594, 599, 146 Ed. Law Rep. 844 (Ind. Ct. App. 2000). It should be noted that the court also made an abbreviated "positional risk" analysis in its opinion. See also Smith v. Bob Evans Farms, Inc., 754 N.E.2d 18 (Ind. Ct. App. 2001).

[16]Conway ex rel. Conway v. School City of East Chicago, 734 N.E.2d 594, 146 Ed. Law Rep. 844 (Ind. Ct. App. 2000).

[17]Conway ex rel. Conway v. School City of East Chicago, 734 N.E.2d 594, 599, 146 Ed. Law Rep. 844 (Ind. Ct. App. 2000). It should be noted that the

cident and resulting injuries "arise out of" employment if the employee is required by his or her job to be in the place where the injury occurs, and the employee is in such a place to discharge the duties of his or her employment. The theory underlying the rule is that the injury would not have occurred if the employee's job had not required him or her to be in the place where the injury occurred. Without specifically stating so, the appellate court has applied the doctrine any number of times in traveling employee cases to uphold an award of compensation.[18] In *Olinger Const. Co. v. Mosbey*,[19] an employee (Mosbey) was murdered by a disgruntled former employee of Olinger while Mosbey was staying in a motel room 150 miles from his home. The facts of the case established that Mosbey was there because his job required him to be at a construction site near the motel. The court found that Mosbey was a traveling employee, that his death arose out of and in the course of his employment, and that his surviving spouse and dependent children were entitled to receive compensation benefits. Interestingly enough, the court stated in its opinion, "We emphasize our conclusion and our resulting holding is limited to traveling employees."[20]

Categories of risks were first enunciated by the Indiana Supreme Court in its opinion in *Evans v. Yankeetown Dock Corp.*,[21] and later discussed by the Court of Appeals of Indiana in *K-Mart Corp. v. Novak*.[22] The latter involved the death of a store clerk murdered by a lunatic during the course of a shooting spree which began away from the store. Novak was at her station inside the store when the gunman entered and killed her. Her husband was awarded death benefits by the board, and K-Mart appealed. In part, K-Mart argued that the risk of being shot by a lunatic was a risk common to the public at large, was in no way peculiar to her employment, and, therefore, her death did not "arise out of" her employment for the company. In striking down K-Mart's arguments and ruling that Novak's death was compensable, the court of appeals stated:

> As a general rule, under Indiana law a risk is incidental to the employment if the risk involved is not one to which the public at

---

Court also made an abbreviated "positional risk" analysis in its opinion. See also Smith v. Bob Evans Farms, Inc., 754 N.E.2d 18 (Ind. Ct. App. 2001).

[18]Lasear, Inc. v. Anderson, 99 Ind. App. 428, 192 N.E. 762 (1934); Business Systems v. Gilfillen, 120 Ind. App. 565, 92 N.E.2d 868 (1950); C. & E. Trucking Corp. v. Stahl, 135 Ind. App. 600, 181 N.E.2d 21 (1962); In re Harraden, 66 Ind. App. 298, 118 N.E. 142 (1917).

[19]Olinger Const. Co. v. Mosbey, 427 N.E.2d 910 (Ind. Ct. App. 1981).

[20]Olinger Const. Co. v. Mosbey, 427 N.E.2d 910, 915 (Ind. Ct. App. 1981).

[21]Evans v. Yankeetown Dock Corp., 491 N.E.2d 969 (Ind. 1986).

[22]K-Mart Corp. v. Novak, 521 N.E.2d 1346 (Ind. Ct. App. 1988).

large is subjected. *E.I. DuPont De Nemours v. Lilly* (1948), 226 Ind.
267, 262, 79 N.E.2d 387, 389; *Segally v. Ancerys* (1985), Ind. App.,
486 N.E.2d 578, 581; *Lincoln v. Whirlpool Corp.* (1972), 151 Ind.
App. 190, 196, 279 N.E.2d 596, 599–600; *Citizens' Independent
Telephone Co. v. Davis* (1950), 121 Ind. App. 20, 25, 94 N.E.2d 495,
498, *trans. denied* 229 Ind. 217, 97 N.E.2d 490). This general rule is
referred to as the "increased risk" test. *Olinger Const. Co. v. Mosbey*
(1981), Ind. App. 427 N.E.2d 910, 913, *trans. denied; Lincoln,* 151
Ind. App. At 196, 279 N.E.2d at 599. Our courts do not always
require proof of an increased risk. For example in assault cases, es-
pecially in those involving traveling employees or employees
subjected to street perils, the "arising out of" element can be satisfied without proof of an increased risk to the employee *Clem v.
Steveco, Inc.* (1983), Ind. App. 450 N.E.2d 550, 553; *Suburban Ready
Mix Concrete v. Zion* (1983), Ind. App., 443 N.E.2d 1241, 1242;
Ference at 737; *Mosbey* at 913; *Burroughs Adding Machine Co. v.
Dehn* (1942), 110 Ind. App. 483, 503, 39 N.E.2d 499, 507; *Lasear v.
Anderson* (1934), 99 Ind. App. 428, 434, 192 N.E. 762, 765. Our
supreme court also appears to have dispensed with the need to
show an increased risk in a recent case in which an employee was
attacked and killed by a lunatic. *Evans,* at 975. These cases allow
proof of a causal connection under the "positional risk" test. *Olinger,*
at 913; 1 Larson, *Workmen's Compensation Law* § 6.50 (1985).

Larson comments on the "positional risk" test, as follows:

"An important and growing number of courts are accepting the
full implications of the positional-risk test: An injury arises out of
the employment if it would not have occurred *but for* the fact that
the conditions and obligations of the employment placed claimant
in the position where he was injured. It is even more common for
the test to be approved and used in particular situations. This
theory supports compensation, for example, in cases of stray bul-
lets, roving lunatics, and other situations in which the only connection of the employment with the injury is that its obligations
placed the employee in the particular place at the particular time
when he was injured by some neutral force, meaning by 'neutral'
neither personal to the claimant nor distinctly associated with
the employment."

1 Larson, at § 6.50.[23]

In a footnote, the court set out Larson's three categories of
risks, along with some additional commentary by him:

(1) risks distinctly associated with employment, (2) risks personal
to the claimant, and (3) risks of neither distinctly employment nor
distinctly personal character (*i.e.,* neutral risks). Larson notes that
the neutral category presents risk of loss problems because
unfortunately the risk of loss of this category does not fall clearly
upon either the industry or the employee. In answering the question of who should bear the burden for neutral risks Larson states,
"[T]he usual answer in the past has been to leave this loss on the
employee, on the theory that he must meet the burden of proof of

---

[23]K-Mart Corp. v. Novak, 521 N.E.2d 1346, 1348–49 (Ind. Ct. App. 1988).

establishing affirmatively a clear causal connection between the conditions under which he worked and the occurrence of the injury. More recently, some courts have reasoned in the following vein: Either the employer or the employee must bear the loss; to show connection with the employment, there is at least the fact that the injury occurred while the employee was working; to show connection with the employee personally there is nothing; therefore, although the work connection is slender, it is at least stronger than any connection with the claimant's personal life."

1 Larson, at §§ 7.00–7.30.[24]

The court then went on to state that Indiana appears to follow the trend of jurisdictions that place the burden on the industry for neutral risks, citing *Evans*. Following that, the court cited with approval Larson's "neutral category of assaults" as including "[t]hose assaults which are in essence equivalent to blind or irrational forces, such as attacks by lunatics, drunks, small children, and other irresponsibles; completely unexplained assaults and assaults by mistake."[25]

Proceeding further, the court found that the risk in the present case should be analyzed using the "positional risk" doctrine and that the facts surrounding Novak's death fit within Larson's "neutral assaults" category. Therefore, the court upheld the award of compensation to her surviving spouse and went on to state:

> *This court notes also that the Board's finding that Margaret's death "arose out of" her employment with K-Mart would be supportable under the "increased risk" test. The facts presented to the Board, although conflicting, indicated that the risk of encountering dangerous people was higher for Margaret than the non-employed general public. Unlike persons who do not work in stores and who would not be required to deal with and encounter potentially dangerous people, because of her job, Margaret was required to deal with the public and encounter potentially dangerous persons including lunatics. Therefore, the Board did not err by concluding that Margaret's death was compensable.*[26]

With the decision in *K-Mart*, the line between the "increased risk" doctrine and the "positional risk" doctrine starts to become blurred. Later decisions from the appellate courts do not provide much clarity.

---

[24]K-Mart Corp. v. Novak, 521 N.E.2d 1346, 1349 (Ind. Ct. App. 1988).

[25]K-Mart Corp. v. Novak, 521 N.E.2d 1346, 1349 (Ind. Ct. App. 1988) (quoting 1 Larson, § 11.30).

[26]K-Mart Corp. v. Novak, 521 N.E.2d 1346, 1350 (Ind. Ct. App. 1988) (emphasis added).

In *Peavler v. Mitchell & Scott Mach. Co., Inc.*,[27] the court of appeals applied the "positional risk" doctrine once again, but this time held that a claim was not compensable under the Act. There, Peavler, while at work, was shot and killed by her former boyfriend. After reiterating Larson's three categories of risk, the court stated:

> Generally, the risks that fall in the first and third categories are covered by the Indiana Worker's Compensation Act. *K-Mart*, 521 N.E.2d 1346, n. 1. However, harms which arise in the second category, from risks personal to the claimant/employee, are universally noncompensable. 1 Larson § 7.00. If the employee has a mortal personal enemy who finds and murders the employee while the employee is at work, the employment cannot be said to have had any causal relationship to the death. 1 Larson § 7.20. When the animosity or dispute that culminates in an assault on the employee is imported into the workplace from the claimant's domestic or private life, and is not exacerbated by the employment, the assault cannot be said to arise out of the employment under any circumstances. 1 Larson § 11.21.

> Indiana follows the general rule that a personal squabble with a third person that culminates in an assault is not compensable under the Worker's Compensation Act. *Wayne Adams Buick, Inc. v. Ference* (1981), Ind. App., 421 N.E.2d 733, *trans. denied.* However, where the assault is one which might be reasonably anticipated because of the general character of the work, or other particular duties imposed on the worker (a "neutral" risk), such injuries or death may be found to arise out of the employment . . . .

> In the present case, Cherlyn was murdered by her ex-boyfriend; the animosity that culminated in the murder at the Employer's plant arose out of Cherlyn's domestic or private life . . . . [T]here has been no contention, or evidence which would reasonably support . . . a contention, that the character of Cherlyn's work or the particular duties imposed upon her through her employment exacerbated the risk she would be assaulted by her former boyfriend at work. As such, Cherlyn's death resulted from a risk personal to her and did not arise out of and in the course of her employment.[28]

Milledge v. Oaks[29] was not an assault case, but one which arose when an employee sprained her ankle upon exiting her vehicle in the employer's parking lot after arriving for work. The board denied her claim for worker's compensation benefits, and the appellate court affirmed the denial. In reversing and remanding the

---

[27]Peavler v. Mitchell & Scott Mach. Co., Inc., 638 N.E.2d 879 (Ind. Ct. App. 1994).

[28]Peavler v. Mitchell & Scott Mach. Co., Inc., 638 N.E.2d 879, 881–82 (Ind. Ct. App. 1994). See also Rogers v. Bethlehem Steel Corp., 655 N.E.2d 73 (Ind. Ct. App. 1995) (death of employee robbed and murdered by co-employee). See also Luong ex rel. Luong v. Chung King Express, 781 N.E.2d 1181 (Ind. Ct. App. 2003).

[29]Milledge v. Oaks, 784 N.E.2d 926 (Ind. 2003).

cause for further proceedings before the board, the Indiana Supreme Court discussed not only the "increased risk" and "positional risk" doctrines, but also "approaches" taken by other states in cases involving unexplained falls. The Court concluded:

> [A]n injury resulting from an unexplained accident falls under the category of a neutral risk, one neither distinctly personal to the claimant nor distinctly associated with the employment . . . . [I]n the case of a neutral risk, the positional risk doctrine applies. As applied in this case, Milledge would not have been at the place where she injured her ankle injury but for the duties of her employment. Consequently, a presumption arises that her injury "arose out of" employment.[30]

The Court went further to state that, under the "positional risk" doctrine, a rebuttable presumption exists that the injury "arose out of employment" once the element is met that the injury occurred "in the course of employment." Also, it is the employer's burden to prove that the employee's injury was actually the result of a cause personal to the claimant, such as a pre-existing illness or condition.[31]

The common question of whether the act of merely bending over at work and injuring one's back arises out of and in the course of employment was addressed in *Baker v. Heartland Food Corp.*[32] In *Baker*, a Burger King employee began stocking product at work and then bent over and felt a pop in her spine. The single hearing member denied compensability, in part because "the parties' exhibits do not contain specific medical reporting or testimony addressing the mechanism of Plaintiff's injury or the issue of causation for purposes of the Worker's Compensation Act."[33] Baker appealed.

The court of appeals analyzed the three categories of risk and held that Baker's risk fell within the "neutral risk" category—an injury which takes place at work with no apparent cause. As such, the employer then has the burden to rebut that presumption. The employer in *Baker* failed to rebut the presumption in the employee's favor and prove that the injury was idiopathic. Therefore, the court reversed the board and remanded with instructions to award benefits to Baker.

---

[30]Milledge v. Oaks, 784 N.E.2d 926, 933–34 (Ind. 2003).

[31]Milledge v. Oaks, 784 N.E.2d 926, 931 (Ind. 2003).

[32]Baker v. Heartland Food Corp., 912 N.E.2d 403 (Ind. Ct. App. 2009), withdrawn from bound volume.

[33]Baker v. Heartland Food Corp., 912 N.E.2d 403, 405 (Ind. Ct. App. 2009), withdrawn from bound volume.

In *Manous v. Manousogianakis*,[34] an employee was murdered by an unknown assailant while at his place of employment. No motive for the killing was ever established. It was the court's belief that the question presented by *Manous* (whether the positional risk doctrine applies to cases involving murdered employees) was a matter of first impression. The court concluded that the doctrine did apply when an employee is murdered without explanation and, in affirming an award of compensation to the employee's spouse and dependents, stated:

> In *Milledge*, our supreme court adopted the positional risk doctrine and thereby shifted the burden of proof on the "arising out of employment" element to employers when the claimant has shown that his injury occurred in the course of employment and was the result of a neutral risk. 784 N.E.2d at 931, 933–34 . . . .
>
> . . . .
>
> This case falls squarely within the holding of *Milledge*. The hallmark characteristic of a neutral risk is its inexplicable nature, and, in that regard, an unexplained murder is no less a neutral risk than is a more commonplace unexplained accident. In neither case can the cause of the injury be attributed to purely personal or purely employment conditions. And, pursuant to *Milledge*, which is binding precedent on this court, the positional risk doctrine must be applied in cases of neutral risks. *Milledge*, 784 N.E.2d at 934. As Professor Larson aptly stated:
>
> > "Occasionally an assault occurs for which no explanation whatever appears. . . . Nothing connects it with the victim privately; neither can it be shown to have had a specific employment origin. If the claimant is in fact exposed to that assault because he or she is discharging employment duties at that time and place, there is no better reason here than in the unexplained fall or death cases to deny an award merely because claimant cannot positively show that the assault was motivated by something connected with the work."
>
> Arthur Larson & Lex Larson, *Larson's Workers' Compensation Law* § 8.03[3], at 8-64 (2004).[35]

The court reiterated the position taken by the Supreme Court in *Milledge* that, since the claimant established that the employee's death occurred in the course of his employment, and since the positional risk doctrine was deemed applicable to the facts of the case, a rebuttable presumption applied that the employee's death "arose out of" his employment and, therefore, the burden of proof shifted to the employer to demonstrate that the murder was actually the result of a cause personal to the employee.[36]

So, in the final analysis, what is to be gleaned from the courts'

---

[34]Manous v. Manousogianakis, 824 N.E.2d 756 (Ind. Ct. App. 2005).

[35]Manous v. Manousogianakis, 824 N.E.2d 756, 764–65 (Ind. Ct. App. 2005).

[36]Manous v. Manousogianakis, 824 N.E.2d 756, 766 (Ind. Ct. App. 2005).

opinions on this issue? It appears that the courts have interpreted the language of the Act quite broadly and in a manner designed to aid claimants in their quest for compensation benefits. While resolution of future disputes will, of course, depend upon the facts of each individual case, it would not be surprising to find that more and more factual situations will be brought within the fold of "neutral risks," and, hence, the "positional risk doctrine" will be applied to make more injuries compensable if it is merely shown that the claimant was at work when the injury occurred.

In *Wright Tree Service v. Hernandez*,[37] the employee injured his neck on October 4, 2005 at approximately 2:00 p.m. He declined his employer's offer for medical treatment, but accepted an offer to be taken home by his foreman. Shortly before 2:30 p.m., Hernandez arrived home and his wife observed that he did not look like he was feeling well. Hernandez told his wife that his employer gave him a pill. He then went upstairs to change his clothes because he had been perspiring. Hernandez's wife heard him yell for her; she found him collapsed on the bed and nonresponsive. Hernandez died around 3:18 p.m. due to severe irreversible hypoxic encephalopathy. Prior to his death, Hernandez appeared to be in good health and had exhibited no signs of a heart attack. At hearing, Hernandez's widow presented medical evidence which supported a causal relationship between the accident and the heart attack. The single hearing member awarded death benefits.

Several issues were presented on appeal. Of most interest, the court of appeals addressed whether Hernandez's medical evidence was presented to a reasonable degree of medical certainty. When medical evidence falls short of a reasonable degree of medical certainty, such evidence by itself cannot support a verdict, but said testimony can serve as probative when considered in conjunction with other evidence. The court concluded that Hernandez's lack of prior symptoms of heart disease, combined with the doctor's opinion, supported the award.

In *Waters v. Indiana State University*,[38] claimant Waters worked for Indiana State University and was attending the annual employee appreciate luncheon sponsored by her employer. She was not required to attend the event, but if she chose to attend, she was paid for her time. The picnic was held on campus. After eating, Waters suffered injury while exiting the booth. She sustained a cracked femur and underwent immediate surgery to have a pin placed at the site of her fracture. The Worker's

---

[37]Wright Tree Service v. Hernandez, 907 N.E.2d 183 (Ind. Ct. App. 2009), transfer denied, (Sept. 11, 2009).

[38]Waters v. Indiana State University, 953 N.E.2d 1108, 271 Ed. Law Rep. 1040 (Ind. Ct. App. 2011), transfer denied, 962 N.E.2d 653 (Ind. 2011).

Compensation Board denied Walter's claim, finding that her pre-existing condition created the risk of injury, not her work. The Court of Appeals reversed the Board's finding of fact holding that medical evidence submitted attributed the injury to the exit from the booth at the picnic. The Court stated that it is error to determine whether an injury is compensable under the Act by asking whether the injury resulted from an everyday activity as opposed as to some unusual event. Rather the proper inquiry is whether the injury itself was unexpected. Even though Waters was performing a personal function at the time of her injury, standing up after lunch is incidental to and therefore considered to arise out of the employment.

In *Burdette v. Perlman-Rocque Co.,*[39] employee Burdette was found unconscious and unresponsive by co-workers while working on a mechanism to a door to a freezer located in a warehouse facility. The co-worker's moved him and he died a few days later at the hospital. The incident report stated that Burdette had fallen and hit his head against the door jamb. There was evidence of Burdette suffering from equilibrium diseases, and that he had complained almost daily to co-workers that he had been having trouble with his balance. The supervisor who stated in the incident report that Burdette had hit his head on a door jamb, testified at hearing that he intended to report that Burdette's head was found on the ground by the door jamb, not that he had knowledge that Burdette had actually hit the door jamb. The Court of Appeals affirmed the Board's decision denying compensation stating that there was evidence in the record to support the Board's finding that the plaintiff failed to prove that the employment increased the risk of the injury.

In *Moorehead Electric Co., Inc. v. Payne,*[40] Payne suffered a compensable shoulder injury at work on September 2, 2008. He had his second surgery for the injury on April 7, 2009. Approximately 11 days after his second surgery, he fell at a wedding reception and reinjured his right shoulder. Specifically, he had to step out of the way of someone coming towards him and he stepped to his right and his foot hit a raised grate surrounding the base of tree causing him to fall. Payne was wearing a shoulder brace at the time and it contributed to his fall because it obstructed his vision including his ability to see his right foot and the raised grate on the sidewalk. The fall at the wedding reception caused the need for a third surgery. A hearing was held on whether the fall at the wedding reception constituted an intervening cause breaking the chain of causation between the original injury and the need for the third shoulder surgery. The

[39]Burdette v. Perlman-Rocque Co., 954 N.E.2d 925 (Ind. Ct. App. 2011).

[40]Moorehead Elec. Co., Inc. v. Payne, 962 N.E.2d 657 (Ind. Ct. App. 2011).

single hearing member found that the original injury contributed to the injury at the wedding reception because the large shoulder brace that plaintiff was wearing at the time of his fall did obstruct his vision. The Board ordered that the disability and medical services surrounding the third surgery be paid under the worker's compensation claim. The Court of Appeals, in affirming the Board, restated the general rule that certain conduct such as negligence or intoxication may constitute an intervening cause of the subsequent injury thereby relieving the employer liability, especially if the injured rationally undertakes a line of action with the knowledge of the risk involved; however, a distinction must be drawn between mere carelessness or errors of judgment which do not break the causative chain.

In *A Plus Home Healthcare, Inc. v. Miecznikowski*,[41] Kathleen Miecznikowski (Kathy) worked for A Plus Home Healthcare, Inc. as a home healthcare registered nurse. While visiting a patient at the patient's home, she returned to her car to retrieve some medical equipment. On her way back inside the patient's house, Kathy lost her footing and injured her left arm and hand. The parties stipulated that Kathy's fall was caused by her tripping. The Single Hearing Member found that Kathy had not fallen due to a mental illness or condition and credited her statement that she simply lost her own footing; however, Single Hearing member further denied benefits because Kathy's own description of the cause of her fall indicated it was a personal risk and therefore not compensable. The Full Board, in reversing, found that Kathy's fall was a neutral risk and therefore compensable.

This case turns on the positional risk doctrine of causation. In *Milledge v. The Oaks.*,[42] the Supreme Court held that where injury results from neutral risks that occurred in the course of employment, a presumption was triggered that the injury also arose out of the employment thus shifting the burden to the employer to prove that the injury was the result of a personal risk. About three years after the decision in *Milledge*, the General Assembly amended the Worker's Compensation Act to provide that "the burden of proof is on the employee. The proof by the employee of an element of the claim does not create a presumption in favor of the employee with regard to another element of the claim." Here, the employer argued that by amending the act, the legislature had also overruled the positional risk doctrine altogether.

In *A Plus Home Healthcare, Inc.*, the Court of Appeals held

---

[41]A Plus Home Health Care Inc. v. Miecznikowski, 983 N.E.2d 140 (Ind. Ct. App. 2012), transfer denied, 985 N.E.2d 338 (Ind. 2013).

[42]Milledge v. Oaks, 784 N.E.2d 926 (Ind. 2003).

that the positional risk doctrine is still the law in Indiana.[43] Even though the legislature overruled the Supreme Court's holding that a neutral risk creates a presumption that the injury arising out of employment, if the worker provides evidence of a neutral risk, the injury is compensable.

Thompson v York Chrysler,[44] Thompson was a parts clerk for York Chrysler. A co-employee, Blackford, became agitated with Thompson when he told him a part was not available. Blackford began verbally attacking Thompson. Thompson had a heart condition requiring a pacemaker. He reported to his employer that the attack affected his heart and he was given permission to leave work early. As he walked to his truck, Blackford confronted him again and continued the verbal altercation. Thompson fell during this argument (either he was pushed by Blackford or Blackford blocked Thompson's "flailing" arm causing him to fall). He was taken to the emergency room with complaints of headache and pain in his left flank and shoulder. He was treated and released. Thompson sought no treatment for eight months, and then he was evaluated for counseling services he related to the incident. Thompson filed a claim with the workers' compensation board claiming the incident caused or aggravated his mood disorder and depression. Thompson passed away from causes unrelated to the claim in the summer of 2011 and his wife continued to pursue his claim for medical expenses, lost wages, permanent partial impairment and permanent total disability benefits. The Board denied her and she appealed.

The Court of Appeals found the argument first began as Thompson was leaving work for the day but before he had left the premises and therefore it occurred within the course of his employment. The Court then considered whether the injury arose out of the employment and noted that an assault by a co-worker may be compensable under the Act, where the applicant was not the aggressor. Here the parties had stipulated to there being one incident. Therefore, the Court of Appeals concluded that the Board's parsing the altercation into an "initial exchange" and a "later exchange" was improper because the Board could not permit a stipulation to stand and then find contrary to it. The Court of Appeals concluded the Blackford was the aggressor and there was no support for a contrary conclusion. The Court concluded the Board was in error in finding that Thompson's injuries did not arise out of or occur in his employment; Thompson's wife had met her burden that Thompson was entitled

---

[43]A Plus Home Health Care Inc. v. Miecznikowski, 983 N.E.2d 140, 143–44 (Ind. Ct. App. 2012), transfer denied, 985 N.E.2d 338 (Ind. 2013).

[44]Thompson v. York Chrysler, 999 N.E.2d 446 (Ind. Ct. App. 2013).

to benefits and reversed and remanded the matter for a determination of the benefits she should receive on his behalf.

In Ward v. Univ. of Notre Dame,[45] Ward, a food service worker, accidently slipped on a floor at work injuring her foot and ankle. Her employer accepted her injuries as work-related and provided workers' compensation benefits. She was diagnosed with Reflex Sympathy Dystrophy ("RSD") or Complex Regional Pain Syndrome ("CRPS") as a result of her work injury. Dr. Graham, Ward's authorized treating physician, opined that she was suffering from CRSP but her injury had reached maximum medical improvement. Dr. Graham assigned a 5% whole body permanent partial impairment ("PPI") for Ward's work injury. Ward disputed Dr. Graham's opinion and was awarded an Independent Medical Examination ("IME") with Dr. Kondamuri by the Workers' Compensation Board. Dr. Kondamuri opined that Ward was not suffering from CRPS and that she had reached maximum medical improvement. Dr. Kondamuri also opined that Ward had been diagnosed with an anxiety disorder. Ward sought her own second opinion with Dr. Schreier who opined she was not suffering from RSD, that her injuries had reached maximum medical improvement and that, while she had a history of anxiety and depression, she appeared to have active depression due to her injuries. Dr. Schreier assessed Ward sustained a 6% whole body impairment as a result of her injuries. Then, Ward was assessed by Dr. Corey who opined she may still have RSD or CRPS and referred her to Dr. Cheng to confirm the diagnosis. Dr. Cheng opined Ward had CRPS. Ward's case was heard before a Single Hearing Member who found she was at maximum medical improvement and awarded a 6% PPI. The Single Hearing Member found that Ward's claim for treatment for depression, anxiety and cardiac related issues was not supported by sufficient evidence. The Single Hearing Member's award was affirmed by the Full Workers' Compensation Board.

On Appeal, Ward argued it was improper for the Single Hearing Member and Full Board to consider the IME report of Dr. Kondamuri because of a reference to Ward as "Oriental." The Court of Appeals found that because the admissibility of the report was stipulated to this argument was waived. The Court noted that "waiver notwithstanding, the descriptive reference had no bearing on Dr. Kondamuri's evaluation of Ward's injury and condition." There was no evidence that the use of the term undermined the validity of the doctor's opinion. Even if it had, it would go to the doctor's credibility which was the task of the Single Hearing Member. Ward also challenged the sufficiency of

---

[45]Ward v. University of Notre Dame, 25 N.E.3d 172 (Ind. Ct. App. 2015), transfer denied, 34 N.E.3d 251 (Ind. 2015).

the evidence supporting the Single Hearing Member's decision and Full Board's affirmation of the same. Applying a deferential standard of review the Court of Appeals found the single hearing member and Full Board considered the medical evidence presented by both sides and found certain evidence more credible. The Single Hearing Member and Full Board found Dr. Kondamuri, Dr. Graham and Dr. Schreier more credible and persuasive than other evidence. The Court found there was sufficient evidence to support the award. As it related to the appeal that Ward had failed to present sufficient evidence that her depression, anxiety and cardiac conditions were work related, the Court noted that they would not reweigh the evidence as Ward requested. In conclusion the Court of Appeals affirmed the Single Hearing Member and Full Board's decision.

§ 3:24   Injuries in the course of employment

In order to be compensable under the Act, an injury must also be sustained "in the course of" employment.[1] The phrase refers to the time, place, and circumstances of the accident.[2] It has been held that "[a]n accident occurs 'in the course of employment' when it takes place within the period of employment, at a place where the employee may reasonably be, and while the employee is fulfilling the duties of employment or while engaged in doing something that is incidental thereto."[3]

In its opinion in *Global Const., Inc. v. March*,[4] the Indiana Supreme Court discussed the difficulties encountered in attempting to fit certain factual situations into the definitional requirements of the Act. There, an employee was injured by striking workers after he pulled his vehicle from an employee parking lot onto a public street. In resisting March's claim for worker's compensation benefits, Global argued that his injuries were not incurred "in the course of" his employment since he was not on the employer's premises, had already completed his work, and was not performing any employment duties at the time he was injured. In finding that March's claim was compensable, the Court reasoned:

In general, to arise "in the course" of employment, an injury must

---

[Section 3:24]

[1]IC 22-3-2-2(a).

[2]Consolidated Products, Inc. v. Lawrence, 521 N.E.2d 1327 (Ind. Ct. App. 1988); Muncie Indiana Transit Authority v. Smith, 743 N.E.2d 1214 (Ind. Ct. App. 2001).

[3]Mueller v. DaimlerChrysler Motors Corp., Transmission Plant, 842 N.E.2d 845, 847–48 (Ind. Ct. App. 2006); Milledge v. Oaks, 784 N.E.2d 926 (Ind. 2003).

[4]Global Const., Inc. v. March, 813 N.E.2d 1163 (Ind. 2004).

occur during work and on the employer's premises. Therefore, most injuries sustained on route to or from the workplace are not covered. Arthur Larson & Lex K. Larson, *Larson's Workers' Compensation Law*, § 13.01, at 13-3 (2004). For example, in *Donahue v. Youngstown Sheet & Tube Co.*, 474 N.E.2d 1013, 1014 (Ind. 1985), this Court affirmed the denial by the Worker's Compensation Board of benefits for an injury an employee sustained on the way home from work. We reasoned that the claimant had completed her duties and clocked out and was crossing a public street when she was injured. Her employer did not expect or compel her to cross that street. *Id.* We explained that because the claimant was on a public street open to and used by members of the general public, she was exposed to the same dangers as any member of the public and her injury therefore fell outside of the employment relationship. *Id.* at 1015.

Despite this general doctrine, courts have in some circumstances allowed compensation for injuries that occur close to, but not on, the employer's premises when an employee was going to or coming from work. As the Indiana Court of Appeals early explained, "employment is not limited to the exact moment when the workman reaches the place where he is to begin his work, or to the moment when he ceases that work. It necessarily includes a reasonable amount of time and space before and after ceasing actual employment, having in mind all the circumstances connected with the accident." *Reed v. Brown*, 129 Ind. App. 75, 82, 152 N.E.2d 257, 259 (1985) (citation omitted). Thus, employer-controlled parking lots and private drives used by employees have been held to be extensions of the employer's operating premises for purposes of coverage under the Act. *Id.* Injuries sustained in public thoroughfares may also be covered under some circumstances. For example, an employee was allowed to recover for injuries sustained when she crossed a public street separating her place of employment from the parking lot her employer provided. *Clemans v. Wishard Mem'l Hosp.*, 727 N.E.2d 1084, 1087 (Ind. Ct. App. 2000), *trans. denied*. The court recognized that ordinarily an injury on a public street in not compensable, but reasoned that the injury was incidental to her employment because she was required to cross the public street to access the employee parking lot. The street "would be used as the most convenient and reasonable means of ingress to and egress from its operating premises." *Id.* at 1088. The same reasoning applies here. March was injured while leaving work using the only available means of egress from the employer's parking lot. That egress exposed him to a danger specifically related to March's employment—passing through a group of agitated striking workers. Global argues that the strikers posed a threat to all who used the street, and therefore were not peculiar to March's employment. We think it obvious that a worker exiting a plant under picketing is at greater risk than a passing motorist. Under these circumstances, *the area where the protesting strikers gathered is for all practical purposes an extension of the workplace and March was not on his own time until freed of the stress of exiting.*[5]

It was unclear from the evidence presented whether March had completed his exit from the employee parking lot, had passed the area where the strikers had gathered, and then backed up to confront them after his vehicle was struck twice by objects presumably thrown at it. It was also unclear whether, after stopping his vehicle, March got out of it voluntarily or was pulled out by one or more picketers. The board concluded that March stopped his vehicle in response to a cracked window and, thereafter, did not initiate the fight that led to his injuries. In passing upon March's actions, the Court stated:

> [I]f, at the time of the injury, the employee was doing what a reasonable person might expect him to do under the circumstances, the employee has not abandoned his employment. *Nat'l Biscuit Co. v. Roth,* 83 Ind. App. 21, 26–27, 146 N.E. 410, 412 (1925). We cannot say as a matter of law March's response to this stressful situation was unreasonable. At any rate, whether March acted personally or as an employee, his injury resulted from a danger specific to his employment. March was required by his employer to cross the picket line at the Foundry. Stopping his truck when the windshield was cracked is within the range of reasonable responses. Even if March disembarked contrary to orders, that is a predictable response to a plainly stressful situation created by the circumstances of his employment. We agree that March may have failed to follow the instructions to ignore the strikers, but no personal motive is apparent in March's conduct. Employees cannot be expected to conform strictly to formal instructions when faced with sudden and intentional wrongful conduct from others. *Although "arising from" and "in the course of" are usually discussed as independent factors, in practice the two "are not, and should not be, applied entirely independently." Larson, supra, § 29.01, at 29-1. The stronger the causal link to employment, the weaker the showing required to find an injury to be incurred in the course of employment . . . The injury was incurred in a chain of events originating in the course of employment. This is sufficient to support coverage under the worker's compensation statute.*[6]

Whether this opinion from the Court is yet one more example of how far the appellate courts of this state are willing to go to find an injury compensable in assault cases, or whether it seeks to diminish the proof requirements which must be met by employees injured in the course of "stressful" situations, has yet to be determined. IC 22-3-2-2(a) specifically states that "[t]he burden of proof is on the employee," but, as demonstrated above, the ap-

---

[5]Global Const., Inc. v. March, 813 N.E.2d 1163, 1166–67 (Ind. 2004) (emphasis added).

[6]Global Const., Inc. v. March, 813 N.E.2d 1163, 1167–68 (Ind. 2004) (citations omitted) (emphasis added).

pellate courts have apparently decided that, at least in certain situations, the employer must bear an even greater degree of responsibility to rebut claims made by its injured or deceased employees.

D.A.L.L. Anointed, Inc. operated a McDonalds Restaurant in the case of *Curry v. D.A.L.L. Anointed, Inc.*[7] Curry was employed at the restaurant at the time of her injury. On the date in question Curry arrived at the restaurant to attend an employee meeting scheduled to begin at 5:00 p.m. However, she arrived at approximately 3:45 p.m. in order to eat a meal before the meeting. Curry was unsure whether the meeting was mandatory or whether she was being paid to attend the meeting. She did attend meetings regularly prior to her shift beginning and would often meet co-employees to eat before the meeting began. At the employee meetings the employer would discuss customer complaints and ways to improve customer service. During the time plaintiff was eating her meal she fell and suffered injury. She filed suit for negligence, along with her husband, against D.A.L.L. D.A.L.L. filed a motion to dismiss stating that her exclusive remedy was with the Worker's Compensation Act. The trial court granted the motion to dismiss. The Court of Appeals, in a affirming the trial court, held that the plaintiff was attending a meeting to improve the employer's business and the meetings usually involved her eating with other co-workers. The Court of Appeals stated that the injured worker's remedy was exclusively with the Worker's Compensation Act.

In *Arnold v. Roseacre Farms Inc.*,[8] Arnold, the claimant, was employed as a night security guard at Roseacre's facility. He drove his automobile from his home to the facility on a public road to a point in front of the gravel road that serves as the only entrance into Roseacre's facility. As he crossed the center line and entered the eastbound lane, his automobile was struck by a pick-up truck. The collision occurred on the public road and the vehicles came to rest partially in the public road and partially in Roseacre's drive-way. The Board denied Arnold's claim for compensation stating that injuries on the public highway are not compensable. The Court of Appeals affirmed distinguishing the case *Clemans v. Wishard Memorial Hospital*[9] by stating that in *Clemans* the employee was entitled to worker's compensation benefits when she was crossing a public highway because she was going from the employer's premises on one side of the

---

[7]Curry v. D.A.L.L. Anointed, Inc., 966 N.E.2d 91 (Ind. Ct. App. 2012), transfer denied, 969 N.E.2d 605 (Ind. 2012).

[8]Arnold v. Rose Acre Farms, Inc., 966 N.E.2d 107 (Ind. Ct. App. 2012).

[9]Clemans v. Wishard Memorial Hosp., 727 N.E.2d 1084 (Ind. Ct. App. 2000).

highway to the employer's premises on the other side of the highway. Here, Arnold was traveling from his home to the workplace and injured on the public highway and therefore the claim is not compensable.

§ 3:25 Bars to compensation

There are certain "affirmative defenses" available to an employer which will bar an employee's claim for compensation. It is the employer's burden to prove these defenses and, in addition, to prove that the injury or death proximately resulted from them. The defenses are an employee's: (1) knowingly self-inflicted injury, (2) intoxication, (3) commission of an offense, (4) knowing failure to use a safety appliance, (5) knowing failure to obey a reasonable written or printed rule of the employer which has been posted in a conspicuous position in the workplace, or (6) knowing failure to perform any statutory duty.[1]

In *Henry v. Schenk Mechanical Contractors, Inc.*,[2] the board and the appellate court found facts sufficient to establish that an employee's attempted suicide, while upon the employer's premises shortly before the work day was to begin, barred his claim for worker's compensation benefits. In *Indiana State Police v. Wiessing*,[3] however, the full board and the court of appeals found that a state trooper's self-inflicted gunshot wound to the head resulting in his death was *not* a "self-inflicted injury" which would bar his dependants from recovering under the Act, since the evidence established that the trooper's suicide resulted from a post-traumatic stress disorder diagnosed five years earlier.

In *Vandenberg v. Snedegar Construction, Inc.*,[4] the employee crashed his company-owned vehicle into another company-owned vehicle following an office party on company premises. Distraught, the employee took a handgun from the console of his truck and tragically committed suicide. The single hearing member denied the widow's claim for death benefits, finding that she had failed to meet her burden to prove that her husband's suicide was an accident arising out of his employment.

Injuries caused by certain types of activities will bar recovery of benefits. IC 22-3-2-8 provides, in part, that no compensation is

---

[Section 3:25]

[1]IC 22-3-2-8; Dane Trucking Co. v. Elkins, 529 N.E.2d 117 (Ind. Ct. App. 1988).

[2]Henry v. Schenk Mechanical Contractors, Inc., 169 Ind. App. 178, 346 N.E.2d 616 (1976).

[3]Indiana State Police v. Wiessing, 836 N.E.2d 1038 (Ind. Ct. App. 2005), transfer denied, 855 N.E.2d 1001 (Ind. 2006).

[4]Vandenberg v. Snedegar Const., Inc., 911 N.E.2d 681 (Ind. Ct. App. 2009).

allowed for injury or death due to the employee's knowingly self-inflicted injury. In another suicide case, *Indiana State Police v. Weissing*,[5] the dependents of a state trooper were awarded death benefits after the trooper, years after taking the life of a motorist during a routine traffic stop and subsequently developing post-traumatic stress disorder (PTSD) due to the shooting, took his own life as a complication of the PTSD. Weissing's suicide was preceded by a work-related injury—PTSD—and his suicide was causally related to the PTSD. In *Vandenberg*, however, no such work injury preceded the suicide. As such, the court of appeals agreed and held that Vandenberg's death was the result of a knowingly self-inflicted injury for which benefits were barred.

In *Deckard v. Bloomington Crushed Stone Co.*,[6] a claimant was denied compensation benefits upon a finding by the board that he was injured while operating his dump truck in an intoxicated condition. In affirming the board's decision, the appellate court stated:

> What the legislature condemns, rather, is the worker who appears at his job in an intoxicated condition and who then is injured in an accident caused by that intoxication. Contrary to Deckard's position, we find the legislative policy to deny worker's compensation benefits in such circumstances sound indeed. That the worker was unaware of his intoxicated condition [Deckard's position, since the accident occurred approximately 8 1/2 hours after he last drank] matters not at all.[7]

In *NAPA/General Automotive Parts v. Whitcomb*,[8] an award of compensation benefits was sustained even though the employer demonstrated that, at the time of his accident, the deceased employee was intoxicated with a .13% blood alcohol level. The court stated that "such a finding, standing alone, does not mandate the denial of compensation unless NAPA has satisfied its burden of proving that Steven's death was due to or proximately caused by his intoxication . . . ."[9] The board, as well as the appellate court, found that NAPA had not met its burden of proof in that regard. No evidence was offered by NAPA as to what effect a .13% blood alcohol level had upon its employee specifically or would have

---

[5]Indiana State Police v. Wiessing, 836 N.E.2d 1038 (Ind. Ct. App. 2005).

[6]Deckard v. Bloomington Crushed Stone Co., 590 N.E.2d 137 (Ind. Ct. App. 1992).

[7]Deckard v. Bloomington Crushed Stone Co., 590 N.E.2d 137, 140 (Ind. Ct. App. 1992). It should be noted that that board heard extensive testimony from a toxicologist regarding the effects of alcohol consumption and impairment.

[8]NAPA/General Automotive Parts v. Whitcomb, 481 N.E.2d 1335 (Ind. Ct. App. 1985).

[9]NAPA/General Automotive Parts v. Whitcomb, 481 N.E.2d 1335, 1337 (Ind. Ct. App. 1985).

had upon an average male of like height, weight, etc. In addition, other possible causes for the accident were not negated by NAPA.[10]

In *Jones v. Pillow Express Delivery, Inc.*,[11] an employee died in a vehicle accident while returning from an out-of-state delivery. At the time, the employee had been diagnosed with fibromyalgia and had been prescribed a Duragesic patch. Testimony at hearing indicated that the patch would make Jones (the employee) feel drugged, exhibit problems walking, and slur his speech, and adversely affected his judgment. The single hearing member denied benefits, concluding that Jones's accident was caused by his intoxication.

On appeal, the board's decision was affirmed. Although not defined in the Act, intoxication is defined within the Indiana Code related to motor vehicles:

> Under the influence of: (1) alcohol; (2) a controlled substance . . .; (3) a drug other than alcohol or a controlled substance; (4) a substance defined in IC 35-46-6-2 or IC 35-46-6-3 [toxic vapors and non-medical nitrous oxide] or (5) a combination of substances described in subdivisions (1) through (4); so that there is an impaired condition of thought and action and the loss of normal control of a person's faculties.

Operating a motor vehicle under the effects of a controlled substance such as a Duragesic patch is not a defense to operating a motor vehicle while intoxicated. When a driver becomes intoxicated by the prescribed controlled substance to the extent that it impairs his thought and actions and he loses normal control of his faculties, it becomes a crime. Since the Duragesic patch caused Jones to become intoxicated and that intoxication ultimately led to his death, according to the appellate court, Jones was not entitled to benefits.

In *Hass v. Schrader's Inc.*,[12] a deliveryman was injured when he attempted to pass another vehicle on the shoulder of the roadway and collided with a parked, unattended semi-tractor trailer. His employer sought to deny his claim for compensation on the ground that Hass committed "an offense," namely a violation of IC 9-4-1-67's "Overtaking on the right," a Class C infraction. The board denied Hass's claim, but the appellate court

---

[10]NAPA/General Automotive Parts v. Whitcomb, 481 N.E.2d 1335, 1337, (Ind. Ct. App. 1985). See also Dane Trucking Co. v. Elkins, 529 N.E.2d 117 (Ind. Ct. App. 1988) (compensation award affirmed where evidence of intoxication was presented, but employer failed to prove employee's accident and injuries were caused by his intoxicated condition).

[11]Jones ex rel. Jones v. Pillow Express Delivery, Inc., 908 N.E.2d 1211 (Ind. Ct. App. 2009).

[12]Hass v. Shrader's Inc., 534 N.E.2d 1119 (Ind. Ct. App. 1989).

reversed. The court noted that the Worker's Compensation Act nowhere defines the term "offense," but it is defined in other sections of the code. The court stated:

> In 1983, the legislature "decriminalized" the traffic code. At that time, many offenses, which had previously been misdemeanors, were reduced to civil infractions. At the same time, the legislature amended the criminal code's definition of "offense" to specifically exclude infractions . . . .
>
> . . . .
>
> . . . Accordingly, we hold that the word "offense" as found in I.C. 22-3-2-8 is defined in I.C. 35-41-1-19 and does not include infractions.[13]

I.C. 35-31.5-2-75 (a) provides the term "crime" means misdemeanor or felony and not infraction and I.C. 35-31.5-2-215 (a) provides the term "offense" means crime.

In *Haskell & Barker Car Co. v. Kay*,[14] a worker was injured while using a power drilling machine in the employer's factory. Two safety appliances were provided by the company for employees using that machine but the employees often used a third device, which was safe for some forms of work but not others, to save time in doing their piecework. The evidence established that, at the time he was injured, and to properly guard against the specific manner in which he was injured, Kay should have been using the safer appliance which the company provided. The appellate court affirmed an award of compensation due to the fact that the employer did not prove that Kay's conduct amounted to a "willful failure or refusal to use a safety appliance" which was required under the predecessor to the current statute. In its opinion, the court stated:

> Two safety appliances are involved here: The clamp and the plug. The latter was used; the former was not used. The evidence was sufficient to sustain a finding, if made, that reasonable care required that the former rather than the latter be used. *We do not believe that a workman satisfies the statute merely by using a safety appliance. The statute contemplates the use of a safety appliance proper for the work being done.* A mere failure to use the proper safety appliance, however, will not defeat a claim for compensation .
> . . .
>
> . . . .
>
> . . . . A mere failure to do a certain thing does not involve action or omission more serious in nature than negligence . . . .
>
> . . . .
>
> . . . . If the evidence here were sufficient to justify a finding that

---

[13]Hass v. Shrader's Inc., 534 N.E.2d 1119, 1120–21 (Ind. Ct. App. 1989).

[14]Haskell & Barker Car Co. v. Kay, 69 Ind. App. 545, 119 N.E. 811 (1918).

appellant had ordered or directed decedent to use a clamp on the particular kind of work which he was doing when injured, or if by virtue of a custom or otherwise decedent knew that only such an appliance should be used on that kind of work, and if the board had so found, and if under such circumstances and with such knowledge decedent had failed to use such appliance, then under any ordinary circumstances, and unless there was something exceptional in the situation, we should feel impelled to sustain a finding of the board, if made, that such a failure was willful.[15]

The current statute requires a showing by the employer of a "knowing," not a "willful," failure to use a safety appliance in order to defeat recovery by an injured employee. " 'Willful misconduct' means a deliberate purpose not to discharge some duty necessary to safety. It implies obstinacy, stubbornness, design, set purpose, and conduct quasi-criminal in nature."[16] Certainly, employers today asserting this defense need not prove facts constituting willfulness, but, on the other hand, need to prove something more than nonconformity, inattention, thoughtlessness, or heedlessness. It would seem reasonable to require employers to prove that a particular safety device was provided for the particular work being performed, that the employee had knowledge of the device, knew how to use it, knew that he or she was expected to use it for the work being done, but failed to do so without some reasonable justification or excuse.

There is no doubt that an employer may defend against a claim for compensation on the ground that the employee was injured while violating a written or printed rule. The theory supporting the defense was aptly stated by the appellate court in *Western Union Telegraph Co. v. Owens*:[17]

> The Legislature evidently had in mind, when this law was enacted, that employers could and would protect themselves against certain dangers—hazards of the employment—by adopting rules for the government of their employees in relation to such hazards. As reasonable men, the employers should anticipate the reasonable hazards of the employment and the natural and probable conduct of the employees with reference thereto. The employer knows that men and boys, when associated together, will, under natural impulse, engage in frolic, in "horseplay," and that injury may result therefrom. It is within the power of the employer to prevent these things, or at least to save himself harmless from the consequences

---

[15]Haskell & Barker Car Co. v. Kay, 69 Ind. App. 545, 119 N.E. 811, 813–14 (1918) (emphasis added).

[16]General American Tank Car Corp. v. Borchardt, 69 Ind. App. 580, 122 N.E. 433, 435 (1919).

[17]Western Union Telegraph Co. v. Owens, 82 Ind. App. 474, 146 N.E. 427 (1925).

thereof, by adopting rules according to the statute, and then enforcing such rule or rules.[18]

Under the current statute, an employer's ability to successfully sustain its burden of proof for an employee's "knowing failure to obey a reasonable written or printed rule of the employer which has been posted in a conspicuous position in the place of work" is difficult. The facts presented must establish that: (1) the rule was written or printed (not verbal); (2) it was reasonable; (3) it was posted; (4) in a conspicuous place; (5) in the workplace; (6) the employee knowingly failed to obey it; and (7) the employer did not, by its conduct, condone or seemingly acquiesce in a violation of its rule. The last element is nowhere contained in the statutory language, but has been applied by the courts interpreting the statute.[19] In *U.S. Steel Corp. v. Mason*,[20] the appellate court reasoned that:

> "If the employer allows violations of the rule or acquiesces therein, he cannot later set up such a violation as a defense to the payment of compensation."
>
> Small, Workmans Compensation Law of Indiana (1950) Sec. 11, P. 320.
>
> We believe that the employer has an obligation to check all infractions of its rules . . . .[21]

In *Motor Freight Corp. v. Jarvis*,[22] the court held that, "[w]here an employer knows that an employee has been violating safety statutes, and has acquiesced in it, he cannot be heard to set up such a violation as a defense to a claim for injury or death growing out of the breach."[23] In *Wimmer Temporaries, Inc. v. Massoff*,[24] the court stated that, "an employer cannot shield itself from liability behind a safety rule that it fails to enforce, and instead displays its acquiescence."[25]

---

[18]Western Union Telegraph Co. v. Owens, 82 Ind. App. 474, 146 N.E. 427, 429 (1925).

[19]U.S. Steel Corp. v. Mason, 141 Ind. App. 336, 227 N.E.2d 694 (1967); Motor Freight Corp. v. Jarvis, 163 Ind. App. 442, 324 N.E.2d 500 (1975); Wimmer Temporaries, Inc. v. Massoff, 740 N.E.2d 886 (Ind. Ct. App. 2000).

[20]U.S. Steel Corp. v. Mason, 141 Ind. App. 336, 227 N.E.2d 694 (1967).

[21]U.S. Steel Corp. v. Mason, 141 Ind. App. 336, 227 N.E.2d 694, 695 (1967).

[22]Motor Freight Corp. v. Jarvis, 163 Ind. App. 442, 324 N.E.2d 500 (1975).

[23]Motor Freight Corp. v. Jarvis, 163 Ind. App. 442, 324 N.E.2d 500, 504 (1975).

[24]Wimmer Temporaries, Inc. v. Massoff, 740 N.E.2d 886 (Ind. Ct. App. 2000).

[25]Wimmer Temporaries, Inc. v. Massoff, 740 N.E.2d 886, 892 (Ind. Ct. App. 2000).

§ 3:26   Bars to compensation—"Horseplay"

Although not an enumerated defense under IC 22-3-2-8, "horseplay" has often been asserted as a defense by employers seeking to challenge a claim for compensation benefits under the Act. The appellate courts have recognized that, "[i]t is a matter of common knowledge to employers of labor that men working together, or in near proximity to other workers, will indulge in moments of diversion from work to play pranks on each other . . . ."[1]

Whether couched in terms that an injury did not "arise out of" or was not "in the course of" employment, or was sustained as the result of a failure to obey a written or posted rule of the employer, the essence of the defense is the same; because of the employee's misconduct, the employee should be denied compensation for injuries arising therefrom.

Certain principals have been established by the appellate courts in cases involving horseplay. If the horseplay, practical joking, or acts done in the spirit of fun, or play, or sport may be expected to occur because of the type of activity the employee is engaged in;[2] or, if the employer has acquiesced in the particular conduct;[3] or, if the injured employee is the innocent victim of another's prank and not actively engaged in horseplay, then the employee may be compensated for his or her injuries.[4] Each situation is, obviously, fact sensitive, but the appellate courts have been fairly consistent in applying the aforestated principals to either award or deny compensation where appropriate.

§ 3:27   Third-party liability

The Indiana Worker's Compensation Act authorizes an injured employee, or, in the case of death, the employee's dependents, to sue someone other than the employer or a co-employee, provided compensation is payable for such injury or death under the Act, and the circumstances giving rise to the injury or death create in that other person a legal liability to pay damages. It is immate-

---

[Section 3:26]

[1]Chicago, I. & L. Ry. Co. v. Clendennin, 81 Ind. App. 323, 143 N.E. 303, 304 (1924).

[2]In re Loper, 64 Ind. App. 571, 116 N.E. 324 (1917); Block v. Fruehauf Trailer Division Fruehauf Corp., 146 Ind. App. 70, 252 N.E.2d 612 (1969).

[3]In re Loper, 64 Ind. App. 571, 116 N.E. 324 (1917); Kokomo Steel & Wire Co. v. Irick, 80 Ind. App. 610, 141 N.E. 796 (1923).

[4]Woodlawn Cemetery Ass'n v. Graham, 149 Ind. App. 431, 273 N.E.2d 546 (1971); Lincoln v. Whirlpool Corp., 151 Ind. App. 190, 279 N.E.2d 596 (1972); Fields v. Cummins Employees Federal Credit Union, 540 N.E.2d 631 (Ind. Ct. App. 1989) (disapproved of by, Wine-Settergren v. Lamey, 716 N.E.2d 381 (Ind. 1999)); DePuy, Inc. v. Farmer, 847 N.E.2d 160 (Ind. 2006).

rial whether or not the employer or its worker's compensation insurance carrier has paid, or has a legal obligation to pay, benefits under the Act on account of such injury or death.[1]

Whether or not an injured employee or the employee's dependents avail themselves of this right to sue a third-party tortfeasor, the Act provides full protection for the employer and its insurance carrier and, in the event suit is brought by the employee or dependents, the Act imposes a number of obligations on them. For example, the injured employee or his or her dependents must file suit against the third party within two years after the cause of action accrues; if they do not, the employer or its carrier has an additional year (three years from the date the cause of action accrued) within which to file suit and seek recovery. In the event the employee or dependents file suit, they must notify the employer or its carrier, by personal service or registered mail, that they have done so within 30 days after the action is filed. The employer, then, has 90 days after receipt of notification to join in the action so that all orders of the court may be made for its protection. If, after filing suit, the action brought by the employee or dependents is dismissed, the employer or its carrier has one year from the date of dismissal to file suit against the third party, assuming the employer has not previously been made a party to the action.[2]

If the injured employee or his or her dependents agree to receive compensation from the employer or its carrier, or they institute proceedings to recover the same, the employer or carrier is entitled to a lien upon any settlement award, judgment, or fund out of which the employee or dependents might be compensated from the third party. As further protection, no release, or settlement, or satisfaction of judgment is valid without the written consent of the employer or its carrier and the employee or his or her dependents. Consent is not required, however, if the employer or its carrier has been fully indemnified or protected by court order.[3]

If the employee or dependents have not received any benefits under the Act from the employer or its carrier and, thereafter, obtain a judgment or settlement from the third party, the employer and its carrier are relieved from its obligations to pay benefits to the employee or his or her dependents. If, however, any benefits are received by the employee or dependents, the employer or its carrier are entitled to reimbursement from any

---

[Section 3:27]

[1]IC 22-3-2-13.

[2]IC 22-3-2-13.

[3]IC 22-3-2-13.

judgment obtained and paid or settlement accepted by them. In that event, any liability of the employer or carrier to pay further compensation or benefits shall terminate. An employer's liability for an employee's benefits terminates if the employee settles a claim against a third party for the same injury without first obtaining the employer's consent to settlement. In *Smith v. Champion Trucking Co., Inc.*,[4] the Indiana Supreme Court concluded that even if the amount of the third party settlement is less than the total value of the worker's compensation claim, an absolute bar to further benefits is in place to prevent employees from settling third party cases without the consent of their employers. This protects the subrogation rights of the employer and prevents double recovery by the employee.[5]

This section of the Act requires the employer or its carrier to pay its pro rata share of all costs and reasonably necessary expenses incurred in connection with asserting the third-party claim or suit, including an attorney fee of 25% (collection of benefits actually repaid without filing suit) or 33% (collection of benefits actually repaid with suit being filed). If the employer or carrier agrees to waive their reimbursement rights under this section of the Act, they will not have to pay the pro rata share of the costs and expenses required to maintain the action against the third party.[6]

In *Barrett v. City of Brazil*,[7] the court looked at the question of whether the court ordered restitution to an injured party from a third party results in the dismissal of the worker's compensation claim. Concluding that the restitution was a payment made "other than by agreement" for less than the value of the worker's compensation claim, the court determined that paragraph three of IC 22-3-2-13 applied, which allows a claimant to either collect the judgment or repay the employer and pursue the worker's compensation claim.[8]

While it is true that the exclusivity provision of the Act (IC 22-3-2-6) "limits an employee whose injury meets the jurisdictional requirements of the Act to the rights and remedies provided by the Act," the Act also "permits actions against third party tortfeasors, so long as the third party is neither the plaintiff's employer

---

[4]Smith v. Champion Trucking Co., Inc., 925 N.E.2d 362 (Ind. 2010).

[5]Smith v. Champion Trucking Co., Inc., 925 N.E.2d 362, 366 (Ind. 2010).

[6]IC 22-3-2-13.

[7]Barrett v. City of Brazil, 919 N.E.2d 1176 (Ind. Ct. App. 2010), transfer denied, 940 N.E.2d 822 (Ind. 2010).

[8]Barrett v. City of Brazil, 919 N.E.2d 1176, 1180-1181 (Ind. Ct. App. 2010), transfer denied, 940 N.E.2d 822 (Ind. 2010).

nor his fellow employee."[9] The appellate courts of Indiana have been called upon repeatedly to decide who employed the plaintiff and defendant at the time of the accident in question, and whether or not the defendant was a co-employee of the injured plaintiff.

Thus, in *State v. Coffman*,[10] an employee of the Indiana State Highway Department was prohibited from asserting a civil action against the State of Indiana for injuries which he received when his truck collided with a vehicle operated by an Indiana State Police officer. The court concluded that the plaintiff and the officer had the same employer, and plaintiff's action sought to impose a legal liability in the state to pay him damages contrary to IC 22-3-2-13.[11] In *Rodgers v. Hembd*,[12] it was found that an officer of a corporation was an employee and a fellow employee of a waitress injured while working at a restaurant owned by the corporation. Hembd sought to impose liability upon Rodgers, and, hence, the corporation for the defective architectural design work which he did relating to the premises upon which she was injured. The court rejected her dual capacity argument and ruled that Rodgers was immune from civil tort liability since his acts, as alleged, were such as to render their mutual employer, the corporation, vicariously liable.[13]

It has been held that whether or not two individuals were "in the same employ" at the time of the accident "is determined by examining whether (the defendant) could obtain compensation benefits under the same or similar circumstances."[14] In *Weldy v. Kline*,[15] a wrongful death action was initiated on behalf of an employee who drowned in a swimming pool accident during the

---

[9]Williams v. R.H. Marlin, Inc., 656 N.E.2d 1145 (Ind. Ct. App. 1995); Campbell v. Eckman/Freeman & Associates, 670 N.E.2d 925 (Ind. Ct. App. 1996).

[10]State v. Coffman, 446 N.E.2d 611 (Ind. Ct. App. 1983).

[11]But see Turner v. Richmond Power and Light Co., 756 N.E.2d 547 (Ind. Ct. App. 2001), on reh'g, 763 N.E.2d 1005 (Ind. Ct. App. 2002) (civil action permitted).

[12]Rodgers v. Hembd, 518 N.E.2d 1120 (Ind. Ct. App. 1988).

[13]See also Witherspoon v. Salm, 251 Ind. 575, 243 N.E.2d 876 (1969); Kottis v. U.S. Steel Corp., 543 F.2d 22 (7th Cir. 1976); Needham v. Fred's Frozen Foods, Inc., 171 Ind. App. 671, 359 N.E.2d 544 (1977); Jackson v. Gibson, 409 N.E.2d 1236 (Ind. Ct. App. 1980). "Dual capacity" arguments advanced in each case were rejected by the courts. Lawhead v. Brown, 653 N.E.2d 527 (Ind. Ct. App. 1995); Tapia v. Heavner, 648 N.E.2d 1202 (Ind. Ct. App. 1995).

[14]Northcutt v. Smith, 642 N.E.2d 254 (Ind. Ct. App. 1994); Ward v. Tillman, 179 Ind. App. 626, 386 N.E.2d 1003 (1979); O'Dell v. State Farm Mut. Auto. Ins. Co., 173 Ind. App. 106, 362 N.E.2d 862 (1977) (disapproved of by, Thiellen v. Graves, 530 N.E.2d 765 (Ind. Ct. App. 1988)), trans. denied.

[15]Weldy v. Kline, 616 N.E.2d 398 (Ind. Ct. App. 1993).

course of an employer-sponsored party. The evidence established that both Weldy and Kline were employed by MPI and worked together in the kitchen of a Holiday Inn at the time of a party given by MPI for its employees. During the course of the party, Weldy and a nonemployee guest threw Kline into a swimming pool located on the premises. Kline's body was found a short time later at the bottom of the pool; he had drowned. Kline's estate sued Weldy, among others, for wrongful death. The court of appeals in its opinion made an extensive analysis of the statutory language on this issue of co-employment:

I.C. 22-3-2-13 is an exception to the general rule limiting an employee's recovery for job-related accidental injuries to the provisions of the Act. *See Skinner v. Martin* (1983), Ind. App., 455 N.E.2d 1168, 1171. I.C. 22-3-2-13 allows the possibility of bringing suit against third parties but limits this exception to suits against individuals other than the employer or fellow employees. *Id.* The language "not in the same employ" specifically preserves a co-employee's immunity from common law liability for accidents found to have arisen out of and in the course of employment. *Id; Tarr v. Jablonski* (1991), Ind. App., 569 N.E.2d 378, 379, *trans. denied.*

Several recent cases have, however, carved out an exception, holding that where a co-employee, normally covered under this exception, engages in horseplay or various other non job-related activities, he forfeits his immunity under I.C. 22-3-2-6. *See e.g. Fields v. Cummins Emp. Fed. Credit Union* (1989), Ind. App., 540 N.E.2d 631, 635, 637–38; *Seiler v. Grow* (1987), Ind. App., 507 N.E.2d 628, 630–31, *trans. denied; Martin v. Powell* (1985), Ind. App., 477 N.E.2d 943, 945, *trans. dismissed.* This conclusion is reached by interpreting the phrase "in the same employ" to mean an *activity "in the course of employment." See Fields, supra,* 540 N.E.2d at 637; *Seiler, supra,* 507 N.E.2d at 631; *Martin, supra,* 477 N.E.2d at 945. Such activities as pulling chairs from under fellow employees and classic sexual harassment are not, under this analysis, "in the course of employment" and therefore are not "in the same employ" for the purposes of immunity under the Act. *See Fields, supra,* 540 N.E.2d at 637–38; *Martin, supra,* 477 N.E.2d at 944–45.

This interpretation causes us several problems. First, the requirement that the injury be sustained "in the course of employment'" refers specifically to the status of the *injured employee.* The Act does not scrutinize the actions of the employer or the co-employee with regard to whether an injury occurred in the course of employment. For us to do so is to create a category of persons subject to liability unaddressed by the statute. Second, these two requirements, "in the same employ" and "in the course of employment," are separate and distinct requirements. They do not mean the same thing. For example, this court has acknowledged on previous occasions that the Act does provide that a claimant may rightfully proceed against a third party tort-feasor not in the same employ, but we have specifically stated that a *co-employee is removed* from liability for accidents *found to have arisen out of and in the course of employment. Ward v. Tillman* (1979), 179 Ind. App. 626, 386 N.E.2d 1003, 1005; *see also Skinner, supra,* 455 N.E.2d at 1171; *O'Dell v. State Farm Mut. Auto. Ins. Co.* (1977), 173 Ind. App. 106, 362 N.E.2d 862, 866. Thirdly, the interpretation contravenes the clear purposes behind the Act. Generally, workmen's compensation is intended to afford employees an adequate and certain remedy independent of any finding of negligence for accidents arising out of and in the course of employment. *O'Dell, supra,* 362 N.E.2d at 864. . . . The court in *O'Dell* noted that this policy confined an injured employee's rights to those available under workmen's compensation if the accident, involving the deceased and his co-employee, arose out of and in the course of their mutual employment. *O'Dell, supra,* at 864. That holding is consistent with several sections of the Act, and the cases construing them, that evince a strong policy against double recovery. *Freel v. Foster Forbes Glass Co.* (1983), Ind. App., 449 N.E.2d 1148, 1151.

For these reasons, we decline to follow those cases which expose a co-employee to liability based upon the non job-related nature of his actions. The Act is concerned with only the *injured employee* and the circumstances surrounding his or her injury. To the extent that the Act does not provide adequate compensation for such injury or death, thereby encouraging injured employees or their representatives to seek other avenues of redress, the legislature should recognize its responsibility to adjust awards to a reasonable level. We are not the appropriate body to make such determinations.

The next question then becomes what does "in the same employ" mean in this context. The test, according to the court in *Ward, supra,* to determine whether Kline and Weldy were "in the same employ" is whether or not the denominated defendant, Weldy, could obtain compensation benefits under the same or similar circumstances. *Ward, supra,* at 1005. The facts in this case reveal that Kline and Weldy both worked in the kitchen at the Holiday Inn and both attended the party given by their mutual employer. As employees they were identically situated. Should the positions have been reversed, Weldy would have been able to obtain compensation benefits to the same extent as Kline. We can think of no clearer case of someone "in the same employ."[16]

The courts have also dealt with this issue in situations involving an alleged dual employment. In *Jennings v. St. Vincent Hosp. and Health Care Center,*[17] it was found that Jennings, a registered nurse, was employed by Star-Med, a company which made temporary assignments to hospitals and emergency rooms. Star-Med had a staffing agreement with St. Vincent which provided, in part, that its nurses were employees of Star-Med and not St. Vincent. Star-Med agreed to provide worker's compensation insurance coverage for the nurses it referred to St. Vincent. Pursu-

---

[16]Weldy v. Kline, 616 N.E.2d 398, 401–03 (Ind. Ct. App. 1993) (footnotes omitted).

[17]Jennings v. St. Vincent Hosp. and Health Care Center, 832 N.E.2d 1044 (Ind. Ct. App. 2005), transfer denied, 855 N.E.2d 1001 (Ind. 2006).

ant to the agreement, Jennings was assigned to work in St. Vincent's emergency room, where he was injured. Star-Med's insurance carrier paid for all medical expenses and worker's compensation benefits related to Jennings' injury. Thereafter, Jennings sued St. Vincent, alleging that his injury was caused by the negligence of a St. Vincent employee, and that he was an employee of Star-Med and not St. Vincent. The trial court held that Jennings was a co-employee of St. Vincent and Star-Med and granted the motion to dismiss filed by St. Vincent. In affirming the trial court's dismissal of Jennings' action, the court of appeals stated:

> The Act establishes that one worker may simultaneously have two employers. *See* I.C. § 22-3-3-31. Where two employers "so associate themselves together that both are in direct control of the employee and he is made accountable to both, he will be considered an employee of both employers . . . ." *GKN*, 744 N.E.2d at 402 (citing *U.S. Metalsource Corp. v. Simpson*, 649 N.E.2d 682, 685 (Ind. Ct. App. 1995).[18]

The essence of the court's opinion was that, after applying the facts of the case to the *Hale* criteria used to resolve this type of issue,[19] St. Vincent had met its burden to establish that an employer-employee relationship existed with Jennings. The court found that St. Vincent had both control over Jennings's performance of his duties and a right to dismiss him from his position. Even though the court noted that the Star-Med/St. Vincent agreement provided that Jennings was to remain an employee of Star-Med, and that "this fact weighs heavily against the conclusion that Jennings was a co-employee of St. Vincent and Star-Med," the result reached by the court was, nonetheless, that he was an employee of both Star-Med and St. Vincent, thus barring his civil tort action against the latter.[20]

The opposite result was reached by the court of appeals in

---

[18]Jennings v. St. Vincent Hosp. and Health Care Center, 832 N.E.2d 1044, 1050 (Ind. Ct. App. 2005), transfer denied, 855 N.E.2d 1001 (Ind. 2006).

[19]Hale v. Kemp, 579 N.E.2d 63 (Ind. 1991).

[20]Jennings v. St. Vincent Hosp. and Health Care Center, 832 N.E.2d 1044, 1055 (Ind. Ct. App. 2005), transfer denied, 855 N.E.2d 1001 (Ind. 2006). See also the dissenting opinion of Judge Barnes, at 1055–57). The court seemed somewhat uncomfortable with the decision which it reached and the denial of relief to Jennings. It noted:

While the worker's compensation scheme fulfills many needs, the rates employer's pay (when they are not otherwise self-insured) will be materially affected by the safety of the workplace they provide to their "employees." Here, we have an employer without a "workplace" and one with. The one with the workplace is shielded from traditional tort liability because it qualifies as a "co-employer." The entire scheme should be reviewed by our General Assembly . . . .

Wishard Memorial Hosp. v. Kerr.[21] There, Kerr was employed by CareStaff, Inc., a temporary staffing agency for nurses. CareStaff had an agreement with Wishard for Kerr to work there, and within the agreement, Kerr was referred to as a "CS Employee." Kerr worked in Wishard's psychiatric emergency room pursuant to the agreement. She was injured upon leaving Wishard after completing her shift one day when she slipped and fell on a freshly waxed floor. She received worker's compensation benefits from CareStaff's insurer, then sued Wishard for negligence. Wishard moved to dismiss her complaint alleging that she was its employee, and, therefore, her exclusive remedy was worker's compensation. The trial court denied Wishard's motion, thus allowing Kerr's cause of action to proceed. The opinion of the court of appeals, affirming the trial court's determination, was written by Judge Barnes, who dissented from the majority opinion in *Jennings*. He acknowledged the inconsistencies involved:

> We note that "dual employment" issues in the worker's compensation context have had a tendency to generate fractured rulings from Indiana's courts. The ad hoc balancing of seven different factors does not seem to lead to predictable results in these types of cases. Here, for example, the Marion County Superior Court found there was no dual employment. In a different case with very similar facts, the same court (though a different judge) found that there was dual employment and dismissed a complaint; that result was affirmed by this court on appeal in a 2-1 decision, and our supreme court denied transfer with one justice not participating and one justice dissenting from the denial of transfer.[22]

After once again applying the *Hale* factors to the facts of this case, the court stated:

> Three factors lead us to affirm the trial court's conclusion that Wishard did not employ Jennings [sic] for purposes of the Act. First, Wishard bore the burden of establishing that Kerr was its employee . . . .

> Second, "the remedies provided in the Worker's Compensation Act are in derogation of common law, and a statute that is in derogation of common law must be strictly construed against limitations on a claimant's right to bring suit." There is a strong public policy favoring the coverage of employees under the Act. "However, . . . this public policy is not advanced where its effect 'immunize[s] third-party tortfeasors and their liability insurers from liability for negligence which results in serious injuries to one who is not in their employ.'"

> Finally, the trial court's ruling in this case must be considered presumptively correct, and Wishard was required to convince us that the balance of the evidence is tipped against that ruling. We

---

[21]Wishard Memorial Hosp. v. Kerr, 846 N.E.2d 1083 (Ind. Ct. App. 2006).

[22]Wishard Memorial Hosp. v. Kerr, 846 N.E.2d 1083, 1088 (Ind. Ct. App. 2006) (citing *Jennings*).

have not analyzed the seven *Hale* factors in this case in precisely the same way as did the trial court, but we may affirm its decision on any basis supported by the evidence of record.

Although the *Hale* factors are nearly evenly split both for and against a finding of dual employment, Wishard has failed to convince us that the trial court ruling was erroneous . . . .[23]

It is interesting to note that no judge dissented to the majority opinion or wrote a separate dissenting opinion in *Kerr*. With the factual situations presented in *Jennings* and *Kerr* practically identical, the ultimate decisions reached by the court in the two cases appear irreconcilable.

A similar issue is raised when an employee seeks to sue the employer's parent corporation for injuries sustained while in the course of employment. The first appellate decision discussing this topic came in *McQuade v. Draw Tite, Inc.*[24] The Indiana Supreme Court concluded that an injured employee may bring a civil action against the employer's parent corporation, provided the action is based upon an alleged breach of duty of care separate and distinct from any vicarious liability attributable to the parent corporation for acts of its subsidiary under principles of agency law.[25] In subsequent decisions, the courts have continued to apply this principle.

Finally, the appellate courts have had to grapple with the "in the same employ" language of the statute in independent contractor cases. In *Wolf v. Kajima Intern. Inc.*,[26] the Indiana Supreme Court ruled that an employee of a subcontractor was permitted to file a negligence action against a general contractor for injuries which he received on a jobsite, even though the general contractor had procured and paid for worker's compensation insurance to cover the subcontractor's employees. The Court reasoned that, "an owner or general contractor does not alter its status concerning potential tort liability to employees of contractors or subcontractors by directly purchasing worker's compensation insurance on behalf of subcontractors."[27]

A more complex situation arises when a subcontractor's employee brings a civil action against a general contractor and/or a separate subcontractor and its employee who injured him. In

---

[23]Wishard Memorial Hosp. v. Kerr, 846 N.E.2d 1083, 1088, (Ind. Ct. App. 2006) (citations omitted).

[24]McQuade v. Draw Tite, Inc., 659 N.E.2d 1016 (Ind. 1995).

[25]McQuade v. Draw Tite, Inc., 659 N.E.2d 1016, 1020 (Ind. 1995). See also Ritter v. Stanton, 745 N.E.2d 828 (Ind. Ct. App. 2001).

[26]Wolf v. Kajima Intern. Inc., 629 N.E.2d 1237 (Ind. 1994).

[27]Wolf v. Kajima Intern. Inc., 629 N.E.2d 1237, 1237 (Ind. 1994).

Riffle v. Knecht Excavating, Inc.,[28] the facts established that Riffle was employed by the general contractor on a highway project. As part of the construction, a large hole had to be dug to set a manhole. Shortly before the incident giving rise to Riffle's claim, the general contractor rented a backhoe and operator from an excavating company to dig the hole and demolish concrete. The backhoe operator dug the hole as he was instructed to do by the job superintendent of the general contractor (Riffle's employer). The accident and Riffle's injuries occurred after he entered the hole to install a wooden form on which to pour concrete. Riffle filed suit against the backhoe operator and the excavating company. The trial court granted summary judgment in favor of the defendants, and the appellate court affirmed. In doing so, the court reasoned that Riffle and the backhoe operator were co-employees since they performed the same type of work on the project, and because the backhoe operator could have received worker's compensation benefits from the general contractor had he been injured under circumstances similar to the manner in which Riffle was injured. Finally, the court found that Riffle's action against the excavating company was based entirely upon the doctrine of respondeat superior. Therefore, since its employee could not be held liable to Riffle, no action based solely upon respondeat superior could be maintained against his employer. Riffle's exclusive remedy was worker's compensation.[29]

However, in *Williams v. R.H. Marlin, Inc.,*[30] an injured employee (Williams) of a subcontractor (Centin) was permitted to pursue his civil action against a crane operator (Hutchinson), the company (Marlin) which provided the crane and operator, the general contractor (PDM) on the project, and the contractor (Real) who hired plaintiff's employer. Williams was injured when a caged basket in which he was being lifted by a crane dropped several feet to the ground. The appellate court utilized the seven-factor *Hale* test and concluded that Williams and Hutchinson were not co-employees, and that the trial court's entry of summary judgment in favor of the defendants was improper. In so ruling, the court stated:

> The only facts which support the proposition that Centin was Hutchinson's employer are that Centin did occasionally use the crane to complete its work, and that on the date of the injuries Centin employees motioned to Hutchinson to lift them up. Work-

---

[28]Riffle v. Knecht Excavating, Inc., 647 N.E.2d 334 (Ind. Ct. App. 1995).

[29]See also Argabright v. R.H. Marlin, Inc., 804 N.E.2d 1161 (Ind. Ct. App. 2004); Verma v. D.T. Carpentry, LLC, 805 N.E.2d 430 (Ind. Ct. App. 2004); Nickels v. Bryant, 839 N.E.2d 1211 (Ind. Ct. App. 2005), transfer denied, 855 N.E.2d 1008 (Ind. 2006).

[30]Williams v. R.H. Marlin, Inc., 656 N.E.2d 1145 (Ind. Ct. App. 1995).

men signaling to a crane operator with a "thumbs up" hardly constitutes an assertion of control.

We conclude that the majority, if not all, of the indicia used to determine the existence of an employer-employee relationship are absent in this case. Therefore, having failed to establish the existence of the requisite employer-employee relationship, Hutchinson is not entitled to immunity under the Act's fellow-employee exemption and Williams is not relegated to the Act for his sole remedy.[31]

In *Kornelik v. Mittal Steel USA, Inc.*,[32] employee Kornelik suffered a compensable injury. The worker's compensation carrier paid over $108,000 in temporary total disability payments and medical expenses. Later, Kornelik filed a negligence against third party tortfeasors. Mediation was held and the third party case settled for $260,000 in full and final settlement of all claims. The agreement further provided that Kornelik was responsible for the payment of all liens including the worker's compensation lien. Finally, the agreement provided that the mediator found the damages could reasonably have exceeded $2 million. The agreement of the third party case was reached without consent of the employer or the employer's worker's compensation carrier.

After the settlement of the third party case, the injured worker petitioned the Court to reduce the worker's compensation lien consistent with the mediator's evaluation of the damages. The worker's compensation carrier filed a motion to intervene, arguing that no lien reduction is allowed, since neither the employer or the worker's compensation carrier consented to the settlement agreement of the third party case. The trial court denied Kornelik's request to have the lien reduced and the Court of Appeals affirmed. The Courts of Appeals held the worker's compensation carrier was entitled to its full recovery minus the usual attorney's fees and pro rata share of costs because it did not consent to the third party settlement.

In *Justice v. American Family Mutual Insurance Co.*,[33] the claimant, Justice, suffered injury while driving a bus for the city of Indianapolis. He received worker's compensation benefits and filed a claim of personal injury against the other driver. The tortfeasor was insured by Geico who had a policy limit of $25,000. Geico paid its policy limits to Justice with AFI's consent. At the time of his injury, Justice had an underinsurance policy with AFI with a limit of $50,000 per person. Justice made a claim against that policy which was denied. The trial court granted AFI's mo-

---

[31]Williams v. R.H. Marlin, Inc., 656 N.E.2d 1145, 1153 (Ind. Ct. App. 1995).

[32]Kornelik v. Mittal Steel USA, Inc., 952 N.E.2d 320 (Ind. Ct. App. 2011), transfer denied, 971 N.E.2d 669 (Ind. 2012).

[33]Justice v. American Family Mut. Ins. Co., 971 N.E.2d 1236 (Ind. Ct. App. 2012).

tion for summary judgment stating that the worker's compensation provision of the underinsurance motorists policy reduced the limits of the liability policy such that AFI's liability was $0. The trial court granted AFI's motion for summary judgment. The Court of Appeals, in reversing the trial court, held that in this case Justice's damages should be reduced by the $25,000 recovery from the tortfeasor and the percentage of the worker's compensation benefits paid to Justice based on the tortfeasor's percentage of comparative fault up to a maximum of $25,000.

§ 3:28   Third-party liability—Subrogation

The current subrogation provisions of the Act allow an injured worker to both proceed under the Act and pursue a civil action asserting third-party liability in tort. However, in a footnote in its opinion in *Rausch v. Reinhold*,[1] the court of appeals stated that "in order to collect both remedies, the injured worker must receive worker's compensation before collecting a tort remedy."[2] That seems to make some sense, especially if the focus of such statement is upon the word "collect" and further in light of the termination of benefits language and the reimbursement requirements contained in IC 22-3-2-13. But it should be noted that this section of the Act does not specifically state that an injured employee must first receive compensation benefits before the employee recovers upon his or her tort remedy. In *Wabash Water & Light Co. v. Home Telephone Co.*,[3] the appellate court held that "an employer against whom compensation has been awarded may recover, not only for the amount of money which he has already paid, but also that for which he has become legally liable."[4] The statutory scheme is designed to protect the employer and its compensation insurance carrier if they have paid worker's compensation benefits to their injured employee *or* if they have a legal obligation to pay pursuant to the Act.

IC 22-3-2-13 is amended by technical changes to remove gender-specific pronouns and to replace the word "evenamount" with "amount"; by replacing "medical, surgical, hospital and nurses' services and supplies" with "services and products"; and by replacing "medical, surgical, hospital or nurses' services and supplies" with "services and products."

[Section 3:28]

[1]Rausch v. Reinhold, 716 N.E.2d 993 (Ind. Ct. App. 1999).

[2]Rausch v. Reinhold, 716 N.E.2d 993, 999 (Ind. Ct. App. 1999). See Lewis v. Lockard, 498 N.E.2d 1024, 1027 (Ind. Ct. App. 1986).

[3]Wabash Water & Light Co. v. Home Telephone Co., 79 Ind. App. 395, 138 N.E. 692 (1923).

[4]Wabash Water & Light Co. v. Home Telephone Co., 79 Ind. App. 395, 138 N.E. 692, 693 (1923).

The subrogation provisions contain a number of other safeguards which serve to protect the interests of employers and insurance carriers as well. They impose notification requirements upon injured employees desirous of filing suit against third parties. They allow employers to join actions in order to be protected by court order. The provisions extend the applicable statutes of limitation for employers to file suit, if necessary. They "make the employee in effect a constructive trustee for the employer of that portion of the settlement [or judgment] necessary to fully reimburse the employer for amounts it expended on the employee's behalf under the Act."[5] They allow for the termination of compensation benefits at the conclusion of the third-party litigation. Lien rights in favor of the employer are established and, in certain circumstances, allow the employee's rights and remedies to be assigned the employer. The provisions recognize the importance of having employers consent to a settlement or a satisfaction of judgment in order for the same to be valid. Most importantly, they prohibit an injured worker from obtaining a windfall as a result of a work-related accident. As stated by the appellate court in *Lewis v. Lockard*,[6] "[t]hese subrogation provisions are consistent with the strong policy within the Act against double recovery by an injured employee for the same injury."[7]

In *Morgan v. Duro Paper Bag Mfg. Co.*,[8] the effect of the notice provision contained within the predecessor to the current statute came into question. The court found:

> [T]he notice provision was inserted to protect the employer; to enable him to be apprised of the pending action so that he may timely assert his lien on any judgment resulting therefrom.
>
> . . . .
>
> . . . . It would thus seem that if plaintiff *files proof of service* of notice upon the employer at a time sufficiently early to enable the employer to protect his rights with regard to his lien, then the duty imposed by the statute has been fulfilled.[9]

In *Strate v. Niagara Mach. and Tool Works*,[10] the "joinder" language contained in the predecessor to the current subrogation section was considered. There, the defendant sought to join the employer's compensation insurance carrier as an additional

---

[5]State v. Mileff, 520 N.E.2d 123, 128 (Ind. Ct. App. 1988).

[6]Lewis v. Lockard, 498 N.E.2d 1024 (Ind. Ct. App. 1986).

[7]Lewis v. Lockard, 498 N.E.2d 1024, 1027 (Ind. Ct. App. 1986).

[8]Morgan v. Duro Paper Bag Mfg. Co., 22 F.R.D. 508 (S.D. Ind. 1957).

[9]Morgan v. Duro Paper Bag Mfg. Co., 22 F.R.D. 508, 511–12 (S.D. Ind. 1957).

[10]Strate v. Niagara Mach. and Tool Works, 160 F. Supp. 296 (S.D. Ind. 1958).

party-plaintiff. In prohibiting the defendant from doing so, the court stated:

> [T]he legislature intended that any "joinder" of an employer in an action brought by an employee against a third party tortfeasor should be limited to intervention, i.e., so that all orders of court after hearing and judgment shall be made for his protection with regard to his statutory lien. This conclusion is dictated by those provisions of § 40-1213 which provide that the employer may only sue the third party tortfeasor for the amount of the compensation paid the injured employee upon the happening of either of two contingencies. These are:
> (1) If the employee brings an action against the third party and said action is dismissed, then the employer may commence an action in his own behalf within one year from the date or such dismissal.
> (2) If the employee fails to bring action against the third party within two years after his cause of action accrues, then the employer may bring an action in his own behalf within one year from the date of expiration of the two-year limitation on the employee's cause of action.
> . . . . If the employee brings an action within two years of the events complained of and does not dismiss same, then by operation of the maxim expressio unius est exclusio alterius, the employer has no right of action as against the third party and is therefore bound by any judgment rendered in the employee's action. Consequently, the employer must be content to take the procedural steps necessary to protect his lien rights with regard to any judgment which the employee might recover. He is not subrogated to the rights of the employee until the employee dismisses his action, since under the statutory scheme of § 40-1213, the employer becomes a subrogee only upon the happening of either of the two contingencies noted.
> . . . .
> The court concludes, therefore, that since American Insurance Co., by operation of Indiana law, is not a partial subrogee at this time, its rights at this time are limited to the right to intervene to protect its statutory lien on any judgment which might inure to the plaintiff. With its rights thus limited, the court holds that American Insurance Co. is not a 'real party in interest' within the terms of Rule 17(a), Federal Rules of Civil Procedure and thus cannot be joined as an additional party plaintiff.[11]

In *Swift v. State Farm Ins. Co.*,[12] an injured employee received medical and compensation benefits from his employer's insurer. He also sued and later settled with the third-party tortfeasor responsible for causing his injuries. The insurer then requested

---

[11]Strate v. Niagara Mach. and Tool Works, 160 F. Supp. 296, 299–300 (S.D. Ind. 1958).

[12]Swift v. State Farm Ins. Co., 819 N.E.2d 389 (Ind. Ct. App. 2004).

repayment of the compensation which it paid, but the employee refused. The insurer filed an application with the board seeking a determination of benefits paid under the Act. The employee sought to defeat the insurer's application, claiming that it was untimely since it was filed more than three years after the accident in which he was injured. The board concluded that the insurer's application was timely filed, and that it was entitled to repayment. In affirming the board's decision, the court of appeals stated:

> In its petition, State Farm did not request compensation; instead, it requested a hearing to determine the amount of the lien it was entitled to for compensation it had already paid to Swift. Therefore, Indiana Code section 22-3-3-3 was not applicable to State Farm's petition.
>
> Because State Farm's petition falls under Indiana Code section 22-3-2-13, we hold the Board properly accepted jurisdiction.[13]

In its opinion in the matter of *McCammon v. Youngstown Sheet and Tube Co.*,[14] the court of appeals strictly construed the language of the first and third paragraphs of IC 22-3-2-13:

> Clearly the statute provides that if an action is brought by an injured employee against a third party and a settlement is made, the liability of the employer or employer's compensation carrier to pay further compensation terminates. Koughn v. Utrad Industries, Inc. (1971), 150 Ind. App. 110, 275 N.E.2d 572. McCammon refers this Court to another portion of I.C. 1971, 22-3-2-13 which gives the employee an option of either collecting a judgment and repaying the employer for compensation previously drawn or of assigning all rights under the judgment to the employer and thereafter receiving from the employer the compensation to which he is entitled. This portion of the statute is inapplicable in the present case however, because it requires that a final judgment, other than by agreement, be received by the injured employee. The evidence is uncontroverted that McCammon did not procure a final judgment, but rather reached an agreed settlement with the third party.[15]

The court would not allow McCammon to conclude a settlement

---

[13]Swift v. State Farm Ins. Co., 819 N.E.2d 389, 392 (Ind. Ct. App. 2004). IC 22-3-3-3 states that "The right to compensation under [the Indiana Worker's Compensation Act] shall be forever barred unless within two (2) years after the occurrence of the accident . . . a claim for compensation thereunder shall be filed with the worker's compensation board."

[14]McCammon v. Youngstown Sheet and Tube Co., 426 N.E.2d 1360 (Ind. Ct. App. 1981).

[15]McCammon v. Youngstown Sheet and Tube Co., 426 N.E.2d 1360, 1363–64 (Ind. Ct. App. 1981). See Carrier Agency, Inc. v. Top Quality Bldg. Products, Inc., 519 N.E.2d 739 (Ind. Ct. App. 1988). See also Waldridge v. Futurex Industries, Inc., 714 N.E.2d 783 (Ind. Ct. App. 1999) (by enacting the Indiana Comparative Fault Act, IC 34-51-2-1, the legislature did not intend to repeal IC 22-3-2-13 by implication.

with a third-party tortfeasor and, thereafter, obtain additional compensation benefits from his employer.

In *Norris v. U.S. Fidelity and Guar. Co.*,[16] the character of the lien granted to the employer's worker's compensation insurance carrier was at issue. The injured employee who settled with the third-party tortfeasor claimed that the lien was an equitable subrogation to his recovery which necessitated a settlement by him for the full value of his claim prior to the compensation carrier's receipt of any reimbursement. At the very least, only a pro rata distribution of the settlement to the carrier was required, according to the employee. In rejecting both arguments, the court of appeals, relying in part upon the U.S. District Court's opinion in *Strate*, stated:

> Only where the insurance carrier may bring suit in its own right is subrogation of the carrier's interest at issue. As the court in Strate implicitly indicated, where the employer's compensation insurance carrier is precluded from bringing suit by a settlement or judgment obtained by the injured employee against a third-party tortfeasor, subrogation is not at issue. The insurance carrier may protect itself via the lien provisions of the Act and is thus a lienholder but is not a subrogee. As a lienholder, the carrier would be entitled to recover for the full value of the lien.[17]

Regarding the plaintiff's pro rata distribution argument, the court wrote:

> Injured employees could conceivably prevent recovery by the compensation carrier by making such an allegation [i.e., that he only recovered one quarter to one third of the value of his action via settlement]. Here, Norris settled his action against the third-party tortfeasor for what he felt he could get. Norris got the full value of what he bargained for and cannot now be heard to complain that the settlement was for less than the actual value of the action.[18]

In *Ansert Mechanical Contractors, Inc. v. Ansert*,[19] the Court of Appeals of Indiana concluded that an employer was entitled to assert a worker's compensation lien upon an underinsured motorist insurance payment made to an injured employee. The court found that a UIM carrier was "some other person than the employer and not in the same employ [who has] a legal liability to pay damages" pursuant to IC 22-3-2-13. The "some other

---

[16]Norris v. U.S. Fidelity and Guar. Co., 436 N.E.2d 1191 (Ind. Ct. App. 1982).

[17]Norris v. U.S. Fidelity and Guar. Co., 436 N.E.2d 1191, 1194 (Ind. Ct. App. 1982).

[18]Norris v. U.S. Fidelity and Guar. Co., 436 N.E.2d 1191, 1194 (Ind. Ct. App. 1982).

[19]Ansert Mechanical Contractors, Inc. v. Ansert, 690 N.E.2d 305 (Ind. Ct. App. 1997).

person" language of the statute is not specifically restricted to a tortfeasor causing injury, the "legal liability" to which the statute refers may extend to a contractual obligation to pay on a UIM insurance policy, and the "damages" contemplated by the statute would include payments made pursuant to UIM coverage, according to the court.

> [T]he clear policy underlying the lien provision of the statute supports our conclusion that such payments would constitute "damages." The purpose of the lien is to prevent double recovery on the part of the injured employee. *Freel v. Foster Forbes Glass Co.,* 449 N.E.2d 1148, 1151 (Ind. Ct. App. 1983). In light of this policy, we find no reason to distinguish between damages paid by a tortfeasor or the tortfeasor's insurance carrier and damages paid by a UIM carrier when the tortfeasor lacks sufficient coverage to fully compensate the injured employee. In essence, uninsured motorist benefits are merely a contractual substitute for funds that would have been available if the tortfeasor had been fully insured. "Although uninsured motorist coverage is provided for the protection of persons injured by uninsured or underinsured tortfeasors, and not for the benefit of such wrongdoers, the statutorily specified coverage guarantees the injured person's recovery of damages as if the tortfeasor had been insured." *See Johnson v. Fireman's Fund Ins. Co.,* 425 So.2d 224, 227 (La. 1982), *reh'g denied.*
>
> The primary goal of the policy is to prevent double recovery. As such, it would not further the purpose of the lien provision to interpret the statute in such a way that a worker's compensation carrier would be reimbursed if the damages are paid out of the tortfeasor's insurance, but not if paid out of the UIM coverage.[20]

In *Pinkerton's Inc. v. Ferguson,*[21] however, the court of appeals ruled that an employer was not entitled to assert a compensation lien on proceeds paid to an injured employee under the uninsured motorist provisions of her husband's personal automobile insurance policy. The court reasoned that, if such recovery were permitted the employer, the underlying humane purposes which the Act seeks to achieve would be emasculated. The court said reasoned:

> Stated otherwise, to rule as Pinkerton's suggests would shift part of the economic burden back from the employer or industry to the employee . . . . Where, however, an employer pays for the uninsured/underinsured motorist coverage, there are not these same concerns about shifting the cost of injury back to the employee and dilution of benefits. Thus, in public policy lies the

---

[20]Ansert Mechanical Contractors, Inc. v. Ansert, 690 N.E.2d 305, 309–10 (Ind. Ct. App. 1997). See also Walkup v. Wabash Nat. Corp., 691 N.E.2d 1282 (Ind. Ct. App. 1998), opinion vacated, 702 N.E.2d 713 (Ind. 1998).

[21]Pinkerton's Inc. v. Ferguson, 824 N.E.2d 789 (Ind. Ct. App. 2005).

justification for distinguishing between employer-paid and employee-paid uninsured/underinsured motorist coverage.[22]

In *Walkup v. Wabash Nat. Corp.*,[23] an injured employee claimed that his employer could not recover under its lien for compensation benefit amounts already paid, since his settlement with the employer's automobile carrier under its UM coverage specifically excluded any amounts for hospital bills and medications. In sustaining the trial court's grant of summary judgment in favor of the employer, the court of appeals stated:

> The plain language of Indiana Code § 22-3-2-13 states that an employer can place a lien on "any" settlement award. "The key word in this provision is the word 'any.' [sic] The legislature did not distinguish between amounts recovered for which the carrier is not responsible such as pain and suffering." *Dearing v. Perry*, 499 N.E.2d 268, 270 (Ind. Ct. App. 1986). Damages, even for pain and suffering, will not be placed outside of the reach of the employer's lien.[24]

The Supreme Court of Indiana vacated the appellate court's decision in *Walkup* and issued a new decision, holding that Walkup's payments from Cincinnati Insurance, under a policy that specifically excluded payments for worker's compensation benefits, was not subject to Wabash's statutory lien under IC 2-3-2-13.[25]

In *Koval v. Simon Telelect, Inc.*,[26] the Indiana Supreme Court dealt with the consent provisions of the statute:

> The reason the legislature required written consent as one alternative is obvious. Because settlement serves as a bar to further recovery against the third party, *State v. Mileff*, 520 N.E.2d 123, 126 (Ind. Ct. App. 1988), without a consent requirement, an employee could settle a lawsuit for an amount well below medical and disability costs and leave the employer with nowhere to turn for the additional money owed. Requiring the written consent of the employer is designed to protect an employer from being short-changed without its advance approval.
>
> In the absence of written consent, a settlement is valid only if the employer is "indemnified or protected by court order." As a substitute for the consent requirement, this language is directed to the same purpose: . . . complete protected assurance that the employer will be paid without further litigation. . . .

---

[22]Pinkerton's Inc. v. Ferguson, 824 N.E.2d 789, 793 (Ind. Ct. App. 2005).

[23]Walkup v. Wabash Nat. Corp., 691 N.E.2d 1282 (Ind. Ct. App. 1998), opinion vacated, 702 N.E.2d 713 (Ind. 1998).

[24]Walkup v. Wabash Nat. Corp., 691 N.E.2d 1282, 1285 (Ind. Ct. App. 1998), opinion vacated, 702 N.E.2d 713 (Ind. 1998).

[25]Walkup v. Wabash Nat. Corp., 702 N.E.2d 713 (Ind. 1998).

[26]Koval v. Simon Telelect, Inc., 693 N.E.2d 1299 (Ind. 1998).

. . . .

[F]or purposes of Indiana Code § 22-3-2-13 it does not constitute "protect[ion] by court order" for a court specifically to preserve an employer's or an employer's insurance carrier's right to bring suit for breach of duty by its agent.[27]

The decision of the Seventh Circuit Court of Appeals in *Schneider Nat. Carriers, Inc. v. National Employee Care Systems, Inc.*,[28] is even more instructive. There, a trucker (Menist) was injured on the job in an accident with another trucker employed by Schneider and received worker's compensation benefits from NECS, the third-party administrator for his employer's compensation carrier (Carolina Casualty Company). Menist sued Schneider in Pennsylvania, where the accident occurred, and the case was removed to federal court. NECS moved to intervene to protect its lien rights, but Schneider opposed the motion. NECS ultimately withdrew its motion after entering into a "Stipulation of Subrogation Lien" with Menist whereby the latter stated that he would "recognize and agree to honor the subrogation lien [of NECS] pursuant to and consistent with the aforementioned Pennsylvania and Indiana law." Menist and Schneider later settled the lawsuit for an amount substantially less than the amount of worker's compensation benefits paid by NECS. NECS was not a party to the settlement agreement, did not participate in the settlement discussions, and did not give its consent to the settlement as required by IC 22-3-2-13. NECS was never paid any portion of the settlement proceeds by either Menist or Schneider; instead, they agreed that Schneider would negotiate with NECS and indemnify Menist against any lien claim which NECS might make against him. The negotiations between NECS and Schneider broke down, and Schneider then filed an action against NECS and Menist seeking a judicial declaration of its rights and obligations regarding the lien. The district court granted NECS's motion for summary judgment and awarded it the amount of the Menist/Schneider settlement minus the attorney fee that would have gone to Menist's attorney if the settlement had been handled properly in the first place. In affirming the district court's decision, the court of appeals, after citing with approval the opinion of the Indiana Supreme Court in *Koval*, stated:

Schneider's first attack on the district court's decision is to argue that NECS waived any lien claim by choosing not to intervene as a party in the Pennsylvania lawsuit . . . .

No doubt in hindsight NECS regrets that it withdrew its interven-

---

[27]Koval v. Simon Telelect, Inc., 693 N.E.2d 1299, 1309–10 (Ind. 1998).

[28]Schneider Nat. Carriers, Inc. v. National Employee Care Systems, Inc., 469 F.3d 654 (7th Cir. 2006).

tion motion in the Pennsylvania action. But there is nothing in the Indiana statute or its interpretive case law that makes intervention anything other than permissive; there is no authority for the proposition that intervention is a *necessary prerequisite* to the operation of the statutory lien rights (although it may be the most efficient way to protect those rights). Indeed, an insurer's lien rights arise by operation of the statute itself without any requirement of a positive act on the part of the insurer. Schneider acknowledged as much in its opposition to NECS's motion to intervene in the Pennsylvania suit . . . .

Schneider cannot have it both ways. NECS's lien rights, and the requirement that Menist and Schneider obtain NECS's written consent to the settlement, were not dependent upon NECS's intervention in the lawsuit. NECS did not waive its lien rights by withdrawing its motion to intervene. Schneider and Menist were in no way relieved of the requirements of § 22-3-2-13 by virtue of NECS's withdrawal of its intervention motion.

. . . .

Menist negotiated a settlement of his Pennsylvania lawsuit with Schneider . . . . This was a "successful conclusion" of the action under any reasonable understanding of the phrase. Schneider cites no authority for the proposition that settling parties' noncompliance with the insurer consent requirement of § 22-3-2-13 extinguishes the insurer's statutory lien rights, leaving only the subrogation remedy. Accepting Schneider's argument would obliterate a central purpose of the statute, which is to establish and protect the reimbursement rights of worker's compensation insurers without the need for additional litigation. *See Koval*, 693 N.E.2d at 1309. If Schneider is right, injured employees and tortfeasors would be encouraged to quietly settle their cases without notifying or consulting the worker's compensation lien holder—in other words, to intentionally disregard the statutory consent requirement—in the hope that the carrier will not discover the settlement in time to intervene to invalidate the settlement or assert a subrogation claim. Approving this interpretation would run counter to the statute's objectives as identified by the Indiana Supreme Court in *Koval*.

. . . .

Schneider contends that any judgment in favor of NECS should have been against Menist alone . . . .

Schneider's arguments are foreclosed by the simple fact that in settling the lawsuit, Schneider bound itself not to assert the very position it now takes. The language of the settlement agreement plainly obligates Schneider to assume all responsibility for satisfying NECS's lien rights, regardless of whether other legal principles would have operated to make Menist liable to NECS . . . .

Having agreed to these terms, with full awareness of the existence and amount of NECS's lien and the fact that NECS was improperly excluded from the settlement negotiations in violation of Indiana law, Schneider cannot now argue that NECS must look to Menist alone. The bottom line is Schneider and Menist knowingly settled the case for less than the amount of the worker's compensation lien without notifying NECS and placed the risk of liability to NECS squarely on Schneider. The planned-for contingency now having arrived, Schneider cannot use its own noncompliance with the consent requirement of the Indiana statute as a sword to defeat its liability to NECS.[29]

Finally, there has been considerable discussion by the appellate courts on the issue of attorney fees and expenses to be paid by the employer or its carrier in the event the employee pursues a third-party claim. In *Calvary Temple Church, Inc. v. Paino*,[30] the employer's worker's compensation insurance carrier claimed that it had no responsibility to pay one-third of the employee's attorney fees based upon the total of the amount it had paid in temporary total disability and medical expenses and the amount it was further obligated to pay for medical expenses and permanent partial impairment. In its opinion affirming the board's order to pay, the court stated:

> The seventh paragraph of Ind. Code Sec. 22-3-2-13 provides that an employer or its compensation insurance carrier pay a pro rata share of the costs and expenses of asserting the third party claim, action, or suit. In *Indiana State Commission v. White* (1973), 259 Ind. 690, 291 N.E.2d 550, our supreme court interpreted an earlier version of the same statute and reasoned that neither the duty of the employer to compensate the injured employee nor the right of the employee to receive compensation was diminished by the existence of a valid damage claim against a third party tort-feasor. The court further reasoned that if the employee failed to sue the third party, the employer could sue the third party based upon the employer's right to subrogation. However, since the employer would have had to pay all of its own attorneys' fees when instituting a subrogation suit, the employer or its compensation insurance carrier benefited, to the full extent of the employer's obligation under the Act, from a judgment or settlement of an action brought by the employee. The court noted the employer or its carrier, when reimbursed by the third party, received not only an amount equal to the payments made to the employee but also the value of having future compensation installments terminated. The court held that attorneys' fees, therefore, should be computed upon the total, after deduction of costs and expenses of the claim, of the amount which the employer or its carrier had already paid and the amount which it remained obligated to pay. *Id.* at 696–97, 291 N.E.2d at 554.[31]

The decision in *Calvary Temple Church* was later abrogated by

---

[29]Schneider Nat. Carriers, Inc. v. National Employee Care Systems, Inc., 469 F.3d 654, 658–61 (7th Cir. 2006).

[30]Calvary Temple Church, Inc. v. Paino, 555 N.E.2d 190 (Ind. Ct. App. 1990) (abrogated by, Christopher R. Brown, D.D.S., Inc. v. Decatur County Memorial Hosp., 892 N.E.2d 642 (Ind. 2008)).

[31]Calvary Temple Church, Inc. v. Paino, 555 N.E.2d 190, 194 (Ind. Ct. App. 1990) (abrogated by, Christopher R. Brown, D.D.S., Inc. v. Decatur County Memorial Hosp., 892 N.E.2d 642 (Ind. 2008)). See also Barclay v. Universal

the Indiana Supreme Court in *Christopher R. Brown, D.D.S., Inc. v. Decatur County Memorial Hosp.*[32] In *Christopher R. Brown, D.D.S.*, an employee of Decatur County Memorial Hospital was injured in an automobile accident. The employee received medical treatment through the authorization of her employer's insurance carrier. Dr. Brown provided some medical treatment and filed an Application for Adjustment of Claim for Provider Fee. Dr. Brown ultimately demanded payment of $17,292.88 in outstanding bills and requested an award of interest of 8% per annum on all unpaid amounts. The insurer paid the outstanding medical bills.

Subsequently, the board held a hearing on the issue of whether Dr. Brown was entitled to interest and the single hearing member awarded prejudgment interest. The full board reversed the single hearing member's decision. On appeal, Dr. Brown argued that he had entered into a contract for services with Decatur County Memorial Hospital's worker's compensation insurer. Thus, he argued, his claim should be treated as any other civil contract for purposes of his claim for prejudgment interest. The hospital argued that the Worker's Compensation Act contains no provision for an award of prejudgment interest.

In affirming the decision of the full board, the court of appeals reasoned that the worker's compensation system is purely statutory in nature and that it was not the intent of the legislature to create rights or obligations that were not specifically imposed in the Act.[33] The Indiana Supreme Court again affirmed, holding that in the absence of express statutory authority, the board could not award interest on worker's compensation benefits including past due medical bills, thereby abrogating *Calvary Temple Church.*[34]

In *Spangler, Jennings & Dougherty P.C. v. Indiana Ins. Co.,*[35] the law firm representing the injured employee claimed that it

---

Underwriters Group, 703 N.E.2d 169 (Ind. Ct. App. 1998) (a worker's compensation insurance carrier, asserting its lien against the proceeds secured by the injured employee pursuant to a settlement reached with the third-party tortfeasor, is bound *only* by the terms of IC 22-3-2-13 as to what it shall pay an attorney chosen by the injured employee). It should be noted, however, that comparative fault was not an issue in Barclay's settlement with the tortfeasor and, therefore, the court refused to consider the applicability of the comparative fault statute.

[32]Christopher R. Brown, D.D.S., Inc. v. Decatur County Memorial Hosp., 892 N.E.2d 642 (Ind. 2008).

[33]Christopher R. Brown, D.D.S., Inc. v. Decatur County Memorial Hosp., 873 N.E.2d 69, 72 (Ind. Ct. App. 2007).

[34]Christopher R. Brown, D.D.S., Inc. v. Decatur County Memorial Hosp., 892 N.E.2d 642 (Ind. 2008).

[35]Spangler, Jennings & Dougherty P.C. v. Indiana Ins. Co., 729 N.E.2d 117

was entitled to an attorney fee of one-third of the amount previously paid by the worker's compensation insurance carrier, plus one-third of the amount which it collected from the third-party tortfeasor but not reimbursed to the carrier, plus one-third of the amount of future medical expenses which the carrier would have paid but for the tort recovery. The lawyers relied upon the Supreme Court's opinion in *Indiana State Highway Commission v. White*,[36] to support their argument that they were entitled to a fee on future medical expenses. In deciding against the lawyers, the Indiana Supreme Court stated:

> The distinguishing factor between the future medical expenses in the present case and the future worker's compensation benefits in *White* is that the benefits in *White* were readily ascertainable. White died while acting within the scope of his employment. His death effectively fixed the amount of medical and funeral expenses and weekly wage benefits. Because Weidenaar was gravely injured, however, his medical expenses will be ongoing. To receive a fee on those unascertained expenses, Spangler would have to prove their value . . . .
>
> . . . The fact that the insurance carrier must pay fees on the whole worker's compensation award does not mean that the injured employee's attorney may keep a fee on the award in addition to the percentage of the third-party judgment he should receive. The attorney's entire fee for a third-party action should be no more than a percentage of the whole third-party judgment or settlement.
>
> Limiting Spangler's recovery from Indiana Insurance to a percentage of the carrier's lien provides Spangler one complete fee for its part of the work: the third-party action that benefits both Weidenaar and Indiana Insurance. If an attorney could keep a percentage of both the entire third-party judgment and a percentage of the future medical expenses the carrier would have paid but for the third-party tort action, that lawyer would be paid twice for the same dollar recovered . . . .
>
> . . . .
>
> Because we presume that Spangler did its job, we assume that the future medical expenses were part of the verdict that Spangler won for Weidenaar, and upon which it negotiated a settlement.
>
> "[T]he purpose the Legislature had in mind [when it enacted § 22-3-2-13] . . . was to free the injured workman . . . from paying attorney['s] fees for legal services for recovering the equivalent of the employer or compensation insurance carrier subrogation claim. In effect, the Legislature intended that the ultimate recovery of the employee should not be diluted by having to pay that portion of the attorney['s] fees required to collect that, which the injured employee . . . [is] entitled to collect under a compensation award, without any suit or settlement.

(Ind. 2000).

[36]Indiana State Highway Commission v. White, 259 Ind. 690, 291 N.E.2d 550 (1973).

White, 259 Ind. at 695–96, 291 N.E.2d at 553–54. In other words, the injured employee should not have to pay attorney's fees on the worker's compensation award, because the employee should get those fixed benefits without doing anything at all."[37]

In a footnote, the Court stated that an injured worker's attorney would not be "double dipping" under those circumstances where the attorney receives a fee, pursuant to IC 22-3-4-12, for litigating a client's case before the board and then performs the separately productive duty of pursuing a third-party tort claim for the benefit of the worker and/or the carrier.[38]

The Court also stated, in pertinent part:

> In worker's compensation third-party actions, as in other tort settings, the comparative fault of the injured employee-plaintiff is factored into the final judgment or settlement. And, while the employee is generally required to repay the worker's compensation carrier for benefits and expenses paid while the employee pursued the third-party action, the amount of that reimbursement is likewise reduced by the amount of the employee's comparative fault. Ind. Code Ann. § 22-3-2-13 (West 1991); Ind. Code Ann. § 34-51-2 19 (West 1999).[39]

Support for the Court's opinion in that regard comes from the decision of the U.S. District Court in *Weidenaar v. Indiana Ins. Co.*[40] There, the Court declared that the carrier's lien on the judgment which Weidenaar obtained must be reduced by the percentage of fault which the jury attributed to Weidenaar for his injuries.

But it must be remembered that these cases were decided prior to the 2000 amendment to IC 22-3-2-13. The current language of the statute provides that the attorney fee is to be computed on "the amount of benefits *actually repaid* after the expenses and costs in connection with the third party claim have been deducted."[41] The statute, in its present form, appears more concise and definite and should provide more certainty with respect to the amount of attorney fees which should be paid by the employer or carrier in any particular case.

Finally, *Tunny v. Erie Ins. Co.*[42] is illustrative of the interplay among many of the paragraphs contained in IC 22-3-2-13. There,

---

[37]Spangler, Jennings & Dougherty P.C. v. Indiana Ins. Co., 729 N.E.2d 117, 123–125 (Ind. 2000) (footnotes omitted).

[38]Spangler, Jennings & Dougherty P.C. v. Indiana Ins. Co., 729 N.E.2d 117, 124 (Ind. 2000).

[39]Spangler, Jennings & Dougherty P.C. v. Indiana Ins. Co., 729 N.E.2d 117, 120 (Ind. 2000).

[40]Weidenaar v. Indiana Ins. Co., 874 F. Supp. 235 (N.D. Ind. 1995).

[41]IC 22-3-2-13 (emphasis added).

[42]Tunny v. Erie Ins. Co., 790 N.E.2d 1009 (Ind. Ct. App. 2003).

Tunny sustained injuries in a work-related motor vehicle accident with Zheng. At the time of the accident, Zheng's employer, Tunny Brothers Masonry, carried underinsured motorist coverage with Erie Insurance Company. Tunny's employer's worker's compensation insurance carrier (GRE) paid his medical bills, temporary total disability, and permanent partial impairment compensation payments, and thus held a lien to the extent of those payment amounts. Prior to suit being filed, Zheng's insurer, American Economy, settled Tunny's claims against Zheng. Tunny used part of the settlement proceeds to reimburse GRE for the payments it had made to him and on his behalf, i.e., he paid 75% of the lien amount to GRE to satisfy its lien and paid 25% to his attorney (Skiles) for protecting GRE's lien rights, as required by IC 22-3-2-13. Thereafter, Tunny arbitrated his entitlement to UIM benefits with Erie, but the parties could not reach an agreement on the amount owed, and Erie then filed a declaratory judgment action in court. The trial court determined that Erie was entitled to a dollar for dollar set-off for the amount of the benefits received by Tunny from GRE but which Tunny did not repay GRE (i.e., the amount of attorney fees he paid to Skiles pursuant to IC 22-3-2-13). In reversing the trial court's decision, the court of appeals stated:

> The basic foundation for resolving the question before us rests upon what payments an injured employee is entitled to after the injury occurs and what requirements are placed upon that employee and his employer or the worker's compensation carrier by I.C. § 22-3-2-13 . . . . [T]he injured employee is entitled to the worker's compensation benefits regardless of whether or not any action is taken against the third party tortfeasor, a settlement or judgment is acquired by the injured employee, or the injured employee is able to collect against the tortfeasor. What is required is that if an injured employee collects an amount from a tortfeasor which exceeds the amount of worker's compensation benefits received by the injured employee, the employee must reimburse to the worker's compensation carrier from the amount received from the tortfeasor the amount of compensation already paid by the worker's compensation carrier. I.C. § 22-3-2-13. Literally, this means that the employee retains the rights to the worker's compensation payments and transfers to the worker's compensation carrier, the rights for the settlement or judgment against the tortfeasor, to the extent that the settlement or judgment satisfies the lien held by the worker's compensation carrier.
>
> . . . The worker's compensation statute requires the worker's compensation carrier to pay to the injured employee's attorney a fixed amount of 25% or 33 1/3%, depending upon whether suit was filed to collect against the third-party tortfeasor. The percentage is computed upon the amount which it receives as reimbursement to fulfill its lien. . . .
>
> . . . .

. . . . [T]he reimbursement to the worker's compensation carrier from the third-party settlement is not a reimbursement of the worker's compensation *payments* . . . but rather, of the *amount* of the payments . . . .

. . . [W]hile the amount reimbursed to GRE was equal to the amount of worker's compensation benefits paid to Tunny (and will be whenever the settlement from the third-party is greater than the amount of the worker's compensation payments), Tunny did not reimburse the worker's compensation benefits to GRE. Instead, GRE is collecting a third-party judgment to satisfy its lien. The fee which GRE must pay to Skiles is not for Tunny receiving worker's compensation benefits, but for Skiles protecting GRE's lien. Tunny had already received his worker's compensation benefits before GRE had a lien, and in the event that Tunny did retain counsel to assist in the collection of worker's compensation benefits, the attorney fees would come from those payments, not from the later reimbursement to GRE.

. . . .

. . . [T]he injured employee retains the entire worker's compensation payment. The worker is entitled to that amount even if no third-party action is taken and does not have to reimburse that amount unless a sufficient recovery is made against a third-party. Stated differently, in the event of a settlement with the third-party tortfeasor, the injured employee retains from the settlement with the third-party only the amount which exceeds that which satisfies the lien of the worker's compensation carrier. The second reason that the injured employee cannot be deemed to have retained the amount which is to be paid to his attorney is that the fee is not for any benefit provided to the injured employee. Rather, the amount is based solely upon the share of the representation which the attorney has done for the worker's compensation carrier in collecting upon its lien. Consequently, to the extent that the *Wildman* decision could be read to hold that the UIM insurer could reduce the policy limit by the amount of the attorney's fees to be paid by the worker's compensation carrier if those fees are not directly paid to the attorney by the worker's compensation carrier, we decline to follow it.

Based upon these considerations, and redirecting our attention to the UIM policy before us, we conclude that Erie may not reduce the policy limit by the amount which GRE was required to reimburse Skiles. . . .

. . . [W]hen calculating attorney fees under I.C. § 22-3-2-13, one should not look at the ultimate percentage which the attorney collects, but instead, one should be concerned that the attorney does not receive a percentage of the reimbursement to the worker's compensation carrier plus a percentage from the injured employee on the amount which is reimbursed to the worker's compensation carrier. *See Spangler, Jennings & Dougherty P.C.,* 729 N.E.2d at 123 (stating that an attorney should not receive a fee on the whole worker's compensation award in addition to a percentage of the third-party judgment he should receive). In this case, the agreement between Tunny and Skiles prevents such a double recovery.[43]

In *Gonzalez v. State*,[44] the Court of Appeals addressed a recovery of workers compensation benefits that resulted from a criminal act under Indiana's restitution provisions. Gonzalez was a prisoner in the Indiana Department of Correction. He beat Miami Corrections Officer Rodney Gahl in the head and face with a padlock in a sock, resulting in serious injuries. He was convicted of attempted murder for the attack and ordered to pay restitution to the third party administrator of the State's workers' compensation benefits including $181,185.43 in medical benefits, $34,901.17 in lost wage benefits and $41,200 for the permanent partial impairment settlement paid to Gahl. On appeal Gonzalez argued he should not be ordered to repay the PPI settlement because it was not a "specific cost" that the trial court should have considered and the Court of Appeals agreed as the restitution provision provided for recovery of already incurred lost wages or medical expenses.

In *Justice v American Family Mutual Insurance Co.*,[45] the Indiana Supreme Court considered whether an uninsured motorist insurer may apply the insured's workers' compensation recovery as a setoff against the policy's liability limit. The American Family policy expressly and unambiguously stated that the "limits of liability of this coverage will be reduced by . . . [a] payment made or amount payable by or on behalf of any person or organization which may be legally liable [and] . . . [a] payment made or amount payable because of bodily injury under any workers' compensation or disability benefits law."[46] The Court reviewed the policy language and concluded that it unambiguously provides for the setoff against the policy limits. However, continuing its analysis, the Court considered whether the language comports with state statute. If not, it was unenforceable. The uninsured/underinsured motorist statute was intended to promote recovery of damages for innocent victims of auto accidents with uninsured or underinsured motorists. The Court noted that, since it was enacted, insurers had tried on many occasions to circumvent its minimum coverage requirement, the outcome of which was unsuccessful. Justice, who received $25,000 from the driver of the vehicle, Wagner, who caused his accident, did not receive the full statutory minimum from the tortfeasor's insurer; minimum was $50,000. Wagner had failed to carry the statutory minimum

---

[43]Tunny v. Erie Ins. Co., 790 N.E.2d 1009, 1014–18 (Ind. Ct. App. 2003).

[44]Gonzalez v. State, 3 N.E.3d 27 (Ind. Ct. App. 2014).

[45]Justice v. American Family Mut. Ins. Co., 4 N.E.3d 1171 (Ind. 2014).

[46]Justice, 4 N.E.3d at 1174.

coverage and if he had Justice would have received $50,000. Given the purpose of the uninsured/underinsured motorist statute was to "put him in that position." The Court concluded that Justice was entitled to recover the remaining $25,000 from American Family and to the extent that the policy provisions were contrary to the uninsured/underinsured motorist statute it was unlawful and unenforceable.

In *Anderson v. Indiana Insurance Co.*,[47] the Court of Appeals considered the offset provisions of an underinsured motorist policy. In October 2010, Anderson, while acting in the course and scope of her employment, was stopped in traffic when she was struck by a vehicle driven by Denise Cox resulting in injuries to her neck and left shoulder. Anderson received $25,000 from Cox's insurer and $81,166.15 in workers' compensation benefits. At the time of the accident Anderson was insured under a policy with Indiana Insurance which included underinsured motorist coverage. Anderson filed a complaint against Cox and Indiana Insurance arguing Indiana Insurance should compensate her for her injuries and damages to the extent that such damages exceeded Cox's insurance coverage. The trial court dismissed her complaint based on a summary judgment motion filed by Indiana Insurance. The Court concluded that the language of the policy allowed for the offset but then went a step further to consider whether this offset was allowed by Indiana Code § 27-7-5. The trial courts order that Anderson could not recover anything from Indiana Insurance because she had received $25,000 from Cox and $81,166.15 in workers' compensation benefits and the sum of those amounts exceeded the policy limits of $100,000 was found in error. Reasoning that if Cox had carried the required amount of liability insurance Anderson might have received $50,000 in addition to the over $81,000 in workers' compensation benefits the Court of Appeals reversed the dismissal of her complaint for underinsured damages against Indiana Insurance. The Court of Appeals, considering the intent of the underinsured motorist statute, found Anderson was entitled to receive the remaining $25,000 from Indiana Insurance (as long as her total damages supported the same).

§ 3:29 Contractor liability; certificates of compliance or exemption

IC 22-3-2-14 and IC 22-3-2-14.5 contain specific liability provisions relating to independent contractors and those who contract with them for the performance of their services. Depending upon the factual circumstances of each particular case, secondary liability may or may not be imposed under these sections.

---

[47]Anderson v. Indiana Ins. Co., 8 N.E.3d 258 (Ind. Ct. App. 2014).

In IC 22-3-2-14(b), it is provided that the state, any political division thereof, any municipal corporation, any corporation, limited liability company, partnership, or person (except one who contracts for work to be performed on his or her owner-occupied residential property), who contracts for the performance of any work exceeding $1,000 in value by a contractor subject to the Act, must obtain from the board a certificate demonstrating that the contractor has complied with the insurance or self-insurance provisions of the Act. If no certificate is obtained from the board, any of the above are liable to the same extent as the contractor for the payment of compensation, physician's fees, hospital fees, nurse's charges, and burial expenses on account of the injury or death of any employee of the contractor, due to an accident arising out of and in the course of the performance of the work covered by the contract.[1]

Pursuant to IC 22-3-2-14(c), a contractor who sublets a contract to a subcontractor subject to the Act has a like duty to exact a certificate from the board showing compliance by the subcontractor and, if the contractor does not, it will be liable to the same extent as the subcontractor for compensable injuries sustained by the subcontractor's employees.

IC 22-3-2-14(d) states that those persons or entities who are compelled to pay worker's compensation benefits under this section may recover the amounts paid, or to be paid, from any person who, independently of these provisions, would have been liable for such payments. In addition, those held secondarily liable may recover the litigation expenses and attorney fees which they incur to both defend the action before the board and pursue collection of the benefits paid.

Finally, IC 22-3-2-14(e) provides that every claim filed with the board under this section shall be brought against all parties liable for payment so that the board may fix the order in which the parties shall be exhausted, beginning with the immediate employer of the injured worker.

IC 22-3-2-14(c) provides:

An contractor who shall sublet any contract for the performance of any work, to a subcontractor subject to the compensation provisions of IC 22-3-2 through IC 22-3-6, without obtaining a certificate from the workers' compensation board showing that such subcontractor has complied with section 5 of this chapter, IC 22-3-5-1, and IC 22-3-5-2, shall be liable to the same extent as such subcontractor for the payment of compensation, physician's fees, hospital fees, nurses charges, and burial expenses on account of the injury or death of

---

[Section 3:29]

[1]IC 22-3-2-14(a) and (b).

any employee of such subcontractor due to an accident arising out of and in the course of the performance of the work covered by such subcontract.

In *Gradex v. Arbuckle*,[2] the full board ordered a general contractor to pay 95% of the plaintiff's medical expenses and permanent impairment compensation. On appeal, Gradex argued that the full board erred in concluding that the subcontractor, M & W, was financially unable to foot the bill.

The court of appeals affirmed the full board, referring to IC 22-3-2-14(e) which provides that the board shall fix the order in which said parties shall be exhausted. The evidence before the board supported its decision to require Gradex to pay a majority of the claimed benefits.

As with other sections of the Act, the appellate courts have attempted to give the wording of this section its plain and ordinary meaning. For instance, in *B & V Distributing, Inc. v. Mayo*,[3] B & V contracted with McCarty's Roofing to reconstruct the roof of a building. McCarty's subcontracted a portion of the work to Patterson. Patterson hired Mayo to work on the job. Mayo was injured while working on the roof. Neither McCarty's nor Patterson carried worker's compensation insurance. Mayo filed a claim with the board naming B & V, McCarty's, and Patterson as his employers. The board held B & V secondarily liable to Mayo, but the appellate court reversed. In doing so, the court reasoned:

> IC 22-3-2-14(a) does not impose liability on B & V for an injured employee of a subcontractor. Moreover, the nature of the relationship between the contractee corporation and the independent contractor inherently limits the control the contractee corporation exerts over the independent contractor's business practices. The corporation also lacks notice or knowledge of the independent contractor's failure to comply with the Worker's Compensation Act when hiring a subcontractor. In the present case, the imposition of liability creates an additional tier of liability not provided for by the General Assembly in IC 22-3-2-14.[4]

In *Howard v. U.S. Signcrafters*,[5] the appellate court noted that IC 22-3-2-14 and its subsections "are intended to provide adequate coverage for *employees* of independent contractors where the contractors have not adequately covered worker's compensation risks. *See* Travelers Ins. Co. v. R.B. Carriers, Inc., 613 N.E.2d

---

[2]Gradex, Inc. v. Arbuckle, 903 N.E.2d 969 (Ind. Ct. App. 2009).

[3]B & V Distributing, Inc. v. Mayo, 613 N.E.2d 499 (Ind. Ct. App. 1993).

[4]B & V Distributing, Inc. v. Mayo, 613 N.E.2d 499, 501 (Ind. Ct. App. 1993).

[5]Howard v. U.S. Signcrafters, 811 N.E.2d 479 (Ind. Ct. App. 2004).

440, 444 (Ind. Ct. App. 1993)."[6] Although Howard sought to bring himself within the coverage of the Act, the court concluded that he did not meet the definitional requirements:

> Howard was the owner of a sole proprietorship called Custom Signs. While sole proprietors may elect to make themselves employees of their sole proprietorships under Indiana Code section 22-3-6-1(b)(4), Howard did not do so. Howard failed to maintain worker's compensation coverage for his business. As a result, he was unable to elect to treat himself as an employee for worker's compensation purposes. Howard is therefore not an employee of Custom Signs under the worker's compensation statute, and Indiana Code section 22-3-2-14 does not apply to his injury.[7]

IC 22-3-2-14.5 contains definitional subsections as well as those more substantive in nature. There is some interplay between this section and IC 22-3-6-1(b)(4) and (5); they must be read together. As referred to in *Howard*, IC 22-3-6-1(b)(4) and (5) provide that owners of sole proprietorships and partners in partnerships may elect to include themselves as employees for coverage under the Act, if they actually are engaged in the proprietorship or partnership business. If they make this election, they must serve written notice of the election upon their insurance carriers and the board. They are not employees under the Act until the notice is received. If the owners or partners also are independent contractors in the construction trades, and they do not make the election allowed by this subsection, they must obtain an affidavit of exemption under IC 22-3-2-14.5.

Independent contractors who do not elect to include themselves as employees are not subject to the compensation provisions of the Act and must file a statement to that effect with, and obtain clearance from, the Indiana Department of Revenue in order to obtain a certificate of exemption. The certificate, along with a filing fee, must be filed with the board, and the certificate so received will be stamped and noted in the database maintained by the board for that purpose. In order to keep their exemption valid, independent contractors must file annual statements of their independent contractor status with the Department of Revenue.[8]

A person (meaning, an individual, a proprietorship, partnership, joint venture, firm, association, corporation, or other legal entity) contracting for services with another person not covered by the Act to perform work must secure a copy of a stamped certificate of exemption from the person hired. The person providing

---

[6]Howard v. U.S. Signcrafters, 811 N.E.2d 479 (Ind. Ct. App. 2004).

[7]Howard v. U.S. Signcrafters, 811 N.E.2d 479, 484 (Ind. Ct. App. 2004).

[8]IC 22-3-2-14.5(c) to (g).

the certificate of exemption cannot be compelled to have worker's compensation coverage, and the compensation insurance carrier for the person who contracts with an independent contractor must accept the certificate of exemption the same as it would a certificate of insurance.[9]

Most importantly, subsection (i) of IC 22-3-2-14.5 provides that a stamped certificate filed under the section is binding upon and holds harmless from all claims a person who contracts with an independent contractor after receiving a copy of the stamped certificate, as well as the person's worker's compensation insurance carrier. Needless to say, an independent contractor may not collect worker's compensation benefits from a person, or his or her carrier, to whom the independent contractor has furnished a stamped certificate of exemption.

The issue in Hood's Gardens, Inc. v. Young,[10] a 2012 case before the Court of Appeals, was essentially whether the state court had jurisdiction to make a threshold determination as to whether the Worker's Compensation Act applied. Hoods entered into an oral contract with D&E that D&E would remove an oak tree for a price of $600 with D&E to clear and haul away the wood and debris. D&E sent Dennis Wyant a subcontractor, to cut the limbs from the trees. A few days later, D&E sent Young (its employee) to finish the job. Young sustained severe injuries while removing the tree resulting in paraplegia. D&E did not have worker's compensation insurance at the time of this injury. Young then demanded Hoods' pay worker's compensation benefits under IC 22-3-2-14(b) which in essence provides that any person contracting for work performance of any work exceeding $1,000 in value without first extracting a certificate of compliance from the Worker's Compensation Board showing the contractor has worker's compensation, will be secondarily liable to pay worker's compensation to the contractor's employees.

Hoods argued that it had no duty to pay worker's compensation because the value of the contract was less than $1,000. Hoods filed a motion for summary judgment with the state court seeking an order that Hoods cannot be held secondarily liable to pay worker's compensation benefits. Young responded by filing a motion to dismiss the state court matter on the grounds that it does not have subject matter jurisdiction to determine the rights and obligations of the parties, and that this case should be heard by the Indiana worker's compensation board.

The state court dismissed Hoods' motion for summary judgment, stating in essence that since IC 22-3-2-14(b) is located

---

[9]IC 22-3-2-14.5(h).

[10]Hood's Gardens, Inc. v. Young, 976 N.E.2d 80 (Ind. Ct. App. 2012).

within the Worker's Compensation Act, the worker's compensation board has exclusive jurisdiction.

In reversing the lower court, The Court of Appeals held that the exclusive jurisdiction provision in the Worker's Compensation Act does not limit a trial court's jurisdiction to make a threshold determination of whether the Worker's Compensation Act applies.

The matter went back to the trial court and thereafter Young appealed to the Court of Appeals again.[11] On appeal from the trial court's decision following the Court of Appeals ruling in 2012,[12] Young challenged the trial court's granting of summary judgment in favor of Hood's as well as its striking of his affidavit. The Court of Appeals first determined that the trial court did not abuse its discretion by striking a portion of Young's affidavit in regards to the value of the wood at issue in the litigation, finding Young failed to establish he was an expert or a "skilled witness" and his opinion was thus a conclusory and speculative lay opinion.

On the issue of the trial court having granted Hood's summary judgment motion, Young argued that there remained a material issue of fact regarding whether the actual value of the contract exceeded $1000.00, and therefore Hood's summary judgment motion was granted in error. The trial court rejected Young's argument that the value of the contract should include the value stated in the contract and the value of the wood to be retained. The Court of Appeals agreed and affirmed that trial court. It found that it was the "up-front" value as stated in the agreement which must exceed $1000 in order to trigger secondary liability under the Act. The trial Court reasoned that "[o]therwise, companies would be unknowingly exposing themselves to liability, depending on the value of 'scrap' that they just want to be removed from their property."

In 2015, Indiana's Supreme Court accepted transfer in *Young v. Hood's Gardens Inc.*[13] to address whether the "value" that triggers secondary liability under Indiana Code § 22-3-2-14(b) is limited to the dollar amount paid in cash or may include the value of other property transferred, in this case fire wood, in performance of the contract. Indiana's Supreme Court reversed the Court of Appeals and found that the "value" includes both direct monetary payment as well as any ancillary consideration in goods and services received by the employer for the work.

It should be noted that transfer to the Supreme Court was not

---

[11]Young v. Hood's Gardens, Inc., 2 N.E.3d 724 (Ind. Ct. App. 2013), transfer granted, opinion vacated, IN RAP 58(A), 7 N.E.3d 992 (Ind. 2014).

[12]Hood's Gardens, Inc. v. Young, 976 N.E.2d 80 (Ind. Ct. App. 2012).

[13]Young v. Hood's Gardens, Inc., 24 N.E.3d 421 (Ind. 2015).

sought in regards to the initial appeal decision which established the trial court's subject matter jurisdiction to determine the threshold issue of whether the Workers' Compensation Act applies.[14]

---

[14]See Hood's Gardens, Inc. v. Young, 976 N.E.2d 80, 84 (Ind. Ct. App. 2012), *trans. not sought.*

Chapter 4

Claims and Benefits

KeyCite®: Cases and other legal materials listed in KeyCite Scope can be researched through the KeyCite service on Westlaw®. Use KeyCite to check citations for form, parallel references, prior and later history, and comprehensive citator information, including citations to other decisions and secondary materials.

---

§ 4:1   Introduction

The claims and benefits section of the Act, IC 22-3-3-1 et seq., not only establishes the pecuniary entitlements which an injured worker or his or her dependents may receive for medical care and treatment, disability, impairment, and/or death, but it also provides the mechanism by which the injury must be reported and the compensation benefits pursued, at least in the initial stages of development of the claim. These sections serve to protect employers against the assertion of stale claims, and impose obligations upon the worker to timely treat his or her injuries with a view toward returning to gainful employment, if possible.

§ 4:2 Notice

The injured employee or his or her dependents are duty bound to give written notice to the employer of the injury or death as soon as practicable after the occurrence of the injury-producing event, unless the employer or its representative already have actual knowledge or acquire actual knowledge of the injury or death afterward.[1] Unless written notice is given or knowledge is acquired within 30 days from the date of injury or death, no compensation shall be paid until and from the date such notice is given or knowledge obtained. However, IC 22-3-3-1 also provides that lack of knowledge or insufficiency of the notice will not bar the right to compensation, unless the employer is able to demonstrate that it is prejudiced, and then only to the extent of such prejudice.[2]

The notice contemplated by the Act must state the name and address of the employee, and the time, place, nature, and cause of the injury or death. The notice must be signed by the injured employee or by someone on the employee's behalf. In the case of death, one or more of the employee's dependents, or someone on their behalf, must sign the notice. The notice may be served on the employer personally, or upon any foreperson, superintendent, or manager of the employer to whose orders the injured or deceased employee was required to conform. It may also be served upon any agent of the employer upon whom a summons in a civil action may be served. In the alternative, the notice may be sent to the employer by registered mail, addressed to his last known residence or place of business.[3]

In *Pirtle v. National Tea Co.*,[4] a worker was injured while picking up a carton weighing 40 to 60 pounds. Pirtle thought that he only "pulled a muscle" in his back, and therefore continued working and did not inform his employer of his injury at the time of the injury. Four days later, while at work, Pirtle could not stand up straight. He told his foreman that he had pain in his back stemming from the incident four days earlier. The foreman sent him home and the following day, the employee telephoned his employer to report the injury. He was advised to seek treatment at the employer's clinic, which he did over a period of weeks. Five months later, he filed his claim for compensation benefits with the board. The board denied his claim based in part upon his fail-

---

[Section 4:2]

[1]IC 22-3-3-1.

[2]IC 22-3-3-1; Bogdon v. Ramada Inn, Inc., 415 N.E.2d 767 (Ind. Ct. App. 1981).

[3]IC 22-3-3-2.

[4]Pirtle v. National Tea Co., 159 Ind. App. 597, 308 N.E.2d 720 (1974).

ure to give notice of the injury to his employer. In reversing the board's decision, the appellate court stated:

An injured employee must give notice to his employer as a condition precedent to receiving compensation under the Workmen's Compensation Act . . . .

This court has long held that an employer seeking to defend against payment of a claim on the ground that he was prejudiced by lack of knowledge or defective notice of the employee's injury has the burden of proof to show such lack of notice or defective notice. And, even if the employer shows lack of notice, compensation is not barred unless the employer can show he is prejudiced by such lack of knowledge. Where such prejudice is shown, the employee's right to compensation is barred only to the extent of the prejudice.

In the case at bar, the employer neither alleged that it was prejudiced by inadequate notice from the claimant, nor attempted to prove to what extent and in what manner claimant's failure to submit a written accident report has prejudiced it.

. . . .

This court has repeatedly held that under our Workmen's Compensation Act actual knowledge of a claimant's injury by another employee who has some supervisory authority over claimant is sufficient to impute that notice to the employer. Fear-Campbell Co. v. Yearion (1928), 88 Ind. App. 382, 164 N.E. 282 . . . .

The court stated in Fear-Campbell Co. at 385 of 88 Ind. App., at 284 of 164 N.E.:

"[The] testimony discloses actual knowledge of the said injury by the appellant, through its foreman Pierce. It is evident that both Pierce and appellee did not regard the injury as being of the serious nature that afterwards developed but this fact can in no way relieve the appellant. A workman had received an injury by accident, arising out of and in the course of his employment, and his foreman had knowledge of these facts and should have reported the same to his superiors. His failure to do so cannot be charged against the appellee."

. . . .

The law on the sufficiency of actual and imputed notice to an employer of an employee's injury is well settled in Small, Workmen's Compensation Law, s12.2, at 372–373 (1950):

"It is readily apparent from the statute that no formal notice of injury or death need be given if the employer has knowledge of it, either actually or by imputation.

"The actual knowledge of any foreman, superintendent, or other person charged with authority over the injured employee's work is sufficient notice upon which to charge the employer. It is immaterial that the information may have been obtained quite informally, or that the supervisory employee failed to relay the knowledge to the employer.

"It is enough if the employer has knowledge, either actual or imputed, that the workman has suffered an injury; he does not have to be fully informed of the consequences." [Footnotes omitted.]

Thus, even upon the facts most favorable to the appellee herein, the conclusion must be reached that the notice given by the claimant in the case at bar was sufficient. The employer was, in fact, aware the claimant had been injured.[5]

In *Roebel v. Dana Corp.*,[6] however, an employee was denied compensation benefits for failing to notify his employer of an injury, who was prejudiced by the employee's lack of notice. The facts established that Roebel had been a Dana employee for 42 years. Approximately a year-and-a-half prior to taking early retirement, Roebel began to complain every two to four weeks that he had been the subject of harassment or practical jokes. Dana was unable to identify a perpetrator. The employer offered to transfer Roebel to a different department, but he refused. Roebel worked a considerable amount of hours right up to his retirement, and was viewed as an excellent employee until the day he left his job.

Approximately eight months prior to his eventual retirement, Roebel did not go home one night, but slept in his car at Dana. The following day, he took a leave of absence and did not return to work for 11 weeks. During that period, Roebel was treated at two separate facilities for depression and stress. His medical records established marital discord, but no reference to the incidents of harassment at work.

Roebel left Dana without telling anyone that he had decided to retire because he could no longer tolerate the pranks. In fact, when he notified Dana of his intent to retire, he said that things in the plant were going well. Dana first learned of Roebel's claimed disability two months after his retirement when his wife notified the company that a worker's compensation claim form had been mailed. Dana had no prior knowledge that Roebel had been treated for stress or the reasons therefor.

In affirming the board's denial of benefits to Roebel, the court of appeals stated:

> At no time did Roebel expressly state that he perceived himself to have been injured by reason of the work environment at Dana or give anyone any reason to suspect that he was suffering emotionally to such an extent that he could no longer work. Roebel did not appear to manifest any symptoms of injury, and Roebel made no showing that anyone at Dana had any knowledge of his pre-existing nonoccupational susceptibility to anxiety and depression. Moreover, there was no single precipitating event which might have been identified by Dana as producing Roebel's injury.
>
> . . . .

---

[5]Pirtle v. National Tea Co., 159 Ind. App. 597, 308 N.E.2d 720, 721–723 (1974) (citations omitted).

[6]Roebel v. Dana Corp., 638 N.E.2d 1356 (Ind. Ct. App. 1994).

. . . The medical evidence offered from Dr. Green established that Roebel suffered from dysthymia, a depression, which, if compensable as an injury by accident at all in this case, is compensable by reason of its aggravation. *See generally, Hansen,* 507 N.E.2d 573. Roebel's failure to give Dana actual notice of his injury precluded Dana from taking any action with respect to Roebel's condition, either to immediately alleviate the stress experienced by Roebel which was attributable to the workplace by putting Roebel into a different kind of employment or by obtaining appropriate medical treatment for him. Dr. Green testified that Roebel had not had appropriate medication prescribed for him; Dana was never given the opportunity to investigate how Roebel might function in his job with proper medication. In short, Roebel's failure to give notice of the injury sustained by him precluded Dana from removing the workplace as a contributing cause of Roebel's disability; further aggravation of Roebel's condition might have been prevented and disability forestalled. The Board's conclusion that Dana has proven that it has been prejudiced by Roebel's failure to give notice is amply substantiated by the record.[7]

Obviously, each claim of prejudice by an employer will necessarily turn upon the facts associated therewith, but those portions of the facts and the court's opinion in *Roebel,* as set forth above, serve to demonstrate the types of factual matters which would serve to assist the board or an appellate court in making its determination in that regard.

§ 4:3   Limitation for filing claim

The Act provides that a right to compensation shall be forever barred unless, within two years after the occurrence of the accident, or, if death results from the accident, within two years from the date of death, a claim for compensation is filed with the board. But in those cases where an accident or death results from the exposure to radiation, a claim for compensation must be filed with the board within two years from the date upon which the employee had knowledge of the injury or, by exercise of reasonable diligence, should have known of the existence of the injury and its causal relationship to his or her employment.[1]

The nature and effect of the predecessor to IC 22-3-3-3 was discussed by the appellate court in its opinion in *Wawrinchak v. U. S. Steel Corp., Gary Works:*[2]

"A statute of limitations should be differentiated from conditions which are annexed to a right of action created by statute. A statute

---

[7]Roebel v. Dana Corp., 638 N.E.2d 1356, 1361–62 (Ind. Ct. App. 1994).

[Section 4:3]

[1]IC 22-3-3-3.

[2]Wawrinchak v. U. S. Steel Corp., Gary Works, 148 Ind. App. 444, 267 N.E.2d 395 (1971).

which in itself creates a new liability, gives an action to enforce it unknown to the common law, and fixes the time within which that action may be commenced, is not a statute of limitations. It is a statute of creation, and the commencement of the action of the time it fixes is an indispensable condition of the liability and of the action which it permits. The time element is an inherent element of the right so created, and the limitation of the remedy is a limitation of the right. Such a provision will control, no matter in what form the action is brought. The statute is an offer of an action on condition that it be commenced within the specified time. If the offer is not accepted in the only way in which it can be accepted, by a commencement of the action within the specified time, the action and the right of action no longer exist, and the defendant is exempt from liability. Whether an enactment is of this nature, or whether it is a statute of limitations, should be determined from a proper construction of its terms."

A nonclaim statute creates a right of action and has inherent in it the denial of a right of action. It imposes a condition precedent—the time element which is a part of the action itself. As noted in Donnella, Admrx. v. Crady (1962), 135 Ind. App. 60, 185 N.E.2d 623, "Unless the claim is filed within the prescribed time set out in the statute, no enforceable right of action is created." The nonclaim statute is self-executing where the general statute of limitations is not. Even the rule of waiver has no application to the nonclaim statute, and the time element is not a defense as in the general statute of limitations. Moreover, such nonclaim statutes may not be extended. As this court pointed out in Donnella v. Crady, supra, at pages 63 and 64, 185 N.E.2d at page 625: "Such statutes are not extended by the disability, fraud, or misconduct of the parties. The time to act cannot be waived by the parties or lengthened by the court. Unless the claim is filed or the action thereon brought within the time prescribed by the said statute, any right of action then existing becomes unenforceable and the claim or action is forever barred."

The final word of this court upon the statute here under consideration was expressed by Judge Sharp in Huffman v. State Sign Co. (1969), Ind. App., 18 Ind. Dec. 770, at page 771, 251 N.E.2d 489, wherein this court stated: "The legislative intent of Sec. 40-1224 is clear. With the exception of radiation injuries, the right is forever barred unless a claim is filed within two years after such death. This interpretation was clearly inferred in Railway Express Agency v. Harrington, 119 Ind. App. 593, 598, 88 N.E.2d 175 (1949), and explicitly stated by this court in Lewis v. Marhoefer Packing Co., Ind. App., [18 Ind. Dec. 346], 250 N.E.2d 375 (1969).

See also Small, Workmen's Compensation Law of Indiana, § 12. 3."

An examination of the statute presently before the court, s 40-1224, supra, leaves no doubt that we are dealing with a nonclaim statute and not a general statute of limitations. Therefore, the questions of waiver and stipulation are laid to rest.

The appellant's claim was barred by s 40-1224, supra, and could not have been resurrected by waiver or stipulation after the expiration of two years from the date of death.[3]

In *Bowles v. General Elec.*,[4] an assembly line worker began to experience pain in her elbows in 1994. In 1995, Bowles underwent ulnar nerve transfers on both elbows, and then returned to work 12 weeks later. The symptoms which she experienced before her surgeries never completely subsided. In 1999, Bowles was diagnosed as having lateral epicondylitis, a condition more commonly known as tennis elbow. In 2000, she left her employment with GE. Thereafter, subsequent surgeries were performed. In 2002, for the first time, Bowles filed an application for worker's compensation benefits. At no time prior thereto did she seek to have her medical expenses paid by her employer, nor did she seek compensation from GE for her time off from work. GE moved to dismiss her application as untimely. The single hearing member granted GE's motion, and the full board adopted his decision. In affirming the dismissal of the claimant's application, the court of appeals stated:

> Once the definition of a compensable worker's compensation injury evolved to encompass repetitive stress injuries, however, the question arose regarding when such a claim accrued . . . .
>
> . . . .
>
> . . . Here, as in *Duvall*, Bowles's work-related repetitive stress injuries were discernible years before she filed an application for worker's compensation. . . . Bowles testified before the Board, and conceded at oral argument, that she *knew* her injuries were work-related. Despite this, she made the conscious choice *not* to submit

---

[3]Wawrinchak v. U. S. Steel Corp., Gary Works, 148 Ind. App. 444, 267 N.E.2d 395, 399–400 (1971) (citations omitted). See also Cox v. American Aggregates Corp., 684 N.E.2d 193 (Ind. 1997). There, an injured worker filed a civil action against his employer alleging an intentional injury. The trial court granted summary judgment for the employer, and the court of appeals affirmed. The injured employee then, seven years after the date of his injury, filed a claim with the board. He relied upon the Journey's Account Statute, which "serves to resuscitate actions that have otherwise expired under a statute of limitations." Cox, 684 N.E.2d at 195. The court concluded that the Journey's Account Statute does not apply to worker's compensation claims, "regardless of how the limitation period was built into the statute." Cox, 684 N.E.2d at 196. Also, in Colburn v. Kessler's Team Sports, 850 N.E.2d 1001 (Ind. Ct. App. 2006), transfer denied, 869 N.E.2d 451 (Ind. 2007), an injured employee's claim, filed more than two years after the date of injury was held to be untimely and thus barred. The employee unsuccessfully argued that since the statute referred to a right to compensation, the two-year limitation period contained therein did not apply to a claim for medical expenses. He further argued that the two-year claim filing requirement is tolled if there is no disagreement between the employee and the employer within two years from the accident date. The court could find no support for claimant's argument.

[4]Bowles v. General Elec., 824 N.E.2d 769 (Ind. Ct. App. 2005).

her claim to worker's compensation because of her negative percep-
tion of GE's doctors . . . . Bowles's injury was discernible, at the
latest, by November 1999 and her Application was untimely.

. . . [S]he urges us to refine the *Duvall* rule and hold that a
claim accrues when the *permanence* of the injury is discernible,
relying on *Union City Body Co. v. Lambdin*, 569 N.E.2d 373. *Union
City*, however, is readily distinguishable. . . . [T]he language relied
upon from *Union City*, 'the statute of limitations will commence to
run when its permanence is discernible,' *id.* at 374, derives from
tort case law discussing application of the continuing wrong
doctrine . . . . The continuing wrong doctrine is a "legal concept
used to define when an act, omission, or neglect took place" and
causes a statute of limitations to begin to run at the end of the
continuing wrongful act . . . . The continuing wrong doctrine,
however, is fundamentally at odds with Indiana's worker's
compensation laws since, as the doctrine's name implies, an initial
wrongful act is required for its application. Worker's compensation,
to the contrary, is designed to provide compensation to injured employees without regard to a determination of fault or wrongful
actions. *See, e.g., Waldridge v. Futurex Indus., Inc.*, 714 N.E.2d 783
(Ind. Ct. App. 1999). As such, we disagree that language in Union
City discussing the permanence of an injury should be used as the
basis of a rule in repetitive stress injury cases regarding when a
claim accrues.[5]

In *Inland Steel Co. v. Pavlinac*,[6] an employer also argued that
the claimant's application for worker's compensation benefits was
untimely, since it was filed more than a decade after his repetitive trauma injury was first discernible. In affirming the board's
award for the injured employee, the court of appeals stated:

When the claim is one for repetitive trauma, this court has held
that an employee's claim for repetitive trauma injuries accrues
when the cumulative effect of the work demands is discernible as
an injury. *Barrett*, 638 N.E.2d at 795.

It is undisputed that Pavlinac suffered several back injuries over
the years and that several of these injuries were sustained in the
scope and course of his employment with Inland while others were
not. As found by the Board, after each injury, Pavlinac was assigned a 0% permanent partial impairment rating and was released
from medical care and returned to work with no restrictions, with
the most recent release being October 23, 1998. Thereafter, Pavlinac
worked on a full-time basis at his usual capacity. The Board further
found that in April, 1999, Pavlinac had a specific, identifiable accident which was deemed by the Board to be the "[s]traw that broke
the camel's back." Given that Pavlinac attempted to return to work
after this last accident, but was unsuccessful because the demands
of the job proved too great given the condition of his back, his last
date of employment essentially represented the culmination of the

---

[5]Bowles v. General Elec., 824 N.E.2d 769, 773–75 (Ind. Ct. App. 2005)
(citations omitted) (footnote omitted).

[6]Inland Steel Co. v. Pavlinac, 865 N.E.2d 690 (Ind. Ct. App. 2007).

repetitive trauma to his back. It was on this date, June 8, 1999, when it became clear that Pavlinac sustained an injury resulting from the cumulative effect of the prior back injuries, the incident in April, 1999, and the repetitive heavy lifting, twisting, turning, and bending which were part of his normal day-to-day job duties. It is this injury from which Pavlinac will never be able to return to work. Thus, Pavlinac's October 20, 2000 application for benefits for "repetitive trauma to back" was timely as it was filed within two years of the date such injury was discernible.

. . . Inland notes Pavlinac's long medical history relating to the problems with his back, specifically noting the numerous surgeries and procedures Pavlinac has undergone. What Inland fails to note, however, is that, although Pavlinac had a long history of back problems, after each previous incident, he ultimately improved to a point where he no longer required medical care and was able to return to work without restrictions. It is this fact which seemingly distinguishes Pavlinac's claim from both *Duvall v. ICI Americas, Inc.*, 621 N.E.2d 1122 (Ind. Ct. App. 1993) and *Bowles v. General Electric*, 824 N.E.2d 769 (Ind. Ct. App. 2005), *trans. denied*, cases cited by Inland.[7]

Separate issues have arisen, however, in those situations where the statute has been applied to injured employees who are minors at the time of injury. Three sections of the Act, and one statute of general application, are called into play under such circumstances. Along with IC 22-3-3-3, consideration must be given to IC 22-3-3-30 (which tolls the time limitation for minors), IC 22-3-6-1(c) (wherein "minor" is defined for purposes of the Act), and IC 1-1-4(a)(8) (wherein "minor" is defined generally). IC 22-3-3-30 provides that, "No limitation of time provided in [the Act] shall run against any person who is mentally incompetent or a minor so long as he has no guardian or trustee." IC 22-3-6-1(c) defines a "minor" as "an individual who has not reached seventeen (17) years of age." IC 1-1-4(a)(8) states that an " 'infant' or 'minor' means a person less than eighteen (18) years of age."

In *Davis v. C. P. Lesh Paper Co.*,[8] a 17-year-old was injured in the course of her employment. She filed her claim for compensation more than two years after the date she was injured, but less than two years after she turned 18. The predecessor to IC 22-3-6-1(c) defined a "minor" as "an individual under the age of seventeen (17) years." The board dismissed her claim, and the appellate court affirmed. In doing so, the court reasoned:

We think our decision is clearly controlled by Reynolds v. Mobile Wash, Inc., (1976) Ind. App., 346 N.E.2d 625. In an almost identical factual situation, the Second District found the language of Ind. Code 22-3-6-1(b) to be "plain and unambiguous" and held that

---

[7]Inland Steel Co. v. Pavlinac, 865 N.E.2d 690, 700 (Ind. Ct. App. 2007) (citations omitted).

[8]Davis v. C. P. Lesh Paper Co., 182 Ind. App. 81, 394 N.E.2d 207 (1979).

section's definition of "minor" to [be] applicable to both the statute of limitations, Ind. Code 22-3-3-3, and the tolling statute, Ind. Code 22-3-3-30, of the Workmen's Compensation Act. We find no basis for questioning that decision.[9]

Likewise, in *Memorial Hosp. v. Szuba*,[10] a 16-year-old sustained a work-related injury. Three-and-a-half-years later, and one month prior to his twentieth birthday, he filed his application with the board. His employer moved to dismiss his application on the ground that the statute of limitations had ended. More specifically, the employer argued that, for purposes of the Act, the age of majority was 17, and, therefore, Szuba had until his nineteenth birthday to file his claim. The board, however, found that the employee's claim was timely filed and the court of appeals affirmed. Interestingly enough, both parties argued that the court's decision in *Davis* supported the position which they advanced.

In a rather strangely reasoned opinion, the court stated:

> In *Davis*, we made the following observation: "Thus, if Davis was a minor at the time of her accident, her claim was timely filed. If she was not a minor, the Industrial Board properly dismissed her application for compensation." *Id.* This clearly supports Szuba's proposition that an injured employee under the age of seventeen has until he is twenty to file his claim. While we recognize that this statement was made in dicta and that there are inherent inconsistencies in its logic, we note that the General Assembly and the Board have presumably been aware of this interpretation and have left it unchanged for over twenty years . . . . Therefore, we find that the Legislature has acquiesced to our previous judicial interpretation in *Davis*, and Szuba had two years from the time he reached the age of eighteen, pursuant to the general definitions of "majority" and "minor" found in Ind. Code § 1-1-4-5, to file his application.[11]

The court obviously chose to ignore the precise language of the statute (i.e., one is no longer a minor on his or her seventeenth birthday) and instead premised its decision upon language from *Davis* which had absolutely nothing to do with the basis for the court's decision and the eventual outcome of that case. In *Davis*, the court found that the definition of "minor," as contained within the Act, was clear and unambiguous. A person 17 years of age was not a minor. Since Davis was 17 at the time she was injured, she had to have had her claim filed within two years after the date of her injury in order to preserve her right to compensation.

---

[9]Davis v. C. P. Lesh Paper Co., 182 Ind. App. 81, 394 N.E.2d 207, 208 (1979).

[10]Memorial Hosp. v. Szuba, 705 N.E.2d 519 (Ind. Ct. App. 1999).

[11]Memorial Hosp. v. Szuba, 705 N.E.2d 519, 522 (Ind. Ct. App. 1999) (footnotes omitted) (citations omitted).

She did not so file, and that is precisely why her action before the board was dismissed. Whether she could or could not have filed her claim at some other point in time should have been irrelevant, and therefore that dicta should not have been interjected into the court's opinion in *Davis*, and definitely should not have formed the basis for the court's opinion in *Szuba*.

In *Harris v. United Water Services, Inc.*,[12] an employee claimed that he was exposed to bacteria that caused illness while in the employ of United Water Services, Inc. He filed his claim with the Worker's Compensation Board and United Water Services file a motion to dismiss arguing that Harris' symptoms all stemmed from a particular incident where he was splashed in the face with waste water more than two years before the filing of his application. As such, the employer's position was that Harris was claiming a worker's compensation, not occupational disease claim, and his application was untimely filed. The Board granted the employer's motion to dismiss finding that in his deposition testimony. Harris admitted that his problems began with the waste water incident more than two years before his application was filed. In reversing the Board, the Court of Appeals held that the Board erred by concluding that Harris admitted that his problems began with the waste water splash incident. The Court pointed to Harris' deposition testimony that he only suspected he first became infected with the splash, but he was always exposed to bacteria and could have contracted it at any time. The Court remanded the case to the Board so that a hearing on the merits could be conducted to determine whether Harris suffered accidental injury on the date that he was splashed in the face by waste water or he suffered disablement by occupational disease giving him two years after his date of disablement, as long as disablement occurs with two years from the last date of exposure, to file his claim with the Board.

§4:4 Medical services

The Act provides that, after an injury and prior to an adjudication of permanent impairment, the employer shall either furnish or cause to be furnished, free of charge to the employee, an attending physician and such medical services and supplies as the physician or the board deem necessary for the treatment of the employee's injuries. In addition, if the employee is requested or required by the employer to submit to treatment outside the county of employment, the employer shall pay the reasonable expense of travel, food, and lodging necessary to obtain the treatment. If the treatment or travel results in lost work by the

---

[12]Harris v. United Water Services, Inc., 946 N.E.2d 35 (Ind. Ct. App. 2011).

employee, the employer shall reimburse the employee for his or her loss of wages, using the employee's average daily wage as the basis for computation.[1]

IC 22-3-3-4(c) provides that, after an employee's injury has been adjudicated by agreement or award on the basis of permanent partial impairment, and within the statutory period for review pursuant to IC 22-3-3-27, the employer may continue to furnish medical services and supplies, and the board, upon proper application of either party, may require that such services and supplies be furnished by or on behalf of the employer as the board may deem necessary to limit or reduce the amount and extent of the employee's impairment. If the employee refuses to accept such medical services and supplies when provided, then the employee shall be barred from all compensation otherwise payable during the period of refusal, and his or her right to prosecute any proceeding under the Act shall be suspended and abated until the refusal ceases. The employee must be served with a notice, in a form prescribed by the board, setting forth the consequences of his or her refusal. Furthermore, no compensation for permanent total impairment, permanent partial impairment, permanent disfigurement, or death shall be paid or payable for that portion of the impairment, disfigurement or death resulting from the employee's refusal to accept the medical treatment, services or supplies required. But an employer may, at any time, permit an employee to treat his or her injuries by spiritual means or prayer in lieu of the medical services and supplies required under this section.[2]

If because of an emergency—or because of the employer's failure to provide the medical treatment, services or supplies, or the treatment by spiritual means or prayer, or because of any other good reason—a physician other than one provided by the employer treats the injured employee, or necessary medical services or supplies are procured during the period of temporary total disability, the reasonable cost of those services and supplies shall, subject to the approval of the board, be paid by the employer.[3]

If a compensable injury results in the amputation of a body part, the enucleation of an eye, or the loss of natural teeth, the

---

[Section 4:4]

[1]IC 22-3-3-4(a). See also Calvary Temple Church, Inc. v. Paino, 555 N.E.2d 190, 193 (Ind. Ct. App. 1990) (abrogated by, Christopher R. Brown, D.D.S., Inc. v. Decatur County Memorial Hosp., 892 N.E.2d 642 (Ind. 2008)); Gregg v. Sun Oil Co., 180 Ind. App. 379, 388 N.E.2d 588, 589 (1979).

[2]IC 22-3-3-4(c).

[3]IC 22-3-3-4(d).

employer must furnish an appropriate artificial member, braces and prosthodontics. Also, the cost of repairs to or replacements for them that result from a compensable injury pursuant to a prior award and are required due to either medical necessity or normal wear and tear, determined according to the employee's individual use, but not abuse, shall be paid from the Second Injury Fund upon order of the board. The employee is not required to meet any other requirement for admission to the Second Injury Fund.[4]

If a compensable injury after June 30, 1997 results in the loss of or damage to an artificial member, brace, implant, eyeglasses, prosthodontics, or other medically prescribed device, the employer shall repair same or furnish an identical or reasonably equivalent replacement.[5]

Nothing in IC 22-3-3-4 prohibits an employer and its employees from agreeing to medical care, both before or after an injury, furnished by health care providers selected by agreement or to the findings of such health care providers, as long as the parties are bound by their agreement and the approval of the board is obtained.[6]

IC 22-3-3-4 is amended as follows: subsection (a) is amended to replace "surgical, hospital, and nursing services and supplies" with "services and products"; subsection (b) is amended to replace "services and supplies" with "services and products"; subsection (c) is amended to replace "medical services and supplies" with, alternately, "medical services and products," and "services and products," replace "services and supplies" with "services and products" and replace "treatment, services and products" with "services and products"; subsection (d) is amended to replace "surgical, hospital, or nursing services and supplies" with "services and products" and replace "services and supplies" with "services and products"; subsection (h)(1) is amended to replace "health care providers" with "medical service providers"; and subsection (h)(2) is amended to replace "health care provider" with "medical service provider."

It is axiomatic that before an employer has an obligation to furnish necessary medical treatment to an injured employee, the employer must have knowledge that such treatment is required. Hence, in *Allen v. United Telephone Co. Inc.*,[7] a claim for reimbursement for the services of a practical nurse was denied. The court of appeals stated:

---

[4]IC 22-3-3-4(d).

[5]IC 22-3-3-4(e).

[6]IC 22-3-3-3(f).

[7]Allen v. United Telephone Co., Inc., 168 Ind. App. 696, 345 N.E.2d 261 (1976).

The Workmen's Compensation Act provides that the employer must furnish nursing services to the injured employee if the attending physician or the Industrial Board deem the services necessary. Ind.Ann.Stat. 22-3-3-4 (Burns Code Ed. 1974). Nothing in the record indicates that a physician ordered the nursing services. Allen and her husband testified that they hired the nurse because Allen was unable to take care of herself or do her chores when she came home from the hospital following the second accident. It was within the board's discretion to find, as it did here, that the services were not proved to be necessary within contemplation of the statute.[8]

In *Richmond State Hosp. v. Waldren,*[9] an injured employee consulted a doctor of her own choosing without first notifying her employer and obtaining its authorization. She testified that she "wanted a more professional opinion" than that presumably rendered by the employer's staff physician. She treated with her personal physician for several months and, at one point, was hospitalized for treatment based upon his advice. The court of appeals expressed its disapproval of the employee's actions:

> The majority rule is set forth in 2 Larson, *Workmen's Compensation Law* § 61.12(c) (1981) as follows:
>
> "[I]t is generally held that the employee should . . . not incur medical expense without first giving the employer a reasonable opportunity to furnish such services, and if he does so, the employee will be liable for that expense himself. The mere fact that claimant has more faith in his family doctor, or lacks confidence in the employer's doctor, is not enough to change the rule."
>
> . . . [T]he Hospital was not given the opportunity to furnish medical aid because it had no knowledge of a need therefor. There can be no failure to provide within the meaning of the statute without knowledge of need.
>
> . . . Our holding is a narrow one: when the employer has no knowledge of the need for medical services and no opportunity to tender the medical services and when no emergency or other good cause is shown, he cannot be held liable for them.[10]

The court of appeals went one step further in its opinion in the matter of *K-Mart Corp. v. Morrison:*[11]

> We do not agree that mere referrals will validate unknown and unauthorized doctors or treatments simply because they descend in a direct line from an authorized doctor or treatment. Each new doctor or treatment should, at the very minimum, be communicated to the

---

[8]Allen v. United Telephone Co., Inc., 168 Ind. App. 696, 345 N.E.2d 261, 264 (1976).

[9]Richmond State Hosp. v. Waldren, 446 N.E.2d 1333 (Ind. Ct. App. 1983).

[10]Richmond State Hosp. v. Waldren, 446 N.E.2d 1333, 1336 (Ind. Ct. App. 1983). See also Perez v. U. S. Steel Corp., 172 Ind. App. 242, 359 N.E.2d 925 (1977).

[11]K-Mart Corp. v. Morrison, 609 N.E.2d 17 (Ind. Ct. App. 1993).

employer in such a way that the employer is put on notice that medical care is needed and the employer is given an opportunity to provide.[12]

In a footnote, the Court said: "We understand that by this we are putting a burden upon the recipients of worker's compensation benefits to communicate with their employers. This is a minimal burden, however, and one already implicit in IC 22-3-3-4 and *Richmond, supra.*"[13]

Once treatment is furnished to the injured employee, the employer has an obligation to pay for the treatment rendered.

In *Young v. Marling*,[14] a worker's compensation carrier referred Marling for pain management, but limited the pain management physician's ability to treat the patient to "medication and no other type of therapy." Marling continued to treat with the pain doctor and permitted the doctor to select the medically necessary treatment, including, but not limited to, medication. The carrier argued that only charges related to the medication should be paid.

The treatments at issue in *Marling* were before the injury was adjudicated. As such, IC 22-3-3-4(a) governed the issue. This section requires that the employer shall furnish to the employee an attending physician and such surgical, hospital, and nursing services and supplies as the attending physician or worker's compensation board shall deem necessary. The medical doctor, and not the carrier, determines care. Thus, the court determined that Marling's unpaid charges were the responsibility of the carrier.

In *Sears Roebuck & Co. v. Murphy*,[15] Sears argued that it should not have to pay to Murphy his statutory medical expenses since 80% of those expenses were paid by a non-party insurance carrier while litigation was pending, and that such an award to Murphy would allow him to obtain an unjustified windfall. In a rather lengthy footnote, the court of appeals stated that:

> [I]t is clear the legislature intended for the employer and its workmen's compensation carrier to *pay* the claims, of its employees who are injured or killed by accident arising out of and in the course of the employment.
>
> In the absence of any provision granting an exception to those employers whose employees receive compensation elsewhere,

---

[12]K-Mart Corp. v. Morrison, 609 N.E.2d 17, 34 (Ind. Ct. App. 1993).

[13]K-Mart Corp. v. Morrison, 609 N.E.2d 17, 34 (Ind. Ct. App. 1993).

[14]Young v. Marling, 900 N.E.2d 30 (Ind. Ct. App. 2009).

[15]Sears Roebuck & Co. v. Murphy, 511 N.E.2d 515 (Ind. Ct. App. 1987).

Sears's argument that it need only make sure an employee's medical expenses are provided by someone is meritless.[16]

The court went further to address Sears' argument in the following language:

Sears is concerned that by awarding Murphy the statutory medical expenses paid by Provident, Murphy will receive an "unowed, unjustified windfall." However, in *Jenkins v. Pullman Standard Car Mfg. Co.* (1957), 127 Ind. App. 173, 139 N.E.2d 566, the Court stated:

". . . Should the [employer] be required to reimburse a third party, a stranger to this litigation, who voluntarily paid medical bills incurred by the appellant as a result of his injury? By the great weight of authority in actions against tort-feasors *an injured person is entitled to recover for medical services rendered him even if gratuitous, or paid for by a third party,* on the theory that, while such services or payment is a gift for his benefit, it is one of the elements of his injury and it is no concern of the tort-feasor that he has benefited by such gift. It would seem at first blush that the elements of legal recovery, having in mind the liberal purposes of the Workmen's Compensation Act, should not be more restricted in cases before the Industrial Board than in the ordinary civil action for damages resulting from the negligence of another." (Emphasis added). *Id.,* 139 N.E.2d at 568.

Our holding not only is mandated by statute and case law, but is supported by strong policy reasons. To hold otherwise would encourage employers to delay payment, waiting for a non-work-related insurance carrier to pay the employee's medical or other expenses. Then, in any subsequent action, the employer could argue that medical care had already been furnished and that its liability to its employee was extinguished.[17]

In *Rayford v. Lumbermens Mut. Cas. Co.,*[18] an employee brought an action against his employer's worker's compensation insurance carriers for their refusal to provide and pay for counseling for psychological problems which he developed as the result of a work-related accident in which his leg was severely damaged. The facts demonstrated that Rayford and his employer filed with the board a compensation agreement shortly after the accident, which provided Rayford with complete coverage for the treatment of his injuries as well as weekly compensation payments. The agreement did not, however, provide for any psychological counseling. Rayford voluntarily began attending counseling sessions on the advice of his attorney. He requested that the insurers pay for the charges rendered by the counselor. Even though the insurers received nothing from Rayford's attending physician

---

[16]Sears Roebuck & Co. v. Murphy, 511 N.E.2d 515, 516 (Ind. Ct. App. 1987).

[17]Sears Roebuck & Co. v. Murphy, 511 N.E.2d 515, 517 (Ind. Ct. App. 1987) (footnotes omitted) (citations omitted).

[18]Rayford v. Lumbermens Mut. Cas. Co., 44 F.3d 546 (7th Cir. 1995).

diagnosing him with psychological problems or recommending psychological counseling, the insurers voluntarily agreed to pay for five counseling sessions. The counselor believed five sessions would be enough, but they weren't. Rayford demanded that the insurers pay for more counseling sessions, but they refused. He only offered the insurers a letter from his counselor stating that more sessions were needed. He neither consulted with the attending physician nor filed an application for benefits with the board. Thereafter, Rayford attempted suicide and was hospitalized. The insurers, once again, refused his request to provide and pay for in-patient psychological services.

In affirming the district court's dismissal of Rayford's complaint, the court of appeals stated that:

> [I]n certain situations, like the one that developed in this case, the employee and the employer (or insurer) disagree over the proper treatment required by the employee. In these instances, the statute provides that the employer must furnish whatever treatment "the attending physician or the worker's compensation board may deem necessary." Ind.Code 22-3-3-4.
>
> In this case, Rayford failed to press his case with either his attending physician or the board before making his request for additional counseling of the insurers. The only evidence of lingering psychological problems presented to the insurers came in the form of a letter from his counselor. The employer is not required to take the employee's word for it when he requests that it furnish treatment in addition to that already provided; nor is it required to act on the request of a third party. Under the statute, to force the insurers to provide his counseling, Rayford had only two options: return to his attending physician for a diagnosis that Rayford required psychological counseling or file an Application for Adjustment of Claim with the board. He did neither at the time of his demand.[19]

However, in *Daugherty v. Industrial Contracting & Erecting*,[20] the Indiana Supreme Court concluded that an employer and its carrier *were* obligated to pay for an injured employee's knee replacement surgery and related medical care, even though he did not obtain authority from either his employer, its carrier, or the board for those medical services. The Court noted that medical treatment for Daugherty's injury was provided from the outset by more than six treating physicians and a number of other health care professionals. One physician determined that his condition was permanent and quiescent, and a permanent partial impairment rating was assigned. An independent medical examiner appointed by the board concluded that Daugherty's

---

[19]Rayford v. Lumbermens Mut. Cas. Co., 44 F.3d 546, 549 (7th Cir. 1995).

[20]Daugherty v. Industrial Contracting & Erecting, 802 N.E.2d 912 (Ind. 2004).

injury had achieved its maximum medical improvement. Nonetheless, in approving Daugherty's conduct in obtaining unauthorized medical care, and in ordering payment for such care, the
Court, citing authority from states other than Indiana, said:

> When an employee seeks treatment other than that provided by
> the employer or the Board, he or she does so at his or her own peril
> and risks not being reimbursed. The mere fact that the unautho-
> rized medical treatment is an acceptable method of treating the
> condition does not mean that the employer should pay for the
> treatment. However as Professor Larson observes:
>
> > "[D]ifficult questions can arise when there is a difference of
> > opinion on diagnosis or appropriate treatment, as when the
> > employer's doctor recommends conservative measures while the
> > claimant thinks he or she should have surgery."

5 Larson, *Larson's Workers' Compensation Law* § 94-02[5], at 94-19
(2002). "One way to settle this kind of controversy is to let the
result turn on whose diagnosis proved to be right." *Id.* Several
jurisdictions have embraced this approach. *See, e.g. Caldwell v.
Joseph W. Vestal & Son, Inc.* 237 Ark. 142, 371 S.W.2d 836, 838
(1963) (noting that claimant "acted at his peril in overriding the
insurer's warning that the proposed operation would be at the
claimant's own expense," but on the strength of hindsight knowledge that the operation was in fact necessary, the court held
employer responsible for paying the incurred medical expenses);
McCoy v. Indus. Accident Comm'n, 64 Cal.2d 82, 48 Cal. Rptr. 858,
410 P.2d 362, 365 (Cal. 1966) (declaring employee entitled to
reimbursement for self-procured treatment from her doctor because
the care was "reasonably required to cure or relieve" the effects of
the injury); *Mattingly v. Okla. Indus. Court,* 382 P.2d 125, 128
(Okla. 1963) (declaring as "mere idle gesture" the medical care
provided by employer and holding employer liable for employee's
successful but self-procured, unauthorized medical expenses); *cf.
Halbert v. U.S. Fid. & Guar. Co.,* 185 Neb. 775, 178 N.W.2d 781,
783 (1970) (awarding employee the costs of an unsuccessful self-
procured surgery because "it was grounded upon a reasonable belief
that improvement would result"), *modified,* 186 Neb. 23, 180
N.W.2d 879 (1970).

We find particularly persuasive the Virginia case of *Shenandoah
Prods., Inc. v. Whitlock,* 15 Va. App. 207, 421 S.E.2d 483 (1992). In
that case . . . the employee sought the advice of a specialist for a
neurosurgical evaluation. At the specialist's suggestion, the employee underwent surgery. Prior to doing so, both the employer and
treating physician refused authorization for treatment . . . .

Construing a Worker's Compensation Statute that is similar to
our own, the Virginia Court of Appeals noted that without a refer-
ral from an authorized treating physician, treatment by an unauthorized physician is allowed in an "emergency" or "for other good
reason." *Id.* In that case there was no question the treatment the
employee received was not required due to an emergency. However,
acknowledging this was a case of first impression in Virginia, and
citing supporting authority from other jurisdictions, the Court
fashioned the following test:

"[I]f the employee, without authorization but in good faith, obtains medical treatment different from that provided by the employer, and it is determined that the treatment provided by the employer was inadequate treatment for the employee's condition and the unauthorized treatment received by the claimant was medically reasonable and necessary treatment, the employer should be responsible, notwithstanding the lack of prior approval by the employer. These legal principles which provide a basis for the payment of unauthorized medical treatment are part of the 'other good reasons test.' "

Id. at 486 (citations omitted); *accord H.J. Holz & Son, Inc. v. Dumas-Thayer,* 37 Va.App. 645, 561 S.E.2d 6 (2002). We agree with Virginia's approach, and adopt the foregoing test as appropriate for evaluating the existence of good reason under Indiana Code section 22-3-3-4 . . . . We hasten to add that reimbursement for medical treatment not authorized by the employer, or the Board, should be the rare exception. Indeed the employee runs a high risk that he or she will not be reimbursed for such treatment. And the employee can avoid that risk simply by obtaining prior approval.

Nonetheless, if an employee can demonstrate good reason for the unauthorized care, then subject to the approval of the Board, the employer will be responsible for paying the cost of certain medical care. Applying the foregoing test, we determine that Daugherty has made such a showing. The record shows that Daugherty submitted to the treatment of Dr. Brooks without obtaining approval of the employer or the Board. However, he did first seek prior approval from the employer's insurance carrier. This fact suggests he acted in good faith. The record also shows that the course of treatment being offered by IC & E was inadequate. Despite the efforts of numerous physicians and other health care professionals Daugherty still suffered pain and was unable to return to work performing his regular duties. Finally, the Board specifically found that Dr. Brooks' recommended care and treatment was "reasonable and appropriate." We think this is the functional equivalent of "reasonable and necessary." In sum, the record before us is sufficient to demonstrate that Daugherty's decision to obtain unauthorized medical care fell under the "other good reason" exception to the general rule that an employee is not free to elect, at the employer's expense, additional treatment or other physicians than those tendered by the employer.[21]

What has become of that portion of the quid pro quo rationale underlying the enactment of the worker's compensation scheme which suggested that the employer's liability would be relatively quantifiable, and that the employer would no longer be subjected to unexpected awards? Is the employer's liability for the payment of medical benefits and compensation now to be viewed only, or mostly, in hindsight? Are injured claimants now free to "doctor-shop" for their own medical care and treatment, and have their

---

[21]Daugherty v. Industrial Contracting & Erecting, 802 N.E.2d 912, 917–19 (Ind. 2004).

employers pay for it, so long as they have a "reasonable belief" that such care is, in their own opinion, appropriate? Is such the case, even if the medical care obtained proves utterly unsuccessful? Does the end now justify the means; and must an employer wait until the employee has concluded his or her search for medical care to cure the condition in order to determine the employer's eventual liability? In the meantime, how is the employee's "good faith" to be measured and by whom? What criteria are to be used to determine whether or not the medical treatment furnished by the employer is "inadequate," and that chosen by the employee is reasonable and necessary? Will the war of words waged by a multitude of physicians offering a variety of opinions escalate far beyond that which already exists? The court's opinion in *Daugherty* offers little, if any, guidance for the resolution of those issues, and it appears that continued litigation will be necessary to attempt to determine the parameters of the decision reached and the effects thereof.

In *Childers v. Central Teaming & Const. Co.*,[22] an injured employee's refusal to accept medical treatment offered by his employer was at issue. It was stipulated that Childers suffered an 80% permanent partial impairment as a result of a work-related back injury. An examining physician testified that this impairment could be reduced to 25% to 30% with surgery. It was his opinion that the chances of a successful operation were 75% to 80%, and, even if it was unsuccessful, Childers would be no worse than his present condition. Finally, the physician testified that the surgery involved no unusual risk or extraordinary pain, and that it was the "textbook" treatment for Childers' condition. Childers did not question the physician's skill or expertise in performing the operation. His sole reason for refusing the surgery was fear; according to Childers, the doctor would not guarantee that he would improve following surgery.

The board's single hearing member awarded Childers compensation for an 80% permanent partial impairment. The full board held that he was entitled to only 30% due to his unreasonable refusal to accept the proffered medical treatment. In affirming the full board's reduction of Childers' compensation benefits, the court of appeals stated the following:

> [W]e first emphasize that it is not every refusal to accept medical treatment, services or supplies that will invoke IC 22-3-3-4 and mandate the reduction or elimination of compensation benefits.
>
> In order for the refusal to justify the reduction or elimination of benefits, the refusal must be unreasonable or without just cause. Witte v. J. Winkler & Sons (1934), 98 Ind. App. 466, 190 N.E. 72.

---

[22]Childers v. Central Teaming & Const. Co., 179 Ind. App. 186, 384 N.E.2d 1116 (1979).

However, the question of whether refusal is reasonable is one of fact to be determined by the board . . . .

The evidence as set forth above is sufficient to sustain the board's finding that Childers' refusal was unreasonable. The operation does not pose a substantial danger to life or health or extraordinary suffering and does offer a substantial prospect of relieving the impairment. See, e.g. Vonnegut Hardware Co. v. Rose (1918), 68 Ind. App. 385, 120 N.E. 608. That a physician would decline to guarantee the success of a major medical procedure certainly does not compel a contrary result, especially since the physician could and did evaluate the substantial prospect for success.

The foregoing, of course, does not mean that Childers is being forced to undergo a recommended medical procedure. That choice is still his. However, the provisions for workmen's compensation relieve an employer from the burden of paying compensation for that portion of his impairment which exists because he has unreasonably refused the proffered treatment.[23]

In *Pipkin v. Continental Steel Corp.*,[24] the claimant sustained a hernia as the result of a work-related accident. He consulted with two doctors furnished by the employer and two doctors he selected himself. Surgery to correct the hernia was offered by the employer, but refused by the employee. His reason for declining the services of the company surgeon was that he thought the doctor "did not know what was the matter with him." Subsequently, he was operated on by a surgeon he chose. He later argued that the medical expenses associated with the surgery should be paid by his employer, since his refusal to accept the employer's proffered medical services was reasonable. In affirming the board's denial of medical benefits, the appellate court stated:

The qualification of the company surgeon and his ability to perform the operation were proven and undisputed. No reason was given for the refusal to accept his services except that appellant did not have confidence in him. To hold such reason sufficient would, in effect, be a holding that the employer must furnish a surgeon satisfactory to the employee. The statute does not give to the employee the privilege of choosing the surgeon. To so hold would be materially changing the effect of the statute and would constitute a precedent upon which fraud and injustice could be logically based.[25]

In *PS2, LLC v. Childers*,[26] the single hearing member ordered the employer to pay for employee's lap band surgery intended to reduce the employee's weight prior to back fusion surgery for his compensable low back injury. The board member's decision was

---

[23]Childers v. Central Teaming & Const. Co., 179 Ind. App. 186, 384 N.E.2d 1116, 1117–18 (1979).

[24]Pipkin v. Continental Steel Corp., 105 Ind. App. 669, 16 N.E.2d 984 (1938).

[25]Pipkin v. Continental Steel Corp., 105 Ind. App. 669, 16 N.E.2d 984, 986 (1938).

[26]PS2, LLC v. Childers, 910 N.E.2d 809 (Ind. Ct. App. 2009).

affirmed on appeal. The employee correctly argued that " '[a]fter an injury and prior to an adjudication of permanent impairment, the employer shall furnish' treatment as deemed necessary by the Board, and that '[d]uring the period of temporary total disability resulting from the injury, the employer shall furnish' treatment deemed necessary by the Board."[27] The board member's interpretation of this statute is given great weight on appeal, unless the interpretation is inconsistent with the statute itself. Since the board holds authority to determine necessary treatment and the weight loss surgery was medically necessary, the court of appeals declined to reverse the award.

The notice which an employer must give an employee refusing proffered medical services was the subject of the opinion of the court of appeals in the matter of *Krause v. Indiana University-Purdue University at Indianapolis*.[28] Krause unilaterally terminated her treatment with the physician selected by the employer to treat her and instead sought medical care from physicians at the Indiana University Pain Clinic. The board concluded that her employer was not obligated to pay for the medical treatment which she sought and obtained on her own. In reversing the board's decision, the court stated:

[I]f an employee refuses to accept "all compensation," including treatment services provided by the employer, the "employee must be served with a notice setting forth the consequences of the refusal . . . in a form prescribed by the worker's compensation board." I.C. § 22-3-3-4(c).

. . . We can appreciate the concern of employers that they not be required to pay for questionable or possibly inappropriate medical treatment. However, such a concern would not appear to be warranted or have any basis where, as here, the "unauthorized" treating physician is part of the employer's corporate entity.

In addition, the required use of a prescribed statutory form further protects the employer from any allegation that the employee was not properly informed of the consequence of refusing medical treatment authorized by the employer. IUPUI has failed to take advantage of such statutory protection.

IUPUI failed to provide the required prescribed statutory notice to Krause. Therefore, the Board erred when it failed to find that IUPUI was required to provide medical services to Krause after . . . she stopped being treated by [the physician selected by the employer].[29]

---

[27]PS2, LLC v. Childers, 910 N.E.2d 809, 818 (Ind. Ct. App. 2009).

[28]Krause v. Indiana University-Purdue University at Indianapolis, 866 N.E.2d 846, 219 Ed. Law Rep. 259 (Ind. Ct. App. 2007), transfer denied, 878 N.E.2d 210 (Ind. 2007).

[29]Krause v. Indiana University-Purdue University at Indianapolis, 866 N.E.2d 846, 853, 219 Ed. Law Rep. 259 (Ind. Ct. App. 2007), transfer denied,

In *Talas v. Correct Piping Co., Inc.*,[30] an employee was rendered a traumatic quadriplegic as the result of a fall from scaffolding while working. After extensive hospitalizations and efforts at rehabilitation, he was returned home where he received around-the-clock nursing care. The parties filed an agreement with the board and therein stipulated that Talas's injury had reached a permanent and quiescent state, and that he had sustained 100% permanent impairment of the man as a whole and 100% total permanent disability. The parties could not agree upon the employer's need to continue to furnish medical services and supplies, and Talas, therefore, filed an emergency petition with the board seeking an award of additional nursing care and services to sustain and maintain his life. The board found that Talas should take nothing by his petition, but the Indiana Supreme Court reversed its decision. In doing so, the Court stated:

> Here it is apparent that Talas's status as a quadriplegic is permanent. No medical remedy is available to cure that affliction; nothing can be done to "limit or reduce the amount and extent" of his quadriplegia. This inability to mitigate or positively influence Talas's quadriplegia formed one basis for the Industrial Board's denial of benefits, as its findings of fact indicate.
>
> Talas's impairment—his loss of physical functions—reaches beyond the mere inability to control his arms and legs, however. He is unable to control his most basic daily bodily functions . . . . In short, absent [of] assistance and care, Talas would be a hopelessly bedridden invalid who, by virtue of circumstance, would be prone to further medical disorders . . . of a life-threatening nature. With assistance and care, on the other hand, Talas can be lifted from bed, take sustenance, bathe, discharge bodily wastes, and enjoy a daily regimen of exercise, postural drainage, respiratory therapy, and assisted coughing, all of which serve to minimize the possibility that additional medical disorders will further complicate his physical condition . . . .
>
> [W]e conclude that the impairment of Talas's physical functions would be limited, if not reduced, by nursing care, as these terms are utilized in the Act. That conclusion follows even though the care will not cure Talas's quadriplegia, *for in the circumstances present here,* any other construction would be inimical to the humanitarian purposes of the Act . . . .
>
> This jurisdiction has tacitly recognized that the nursing services available under our Workmen's Compensation Act include practical nursing, as well as the services of a professional or registered nurse. *Allen v. United Tel. Co., Inc.,* (1976), 168 Ind. App. 696, 345 N.E.2d 261 (evidence indicated practical nursing services were not necessary within contemplation of statute) . . . .
>
> Here, the circumstances include an injured employee whose spouse is actively engaged in gainful employment; the record reveals no other family members or persons reside in the home.

---

878 N.E.2d 210 (Ind. 2007).

[30]Talas v. Correct Piping Co., Inc., 435 N.E.2d 22 (Ind. 1982).

We are unable to conclude that our Workmen's Compensation Act was intended to require a spouse to quit his or her employment when, by virtue of a work-related accident, the fellow spouse is rendered bedfast and wholly dependent upon others . . . .

The proposition that the spouse's employment, which constitutes the sole continuing income for the couple, must be forsaken is so at odds with the spirit and purposes of the Act that it must be rejected.

Consequently, we conclude that Talas is entitled to an award of the expenses necessary to employ nonprofessional nursing care . . . . Included within the award must be the medical expenses Talas incurs via periodic maintenance checkups at the hands of professional medical personnel . . . .[31]

Likewise, in *Jones & Laughlin Steel Corp. v. Kilburne*,[32] the court was called upon to decide whether or not the board may award prospective non-curative relief to an injured employee. After noting the language contained in IC 22-3-3-4, the court stated:

This code section clearly speaks of limiting or reducing the amount and extent of the impairment, not reducing the permanency of that impairment. *See Mousley v. Curry* (1954) 124 Ind. App. 280, 117 N.E.2d 280. "Impairment," within the context of the Workmen's Compensation Act, refers to the employee's loss of physical function(s) as a result of the injury. *Talas v. Correct Piping Co., Inc.* (1982) Ind., 435 N.E.2d 22, and cases cited therein. Therefore, this code section permits awards which will limit or reduce the extent or effect of Kilburne's loss of physical function. As was explained in *Gregg v. Sun Oil Co.* (1979) 3d Dist., 180 Ind. App. 379, 388 N.E.2d 588, 589:

"The legislature, cognizant of the fact that a permanent impairment oftentimes requires continuing medical treatment, also provided that medical expenses incurred by the employee subsequent to the original award could be imposed on the employer."

See also Talas, supra, 435 N.E.2d 22. Board awards may, theoretically, be unlimited in duration and amount. *Gregg, supra,* 388 N.E.2d at 591, n. 5. Therefore, it was not improper for the Board to award prospective relief which would tend to limit the extent or effect of his impairment.

J & L argues, however, that the Indiana Supreme Court's decision in *Talas, supra,* limits the grant of any prospective non-curative relief to unique and compelling factual situations . . . . J & L is correct that the court in *Talas* described the situation as unique and warned against any unwarranted extension of the decision . . . .

. . . [T]he court in *Talas, supra,* focused upon the fact that the award would tend to protect against a worsening of the physical condition and against future medical complications. This aspect was also present in the Board's award to Kilburne. Added mobility

---

[31]Talas v. Correct Piping Co., Inc., 435 N.E.2d 22, 28-31 (Ind. 1982).

[32]Jones & Laughlin Steel Corp. v. Kilburne, 477 N.E.2d 345 (Ind. Ct. App. 1985).

increases Kilburne's ability to fend for himself, particularly in an emergency situation. In this sense, *Talas* supports the award in the case before us.[33]

Essentially the same argument was presented to the court of appeals by an employer in *Grand Lodge Free & Accepted Masons v. Jones*.[34] There, an injured employee used a TENS unit, prescribed by the employer's physician, to control pain in her back following a work-related accident. The physician testified that the unit was a device used solely to reduce a patient's pain and reduce a patient's reliance upon oral medications. It would not cause a cure or alter the percentage of impairment in a patient. After her injury became permanent and an impairment rating was issued, the board ordered that the employer be responsible for Jones' rehabilitation, including payment for the TENS unit which she used, and related medical supplies. In affirming the board's order, the court stated:

> Whether medical benefits extend to palliative steps useful only to prevent pain and discomfort after all hope of cure is gone has produced a split of opinion throughout the states . . . .
>
> However, our supreme court has determined even under Indiana's restrictive statute, palliative treatment methods are allowed. *Talas v. Correct Piping Co.* (1982), Ind., 435 N.E.2d 22, 27. As a result of an industrial accident, the claimant in *Talas* became a permanent quadriplegic. Although his condition remained stable, no hope of cure existed. Our supreme court reversed the Board and awarded benefits for continuing palliative care. *Id.*
>
> Our supreme court concluded nursing care which was required to prevent the development of life-threatening diseases could be said to limit the claimant's impairment by keeping him from 100% impairment, or death. *Id.* Thus, it allowed palliative methods under IC 22-3-3-4.
>
> Here, as in *Talas,* the Board had discretion to award an employee continuing medical expenses for a time period which it deemed necessary to limit or reduce the amount and extent of such impairment. *Gregg v. Sun Oil Co.* (1979), Ind. App., 388 N.E.2d 588, 591.
>
> The Board found Jones's pain could be reduced by use of the TENS unit and such pain reduction would limit the extent of her impairment. (R. 30). IC 22-3-3-4 allows the Board to award prospective noncurative relief to limit or reduce the amount and extent of impairment. The Board determined to the extent Jones's pain is reduced, the "amount" of her impairment is reduced. (R. 30–31). Such pain relief may result in Jones's restored ability to perform tasks and functions she may have been previously unable to perform. Thus, the Board's award to Jones was not contrary to law.

---

[33]Jones & Laughlin Steel Corp. v. Kilburne, 477 N.E.2d 345, 350–51 (Ind. Ct. App. 1985).

[34]Grand Lodge Free & Accepted Masons v. Jones, 590 N.E.2d 653 (Ind. Ct. App. 1992).

Finally, Grand Lodge complains the Board lacks authority to order a particular pain medication or require a particular physician to treat an employee indefinitely. Grand Lodge's argument is without merit. The Board held:

"It is further found that the defendant should be responsible for the ongoing cost of the use of said TENS unit so long as Dr. Silbert or his appointed successor shall so prescribe the use of the unit. (R. 30). The order's language is clear and unambiguous. Such treatment is to continue only so long as it is prescribed, not indefinitely."[35]

However, in *Jackel v. Peter Eckrich & Sons*,[36] both the board and the appellate court denied an injured worker's request for payment for the cost of prescription work shoes. He suffered a malformation of his foot as the result of a work-related injury. His physician testified that he could not relieve the malformation or alleviate Jackel's pain with further surgery. However, he did prescribe custom-made work shoes to make Jackel more comfortable. He stated that he believed Jackel would always require the prescription shoes for work, but that they would not limit or reduce Jackel's impairment. The court affirmed the board's finding that the cost of the shoes was speculative and would not limit or reduce Jackel's impairment.

The court's opinion is silent with respect to whether or not the prescription work shoes would alleviate pain in Jackel's malformed foot or make him more mobile or more able to perform certain tasks than if he were to wear non-prescription shoes. The value of the court's holding may have more to do with the claimant's failure to present evidence than with the actual conclusion reached by the court.

In *Gregg v. Sun Oil Co.*,[37] the court of appeals discussed the interplay between IC 22-3-3-4 and IC 22-3-3-27, which it incorporates by reference. The court found that applications for the modification of an award of medical expenses must be filed within one year from the last day for which compensation was paid. The court further stated:

Consequently, no limitation is placed on the number of modifications which can be sought on the basis of an increase in permanent partial impairment or a continuation of medical expenses. *Luker v. Starcraft Co.* (1976), Ind. App., 358 N.E.2d 231, 233, fn.9; *Bagwell v. Chrysler Corporation* (1976), Ind. App., 341 N.E.2d 799, 803. So long as the application is filed within one year from the last day on which compensation was paid, whether under the original award or a previous modification, the Industrial Board has jurisdiction to adjudicate the applicant's claim.

---

[35]Grand Lodge Free & Accepted Masons v. Jones, 590 N.E.2d 653, 655–56 (Ind. Ct. App. 1992).

[36]Jackel v. Peter Eckrich & Sons, 516 N.E.2d 1082 (Ind. Ct. App. 1987).

[37]Gregg v. Sun Oil Co., 180 Ind. App. 379, 388 N.E.2d 588 (1979).

. . . If Gregg's application for such modification is filed within the one year period of review, the Industrial Board is bound by IC 1971, 22-3-3-4, supra, to adjudicate his claim on the merits. *Furthermore, the opportunity for successive modifications which is provided to Gregg could conceivably result in Sun Oil bearing the costs incurred by Gregg for injury-related medical expenses throughout the duration of his life.*[38]

In *Perkins v. Jayco*,[39] the employee suffered a compensable back injury which resulted in a stipulated 10% permanent partial impairment. He claimed entitlement to "additional medical care." The single hearing member declined the request and found that any future medical treatment was due to Perkin's pre-existing condition. The full board subsequently found that Perkins was at maximum medical improvement.

Under IC 22-3-3-4 and longstanding case law interpreting that provision, the board could have awarded Perkins certain palliative care upon a finding that such care would reduce his pain and limit the extent of the impairment. Perkins presented evidence of his need for future care but the board made no findings on this issue. The appellate court, therefore, remanded the case for a finding on the issue of palliative care.

In *Perkins v. Jayco Inc.*,[40] the Court of Appeals affirmed the Board's decision to not award palliative care to the injured worker. However, the Court stated the Board did not apply the correct standard to determine whether palliative care was indeed indicated. The Court stated that the Board erred in concluding that a finding of maximum medical improvement allows an inference that palliative care is not needed. The Court explained that MMI relates to a curative state and palliative care does not. Palliative care instead relates to reducing the effects of an impairment, not to cure the condition causing the impairment. Nevertheless, the Court affirmed the Board's denial of treatment because the Board also found that the treatment requested was unrelated to the compensable injury.

In *Albright v. Four Winds International*,[41] claimant Albright suffered a compensable injury to her neck that required fusion

---

[38]Gregg v. Sun Oil Co., 180 Ind. App. 379, 388 N.E.2d 588, 590–591 (1979) (footnotes omitted) (emphasis added). See also Berry v. Anaconda Corp., 534 N.E.2d 250 (Ind. Ct. App. 1989); Halteman Swim Club v. Duguid, 757 N.E.2d 1017 (Ind. Ct. App. 2001); Krause v. Indiana University-Purdue University at Indianapolis, 866 N.E.2d 846, 853–55, 219 Ed. Law Rep. 259 (Ind. Ct. App. 2007), transfer denied, 878 N.E.2d 210 (Ind. 2007).

[39]Perkins v. Jayco, 905 N.E.2d 1085 (Ind. Ct. App. 2009).

[40]Perkins v. Jayco, Inc., 956 N.E.2d 1151 (Ind. Ct. App. 2011).

[41]Albright v. Four Winds Intern., 950 N.E.2d 1251 (Ind. Ct. App. 2011), transfer denied, 963 N.E.2d 1121 (Ind. 2012).

surgery. She accepted the compensation for the 18% permanent partial impairment of the body as a whole. At the time she accepted the compensation the attending physician noted that Albright suffered persistent weakness in her hand and some dysesthetic pain. Approximately one year after the agreement was approved for payment of the permanent partial impairment, Albright's family doctor noted parenthesis, and she recommended Albright increase Cymbalta from 30 to 60 mg. Approximately five months later, the family doctor stated that Albright might need Cymbalta or some other similar medication for the next 20 plus years. The doctor also noted that the increase in Cymbalta seemed to be helping the patient with sleeping but she still had significant pain during the day. Albright eventually filed an Application for Adjustment of Claim with the Worker's Compensation Board and requested a hearing to determine her future medical expense. The defendant's reviewing physician determined Cymbalta was helping the patient with neuropathic pain and depression associated with chronic pain. The physician then recommended Cymbalta for two months, and that the family doctor submit a more detailed report indicating exactly how much pain relief the patient has had with Cymbalta. The employer apparently authorized the use of Cymbalta for another two months. After that time, the family doctor did report that the patient's pain improved 60-70%, and that her quality of life had significantly improved on the medication. The family doctor opined that the patient will only continue to have improvement in her pain if she continues on Cymbalta and that the patient will need the medication long-term. A hearing was held on whether the employer was obligated to provide the Cymbalta and if so for what period of time. The Board found that the family doctor's response to the employer's physician's inquiry was insufficient and that the Cymbalta was being primarily prescribed for depression and anxiety and not for reducing the impairment to the cervical injury that was the compensable injury in this claim. The Court of Appeals reviewed the specific findings from the Board and held that the family doctor's reports were sufficient in providing evidence that Cymbalta was assisting the patient's reduction of pain and improving her ability to function. The Court also pointed to the employer's physician's statement that Cymbalta can be used to treat pain condition such as the plaintiff was experiencing. The Court reversed the Board's decision, and ordered the defendant to provide the Cymbalta as recommended by the family physician. The Court also remanded the case to the Board for determination on the length of time necessary for the patient to receive the medication.

In *Reeves v. Citizens Financial* Services,[42] plaintiff Reeves suffered a compensable injury and received a permanent partial impairment of 5%. The issue was whether he was entitled to palliative care. The Board pointed to evidence that an independent medical examiner, chosen by the Board pursuant to IC 22-3-3-7 recommended treatment from a pain management specialist. That treatment was provided for nearly four months after which pain management specialist reported the plaintiff's injury resulted in a 5% impairment and that he had reached maximum medical improvement as far as pain management was concerned. As such, the Board denied plaintiff's claim for ongoing palliative treatment. The Court of Appeals noted that it would not disturb the Board's findings of fact unless it concludes that the evidence is undisputed and leads inescapably to a contrary result, considering only the evidence that tends to support the Board's determination together with any adverse evidence. The Court affirmed the Board's denial of palliative care.

§ 4:5 Medical services—Liability

The employer's liability for medical services and supplies furnished to its injured employee is limited to such charges as prevail in the same community for a like service or product to injured persons. All claims by health care providers for the payment of services must be made with the board. The board may withhold approval of the fees of an attending physician until the physician files a report with the board.[1]

Neither the employee nor his or her estate is liable to a health care provider for payment for services rendered pursuant to the Act. All such clams are against the employer or its compensation insurance carrier, if any.[2] If a health care provider or anyone on its behalf knowingly attempts to collect payment of a charge for medical services or products covered by the Act, the board, after holding a hearing, may assess a civil penalty against the provider in a sum not less that $100 but not more than $1,000, unless the

---

[42]Reeves v. Citizens Financial Services, 960 N.E.2d 860 (Ind. Ct. App. 2012), transfer denied, 968 N.E.2d 232 (Ind. 2012).

[Section 4:5]

[1]IC 22-3-3-5. See also IC 22-3-6-1(j) (the charge for each specific medical service or product in a defined community must be equal to or less than the charges made by medical service providers at the 80th percentile in the same community for like services or products. IC 22-3-6-1(h) defines communities as geographic service areas based upon zip code districts established by the U.S. Postal Service. IC 22-3-3-5.2 establishes criteria to be used by billing review services and provides for civil penalties to be imposed by the board if a billing review standard other than that authorized is used).

[2]IC 22-3-3-5.

board finds that the provider's attempt to collect the charges was the result of a good faith error.[3]

IC 22-3-3-5 is amended to provide that a health care provider must file an Application for Adjustment of Claim for Health Provider's Fee with the Board no later than two (2) years after the receipt of an initial written communication from the employer, the employer's insurance carrier, if any, or an agent acting on behalf of the employer after the health care provider submits a bill for services. IC 22-3-7-9(g) is amended to provide the same time period for medical providers to file their claims for medical services and supplies with the Board in occupational disease cases.

IC 22-3-3-5 is amended as follows: subsection (a) now reads:

(a) The pecuniary liability of the employer for a service or product herein required shall be limited to the following:

(1) This subdivision applies before July 1, 2014, to all medical service providers, and after June 30, 2014, to a medical service provider that is not a medical service facility. Such charges as prevail as provided under IC 22-3-6-1(k)(1), in the same community (as defined in IC 22-3-6-1(h)) for a like service or product to injured persons.

(2) This subdivision applies after June 30, 2014, to a medical service facility. The amount provided under IC 22-3-6-1(k)(2).

and subsection (c) and (d) now read:

(c) The right to order payment for all services or products provided under IC 22-3-2 through IC 22-3-6 is solely with the board.

(d) All claims by a medical service provider for payment for services or products are against the employer and the employer's insurance carrier, if any, and must be made with the board under IC 22-3-2 through IC 22-3-6. After June 30, 2011, a medical service provider must file an application for adjustment of a claim for a medical service provider's fee with the board not later than two (2) years after the receipt of an initial written communication from the employer, the employer's insurance carrier, if any, or an agent acting on behalf of the employer after the medical service provider submits a bill for services or products. To offset a part of the board's expenses related to the administration of medical service provider reimbursement disputes, a medical service facility shall pay a filing fee of sixty dollars ($60) in a balance billing case. The filing fee must accompany each application filed with the board. If an employer, an employer's insurance carrier, or an agent acting on behalf of the employer denies or fails to pay any amount on a claim

_____

[3]IC 22-3-3-5.1.

submitted by a medical service facility, a filing fee is not required to accompany an application that is filed for the denied or unpaid claim. A medical service provider may combine up to ten (10) individual claims into one (1) application whenever:

(1) all individual claims involve the same employer, insurance carrier, or billing review service; and

(2) the amount of each individual claim does not exceed two hundred dollars ($200).

IC 22-3-3-4.5 is created and provides that whenever a prescription covered by the worker's compensation act is filled with a repackaged legend drug as defined IC 25-26-14-7 and IC 25-26-14-9.3, (1) the reimbursement amount for the repackaged legend drug must be computed using the average wholesale price set by the original manufacturer for the legend drug; (2) the medical service provider may not be reimbursed for more than one office visit for each repackaged legend drug prescribed; and (3) the maximum period during which a medical service provider may receive reimbursement for a repackaged legend drug begins on the date of the injury and ends at the beginning of the eighth day after the date of the injury. It further provides that if the National Drug Code for a legend drug cannot be determined from the medical service provider's billing or statement, the maximum reimbursement is the lowest cost generic for that legend drug.

IC 22-3-4-5 is amended to provide a different pecuniary liability for employers or their worker's compensation carrier for covered medical services provided by a medical service provider and those provided by a medical service facility. The pecuniary liability for an employer or its worker's compensation carrier for medical services covered under worker's compensation provided by a medical service provider is unchanged. After June 30, 2014, the pecuniary liability of an employer or its worker's compensation carrier for medical services covered under worker's compensation provided by a medical service facility may be negotiated by the employer or its carrier and the medical service facility; a billing review service and an employer or its carrier; or a direct provider network and the employer or its carrier. If an amount has not been negotiated, the pecuniary liability of an employer or its worker's compensation carrier is 200% of the amount that would be paid to the medical service facility on the same date for the same service or product under the medical service facility's Medicare reimbursement rate. Effective July 1, 2013, the payment to a medical service provider for an implant furnished to an employee under the worker's compensation act may not exceed the invoice amount plus 25%.

IC 22-3-6-1 is amended to provide that medical service facility means a hospital (as defined in IC 16-18-2-179); a hospital based health facility (as defined in IC 16-18-2-180); and a medical center (as defined in IC 16-18-2-223.4). The term does not include a professional corporation (as defined in IC 23-1.5-1-10) comprised of health care professionals (as defined in IC 23-1.5-1-8) who render professional services or to a health care professional who bills for a service or product provided under worker's compensation as an individual or a group practice.

IC 22-3-7-9 of the Occupational Diseases Act has been amended to reflect the same provisions for the pecuniary liability of an employer or its worker's compensation carrier for medical services or products.

IC 22-3-7-17.4 is added to the Occupational Diseases Act providing the identical provision.

In *Danielson v. Pratt Industries, Inc.*,[4] Dr. Danielson filed his application for adjustment of claim for provider fee with the board and therein claimed that Pratt owed him a fee for emergency medical services performed on Tien Hsiao. The board denied his claim, and the court of appeals affirmed the denial. In doing so, the court stated:

> [T]he Board dismissed Dr. Danielson's claim because Tien Hsiao never filed a claim for Worker's Compensation upon which Dr. Danielson could base his claim. In order to collect the costs of reasonable medical services from the "Employer" a physician must provide services, treatment, or supplies to an "Employee." *See* I.C. §§ 22-3-3-4(d) and 22-3-6-1(i). In the instant case, at no point in either of the Board hearings was a determination that Tien Hsiao was an "Employee" of Pratt, or that Pratt was the "Employer" of Tien Hsiao as those definitions are codified in I.C. §§ 22-3-6-1(a) and (b). Without those determinations being made, Dr. Danielson does not qualify as a "Medical Service Provider." *See* I.C. § 22-3-6-1(i). Dr. Danielson failed to file this Application, seeking to have the Board reimburse him for medical costs, without first determining that Pratt was the employer of Tien Hsiao, or that Tien Hsiao was the employee of Pratt, as required under the Worker's Compensation Act. Claims which do not meet any one of the jurisdictional prerequisites do not fall within the Act and may be pursued in court.[5]

In *Christopher R. Brown, DDS, Inc. v. Decatur County Memorial Hosp.*,[6] a dentist filed a provider fee claim with the board for unpaid services rendered to an injured employee of the hospital.

---

[4]Danielson v. Pratt Industries, Inc., 846 N.E.2d 244 (Ind. Ct. App. 2006).

[5]Danielson v. Pratt Industries, Inc., 846 N.E.2d 244, 247 (Ind. Ct. App. 2006).

[6]Christopher R. Brown, DDS, Inc. v. Decatur County Memorial Hosp., 873 N.E.2d 69 (Ind. Ct. App. 2007), transfer granted, opinion vacated, IN RAP 58(A), 878 N.E.2d 220 (Ind. 2007) and opinion vacated, 892 N.E.2d 642 (Ind. 2008).

As a part of his claim, he requested interest on all unpaid amounts. The single hearing member awarded him prejudgment interest, but the full board reversed. In upholding the decision of the full board denying Brown prejudgment interest, the court of appeals, after citing with approval its decisions in the cases of *Bowles v. Griffin Industries,*[7] and *Joseph E. Seagram & Sons v. Willis,*[8] stated:

> Significantly, in the quarter century since *Seagram* was decided, the Legislature has amended the Act numerous times, but has never added a provision requiring prejudgment interest on a Worker's Compensation award. *Bowles,* 855 N.E.2d at 321.We have no authority to read in such a requirement. *Id* . . . .

> Brown claims that because he is not employed by the Hospital a contract outside the purview of the Act was created between him and the hospital. We cannot agree because he is seeking prejudgment interest pursuant to a Worker's Compensation claim and because we have no authority to read into a statute a provision that the Legislature has purposely omitted, *i.e.,* a provision for prejudgment interest, we cannot find the Board incorrectly interpreted the Act.[9]

In *Indiana Spine Group v. Pilot Travel Centers, LLC,*[10] the appellate court looked at the question of the statute of limitations for the filing of a Provider Fee claim before the Board. The Board dismissed the Provider Fee Application filed by the Indiana Spine Group pursuant to IC 22-3-3-7 because it was filed more than two years after the last date for which compensation was paid.[11] However, the court concluded that this statute does not apply and that the Act is silent on the statute of limitations applicable to claims involving the pecuniary liability of employers to medical service providers. Applying this statute could result in "absurd results" with medical service providers potentially having little or no time enforce its right to payment for services. This would result in leaving medical providers little incentive to treat injured workers.[12]

---

[7]Bowles v. Griffin Industries, 855 N.E.2d 315 (Ind. Ct. App. 2006), transfer denied, 869 N.E.2d 449 (Ind. 2007).

[8]Joseph E. Seagram & Sons, Inc. v. Willis, 401 N.E.2d 87 (Ind. Ct. App. 1980).

[9]Christopher R. Brown, DDS, Inc. v. Decatur County Memorial Hosp., 873 N.E.2d 69, 72 (Ind. Ct. App. 2007), transfer granted, opinion vacated, IN RAP 58(A), 878 N.E.2d 220 (Ind. 2007) and opinion vacated, 892 N.E.2d 642 (Ind. 2008).

[10]Indiana Spine Group, PC v. Pilot Travel Centers, LLC, 931 N.E.2d 435 (Ind. Ct. App. 2010).

[11]Indiana Spine Group, PC v. Pilot Travel Centers, LLC, 931 N.E.2d 435, 437 (Ind. Ct. App. 2010).

[12]Indiana Spine Group, PC v. Pilot Travel Centers, LLC, 931 N.E.2d 435,

In *Indiana Spine Group, P.C. v. Pilot Travel Centers, LLC,*[13] the Supreme Court granted transfer in the case to hold that the Indiana Worker's Compensation Act does not provide (before July 1, 2011) a specific statute of limitations for medical providers to file their claims with the Board for payment of medical services and supplies.

In two cases, *Indiana Spine Group, P.C. v. International Entertainment Consultants*[14] and *Indiana Spine Group, P.C. v. Handleman Co.,*[15] the Court of Appeals held that the Worker's Compensation Act was silent with respect to the statute of limitations for a medical provider to file a claim for payment with the Worker's Compensation Board. These cases were decided prior to July 1, 2011 when the legislature amended IC 22-3-3-5(c) by providing that a health care provider must file an Application for Adjustment of Claim for Provider Fee with the Board not later than two years after the receipt of an initial written communication from the employer, the employer's insurance carrier, if any, or an agent acting on behalf of the employer denying payment of a medical bill submitted for services. As such, these cases have been legislatively overruled effective July 1, 2011.

§ 4:6 Medical services—Examinations

If requested by an employer, or ordered by the board, an injured employee must submit to an examination by a duly qualified physician or surgeon. The examination must be conducted at a reasonable time and place and during the period of disability or impairment resulting from the injury. The employee has the right to have present a duly qualified physician or surgeon of the employee's own choosing. No fact communicated to or learned by any physician present at the examination is privileged. If the employee refuses to submit to, or in any way obstructs, the examination, the employee's right to compensation and his or her right to prosecute any further proceedings under the Act will be suspended until the refusal or obstruction ceases. No compensation is payable for the period of suspension unless the board finds that the circumstances justified the employee's refusal or obstruction. The employee must be served with a notice, in a

---

438-439 (Ind. Ct. App. 2010).

[13]Indiana Spine Group, PC v. Pilot Travel Centers, LLC, 959 N.E.2d 789 (Ind. 2011).

[14]Indiana Spine Group, P.C. v. International Entertainment Consultants, 940 N.E.2d 380 (Ind. Ct. App. 2011), transfer denied, 962 N.E.2d 652 (Ind. 2011).

[15]Indiana Spine Group, P.C. v. Handleman Co., 944 N.E.2d 497 (Ind. Ct. App. 2011), transfer denied, 962 N.E.2d 652 (Ind. 2011).

form prescribed by the board, setting forth the consequences of the refusal.[1]

If the employer requests an examination of an employee residing in Indiana, the employer must pay in advance the necessary expenses of travel, meals and lodging for the employee to attend the examination. The employer must also reimburse the employee's lost wages, if the same result from attending the examination. If an employee who was injured in Indiana moves outside the state, the travel expense and the cost of meals and lodging is to be computed from the point in Indiana nearest to the employee's residence to the place of examination.[2]

If the employee has no physician present at the examination, the physician or surgeon conducting the examination must deliver to the employee or the employee's representative (attorney or agent), as soon as practicable, but no later than 30 days in advance of the hearing, a written statement of the conditions evidenced by the examination. The statement must disclose all facts that are reported to the employer by the physician. If the physician fails or refuses to timely furnish the statement, it may not be submitted as evidence at the hearing, and such physician will not be permitted to testify at the hearing as to any facts learned during the course of the examination. The same rules pertain to examinations made by physicians or surgeons engaged by the employee where no physician or surgeon representing the employer is present.[3]

All statements of physicians or surgeons, whether they are engaged by the employee or the employer, must contain the following information: (1) the history of the injury as given by the claimant, (2) the physician's diagnosis of the patient's physical or mental condition, (3) the physician's opinion of the causal relationship, if any, between the injury and the patient's condition, including the reasons therefore, (4) the physician's opinion concerning whether the injury resulted in a disability or impairment and, if so, the extent of the disability or impairment, including the reasons therefore, and (5) the original signature of the physician or surgeon. Notwithstanding any hearsay objection, the board shall admit into evidence a statement that meets these requirements, unless the statement is ruled inadmissible on other grounds. Any party may object to a statement on the basis that it

---

[Section 4:6]

[1]IC 22-3-3-6(a). See also Pedigo v. Miller, 175 Ind. App. 97, 369 N.E.2d 1100, 1102 (1977) ("it is clear that the legislature intended to provide an avenue for the employer to discover the true physical condition of a claiming employee.").

[2]IC 22-3-3-6(b).

[3]IC 22-3-3-6(c), IC 22-3-3-6(d), IC 22-3-3-6(f).

does not meet these requirements. However, the objecting party must give notice, no later than 20 days in advance of the hearing, to the party providing the statement, specifying the basis for the objection. Failure to object, as provided, precludes any further objection as to the adequacy of the statement.[4]

The employer, or the board, upon proper application, has the right in any case of death to require any autopsy at the expense of the party requesting same. If, after a hearing, the board orders an autopsy and the surviving spouse or next-of-kin refuses, any claim for compensation on account of the death is suspended and abated during the period of such refusal. The surviving spouse or dependant must be served with a notice, in a form prescribed by the board, setting forth the consequences of the refusal. No autopsy, except one performed by or upon the authority of the coroner in the discharge of his or her duties, shall be held in any case by any person without notice first being given to the surviving spouse or next-of-kin. The notice must state the time and place of the autopsy and must provide reasonable time and opportunity for the surviving spouse or next-of-kin to have a representative present to witness the autopsy. If the requisite notice is not given, all evidence obtained in the autopsy will be suppressed on motion made to the board.[5]

While IC 22-3-3-6 is rather self-explanatory, an interesting situation was presented in *Borgman v. Sugar Creek Animal Hosp.*[6] There, the employer's insurer sent the employee's medical records to a physician and sought his opinion regarding causation. Without ever examining the claimant, he "unequivocally" concluded that her medical conditions were not related to her work accident. The physician's statement was admitted into evidence, and the appellate court found that the board properly admitted it since the report met the requirements of IC 22-3-3-6(e). Even though the court set out the text of the subsection in its opinion, there was no discussion by the court of the language contained therein regarding the physician's statements "required by this section." "This section" relates to the physician's statements prepared as the result of and following an examination of an injured employee. It would, therefore, seem that the medical report offered by the employer was beyond the scope of the statute and was thus inadmissible.[7]

Little litigation has developed with respect to the interpreta-

---

[4]IC 22-3-3-6(e), IC 22-3-3-6(g). See also IC 22-3-3-6(c) and (d).

[5]IC 22-3-3-6(h).

[6]Borgman v. Sugar Creek Animal Hosp., 782 N.E.2d 993 (Ind. Ct. App. 2002).

[7]Borgman v. Sugar Creek Animal Hosp., 782 N.E.2d 993, 997–998 (Ind. Ct. App. 2002).

tion of the autopsy requirements set forth in subsection (h) of IC 22-3-3-6. Even though *McDermid v. Pearson Co.*,[8] dealt with a predecessor to the current subsection, the following language from the court's opinion is instructive, especially since it formed the basis for subsequent amendments to the statute:

> This section of the statute does not provide unconditionally the right to an autopsy in all events. It recognizes by implication that there must be a necessity for such autopsy and that a demand therefor should be made at a reasonable time and place. Vonnegut Hardware Co. v. Rose (1918), 68 Ind. App. 385, 120 N.E. 608.
>
> Obviously, it is not every case in which there is need for an autopsy. Furthermore, such right should be exercised with the greatest of caution on cases where the request for the autopsy has been made after interment has taken place, so that relatives of the deceased may not be caused any more mental distress than is absolutely necessary in view of all the circumstances.
>
> . . . .
>
> Generally speaking, it is usually a question of fact and is, in the first instance, within the province of the Board to determine whether or not the demand for an autopsy was made at a reasonable time and place.[9]

§ 4:7 Temporary disability

If an injury produces only a temporary total or partial disability to work, compensation under the Act will be allowed, but only from the eighth day of the disability. However, if the disability continues for longer than 21 days, compensation will be allowed for the first seven days. The waiting period has no application to the employer's obligation to furnish medical benefits.[1]

The first weekly installment of compensation for temporary disability is due to be paid 14 days after the disability begins. Not later than 15 days thereafter (or 29 days after the disability begins), the employer or its insurance carrier must tender to the employee or his or her dependents, with all compensation due, a properly prepared compensation agreement in a form prescribed by the board. Whenever an employer or its carrier denies or is unable to determine its liability to pay compensation or benefits, it must so notify the board and the employee in writing, on a form prescribed by the board, within 30 days after the employer's knowledge of the claimed injury. If a determination of liability

---

[8]McDermid v. Pearson Co., 107 Ind. App. 96, 21 N.E.2d 80 (1939).

[9]McDermid v. Pearson Co., 107 Ind. App. 96, 21 N.E.2d 80, 81–82 (1939). See also Delaware Machinery & Tool Co. v. Yates, 170 Ind. App. 6, 351 N.E.2d 67 (1976).

[Section 4:7]

[1]IC 22-3-3-7(a).

cannot be made within 30 days, the board may approve an additional 30 days, upon written request of the employer or carrier. Such request must set forth the reasons why a determination could not be made within 30 days and those facts or circumstances necessary to determine liability within the additional 30 days. More than 30 days of additional time may be approved by the board, but a petition therefor must be filed by the employer or carrier, and the following must be set forth in the petition: (1) a statement of the extraordinary circumstances which have precluded a determination of liability within the first 60 days; (2) the status of the investigation on the day the petition is filed; (3) the facts or circumstances necessary to make a determination of liability; and (4) a timetable for the completion of the investigation. An employer who fails to comply is subject to a civil penalty of $50 to be assessed and collected by the board upon notice and hearing.[2]

Once begun, temporary total disability (TTD) benefits may not be terminated by the employer unless the employee: (1) has returned to any employment; (2) has died; (3) has refused to undergo a medical examination or has refused to accept suitable employment; (4) has received 500 weeks of TTD benefits or has been paid the maximum compensation allowed under IC 22-3-3-22; or (5) is unable or unavailable to work for reasons unrelated to the compensable injury. In all other cases, the employer must notify the employee in writing of its intent to terminate the payment of TTD benefits and of the availability of employment, if any, on a form approved by the board. If the employee disagrees with the proposed termination, he or she must give written notice of disagreement to the board and the employer within seven days of receipt of the notice of intent to terminate benefits. If the board and employer do not receive the employee's notice of disagreement, TTD benefits will be terminated. Upon receipt of the notice of disagreement, the board must immediately contact the parties and attempt to resolve the disagreement. If the board cannot resolve the disagreement within 10 days of receipt of the employee's notice, it must immediately arrange for the employee to be evaluated by an independent medical examiner. The physician will be appointed by the board if the parties are unable to select one by mutual agreement. If the physician determines that the employee is no longer temporarily disabled; is still temporarily disabled but can return to employment that the employer has made available; or if the employee fails or refuses to appear for the independent medical examination, TTD benefits may be terminated. If either party disagrees with the opinion of the inde-

---

[2]IC 22-3-3-7(b).

pendent medical examiner, the party shall apply to the board for a hearing.[3]

An employer is not required to continue the payment of TTD benefits for more than 14 days after its proposed termination date unless the independent medical examiner determines that the employee is temporarily disabled and unable to return to any employment that the employer has made available.[4]

If it is determined that TTD benefits were overpaid, the overpayment must be deducted from any benefits due the employee under the compensation schedule for impairment. If there are no such benefits due to the employee or if the benefits due to the employee do not equal the amount of the overpayment, the employee is responsible for paying any overpayment which cannot be deducted from benefits due him or her.[5]

In its opinion in *Spangler, Jennings & Dougherty P.C. v. Indiana Ins. Co.*,[6] the Indiana Supreme Court stated, in part, that: "Compensation benefits are not awarded as 'damages for pain, suffering or other monetary loss.' . . . The 'benefits are intended to replace the future wages that the employee would earn if he were able to continue to work.' *Leisure v. Leisure*, 605 N.E.2d 755, 758–59 (Ind. 1993)."[7]

In *Perry v. Stitzer Buick GMC, Inc.*,[8] the Supreme Court defined "disability" as "an injured employee's inability to work. *Talas*, 435 N.E.2d at 26. The extent of a disability is determined by a worker's physical and mental fitness for various employment opportunities. *Rork v. Szabo Foods*, 439 N.E.2d 1338 (Ind. 1982)."[9]

> Temporary total disability payments are intended to compensate an employee for the treatment period following a work-related injury, and during this treatment period it is relevant whether the injured workman has the ability to return to work of the same kind or character. Covarubias v. Decatur Casting; Division of Hamilton Allied Corp., (1976) Ind. App., 358 N.E.2d 174. If he does not have the ability to return to work of the same kind or character during

---

[3]IC 22-3-3-7(c).

[4]IC 22-3-3-7(d).

[5]IC 22-3-3-7(e).

[6]Spangler, Jennings & Dougherty P.C. v. Indiana Ins. Co., 729 N.E.2d 117 (Ind. 2000).

[7]Spangler, Jennings & Dougherty P.C. v. Indiana Ins. Co., 729 N.E.2d 117, 121 (Ind. 2000); Cavazos v. Midwest General Metals Corp., 783 N.E.2d 1233 (Ind. Ct. App. 2003).

[8]Perry v. Stitzer Buick GMC, Inc., 637 N.E.2d 1282 (Ind. 1994).

[9]Perry v. Stitzer Buick GMC, Inc., 637 N.E.2d 1282, 1288 (Ind. 1994). See also Borgman v. Sugar Creek Animal Hosp., 782 N.E.2d 993, 996 (Ind. Ct. App. 2002).

the treatment period, he is temporarily totally disabled. Covarubias, supra.[10]

In *Ballard v. Book Heating & Cooling, Inc.*,[11] the court of appeals had to decide whether a claimant was entitled to receive temporary total disability payments while simultaneously drawing unemployment compensation benefits. In deciding that he was not entitled to do so, the court stated:

> In the instant case, Ballard represented to the Unemployment Insurance Division (Unemployment Division) in March of 1996, that he was ready, willing and able to return to work. Thereafter, the Division determined that Ballard had fully satisfied all the eligibility requirements of I.C. § 22-4-14-3, and entered an award for unemployment benefits. R. at 6. At the same time, Ballard represented in his application for worker's compensation benefits that he was temporarily totally disabled and was no longer able to work. As Ballard was bound to establish that he was physically able to work in order to receive unemployment compensation under I.C. § 22-4-14-3, it logically follows that he may not also claim that he was incapacitated from his work-related injury, with the exception of receiving workers' compensation benefits for that same period of time.
>
> Although our statutes do not expressly prohibit a claimant from receiving both types of benefits, we conclude that our legislature could not have intended for an employee to recover dual benefits under these circumstances. To suggest that one who was physically and mentally able to work, available for work, and was making an effort to secure full-time work was at the same time totally disabled, would be contrary to law . . . . Therefore, we conclude that the Board properly determined that Ballard was not entitled to receive temporary total disability benefits for the same period of time that he drew unemployment benefits.[12]

The effect of IC 22-3-3-7(c) and the duties and responsibilities of the parties the board contained therein has been the subject of recent litigation. In *Cavazos v. Midwest General Metals Corp.*,[13] the court of appeals found that "TTD benefits can be suspended or terminated based on an employee's unreasonable refusal of medical services," and that an employer may terminate TTD benefits "when an injury has stabilized to a permanent and quiescent state." The court went further to state:

---

[10]White v. Woolery Stone Co., Inc., 181 Ind. App. 532, 396 N.E.2d 137, 139 (1979). See also Tanglewood Trace v. Long, 715 N.E.2d 410, 414 (Ind. Ct. App. 1999) ("lay evidence, such as claimant's own testimony is sufficient to support an initial award of temporary total disability payments").

[11]Ballard v. Book Heating & Cooling, Inc., 696 N.E.2d 55 (Ind. Ct. App. 1998).

[12]Ballard v. Book Heating & Cooling, Inc., 696 N.E.2d 55, 57–58 (Ind. Ct. App. 1998).

[13]Cavazos v. Midwest General Metals Corp., 783 N.E.2d 1233 (Ind. Ct. App. 2003).

However, while the employer may terminate temporary total disability benefits without notice to the employee in certain instances (for example, death or reemployment), in all other circumstances, such as in this one, the employer must notify the employee and the Board of its intent to terminate benefits. *Cox v. Worker's Compensation Bd. of Ind.*, 675 N.E.2d 1053, 1056 (Ind. 1996). Thus, Indiana Code § 22-3-3-7 requires that the employer notify the employee of the consequence of refusing medical services- benefit termination.

. . . As TTD benefits in this case could not be terminated until Cavazos was notified in writing on a form approved by the Board of Midwest's intent to terminate the payments, we find that Midwest could not terminate Cavazos's TTD benefits until June 4, 1998, when it sent a State Form 38911. *See Woehnker,* 764 N.E.2d at 689 . . . .

. . . .

Midwest's third termination of Cavazos's TTD benefits was based on evidence that Cavazos's injury had reached a permanent and quiescent state. The evidence before the Board reveals that Midwest terminated Cavazos's TTD benefits on May 28, 2000, after Dr. Javors issued his opinion that Cavazos had a . . . permanent partial impairment due to the injury he received and after treatment ended for the psychological component of Cavazos's injury. On June 4, 2000, Midwest sent Cavazos a State Form 38911 notifying him of the termination and a few days later Cavazos requested an independent medical examination. The independent medical examiner found that Cavazos was still not able to return to work as a result of the injury which he received, that he considered Cavazos to be disabled for an indefinite period of time, and that there was a strong psychological component to Cavazos's condition. On October 6, 2000, the Ombudsmen of the Worker's Compensation Board ordered that Cavazos's "(TTD) benefits should be reinstated from the date of termination and paid until he reaches medical quiescence." Appellee's App. p. 67. However, Midwest only reinstated Cavazos's TTD benefits starting October 6, 2000; it did not reinstate them from the date of termination, May 28, 2000. The record does not reveal that Midwest ever applied to the Board for a hearing in order to dispute the opinion of the independent medical examiner. Therefore, we find that the Board erred in finding that Midwest properly withheld Cavazos's TTD benefits from May 29, 2000, to October 5, 2000.[14]

In *Woehnker v. Cooper Tire & Rubber Co.*,[15] a dispute arose over the termination of TTD benefits and the injured employee's request for an independent medical examination. The court of appeals had the following to say:

Here, Cooper terminated Woehnker's temporary total disability benefits because he had reportedly reached MMI—one of the "other

---

[14]Cavazos v. Midwest General Metals Corp., 783 N.E.2d 1233, 1242–43 (Ind. Ct. App. 2003).

[15]Woehnker v. Cooper Tire & Rubber Co., 764 N.E.2d 688 (Ind. Ct. App. 2002).

cases" contemplated by the statute—but failed to notify him in writing before doing so. Woehnker notified both Cooper and the Board of his disagreement with the termination of his benefits in his IME petition . . . .

. . . .

The purpose of an IME is to determine expeditiously whether an employee is entitled to continue receiving temporary total disability benefits notwithstanding their proposed termination by an employer. Should the Board be unable to resolve a disagreement between the employer and the employee, an IME is the only avenue for an employee to challenge the employer's proposed termination of benefits. Absent any indication of contrary legislative intent, and consistent with the humanitarian purpose of the Act, we construe the legislature's usage of "shall" in this instance as being of mandatory import and therefore as requiring the Board to immediately arrange for an IME if it is unable to resolve a disagreement between an employer and an employee within ten days of receipt of the employee's notice of disagreement . . . .

. . . In the instant case, the Board denied Woehnker's IME request because of his alleged failure to comply with medical treatment. There is no evidence, however, that Cooper ever served Woehnker a notice setting forth the consequences of his refusal to comply or that Woehnker was refusing to comply at the time he requested an IME. Thus, the Board incorrectly concluded that Woehnker had forfeited his right to request an IME under section 22-3-3-7(c).[16]

Currently, with respect to injuries causing temporary total disability or total permanent disability for work, an injured employee is entitled to receive during the total disability a weekly compensation equal to 66 2/3% of his or her average weekly wages, as defined in IC 22-3-3-22, for a period not to exceed 500 weeks.[17]

Similarly, at the present time and with respect to injuries causing temporary partial disability for work, the employee is entitled to receive a weekly compensation during such disability equal to 66 2/3% of the difference between his or her average weekly wages and the weekly wages at which he or she is actually employed after the injury, for a period not to exceed 500 weeks. In case the partial disability begins after the period of temporary total disability, the latter period must be included as a part of the maximum period allowed for partial disability.[18]

At the present time, in computing compensation for temporary total, temporary partial, and total permanent disability, the employee's average weekly wage is considered to be not more than

---

[16]Woehnker v. Cooper Tire & Rubber Co., 764 N.E.2d 688, 691–692 (Ind. Ct. App. 2002) (footnotes omitted).

[17]IC 22-3-3-8.

[18]IC 22-3-3-9.

$1,040 and not less than $75. However, the weekly compensation payable must not exceed the average weekly wages of the employee at the time of injury.[19]

In *Bowles v. Griffin Industries*,[20] the claimant sought an award of interest upon TTD and PTD weekly payments that he alleged were paid late. Both the single hearing member and the full board denied his request. In affirming, the court of appeals wrote:

> While we understand Bowles' time value of money argument, as we outline below, neither the Act nor the case law mandates the payment of interest under the circumstances presented.
>
> . . . .
>
> . . . Griffin did not pay "very belatedly." To the contrary, along the way, whenever agreements were reached, Griffin swiftly made payment . . . . Griffin did not appeal or contest those certain amounts. Of additional importance, Bowles received medical benefits from the day of the incident and for three years thereafter. Given these circumstances, we conclude that interest is not appropriate.
>
> Having reached our conclusion, we stress that we do not disagree with either the case law permitting *post*-judgment interest in certain situations or the separate statutory authority to award such interest. *See Paino,* 555 N.E.2d 190; *see also Hatfield v. Higgins,* 31 N.E.2d 650, 651, 108 Ind. App. 681, 683 (1941) (reversing denial of motion for "interest on the deferred installments *from and after the time they became due under the judgment* of the Circuit Court until the time that they were actually paid"; and citing then-current statute that authorized post-judgment interest) (emphasis added); *see* Ind. Code § 4-4.6-1-101 . . . . However, even if one could characterize the amounts determined here as "judgments," Griffin's insurer paid them immediately as they arose. Therefore, interest is not merited.[21]

There is authority for the proposition that, when a partially disabled employee is earning an amount equal to or greater than the amount he or she would otherwise be entitled to receive under this section of the Act, the employee cannot be awarded any compensation for temporary partial disability.[22]

---

[19]IC 22-3-3-22(j)(11)(A) and (B). The remaining subsections, (a) through (j)(13)(A) and (B), set forth maximum and minimum values for average weekly wages for periods from July 1, 1985, to June 30, 2014, and July 1, 2015, through and after July 1, 2016, respectively.

[20]Bowles v. Griffin Industries, 855 N.E.2d 315 (Ind. Ct. App. 2006), transfer denied, 869 N.E.2d 449 (Ind. 2007).

[21]Bowles v. Griffin Industries, 855 N.E.2d 315, 320, (Ind. Ct. App. 2006), transfer denied, 869 N.E.2d 449 (Ind. 2007).

[22]In re Dove, 65 Ind. App. 299, 117 N.E. 210 (1917).

In *Kohlman v. Indiana University*,[23] the court of appeals
decided that an employer has the right to deny temporary partial
disability (TPD) benefits to an employee after her injuries have
reached a permanent and quiescent state. There, Kohlman's
treating physician issued a permanent partial impairment rating
and released her to return to work but with restrictions. Because
of the physical restrictions placed on her, she could not return to
her previous job as a bus driver, but she did return to work for
her same employer as a receptionist which paid her less money.
She sought, but was denied, TPD benefits. In affirming the
board's denial of compensation, the court stated:

> This court has determined that an employer may terminate
> temporary disability benefits once the permanency of the employ-
> ee's injury has been established. In *Covarubias v. Decatur Casting,
> etc.,* 171 Ind. App. 533, 358 N.E.2d 174 (1976), we stated:
>
> "[O]nce the injury has stabilized to a permanent and quiescent
> state, *temporary* disability ceases, and the extent of *permanent*
> injury resulting in a degree of impairment *or* total disability is
> determined pursuant to the schedules in Ind. Ann. Stat. 22-3-3-10 .
> . . ."
>
> . . . .
>
> While the *Covarubias* panel confronted the question in the context
> of total, as opposed to partial, disability benefits, the principle
> underlying that decision is equally applicable, and dispositive, in
> the instant case: once the physical condition is quiescent, temporary
> disability ceases and the only compensation available is that
> prescribed for permanent impairment, as set out in IC § 22-3-3-10.
> . . .
>
> . . . .
>
> . . . The Act, whether in Section 10 or elsewhere, simply does not
> provide claimants with the right to receive temporary disability
> benefits for the permanent effects of an injury. Because Kohlman's
> condition was permanent and she was admittedly not permanently
> and totally disabled, her only remedy under the Act was to receive
> benefits for permanent partial impairment, which were awarded.
> *Covarubias,* 171 Ind. App. 533, 358 N.E.2d 174.
>
> In summary, no provision in the Act indicates that an employer
> is obligated to pay temporary partial disability benefits after the
> claimant's condition becomes permanent and quiescent. Therefore,
> we reaffirm the *Covarubias* panel's holding that the right to receive
> temporary benefits ceases when the worker's physical condition
> reaches a quiescent state.[24]

In applying IC 22-3-3-7(c)(5) to a claim for TPD benefits, the
court of appeals in *Borgman v. Sugar Creek Animal Hosp.*[25]
stated:

---

[23]Kohlman v. Indiana University, 670 N.E.2d 42 (Ind. Ct. App. 1996).

[24]Kohlman v. Indiana University, 670 N.E.2d 42, 43–44 (Ind. Ct. App. 1996).

[25]Borgman v. Sugar Creek Animal Hosp., 782 N.E.2d 993 (Ind. Ct. App.

. . . Borgman asserts entitlement to temporary partial disability benefits (TPD) because Sugar Creek did not offer her any work in accordance with her ability to perform sedentary work. Borgman, however, did not preserve the issue of her entitlement for such benefits at the . . . hearing. Also, because Borgman voluntarily terminated her employment with Sugar Creek due to reasons unrelated to her work injury [personal difficulties that she had experienced with a co-worker], Sugar Creek did not have a duty to offer her work according to medical restrictions or to remit any TPD benefits to her. Thus, the Board properly determined that Borgman was unavailable for work for reasons that were not related to her work injury. Indiana Code section 22-3-3-7(c)(5), which provides that TTD benefits "may not be terminated by the employer unless the employee is unable or unavailable to work for reasons unrelated to the compensable injury," commands such a result in this instance.[26]

As peripherally alluded to in *Borgman*, there is a provision in the Act which allows the employer to suspend or terminate the payment of compensation if an injured employee who is only partially disabled unjustifiably refuses to accept employment, suitable to his or her capacity, which the employer has procured for the employee. The suspension of compensation continues for as long as the employee refuses the employment. It is for the board to decide whether or not the employee's refusal of the employment proffered is justified.[27]

However, before compensation can be denied for refusing the employer's offer of suitable employment, the employee must be served with a notice, in a form prescribed by the board, setting forth the consequences of the refusal.[28]

The court of appeals had an opportunity to discuss IC 22-3-3-11 of the Act in its opinion in *Jones & Laughlin Steel Corp. v. Kilburne*.[29] The court stated:

> Under I.C. 22-3-3-11, an employer is permitted to reduce its workmen's compensation obligation by procuring for the injured employee employment by which he can earn some wages without injury to himself. *Bruce v. Stutz Motor Car Co. of America, Inc.* (1925) 83 Ind. App. 257, 148 N.E. 161. If the injured employee refuses the procured employment the employer's workmen's compensation obligation is suspended unless the board determines that the refusal was justified. *Silvey v. Panhandle Coal Co. No. 5* (1927), 86 Ind. App. 111, 154 N.E. 778 (*en banc*). Until suitable employment

---

2002).

[26]Borgman v. Sugar Creek Animal Hosp., 782 N.E.2d 993, 997 (Ind. Ct. App. 2002).

[27]IC 22-3-3-11(a).

[28]IC 22-3-3-11(b).

[29]Jones & Laughlin Steel Corp. v. Kilburne, 477 N.E.2d 345 (Ind. Ct. App. 1985).

has actually been procured by the employer and refused by the employee I.C. 22-3-3-11 does not apply. *Bruce, supra,* 148 N.E. at 163. Furthermore, I.C. 22-3-3-11 only applies where the employee is partially disabled. Kilburne is totally disabled and the mere request for pension benefits does not constitute a refusal to be otherwise employed. Therefore, I.C. 22-3-3-11 is wholly inapplicable.[30]

In *Platinum Construction Group, LLC v Christopher Collings,*[31] Christopher Collings, an employee of Platinum Construction Group, LLC (Platinum), suffered a work related injury that caused him to be off work 37 days. He was paid TTD benefits during that time. He was released to return to work by the employer's physician with no restrictions. Around the same time, Platinum laid-off its employees and closed its doors. Collings filed a claim for unemployment compensation. Collings attempted to work for two other contracting companies and even started his own construction company, but he was unable to earn any income other than about $1,200 due to his ongoing physical limitations. He never completed any of his projects.

Collings was released from medical treatment about eight months after his return to work and given a 7% PPI rating. He continued to treat for pain with Dr. Martino who determined that additional treatment was necessary. The Worker's Compensation Board appointed an independent medical examiner (IME) who determined that Collings had been disabled since the time of accident, and that he was not at maximum medical improvement. The IME also recommended a work hardening program.

At hearing, the Board awarded TTD for the entire period of temporary disability identified by the Board IME; however, the Board subtracted the amount of unemployment compensation Collings earned from the total award of TTD. The Full Board unanimously affirmed the Single Hearing Member's decision. On appeal, the Court of Appeals affirmed the Board's decision holding that TTD is due when the worker is unable to perform work of the same kind and character due to the injury and that unemployment is payable where worker is available to work in a less taxing position. As such, Collings is theoretically available for both benefits but may not receive both. As such, the court held that the Board, by subtracting amounts paid for unemployment, did not award a windfall to the injured worker.

---

[30]Jones & Laughlin Steel Corp. v. Kilburne, 477 N.E.2d 345, 350 (Ind. Ct. App. 1985).

[31]Platinum Const. Group, LLC v. Collings, 988 N.E.2d 1153 (Ind. Ct. App. 2013).

The *Collings* case seems to conflict with the court's previous hearing in *Ballard v. Book Heating and Cooling, Inc.*,[32] That is, in *Ballard* the court affirmed the Board's denial of TTD to a claimant who was also receiving unemployment benefits where the findings of facts stated that the claimant was physically and mentally able to work. In *Platinum*, the court observed that the *Ballard* court noted that the worker's compensation statutes do not specifically prohibit a claimant from being eligible for both benefits, but the *Ballard* court seemed most concerned that the claimant does not receive a windfall in the form of dual benefits.

In Gordon v. Toyota Motor Manufacturing,[33] William Gordon suffered an injury to his left shoulder and neck. The employer, Toyota, acknowledged his injury and paid for certain medical services and supplies. On July 24, 2008, the Toyota's specialist took Gordon off work; however, on August 5, 2008, the Toyota's in-house physician released the employee to work with restrictions. Gordon attempted to return to work but was unable to continue due to pain, and he resigned his employment on August 8, 2008 to avoid being fired. Both parties obtained medical opinions on whether Gordon needed more treatment. Toyota refused to provide the additional treatment recommended by Gordon's physician, so, on June 7, 2010, Gordon proceeded with surgery on his own. The surgery was successful, and resulted in a complete recovery without impairment after six months. At hearing, the Board found that Gordon was entitled to the cost of the June 7, 2010 surgery, TTD for the period of time he was taken off work from July 24, 2008 until August 5, 2008, and TTD from the date of the surgery (June 10, 2010) for 26 weeks until December 10, 2010. Gordon appealed claiming the evidence was clear that he should have been awarded additional TTD from August 5, 2008 until June 10, 2010. The Full Board affirmed the Single Hearing Member's decision adding that Gordon was not allowed to argue that no notice of the consequences of refusing light duty was served at the Full Board argument when it was not argued at the Single Member hearing level.

The Court of Appeals vacated the Board's decision holding that the findings were insufficient to explain, so the Single Hearing Member issued new findings which were again affirmed by the Full Board.

In the second appeal, the Court of Appeals reversed the Board and ordered TTD for the period Gordon claimed. The Court held that because the undisputed evidence shows Gordon's work re-

---

[32]Ballard v. Book Heating & Cooling, Inc., 696 N.E.2d 55 (Ind. Ct. App. 1998).

[33]Gordon v. Toyota Motor Mfg. of Indiana, 53 N.E.3d 477 (Ind. Ct. App. 2016).

lated injuries prevented him from doing even the sedentary work he was offered on August 5, 2008, IC 22-3-3-11 controls this case. IC 22-3-3-11(a) in sum provides that if an employer procures suitable work within temporary restrictions, and the employee refuses said work, TTD is not owed, unless the refusal is justifiable. IC 22-3-3-11(b) provides that the employer must first provide notice on a form prescribed by the Board (state Form 38911) of the consequences of refusing suitable work before TTD can be withheld. The Court stated the Board's findings were inadequate to determine whether it found Gordon's refusal of light duty work justifiable; however, the Court held once Gordon offered evidence that his refusal of light duty work was justifiable, the burden shifted to Toyota to show it complied with the notice requirement. The Court stated Gordon was not required to point out to the Single Hearing Member that Toyota had not met its burden under IC 22-3-3-11(b) which requires employers to serve notice of the consequences of refusing light duty work.

In Bush v. Robinson Engineering and Oil Co.,[34] the employee suffered an injury he believed was to his low back. He received benefits and was paid TTD. At the end of his period of TTD he requested and received an independent medical examination which was performed by Dr. Sasso. Dr. Sasso noted that all of symptoms complained of were related to the work injury, and he ordered an MRI of the cervical and lumbar spines. The lumbar spine was negative; however, the cervical spine showed a need for further evaluation. The employer refused to provide the additional evaluation arguing there had been no mention of a neck injury in the record before the independent medical examination. The employee argued that Dr. Sasso was in the best position to determine whether a particular symptom is related to a work incident, and that the Board should defer to its duly appointed physician. The Board found that the employee was not entitled to the evaluation and treatment recommended by the Board IME.

At the Court of Appeals, the employee argued that an independent medical examination, when it is appointed pursuant to IC 22-3-3-7(c), creates a rebuttable presumption that the opinion of the independent medical examiner is correct. Further, the employer did not offer any post IME opinion rebutting Dr. Sasso's report. The Court, in affirming the Board, held that IC 22-3-3-7(c), (d) do not create rebuttable presumption in favor of the opinion of the independent medical examination because the plain language of the statute establishes the right of either party to disagree with the opinion and request a hearing.

---

[34]Bush v. Robinson Engineering & Oil, Co., Inc., 54 N.E.3d 1073 (Ind. Ct. App. 2016).

§ 4:8 Impairment

The schedules for the payment of compensation for impairment are contained in IC 22-3-3-10. Currently, the injured employee is entitled to receive, in addition to TTD benefits not exceeding 125 weeks, weekly compensation of 66 2/3% of his or her average weekly wages during the 52 weeks immediately preceding the week in which he or she was injured.[1] The schedules list degrees of impairment for injuries resulting in amputations or loss of use of body parts, loss or reduction of vision, loss or reduction of hearing, permanent partial impairment, permanent disfigurement, and total permanent disability.[2]

IC 22-3-3-10(i)(2) contains a "doubling" provision for certain amputations occurring on or after July 1, 1997 (those described in subsection (i)(1)), and amputations occurring on and after July 1, 1999 (those described in subsection (i)(3), (5), or (8)). The dollar values per degree, as set forth in subsection (j), are to be multiplied by two (2); however, this doubling provision does not apply to a loss of use that is not a loss by separation.

IC 22-3-3-10(i)(9) provides:

> Loss of use: the total permanent loss of the use of an arm, a hand, a thumb, a finger, a leg, a foot, a toe, or a phalange shall be considered as the equivalent of the loss by separation of the arm, hand, thumb, finger, leg, foot, toe, or phalange, and compensation shall be paid in the same amount as for the loss by separation. *However, the doubling provision of subdivision (2) does not apply to a loss of use that is not a loss by separation.* (Emphasis added).

So, even though these total, permanent losses of use are considered to be the equivalent of a loss by separation, an injured employee will not receive the benefit of the doubling provision with respect to such a loss.

IC 22-3-3-10(i)(14) contains a residual provision, which reads, as follows: "In all other cases of permanent partial impairment, compensation proportionate to the degree of a permanent partial impairment, in the discretion of the worker's compensation board, not exceeding one hundred (100) degrees of permanent impairment." Therefore, if a loss does not appear elsewhere in the compensation schedules (for example, a percentage loss to the body as a whole), the board has the discretion to make an award pursuant to this subsection.

IC 22-3-3-10(i)(15) states the following with respect to disfigurement:

[Section 4:8]

[1]IC 22-3-3-10(i).

[2]IC 22-3-3-10(i)(1) to (15).

In all cases of permanent disfigurement *which may impair the future usefulness or opportunities of the employee,* compensation, in the discretion of the worker's compensation board, not exceeding forty (40) degrees of permanent impairment *except that no compensation shall be payable under this subdivision where compensation is payable elsewhere in this section.* (emphasis supplied).

It is the claimant's burden to prove that the disfigurement is such as to impair his or her future usefulness or opportunities.

With respect to injuries occurring on and after July 1, 2007, and before July 1, 2008, for each degree of permanent impairment from one (1) to ten (10), an injured employee is entitled to receive $1,340 per degree; for each degree of permanent impairment from 11 to 35, $1,545 per degree; for each degree of permanent impairment from 36 to 50, $2,475 per degree; and for each degree of permanent impairment above 50, $3,150 per degree.[3]

IC 22-3-3-10 is amended to provide an increase in compensation payable for permanent impairment for injuries occurring on and after July 1, 2014, for injuries occurring on and after July 1, 2015, and for injuries occurring on and after July 1, 2016:

Degrees of impairment:	July 1, 2014:	July 1, 2015:	July 1, 2016
1 to 10	$1,517 per degree	$1,633 per degree	$1,750 per degree
11 to 35	$1,717 per degree	$1,835 per degree	$1,952 per degree
36 to 50	$2,862 per degree	$3,024 per degree	$3,186 per degree
Above 50	$3,687 per degree	$3,873 per degree	$4,060 per degree

The maximum average weekly wage for determining compensation of permanent impairment, temporary total disability and temporary partial disability has been increased for injuries occurring on and after July 1, 2014, occurring on an after July 1, 2015, and occurring on and after July 1, 2016:

Maximum average weekly wage:

July 1, 2014	July 1, 2015	July 1, 2016
$1,040	$1,105	$1,170

---

[3]IC 22-3-3-10(j)(9). The remaining subsections, (1) to (8) and (10) to (12), value degrees of impairment for injuries occurring from July 1, 1991, to June 30, 2007, and July 1, 2008, through July 1, 2010, and after, respectively.

The maximum compensation payable, exclusive of medical benefits, has been increased of injuries occurring on and after July 1, 2014, occurring on and after July 1, 2015, and occurring on and after July 1, 2016:

Maximum compensation, exclusive of medical benefits:

July 1, 2014	July 1, 2015	July 1, 2016
$347,000	$368,000	$390,000

IC 22-3-7-16 and IC 22-3-7-19 of the Occupational Diseases Act have been amended to provide the same increase in benefits for disablements occurring on and after July 1, 2014, on and after July 1, 2015, and on and after July 1, 2016.

IC 22-3-6-1(d)(1) to (4) define an individual's "average weekly wage." Generally, it is "the earnings of the injured employee in the employment in which he was working at the time of the injury during the period of 52 weeks immediately preceding the date of injury, divided by 52." If the employee lost seven or more calendar days during that period, the time lost should be deducted and then the earnings for the remainder of the 52 weeks are to be divided by the number of weeks and parts thereof remaining. However, the computation must be just and fair to both the employee and the employer. If, because of the shortness of time for which the employee has worked for his or her employer, or because of the casual nature or terms of the employment, it is impracticable to compute the average weekly wage in the manner set forth above, the parties should give due regard to the average weekly amount which, during the 52 weeks previous to the injury, was being earned by a person in the same grade employed at the same work by the same employer. If there is no person so employed, then regard should be given to a person in the same grade employed in the same class of employment in the same district. If allowances of any character made to an employee if lieu of wages are a specified part of the wage contract, they shall be deemed a part of the employee's earnings.

At present, the average weekly wages used to determine compensation for permanent partial impairment shall not exceed $930 for injuries occurring on or after July 1, 2007, and before July 1, 2008.[4]

Although this section of the Act is rather self-explanatory, and

---

[4]IC 22-3-3-10(k)(12). The remaining subsections, (1) to (11) and (13) to (14), set forth maximum average weekly wage values for the periods from July 1, 1991, to June 30, 2007, and July 1, 2008, through July 1, 2009, and after, respectively.

the mathematical computations are relatively easy to make, some interpretive decisions by the appellate courts of Indiana have been required. At the outset, it must be remembered that there is a distinction in the Act between the concepts of disability and impairment. As stated by the appellate court in its decision in *Sumpter v. Colvin*,[5] and repeated often thereafter: "The term 'disability' as used in the act means inability to work, while the term 'impairment' means the partial or total loss of the function of a member or members of the body or of the body as a whole."[6]

In its opinion in *East Asiatic/Plumrose v. Ritchie*,[7] the court of appeals stated, in pertinent part:

> Once an injury reaches a permanent and quiescent state, an assessment may be made as to the extent of the permanent injury and the injured employee can be compensated. *Duncan v. George Moser Leather Co.* (1980), Ind. App., 408 N.E.2d 1332, 1337. If neither the employee or the employer appeals the award of permanent compensation, "it becomes a full and final determination of the condition of the injured worker at that time and of the employer's liability to pay, subject only to a petition for modification." *Id.* The award is not an adjudication as to the claimant's future condition, and the employee "may seek modification of the original award . . . ." *Id.*
>
> . . . .
>
> . . . Typically a TTD award entered at the initial stages of the case contains no fixed compensation period because the extent of the injury is unknown. It is a continuous award providing benefits until the worker returns to work or reaches a permanent and quiescent state. It is the PPI award that usually adjudicates the injured employee's right to compensation up to that point in time. . . . In essence, the TTD and PPI benefits are the two halves of the whole award.[8]

Going one step further, in *Perez v. U. S. Steel Corp.*,[9] the court of appeals discussed the concept of permanent total disability:

> *Permanent total disability* is not the subject of a separate section. Instead, it appears under subparagraph (b)(3) of the impairment section. This underscores a basic distinction between the *disabilities* for which recovery may be had under the act, *i.e.*, a distinction between temporary total disability and permanent total disability.
>
> . . . .
>
> Speaking of permanent total disability under § 10, Dean Small stated:

---

[5]Sumpter v. Colvin, 98 Ind. App. 453, 190 N.E. 66 (1934).

[6]Sumpter v. Colvin, 98 Ind. App. 453, 190 N.E. 66, 67–68 (1934).

[7]East Asiatic/Plumrose v. Ritchie, 655 N.E.2d 87 (Ind. Ct. App. 1995).

[8]East Asiatic/Plumrose v. Ritchie, 655 N.E.2d 87, 89–90 (Ind. Ct. App. 1995).

[9]Perez v. U. S. Steel Corp., 172 Ind. App. 242, 359 N.E.2d 925 (1977).

"A total disability to be permanent must be one which so destroys or shatters a workman's wage earning capacities as to leave him *unable to resume reasonable types of employment* for the remainder of his life. Since this form of disability is treated in the same section with other harms comprising threats to wage-earning power such as impairments and lost uses, total permanent disability *must be taken to require a greater incapacity than that produced by any other of the scheduled harms.* However, it is not necessary to a showing of total permanent disability that the workman prove an utter inability to do anything with the remains of his body. The believe-it-or-nots demonstrate that even the most hopeless human wrecks have on occasion developed obscure means for obtaining livelihood. It is sufficient if the workman can show that he has been so incapacitated by his injuries that *he cannot carry on reasonable types of employments.* The reasonableness of the workman's opportunities will be measured by his physical and mental fitness for them and by their availability." (emphasis added)

Small, *Workmen's Compensation Law of Indiana,* § 9.4, p. 244.

. . . .

. . . [T]he principle of § 10 is to provide a fixed amount of recovery for a permanent loss. In this context, a provision for permanent disability, *i.e.,* inability to work for the remainder of one's life, naturally carries the connotation of the inability to reasonably earn a livelihood. Accordingly, we adopt Dean Small's definition of the proof necessary to establish "permanent total disability" under § 10.

. . . .

Despite the definitional difference we have drawn between that inability which constitutes temporary total disability and the inability which constitutes permanent total disability, the basic distinction between disability (the inability to work) and impairment (loss of physical function) remains. The terms do *not* describe results that necessarily are mutually exclusive.[10]

In *Bowles v. Griffin Industries,*[11] the court of appeals stated:

[T]he touchstone for PTD is the extent to which the employee's ability to work has been compromised, while the aim of a PPI determination is to decide what parts of an employee's body have lost their proper function and to what extent. *Van-Scyoc v. Mid-State Paving,* 787 N.E.2d 499, 508 (Ind. Ct. App. 2003) . . . .

. . . .

. . . "[T]he issue of physical impairment concerns medical evidence relating to the loss of *bodily function,* whereas a disability determi-

---

[10]Perez v. U. S. Steel Corp., 172 Ind. App. 242, 359 N.E.2d 925, 927–29 (1977) (footnotes omitted) (emphasis added). Currently, injuries resulting in total permanent disability are compensated under IC 22-3-3-8 and IC 22-3-3-10(i)(11) of the Act.

[11]Bowles v. Griffin Industries, 798 N.E.2d 908 (Ind. Ct. App. 2003).

nation rests on *vocational factors* relating to the ability of an individual to engage in reasonable forms of work activity."[12]

In *Walker v. State, Muscatatuck State Development Center*,[13] the Indiana Supreme Court further amplified the issues involved in making determinations of permanent total disability. The Court stated:

> Once plaintiff has established the degree of obvious physical impairment, coupled with other facts such as the claimant's capacity, education, training, or age, and has established that she has attempted unsuccessfully to find work or that it would be futile to search for work in light of her impairment and other characteristics, the burden of producing evidence that reasonable employment is regularly and continuously available then rests on the employer. *See generally* 4 Arthur Larson, *Larson's Workers' Compensation Law* § 57.51, at 10-283 to -378, § 57.61(c), at 10-405 to -439 (1997) . . . Shifting the burden of production to the employer under these circumstances is justified because it is much easier for the employer, by virtue of its contact with the labor market, to prove the claimant's employability than it is for the employee to attempt to prove the universal negative of being totally unemployable.

> . . . .

> While what constitutes reasonable employment is often a question of fact, at the outer perimeters, the question is one of law. . . .

> . . . [W]e conclude, as a matter of law, that plaintiff has met her burden of establishing that, in light of her impairment, her age, her prior experience, and her lack of education, there are no general kinds of employment that would be suitable for her, and that it likely would be futile for her to seek employment in the general competitive labor market. Although the State did put forth evidence that it had offered her a position as a seamstress, that position cannot constitute "reasonable employment" for at least two reasons, either of which, standing alone, is sufficient to demonstrate that the offered employment is not reasonable employment as a matter of law.

> First, the temporary nature of the employment is in itself sufficient reason to conclude that it cannot constitute reasonable employment such that it defeats a claim of total permanent disability. If the post-injury employment lacks permanence and if it can fairly be said that, should the claimant lose that job, the claimant would have a hard time getting new work of a regular and continuous nature, a finding of total permanent disability is in order. *See generally* Larson, § 57.35, at 10-247 to -251, § 57.51(c), at 10-331 to -336 . . . .

> Second, work that is highly accommodated to suit the needs and disabilities of a particular claimant cannot defeat a claim of total permanent disability where it is clear that the claimant could not

---

[12]Bowles v. Griffin Industries, 798 N.E.2d 908, 910, (Ind. Ct. App. 2003).

[13]Walker v. State, Muscatatuck State Development Center, 694 N.E.2d 258 (Ind. 1998).

find similar work under normally prevailing market conditions. "Wages paid an injured employee out of sympathy, or in consideration of his long service with the employer" do not reflect his actual earning capacity under normal market conditions and are to be discounted for the purposes of determining permanent disability. *See* Larson, § 57.34, at 10-239. "The same is true if the injured man's friends help him to hold his job by doing much of his work for him, or if he manages to continue only by delegating his more onerous tasks to a helper, or if the work for which claimant is paid is 'made work' or 'sheltered work.' "*Id.* § 57.34, at 10-239 to 245. Similarly, an employer cannot avoid deliberately its duty to pay worker's compensation benefits simply by offering the employee work that is so highly accommodated to the employee's needs that it would not ordinarily be available under normally prevailing market conditions.[14]

The claimant's competency to testify regarding matters of impairment was at issue in *Kenwood Erection Co. v. Cowsert.*[15] The appellate court stated that a claimant in a worker's compensation proceeding was not qualified to testify to the permanency of his condition of impairment. That, said the court, was a medical question upon which only expert testimony was competent. However, the court went on to state:

> *Impairment,* within the confines of the Workmen's Compensation Act, relates to the functional use of the body. This is a fact regarding which the injured party has personal knowledge and experience. He is, therefore, qualified to speak upon the subject within the scope of the knowledge existent in each individual case. Therefore, the Industrial Board was entitled to receive appellee's testimony and weigh the same with that of medical experts upon the subject.[16]

In *Justiniano v. Williams,*[17] the application of the schedules to multiple injuries was brought before the court of appeals. There, Justiniano suffered severe injuries to both of his legs when he fell from scaffolding while hanging drywall. The treating physician determined that his permanent partial impairment was "18% of the lower extremity, bilaterally" or a total of 16% "whole body impairment." Justiniano argued that his compensation amount should have been computed upon the basis of his proportional loss of use of his legs, not the impairment to his whole body, which would have resulted in a greater dollar amount of benefit

---

[14]Walker v. State, Muscatatuck State Development Center, 694 N.E.2d 258, 265–267 (Ind. 1998) (footnotes omitted) (citations omitted).

[15]Kenwood Erection Co. v. Cowsert, 124 Ind. App. 165, 115 N.E.2d 507 (1953).

[16]Kenwood Erection Co. v. Cowsert, 124 Ind. App. 165, 115 N.E.2d 507, 509 (1953). See also Coachmen Industries, Inc. v. Yoder, 422 N.E.2d 384 (Ind. Ct. App. 1981).

[17]Justiniano v. Williams, 760 N.E.2d 225 (Ind. Ct. App. 2001).

to him. The board rejected his argument, and the court of appeals affirmed. In doing so, the court stated:

> In calculating the amount of compensation that is due an injured employee under the Act, this court determined in *Superior Construction Co. v. Day,* 127 Ind. App. 84, 91, 137 N.E.2d 543, 547 (1956), that where multiple injuries are sustained, the measure of compensation should be the degree of impairment of the man as a whole, and not the value of the individual injuries. *See also Custer v. Fougerhousse,* 123 Ind. App. 559, 562, 112 N.E.2d 584, 585 (1953) (same).
>
>   . . . .
>
> Thus, because Justiniano's physician determined that he lost 18% of the use of each leg, the figure representing the value of an entire leg, which is $41,000, should be multiplied by 18% and yield an amount of $7,380. Justiniano then argues that because he suffered an 18% partial loss of use impairment to both legs, the award becomes $14,760. Justiniano arrives at this figure by urging that the Board's improper assignment of degrees of impairment calculation and analysis contradicts the plain language of the act. We reject this contention, however, in accordance with the Board's exercise of discretion to adopt the physician's determination that Justiniano suffered a 16% "whole body impairment." Inasmuch as this court has determined that the proper measure of compensation should be the degree of impairment of the person "as a whole," there was no error in the Board's calculation of benefits in this fashion.[18]

§ 4:9   Subsequent permanent injuries

If an employee sustains a permanent injury, either in another employment or from another cause than the employment in which he or she received a subsequent permanent injury by accident, the employee is entitled to receive compensation for the subsequent permanent injury in the same amount as if the previous injury had not occurred. However, if the permanent injury for which compensation is claimed results only in an aggravation or increase of a previously-sustained permanent injury or physical condition, regardless of the source or cause of the previously-sustained injury or physical condition, the board must determine the extent of both the previously-sustained permanent injury or physical condition as well as the aggravation or increase resulting from the subsequent permanent injury. The board must then award compensation only for that part of such injury or physical condition resulting from the subsequent permanent injury. Amputation of any body part or loss of any or all of the vision of

---

[18]Justiniano v. Williams, 760 N.E.2d 225, 228–29 (Ind. Ct. App. 2001) (footnote omitted). See also Coachmen Industries, Inc. v. Yoder, 422 N.E.2d 384 (Ind. Ct. App. 1981).

one or both eyes shall be considered a permanent injury or physical condition.[1]

This section of the Act, IC 22-3-3-12, is often referred to as the Apportionment Statute. It has been the subject of some consternation and litigation, due primarily to the General Assembly's insertion of the phrase "or physical condition," and subsequent attempts by employers to attribute percentages of disability or impairment to an employee's pre-existing physical condition which neither previously disabled nor impaired his or her ability to function. One such case was *Bethlehem Steel Corp. v. Cummings*.[2] There, prior to his industrial accident, the claimant had not experienced any problem with his back, even though he had a partial lumbarization of the first sacral segment of his spine together with a slight curvature of the spine. He was injured while attempting to carry a heavy bucket of material. He felt a sharp pain in his low back which caused him to drop the bucket and fall to the floor. For months thereafter, his condition waxed and waned, and during that period he occasionally complained of discomfort in his back. Finally, four months after his initial accident, he reported to the company clinic that he had, once again, injured his back while trying to lift a large ladle at work. The following day, he awoke with a severe pain in his back and went to the hospital where it was discovered that he had herniated a disc at the L5-S1 level. A laminectomy and spinal fusion were subsequently performed.

The employer argued that the board should have determined the extent of Cummings' congenital back defects and the extent of the aggravation caused by his industrial accident, and then should have awarded him compensation only for such aggravation. The board refused to do so, and the court of appeals affirmed the board's award for Cummings. In its affirmation, the court stated:

> Our prior decisions make it clear that the concern of this statute lies in those instances where a claimant at the time of the complained of incident is already suffering an impairment or disability in the affected members. Where he merely has a physical condition which renders him more susceptible to being injured, he is entitled to recover for the full extent of the injury received. *Magazine v. Shull* (1945), 116 Ind. App. 79, 60 N.E.2d 611; *Bendix Products Div. v. Kolberg* (1961), 133 Ind. App. 405, 172 N.E.2d 589; *Steel v. Anderson Company* (1956), 126 Ind. App. 445, 133 N.E.2d 896. See also Small, *Workmen's Compensation Law*, pp. 216, 217.

[Section 4:9]

[1]IC 22-3-3-12.

[2]Bethlehem Steel Corp. v. Cummings, 160 Ind. App. 160, 310 N.E.2d 565 (1974).

The Board found that "plaintiff never injured his back in any accident or by any other means prior to January 30, 1970." We have consistently held that the term "injury" as used in Industrial Board proceedings refers to the occurrence of disability or impairment. *Earhart v. Cyclone Fence Co.* (1934), 99 Ind. App. 48, 190 N.E. 558; *Hornbook-Price Co. v. Stewart* (1918), 66 Ind. App. 400, 118 N.E. 315. Accordingly, if supported by the evidence, this finding by the Board is sufficient to determine that there was no pre-existing impairment such as to invoke the proviso of Section [22-3-3-12].[3]

In *Goodman v. Olin Matheison Chemical Corp.*,[4] the claimant sprained her low back while performing her normal duties at work. Prior to the date of her accident, she had several preexisting conditions in her back, including kyphosis, spondylosis (osteoarthritis), and lardosis, all of which contributed to a weakened and degenerating condition in her back. The board found that the claimant was permanently totally disabled, and apportioned her disability between her work accident and her pre-existing back condition. In reversing the board's award, the court of appeals stated:

Such an apportionment had no Indiana precedent and is not authorized by any provision in the Indiana Workmen's Compensation Act.

"Apart from special statute, apportionable 'disability' does not include a prior nondisabling defect or disease that contributes to the end result. Nothing is better established in compensation law than the rule that, when industrial injury precipitates disability from a latent prior condition, such as heart disease, cancer, back weakness and the like, the entire disability is compensable, and, except in states having special statutes on aggravation of disease, no attempt is made to weigh the relative contribution of the accident and the pre-existing condition to the final disability or death. Apportionment does not apply in such cases, nor in any case in which the prior condition was not a disability [Indiana would say "impairment"] in the compensation sense." Larson *Workmen's Compensation Law* § 59.20, p.10-270.

Indiana does have an apportionment statute, Ind. Ann. Stat. § 22-3-3-12 (Burns Code Ed., 1974), also known as "section 33" (of the 1929 Act), but it applies only to "those instances where a claimant at the time of the complained of incident [i.e., his or her industrial accident] is already suffering an impairment or disability in the affected members." *Bethlehem Steel Corporation v. Cummings* (1974), Ind. App., 310 N.E.2d 565, 567. In other words, it applies to those instances in which an employee has a pre-existing impairment which combines with the impairment resulting from his subsequent compensable accidental injury to render him either

---

[3]Bethlehem Steel Corp. v. Cummings, 160 Ind. App. 160, 310 N.E.2d 565, 566–67 (1974).

[4]Goodman v. Olin Matheison Chemical Corp., 174 Ind. App. 396, 367 N.E.2d 1140 (1977).

permanently totally disabled or permanently partially impaired in a greater degree than would have resulted from the subsequent injury had there been no pre-existing impairment. This, of course, is something quite different from the exacerbation or aggravation of a pre-existing, but non-impairing and non-disabling condition of the body. As both the 1968 and 1976 supplements to Small's *Workmen's Compensation Law of Indiana* point out:

"The procedures of Section 33 . . . [Ind. Ann. Stat. § 22-3-3-12 (Burns Code Ed., 1974)] should not be confused with those of the ordinary case of employment aggravation of a pre-existing disease or weakness . . . While it is not too clear in its scope, Section 33 . . . has always related to successive permanent injuries of the type scheduled in Section 31 . . . . (Ind. Ann. Stat. § 22-3-3-10 (Burns Code Ed., (1974)). Before 1945, this was apparent on the face of the statute itself. Then, in 1945, the present proviso concerning apportionment was added, and with the 1945 amendment came the new words 'physical condition' in addition to the old 'permanent injury,' so that it might seem that the proviso would apply to any case of aggravation of pre-existing condition. However, the case precedents, as well as the legislative history, do not warrant such a conclusion. The cases decided under Section 33 . . . have always been ones involving successive harms of the type set out in the schedules of Section 31 . . . . (Ind. Ann. Stat. § 22-3-3-10 (Burns Code Ed., 1974)), while the cases dealing with the other types of aggravation of pre-existing condition have involved unscheduled harms—hernia, cardio-vascular weakness, infection, etc.—not permanent injuries." *Small, supra,* 1968 Supp. at 73, 1976 Supp. at 92 . . . .

. . . The employer takes his employees as he finds them, if he takes them at all, and if they sustain injuries by accident arising out of and in the course of their employment they are entitled to compensation for their own injuries, not for the injuries physically and mentally perfect employees would have sustained in like accidents. *Heflin v. Red Front Cash & Carry Stores, Inc.* (1947), 225 Ind. 517, 521, 75 N.E.2d 662, 664; *Rankin v. Industrial Contractors* (1969), 144 Ind. App. 394, 401, 246 N.E.2d 410, 414; *Noble County Highway Department v. Sorgenfrei* (1975), Ind. App., 321 N.E.2d 766, 768.[5]

In *U.S. Steel Corp. v. Spencer,*[6] the claimant sustained a back injury while at work. Ten years earlier, he injured his back playing baseball. He developed spondylolisthesis as a result of that earlier injury and was required to undergo a lumbar spinal fusion which proved unsuccessful. He developed pseudarthrosis of the fusion and a secondary infection of the spine which forced him to take a one-year leave of absence from work. Thereafter he returned to work, but with restrictions. For the eight years prior

---

[5]Goodman v. Olin Matheison Chemical Corp., 174 Ind. App. 396, 367 N.E.2d 1140, 1143–45, (1977).

[6]U.S. Steel Corp. v. Spencer, 655 N.E.2d 1243 (Ind. Ct. App. 1995).

to his latest accident, he received continual treatments to and for his back and intermittently took time off from work due to complaints of back pain. The board found Spencer to be permanently totally disabled and, more specifically, that he did not suffer from a disabling condition prior to his accident at USX. The court of appeals affirmed, in pertinent part:

> [F]airness dictates that the employer should only be responsible for compensating those injuries which result solely from events within its employ. The Apportionment Statute furthers this policy by providing that if an employee comes to an employer with a pre-existing impairment or disability which combines with a subsequent accident to result in further impairment or disability, the employer will not be liable for that portion of the injury not directly related to its employment. On the other hand, if an employee has merely common ailments, *i.e.,* back pain as Spencer was found by the Board to suffer from here, but thereafter falls victim to a workplace accident, it would not be just to deny such employee compensation for his injury because he did not come to his employer as a mentally and physically perfect employee even if such perfect employee would not have sustained the same injury. In sum, the statute attempts to separate those injuries which merely combine with pre-existing impairments or disabilities to render an employee disabled, and those disabilities which are, in fact, merely aggravations of pre-existing impairments or disabilities, from those injuries which occur, perhaps to mentally and physically imperfect employees, solely from events at the current employer's workplace. *See Rockwell Intern. v. Byrd* (1986), Ind. App., 498 N.E.2d 1033, 1038 (although employee had susceptibility to back injury, apportionment not proper where Board found employee did not have pre-existing back impairment or disability); *Bethlehem Steel Corporation v. Cummings* (1974), 160 Ind. App. 160, 310 N.E.2d 565, 567 (where claimant has physical condition which renders him more susceptible to being injured rather than an existing impairment or disability in affected member, claimant entitled to recover for full extent of injury).
>
> That Spencer's condition was not of the sort which would normally progress to disability on its own, merely supports the Board's finding that although Spencer was an employee with back pain and was susceptible to back injury, it was the June 15, 1983, injury which rendered him disabled, not some pre-existing impairment or partial disability which did so. Likewise, that Spencer was able to work with such back pain, or as Dr. Frank found, was able to work at "hard arduous labor" for ten years following his 1973 injury, supports the same conclusion. The Board's use of these factors in its I.C. § 22-3-3-12 analysis neither compromises the purpose of the Apportionment Statute nor places insurmountable burdens on employers in seeking its application.[7]

---

[7]U.S. Steel Corp. v. Spencer, 655 N.E.2d 1243, 1247–1248 (Ind. Ct. App. 1995). See also Luz v. Hart Schaffner & Marx, 771 N.E.2d 1230, 1233–1234 (Ind. Ct. App. 2002).

In *Bowles v. Griffin Industries*,[8] the board concluded that a permanent total disability award should be apportioned between the claimant's prior active back condition and his later work injury in the same percentage as was his permanent partial impairment award. The court of appeals disagreed:

> Bowles contends, correctly, that there is no statutory procedure to reduce a *disability* award by using *impairment* statistics . . . . It is evident to us that the Board did not consider that "the issue of physical impairment concerns medical evidence relating to the loss of bodily function, whereas a disability determination rests on vocational factors relating to the ability of an individual to engage in reasonable forms of work activity." *Spencer,* 645 N.E.2d at 1109. Instead, the Board simply applied the *impairment* ratio to determine the allocation of a *disability* award. Because such a procedure is not within the language of the Apportionment Statute, we must reverse and remand.
>
> We note that the use of *impairment* rates provided by physicians . . . may be used to apply the Apportionment Statute to reduce PPI awards. However, to reduce a disability award through the use of the Apportionment Statute, evidence of vocational factors—such as testimony by a vocational rehabilitation specialist—is necessary. *See Spencer,* 645 N.E.2d at 1109. In some situations, both PPI and PTD awards will undoubtedly be reduced by the same amounts. However, to reduce a disability award, the correct factors—vocational factors—must be part of the record. Such was not the case here.[9]

§ 4:10   Subsequent permanent injuries—Second Injury Fund

Matters pertaining to the Second Injury Fund are found in IC 22-3-3-13. The section is rather lengthy and will not be reproduced here. Suffice it to say that if an employee who, from any cause, has lost the use of one hand, arm, foot, leg, or eye, and, in a subsequent industrial accident, becomes permanently and totally disabled because of the loss of use of another such member of the body or eye, the employer is liable only for the compensation payable for such second injury. But in addition to such compensation, and after the payment is completely made, the employee shall be paid the remainder of the compensation that would be due him or her for such permanent total disability out of the Second Injury Fund.[1]

The section sets forth the manner in which the Second Injury Fund is to be funded—by assessments charged to and paid by

---

[8]Bowles v. Griffin Industries, 798 N.E.2d 908 (Ind. Ct. App. 2003).

[9]Bowles v. Griffin Industries, 798 N.E.2d 908, 912 (Ind. Ct. App. 2003).

[Section 4:10]

[1]IC 22-3-3-13(b).

self-insured employers and worker's compensation insurance carriers—and administered by the board. It is specifically provided that all sums deposited in the Second Injury Fund are to be used only for the payment of awards of compensation ordered by the board and chargeable against the fund.[2]

Subsections (h) to (j) of IC 22-3-3-13 establish the prerequisites for and the procedures to be followed by an injured employee seeking benefits from the Second Injury Fund. Before an employee may apply to the board for compensation from the Second Injury Fund, the employee must establish that: (1) he or she is entitled to compensation under the Act, and (2) he or she has either exhausted the maximum benefits allowed under IC 22-3-3-22 without having received the full amount of award to which he or she is entitled under IC 22-3-3-10, or (3) he or she has exhausted the benefits payable under IC 22-3-3-10.[3]

If the employee has exhausted the maximum benefits payable under IC 22-3-3-10, the employee may be awarded additional compensation equal to 66 2/3% of his or her average weekly wage at the time of the injury (not to exceed the maximum then applicable under IC 22-3-3-22) for a period not to exceed 150 weeks. However, in order to be entitled to such an award by the board, the employee must establish that: (1) he or she is permanently totally disabled from causes and conditions that are or have been objectively proven (i.e., purely subjective complaints by the employee are not sufficient), and (2) he or she is unable to support himself or herself in any gainful employment, not associated with rehabilitative or vocational therapy.[4]

Any additional award received by the employee may be renewed during the period of his or her permanent total disability for successive periods not to exceed 150 weeks each, upon appropriate hearings by the board.[5]

Even if an employee seemingly meets the prerequisites established by this section, it is ultimately for the board to decide, upon proper application, whether or not he or she is entitled to an award of additional benefits from the Second Injury Fund. The case of *Bowles v. Second Injury Fund*,[6] is illustrative. There, Bowles sought—and the board denied—retroactive entry into the Second Injury Fund. The court of appeals affirmed, preliminarily stating that:

One of the purposes of the Second Injury Fund is to provide

---

[2]IC 22-3-3-13(c) to (g), (k).

[3]IC 22-3-3-13(h).

[4]IC 22-3-3-13(i).

[5]IC 22-3-3-13(j).

[6]Bowles v. Second Injury Fund, 827 N.E.2d 142 (Ind. Ct. App. 2005).

monetary benefits to employees who are permanently and totally disabled and have received the maximum compensation they are entitled to under the Worker's Compensation Act . . . .

. . . .

The workings of the Second Injury Fund are further explained in Title 631, § 1-1-31 of the Indiana Administrative Code, which states that

"[a]wards for the payment of compensation from the second injury fund shall set forth that no payments out of the second injury fund will be made to a claimant until the full amount due from the employer for whom he was working when he received his second injury shall have been fully paid; *said payments of compensation from the second injury fund shall commence on the filing date of claimant's application for said benefits . . . .*"[7]

The facts of the case established that Bowles was injured in October, 1990, and filed his original application for adjustment of claim in 1993. After multiple delays, his case was finally heard by the board in 2000. In 2002, an award in Bowles' favor was made by a single hearing member, which was affirmed by the full board later that year. Bowles appealed the full board award, and in 2003 the court of appeals reversed it and remanded the case to the board. Before the board could act upon remand, the employer's insurer paid—in January, 2004—Bowles the remainder of the benefits he was entitled to for his permanent total disability. Bowles then applied for benefits from the Second Injury Fund. His application included a request that he be granted retroactive entry into the fund as of November, 2001, when, as he claimed, his benefits would have been exhausted. In denying his request for retroactive entry into the Fund, the court stated:

[I]n its order denying Bowles retroactive entry into the Second Injury Fund, the Board listed two pages of various delays in Bowles' case that it attributed to Bowles. Delays in Bowles' case began in 1993 shortly after Bowles filed his Application for Adjustment of Claim and continued up through 2001 when the parties completed their post-hearing briefs. The Board found that Bowles' case had to be continued multiple times for multiple reasons including Bowles' failure to "timely respond to discovery requests." Appellant's App. at 28. We agree with the Board that absent the delays attributable to Bowles, the Board could have resolved this case several years before Bowles became eligible for benefits from the Second Injury Fund. Therefore, we conclude that any delay in exhausting the benefits available to him under Indiana Code § 22-3-3-10 is principally attributable to Bowles rather than the Board . . . . Therefore, the Board properly concluded that Bowles . . . was not entitled to retroactive entry into the Second Injury Fund.[8]

---

[7]Bowles v. Second Injury Fund, 827 N.E.2d 142, 147 (Ind. Ct. App. 2005).

[8]Bowles v. Second Injury Fund, 827 N.E.2d 142, 147–148 (Ind. Ct. App.

In *Cincinnati Ins. Co. ex rel. Struyf v. Second Injury Fund*,[9] Struyf sustained a work-related injury which rendered him a quadriplegic. Thereafter, his employer's insurance carrier, Cincinnati, paid Struyf 500 weeks of compensation, and his medical expenses up to that point in time. Cincinnati, on behalf of Struyf, then requested that the Second Injury Fund take over the payment of compensation and ongoing medical expenses for Struyf. On three separate occasions, a single hearing member awarded Struyf compensation from the Fund, but made no finding as to his request for the payment of medical expenses. Cincinnati continued to pay the medical expenses. Ultimately, a single hearing member—and upon review, the full board—dismissed a subsequent application by Struyf due to the fact that all filings on his behalf had been made by the attorney representing Cincinnati, and the board concluded that it was a conflict of interest for the attorney to effectively represent both parties. Cincinnati appealed the board's order of dismissal. In affirming the board's order, the court of appeals stated:

> The repeated reference to "compensation" in the Second Injury Fund statute suggests that the legislature intended the Fund to serve mainly as a source of compensation payments, not medical expense payments . . . .

> Second, and perhaps more importantly, Cincinnati Insurance's view of the Second Injury Fund's liability for medical expenses conflicts with that of the Worker's Compensation Board. In the final paragraph of its order below, the Board wrote:

> "IT IS HEREBY CONCLUDED as a matter of law that IC 22-3-3-13(f) in its pertinent part states as follows: 'The funds shall be used only for the payment of awards of compensation and expense of medical examination[s] [or] treatment made and ordered by the Board . . .' It is hereby interpreted to mean that the Board, in its discretion, may order treatment for injured employees or recipients of Second Injury Fund compensation, but such treatment, and cost for the same, is not designed to supplant or take the place of the employer's or the employer's worker's compensation insurance company's obligation to provide medical benefits to the injured employee."

Appellant's App. P. 186–87. It is apparent that the Board believes the legislature never intended for the Second Injury Fund to be liable for all of an injured worker's medical expenses. The Board's interpretation of Indiana Code Sec. 22-3-3-13 is entitled to great weight . . . .

In sum, we conclude that the legislature, in enacting Indiana Code Sec. 22-3-3-32, did not intend to shift the obligation for a permanently totally disabled worker's medical expenses to the Second Injury Fund after 500 weeks.

2005).

    [9]Cincinnati Ins. Co. ex rel. Struyf v. Second Injury Fund, 863 N.E.2d 1242 (Ind. Ct. App. 2007).

Cincinnati Insurance also contends that in adopting Indiana Code Sec. 22-3-3-32, the legislature intended to limit an employer's liability for an injured worker's medical expenses to 500 weeks. The Attorney General's Office, on behalf of the Second Injury Fund, agrees with this contention. We do not . . . .

We first observe that nowhere in the Worker's Compensation Act is the payment of medical expenses discussed in terms of a "number of weeks." . . . The portions of the Act concerning compensation payments, on the other hand, speak largely in terms of "weekly compensation," "weeks of compensation," and "average weekly wages.". . . Though the legislature used the term "benefits" instead of "compensation" in Indiana Code Sec. 22-3-3-32, its reference to "the number of weeks paid and to be paid" indicates that it was creating a limitation on compensation payments, not medical expense payments.

In addition, Indiana Code Sec. 22-3-3-32 pertains to "benefits . . . paid and to be paid for temporary total *disability*, temporary partial *disability,* or permanent total *disability*[.]" As the Indiana Supreme Court has noted, " 'Disability' in its general sense refers to the injured employee's inability to work[.]" *Talas,* 435 N.E.2d at 26. An injured worker does not receive compensation payments for medical expenses; rather, she receives compensation payments due to her inability to work. Therefore, to the extent that Indiana Code Sec. 22-3-3-32 limits the "benefits" for an injured worker's disability, i.e., inability to work, it limits compensation payments, not medical expense payments . . . .

Furthermore, we note that the second sentence of Indiana Code Sec. 22-3-3-32 directs claimants seeking continuing benefits to Indiana Code Sec. 22-3-3-13, the Second Injury Fund statute . . . . It would be absurd for the legislature to refer an injured worker in search of significant medical expense coverage to a statute intended to provide only very limited medical expense payments . . . .

[I]f we were to construe Indiana Code Sec. 22-3-3-32 the way Cincinnati Insurance proposes, that is, determine that the term "benefits" includes the payment of medical expenses and hold that Cincinnati Insurance's liability for Struyf's medical expenses ended at 500 weeks, Struyf would be left to his own devices to pay for his medical expenses. We are to resolve doubts in the application of terms in the Worker's Compensation Act in favor of the employee . . . .

We acknowledge that the payment of Struyf's medical expenses has placed and will continue to place a heavy burden on Cincinnati Insurance. But the extent of Struyf's medical expenses . . . makes the case for continuing coverage stronger, not weaker. Our legislature's decision to make worker's compensation insurers and self-insured employers, rather than the Second Injury Fund, liable for long-term medical expenses may represent a policy determination that worker's compensation insurers and employers are in the best position to ensure safe working conditions, given the insurers'

ability to set premium rates and, in certain cases, to refuse coverage, and the employer's direct oversight of working conditions.[10]

In *Linville v. Hoosier Trim Products*,[11] Linville had previously
sustained a work-related injury which resulted in an 11% permanent partial impairment of her right hand. Thereafter, she suffered a second work-related injury which resulted in a 37% permanent partial impairment of her left hand. After her second
injury, she sought benefits from the Second Injury Fund, but her
claim was denied by the board. In affirming the board's decision,
the court of appeals stated:

> When analyzed within the context of I.C. 22-3-3-13(a), the word
> "lost" connotes total deprivation of a body part, or the total depriva-
> tion of the use of a body part. The word "lost" simply does not sug-
> gest the mere diminution of the use of a body part. Our interpreta-
> tion is supported by the legislature's list of scheduled injuries and
> corresponding compensation rates found at Ind. Code 22-3-3-10(c)
> which distinguishes between accidents causing "loss by separation,"
> "loss of use," and "partial loss of use."

> Thus, the language of I.C. 22-3-3-13(a) clearly and unambigu-
> ously refers to those workers who no longer possess a certain body
> part, or to those who no longer possess the use of a certain body
> part. Had the legislature intended the Second Injury Fund to bene-
> fit those who retain partial use of a body part, it could easily have
> so specified . . . .

> Linville did not lose either of her hands, nor did she lose the use
> of either of her hands. Thus, the Board did not err in denying her
> request for benefits from the Second Injury Fund.[12]

In *Munster Med Inn v. Banks*,[13] the novel question of responsibility for permanent total disability benefits for an injured worker
with a pre-existing vision loss was addressed. In *Banks*, a licensed
practical nurse had diabetes for several years and had vision
problems related to that condition. Due to a compensable fall at
work, Banks's visual acuity decreased to the point that the single
hearing member found her permanently and totally disabled and
ordered the employer responsible for paying the benefits. On appeal, the employer cited IC 22-3-3-13(b), which provides:

> If an employee who from any cause, had lost, or lost the use of, one
> (1) hand, one (1) arm, one (1) foot, one (1) leg, or one (1) eye, and in
> a subsequent industrial accident becomes permanently and totally
> disabled by reason of the loss, or loss of use of, another such member

---

[10]Cincinnati Ins. Co. ex rel. Struyf v. Second Injury Fund, 863 N.E.2d 1242,
1248–1252 (Ind. Ct. App. 2007).

[11]Linville v. Hoosier Trim Products, 664 N.E.2d 1178 (Ind. Ct. App. 1996).

[12]Linville v. Hoosier Trim Products, 664 N.E.2d 1178, 1179–1190 (Ind. Ct.
App. 1996).

[13]Munster Med Inn v. Banks, 913 N.E.2d 773 (Ind. Ct. App. 2009).

or eye, the employer shall be liable only for the compensation payable for such second injury. However, in addition to such compensation and after the completion of the payment therefor, the employee shall be paid the remainder of the compensation that would be due for such total permanent disability out of a special fund known as the second injury fund, and created in the manner described in subsection (c).

The *Banks* court held that the Second Injury Fund's liability may be triggered where the injury results in vision that meets the widely recognized definition of legal blindness and a total, permanent injury.

In *Mayes v. Second Injury Fund*,[14] the claimant, an employee of Main Tech Corporation, was rendered permanently and totally disabled as the result of a work-related accident. He was awarded compensation and began receiving said compensation from Main Tech's insurance carrier (Reliance), then from the Indiana Guaranty Fund (when Reliance became insolvent), and, finally, from Main Tech (after the Guaranty Fund had awarded Mayes its statutory maximum). Mayes then filed a civil action against the tortfeasor who, he alleged, caused his injuries, Federal Express Corporation (and others). Three years later, Mayes and Main Tech filed with the board an agreed statement of facts, which the board approved. Therein, it was stated that Mayes and Federal Express had settled the third-party action for a confidential, and therefore undisclosed, amount of money. Main Tech consented to the settlement and agreed to "continue to pay all statutory worker's compensation benefits pursuant to Indiana's Worker's Compensation law." Later the following year, Main Tech filed for bankruptcy protection. Mayes then filed for entry into the Second Injury Fund, but his petition was denied. The single hearing member found that Mayes had not exhausted his maximum benefit, but that he had exhausted all of his remedies against Reliance, and any further action on his behalf would be futile. The reason Mayes' petition was denied, according to the single hearing member, was:

> because of his acceptance of a third party settlement with Federal Express Corporation in 2000. This settlement under Ind. Code § 22-3-2-13 would have alleviated [Main Tech] from paying any further compensation and therefore alleviates the Second Injury Fund. The fact that [Main Tech] voluntarily agreed to continue paying [Mayes] is outside the purview of the Indiana Worker's Compensation Act.[15]

The full board affirmed the single member's order. In affirming the decision of the full board, the court of appeals stated:

---

[14]Mayes v. Second Injury Fund, 873 N.E.2d 136 (Ind. Ct. App. 2007), transfer granted, opinion vacated, IN RAP 58(A), 891 N.E.2d 41 (Ind. 2008) and opinion vacated, 888 N.E.2d 773 (Ind. 2008).

[15]Mayes v. Second Injury Fund, 873 N.E.2d 136, 140, 141, (Ind. Ct. App.

The parties disagree over the impact of Indiana Code § 22-3-2-13 on Mayes's petition for compensation from the Second Injury Fund . . . . Mayes argues that he is entitled to compensation from the Second Injury Fund in spite of his third-party settlement with Federal Express. Specifically, he argues that the language of § 22-3-2-13 is "not ambiguous. It clearly states that the liability that terminates . . . is that of the 'employer or the employer's compensation insurance carrier.' The liability of the Second Injury Fund does not terminate." . . . .

The effect of a third-party settlement on an employee's petition for compensation from the Second Injury Fund is an issue of first impression. However, as previously noted, the burden is on Mayes to prove that he is entitled to compensation for [sic] the Second Injury Fund. *Burton*, 360 N.E.2d at 39. An employee who successfully petitions for compensation from the Second Injury Fund is not entitled to unlimited compensation; instead the employee "may be awarded additional compensation equal to sixty-six and two-thirds percent (66 2/3%) of the employee's average weekly wage at the time of the employee's injury . . . for a period of not to exceed one hundred fifty (150) weeks." I.C. Sec. 22-3-3-13(i). And, as our Supreme Court recognized in *DePuy*, Indiana Code § 22-3-2-13 is designed to prevent double recovery. 847 N.E.2d at 170–71. Therefore, even if we assume for the sake of the argument that Mayes was entitled to compensation from the Second Injury Fund in spite of the third-party settlement, he still must prove that such compensation would not result in double recovery.

Here, Mayes's settlement with Federal Express remains "confidential" and is not included in the record . . . . Based on the limited information in the record, we cannot discern the amount of compensation Mayes obtained from the third-party settlement. Because it is his burden to prove that he is entitled to compensation from the Second Injury Fund and we cannot conclude that he has not already been compensated, Mayes has failed to carry his burden . . . . [H]e has failed to prove that further compensation would not result in double recovery.[16]

Transfer on *Mayes* was granted to the Indiana Supreme Court. The Court vacated the opinion of the appellate court and granted Mayes entry into the Second Injury Fund. The Court held that because the board approved the agreement between Mayes and Main Tech, the Second Injury Fund had waived the right to now claim that the risk of double recovery should prohibit Second Injury Fund liability. The board was advised that, in the future, any concern about double recovery should be solved by refusing to approve agreements involving confidential settlements or

---

2007), transfer granted, opinion vacated, IN RAP 58(A), 891 N.E.2d 41 (Ind. 2008) and opinion vacated, 888 N.E.2d 773 (Ind. 2008).

[16]Mayes v. Second Injury Fund, 873 N.E.2d 136, 140, 141, (Ind. Ct. App. 2007), transfer granted, opinion vacated, IN RAP 58(A), 891 N.E.2d 41 (Ind. 2008) and opinion vacated, 888 N.E.2d 773 (Ind. 2008).

insisting that the agreements contain a provision releasing the Second Injury Fund from liability.[17]

Mayes' claim returned to the appellate court in *R.M. v. Second Injury Fund*.[18] After this matter was remanded, the Second Injury Fund determined that Mayes was not entitled to benefits until week 501 despite the fact that his benefits had stopped at week 264.[19] The court found that IC 22-3-3-13(h) provides that an individual is eligible for benefits from the Second Injury Fund after he has exhausted the benefits available to him under IC 22-3-3-10. Due to the bankruptcy of both the carrier and employer, Mayes was only able to recover benefits for 264 weeks. The court concluded that Mayes had effectively received the maximum benefits possible and was thus entitled to Second Injury Fund benefits starting with week 265.[20] In *R.M. v. Second Injury Fund*,[21] R.M. suffered a serious workplace injury. He was provided medical care and temporary total disability through the employer's worker's compensation insurance carrier until it became insolvent. At that point the Indiana Guarantee Fund continued the benefits until it reached its maximum of $100,000. Then the employer started paying medical services and temporary total disability until it faced bankruptcy. R.M. did settle a third party case against the tortfeasor during the course of his worker's compensation matter. That settlement agreement included a term that the employer would remain responsible for paying worker's compensation. R.M. appealed the Board's denial into the Second Injury Fund to the Court of Appeals which affirmed the denial; however, the Supreme Court reversed stating that since the Worker's Compensation Board approved the agreement that the employer would continue worker's compensation payments R.M. would allowed into the Second Injury Fund. The case at bar arose when the Board then determined that R.M. would be entitled to the Second Injury Fund only after the 501st week after his workplace injury. The Board's decision was appealed to the Court of Appeals which held that although R.M. only received 264 weeks of compensation, denial of entry in the Second Injury Fund until the 501st week would result in an unjust and absurd result.

§ 4:11 Subsequent permanent injuries—Double compensation prohibited

In IC 22-3-3-14, it is provided that, if an employee receives an

---

[17]Mayes v. Second Injury Fund, 888 N.E.2d 773 (Ind. 2008).

[18]R.M. v. Second Injury Fund, 943 N.E.2d 811 (Ind. Ct. App. 2011).

[19]R.M. v. Second Injury Fund, 943 N.E.2d 811, 814 (Ind. Ct. App. 2011).

[20]R.M. v. Second Injury Fund, 943 N.E.2d 811, 816 (Ind. Ct. App. 2011).

[21]R.M. v. Second Injury Fund, 943 N.E.2d 811 (Ind. Ct. App. 2011).

injury for which compensation is payable while he or she is still receiving or entitled to receive compensation for a previous injury in the same employment, the employee is not at the same time entitled to compensation for both injuries, unless it be for a permanent injury such as specified in IC 22-3-3-10. The employee shall be entitled to compensation for that injury and from the time of that injury which will cover the longest period and largest amount payable under the Act.[1]

If an employee receives a permanent injury such as specified in IC 22-3-3-10 after having sustained another permanent injury in the same employment, he or she is entitled to compensation for both injuries, but the total compensation shall be paid by extending the period and not by increasing the amount of weekly compensation. If the two permanent injuries in combination result in permanent total disability or permanent total impairment, compensation is payable for such, but the payments made for the previous injury are to be deducted from the total payment of compensation due.[2]

These sections of the Act should be viewed in harmony with one another. They both pertain to prior and subsequent injuries sustained in the same employment for the same employer. The latter section (IC 22-3-3-15) applies to permanent injuries such as those specified in IC 22-3-3-10. It is unclear, however, what the General Assembly intended by use of the phrase "permanent total impairment," since, as applied to the whole person, that would equate to a 100% loss of physical function, or death.

The former section (IC 22-3-3-14) seems to apply, for the most part, to nonpermanent injuries. If the injury is of a permanent nature, then resort to IC 22-3-3-15 would seem appropriate. The compensation scheme set forth in this section suggests that the employee is entitled to receive compensation for whichever injury would afford him or her the most money for the longest period of time. As stated by the appellate court in its opinion in *Hollerback v. Blackfoot Coal Corp.*:[3]

> It is intended only to forbid double compensation. It is not intended to deprive a workman of full compensation for permanent injuries received in an unconnected accident following another which has caused permanent injuries, to deprive a workman of full compensation for permanent injuries received in an unconnected accident following one which has caused temporary partial disabil-

---

[Section 4:11]

[1]IC 22-3-3-14. See also Hollerback v. Blackfoot Coal Corp., 113 Ind. App. 614, 49 N.E.2d 973 (1943).

[2]IC 22-3-3-15.

[3]Hollerback v. Blackfoot Coal Corp., 113 Ind. App. 614, 49 N.E.2d 973 (1943).

ity or temporary total disability nor to deprive him of full compensation for injuries received in an unconnected accident causing temporary partial disability or temporary total disability following another which has caused permanent injuries. It is intended only that compensation for the greater non-permanent injury, from the standpoint of the period and amount of compensation payable, shall include compensation payable for the lesser non-permanent injury viewed from the same standpoint. This was the construction given to this section in the case of *In re Denton (In re Good)* 1917, 65 Ind. App. 426, 117 N.E. 520.[4]

§ 4:12 Death

If an employee has been awarded, or is entitled to an award of compensation under the Act, and he or she dies from *any* cause *other than the industrial injury*, the employee's dependents of the first class will receive payment of the unpaid balance of such compensation up to a maximum of 500 weeks. The employee's dependents of the second or third classes will receive payment of the unpaid balance of such compensation not exceeding 350 weeks.[1]

If death results from an injury within 500 weeks of the occurrence, the total and, if applicable, partial dependents of the deceased are entitled to receive weekly compensation of 66 2/3% of his or her average weekly wage, until the compensation so paid, when added to the compensation paid to the deceased employee, equals 500 weeks.[2]

Burial expenses, up to a maximum of $7,500, must be paid by the employer, if the employee dies from an otherwise compensable injury under the Act.[3]

There are three (3) classes of dependents under the Indiana Worker's Compensation Act. "Presumptive dependents" are entitled to compensation, in equal shares, to the complete exclusion of "total dependents in fact" and "partial dependents in fact."[4] "Presumptive dependents" are conclusively presumed to be wholly dependent for support upon a deceased employee.[5] The class of "presumptive dependents" includes:

(1) A wife upon a husband with whom she is living at the time of his death, or upon whom the laws of the state impose

---

[4]Hollerback v. Blackfoot Coal Corp., 113 Ind. App. 614, 49 N.E.2d 973, 975–76 (1943).

[Section 4:12]

[1]IC 22-3-3-16.

[2]IC 22-3-3-17.

[3]IC 22-3-3-21.

[4]IC 22-3-3-18 (a)(1) and (b).

[5]IC 22-3-3-19(a).

the obligation of her support at such time. The term "wife" excludes a common law wife, unless the common law relationship was entered into before January 1, 1958, and, in addition, existed openly and notoriously for at least five (5) years immediately preceding the employee's death.

(2) A husband upon his wife with whom he is living at the time of her death. The term "husband" excludes a common law husband, unless the common law relationship was entered into prior to January 1, 1958, and, in addition, existed openly and notoriously for at least five (5) years immediately preceding the employee's death.

(3) An unmarried child under 21 years of age upon the parent with whom the child is living at the time of the death of such parent.

(4) An unmarried child under 21 years of age upon the parent with whom the child may not be living at the time of such parent's death, but upon whom, at such time, the laws of the state impose the obligation to support such child.

(5) A child over the age of 21 who has never been married and who is physically or mentally incapacitated from earning the child's own support, upon a parent upon whom the laws of the state impose the obligation of the support of such unmarried child.

(6) A child over the age of 21 who has never been married and who at the time of the death of the parent is keeping house for and living with such parent and is not otherwise gainfully employed. Such dependency shall be terminated at such time as the dependent becomes gainfully employed or marries.[6]

For purposes of this section of the Act, the term "child" includes stepchildren, legally adopted children, posthumous children, and acknowledged children born out of wedlock. The term "parent" includes stepparents and parents by adoption.[7]

The dependency of any person as a presumptive dependent terminates upon the marriage of such dependent subsequent to the death of the employee, and such dependency is not reinstated by divorce. However, for deaths from injuries occurring on and after July 1, 1977, a surviving spouse who is a presumptive dependent and who is the only surviving dependent of the deceased employee is entitled to receive, upon remarriage before the expiration of the maximum statutory compensation period, a lump sum settlement equal to the smaller of 104 weeks of

---

[6]IC 22-3-3-19(a)(1) to (b), IC 22-3-3-19(e).

[7]IC 22-3-3-19(b).

compensation or the compensation for the remainder of the maximum statutory compensation period.[8]

A "total dependent in fact" is entitled to compensation to the complete exclusion of "partial dependents in fact" and, if more than one such dependent exists, they are entitled to receive such compensation in equal shares. The question of total dependency is to be determined as of the time of death.[9]

"Partial dependents in fact" are not entitled to any compensation if any other class of dependents exists. The weekly compensation to partial dependents in fact is in the same proportion to the weekly compensation of persons wholly dependent as the average amount contributed weekly by the deceased to such partial dependents bears to his or her average weekly wages at the time of the occurrence of the accident. The question of partial dependency in fact shall be determined as of the time of the occurrence of the accident.[10]

Total or partial dependents in fact include only those persons related to the deceased employee by blood or by marriage, except for an unmarried child under 18 years of age. Any such person who is actually totally or partially dependent upon the deceased employee is entitled to compensation as such dependent in fact. However, the right to compensation is terminated by the marriage of such dependent subsequent to the death of the employee, and such dependency shall not be reinstated by divorce.[11]

In *Pedigo v. Miller*,[12] the claimant later died from a cause unrelated to his industrial injury. Upon the employer's motion, the board dismissed his claim. In reversing the board's order of dismissal, the court of appeals stated the following:

> IC 1971, 22-3-3-16, Ind. Ann. Stat. Sec. 40-1401 (*Burns Code Ed.*) allows payment of benefits to a claimant's dependents if the claimant dies. This right to benefits transfers to the dependents even if the claim is merely pending at the time of the claimant's death. *Weber Milk Co. v. Dunn* (1940), 108 Ind. App. 463, 29 N.E.2d 797. In fact, the claim need not have even been filed before the employee's death; an action for compensation could be instituted independently by the eligible dependent. *Snyder Construction Co. v. Thompson* (1969), 145 Ind. App. 103, 248 N.E.2d 560. If the injured employee would have been eligible for compensation, his death should not extinguish his claim.[13]

---

[8]IC 22-3-3-19(d).

[9]IC 22-3-3-18(c).

[10]IC 22-3-3-18(d).

[11]IC 22-3-3-20.

[12]Pedigo v. Miller, 175 Ind. App. 97, 369 N.E.2d 1100 (1977).

[13]Pedigo v. Miller, 175 Ind. App. 97, 369 N.E.2d 1100, 1102 (1977). See also

In *Federal Cement & Tile Co. v. Pruitt*,[14] an employee died from a cause unrelated to his work injury within two years thereof. Prior to his death, he received medical benefits to treat his injury and compensation during the period that he was off work. By the time of his death, he had not reached any agreement regarding additional compensation to which he might be entitled, nor did he file any claim with the board. No widow, children under 18 years of age, or dependents survived him. Following his death, the administratrix of his estate filed a claim with the board alleging that dependents did survive the employee, and that they were entitled to compensation for the deceased's injury. The full board found that compensation should be paid to his administratrix regardless of the fact that the employee left no dependents surviving him. In reversing the full board's award, the appellate court stated:

> [T]he Act specifically provide(s) that the compensation therein denoted shall be made to his dependents as defined in the Act . . . . [O]ur Supreme Court, in the case of *Russell v. Johnson*, 1942, 220 Ind. 649, 663, 46 N.E.2d 219, held that a dependent is one who looks to another for support and maintenance; one who is in fact dependent; one who relies on another for the reasonable necessities of life.
>
> Our review of the Workmen's Compensation Act fails to disclose any provision for the survival of an action for compensation benefits in those cases where the employee leaves no dependents. The appellee cites us to no such provision. We find no provision that any compensation due, or which may be collectible, shall belong or be paid to the personal representative, estate, or heirs of a deceased employee, without dependents.
>
> The Workmen's Compensation Act, as our courts have many times said, is given a liberal construction in favor of the employee, to carry out the humane purposes of the Workmen's Compensation Act, but such construction does not authorize the Industrial Board or this court to judicially legislate or interpret the law so that compensation will be granted without specific statutory provision therefor.[15]

Wanatah Trucking v. Baert, 448 N.E.2d 48 (Ind. Ct. App. 1983) (widow and dependants entitled to receive balance of claimant's PTD award following his death from cause unrelated to work injury).

[14]Federal Cement & Tile Co. v. Pruitt, 128 Ind. App. 126, 146 N.E.2d 557 (1957).

[15]Federal Cement & Tile Co. v. Pruitt, 128 Ind. App. 126, 146 N.E.2d 557, 560 (1957). See also Wenning v. Turk, 78 Ind. App. 355, 135 N.E. 665 (1922). See also Blue Ribbon Pie Kitchens v. Long, 230 Ind. 257, 103 N.E.2d 205, 207 (1952) ("Dependency . . . is not restricted to the payment of a sum sufficient to provide dependants with the bare necessities of life, but may include keeping the family and home in a condition and with surroundings suitable to their station in life.").

In the matter of *Reeve v. Georgia-Pacific Corp.*,[16] an employee, Carey, was killed in the course of his employment. He was survived by his widow and six children, two of whom remained dependent. His youngest son, Allen, lived with his parents at the time. Following Carey's death, Georgia-Pacific entered into an agreement, approved by the board, to pay compensation for 500 weeks. Approximately four years later, Mrs. Carey remarried, and, when Allen reached 18 years of age a few months later, Georgia-Pacific terminated compensation. Later that same year, Allen graduated from high school and enrolled in college as a full-time student. His mother, Carey's widow, then filed her application seeking a continuation of compensation for Allen. The single Hearing Member granted compensation for Allen, but the full board reversed and terminated compensation. In commenting upon IC 22-3-3-18, 22-3-3-19, and 22-3-3-20, the court of appeals stated:

> Dorothy argues that pursuant to the above statutes, Allen was a dependent-in-fact, as well as a presumptive dependent, and he is entitled to receive compensation after the age of 18. We disagree. Dependency is determined at the date of death of the employee. Once the right to dependent's benefits is established, payments are thereafter terminated if the conditions enumerated in the statute occur. Those conditions are absolute and there is no provision in the statute for a redetermination of actual dependency. *Sam Winer & Co. v. Spelts* (1976), 169 Ind. App. 392, 348 N.E.2d 670; *Studebaker Corp. v. Anderson* (1932), 96 Ind. App. 215, 183 N.E. 408. *See also B. Small, Workmen's Compensation Law,* sec. 10.9 at 287 (1950) (if conditions are met, presumption is conclusive); *Carnegie-Illinois Steel Corp. v. Papuschak* (1943), 114 Ind. App. 233, 51 N.E.2d 875 (where facts are uncontroverted, dependency is a question of law).
>
> Dorothy presents no authority to support her position. We are of the opinion that the statute is clear and there is no need for statutory construction. Her argument on this issue is not well taken.[17]

In *First Student, Inc. v. Estate of Meece*,[18] a question arose regarding the nature and quantum of proof necessary to establish that a child is an "acknowledged (child) born out of wedlock" and, thus, a presumptive dependent under IC 22-3-3-19(b). The court of appeals stated:

> In support of their position that a paternity determination in a worker's compensation case is not the equivalent of a paternity finding under the intestacy statutes, the Defendants refer to *Goins v. Lott,* 435 N.E.2d 1002 (Ind. Ct. App. 1982). In that case, the decedent was killed in an industrial accident and the mother of his

---

[16]Reeve v. Georgia-Pacific Corp., 510 N.E.2d 1378 (Ind. Ct. App. 1987).

[17]Reeve v. Georgia-Pacific Corp., 510 N.E.2d 1378, 1381 (Ind. Ct. App. 1987).

[18]First Student, Inc. v. Estate of Meece, 849 N.E.2d 1156 (Ind. Ct. App. 2006), transfer denied, 860 N.E.2d 596 (Ind. 2006).

legitimate child and the mother of his illegitimate child filed claims on behalf of their respective children for dependency benefits under the worker's compensation statutes. The Industrial Board of Indiana . . . awarded benefits to both children as presumptive beneficiaries. Goins, the mother of the legitimate child, appealed the Board's decision, claiming that the Board was without authority to award benefits to the illegitimate child without a judicial finding of paternity. Upon appeal, . . . the court concluded that the Board had the authority to decide the issue of paternity for purposes of the worker's compensation claim. *Id.* at 1007 . . . .

In a footnote, the court explained:

"In order to establish paternity in a proceeding brought specifically for that purpose a mother need not show the putative father acknowledged the illegitimate child. *[The] argument that the Workmen's Compensation statute under construction here is analogous to the Act delineating an illegitimate's right under the descent and distribution statutes is unpersuasive.* Under Ind. Code 29-1-2-7(b) an illegitimate may share in the estate 'if but only if (1) the paternity of such child has been established by law, during the father's lifetime; or, (2) if the putative father marries the mother of the child and acknowledges the child to be his own . . .' The Workmen's Compensation Act does not contain a similar provision. Had the legislature meant to exclude all acknowledged illegitimate children except those who had their paternity judicially established it could have easily indicated such an intention in a similar fashion. Further, the version of the Act under consideration here makes no reference to the descent distribution statutes." *Id.* at 1009 n. 6 (emphasis supplied).

[W]e read *Goins* to mean that there are more ways of proving paternity in a judicial paternity action than that which is required for an illegitimate child to be considered a presumptive dependent under the worker's compensation statutes. For a child to be a presumptive dependent under the worker's compensation statutes, both the fact of paternity and acknowledgement must be established. *See Goins*, 435 N.E.2d at 1008 . . . .

We are unable to find any specific definition of precisely what is required to prove the fact of paternity in a worker's compensation case. However, in reviewing the sufficiency of the evidence in that case, the court in *Goins* referred to cases involving the paternity statutes . . . .

To us, this indicates that the standard of proof for the factual determination of paternity in a worker's compensation claim is effectively the same as that used under the paternity statutes. The standard of proof under the paternity statutes requires some corroboration of the mother's testimony, *i.e.,* circumstances suggesting a probability of paternity. We therefore conclude that the standard of proof required for the factual determination of paternity in a worker's compensation action requires that the mother's testimony be corroborated in some way.[19]

One claiming worker's compensation benefits as a dependent-in-fact has the burden of proving such dependency.[20] The Indiana Court of Appeals, in *In re Carroll*,[21] said the following on that issue:

> Our act does not define dependency, and does not specifically indicate who are dependents, except as to persons included within the conclusive presumption of total-dependency features of the act. Courts as a rule, in determining questions of dependency and who are dependents, resort to description, to an outlining of the elements rather than to definition. Stated generally, a dependent is one who looks to another for support and maintenance; one who is in fact dependent; one who relies on another for the reasonable necessities of life . . . .
>
> Among the elements that are indicia of a state of dependency are: an obligation to support; the fact that contributions have been made to that end; that the claimant in any case is shown to have relied on such contributions and their continuing; and the existence of some reasonable grounds as a basis for probability of their continuance or of a renewal thereof if interrupted. We would not be understood as indicating that all these elements must exist in each case in order that there may be a state of dependency. As a rule, to which there are exceptions, however, the fact that contributions have been made is an essential element of a state of dependency within the meaning of the act.[22]

The manner in which partial dependents-in-fact are to be compensated was set forth in the opinion of the appellate court in the matter of *Hymera Coal Co. v. Houpt*.[23] There, Paul Houpt died as the result of a work injury. He was survived by his father, Claude; his mother, Belle; his sister, Laura; and two half-brothers, Harold and Ralph, all of whom claimed that they were partially dependent upon him for their support. They filed an application for compensation and, following a hearing, the board determined that Belle, Laura, Harold, and Ralph were each partially dependent, in equal degree, upon Paul for support, and there was an award to them in equal shares. Thereafter, Laura married, and, upon application filed by Belle, Harold, and Ralph, the board found that her dependency had terminated. Therefore,

---

[19]First Student, Inc. v. Estate of Meece, 849 N.E.2d 1156, 1163–1165 (Ind. Ct. App. 2006), transfer denied, 860 N.E.2d 596 (Ind. 2006) (DNA evidence supporting the mother's claim was produced).

[20]Stoner v. Howard Sober, Inc., 128 Ind. App. 371, 149 N.E.2d 121 (1958), DeArmond v. Myers Gravel & Sand Corp., 142 Ind. App. 60, 231 N.E.2d 864 (1967).

[21]In re Carroll, 65 Ind. App. 146, 116 N.E. 844 (1917).

[22]In re Carroll, 65 Ind. App. 146, 116 N.E. 844, 846 (1917).

[23]Hymera Coal Co. v. Houpt, 83 Ind. App. 131, 147 N.E. 813 (1925).

her share of compensation, previously awarded, should be redistributed and paid, in equal shares, to Belle, Harold, and Ralph. The employer appealed, and the appellate court reversed. In its reversal, the court focused upon the language contained in the predecessor to IC 22-3-3-18(d), which was substantially the same as the current section. The court stated:

> This section definitely fixes the amount to which any person who is a partial dependent may be entitled; it treats partial dependents singly; makes the amount of compensation to which each of such persons shall be entitled proportionate to the "amount contributed weekly by the deceased to such partial dependent;" and there is no provision in the statute which would authorize a "redistribution" to partial dependents. It will also be noted that section 38 of said act, which deals with persons who are wholly dependent, contains no such provision for measuring the amount of the award of compensation . . . .

> We hold that, as to partial dependents, there is no authority of law for a redistribution after the payments to one of such partial dependents has ceased.

> We further note that there was no provision in the award herein governing the payment of the money severally awarded to the two minor children, and thereby protecting the appellant in making such payments. The Board should make an order specifying the person or persons to whom this money should be paid, and thereby protect said employer in the making of the payments required to be made.[24]

§ 4:13 Payments

There are a number of payment provisions contained in Chapter 3 of the Act. They govern the manner in which payments are to be made to, or for the benefit of, injured employees or dependents, and for the protection of employers. These provisions also provide for lump sum payments in certain circumstances, and establish minimum and maximum benefits to be paid.

§ 4:14 Payments—Deductions; credits

The General Assembly has provided that any payments made by an employer to an injured employee, or his or her dependents, during the period of the employee's disability which, by the terms of the Act, were *not* due and payable when made, may, subject to the approval of the board, be deducted from the amount to be paid as compensation. However, the deduction, except as to

---

[24]Hymera Coal Co. v. Houpt, 83 Ind. App. 131, 147 N.E. 813, 814 (1925). See also Consolidated Perry Corp. v. Moore, 145 Ind. App. 139, 249 N.E.2d 524 (1969).

temporary disability, must be made from the distal end of the period during which the compensation is to be paid.[1]

A special rule applies to state employees. Payments to state employees under the terms of IC 5-10-8-7(d)(5) (certain disability plans for state employees, other than those who hold elective office) are to be taken as a credit by the state against payments of compensation for temporary total disability during the time period in which the employee is eligible for compensation under both the plan and the Act. Such plan payments are not to be deducted from compensation payable under IC 22-3-3-10. But, if a state employee becomes ineligible for payments under the plan, and if he or she is still eligible for payments of TTD under the act, any TTD payments made are to be deducted from the amount of payable under IC 22-3-3-10.[2]

In *Freel v. Foster Forbes Glass Co.,*[3] an employee received a compensable injury, and the employer paid all statutory medical expenses resulting therefrom. Additionally, the employer continued to pay the employee's regular wages while he was unable to work, pursuant to a "wage continuation plan" which the employer offered some of its employees. The employer made no TTD payments to its injured employee. After he filed his application for compensation, the employee died and his dependents continued to pursue the action. At the hearing upon the application, the Hearing Member awarded TTD benefits, but no award was made for PPI or any unpaid medical expenses. The employer received a credit against the award for its wage continuation payments leaving the dependents with nothing, since the amount of the wage continuation payments made exceeded the amount of the TTD benefits to which the injured employee was entitled. The full board affirmed, as did the court of appeals. The court stated:

[S]everal sections of the act and the cases construing them evince a strong policy against double recovery. See Ind. Code 22-3-2-13, 22-3-3-10, 22-3-3-23, 22-3-3-31; *Bethlehem Steel Corporation v. Dipolito,* (1976 168 Ind. App. 417, 344 N.E.2d 67; *Snow Hill Coal Corporation v. Cook,* (1952) 123 Ind. App. 240, 109 N.E.2d 110; *Bebout v. F.L. Mendez & Company,* (1941) 110 Ind. App. 28, 37 N.E.2d 690. If Foster Forbes is not given credit for its earlier wage continuation payments, the Freels not only will recover twice for the same injury, but will receive from the employer more money for the period of disability than could have been earned if there had been no injury. We do not believe that such a result is consistent with the purposes of the act. In *Cowan v. Southwestern Bell*

[Section 4:14]

[1]IC 22-3-3-23(a).

[2]IC 22-3-3-23(b).

[3]Freel v. Foster Forbes Glass Co., 449 N.E.2d 1148 (Ind. Ct. App. 1983).

Telephone Co., (1975) Mo. App., 529 S.W.2d 485, the employer had paid the injured employee $9,266.68 under its disability plan which specifically included Workmen's Compensation benefits. The employer was given credit for these payments, and although the case is distinguishable from this one, the following discussion applies equally well to our facts:

"An employer who has paid an employee at the time of that employee's greatest need more than he was obligated to pay should not be penalized by being denied full credit for the amount paid above the requirements of the act as against the amount which might subsequently be determined to be due the employee. To do so would inevitably cause employers to be less generous. By limiting the payments the employer can safely make to the amount of temporary total disability the result would be that the employee would lose his full salary at the very moment he needs it most. Such a construction is neither liberal nor one made with a view to the public welfare." *Id.,* 529 S.W.2d at 488.[4]

Although there are no Indiana cases exactly on point, one is sufficiently similar to the case at bar to influence our decision. In *Underhill v. Central Hospital for the Insane,*[5] the injured employee received his full salary, room, board, and laundry (benefits that were part of his regular compensation) for nearly 11 months after he was injured. He performed no services after his injury, and the opinion mentions no contract requiring the employer to make such payments. The board allowed the employer a deduction for the amount of cash paid the employee after the initial month following his injury. The court found the deduction was justified based on Section 41 of the Workmen's Compensation Act, Acts 1915, p. 392, (repealed) the predecessor of IC 22-3-3-23.[6]

In *Rockwell Intern. v. Byrd,*[7] the board found that the claimant was permanently totally disabled as the result of a work-related injury. However, the evidence established that following his work injury, he received and accepted sickness and accident benefits and extended disability benefits for five years from his employer's insurance carrier for a non-work related injury which, it was al-

---

[4]Freel v. Foster Forbes Glass Co., 449 N.E.2d 1148 (Ind. Ct. App. 1983).

[5]Underhill v. Central Hospital for the Insane, 66 Ind. App. 44, 117 N.E. 870 (1917).

[6]Freel v. Foster Forbes Glass Co., 449 N.E.2d 1148, 1151 (Ind. Ct. App. 1983). See also Inland Steel Co. v. Brown, 496 N.E.2d 1332 (Ind. Ct. App. 1986) (an employer, which had a self-insurance plan for worker's compensation purposes, which was registered with the board, and which voluntarily paid the claimant all that he was entitled to under the Act, was entitled to credit against a PPI award for payments made to the claimant during his period of disability. The court stated: "The important thing in *Freel* is that so long as the employer has paid the employee all that he is entitled to under the workmen's compensation law, he is entitled to credit therefor." Inland Steel Co., 496 N.E.2d at 1336.

[7]Rockwell Intern. v. Byrd, 498 N.E.2d 1033 (Ind. Ct. App. 1986).

leged, occurred five days following his work injury. In any event, the employer claimed that it was entitled to a credit for the payments made to the employee by its carrier. In affirming the board's denial of such credit, the court of appeals stated:

As this statutory section [IC 22-3-3-23] clearly indicates, it is payments *made by the employer* which are subject to a credit, not payments made by an insurance carrier under terms of a specific policy. The record is clear that all payments were made to Byrd by Metropolitan Life Insurance Company, not Rockwell. Therefore, while Metropolitan may wish to seek reimbursement from Byrd, the board was without jurisdiction to allow any form of credit for payment of these benefits against amounts awarded Byrd under terms of the Indiana Worker's Compensation Act. Case authority supports the conclusion that Rockwell cannot be allowed any form of credit under the circumstances of this case. In *Inland Steel Corp. v. Almodovar* (1977), 172 Ind. App. 556, 361 N.E.2d 181, this court specifically addressed this issue. The claimant received "non-occupational" group insurance benefits for which the employer claimed a credit against worker's compensation benefits. In determining that the Board had no jurisdiction to allow such a credit, this Court specifically held:

"If Inland, and not some insurance company, paid these 'non-occupational' benefits to or on behalf of Plaintiff pursuant to some contract which gives Inland a right to deduct them from its liability to Plaintiff under this compensation award, then it may be that the Board has jurisdiction to make provision therefore in the award. But if the benefits were paid by an insurance company which is not Inland's workman's compensation carrier . . . it appears to be, without question, beyond the Board's jurisdiction to adjudicate Plaintiff's liability or non-liability to such insurer." 361 N.E.2d at 188.

The threshold inquiry is whether the employer paid the benefits to the employee. In those instances where the benefits were paid by an insurance company as opposed to the employer itself, no credit may be allowed because the Industrial Board lacks jurisdiction to consider there matters . . . .

In support of its assertion that a credit should be allowed, Rockwell cites the case of *Freel v. Foster Forbes Glass Co.* (1983), Ind. App., 449 N.E.2d 1148. While Rockwell asserts this case supports its conclusion that a credit is allowable, Rockwell fails to point out that the "wage continuation" payments made to Freel were *paid by the employer* from its payroll account. The importance of the employer having paid these benefits, as opposed to an independent insurance company, is well illustrated in the court's discussion of the *Inland Steel* case. In distinguishing *Inland Steel,* the *Freel* Court stated:

"In *Inland,* the Court focused on the issue of Plaintiff's liability to *an insurer* who may have paid benefits under a non-occupational group insurance plan. In the case at bar, it is the *employer* who has made payments from its payroll account, and any worker's compensation payments due the Freels would come from the same source since Foster Forbes is self-insured." *Freel, supra,* 449 N.E.2d at 1150 (emphasis added).

This language, taken from the Rockwell's own cited authority, reinforces the statutory rule that if payments are made not by the employer, but by an insurance carrier, the Board may not properly allow a credit in that it lacks jurisdiction to do so. The issue of Byrd's liability or non-liability to Metropolitan for benefits paid is clearly outside the scope of this worker's compensation action, and the Board lacked jurisdiction to consider or allow such credit.[8]

In *State v. Doody,*[9] a state employee was totally disabled as the result of a work injury. The state paid him his full salary for one year pursuant to the state pay plan requirements of IC 4-15-2-6, commonly referred to as Public Law 35. At the end of the first year of his disability, the state paid him 13 weeks of TTD payments. After he filed his application for compensation, the board, upon hearing the matter, ordered the state to pay him PTD benefits commencing with the date of his injury. Doody thereafter filed a copy of the board's award with a trial court and requested judgment thereon. He alleged that the state had unlawfully refused to pay him his disability payments for the year during which he received his full salary Public Law 35 benefits, and, therefore, the state should be required to pay him those disability benefits in addition to his salary for the first year of his disability. Doody also asserted that the state was not entitled to a credit for the Public Law 35 benefits that he received. Doody died while the litigation was pending, and his wife was substituted as plaintiff. The trial court granted partial summary judgment in plaintiff's favor, and the state appealed. In concluding that the state was entitled to a credit for the Public Law 35 benefits paid to Doody against the PTD benefits which the board ordered it to pay, the court of appeals stated:

> Moreover, were the State not allowed a credit, Doody would recover more than her deceased husband's salary for the first year of his disability. The statutes and courts of this state have long evinced a strong policy against double recovery. *Freel v. Foster Forbes Glass Co.* (1983), Ind. App., 449 N.E.2d 1148.[10]

The court noted the difficulty involved in applying the provisions of IC 22-3-3-23(b) to those contained in IC 22-3-3-8 and IC 22-3-3-10, as they relate to compensation for permanent total disability. Analyzing the board's award became absolutely necessary since compensation for PTD could have been awarded under either Section 8 or Section 10, and the resulting consequences to the employer are radically different depending upon the section

---

[8]Rockwell Intern. v. Byrd, 498 N.E.2d 1033, 1040–41 (Ind. Ct. App. 1986).

[9]State v. Doody, 556 N.E.2d 1357 (Ind. Ct. App. 1990).

[10]State v. Doody, 556 N.E.2d 1357, 1361 (Ind. Ct. App. 1990).

chosen. Thus, if Doody's PTD benefits were awarded under IC 22-3-3-8, the state would be entitled to a credit for the Public Law 35 benefits which it paid. If, however, Doody's PTD benefits were awarded under IC S22-3-3-10, the state would be prohibited from deducting the Public Law 35 salary benefits which it paid from Doody's award of PTD compensation. After making multiple mathematical computations, the court concluded, based upon the board's award, that Doody's PTD benefits were awarded pursuant to IC 22-3-3-8, not IC 22-3-3-10, and, therefore, the state was entitled to the credit.

It would seem prudent for the General Assembly to at least consider the dilemma facing employees and their dependents, employers, the board, and the courts when attempting to harmonize these sections of the Act. There seems to be little, if any, rational basis for continuing to provide for the payment of compensation for permanent total disability in two separate sections of the Act. If disability and impairment are, indeed, distinct and unrelated concepts for purposes of worker's compensation law, as the appellate courts have often concluded, then it would seem logical that payment of PTD benefits should be delineated in only the disability section of Chapter 3 of the Act (IC 22-3-3-8), and not also in the impairment section (IC 22-3-3-10).

§ 4:15 Payments—Lump sum payments

Compensation may be redeemed, in whole or in part, by the cash payment, in a lump sum, of the commutable value of the installments to be redeemed. However, such lump sum payments are to be made *only* in unusual cases, and then only with the agreement of the employee or his or her dependents, the employer, its insurer, and with the approval of the board.[1] In the case of permanently disabling injuries sustained by a minor, the board may, at any time, require that the minor be compensated by the cash payment in a lump sum of the commutable value of the unredeemed installments of the compensation to which he or she is entitled.[2] In all such cases, the commutable value of the future unpaid installments shall be the present value thereof, at the rate of 3% interest, compounded annually.[3]

§ 4:16 Payments—Guardians; trustees

If ever the board deems it expedient, it may order the employer

---

[Section 4:15]

[1]IC 22-3-3-25(a).

[2]IC 22-3-3-25(b).

[3]IC 22-3-3-25(c). See K-Mart Corp. v. Novak, 521 N.E.2d 1346 (Ind. Ct. App. 1988) (the pre-conditions necessary for lump sum award were absent and therefore the board erred in ordering the same).

to pay compensation in a lump sum payment to a trustee, appointed by the circuit or superior court, to administer the funds for the benefit of the person entitled thereto in the manner authorized by the court making the appointment. Once the trustee receives the amount so paid, the employer or anyone else liable for the payment is discharged.[1]

Whenever the aggregate payments of compensation due to any person under 18 years of age exceed $100, the payment thereof must be made to a trustee, appointed by the circuit or superior court; to a duly qualified guardian; or to a parent, upon the order of the board. If the aggregate payments do not exceed $100, or if the payments are due to a person 18 years of age or older, such payments may be made directly to that person, unless the board orders otherwise.[2]

If any injured employee or a dependent is under guardianship at the time when any right or privilege under the Act accrues to him or her, the guardian shall claim and exercise such right or privilege.[3] Furthermore, no time limitation contained in the Act shall run against any person who is mentally incompetent or a minor, so long as he or she has no guardian or trustee.[4]

In *Memorial Hosp. v. Szuba*,[5] the employer claimed that a time limitation contained in the Act was not tolled because the minor employee lived with his parents as their dependent. The employer further argued that parents are the natural guardians of their children, and, therefore, the parents should have exercised their child's rights to obtain compensation. The court of appeals concluded that the hospital's argument was not well founded in the following pertinent language:

> An examination of other statutes within the Act reveals that when the Legislature intended to include parents, it specifically used the term "parent" . . . . With these statutes in mind, we observe that the Legislature did not refer to "parent" in IC § 22-3-3-30 . . . . Thus, we find that the Legislature did not intend for parents to be considered guardians for purposes of IC § 22-3-3-30.[6]

§ 4:17 Payments—Distribution of liability

If an employee, for whose injury or death compensation is pay-

---

[Section 4:16]
[1]IC 22-3-3-26.
[2]IC 22-3-3-28(a) and (b).
[3]IC 22-3-3-29.
[4]IC 22-3-3-30.
[5]Memorial Hosp. v. Szuba, 705 N.E.2d 519 (Ind. Ct. App. 1999).
[6]Memorial Hosp. v. Szuba, 705 N.E.2d 519, 523 (Ind. Ct. App. 1999).

able, is at the time of the injury in the joint service of two or more employers subject to the Act, such employers shall contribute to the payment of such compensation in proportion to their wage liability to the employee. However, nothing in this section prevents such employers from reaching a reasonable arrangement between or among themselves for a different distribution regarding the ultimate burden to pay compensation to such employee.[1]

In its opinion in *Nickels v. Bryant*,[2] the court of appeals reaffirmed the principles that:

> [T]he Act contemplates one worker may simultaneously have two employers. *See* Ind. Code § 22-3-3-31 (where employee is in joint service of two or more employers, both are obliged to contribute to payment of compensation in proportion to their wage liability to the employee). However, even where an employee has multiple employers, the Act remains the employee's exclusive remedy. *Degussa Corp. v. Mullens,* 744 N.E.2d 407, 412 (Ind. 2001), *reh'g denied.*[3]

In *Motor Dispatch, Inc. v. Snodgrass*,[4] the decedent was fatally injured while driving a truck, owned by the Austins and under a trip-lease to Motor Dispatch. The court of appeals discussed the applicability of IC 22-3-3-31, as follows:

> [A]t the time of his fatal accident decedent was operating employer Waymon Austin's truck for employer, Motor Dispatch, Inc., under a written "trip-lease" which decedent executed as Austin's agent and which provided for Motor Dispatch to pay a stated sum to Austin for the use of the truck and driver to transport a cargo to its destination, but which made no provision for anyone to pay decedent anything for his service as driver. However, there was a wage arrangement between Austin and decedent whereby Austin paid decedent twenty-five percent of the truck's earnings each week and Austin retained the rest, less trip expenses. Thus, as in any successful business, the wages Austin paid his employee came from the money paid to him by his customer, Motor Dispatch, but there is no evidence of wage liability by Motor Dispatch to decedent.
>
> It is true, of course, that the trip lease agreement gave Motor Dispatch sufficient right of control over decedent driver to justify the finding that Motor Dispatch was a joint employer with Austin, but nothing in the evidence made Motor Dispatch responsible for

---

[Section 4:17]

[1]IC 22-3-3-31.

[2]Nickels v. Bryant, 839 N.E.2d 1211 (Ind. Ct. App. 2005), transfer denied, 855 N.E.2d 1008 (Ind. 2006).

[3]Nickels v. Bryant, 839 N.E.2d 1211, 1215 (Ind. Ct. App. 2005), transfer denied, 855 N.E.2d 1008 (Ind. 2006).

[4]Motor Dispatch, Inc. v. Snodgrass, 173 Ind. App. 68, 362 N.E.2d 489 (1977).

decedent's wage. Under the undisputed evidence the only wage liability to decedent was Austin's. (*E.g.* if decedent had lived and Austin had not paid him his twenty-five percent for that week, he would have had no cause of action to recover it from Motor Dispatch.) Under these facts § 22-3-3-31 makes it Austin's duty, at least as between Austin and Motor Dispatch, to contribute 100% to the payment of compensation to decedent's dependents. Whether the apportionment provisions of § 22-3-3-31 also apply as between Motor Dispatch and decedent's dependents is a question we have not been asked to decide. We therefore express no opinion as to whether Motor Dispatch is secondarily liable in event execution against Austin should be returned unsatisfied.[5]

§ 4:18   Payments—Benefit limits

An award of benefits in which the number of weeks paid and to be paid for TTD, TPD, or PTD combined must not exceed 500 weeks. However, a person who is permanently totally disabled may apply for additional awards from the Second Injury Fund pursuant to IC 22-3-3-13. For permanent total disability resulting from an injury which occurred on or after January 1, 1998, the minimum total benefit therefor shall not be less than $75,000.[1]

The promulgation of this section of the Act was a direct result of the decision of the court of appeals in *Lowell Health Care Center v. Jordan.*[2] There, the claimant applied for and received 78 weeks of temporary total disability benefits and, in addition, 500 weeks of permanent total disability benefits—a total of 578 weeks of benefits. Once again, the court noted the conflict between IC 22-3-3-8 and IC 22-3-3-10, as they both pertain to injuries resulting in permanent total disability. The court reasoned that, since the last legislative action was an amendment to Section 10, it, not Section 8, should control. By the amendment, the General Assembly provided that the 500-week benefit period for PTD was in addition to the 78-week period for TTD benefits. It would now seem that, with the enactment of IC 22-3-3-32 in 1997, there is no longer an issue with respect to the maximum period for which disability payments are to be made.

§ 4:19   Payments—Modifications of awards

The Act specifically provides that the power and jurisdiction of the board over each case is continuing and from time to time it

---

[5]Motor Dispatch, Inc. v. Snodgrass, 173 Ind. App. 68, 362 N.E.2d 489, 491 (1977).

[Section 4:18]

[1]IC 22-3-3-32.

[2]Lowell Health Care Center v. Jordan, 641 N.E.2d 675 (Ind. Ct. App. 1994).

may, either upon its own motion or upon application of either party, on account of a change in conditions, make a modification to or change in an award ending, lessening, continuing, or extending the payments previously awarded, as it may deem just, and subject to the minimum and maximum compensation requirements of the Act.[1] If the board makes any such change, it must immediately send to each of the parties a copy of the modified award.[2] Two years from the last day for which compensation was paid is the deadline for the board to timely make a modification upon its own motion or for either party to file an application seeking a modification of a prior award.[3]

Preliminarily, it should be stated that:

[A]n agreement for compensation, made in compliance with the statute and approved by the board, has the force and effect of an award. *Indiana University Hospitals v. Carter* (1984) 1 Dist. Ind. App., 456 N.E.2d 1051; *In re Stone* (1917) 66 Ind. App. 38, 117 N.E. 669. Where neither party takes any step to have an award set aside or superseded and no appeal is taken, the award becomes a full and final determination of the employee's condition at the time it is made and of the employer's liability to pay compensation to him. This finality is subject only to the right of either party within the time allowed by law to seek a modification thereof on account of a change in the employee's condition. *Sumpter v. Colvin* (1934) 98 Ind. App. 453, 190 N.E. 66.[4]

The appellate courts have had some difficulty with the requirement that a modification of a prior award must be predicated upon a change in conditions. Although not defined, the "change in conditions" to which the section refers more than likely relates to the physical condition of the injured employee.[5] However, in *Swift & Co. v. Neal*,[6] the appellate court took the opposite view, due primarily to the wholly conditional and open-ended nature of the board's original award and order. The dissent to the majority opinion, written by Judge Dudine, seems the more well reasoned. He stated, in pertinent part, the following:

Such reasoning [of the majority of the court] is also necessarily

---

[Section 4:19]

[1]IC 22-3-3-27(a).

[2]IC 22-3-3-27(b).

[3]IC 22-3-3-27(c).

[4]State v. Puckett, 531 N.E.2d 518 (Ind. Ct. App. 1988).

[5]Jackson Hill Coal & Coke Co. v. Gregson, 84 Ind. App. 170, 150 N.E. 398, 399 (1926) ("it has no reference to such change of conditions as may affect the financial needs of one found to be a dependent at the time the award was made"). See also Morgan v. Wooley, 103 Ind. App. 242, 6 N.E.2d 717 (1937); Indianapolis Pump & Tire Co. v. Surface, 86 Ind. App. 55, 155 N.E. 835 (1927).

[6]Swift & Co. v. Neal, 106 Ind. App. 139, 18 N.E.2d 491 (1939).

based upon the assumption that a proceeding to review an award on account of a change in conditions is, in its nature, a proceeding supplementary to an award, to determine whether or not the award should be modified. Such assumption is not founded in law. A proceeding to review an award on account of a change in conditions is not in its nature a proceeding supplementary to the award sought to be reviewed. In such proceedings "the original award stands as an adjudication upon *all matters in dispute up to the time such award was made,* and neither party may thereafter be heard to say that such award was wrong *in any respect,* or that in any subsequent hearing evidence is proper to show that either the injury or disability was greater or less than that *indicated by such award."* Pedlow v. Swartz Electric Co.,1918, 68 Ind. App. 400, 120 N.E. 603, 604.

Whether or not there has been a "change in conditions" in a given cause is a question of fact to be determined in the first instance by the Industrial Board. It is a fact which is essential to sustain an award which increases a previous award on account of a "change in conditions." The burden of proving such fact in the instant case was upon appellee. The Industrial Board did not find in the instant case that there was a "change in conditions." The failure of the Industrial Board to find such fact is equivalent to a finding that there was no change in conditions. See Lukich v. West Clinton Coal Co., Ind. App. 1937, 10 N.E.2d 302, and numerous authorities there cited.

There is in my opinion a complete lack of evidence to show a "change in conditions" within the meaning of said term as used in . . . the Workmens Compensation Act . . . . The only thing, if anything, which the evidence shows, that changed since the first award was made, was appellee's mind as to whether or not he would accept the medical services (surgery to remove cataract which would lessen impairment in claimant's injured eye). That does not constitute a "change in conditions." If it were held that such a fact would constitute "a change in conditions" the employer's liability to have an award increased on account of a "change in conditions" would be dependent upon the wishes of the employee.[7]

Thus, in *Duncan v. George Moser Leather Co.,*[8] the court of appeals concluded that, upon a showing of a change in condition, IC 22-3-3-27 would authorize a recovery for permanent total disability following an award for permanent partial impairment. But, as the court stated, "Duncan was thus required to prove that he was permanently totally disabled and that this constituted a change in condition since the previous award."[9]

---

[7]Swift & Co. v. Neal, 106 Ind. App. 139, 18 N.E.2d 491, 494–95 (1939) (emphasis added).

[8]Duncan v. George Moser Leather Co., 408 N.E.2d 1332 (Ind. Ct. App. 1980).

[9]Duncan v. George Moser Leather Co., 408 N.E.2d 1332, 1338 (Ind. Ct. App. 1980).

R.L. Jeffries Trucking Co., Inc. v. Cain,[10] was a case concerned primarily with the timeliness of a claim for permanent total disability benefits. In reaching its conclusion, the court of appeals discussed the requirement that a modification of a previous award need be predicated upon a change in condition. The court stated:

> Similarly, in *Coachmen, supra,* the court, quoting *Pettiford v. United Department Stores* (1935), 100 Ind. App. 471, 196 N.E. 342, stated the distinction between direct and resulting harms in terms of impairment:
>
> "If an *impairment* . . . occurs at the time of the accident, and if the award of compensation is based upon disability alone then it is obvious that a right of action still lies for the impairment, which may be prosecuted at any time within 2 years after the accident [under IC 22-3-3-3]. . . If, however, the *impairment* does not directly flow from the accident but is resultant at a later time, then if there be an award for the disability the cause of action for the *resultant impairment* must be commenced within one year [now two years] from the termination of the period of disability as fixed in the award for the reason that [IC 22-3-3-27] controls as to the time to bring such action. Such resultant *impairment* in the case last supposed amounts to a *change of conditions* as contemplated in [IC 22-3-3-27]." 196 N.E. at 345.

> In spite of these holdings suggesting that I.C. 22-3-3-27 controls when an *impairment* does not directly flow from the accident, we are convinced that a resultant *disability* also invokes I.C. 22-3-3-27. The statute governing modifications gives the Board continuing jurisdiction to modify an award on account of a change in conditions. I.C. 22-3-3-27. Form 14, the application for review of an award, includes among the reasons for review upon change of conditions, that the disability of the employee has recurred, increased, diminished, or ended since the date of the original award. It is entirely consistent with the humanitarian purposes of the act to construe section 27 to mean that Cain's increased disability resulting from the loss of his leg at the hip, is resultant, and therefore section 27 would apply. We hold that the board's findings and conclusions are supported by the evidence. Cain's lingering medical problems which resulted in his permanent total disability were not a direct result of the accident, but resulted from the condition on which the original disability was based. Therefore, the filing of Form 14 within two years of the last temporary disability payment, was timely.[11]

As may be gleaned from the court's opinion in the *R.L. Jeffries* case, much of the discussion on IC 22-3-3-27 in prior years dealt with the limitation provisions of the section. Prior to the 2006 amendment, the statute contained not only a general two-year

---

[10]R.L. Jeffries Trucking Co., Inc. v. Cain, 545 N.E.2d 582 (Ind. Ct. App. 1989).

[11]R.L. Jeffries Trucking Co., Inc. v. Cain, 545 N.E.2d 582, 589 (Ind. Ct. App. 1989) (emphasis added).

limitation period for the filing of an application to modify an award, but also a specific one-year limitation period for filing a modification request for increased permanent partial impairment benefits. With the deletion of the latter in 2006, the statute became more certain and less cumbersome to apply.

In *Luz v. Hart Schaffner & Marx*,[12] the claimant argued that the two year limitation provision in IC 22-3-3-27 should not have been invoked to bar her claim for modification of earlier award based upon an agreement as to compensation filed with and approved by the board. Her argument was based upon the fact that she did not receive two medical reports containing permanent partial impairment ratings and had no knowledge of the permanence of her injuries. Thus, the limitation period provided by the statute should not have begun to run until the permanency of her injuries was discernible. In dismissing her arguments, the court of appeals stated:

> We are unconvinced by Luz's argument that because the results of the . . . reports were not provided to her, and she had no knowledge of the permanence of her injuries, the two-year statute of limitations should not bar her claim. We decline to hold that a claimant can avoid the time limitations imposed by IC § 22-3-3-27 merely by avoiding or failing to affirmatively obtain the results of her diagnosis. Such an interpretation would eviscerate the purpose and intent of the two-year statute of limitation provided by IC § 22-3-3-27. The language of the statute is clear that while the Board has the power to modify awards, applications for such modification must be filed within two years from the last day of compensation paid under the original award.

> The evidence shows that from February 1996 through August 1997, Luz sought treatment for her injury and was placed on various work restrictions. Based on consultations with numerous doctors, it was evident that Luz was aware that the cumulative effects of her work had resulted in her injury. Luz further entered into an Agreement as to Compensation with Hart Schaffner for TTD payments. The payments ended on October 2, 1996, and Luz had two years from that date to file an application for modification of benefits.

> The Board correctly concluded that Luz's adjusted claim was barred.[13]

Finally, in *Gayheart v. Newnam Foundry Co. Inc.*,[14] an injured employee claimed that he did not comply with the limitation provision of IC 22-3-3-27 because of fraud on the part of his

---

[12]Luz v. Hart Schaffner & Marx, 771 N.E.2d 1230 (Ind. Ct. App. 2002).

[13]Luz v. Hart Schaffner & Marx, 771 N.E.2d 1230, 1233–1234 (Ind. Ct. App. 2002).

[14]Gayheart v. Newnam Foundry Co., Inc., 271 Ind. 422, 393 N.E.2d 163 (1979).

employer's personnel manager. In deciding the issues presented in favor of the employee, the Indiana Supreme Court stated:

> [W]e hold that where a party alleges that he has been fraudulently induced into foregoing the filing of an application for modification under I.C. § 22-3-3-27, the Industrial Board has the authority to determine whether there has in fact been fraud. If such is found, the two-year statute of limitations for applying for a modification shall be deemed tolled at the moment the fraud was perpetrated . .
>
> . .
>
> A finding of fraud as to toll the statute of limitations is not a pure question of law. It requires a factfinding process before the question of whether the statute has been tolled can be determined . . . . [F]inding facts and applying the law to such facts is the gravamen of the work of the Industrial Board. Thus, we find no basis for requiring the Board to certify such question to the Court of Appeals without a prior fact-finding procedure.[15]

---

[15]Gayheart v. Newnam Foundry Co., Inc., 271 Ind. 422, 393 N.E.2d 163, 166 (1979).

Chapter 5

Administration of the Indiana Worker's Compensation Act

§ 5:1   Administration
§ 5:2   —Compensation agreements
§ 5:3   —Hearings; review
§ 5:4   —Appeals
§ 5:5   —Civil court judgments
§ 5:6   —Independent medical examinations
§ 5:7   —Fees of attorneys and physicians
§ 5:8   —Bad faith
§ 5:9   —Records and reports

> **KeyCite®:** Cases and other legal materials listed in KeyCite Scope can be researched through the KeyCite service on Westlaw®. Use KeyCite to check citations for form, parallel references, prior and later history, and comprehensive citator information, including citations to other decisions and secondary materials.

§ 5:1   Administration

Chapter 4 of the Act provides for its effective administration by the Worker's Compensation Board of Indiana. The General Assembly has granted to the board the authority to make and enforce its own rules, and to establish and implement those practices and procedures which will enable it to properly fulfill its duties.[1]

It seems apparent that the statutory authorization given to the Board to adopt rules has for its purpose the enabling of the Board to provide by needed or necessary rules for the prompt and efficient handling and carrying out of its functions and duties in the administration of the provisions of the Workmen's Compensation Act, Burns' Ann. St. § 40-1201 et seq., including the hearing, determination, and review by the full board of all claims for compensa-

---

[Section 5:1]

[1]IC 22-3-1-3, IC 22-3-4-2(a). The rules of the Worker's Compensation Board of Indiana are found in 631 IAC 1-1-1 to 631 IAC 1-1-31.

tion under said act and the Workmen's Occupational Disease Act, Burns' Ann. St. § 40-2201.[2]

Processes and procedures of the board must be as summary and simple as reasonably possible. As stated by the Indiana Court of Appeals in the matter of *Davis v. Webster*:[3]

> The Industrial Board of Indiana is an administrative body and not a court. Rhoden et al. v. Smith, etc. Elec. Co. (1939), 107 Ind. App. 152, 23 N.E.2d 306. We think the rule to be well settled that the Industrial Board is not bound by the rules of court procedure. It has a procedure of its own and the Board borrows nothing by implication from the civil code or the common law. We believe it to be well settled that the Board may prescribe its own procedures which may be summary in nature and should be as simple and informal as possible. Terre Haute Paper Co. v. Price (1943), 113 Ind. App. 578, 47 N.E.2d 166.[4]

The board, or any member thereof, has the power to subpoena witnesses, examine books and records of the parties, and administer oaths.[5] Subpoenas are to be served by the county sheriff[6] and, upon application of the board, the circuit or superior court is to enforce, by proper proceedings, the attendance and testimony of witnesses and the production and examination of books, papers, and records.[7]

It is the board's duty and responsibility to prepare, cause to be printed, and furnish free of charge to any employer or employee, such forms and literature as it deems necessary to facilitate the efficient administration of the Act. Accident reports and reports of attending physicians are the private records of the board; they may be inspected by the employer and the employee, and their legal representatives, but not the public, unless the board determines that the public interest requires such inspection.[8] The board has been given the authority to destroy or dispose of all papers which have been on file for more than two years. However, before such destruction or disposal takes place, it must be determined that either no claim for compensation is pending or, when compensation has been awarded, more than one year has

---

[2]U.S. Steel Corp. v. Douglas, 125 Ind. App. 212, 123 N.E.2d 899, 901 (1955).

[3]Davis v. Webster, 136 Ind. App. 286, 198 N.E.2d 883 (1964).

[4]Davis v. Webster, 136 Ind. App. 286, 198 N.E.2d 883, 885 (1964). See IC 22-3-3-2(a).

[5]IC 22-3-4-2(a).

[6]IC 22-3-4-2(b).

[7]IC 22-3-4-2(c).

[8]IC 22-3-4-3(a).

elapsed since the termination of the compensation period fixed by the board.[9]

§ 5:2 Administration—Compensation agreements

If, after seven days from the date of injury, or at any time in the case of death, the employer and the injured employee or the employee's dependents reach an agreement in regard to compensation, a memorandum of the agreement, in the form prescribed by the board, shall be filed with the board. Unless and until filed, the agreement is voidable by the employee or his or her dependents. Once approved by the board, the memorandum agreement is, for all purposes, enforceable by court order.[1]

It has consistently been held that an agreement, made in compliance with the Act and approved by the board, has the force and effect of a worker's compensation award and is binding upon the parties to the agreement.[2]

In its opinion in *Indiana University Hospitals v. Carter*,[3] the court of appeals had an opportunity to discuss the effect of agreements for compensation. There, Carter sustained a work-related injury, received medical treatment at the hospital, and, thereafter, she and a representative of the hospital signed a Form 12 agreement. The agreement was filed with and approved by the board. Pursuant to the approved agreement, the hospital paid Carter compensation benefits until she returned to work. Carter later filed suit against the hospital seeking damages for the same injuries giving rise to the compensation agreement. In opposing the hospital's motion for summary judgment, Carter claimed that she was misled into signing the agreement. According to her, she had no intention of applying for worker's compensation benefits, and she thought the agreement was only for salary reimbursement. In concluding that the hospital's motion for summary judgment was well taken, the court of appeals stated:

> An agreement, when filed with and approved by the Industrial Board has the force and effect of an award, and adjudicates the facts involved therein.

---

[9]IC 22-3-4-3(b).

[Section 5:2]

[1]IC 22-3-4-4.

[2]Evans v. Enoco Collieries, Inc., 137 Ind. App. 11, 202 N.E.2d 595 (1964); State v. Puckett, 531 N.E.2d 518 (Ind. Ct. App. 1988); Lackey v. Duhadway Co., Inc., 560 N.E.2d 671 (Ind. Ct. App. 1990) (disapproved of by, Wolf v. Kajima Intern. Inc., 629 N.E.2d 1237 (Ind. 1994)) and (abrogated by, Rausch v. Reinhold, 716 N.E.2d 993 (Ind. Ct. App. 1999)).

[3]Indiana University Hospitals v. Carter, 456 N.E.2d 1051 (Ind. Ct. App. 1983).

. . . .

Where there is no fraud on the part of the employer or an attempt to take advantage of an employee, the fact that the employee is ignorant of the provisions of the Workmen's Compensation Act at the time he accepts compensation from his employer with full knowledge of all the facts does not defeat the effect of such acceptance as an election to take compensation. *Talge Mahogany Company v. Burrows,* (1921) 191 Ind. 167, 130 N.E. 865. An agreement between parties providing for compensation payments, once approved by the Industrial Board, is binding on the parties. An award, once approved, cannot be set aside in the absence of showing mistake, fraud, trickery or duress. The Industrial Board has the power in the case of fraud to vacate its approval of a compensation agreement, and to entertain an application for that purpose.

In *Cahill, supra,* the court rejected an employer's attempt to undo an approved compensation agreement by bringing a subsequent civil action. The *Cahill* court said:

". . . It would seem that an award resting on an agreement ought not to be set aside for the mere purpose of permitting an employer to try out the merits of his confession of liability. It may be proper in a proceeding of this character to show that there was a mistake as to some specific fact which would result in modifying the award in some particular; but we are of the opinion that the question of liability cannot be raised in this manner. It is doubtful, also, whether the statute contemplates an appeal from the action of the board with respect to petitions of this kind. The action of the Industrial Board is affirmed."

71 Ind. App. 248–249, 123 N.E. 415.

Likewise, in the present case, the Industrial Board's approval of the parties' mutual compensation agreement is a determination that the incident did arise out of and in the course of her employment. In addition, Carter signed the agreement and received the benefit payments. She cannot now complain that the incident did not occur in the scope of her employment. Carter made a binding election of remedies, precluding her from pursuing another separate remedy.[4]

In *Hill v. Bethlehem Steel Corp.,*[5] the wife of a comatose employee (who later died) and his employer signed a Form 12 agreement for compensation. The agreement was filed with and approved by the board. Thereafter, the employer filed a motion to vacate the agreement, which the board granted. In affirming the board's denial of compensation benefits to the employee's widow, the court of appeals stated:

The Form 12 agreement executed by Hill and BSC . . . was a nullity because Hill did not have the legal capacity to execute the agreement. In *Casualty Reciprocal Exch. v. Methodist Hosp. of Ind.*

---

[4]Indiana University Hospitals v. Carter, 456 N.E.2d 1051, 1054–56 (Ind. Ct. App. 1983) (citations omitted) (footnote omitted).

[5]Hill v. Bethlehem Steel Corp., 690 N.E.2d 1191 (Ind. Ct. App. 1997).

(1969) 146 Ind. App. 32, 252 N.E.2d 517, 523, the court held that a Form 12 agreement executed by the wife of an incapacitated employee, who was not his legally appointed guardian, was a "nullity" and "had no force or effect." The court noted that, under the Worker's Compensation Act, only an employee or his dependent, if the employee is deceased, may exercise an unchecked right to enter into a Form 12 compensation agreement. Because the employee here was still alive, the employee's wife could have validly executed an agreement for her incapacitated spouse only if she was the legally appointed guardian. *Id.* at 523.

In our case, Mr. Hill was incapacitated at the time Hill executed the Form 12 agreement. Therefore, because Hill had not yet been appointed her husband's legal guardian at the time of execution, her Form 12 agreement, just as in *Casualty, supra,* 252 N.E.2d at 523, was a nullity. Because Hill's agreement was not merely voidable, but void ab initio, BSC did not waive the argument by failing to present it at the hearing stage.

. . . .

Although Hill's particular Form 12 agreement was a nullity, we note that had she executed the agreement as the duly appointed guardian, the Board would have been unable to vacate the award on the basis of mistake of fact. An agreement to compensation carries with it the same force and effect as an award. *See State v. Puckett* (Ind. App. 1988), 531 N.E.2d 518, 522. An award, once approved, may not be set aside in the absence of mistake, fraud, trickery or duress. *Indiana Univ. Hosps. v. Carter* (Ind. App. 1983), 456 N.E.2d 1051, 1055. The Board has full power to vacate awards for *mistake of fact* and to entertain an application for that purpose at any time such application is made by the employee or employer. *Terre Haute Paper Co. v. Price* (1943), 113 Ind. App. 578, 47 N.E.2d 166, 169; *Aetna Life Ins. Co. v. Shiveley* (1918), 75 Ind. App. 620, 121 N.E. 50; *E.J. Albrecht Co. v. Michaw* (1940) 108 Ind. App. 407, 29 N.E.2d 334.

A mistake of fact occurs either "when some fact which really exists is unknown, or, some fact is supposed to exist which really does not." *Terre Haute, supra,* 47 N.E.2d at 170. Because BSC *knew that they were not aware of* all the relevant medical evidence at the time it executed the agreement, it was not operating under a mistake of fact, and the original award based on the Form 12 agreement would have been valid.

Finally, today's decision in no way suggests that a valid Form 12 agreement could not be executed by an agent of an injured, yet competent, employee. Additionally . . . we recognize that agents might, under certain circumstances, be able to execute valid Form 12 agreements on behalf of incapacitated employees. When all parties are aware of the employee's incapacity, a hard line rule that all Form 12 agreements are nullities in executed by a non-guardian may lead to very harsh and inequitable results. For instance, if an agent who was acting under the directions of a competent employee leaves to execute an agreement, but the employee becomes incapacitated before she can sign the agreement, a strict reading of *Casualty, supra,* 252 N.E.2d at 517, would result in an unduly harsh, if not absurd, result that the agreement was a nullity and of no force or effect.[6]

§ 5:3 Administration—Hearings; review

If the employer and the injured employee or his or her dependents disagree regarding the compensation payable; the continuation of payments pursuant to an approved agreement; the period for which payments are to be made; or to the amount to be paid because of a change in conditions, either party may apply to the board for the determination of the matters in dispute.[1] Once the application is filed, the board must set a hearing date, as early as practicable, and notify the employer, employee, and their attorneys of record of the time and place of all hearings and requests for continuance. The hearing must be held in the county in which the injury occurred, or in an adjoining county, unless the parties agree otherwise. Claims assigned to an individual board member, which he or she considers to be of an emergency nature, may be heard in any county within that board member's jurisdiction.[2]

The board, by any or all of its members, shall hear the parties at issue, their representatives and witnesses, and, thereafter, determine the dispute in a summary manner. The award must be filed with the record of the proceedings and a copy thereof immediately sent to the employee, employer, and the attorneys of record.[3]

If an application for review is made to the board within 30 days from the date of the award made by less than all of the members, the full board shall review the evidence, or if deemed advisable, hear the parties at issue, or their representatives and witnesses as soon as practicable, and shall make an award and file it with the findings of the facts upon which it is based and send a copy thereof to each of the parties and the attorneys of record.[4]

IC 22-3-4-4.5 is created and provides that the Board may, with the consent of all parties, order mediation in worker's compensation claim using a mediator certified by the Indiana Continuing Legal Education forum. The Board shall establish by rules, sched-

---

[6]Hill v. Bethlehem Steel Corp., 690 N.E.2d 1191, 1192–94 (Ind. Ct. App. 1997) (footnote omitted).

[Section 5:3]

[1]IC 22-3-4-5(a).

[2]IC 22-3-4-5(b).

[3]IC 22-3-4-6.

[4]IC 22-3-4-7.

ule of fees and charges for a mediation conducted to resolve a claim for compensation under the Act.

In *Globe Valve Corp. v. Thomas*,[5] an employee injured her back while working on an assembly line. She went to the plant nurse, received some pain pills, and returned to work. She stayed home the next day, but returned to work the following day. She worked a week or two, but was then hospitalized. She eventually required back surgery, and did not return to work for almost two years. During this period of time she received disability checks from her employer's group disability insurance carrier, and part of her medical bills were paid by the employer's group health insurance carrier. She never requested from her employer any worker's compensation claim forms, nor did she submit any such forms to her employer, and Globe had no notice from her that she had a claim to present. She timely filed an application for worker's compensation benefits, and Globe moved to dismiss it, arguing that no dispute had arisen between the parties prior to the filing of her application. The board denied Globe's motion, awarded benefits to Thomas, and Globe appealed. In reversing the award, the court of appeals stated:

> The court in In re Moore, (1932) 79 Ind. App. 470, 138 N.E. 783 analyzed the purpose and application of Burns § 9506 (1926) which is now IC 22-3-4-5.
>
> "It is fundamental that, as to governmental administrative boards, such as our Industrial Board, they have no powers other than those granted either expressly or by necessary implication. By the plain wording of the statute our Industrial Board is given authority to settle disputes; to act as an arbitrator when the parties themselves—the employer and the injured employee or his dependents—cannot agree. The statute says, if the parties "fail to reach an agreement" regarding the payment of compensation, in the first instance, or, if having made an agreement, they "disagree as to continuance of payments," then either party may apply to the Industrial Board for a determination of the controversy. The word "failure" connotes an attempt, an effort, a trial, and the language of the statute, if it is to be given any force and effect, certainly implies that there shall at least be a good faith effort by the parties to settle the dispute, and an actual disagreement between them as to the rights of the parties. Then, and only then, are they at liberty to ask for the help of the Industrial Board, and then, and only then, is the Industrial Board authorized to hear and decide the matter in dispute. These provisions of our statute are in harmony with the rule, founded in a sound public policy, that the law abhors litigation, and favors the settlement of disputes by the parties interested, where that can be done without the surrender of any right."
>
> Id., at 784. Accordingly, a good faith *effort* to agree on the amount

---

[5]Globe Valve Corp. v. Thomas, 424 N.E.2d 155 (Ind. Ct. App. 1981).

of workmen's compensation due and a failure to agree are conditions precedent to the filing of an application. Skinner v. Flat Rock Canning Co., (1941) 109 Ind. App. 131, 33.E.2d 359.

It is clear from the record that there was not a good faith effort to agree on Thomas' workmen's compensation claim prior to the filing of the application. Hearing Judge Rader found as a conclusion of law that Globe Valve's failure to affirmatively offer workmen's compensation forms to Thomas constituted a dispute as to liability between the parties. Assuming only arguendo the tenuous legal conclusion that an employer must offer such forms to injured employees, we do not agree that the failure to do so constitutes a dispute as contemplated by IC 22-3-4-5 nor does it fulfill the good faith effort to agree on compensation requirement. We find no dispute prior to the filing of the application.[6]

No better discussion regarding the conduct of hearings before the board can be found than that in the opinion of the Indiana Court of Appeals in *Rhoden v. Smith & Decker Electric Co.*[7] There, the court stated:

> The Industrial Board of Indiana is an administrative body and not a court, and under the statute can promulgate rules of procedure in hearings before it.
>
> In the case of Northern Indiana Power Co. v. Hawkins, 1925, 82 Ind. App. 552, 556, 146 N.E. 879, 880, the court said: "The Legislature never intended that all rules of law relative to orderly procedure should be ignored. This is indicated by the fact that it is specifically provided that at least two members of the Industrial Board shall be attorneys, and that the chairman of the Board shall be an attorney of recognized qualifications. The evident idea being that these men, by reason of their professional training, will be able to, in a way, direct and mold the proceedings before the Board so that an award when made will be based upon a proper finding of facts and conform to the law."
>
> . . . .
>
> In the case of Munson v. Scheid, 1924, 82 Ind. App. 258, 261, 145 N.E. 840, 841, . . . this court said: "It thus appears that, when an application for compensation is filed and the matter is taken up for determination by any or all of the members of the board, as provided in said section 59, that a hearing of 'the parties at issue, their representatives and witnesses,' shall be had. This evidently means that the member or members of the board conducting such hearing, although not constituting a court, and hence not bound by all the rules of civil procedure, nevertheless must grant what the statute evidently intends, *viz.* such a hearing of the parties and their wit-

---

[6]Globe Valve Corp. v. Thomas, 424 N.E.2d 155, 157 (Ind. Ct. App. 1981). See also Colburn v. Kessler's Team Sports, 850 N.E.2d 1001 (Ind. Ct. App. 2006), transfer denied, 869 N.E.2d 451 (Ind. 2007) (the lack of a dispute between the employer and an injured employee does not extend or toll the statute of limitations).

[7]Rhoden v. Smith & Decker Electric Co., 107 Ind. App. 152, 23 N.E.2d 306 (1939).

nesses as will enable such member or members to arrive at the truth concerning the material issues, in order to apply the law properly, and thereby do justice between the contending parties."

. . . While the Industrial Board is an administrative board, the litigants are not relieved from all responsibility at the hearings thereof and it is not incumbent on such board to call witnesses and propound questions favorable to either of the litigants, but that burden is upon the parties to the dispute.[8]

In the same vein, the appellate court in *Milholland Sales & Engineering Co. v. Griffiths*[9] stated:

[T]he strict rules of law as to the admissibility of evidence are not binding on the Industrial Board, it being an administrative body.

. . . .

We must also remember that the law puts the burden on the applicant of establishing each fact necessary to a legal award of compensation, and that the proof by which such burden is discharged must be based on something more than mere guess, conjecture, surmise, or possibility. Swing v. Kokomo Steel, etc., Co. (1919), 75 Ind. App. 124, 125 N.E.471; Pioneer Coal Co. v. Hardesty (1921) 77 Ind. App. 205, 133 N.E. 398., 94 Ind. App. 62, 178 N.E. 458, 459–460 (1931).[10]

Hence, it has been held that the board may admit hearsay evidence. However, an award may not be based solely upon such hearsay, unless the party against whom the evidence is offered fails to object to its admission and fails to preserve the issue for review and appeal.[11]

The "summary manner" in which the board is to determine the dispute between the parties was defined by the appellate court in its opinion in the matter of *Matlon v. Matlon*:[12]

The word "summary" means concise, condensed to the utmost possible degree, performed without ceremony. From the entire act it

---

[8]Rhoden v. Smith & Decker Electric Co., 107 Ind. App. 152, 23 N.E.2d 306, 308–309 (1939). See also 631 IAC 1-1-3: "[T]he industrial board will not be bound by any technical rules of practice in conducting hearings but will conduct such hearings and make such investigations in reference to the questions at issue in such manner as in its judgment are best adapted to ascertain and determine expeditiously and accurately the substantial rights of the parties as to carry out justly the spirit of [the Act]."

[9]Milholland Sales & Engineering Co. v. Griffiths, 94 Ind. App. 62, 178 N.E. 458 (1931).

[10]Milholland Sales & Engineering Co. v. Griffiths, 94 Ind. App. 62, 178 N.E. 458, 459–60 (1931). See also Patton Park, Inc. v. Anderson, 222 Ind. 448, 53 N.E.2d 771 (1944). Pike County Highway Dept. v. Fowler, 180 Ind. App. 438, 388 N.E.2d 630 (1979).

[11]See C. T. S. Corp. v. Schoulton, 270 Ind. 34, 383 N.E.2d 293 (1978) and cases cited therein.

[12]Matlon v. Matlon, 92 Ind. App. 350, 175 N.E. 369 (1931).

can be seen that the Legislature intended that speed should stand out boldly. Injured employees unable to work should not be compelled to wait for sustenance while boards write out long and detailed special findings of fact.[13]

In like manner, the Indiana Supreme Court, in *Rork v. Szabo Foods*,[14] stated:

> The summary approach outlined by the legislature effectuates a desirable and pragmatic goal in the administration of the Workmen's Compensation Act—the speedy disposition of claims. The economic impact on the family which suffers a disabling work-related injury to one of its income-producing members, or to its sole breadwinner, is immediate; a speedy disposition of a compensation claim alleviates that impact. At the same time, a heavy case load composed of claims with significant economic ramifications for the parties confronts the Industrial Board. The summary approach established for the initial disposition of claims provides the Industrial Board with a vehicle by which it may fully utilize its members as single person hearing officers, thereby expediting the processing and administration of claims.[15]

Toward that end, 631 IAC 1-1-10 provides, in pertinent part, that "[t]he policy of the industrial board, implementing the spirit of the [Act] . . ., is to determine all questions brought before it as speedily and expeditiously as possible. Therefore, proceedings before the industrial board shall be conducted with the least possible expense and with the greatest possible dispatch."

The nature of a review of an award made by less than the full board was discussed by the Supreme Court in *Russell v. Johnson*:[16] "A review by the full board is on the merits and is not for errors. The hearing is *de novo* as to all parties to the proceeding and the award of the full board supercedes for all purposes the award of the hearing member."[17]

The full board has every right to adopt the hearing member's decision as its own.[18] As the Supreme Court stated in *Rork*:

> Initially, we note that the Full Industrial Board did not draft its own findings of basic fact; rather, it adopted and incorporated by reference the statements denominated by the hearing officer as his

---

[13]Matlon v. Matlon, 92 Ind. App. 350, 175 N.E. 369, 370 (1931). See also American Employers' Ins. Co. v. Huffman, 97 Ind. App. 548, 187 N.E. 410, 413 (1933) ("the proceedings should be expeditious to the end that the purposes of the act be not defeated by delays").

[14]Rork v. Szabo Foods, 436 N.E.2d 64 (Ind. 1982).

[15]Rork v. Szabo Foods, 436 N.E.2d 64, 67 (Ind. 1982).

[16]Russell v. Johnson, 220 Ind. 649, 46 N.E.2d 219 (1943).

[17]Russell v. Johnson, 220 Ind. 649, 46 N.E.2d 219, 221 (1943).

[18]Dial X-Automated Equipment v. Caskey, 826 N.E.2d 642 (Ind. 2005).

"Findings of Fact and Conclusions of Law." In and of itself, that practice is neither prohibited by statute nor judicially condemned.[19]

However, whether the full board adopts the hearing member's findings and conclusions or drafts its own, the findings upon which its decision rests must be specific and thorough enough to allow for intelligent review by the appellate courts. Once again, as the Court in *Rork* stated:

> It is the Full Industrial Board which, by statute, is required to enter the findings of fact upon which its decision is based. Ind. Code s 22-3-4-7, *supra* ('the board . . . shall make an award and file the same with the findings of fact on which it is based . . .'). It is the Full Industrial Board's opinion which the legislature has required; the requirement that the seven members of the Board enumerate their findings of fact is a prophylactic measure against arbitrary or hastily drawn decisions, as we explained in Perez v. United States Steel Corporation, (1981), Ind., 426 N.E.2d 29, 32.

> "Additionally, the statutory requirement serves to protect against careless or arbitrary administrative action. Answers to difficult questions may easily be stated, but the validity and respect to be accorded the answer lies in the rationale and facts upon which it is founded. The requirement that findings of fact be entered insures that a careful examination of the evidence, rather than visceral inclinations, will control the agency's decision. Davis, 2 Administrative Law Treatise, supra (s 16.05 (1958))."

> These considerations warrant that the Full Industrial Board cautiously scrutinize any statements or rationale offered by a hearing officer in the initial and summary disposition of a workmen's compensation claim. Where those statements or findings are supported by the evidence and embody the requisite specificity to satisfy the various purposes of the requirement, the Board should not hesitate to adopt and incorporate by reference the hearing officer's work.

> . . . .

> The statutory fact-finding requirement—if it is to mean anything—requires that the Industrial Board reveal the factual bases for its "determination of the various relevant sub-issues and the factual disputes which, in their sum, are dispositive of the particular claim or ultimate factual question before the Board." Perez v. United States Steel Corporation, supra, at 33. That is not to say the Board is required to "restate in its findings all pieces of medical testimony both in favor of and contrary to the Board's decision" or that the Board should make "findings of non-existent facts" . . . . Rather, it is to acknowledge that when the evidence is conflicting, the Board should delineate that evidence upon which its analysis and ultimate factual conclusion is based; when the Board denies compensation for the reason that the claimant has failed to sustain his burden of proof, the Board should designate which of the material element(s) of the claim the injured worker has failed to prove.

---

[19]Rork v. Szabo Foods, 436 N.E.2d 64, 67 (Ind. 1982).

Absent such adequate findings of fact, parties are left uninformed as to the evidentiary bases for the Board's ultimate disposition; operating in a vacuum, they are hampered, if not precluded, from formulating specific arguments for judicial review. In turn, the disposition of appeals in our appellate tribunals is delayed by the necessity of resolving broadside claims and searching the entire record. The expertise of the Industrial Board in dealing with the technical medical questions it regularly confronts is lost when its findings are perfunctorily made, and the integrity of its decision is threatened when the reviewing court must search the record and speculate as to the Board's factual analysis and rationale.[20]

However, in *Wicker v. Community Media Group*,[21] a majority of the members of the full board reversed a single hearing member's decision, awarding benefits to the claimant, without issuing findings of fact to support the reversal. In *affirming* the decision of the full board, the court of appeals reasoned:

We acknowledge that the Board's approach was inconsistent with Ind. Code § 22-3-4-7 of the Worker's Compensation Act which provides that the Board "shall make an award and file the same with the finding of the facts on which it is based . . . ." Moreover, on numerous occasions, we have stated that the Board must set out written findings of fact in support of its decision so that we may intelligently review the decision without speculating as to the Board's rationale. Further, we recently held in *Wayman* that the Board's reversal of the Single Hearing Member's award without issuing any findings left us with "no way to review the Board's determination as presently written," and, therefore, we reversed the decision and remanded with instructions to enter specific findings of fact. *Wayman,* 694 N.E.2d 767, 770 (noting that by disposing of the case in such a way, "the Board thwarted the goals of expeditious and effective review of Board determinations and protection against careless or arbitrary administrative action").

While we do not condone the Board's abbreviated disposition of the instant case, which in most instances would warrant reversal and remand, we find that remand would be superfluous here because no speculation as to the Board's rationale is required. Specifically, we note that the medical evidence indisputably demonstrates that Wicker's current hip problems are a result of a preexisting injury, that being Perthes' disease, which has entered its chronic end stage. Moreover, it is apparent to us that the Single Hearing Member simply overlooked the medical records, which were not discussed during witness testimony but were stipulated into evidence by the parties, when it found that Republican "wholly failed to produce any testimony or medical evidence to substantiate

---

[20]Rork v. Szabo Foods, supra, at pages 67–69. See also Wayman v. J & S Petroleum, Inc., 694 N.E.2d 767 (Ind. Ct. App. 1998); Wanatah Trucking v. Baert, 448 N.E.2d 48 (Ind. Ct. App. 1983); Outlaw v. Erbrich Products Company, Inc., 742 N.E.2d 526 (Ind. Ct. App. 2001).

[21]Wicker v. Community Media Group, 717 N.E.2d 596 (Ind. Ct. App. 1999).

the statement to [Wicker's] girlfriend . . . that 'Carlos had a pre-existing injury . . . .' " R. at 25.

. . . Here, the medical evidence does not conflict, as it all points to a preexisting condition. We note that Wicker offered absolutely no medical evidence to show that his injury arose from a work-related accident. . . . From the evidence in the record, reasonable persons would be bound to reach the conclusion that Wicker suffered from a preexisting injury. Therefore, we hold that remand is unnecessary, as Wicker would not be entitled to dispositive findings in his favor. Consequently, we find that the Board's reversal is supported by substantial evidence.[22]

In *ACLS d/b/a Nations Transp. v. Bujaroski*,[23] an interesting question was addressed. A single board member held that Bujaroski was an employee, not an independent contractor, and that because he died as a result of work-related activity, his employer was obligated to pay worker's compensation death benefits. The employer then requested a review by the full board. Typically, the full Indiana Worker's Compensation Board consists of a panel of seven board members. However, in *Bujaroski*, a full board hearing occurred with an absent member. The remaining members issued a 3-3 opinion.

On appeal, the court reminded that to conduct a hearing, only a majority of the full board needs to participate. In addition, a full board hearing is on the merits and the hearing is de novo. As such, when the full board accepted employer's application for review, the opinion of the single hearing member was vacated, and the burden was on Bujaroski to prove his entitlement to compensation. With a tie vote, Bujaroski failed in his burden. The court of appeals thus remanded the case to the board for further action.

Thompson v York Chrysler,[24] Thompson was a parts clerk for York Chrysler. A co-employee, Blackford, became agitated with Thompson when he told him a part was not available. Blackford began verbally attacking Thompson. Thompson had a heart condition requiring a pacemaker. He reported to his employer that the attack affected his heart and he was given permission to leave work early. As he walked to his truck, Blackford confronted him again and continued the verbal altercation. Thompson fell during this argument (either he was pushed by Blackford or Blackford blocked Thompson's "flailing" arm causing him to fall). He was taken to the emergency room with complaints of headache and

---

[22]Wicker v. Community Media Group, 717 N.E.2d 596, 599–600 (Ind. Ct. App. 1999) (citations omitted).

[23]ACLS d/b/a Nations Transp. v. Bujaroski, 904 N.E.2d 1291 (Ind. Ct. App. 2009).

[24]Thompson v. York Chrysler, 999 N.E.2d 446 (Ind. Ct. App. 2013).

pain in his left flank and shoulder. He was treated and released. Thompson sought no treatment for eight months, and then he was evaluated for counseling services he related to the incident. Thompson filed a claim with the workers' compensation board claiming the incident caused or aggravated his mood disorder and depression. Thompson passed away from causes unrelated to the claim in the summer of 2011 and his wife continued to pursue his claim for medical expenses, lost wages, permanent partial impairment and permanent total disability benefits. The Board denied her and she appealed.

The Court of Appeals found the argument first began as Thompson was leaving work for the day but before he had left the premises and therefore it occurred within the course of his employment. The Court then considered whether the injury arose out of the employment and noted that an assault by a co-worker may be compensable under the Act, where the applicant was not the aggressor. Here the parties had stipulated to there being one incident. Therefore, the Court of Appeals concluded that the Board's parsing the altercation into an "initial exchange" and a "later exchange" was improper because the Board could not permit a stipulation to stand and then find contrary to it. The Court of Appeals concluded the Blackford was the aggressor and there was no support for a contrary conclusion. The Court concluded the Board was in error in finding that Thompson's injuries did not arise out of or occur in his employment; Thompson's wife had met her burden that Thompson was entitled to benefits and reversed and remanded the matter for a determination of the benefits she should receive on his behalf.

§ 5:4   Administration—Appeals

An award by less than all of the members, if not reviewed by the full board, is final and conclusive.[1]

A full board award shall be conclusive and binding as to all questions of fact; however, within 30 days from the date of the award, either party may appeal to the court of appeals for errors of law in the same manner as govern appeals in ordinary civil cases.[2]

In its opinion in *Coachmen Industries, Inc. v. Yoder*,[3] the court of appeals stated:

By "conclusive" we mean that this court does not weigh the evi-

---

[Section 5:4]

[1]IC 22-3-4-8(a). See also Lee v. Center Tp. Trustee, 597 N.E.2d 312 (Ind. Ct. App. 1992).

[2]IC 22-3-4-8(b).

[3]Coachmen Industries, Inc. v. Yoder, 422 N.E.2d 384 (Ind. Ct. App. 1981).

dence—only if reasonable men would be bound to reach the opposite conclusion from evidence in the record may the decision of the Board be reversed. Affirmance is required when the evidence is conflicting because only evidence favorable to the Board may be considered. Blue Ribbon Pie Kitchens, Inc. v. Long, (1952) 230 Ind. 257, 103 N.E.2d 205; Bohn Aluminum & Brass Co. v. Kinney, supra. So if the evidence supports the award, we affirm. Penn-Dixie Corp. v. Savage, (1979) Ind. App., 390 N.E.2d 203; Hilltop Concrete Co. v. Roach, (1977) Ind. App., 366 N.E.2d 218.[4]

In *Square D Company v. O'Neal*,[5] the court of appeals further stated:

[I]t was the exclusive province of the Industrial Board, as the trier of the facts, to weigh the evidence, *determine the credibility of the witnesses and decide with whom the truth lay,* and its finding upon the questions of fact cannot be disturbed on appeal, or our judgment as to the weight of the evidence substituted for that of the Industrial Board.[6]

With respect to the 30-day filing requirement contained in IC 22-3-4-8, the opinion of the Indiana Supreme Court in *Sheets v. Disabilities Services, Inc.*[7] is instructive. There, the claimant, Sheets, attempted to appeal an award of the board, but the clerk refused her tender of the record of the proceedings as untimely. She argued that her filing of the record was timely and should have been accepted, since it followed the procedures outlined in the Indiana Rules of Appellate Procedure, even though her filing was made later than the 30 days required by IC 22-3-4-8(b). In affirming the dismissal entered by the court of appeals, the Supreme Court stated:

Technically, there is no such thing as an 'appeal' from the decision of an administrative agency; such decisions are subject to judicial review for errors of law. *Warren v. Indiana Telephone Co.* (1940), 217 Ind. 93, 26 N.E.2d 399.

The foregoing provision for review has been part of Indiana's worker's compensation law since it was first enacted in 1915. 1915 Ind. Acts, c. 106, Sec. 61, pp. 410 to 11. The Appellate Court held early on that this statute required filing a record of proceedings and an assignment of errors within thirty days of the board's decision . . . .

---

[4]Coachmen Industries, Inc. v. Yoder, 422 N.E.2d 384, 389 (Ind. Ct. App. 1981); Duvall v. ICI Americas, Inc., 621 N.E.2d 1122 (Ind. Ct. App. 1993).

[5]Square D Co. v. O'Neal, 117 Ind. App. 92, 66 N.E.2d 898 (1946).

[6]Square D Co. v. O'Neal, 117 Ind. App. 92, 66 N.E.2d 898, 900 (1946) (emphasis added). See Ken Schaefer Auto. Auction, Inc. v. Tustison, 136 Ind. App. 174, 198 N.E.2d 873 (1964); Overshiner v. Indiana State Highway Com'n, 448 N.E.2d 1245 (Ind. Ct. App. 1983).

[7]Sheets v. Disabilities Services, Inc., 602 N.E.2d 506 (Ind. 1992) (disapproved of by, Sneed v. Associated Group Ins., 663 N.E.2d 789 (Ind. Ct. App. 1996)).

Consistent with those rulings, this Court later observed that the rules of appellate procedure do not apply to reviews of worker's compensation claims . . . . [T]he statute still governed and the failure to file the record within thirty days of a decision by the board constituted a failure to invoke the jurisdiction of the appellate courts. *Clary v. National Friction Products* (1972), 259 Ind. 581, 290 N.E.2d 53.[8]

The Act provides that the board, of its own motion, may certify questions of law to the court of appeals for its decision and determination.[9]

An assignment of errors that the full board award is contrary to law is sufficient to present both the sufficiency of the facts found to support the award and the sufficiency of the evidence to sustain the findings of facts.[10] All appeals and certified questions of law shall be submitted on the date filed in the court of appeals, shall be advanced on the court's docket, and shall be determined at the earliest practicable date without any extensions of time for filing briefs.[11]

An award of the full board affirmed on appeal by the employer shall be increased thereby by 5%, and by order of the court may be increased 10%.[12]

In its opinion in *Tanglewood Trace v. Long*,[13] the court of appeals stated:

> Where this court affirms an award by the Board, the appeal was not frivolous, and appellate review was not thwarted by the actions of the employer, the award should be increased by 5%, but not by 10%. *See Calvary Temple Church, Inc. v. Paino,* 555 N.E.2d 190 (Ind. Ct. App. 1990).[14]

In *Wholesalers, Inc. v. Hobson*,[15] the claimant sought a 10% increase in her award on appeal. In denying her the same, the court of appeals:

---

[8]Sheets v. Disabilities Services, Inc., 602 N.E.2d 506, 507 (Ind. 1992) (disapproved of by, Sneed v. Associated Group Ins., 663 N.E.2d 789 (Ind. Ct. App. 1996)).

[9]IC 22-3-4-8(c).

[10]IC 22-3-4-8(d).

[11]IC 22-3-4-8(e).

[12]IC 22-3-4-8(f).

[13]Tanglewood Trace v. Long, 715 N.E.2d 410 (Ind. Ct. App. 1999).

[14]Tanglewood Trace v. Long, 715 N.E.2d 410, 416 (Ind. Ct. App. 1999). See also Manous v. Manousogianakis, 824 N.E.2d 756 (Ind. Ct. App. 2005). But in Graycor Industrial v. Metz, 806 N.E.2d 791, 801–02 (Ind. Ct. App. 2004), an award was increased 10% due to "the extended period [almost four years that Metz has been prevented from obtaining worker's compensation benefits, and Graycor's patent disingenuity with regard to some of its arguments."

[15]Wholesalers, Inc. v. Hobson, 874 N.E.2d 622 (Ind. Ct. App. 2007).

In general, "in the absence of substantive or procedural bad faith a claimant's award should be increased by the required 5%." . . . We have held in the past, however, that if the employee has been prevented from obtaining worker's compensation benefits for an extended period of time, it is appropriate to increase the award by 10%. See *DePuy, Inc. v. Farmer*, 847 N.E.2d 160, 172 (Ind. 2006) (increasing employee's award by 10% even though appeal was not frivolous or in bad faith because of a ten-year delay in employee's receipt of worker's compensation benefits, noting that the delay "'is nearly twice the time consumed by most cases from injury to final determination on appeal"); *Graycor*, 806 N.E.2d at 801 (same following a four-year delay); *but see Manous v. Manousogianakis*, 824 N.E.2d 756, 769 (Ind. Ct. App. 2005) (refusing to award a 10% increase where appeal was not frivolous or in bad faith even though there was a five-year delay between filing of employee's claim and decision on appeal).

Here, we have found that Shangri-La has exhibited neither substantive nor procedural bad faith in this appeal. Notwithstanding a lack of bad faith, Hobson insists that the delay she has experienced in receiving her worker's compensation benefits entitles her to receive a 10% increase in the award. Although Hobson was injured in December 2001, she did not file her claim until October 2003. Thus, six years have passed since her injury and only four years have passed since she filed her claim. Given our Supreme Court's statement in *DePuy* that the average time consumed by most cases between injury and determination on appeal is approximately five years, 847 N.E.2d at 172, we cannot conclude that the four—to six-year delay herein warrants a 10% increase in Hobson's award. Thus, we find that Hobson is entitled only to a 5% increase in the award as provided by Indiana Code § 22-3-4-8(f).[16]

In *Stewart v. Richmond Community Schools*,[17] the claimant Stewart suffered a compensable injury while assisting a student in a gymnastic maneuver that caused her to break her right leg. Approximately one year later she was continuing to experience pain and difficulty putting weight on her leg and she fell at home breaking her right hip. She contended that the fall at home was caused by continuing problems with her right leg. She did not return to work at the school after the hip injury. A hearing was held on the issue of whether the hip injury was related to her work related leg injury and whether she was permanently and totally disabled. The single hearing member found that the hip injury was related and had resulted in permanent total disability. The school appealed the decision to the full board which held that the hip injury was related; however, the Board reversed the single hearing member's determination that the plaintiff is permanently and totally disabled. The board remanded the claim

---

[16]Wholesalers, Inc. v. Hobson, 874 N.E.2d 622, 628 (Ind. Ct. App. 2007).

[17]Stewart v. Richmond Community Schools, 964 N.E.2d 927, 278 Ed. Law Rep. 1111 (Ind. Ct. App. 2012).

to the single hearing member for a determination of permanent partial impairment. Neither party appealed the board's decision. On remand the parties filed Facts of Stipulations and Statements of Contentions. Stewart again argued that she was permanently and totally disabled or in the alternative suffered a 39% permanent partial impairment. The single hearing member awarded the 39% permanent partial impairment and Stewart appealed to the full board. The full Board affirmed the single hearing member's award of the permanent impairment. The Court of Appeals held that, in affirming the Board's award of the 39% impairment, that the plaintiff had waived her right to appellate review of the determination that she was permanently and totally disabled by not appealing the full board's first decision. The Court pointed to Cox v. Worker's Compensation Bd. of Indiana, 675 N.E.2d 1053 (Ind. 1996) where the Supreme court held that awards of temporary total disability are enforceable in court and subject to appellate review. The Court of Appeals then held that the Board's ruling that Stewart was not permanently and totally disabled is more definite than the determination of temporary total disability so therefore the board's determination that she was not permanently and totally disabled was a final award.

In Ward v. Univ. of Notre Dame,[18] Ward, a food service worker, accidently slipped on a floor at work injuring her foot and ankle. Her employer accepted her injuries as work-related and provided workers' compensation benefits. She was diagnosed with Reflex Sympathy Dystrophy ("RSD") or Complex Regional Pain Syndrome ("CRPS") as a result of her work injury. Dr. Graham, Ward's authorized treating physician, opined that she was suffering from CRSP but her injury had reached maximum medical improvement. Dr. Graham assigned a 5% whole body permanent partial impairment ("PPI") for Ward's work injury. Ward disputed Dr. Graham's opinion and was awarded an Independent Medical Examination ("IME") with Dr. Kondamuri by the Workers' Compensation Board. Dr. Kondamuri opined that Ward was not suffering from CRPS and that she had reached maximum medical improvement. Dr. Kondamuri also opined that Ward had been diagnosed with an anxiety disorder. Ward sought her own second opinion with Dr. Schreier who opined she was not suffering from RSD, that her injuries had reached maximum medical improvement and that, while she had a history of anxiety and depression, she appeared to have active depression due to her injuries. Dr. Schreier assessed Ward sustained a 6% whole body impairment as a result of her injuries. Then, Ward was assessed by Dr. Corey who opined she may still have RSD or CRPS and referred her to

---

[18]Ward v. University of Notre Dame, 25 N.E.3d 172 (Ind. Ct. App. 2015), transfer denied, 34 N.E.3d 251 (Ind. 2015).

Dr. Cheng to confirm the diagnosis. Dr. Cheng opined Ward had CRPS. Ward's case was heard before a Single Hearing Member who found she was at maximum medical improvement and awarded a 6% PPI. The Single Hearing Member found that Ward's claim for treatment for depression, anxiety and cardiac related issues was not supported by sufficient evidence. The Single Hearing Member's award was affirmed by the Full Workers' Compensation Board.

On Appeal, Ward argued it was improper for the Single Hearing Member and Full Board to consider the IME report of Dr. Kondamuri because of a reference to Ward as "Oriental." The Court of Appeals found that because the admissibility of the report was stipulated to this argument was waived. The Court noted that "waiver notwithstanding, the descriptive reference had no bearing on Dr. Kondamuri's evaluation of Ward's injury and condition." There was no evidence that the use of the term undermined the validity of the doctor's opinion. Even if it had, it would go to the doctor's credibility which was the task of the Single Hearing Member. Ward also challenged the sufficiency of the evidence supporting the Single Hearing Member's decision and Full Board's affirmation of the same. Applying a deferential standard of review the Court of Appeals found the single hearing member and Full Board considered the medical evidence presented by both sides and found certain evidence more credible. The Single Hearing Member and Full Board found Dr. Kondamuri, Dr. Graham and Dr. Schreier more credible and persuasive than other evidence. The Court found there was sufficient evidence to support the award. As it related to the appeal that Ward had failed to present sufficient evidence that her depression, anxiety and cardiac conditions were work related, the Court noted that they would not reweigh the evidence as Ward requested. In conclusion the Court of Appeals affirmed the Single Hearing Member and Full Board's decision.

§ 5:5 Administration—Civil court judgments

Upon order of the board, made after five days' notice is given to the opposing party, any party in interest may file in the circuit or superior court of the county in which the injury occurred a certified copy of an approved memorandum of agreement, or of an order or decision of the board, or of an unappealed full board award, or of a full board award affirmed on appeal, and, upon the filing of the same, the court shall render judgment in accordance therewith and notify the parties.[1] Any such judgment unappealed from, or affirmed on appeal, or modified per the mandate of the court of appeals, shall be modified to conform to any decision of the board ending, diminishing, or increasing any weekly payment, pursuant to IC 22-3-3-27, upon presentation to it of a certified copy of such decision.[2] Costs are to be awarded and taxed as provided by law in ordinary civil actions.[3]

The scope of IC 22-3-4-9 of the Act was addressed by the Indiana Supreme Court in *Cox v. Worker's Compensation Bd. of Indiana*.[4] There, a federal district court posed a certified question to the Court with respect to whether the Act empowered the board to issue enforceable and appealable decisions on limited issues without disposing of the entirety of the issues between the parties. The Court responded, in pertinent part:

> Any party in interest may enforce "orders," "decisions," or "awards" of the Board pursuant to Ind. Code § 22-3-4-9(a) (1993) . . . . The trial court is authorized merely to enter the award or order of the Board as its own judgment when it receives such an application. *Kuhr v. Willan,* 90 Ind. App. 567, 570, 169 N.E. 475, 476–77 (1930). The trial court has no jurisdiction to review the decision of the Board or determine whether the decision is correct. *Grasselli Chemical Co. v. Simon,* 201 Ind. 41, 52, 166 N.E. 2, 6 (1929). Thus, Ind. Code § 22-3-4-9 provides for a party to enforce a temporary total disability award by having it incorporated into a judgment of the trial court . . . .

> "[A]ward" is not limited to awards that terminate the entire controversy. The statutory scheme makes clear that "disputes," including those regarding termination of temporary total disability benefits, are to result in "awards," and those awards are enforceable and appealable . . . .

> We now address the question whether the Board may enter an enforceable and appealable order determining a claim to be compensable under the Act. This question is not readily resolved by reference to the statute alone. We find nothing in the language of the Act that either demands or rebuts the conclusion that an abstract issue of compensability can be resolved by the Board. Such a decision by the Board presumably would require that the Board resolve subsidiary issues such as whether the injury was work-related, whether the applicant was a covered employee, etc. However, it appears that the additional qualification to the question that the decision be "enforceable" necessarily entails that some award has been

---

[Section 5:5]

[1]IC 22-3-4-9(a).

[2]IC 22-3-4-9(b).

[3]IC 22-3-4-10. See Rickert v. Schreiber, 116 Ind. App. 621, 66 N.E.2d 769 (1946).

[4]Cox v. Worker's Compensation Bd. of Indiana, 675 N.E.2d 1053 (Ind. 1996).

entered. This could take several forms, including an award of specified medical treatment. If so, it becomes an award subject to the same analysis described above.

If, however, the question contemplates a resolution of compensability of injuries resulting from a given accident without accompanying resolution of what remedial action (i.e., benefits, treatment, etc.) is appropriate, there is no award as contemplated by the statute, and nothing for a court to enforce pursuant to Ind. Code § 22-3-4-9. Similarly, there is no appealable order at that point because no one has been directed to reimburse (or declared to be without right to compensation for) any specific benefit. We find nothing in the statute to preclude the Board from ruling on issues such as whether the injury is work-related or whether the applicant is a covered employee, if it wishes to do so. However, until that ruling becomes the predicate of an award, there is no enforceable or appealable order. We are uncertain what other limited issues may be contemplated by the question. The foregoing analysis hopefully provides some guidance.[5]

In *Nishikawa Standard Co. v. Van Phan*,[6] the court of appeals concluded that a trial court lacks jurisdiction over an award which is pending review by the full board. The court stated:

Indiana Code § 22-3-4-9 does not provide that trial courts may exercise jurisdiction over an award that is pending on review before the full Board .... Indiana Code § 22-3-4-9 provides a list of orders and awards that may be presented to a trial court for entry of judgment. That list includes: (1) a certified copy of the memorandum of agreement approved by the Board, (2) an order or decision of the Board, (3) an award of the full Board unappealed from or (4) an award of the full Board affirmed upon appeal. Ind. Code § 22-3-4-9. The use of the phrases "an award of the full board unappealed from" and "an award of the full board affirmed on appeal" indicate that the legislature did not intend for trial courts to exercise jurisdiction over worker's compensation awards that have not yet become final. *Id.* Further, the Act as a whole implies that a trial court's authority to transform the Board's award into a binding legal judgment does not exist unless and until the administrative remedies within the Act have been exhausted, i.e. when the Board has issued a final decision ....

In sum, we conclude that in order for a party to seek enforcement of an award under Indiana Code § 22-3-4-9, regardless of whether the award was rendered by a single hearing member or the full Board, the award must be a final and conclusive determination. While review of a single hearing member's award is pending before the full Board, a trial court lacks subject matter jurisdiction to enter a judgment under Indiana Code § 22-3-4-9 because the par-

---

[5]Cox v. Worker's Compensation Bd. of Indiana, 675 N.E.2d 1053, 1056–57, (Ind. 1996).

[6]Nishikawa Standard Co. v. Van Phan, 703 N.E.2d 1058 (Ind. Ct. App. 1998).

ties have not yet exhausted their administrative remedies under the Act.[7]

§ 5:6   Administration—Independent medical examinations

The board may, upon application of either party or upon its own motion, appoint a disinterested and duly qualified physician or surgeon to perform any necessary medical examination of the employee, and to testify regarding such examination. The physician is entitled to receive a reasonable fee to be determined by the board and reimbursement for travel expenses. The state is not obligated to pay such fees and expenses unless the board specifically orders it to do so.[1]

The board has wide discretion in deciding whether or not to appoint a disinterested physician to examine the injured employee and receive testimony from the physician.[2] However, at least one appellate decision seems to suggest that, if the board appoints an independent medical examiner on its own, the physician should testify regarding his or her examination and findings. In its opinion in *Boyer v. Overhead Door Corp.*,[3] the appellate court had the following to say on this subject:

> This statute should receive a reasonable construction consistent with orderly procedure. It authorizes the board, or any member thereof who has heard the evidence on an application for compensation, to appoint a duly qualified physician or surgeon to make a "medical examination" of the applicant for the further information of the board, but, if this be done, we are of the opinion that, in view of the provisions of the statute, the information thus obtained and the facts disclosed by the examination can only be properly brought to the attention of the board in a manner authorized by proper legal procedure. The board should fix a time and place, when and where it will hear the testimony of the physician or surgeon appointed, giving due notice thereof to such person and to the parties to the proceedings, or, if this be impracticable for any legal reason, then the board should arrange for the taking and transmission to it of the deposition of the examiner appointed, in manner and form as provided by statute, thus giving the parties interested an opportunity to examine such witness. The context of the statute is such that it seems apparent if an examination is made upon the order of the board of its own motion pursuant to the authority conferred, the one making such examination shall "testify in re-

---

[7]Nishikawa Standard Co. v. Van Phan, 703 N.E.2d 1058, 1060–61 (Ind. Ct. App. 1998).

[Section 5:6]

[1]IC 22-3-4-11.

[2]Hilltop Concrete Corp. v. Roach, 174 Ind. App. 100, 366 N.E.2d 218 (1977).

[3]Boyer v. Overhead Door Corp., 107 Ind. App. 679, 26 N.E.2d 572 (1940).

spect thereto." To testify, in the meaning of the term as used in this statute, means that the person appointed shall, after due notice to him and to the parties, appear before the board, or before some officer authorized to take depositions, as a witness, and there subject himself under oath to any pertinent inquiry concerning the material facts involved in the controversy pending which may be addressed to him by any party whose rights will be affected by his testimony, or by the board, or any member thereof . . . .

We hold that such is the plain import of the statute, and that the facts ascertained and discovered by any such medical examination should be imparted to the Industrial Board only after an open hearing where both the employee and the employer shall have an opportunity to examine the witness. It was the duty of the board to provide for such an examination of the person appointed, and this it did not do.[4]

In Ward v. Univ. of Notre Dame,[5] Ward, a food service worker, accidently slipped on a floor at work injuring her foot and ankle. Her employer accepted her injuries as work-related and provided workers' compensation benefits. She was diagnosed with Reflex Sympathy Dystrophy ("RSD") or Complex Regional Pain Syndrome ("CRPS") as a result of her work injury. Dr. Graham, Ward's authorized treating physician, opined that she was suffering from CRSP but her injury had reached maximum medical improvement. Dr. Graham assigned a 5% whole body permanent partial impairment ("PPI") for Ward's work injury. Ward disputed Dr. Graham's opinion and was awarded an Independent Medical Examination ("IME") with Dr. Kondamuri by the Workers' Compensation Board. Dr. Kondamuri opined that Ward was not suffering from CRPS and that she had reached maximum medical improvement. Dr. Kondamuri also opined that Ward had been diagnosed with an anxiety disorder. Ward sought her own second opinion with Dr. Schreier who opined she was not suffering from RSD, that her injuries had reached maximum medical improvement and that, while she had a history of anxiety and depression, she appeared to have active depression due to her injuries. Dr. Schreier assessed Ward sustained a 6% whole body impairment as a result of her injuries. Then, Ward was assessed by Dr. Corey who opined she may still have RSD or CRPS and referred her to Dr. Cheng to confirm the diagnosis. Dr. Cheng opined Ward had CRPS. Ward's case was heard before a Single Hearing Member who found she was at maximum medical improvement and awarded a 6% PPI. The Single Hearing Member found that Ward's claim for treatment for depression, anxiety and cardiac

---

[4]Boyer v. Overhead Door Corp., 107 Ind. App. 679, 26 N.E.2d 572, 575 (1940).

[5]Ward v. University of Notre Dame, 25 N.E.3d 172 (Ind. Ct. App. 2015), transfer denied, 34 N.E.3d 251 (Ind. 2015).

related issues was not supported by sufficient evidence. The Single Hearing Member's award was affirmed by the Full Workers' Compensation Board.

On Appeal, Ward argued it was improper for the Single Hearing Member and Full Board to consider the IME report of Dr. Kondamuri because of a reference to Ward as "Oriental." The Court of Appeals found that because the admissibility of the report was stipulated to this argument was waived. The Court noted that "waiver notwithstanding, the descriptive reference had no bearing on Dr. Kondamuri's evaluation of Ward's injury and condition." There was no evidence that the use of the term undermined the validity of the doctor's opinion. Even if it had, it would go to the doctor's credibility which was the task of the Single Hearing Member. Ward also challenged the sufficiency of the evidence supporting the Single Hearing Member's decision and Full Board's affirmation of the same. Applying a deferential standard of review the Court of Appeals found the single hearing member and Full Board considered the medical evidence presented by both sides and found certain evidence more credible. The Single Hearing Member and Full Board found Dr. Kondamuri, Dr. Graham and Dr. Schreier more credible and persuasive than other evidence. The Court found there was sufficient evidence to support the award. As it related to the appeal that Ward had failed to present sufficient evidence that her depression, anxiety and cardiac conditions were work related, the Court noted that they would not reweigh the evidence as Ward requested. In conclusion the Court of Appeals affirmed the Single Hearing Member and Full Board's decision.

§ 5:7 Administration—Fees of attorneys and physicians

The fees of attorneys and physicians, and the charges for services by hospitals and nurses, shall be subject to the approval of the board. When any claimant is awarded compensation and is represented by an attorney, the board shall fix and state in the award the amount of the claimant's attorney fees. The fee so fixed is binding upon the claimant and the attorney, and the employer is to pay, out of the award, the attorney fee so fixed. The receipt of the fee by the attorney acquits the employer for an equal portion of the award. However, if upon hearing the board determines that the employer has acted in bad faith, or has not pursued settlement of a claim with diligence, the attorney fees shall not be charged against the award to the claimant.[1]

It should be stated at the outset that any contract or agree-

---

[Section 5:7]

[1]IC 22-3-4-12.

ment for the payment of attorney fees contrary to the provisions of this section of the Act is illegal, void, and unenforceable.[2] It is the board alone, and not the employee and/or his or her attorney, which shall determine the amount, if any, of the attorney fees to be awarded in any particular case.

With respect to claims for the payment of attorney fees, the opinion of the court of appeals in *K-Mart Corp. v. Novak*,[3] established:

> The proper statutory provision for attorney's fees in workmen's compensation cases is Indiana Code § 22-3-4-12. To collect fees under this section the claimant first must request them from the Board and present evidence thereon, then the Board must make a determination on the request. None of the foregoing conditions precedent to an award of attorney's fees exists in the present case. Thus, an award of fees cannot be sustained by this court under this statute.[4]

In *E.F.P. Corp. v. Pendill*,[5] the claimant/appellee sought remand to the board with an order from the court of appeals that attorney fees be awarded in addition to the compensation awarded to him, rather than charged against the award. In denying his request, the court stated, "(a)part from this appeal, Pendill has not alleged any facts indicating dilatory action or bad faith by E.F.P., and we do not think E.F.P.'s pursuit of a rightful appeal, without more, warrants punitive fees."[6]

The case of *Wernle, Ristine & Ayers v. Yund*[7] demonstrates that the board has the authority to determine whether or not a physician is to be paid a fee for his or her services and, if so, in what amount. There, the claimant's attorney hired Dr. Nash who conducted a five to eight minute medical examination of Yund in her attorney's office. At the hearing, Dr. Nash testified briefly regarding the AMA Guides for evaluating impairment. He did not testify regarding his examination of Yund, nor did he offer an opinion with respect to her impairment. Dr. Nash submitted a bill for $1,486 for his examination of Yund and his testimony at her hearing. When the claimant refused to pay Dr. Nash's charges, her attorney petitioned the board for an award of same. The board ordered that "no expenses of Dr. Nash as they relate to the plaintiff shall be paid by the plaintiff." The attorney ap-

---

[2]Rickert v. Schreiber, 116 Ind. App. 621, 66 N.E.2d 769 (1946); Buckler v. Hilt, 209 Ind. 541, 200, 200 N.E. 219, 103 A.L.R. 901 (1936); Bauer v. Biel, 132 Ind. App. 224, 177 N.E.2d 269 (1961).

[3]K-Mart Corp. v. Novak, 521 N.E.2d 1346 (Ind. Ct. App. 1988).

[4]K-Mart Corp. v. Novak, 521 N.E.2d 1346, 1352 (Ind. Ct. App. 1988).

[5]E. F. P. Corp. v. Pendill, 413 N.E.2d 279 (Ind. Ct. App. 1980).

[6]E. F. P. Corp. v. Pendill, 413 N.E.2d 279, 281 (Ind. Ct. App. 1980).

[7]Wernle, Ristine & Ayers v. Yund, 790 N.E.2d 992 (Ind. 2003).

pealed, and eventually the Indiana Supreme Court granted transfer, vacated an opinion of the court of appeals, and affirmed the board's decision to deny the attorney reimbursement for Dr. Nash's fees and litigation expenses. In doing so, the Court stated:

> Neither the Act nor the Indiana Administrative Code expressly refers to litigation expenses, nor do they address a claimant-employee's liability to reimburse her attorney for litigation expenses. *See* 631 IAC 1-1-24.

> The Act does not distinguish between the fees of treating physicians and those of non-treating physicians whose services may include examinations, evaluations, expertise, testimony, etc. It expressly provides that "the fees of attorneys and physicians" are subject to the approval of the Board. I.C. 22-3-4-12 . . . . In the absence of contrary statutory language, we conclude that the Board's authority to limit physicians' fees in worker's compensation cases encompasses all fees of physicians, including those of non-treating physicians.

> We hold that the effect of the Board's order was to determine that Dr. Nash is entitled to no fee for his services in this case, and that such a determination is within the Board's authority to approve the fees of physicians.

> WR & A next contends that its attorney/client contract with Yund is controlling, is not subject to the Board's approval authority, and should have been enforced by the Board . . . . WR & A . . . argues that the Board may not invalidate other terms of the attorney-client agreement wherein Yund expressly agreed to be responsible for all medical and other litigation expenses. Because Dr. Nash is entitled to no fees in this matter, however, WR & A is not obligated to pay Dr. Nash and thus Yund has no contractual responsibility to WR & A for these fees. The Board's order does not improperly conflict with the attorney-client agreement.[8]

§ 5:8   Administration—Bad faith

The board, upon hearing a claim, has the exclusive jurisdiction to determine whether the employer, its worker's compensation administrator, or its insurance carrier has acted with a lack of diligence, in bad faith, or has committed an independent tort in adjusting or settling the claim for compensation.[1] If the same is proven, the board must award the claimant an amount, not less than $500, and never more than $20,000 during the life of the claim, depending upon the degree of culpability and the actual

---

[8]Wernle, Ristine & Ayers v. Yund, 790 N.E.2d 992, 994–996 (Ind. 2003). Note: the initial appellate opinion in this case is found at 758 N.E.2d 558 (Ind. Ct. App. 2001). A subsequent opinion, following a petition for rehearing, is at 764 N.E.2d 716 (Ind. Ct. App. 2002). That opinion was vacated by the Indiana Supreme Court at 790 N.E.2d 992 (Ind. 2003).

[Section 5:8]

[1]IC 22-3-4-12.1(a).

damages sustained.[2] In addition to any such award, the board shall fix the amount of attorney fees payable, which must be no more than 33 1/3% of the amount of the award.[3] The award is to be paid by the party responsible for the wrongful act.[4] If the board makes an award under this section, it must reduce the award to writing and forward a copy to the Department of Insurance.[5]

This section of the Act became effective in 1997, however, it has been applied retroactively by the appellate courts.[6] At the outset, it should be noted that the statute does not define the terms "lack of diligence," "bad faith," "independent tort," "adjusting and settling the claim," and "actual damages sustained." In its opinion in *Samm v. Great Dane Trailers*,[7] the court of appeals concluded that "the legislature, in enacting the statute, did not intend to include as an 'independent tort' claims for retaliatory discharge, where such claims are based upon an employee's allegation that he or she was terminated for filing, or expressing an intent to file, a request for worker's compensation benefits." The court, further, held that defamation is an "intentional tort" within the meaning of this section, but, in order for such claim by an employee to be subject to the board's exclusive jurisdiction, it must be demonstrated that the employer's actions were part of (and not separate and independent from) its procedure for adjusting or settling the employee's claim for worker's compensation benefits.[8]

The court's rationale in *Samm* was relied upon by the Seventh Circuit Court of Appeals in *Goetzke v. Ferro Corp.*[9] There, an injured employee sued his employer (Ferro) and a third-party administrator (Crawford) in state court. Crawford was retained through Ferro's insurance carrier to administer worker's compensation claims. Goetzke alleged that Ferro terminated him in retaliation for filing a worker's compensation claim, and that Crawford had tortiously interfered in his employment relationship with Ferro. The case was removed to federal court, and

---

[2]IC 22-3-4-12.1(b) and (f).

[3]IC 22-3-4-12.1(d).

[4]IC 22-3-4-12.1(c).

[5]IC 22-3-4-12.1(c).

[6]Borgman v. State Farm Ins. Co., 713 N.E.2d 851 (Ind. Ct. App. 1999); Samm v. Great Dane Trailers, 715 N.E.2d 420 (Ind. Ct. App. 1999) (abrogated by, Martin v. State, 774 N.E.2d 43 (Ind. 2002)).

[7]Samm v. Great Dane Trailers, 715 N.E.2d 420 (Ind. Ct. App. 1999) (abrogated by, Martin v. State, 774 N.E.2d 43 (Ind. 2002)).

[8]Samm v. Great Dane Trailers, 715 N.E.2d 420, 427 (Ind. Ct. App. 1999) (abrogated by, Martin v. State, 774 N.E.2d 43 (Ind. 2002)).

[9]Goetzke v. Ferro Corp., 280 F.3d 766 (7th Cir. 2002).

thereafter the court granted summary judgment for the defendants. In affirming the order of the district court, the court of appeals wrote:

The Indiana statute bars suits in state court that allege a worker's compensation administrator such as Crawford has committed an independent tort "in adjusting or settling a claim for compensation." Ind. Code 22-3-4-12.1(a). Notably, two elements must exist before this statute is implicated. First, the tort must constitute an "independent tort" within the meaning of the exclusivity provision. *See Samm v. Great Dane Trailers,* 715 N.E.2d 420, 424, 426 (Ind. Ct. App. 1999), *transfer denied,* 735 N.E.2d 221 (Ind. 2000). Second, the worker's compensation administrator must have committed the tort in the context of adjusting or settling a claim for benefits. *See Samm,* 715 N.E.2d at 427.

Mr. Goetzke's claim appears to satisfy the first element of the statute. In particular, the few Indiana courts to construe the statutory phrase "intentional tort" have given it a broad meaning. *See Sims v. United States Fid. & Guar. Co.,* 730 N.E.2d 232, 236 (Ind. Ct. App. 2000) (stating that gross negligence and intentional infliction of emotional distress are independent torts within meaning of the statute), transfer granted on another question, May 4, 2001; *Samm,* 715 N.E.2d at 426 (finding defamation is an independent tort within the meaning of the statute). But *see Samm,* 715 N.E.2d at 424 (finding that the tort of retaliatory discharge is not an "intentional tort" within the meaning of the statute). Mr. Goetzke undoubtedly alleges a tort claim against Crawford. *See, e.g., Winkler v. V.G. Reed & Sons, Inc.,* 638 N.E.2d 1228, 1234 (Ind. 1994) ("Indiana has long recognized that intentional interference with a contract is an actionable tort."). Given the backdrop of the *Sims* and *Samm* cases, Mr. Goetzke's tortious interference claim most likely constitutes an independent tort within the meaning of the exclusivity provision of the Indiana statute.

However, a second component is necessary before the claim falls within the scope of the statute. Specifically, the independent tort must have been committed by the worker's compensation administrator in adjusting or settling a compensation claim. *See* Ind. Code 22-3-4-12.1(a). One Indiana court has provided some elaboration on this element.

In *Samm v. Great Dane Trailers,* 715 N.E.2d 420, 427 (Ind. Ct. App. 1999) . . . the Court of Appeals of Indiana emphasized that the independent tort must have been "part of [the worker's compensation administrator's] procedure for 'adjusting or settling' [a plaintiff's] claim for worker's compensation benefits." *Samm,* 715 N.E.2d at 427. As such, if the defamatory statements "were made within the context of the benefits denial . . . the complaint would seem to allege an independent tort which falls within the exclusive jurisdiction of the Board." *Id.* at 427. However, had the defamatory statement followed the denial of benefits, the claim would fall outside of the exclusivity provision because the "defamatory action would appear to be related to but separate and independent from [the defendant's] procedure for 'adjusting or settling' a request for benefits." *Id.* As the court could not determine whether the defamation claim was intertwined with or separate from the procedure for adjusting or settling the plaintiff's worker's compensation claim, it remanded the case for further fact finding.

As *Samm* makes clear, to fall within the ambit of the statute, Crawford's alleged tortious conduct must have occurred as part of its procedure for adjusting or settling Mr. Goetzke's claim for worker's compensation benefits. This element is simply not present in this case. Specifically, Mr. Goetzke contends that Crawford engaged in a pattern of conduct designed to oust him from his job at Ferro. If Crawford actually engaged in such conduct, such actions would not form part of Crawford's procedure for adjusting or settling Mr. Goetzke's claims. Because the tortious interference claim falls outside of the scope of the exclusivity provision, Mr. Goetzke has stated a claim upon which relief could be granted. Thus, the district court properly addressed the merits of this count of Mr. Goetzke's complaint.[10]

The Indiana courts recently took a look at both bad faith and lack of diligence claims. In *Ag One Co-Op v. Scott*,[11] the appellate court considered whether an insurance carrier can be held in bad faith if the claim is ultimately found to not be compensable. The court stated that, "In the context of the denial of insurance claims, a finding of bad faith requires evidence of a state of mind reflecting a dishonest purpose, moral obliquity, furtive design, or ill will."[12] Citing Borgman v. Sugar Creek Animal Hosp., 782 N.E.2d 993 (Ind. Ct. App. 2002),[13] the court found that there can be no bad faith in denying benefits if, in fact, the employer did not act improperly in denying benefits.[14] Since Ag-One was properly found to have denied Scott's claim, a bad faith finding could not be upheld.[15]

Eastern Alliance Ins. Group v. Howell,[16] is another case involving a dispute between two insurance carriers. Howell suffered a work-related injury and an aggravation of that injury during time periods with insurance coverage by two different carriers, Eastern Alliance and Chubb. Both carriers asserted that the other was responsible to pay for Howell's treatment. Due to this dispute, Howell's treatment was delayed for over two years. Chubb was ultimately found the responsible carrier. The Board assessed lack of diligence penalties against both carriers. The ap-

---

[10]Goetzke v. Ferro Corp., 280 F.3d 766, 779–780 (7th Cir. 2002).

[11]Ag One Co-op v. Scott, 914 N.E.2d 860 (Ind. Ct. App. 2009).

[12]Ag One Co-op v. Scott, 914 N.E.2d 860, 864 (Ind. Ct. App. 2009).

[13]Borgman v. Sugar Creek Animal Hosp., 782 N.E.2d 993 (Ind. Ct. App. 2002).

[14]Ag One Co-op v. Scott, 914 N.E.2d 860, 863 (Ind. Ct. App. 2009).

[15]Ag One Co-op v. Scott, 914 N.E.2d 860, 864 (Ind. Ct. App. 2009).

[16]Eastern Alliance Ins. Group v. Howell, 929 N.E.2d 922 (Ind. Ct. App. 2010).

pellate court considered whether the penalties against Eastern Alliance were proper.[17]

Eastern Alliance argued that since it was not ultimately responsible for the claim, lack of diligence penalties could not be assessed against it in following *Ag One Co-Op v. Scott*. However, the court rejected this argument because unlike a bad faith claim, a lack of diligence requires no conscious wrongdoing by the actor. A lack of diligence is a failure to exercise the degree of attention and care required that a prudent person would exercise or to act negligently.[18] The court concluded that Eastern Alliance's actions in the handling of the claim did not amount to a lack of diligence and reversed the Board's finding.[19]

Although it was decided prior to the advent of IC 22-3-4-12.1 and was not an action before the board, the case of *Stump v. Commercial Union*,[20] is most instructive regarding some of the issues raised by this section of the Act. In fact, it could be argued that IC 22-3-4-12.1 is an outgrowth of the opinion of the Indiana Supreme Court in that case. There, the Court was presented a number of certified questions by a federal district court. It was asked to instruct the court with respect to the "type of causes of action Indiana law will permit against a worker's compensation insurance carrier arising out of its dealing with an injured worker and the processing of the worker's compensation claim."[21] In response, the Court cited the following language from the opinion of the court of appeals in *Baker v. American States Ins. Co.*:[22]

> [IC] 22-3-2-6 speaks to personal injury or death by accident on the job, but it does not purport to prohibit actions by an employee against his employer's workmen's compensation insurance carrier for fraudulent misrepresentations made while the employee and the insurer are attempting to settle the claim . . . . [T]he alleged fraudulent misrepresentation . . . is not the kind of harm for which the Workmen's Compensation Act was calculated to compensate . . . . The alleged fraudulent misrepresentation did not arise "out of and in the course of the employment . . . ." Instead, it arose after Baker had been temporarily but totally disabled from working for a period of time. If Baker's allegations regarding the behavior of the adjusters for American States prove to be true, then it is in the public interest of this state to discourage such activities and to

---

[17]Eastern Alliance Ins. Group v. Howell, 929 N.E.2d 922, 924-925 (Ind. Ct. App. 2010).

[18]Eastern Alliance Ins. Group v. Howell, 929 N.E.2d 922, 926-927 (Ind. Ct. App. 2010).

[19]Eastern Alliance Ins. Group v. Howell, 929 N.E.2d 922, 928 (Ind. Ct. App. 2010).

[20]Stump v. Commercial Union, 601 N.E.2d 327 (Ind. 1992).

[21]Stump v. Commercial Union, 601 N.E.2d 327, 329 (Ind. 1992).

[22]Baker v. American States Ins. Co., 428 N.E.2d 1342 (Ind. Ct. App. 1981).

compensate the victim for resulting injury. We hold that the Workmen's Compensation Act does not preclude Baker's suit for damages, except to the extent that he claims attorney's fees as an element of damages.[23]

The Court went on to conclude that "Indiana law will permit a cause of action by an injured employee against a worker's compensation insurance carrier for injuries proximately caused by the insurance carrier's tortious conduct such as gross negligence, intentional infliction of emotional distress, and constructive fraud."[24]

Undoubtedly, there will be further interpretations of the phrases contained in IC 22-3-4-12.1 from the appellate courts. While they have had some difficulty deciding what is and what is not an intentional tort, they have not even begun to scratch the surface on what behavior is required to constitute "bad faith."

In *Amerisafe Risk Services, Inc. v. Estate of Wadsack ex rel. Wadsack*,[25] Matthew Wadsack was electrocuted and severely burned while working for Mille Tree Service. He was 19 years old at the time. He was in the hospital and induced into a coma for an extended period of time. While he was in the hospital his parents were appointed temporary guardians.

At the time of Matthew's injury, Amerisafe was the worker's compensation insurance carrier for the employer and Riggs was the adjuster assigned to handle his claim. The parents filed an action in state court alleging that Riggs intentionally or recklessly undertook a course of extreme and outrageous conduct that was intended to deny Matthew of worker's compensation benefits to which he was entitled, and to deprive Matthew from receiving necessary medical care. The parents also alleged that Riggs interfered with the parents' obligations as guardians. Amerisafe argued the state court had no subject matter jurisdiction. The state court denied the motion to dismiss without issuing any explanation or issue findings of fact.

On appeal, the Court of Appeals reversed the state court's denial of motion to dismiss holding that the Worker's Compensation Board has exclusive jurisdiction to determine whether an insurance carrier or employer has adjusted or settled a claim for compensation in bad faith, with a lack of diligence, or committed an independent tort in the settlement or adjustment of a claim. The parents argued that the Board does not have jurisdiction because their claims are not on behalf of Matthew; however, the

---

[23]Stump v. Commercial Union, 601 N.E.2d 327 (Ind. 1992).

[24]Stump v. Commercial Union, 601 N.E.2d 327, 330, (Ind. 1992).

[25]Amerisafe Risk Services, Inc. v. Estate of Wadsack ex rel. Wadsack, 980 N.E.2d 842 (Ind. Ct. App. 2012), transfer denied, 984 N.E.2d 1253 (Ind. 2013).

Court answered by stating the Board's jurisdiction to hear claims of improper claim handling extends not only to the injured employee but to his personal representatives and next of kin.

§ 5:9 Administration—Records and reports

Every employer must keep a record of all injuries, fatal or otherwise, received, or claimed to have been received, by its employees in the course of employment. Within seven days after the occurrence and knowledge of any injury causing an employee's death or absence from work for more than one day, a written report must be mailed to the employer's insurance carrier, or, if the employer is self-insured, to the board. The insurance carrier must then deliver the report to the board within seven days after receipt or 14 days after the employer's knowledge of the injury, whichever is later. If the employer or the insurer fails to comply with these requirements, a civil penalty of $50 may be imposed.[1]

The report required by IC 22-3-4-13 must include the name, nature, and location of the employer's business; the name, age, sex, wages, and occupation of the injured employee; the date and hour of the accident; the nature and cause of the injury; and such other information as the board may require.[2]

If a person violates any provision of the Act (except for IC 22-3-5-1 or IC 22-3-7-34(b) or (c)), he or she commits a Class C infraction. If the person violates IC 22-3-5-1 or IC 22-3-7-34(b) or (c), he or she commits a Class A infraction. The board, in the name of the state, may seek relief from any court of competent jurisdiction to enjoin any violation of the Act.[3]

The venue of all criminal actions under this section is in the county in which the employee was injured. If the board so requests, the county prosecutor shall prosecute all such violations, and the action is to be brought in the name of the state.[4]

In an action before the board against an employer who, at the time of the injury to or occupational disease of an employee, failed to comply with IC 22-3-5-1 or IC 22-3-7-34(b) or (c), the board may award to the employee or the dependents of a deceased employee: (1) compensation not to exceed double the compensation provided by the Act; (2) medical expenses; and (3) reasonable attorney fees. These penalty provisions apply only to the employer

---

[Section 5:9]

[1]IC 22-3-4-13(a).
[2]IC 22-3-4-13(c).
[3]IC 22-3-4-13(d).
[4]IC 22-3-4-13(e).

and do not apply for a failure to exact a certificate of insurance under IC 22-3-2-14 or IC 22-3-7-34(i) or (j).[5]

In actions prosecuted under subsections (d) and (e), the court may: (1) order the employer to cease doing business in Indiana until it furnishes proof of insurance as required; (2) require satisfactory proof of the employer's financial ability to pay any compensation or medical expenses in the amount and manner and when due for any injuries which occurred during any period of noncompliance; and (3) require the employer to deposit with the board an acceptable security, indemnity, or bond to secure the payment of such compensation and medical expenses liabilities.[6]

Every employer or insurance carrier paying compensation must, within 10 days from the termination of the compensation period fixed in any award, and within 10 days from the full redemption of any such award by the cash payment thereof in a lump sum, make whatever report the board requires.[7]

It has been held that the penalty provisions contained in subsection (f) of IC 22-3-4-13 are purely discretionary, and the board has the discretion to either award penalties or refuse to award them depending upon the facts and circumstances of the individual case before it.[8]

IC 22-3-4-13(a) is amended to allow the Board to require an employer to provide a record of all injuries fatal or otherwise received by or claimed to have been received by the employer's employees in the course of their employment. IC 22-3-7-37 is amended to require employers to keep a record of all disablements by occupational disease, fatal or otherwise, and the employer shall provide a copy of the record to the Board upon request.

IC 22-3-4-15 is created to provide penalty for failure to comply with the requirement to post notice of insurance and file an injury record with the Board. The penalty shall be $50 for the first violation, second unrelated violation of the same offense is $150 and

---

[5]IC 22-3-4-13(f) and (h). Note: It is assumed that subsection (h) contains a typographical mistake. It refers to "the penalty provisions of subsection (e)," but the penalty provisions are, actually, contained in subsection (f).

[6]IC 22-3-4-13(g). Note: It is assumed that this subsection contains a typographical mistake. It refers to "an action under subsection (c)," however, that subsection deals exclusively with the information which must be contained in the employer's first report of the accident and injury. Since subsection (g) refers to the actions which "the court" may take, it seems logical that this subsection refers to the prosecution of violations as set forth in subsections (d) and (e).

[7]IC 22-3-4-14.

[8]Rayburn v. Johnson, 505 N.E.2d 478 (Ind. Ct. App. 1987).

third or subsequent unrelated violation of the same offense the Board may assess a civil penalty not to exceed $300. The Board shall deposit these penalties in a worker's compensation supplemental administrative fund.

Chapter 6

Worker's Compensation Insurance Policies

§ 6:1   Insurance requirements
§ 6:2   —Policy forms; scope of coverage

> **KeyCite®:** Cases and other legal materials listed in KeyCite Scope can be researched through the KeyCite service on Westlaw®. Use KeyCite to check citations for form, parallel references, prior and later history, and comprehensive citator information, including citations to other decisions and secondary materials.

§ 6:1   Insurance requirements

As stated previously, it is required by the Act that employers insure, and keep insured, their liability to pay compensation benefits in some corporation, association, or organization authorized to transact the business of worker's compensation insurance in the state of Indiana.[1] An employer may, in the alternative, furnish to the board satisfactory proof of its financial ability to pay directly the compensation in the amount and manner and when due as provided in the Act.[2] With respect to the latter, the board may require the employer to deposit an acceptable security, indemnity, or bond to secure the payment of compensation liabilities as they are incurred.[3] If an employer is self-insured, it must pay the board the following fees: (1) an initial application fee of $500, (2) a renewal fee of $250, and (3) a late filing fee of $250.[4]

If an employer's worker's compensation insurance expires or is cancelled, the employer must, within 10 days after the termination, file with the board on a proscribed form evidence of the employer's compliance with the insurance or self-insurance

---

[Section 6:1]
[1]IC 22-3-5-1(a)(1).
[2]IC 22-3-5-1(a)(2).
[3]IC 22-3-5-1(b).
[4]IC 22-3-5-1(b)(1) to (3).

requirements of the Act. Proof of renewal of an existing insurance policy may be filed every three years.[5]

In *Jones v. Indiana Farmers Mut.Ins. Co.*,[6] the appellate court affirmed the Board's determination that the policy in question's cancellation was effective 10 days after the Board received notice of the cancellation. IC 22-3-5-5(c)(5) provides that any termination of a policy by cancellation shall not be effective as to employees of the insured covered unless at least ten days prior to the taking effect of such cancellation, a written notice giving the date upon which such termination is to become effective has been received by the Board.[7] Although the cancellation notice gave a cancellation date less than 10 days after the issuance of the notice, the policy was canceled after the ten days. The "purpose of the statute is effectuated by running the cancellation ten (10) days from the date the Board receives notice because it allows the employer time to secure coverage and allows the Board an opportunity to insure that the employer purchases replacement coverage."[8]

A self-insured employer who has complied with the Act will be issued a certificate by the board which will remain in effect for a period fixed by the board; but, upon 10 days' notice and a hearing, the board may revoke the certificate if it receives evidence sufficient to cause such a revocation. At any time after the revocation, the board may issue a new certificate upon the employer's application and satisfactory proof of financial ability to pay its liabilities under the Act.[9]

Subject to board approval, an employer may enter into or continue any agreement with its employees to provide a system of compensation, benefits, or insurance in lieu of the compensation and insurance provided by the Act. However, no such substitute system will be approved unless it confers benefits upon injured employees and their dependents at least equivalent to the benefits provided by the Act, nor if it requires contributions from the employees, unless the system confers benefits in addition to those provided in the Act at least commensurate with such contributions.[10] The board may terminate such a substitute system on reasonable notice and hearing to the interested parties

---

[5]IC 22-3-5-2.

[6]Jones v. Indiana Farmers Mut. Ins. Co., 926 N.E.2d 116 (Ind. Ct. App. 2010).

[7]IC 22-3-5-5(c)(5).

[8]Jones v. Indiana Farmers Mut. Ins. Co., 926 N.E.2d 116, 122 (Ind. Ct. App. 2010).

[9]IC 22-3-5-3.

[10]IC 22-3-5-4(a).

if it appears that it is not fairly administered, its operation discloses latent defects threatening its solvency, or if for any substantial reason it fails to accomplish the purpose of the Act. If the substitute system is terminated, the board must determine the proper distribution of all remaining assets, if any, subject to the right of any party in interest to take an appeal to the court of appeals.[11]

The insurance (or self-insurance) requirements contained within the Act are matters between employers and the board, and they do not expand the rights or remedies otherwise available to employees should their employers fail to comply. In *Landers v. Pickering*,[12] an employee claimed that she was entitled to seek civil damages against her employer for a work-related injury because the employer did not comply with the Act's insurance and reporting requirements. The trial court granted summary judgment in favor of the employer and the court of appeals affirmed, writing:

> It is well established that in the absence of a specific rejection of the Workmen's Compensation Act by either the employee or the employer, the provisions of the Act govern and the remedies included therein are exclusive. *Stainbrook v. Johnson County Farm Bureau,* (1955) 125 Ind. App. 487, 122 N.E.2d 884, *trans. denied* . . . Moreover, this question was raised in *Hickman v. Western Heating and Air Conditioning Co., Inc.,* (D.C. Ind. 1962) 207 F. Supp. 832, where it was held that an injured employee is limited to the remedies contained in the Act even though the employer failed to comply with the insurance provisions of the Act.

> Landers asks this court to re-examine the *Hickman* decision and to allow a remedy independent from the Act. The legislative history does not support this request. The Act contains a [sic] specific sections penalizing those who violate its requirements in Ind. Code 22-3-4-13.[13]

§ 6:2   Insurance requirements—Policy forms; scope of coverage

An insurer is prohibited from issuing a policy of worker's compensation insurance until its policy form has been submitted to and approved by the Department of Insurance.[1] All worker's compensation insurance policies are conclusively presumed to cover all employees and the entire compensation liability of the

---

[11]IC 22-3-5-4(b).

[12]Landers v. Pickering, 427 N.E.2d 716 (Ind. Ct. App. 1981).

[13]Landers v. Pickering, 427 N.E.2d 716, 717–718 (Ind. Ct. App. 1981).

[Section 6:2]

[1]IC 22-3-5-5(a).

insured. Any provision in any such policy attempting to limit or modify the liability of the one issuing it is wholly void.[2]

Subsection (c) of IC 22-3-5-5 provides that every policy of worker's compensation insurance is deemed to include certain enumerated provisions and any change in the policy which may be required by any statute, as fully as if they were written in the policy. For all intents and purposes, these enumerated provisions simply state in greater detail that which is required by subdivision (b), i.e., an insurer's liability for "all the employees and the entire compensation liability of the insured."

All claims for, and board awards of, worker's compensation benefits may be made directly against either the employer, the insurer, or both. If an insurer fails or refuses to pay a final award or judgment (except during the pendency of an appeal), or if it fails or refuses to comply with any provision of the Act, the board will not accept any further proofs of insurance from it until the award or judgment has been paid or the violated provision complied with.[3]

IC 22-3-5-5.5 includes rules covering deductibles and co-insurance which an insurer is authorized to offer its insured. Where the policy provides for a deductible, the insurer must pay all or part of the deductible amount to the person or medical service provider entitled to the benefit, and then seek reimbursement from the employer.[4] An employer is prohibited from using its election or payment of a deductible or co-insurance in negotiating with its employees on any terms of employment and, if it does so knowingly, it is subject to a civil penalty.[5]

---

[2]IC 22-3-5-5(b).

[3]IC 22-3-5-5(d).

[4]IC 22-3-5-5.5(c)(1)(A) and (B).

[5]IC 22-3-5-5.5(h).

Chapter 7

The Indiana Occupational Diseases Act

> **KeyCite®:** Cases and other legal materials listed in KeyCite Scope can be researched through the KeyCite service on Westlaw®. Use KeyCite to check citations for form, parallel references, prior and later history, and comprehensive citator information, including citations to other decisions and secondary materials.

§ 7:1   Occupational diseases

The Indiana Occupational Diseases Act was enacted in 1937, but repealed in 1988. The current "Occupational Diseases" sections of the Indiana Worker's Compensation Act (IC 22-3-7-2 to IC 22-3-7-38) took its place. In most respects, these sections mirror their counterparts in the Act (IC 22-3-2 to IC 22-3-6). There are some differences—some rather substantial, some more subtle—and those differences will be discussed in the following paragraphs. If a particular occupational disease section is essentially the same as one within the worker's compensation law, that fact will simply be noted.

Initially, it must be kept in mind that "[t]he Workmen's Compensation Act and the Occupational Diseases Act contain separate and distinct provisions, and it is well settled that a legal interpretation of one act cannot force a similar conclusion when a

different act with different provisions is under consideration."[1]
The appellate courts have tended to apply this principle, even
though there are no longer two separate acts and there are
similarities in certain sections.

The general purpose underlying the enactment of the Occupational Diseases Act was set forth in the opinion of the court
of appeals in *Gray v. Daimler Chrysler Corp.*,[2] There, the court
stated:

> The Occupational Diseases Act, Indiana Code chapter 22-3-7,
> introduced more than twenty years after the Worker's Compensa-
> tion Act, was enacted by our General Assembly in order to protect
> employees by providing compensation, without regard to fault, for
> those who contracted occupational diseases which were generally
> not covered under the Worker's Compensation Act. *Roberts v.*
> *AcandS, Inc.,* 806 N.E.2d 1, 3 (Ind. Ct. App. 2004). Therefore, as
> with provisions of the Worker's Compensation Act, provisions of the
> Occupational Diseases Act should be liberally construed in favor of
> the employee to effectuate the act's humanitarian purpose to
> provide injured workers with an expeditious and adequate remedy.
> *Id.*[3]

§ 7:2   Occupational diseases—Essential elements to claim for compensation

IC 22-3-7-2 is, in many respects, similar to IC 22-3-2-2. It
provides that every employer and every employee, except as
stated in these sections of the Act, are bound to and must pay
and accept compensation for *disablement* or death *by occupational*
disease arising out of and in the course of employment,
respectively. The burden of proof is on the employee, and the employee's proof of one element of the claim does not create a
presumption in his or her favor with regard to other elements of
the claim. Certain individuals are not covered by this section, as
discussed below.

The term "occupational disease" is defined in IC 22-3-7-10(a),
as "a disease arising out of and in the course of the employment.
Ordinary diseases of life to which the general public is exposed
outside of the employment shall not be compensable, except
where such diseases follow as an incident of an occupational disease as defined in this section." Subsection (b) of IC 22-3-7-10

[Section 7:1]

[1]Snyder Const. Co. v. Thompson, 145 Ind. App. 103, 248 N.E.2d 560, 563
(1969).

[2]Gray v. Daimler Chrysler Corp., 821 N.E.2d 431 (Ind. Ct. App. 2005).

[3]Gray v. Daimler Chrysler Corp., 821 N.E.2d 431, 434–35 (Ind. Ct. App.
2005). See also Harbison-Walker Refractories Co. v. Turks, 110 Ind. App. 563, 39
N.E.2d 791 (1942).

provides that a disease arises out of the employment *only* if there is apparent "to the rational mind upon consideration of all of the circumstances" a direct causal connection between the conditions under which the work is performed and the occupational disease; and which:

(1) can be seen to have followed as a natural incident of the work as a result of the exposure occasioned by the nature of the employment;

(2) can be fairly traced to the employment as the proximate cause; and

(3) do not come from a hazard to which workers would have been equally exposed outside of the employment.

The disease must be incidental to the character of the business and not independent of the relation of employer and employee. The disease need not have been foreseen or expected, but after its contraction it must appear to have had its origin in a risk connected with the employment and to have flowed from that source as a rational consequence.

It has not been easy for the appellate courts to determine those conditions of the mind and body which constitute an occupational disease, and those which do not. They have shown a reluctance to extend the benefits of the Act to conditions resulting from repetitive trauma and those rising from psychological disorders. In *Duvall v. ICI Americas, Inc.*,[1] the court of appeals concluded, in the following language, that carpal tunnel syndrome was not an occupational disease:

The definition of an "occupational disease" found in Indiana Code § 22-3-7-10 is incomplete because it assumes that the employee suffers from a "disease" and focuses on whether the disease is causally connected to workplace conditions. "Disease" is not defined in the Indiana Occupational Diseases Act, nor have our cases squarely confronted what constitutes a disease under the Act. Duvall has established by stipulation that her carpal tunnel syndrome is causally connected to her occupation, but that causal relationship does not require the conclusion that carpal tunnel syndrome is an occupational disease . . . .

The statutory definition describes an occupational disease in terms of a worker's "exposure" to conditions in the workplace. Specifically, the definition provides that a disease is an occupational disease when it results from "*exposure* occasioned by the nature of the employment." I.C. § 23-3-7-10(b) (emphasis added). The term "exposure" indicates a passive relationship between the worker and his work environment rather than an event or occurrence, or series of events or occurrences, which constitute injury under the Worker's

---

[Section 7:2]

[1]Duvall v. ICI Americas, Inc., 621 N.E.2d 1122 (Ind. Ct. App. 1993).

Compensation Act. Duvall's carpal tunnel syndrome did not result from exposure to workplace conditions at ICI but resulted from the hand and wrist mechanics associated with Duvall's work on ICI's production line. Her carpal tunnel syndrome did not result from where she worked but from the work she did.

Moreover, carpal tunnel syndrome is in a class of disorders described as "cumulative trauma disorders." As a disorder caused by trauma, carpal tunnel syndrome is not a disease. A trauma is defined as a "wound, especially one produced by sudden *physical injury.*" American Heritage Dictionary of the English Language at 1366 (1981) (emphasis added). Similarly, a "traumatism" is an "injury" or a "wound produced by injury; trauma." *Id.* Thus, by definition, the term trauma is synonymous with injury, and the cumulative effect of more than one trauma is likewise an injury ...

Further, "injury" is defined by the Indiana Worker's Compensation Act as "only injury by accident arising out of and in the course of the employment and do[es] not include a disease in any form *except as it results from injury.*" IND. CODE § 22-3-6-1(e) (emphasis added). Thus, even assuming carpal tunnel syndrome were a disease, it would properly be designated as an "injury" under the Worker's Compensation Act because it results from injury, which is trauma to the carpal tunnel of the wrist.

Although we should construe the Occupational Diseases Act liberally, we should not extend the Act to embrace cases which cannot reasonably be interpreted to fall within its scope. *See Reid v. Ontario Manufacturing Co.* (1947), 117 Ind. App. 273, 275, 70 N.E.2d 357, 358, *trans. denied.* Further, we note that our legislature enacted the Occupational Diseases Act to compensate employees who contract occupational diseases but who are generally not covered under the Worker's Compensation Act. *Spaulding,* 550 N.E.2d at 309. Here, our resolution of this appeal is consistent with the original purpose of the Occupational Diseases Act. Duvall's carpal tunnel syndrome, while not compensable as an occupational disease under the Occupational Diseases Act, is compensable as an injury under the Worker's Compensation Act.[2]

In *Star Pub. Co. v. Jackson,*[3] the board found that the employee was disabled due to an occupational disease (neurosis) which was brought about and caused by his employment as a linotype operator. Apparently, all of the medical witnesses who testified agreed that the claimant was suffering from a neurosis. His physician testified that he attributed it to chronic fatigue of the nerve centers controlling the muscles of the upper left extremity. The other medical witnesses attributed the claimant's neurosis to a condition of his mind resulting from confrontations

---

[2]Duvall v. ICI Americas, Inc., 621 N.E.2d 1122, 1125–27 (Ind. Ct. App. 1993).

[3]Star Pub. Co. v. Jackson, 115 Ind. App. 221, 58 N.E.2d 202 (1944).

with his foreman extending over a 10-year period. In reversing the board's award to Jackson, the appellate court stated:

> Neurosis has been defined as: "A functional nervous disorder, without demonstrable physical lesion." *Webster's New International Dictionary*, 2d Ed., 1942 and as: "A change in the nervous system of the individual that produces symptoms, but in which on examination of the nerve organs, after death, at an autopsy, for instance, no physical symptoms could be found." 45 C.J. 1390.
>
> The evidence and scientific books on the subject agree that the risk of becoming disabled as the result of a neurosis is not peculiar to any particular employment or necessarily to employment at all; that it may occur in countless occupations, gainful or otherwise, for it appears generally to be a defense reaction which may arise in connection with any kind of work, or even play, as the result of an accident or injury, a clash of personalities, a feeling of frustration, inadequacy, aversion for the occupation and the like. It is thus an ordinary disease of life to which the general public is exposed outside the employment, and, therefore, not compensable in this case unless it followed as an incident of an occupational disease as defined by our statute . . . .
>
> It is well known that fatigue, whether of the nerve centers, muscles or other cells or organs of the body, is in its very nature common to nearly all employments and to countless other of the ordinary activities of life. People of all ages and in all walks of life are affected by it, and the causes are so numerous that it cannot be said they are peculiar to or result from an exposure occasioned by and naturally incidental to any particular employment.
>
> We therefore hold that chronic fatigue, if a disease at all, was not in this case shown to be an occupational disease as defined by law.[4]

A nearly identical claim was made in *McGill Mfg. Co., Inc. v. Dodd*,[5] Once again, the board found the claim compensable, and the appellate court reversed. After citing its opinion in *Star Pub. Co.*, the court stated:

> While in the instant case objective symptoms were present, the evidence that they resulted from neurosis was positive and undisputed, appellee's physician further testifying that the services of a psychiatrist would have been good for appellee, had such services been available.
>
> In the light of such testimony rationality can be strained to the breaking point without avail in the effort to sustain the proposition that appellee's disease was incidental to the character of the business in which he was employed.
>
> While not denying that, under the rules governing the review of causes appealed from the Industrial Board, the evidence in the instant case, though conflicting, is sufficient to sustain a finding that there existed some causal connection between appellee's dis-

---

[4]Star Pub. Co. v. Jackson, 115 Ind. App. 221, 58 N.E.2d 202, 203–204 (1944).

[5]McGill Mfg. Co. v. Dodd, 116 Ind. App. 66, 59 N.E.2d 899 (1945).

ease and the work performed by him, we cannot hold it probative of a finding that appellee was suffering from an occupational disease as defined by Acts 1937, ch. 69, p. 334, § 6, § 40-2206, *Burns' 1940 Replacement*.

The Indiana Workmen's Occupational Disease Act is a humane enactment designed and intended for the protection of workmen who come within its provisions, which are and ought to be liberally construed and applied, so as to extend that protection to the ultimate good of the greatest possible number of our workers; but the extent and limitation of its applicability also are fixed by those provisions and we cannot, by judicial pronouncement, enlarge these beyond the very obvious intent of the Legislature which was, not to provide general health insurance to the workman, but to compensate him for disability resulting only from a disease incidental to the character of the business in which he is employed and having its origin in a risk connected with the employment, and to exclude from the protection of the Act workmen suffering from diseases arising out of a hazard to which workmen would have been equally exposed outside their employment and independent of the relation of employer and employee.

Indulging all liberality, we cannot perceive in the Act a legislative intent and purpose to extend its protection to those workmen who suffer, unfortunately, from outward manifestations and symptoms of many possible vagaries and aberrations of the human mind which, though having some causal connection with an employment are, nevertheless, ills all human flesh is heir to; unless, in such cases, the causative inducing the mental condition be an intervening occupational disease, as defined by the Act, of which there is no evidence in the instant cases.[6]

The most definitive and exhaustive discussion of the Indiana Occupational Diseases Act is contained in the opinion of the Indiana Court of Appeals in *Schwitzer-Cummins Co. v. Hacker*.[7] There, the board found that the inhalation of dust by Hacker while operating a milling machine caused inflammation of his lungs which resulted in a disease known as bronchiectasis. In affirming the board's award of compensation benefits to the worker, the appellate court concluded:

Prior to the enactment of this legislation it was difficult to find coverage of ailments and disease under the Workmen's Compensation Law because of the requirement of establishing definite dates and circumstances to support accident and injury cases; further, where relief for disease disability was sought under the Indiana Employers' Liability Law, many obstacles were encountered to the satisfactory proof of the negligence of the employer . . . .

---

[6]McGill Mfg. Co. v. Dodd, 116 Ind. App. 66, 59 N.E.2d 899, 900–901 (1945). See also Collins v. Evansville State Hospital, 134 Ind. App. 471, 189 N.E.2d 106 (1963).

[7]Schwitzer-Cummins Co. v. Hacker, 123 Ind. App. 674, 112 N.E.2d 221 (1953).

It seems safe to assume that the legislative mind became cognizant of the circumstances that the slow, creeping, insidious progress of disease often may be more devastating, crippling and lethal to a workman than the disablement resulting from accidental physical injury, and that humane considerations demanded the proffer of an opportunity for compensation to those who contract disease as a result of being compelled to toil for a livelihood in the surroundings and under the conditions furnished by and at the will of an employer wherein may lurk the risks and inherent hazards of disease . . . .

One eminent authority, in speaking of our Occupational Diseases Act, says:

"The Indiana Workmen's Occupational Diseases Act is a good one so far as its general aims and objects are concerned. *It embraces every true occupational disease,* yet provides standards sufficient to exclude pretenders. However, the act is poorly drafted . . . . Its sentences are grammatically intolerable and its sections are inordinately long, all resulting in confusions and contradictions . . . . The statute's high purpose deserves a better mold than that in which it has been cast . . . ." [Our emphasis]. Small's *Workmen's Compensation Law of Indiana,* pages 421–422, § 13-1 . . . .

A complexity has been thereby created out of a simplicity. The Act, when it's [sic] verbiage is assembled in logical sequence and common language, merely provides that where the diseased workman works in surroundings and conditions which are usual, common, and ordinary in all employments, he cannot, simply because he becomes a victim of a disease while working for his employer, claim compensation therefor. But when his surroundings and conditions of work possess within themselves inherent risks, dangers, and hazards which are *not* present in other employments, and he contracts a disease due to his working amid and exposure to such risks and hazards which furnish the roots or cause of the disease from which he suffers, resulting in his disablement, compensation therefor is afforded. The employee's disease may be of a class or nature which the members of the general public may acquire under ordinary and usual circumstances and conditions but, if the disease from which he suffers *did not in fact* arise out of such usual and ordinary circumstances and conditions and *was in fact* occasioned as a result of being subjected to risks and hazards afforded by the particular, peculiar, or unusual conditions of work in his employment, he would be entitled to the benefits of the statute upon the proper legal establishment of such facts in accordance with the procedure required for an appropriate finding of the Industrial Board. The question is not whether the workman has a disease which is more or less common to others of the general public, but whether the *particular conditions* of his work were such as to cause and did cause him to acquire the disease.

It may be urged that these expressions savor too much of the same principles that have been applied to the Workmen's Compensation Law. The fact is that we *are* dealing with a *compensation law* for workmen. The original Workmen's Compensation Law was restricted to injuries occasioned by accidents or mishaps in the employment resulting in a physical personal injury or death. No provision was made therein for disablement by disease. The Occupational Diseases Act undertook to supply the deficiency. It contains much of the substance of the Workmen's Compensation Act . . . .

In determining whether a disease suffered by the workman is one "to which the general public is exposed,"consideration must be given to the circumstances and conditions under which he is required to labor. As heretofore stated, the disease itself may be "ordinary" in the sense that it is an ailment to which many people are exposed to and suffer from, but the conditions of employment of the workman may involve a *special* or *inherent* risk or hazard of disease to which he is exposed but to which the public is not exposed. The Act provides that an occupational disease must "arise out of and in the course of the employment." These are not idle words and seem logically to convey the legislative intent that the employment must furnish or involve some *feature, condition, nature, or character* which subjects the workman to a risk or hazard of disease which is not common to the public outside the employment. For a disease to *arise out* of the employment imports that the nature and conditions of the employment are such that the contracted disease was one likely to be acquired by the workman in that employment. Where it appears that the causative danger is inherent in or peculiar to the work performed under the then prevailing conditions which are not common to the general public outside the employment, the disease *arises* from the employment if it is causally connected therewith . . . .

There is nothing in our Act which requires or implies that the work conditions must subject all the employees as a "class" to the same exposure . . . . All members of the human family are not physically constituted alike. Some are more susceptible to a given disease than are others. Some have greater powers of resistance to disease elements of a given nature . . . . Some carry within themselves latent or dormant seeds of disease which are subject to be activated by certain conditions and to progress to the point of disablement or even death. Some are "allergic" to certain substances, conditions, or gases. It may be conceded that under the conditions of work the "exposure" may be common to all the employees, whether by class or otherwise, but it does not result that *all* of the employees would necessarily become afflicted with the disease . . . .

The Act does not demand "a long period of exposure." In fact, the Act expressly provides against such a requirement. In § 26 of the Act, *Burns' 1952 Replacement*, § 40-2226, it is provided:

"An employee shall be conclusively deemed to have been exposed to the hazards of an occupational disease when *for any length of time, however short,* he is employed in an occupation or process in which the hazard of the disease exists." (Our emphasis)

The Act does not provide that the disease need be an expected one. On the contrary, subdivision (b) provides that "The disease need not have been foreseen or *expected* . . ." [Our emphasis] . . . .

The *Star* case and the *McGill* case both involved a consideration of nerve and mental afflictions. In the Star case, the court held the evidence did not show the neurosis to be an occupational disease, but rather a "chronic fatigue" which "in its very nature" is common to all employments. In the McGill case, the majority of the court held there was no evidence that the causative inducing the mental condition was an occupational disease within the definition of the statute. None of these cases offer support to appellant's insistence that, in this case, we declare a rule which would, in effect, deny protection to all claimants except those suffering from diseases which are commonly known to result from particular or exclusive types of businesses. As heretofore pointed out, if such had been the intent of the Legislature, it would have scheduled or specifically named such diseases with an excluding clause as to all others. It cannot be presumed that the Legislature intended to grant relief to all sufferers of personal injury, or their dependents in case of death, who come within the provisions of the Workmen's Compensation Law, but to deny like relief to sufferers of disease, or their dependents in case of death, except in the case of unusual, uncommon, or special diseases . . . .

It is not the aim or purpose of the Act to set up an insurance plan or make the employer an insurer. *McGill Manufacturing Company (sic) v. Dodd, supra.* We cannot, by judicial pronouncement, declare it a source of employee compensation for all the "ills all human flesh is heir to." The interpretation we have herein placed upon the Act seems to us to be consonant with justice and the intent of the Legislature as expressed by the written Act, and in accord with the apparent leanings of our courts as indicated in their previous holdings. In all cases the claimant must establish that the disease of which he complains arose out of and in the course of his employment *under circumstances consistent with the requirements of subdivision (b) of § 6 of the Act.*[8]

The terms "disablement" and "disability" are defined in IC 22-3-7-9(e) as follows: " 'disablement' means the event of becoming disabled from earning full wages at the work in which the employee was engaged when last exposed to the hazards of the occupational disease by the employer from whom the employee claims compensation, or equal wages in other suitable employment; and 'disability' means the state of being so incapacitated."

It has repeatedly been held that "the mere contraction of an occupational disease does not entitle an employee to compensation. Disablement must ensue."[9] In its opinion in *McGinnis v. American Foundry Co.,*[10] the Indiana Court of Appeals discussed the nature of the term "disablement" within the context of this section of the Act. The court stated:

---

[8]McGinnis v. American Foundry Co., 128 Ind. App. 660, 149 N.E.2d 309, 312 (1958).

[9]Durham Mfg. Co. v. Hutchins, 115 Ind. App. 479, 58 N.E.2d 444 (1945).

[10]McGinnis v. American Foundry Co., 128 Ind. App. 660, 149 N.E.2d 309 (1958).

[T]he test of disablement prescribed by said § 40-2205(d) lies in the *disability to earn full wages* either at the work last engaged in by the employee for the employer from whom compensation is claimed or at other suitable employment affording equal wages with those paid by said charged employer. In other words, if the employee becomes so far disabled that he cannot work sufficiently to earn the full wages paid for the work in which he was last engaged for the employer liable for the compensation, or is so far disabled that he cannot work sufficiently in other suitable employment offering at least equal wages, said employee has suffered a disablement.

The time or date of such disablement, as provided in the Act, is the "event" of becoming so disabled . . . . (I)t seems clear that the event of disablement denotes the time when the happening of the inability of the employee to work and earn full wages occurs. The cause of the disability may be the occupational disease but the time or event of disability, as referred to in the statute, is not the time when the nature or kind of the occupational disease is discovered or made known, but the time or event when the employee becomes unable to earn full wages at the work in which he was last engaged or at other suitable work with equal wages.[11]

In *Spaulding v. International Bakers Services, Inc.*,[12] the Indiana Supreme Court discussed the differences in the term "disability" as it is applied to the Worker's Compensation Act, as opposed to its application in the Occupational Diseases Act. The Court stated:

Unlike the Worker's Compensation Act, the Occupational Diseases Act defines the terms "disablement" and "disability.". . .

It is evident that the legislature intended "disability" as defined in subsection 9(e) to be applied throughout chapter 7, which is the Occupational Diseases Act . . . . The intended meaning and application of "disability," however, require a closer examination of the Act . . . .

Subsection 9(e) defines "disability" only as the state of being disabled from earning full wages or equal wages in other suitable employment. This somewhat circular definition does not of itself indicate whether "disability" was intended to have an element of severity relevant to determining compensation.

We find that "disability" as used in the Occupational Diseases Act means a loss of wage-earning ability which has two distinct aspects: severity and duration. Clearly, temporary *total* disability and temporary *partial* disability are distinguishable in the severity of the loss of wage-earning ability. Likewise, *temporary* total disability differs from total *permanent* disability in duration.

We therefore conclude that, under the Occupational Diseases Act,

---

[11]McGinnis v. American Foundry Co., 128 Ind. App. 660, 149 N.E.2d 309, 312 (1958).

[12]Spaulding v. International Bakers Services, Inc., 550 N.E.2d 307 (Ind. 1990).

"disability" refers to the loss of wage-earning ability and that entitlement to compensation for "total permanent disability" rests upon a showing that a claimant is permanently unable to earn any wages at his or her last work or in "other suitable employment." Ind. Code § 22-3-7-9(e).

While such a determination may involve considerations similar to those used in assessing "total permanent disability" under the Worker's Compensation Act, they need not be identical. Under the Worker's Compensation Act, "disability" relates to the capacity to work, but as defined in the Occupational Diseases Act its *sine qua non* is the capacity to earn wages. While barely distinguishable, we are not prepared to declare that these standards will never require different results under appropriate facts.[13]

Mark May worked at Ashley Ward, a machine shop, from 1997 to 2005. In 2004 he began having headaches and coughing up blood. In early 2005 a large tumor was discovered in his sphenoid sinus. May underwent chemotherapy and radiation therapy. His treatment and the side effects of his illness left him totally disabled. The Worker's Compensation Board denied his Application for Adjustment of Claim, stating that he did not prove that his sphenoid cancer was the result of an accident which arose out of and in the course of employment with the defendant, and that this was not an occupational disease situation. The Court of Appeals, in reversing the Board,[14] stated the evidence pointed to the fact that the only expert who testified in the case opined that May's cancer resulted from exposure to the heavy metal during the grinding process at work. The employer argued May could not have seen any airborne dust particles and had no evidence that he inhaled the metal dust particles through his nose during the course of employment. However, the Court of Appeals held that "it strains reason" to conclude that May failed to establish he was exposed to activated heavy metals in the work place. The evidence revealed that for the first several years May worked at the facility with no ventilation or vacuum system and the whole room was covered with dust even after new grinders were obtained the employer took about six months to install a vacuum system. Further, the employees were never required to wear respirators. The Court of Appeals next pointed to evidence that Plaintiff provided expert testimony linking the workplace exposure to the sinus cancer which is an uncommon type of cancer. As such, the Court of Appeals reversed the Board's finding of fact and awarded benefits in this matter.

---

[13]Spaulding v. International Bakers Services, Inc., 550 N.E.2d 307, 309–10 (Ind. 1990). See also Zike v. Onkyo Mfg., Inc., 622 N.E.2d 1055 (Ind. Ct. App. 1993); Hurd v. Monsanto Co., 908 F. Supp. 604 (S.D. Ind. 1995), aff'd in part, 107 F.3d 873 (7th Cir. 1997).

[14]May v. Ashley F. Ward, Inc., 952 N.E.2d 224 (Ind. Ct. App. 2011), transfer denied, 962 N.E.2d 651 (Ind. 2011).

§ 7:3 Occupational diseases—Applicability of chapter

The occupational disease sections of the worker's compensation laws have a slightly different application than do their counterparts in the Worker's Compensation Act. The definition of "employer" contained in IC 22-3-7-9(a) is the same as that contained in IC 22-3-6-1(a). However, the definition of "employee" contains a few notable differences. While the essential definition of an "employee," contained in IC 22-3-7-9(b), is the same as that contained in IC 22-3-6-1(b), there is no mention in the former of an executive officer of a corporation or municipal corporation, or of a member or manager of a limited liability corporation. Members of the Indiana General Assembly and field examiners of the state Board of Accounts are not specifically included within the coverage of the occupational disease sections as they are in the Worker's Compensation Act, pursuant to IC 22-3-2-2(h). Volunteer workers are not mentioned in the occupational disease sections.

As with the worker's compensation sections, the same railroad employees engaged in train service, enumerated in IC 22-3-2-2(b)(1) to (7), are excluded from coverage under the occupational disease sections, but, in addition, so are "their employers with respect to these employees."[1] The occupational disease sections do not apply to casual laborers, farm or agricultural employees, household employees, nor to "employees or their employers with respect to employments in which the laws of the United States provide for compensation or liability for injury to the health, disability, or death by reason of diseases suffered by these employees."[2] Police and fire department employees of municipal corporations are treated similarly under the occupational disease sections and the Worker's Compensation Act.[3]

The occupational disease sections do apply to school-to-work students under the School to Work Opportunities Act, and, in that respect, the provisions of IC 22-3-7-2.5 mirror IC 22-3-2-2.5. In addition, an "unpaid participant" in the federal program is an "employee to the extent set forth under section 2.5 of this chapter."

The waiver of exemption and notice provisions contained in IC 22-3-7-3(a) and (b) are essentially the same as those found in IC 22-3-2-9(b), (c), and (d). IC 22-3-7-5, which makes the chapter compulsory to the state, all political divisions thereof, coal mine

---

[Section 7:3]

   [1]See IC 22-3-7-9(d).

   [2]IC 22-3-7-9(d).

   [3]See IC 22-3-7-2(c) to (f), IC 22-3-2-2(c), (e), (f), and (g).

operators, and their respective employees, is essentially the same as IC 22-3-2-18 of the Worker's Compensation Act.

§ 7:4 Occupational diseases—Exclusivity

The exclusivity provision of the Worker's Compensation Act (IC 22-3-2-6) and the exclusivity provision contained in the occupational disease sections (IC 22-3-7-6) read essentially the same. The provisions have, however, received a different application by the Indiana Supreme Court. In *Baker v. Westinghouse Elec. Corp.*,[1] a federal district court asked whether there is an intentional tort exception to the exclusivity provisions of the Worker's Compensation Act and the Occupational Diseases Act. The Court responded by holding that the Worker's Compensation Act, by its terms, does not bar certain intentional tort actions, but the Occupational Diseases Act does. The Court stated:

> The Indiana General Assembly has established worker's compensation as an exclusive remedy for employment-related personal injury or death which occurs "by accident." It has not, however, placed such a limitation on the scope of the Occupational Diseases Act. Because injuries intentionally inflicted by an employer are not "by accident," suits arising therefrom are not barred by the compensation act. Conversely, intentionally injured employees who otherwise satisfy the requirements of the Occupational Diseases Act have their exclusive remedy therein. That act contains no "by accident" requirement, and it is beyond the province of the courts to create one . . . .

> This language [of IC 22-3-7-6] essentially tracks that of the Worker's Compensation Act, with the obvious exception that the "by accident" requirement has been omitted and "by occupational disease" substituted in its place. We have concluded that the "by accident" language in the compensation act embodies the legislature's decision that intentionally inflicted personal injuries may be remedied through common law litigation. The absence of this language from the ODA, coupled with the nature of the injuries recognized therein, suggest that the legislature viewed the occupational diseases scheme as the only forum in which those injuries, intentionally inflicted or not, might be compensated.

> In reaching this conclusion, we have considered the possibility that the phrase "by occupational disease" contains a non-intentionality requirement, a possibility which might complement the remedial purposes of the ODA and harmonize it with various components of the worker protection scheme . . . .

> [W]e conclude that the section's "by occupational disease" language is designed to reinforce and explain the requirement that there be a causal connection between any disablement or death suf-

---

[Section 7:4]

[1]Baker v. Westinghouse Elec. Corp., 637 N.E.2d 1271 (Ind. 1994).

fered and the employment, a requirement which is also embodied in the exclusivity section's "arising out of and in the course of employment" component. This causation requirement exists independent of the circumstances by which any given pathogen came to be present in the workplace, including the fact that it was intentionally introduced. Thus, where an employee's disease *was in fact* caused by exposure to the hazards actually posed by a given employment situation, this requirement has been satisfied. *Id.* at page 687, 112 N.E.2d at 225; *see also House v. D.P.D., Inc.* (1988), Ind. App., 519 N.E.2d 1274. This is so even where the employer knows to a certainty that disease will eventually result from a hazard, at least so long as that hazard is incidental to the character of the business and not outside the employer-employee relationship. *Cf.* Ind. Code Ann. § 22-3-7-10(b) (West 1991).

The plaintiffs in the action before the District Court assert in their brief to us that "there is no logical rationale which would warrant a preemption of the cause of action for an intentional tort which results in a disease, while preserving the same cause of action in cases of injury." This is an argument for amending the statute. The legislature might have considered a specialized administrative body better able to resolve questions of liability for occupational disease, whether intentionally caused or not, given the "slow, creeping, insidious" nature of the injury at issue. Moreover, the sheer improbability that a corporate employer would adopt policies through its regular decision-making channels which were intentionally calculated to disease its employees may explain the failure to provide for such an eventuality.

The Occupational Diseases Act does not make any exception for diseases intentionally occasioned, and it was within the authority of the legislature to formulate such a scheme.[2]

IC 22-3-7-7 (Employers and employees not relieved from statutory duties or penalties) and IC 22-3-7-8 (Injury or death occurring outside state) contain essentially the same language as IC 22-3-2-7 and IC 22-3-2-20, respectively.

§ 7:5 Occupational diseases—Definitions; statutes of repose

As stated previously, comparisons between the language employed in IC 22-3-7-9 and IC 22-3-6-1 will show some similarities (the definition of "employer," for example) and some differences. The definition of "minor" in IC 22-3-7-9(c) is essentially the same as that contained in IC 22-3-6-1(c), however, there are a few subtle distinctions. For occupational disease purposes, there is no qualification of "unless otherwise provided in this subsection" prior to the statement that "a minor employee shall be considered as being of full age for all purposes of this

---

[2]Baker v. Westinghouse Elec. Corp., 637 N.E.2d 1271, 1272, (Ind. 1994). See also Buford v. American Tel. & Tel. Co., 881 F.2d 432 (7th Cir. 1989).

chapter." Furthermore, if a minor is employed in violation of the Indiana child labor laws (i.e., IC 20-33-3-35), the employer shall be *wholly* liable for one-half of the compensation or benefits that may be payable on account of the minor's disability or death. The phrase "wholly liable" does not appear in IC 22-3-6-1(c). Finally, the definition of "minor" for worker's compensation purposes specifically includes "a minor employee who, at the time of the accident, is a student performing services for an employer as part of an approved program under IC 20-37-2-7," which relates to certain educational, vocational, or technical training programs.[1] That particular category of individuals is not mentioned in the definition of "minor" for purposes of occupational disease coverage.

IC 22-3-7-9(f) contains specific statutes of repose not found in the Worker's Compensation Act. It is provided therein that no compensation shall be payable for or on account of any occupational diseases unless disablement occurs within two years after the last day of the last exposure to the hazards of the disease, except for the following:

(1) In all cases of occupational diseases caused by the inhalation of silica dust or coal dust, disablement must occur within three years after the last day of the last exposure to the hazards of the disease.

(2) In all cases of occupational disease caused by the exposure to radiation, disablement must occur within two years from the date on which the employee had knowledge of the nature of his or her occupational disease or, by exercise of reasonable diligence, should have known of the existence of such disease and its causal relationship to his or her employment.

(3) In all cases of occupational diseases caused by the inhalation of asbestos dust, disablement must occur within three years after the last day of the last exposure to the hazards of the disease if the last day of the last exposure was before July 1, 1985.

(4) If the last date of the last exposure to the hazards of the disease resulting from the inhalation of asbestos dust occurred on or after July 1, 1985, and before July 1, 1988, disablement must occur within 20 years after the last day of the last exposure.

(5) If the last date of the last exposure to the hazards of the disease resulting from the inhalation of asbestos dust occurred on or after July 1, 1988, disablement must occur within 35 years after the last day of the last exposure.

[Section 7:5]

[1]See IC 22-3-6-1(c)(3).

The case of *Stytle v. Angola Die Casting Co.*,[2] presented a constitutional challenge to the two-year statute of repose contained in the Occupational Diseases Act. There, Stytle alleged that he suffered from aluminum poisoning which arose out of and in the course of his employment. It was not disputed that he was disabled, that his disablement occurred more than two years after the last day of his last exposure to the hazards of his disease, and that his claim was barred by the application of IC 22-3-7-9(f). The board, thus, dismissed his claim, and the court of appeals affirmed. In doing so, the court stated the following:

> Strictly speaking, Indiana Code § 22-3-7-9(f) is a statute of repose, rather than a statute of limitation. As we explained in *Kissel v. Rosenbaum,* 579 N.E.2d 1322 (Ind. Ct. App. 1991).

> "A statute of limitation requires a lawsuit to be filed within a specified period of time after a legal right has been violated. In contrast, a statute of repose is designed to bar actions after a specified period of time has run from the occurrence of some event other than the injury which gave rise to the claim. A statute of repose might theoretically bar a claim filed within the period allowed by the applicable statute of limitation. A statute of limitation extinguishes a remedy while a statute of repose may bar a cause of action even before it arises. In practical terms, a statute of repose marks the boundary of a substantive right whereas a statute of limitation interposes itself only procedurally to bar a remedy after a substantive right has vested. A statute of limitation implicitly seeks to punish those who sleep on their rights, while a statute of repose operates to bar some recoveries no matter how diligently the claim may have been asserted . . . . The statute of repose appears to bar claims, not because of disappearance of evidence but because of the passage of a stated amount of time within which the legislature has, for public policy reasons, deemed it appropriate to bring the claim, regardless of when the claim accrues. In this manner, the statute of repose also advances the statute of limitations policies of the peace, welfare, convenience, necessity, and well-being of society . . . .

> Statutes of repose are based upon considerations of the economic best interests of the public as a whole and are substantive grants of immunity based upon a legislative balance of the respective rights of potential plaintiffs and defendants struck by determining a time limit beyond which liability no longer exists. Thus, a statute of repose is typically an absolute time limit beyond which liability no longer exists and is not tolled for any reason because to do so would upset the economic balance struck by the legislative body." *Id.* at 1326–28 (citations omitted).

The requirement of Indiana Code § 22-3-7-9(f) that disablement occur within two years "after the last day of the last exposure to the hazards of the disease" is a condition precedent to the right to seek compensation under the ODA. *Cf. Durham Mfg. Co. v. Hutchins,* 115 Ind. App. 479, 483, 58 N.E.2d 444, 446 (1945) ("[T]he mere

---

[2]Stytle v. Angola Die Casting Co., 806 N.E.2d 339 (Ind. Ct. App. 2004).

contraction of an occupational disease does not entitle the workman to compensation. The *sine qua non* is disablement."), *trans. denied.*

Indiana Code § 22-3-7-32(c), a statute of limitation, bars the bringing of a compensation claim more than two years after disablement occurs . . . .

Our court is ill-equipped to determine as a matter of law whether a discovery rule for work-related exposure to certain substances is warranted on the basis of a cold and meager administrative record, and we are likewise ill-equipped to determine an appropriate period of repose. As the *Bunker* court astutely observed, such determinations are properly reserved for the legislature. In light of these considerations and the circumstances of this case, we cannot conclude that a two-year period of repose is so manifestly insufficient that it represents a denial of justice.

We therefore hold that Indiana Code § 22-3-7-9(f) is not unconstitutional as applied to Stytle, who did not become disabled from alleged work-related aluminum poisoning until eight years after he was last exposed to aluminum as an Angola employee. Consequently, we affirm the Board's dismissal of Stytle's application as time-barred.[3]

In Harris v. United Water Services, Inc.,[4] an employee claimed that he was exposed to bacteria that caused illness while in the employ of United Water Services, Inc. He filed his claim with the Worker's Compensation Board and United Water Services filed a motion to dismiss arguing that Harris' symptoms all stemmed from a particular incident where he was splashed in the face with waste water more than two years before the filing of his application. As such, the employer's position was that Harris was claiming a worker's compensation, not occupational disease claim, and his application was untimely filed. The Board granted the employer's motion to dismiss finding that in his deposition testimony. Harris admitted that his problems began with the waste water incident more than two years before his application was filed. In reversing the Board, the Court of Appeals held that the Board erred by concluding that Harris admitted that his problems began with the waste water splash incident. The Court pointed to Harris' deposition testimony that he only suspected he first became infected with the splash, but he was always exposed to bacteria and could have contracted it at any time. The Court remanded the case to the Board so that a hearing on the merits could be conducted to determine whether Harris suffered accidental injury on the date that he was splashed in the face by waste water or he suffered disablement by occupational disease giving him two years after his date of disablement, as long as

---

[3]Stytle v. Angola Die Casting Co., 806 N.E.2d 339, 342–43, (Ind. Ct. App. 2004). See also Bunker v. National Gypsum Co., 441 N.E.2d 8 (Ind. 1982).

[4]Harris v. United Water Services, Inc., 946 N.E.2d 35 (Ind. Ct. App. 2011).

disablement occurs with two years from the last date of exposure, to file his claim with the Board.

§ 7:6 Occupational diseases—Death

IC 22-3-7-9(g) provides that no compensation is payable for or on account of death resulting from any occupational disease unless death occurs within two years after the date of disablement. However, compensation for death is not barred: (1) where an employee has filed a claim within two years after the date of disablement and death occurs during the pendency of the claim; or (2) where, by agreement filed or decision rendered, a compensable period of disability has been fixed and death occurs within two years after the end of such fixed period, but in no event later than 300 weeks after the date of disablement.

The current provision relating to the payment of death benefits occasioned by occupational disease, found in IC 22-3-7-11, is essentially the same as the death benefit provision found in IC 22-3-3-17 of the Worker's Compensation Act. The classifications of dependents, and definitions of dependency, and the respective rights of dependents to receive compensation, as set forth in IC 22-3-7-12, IC 22-3-7-13, and IC 22-3-7-14, are the same as those set forth in IC 22-3-3-18, IC 22-3-3-19, and IC 22-3-3-20. The question of partial dependency is to be determined at the time of disablement under the occupational disease sections.

The burial expense benefit provided in IC 22-3-7-15 is the same as the benefit set forth in IC 22-3-3-21.

§ 7:7 Occupational diseases—Disability; impairment; payments

The occupational disease compensation schedules for disability and impairment are set forth in IC 22-3-7-16. This one section of the Act is comprised of 11 consecutive pages of text, and it includes matters extending beyond the compensation schedules. The provisions contained therein are, for the most part, similar to those contained in the following sections of the Worker's Compensation Act: IC 22-3-3-7 to IC 22-3-3-12; IC 22-3-3-14 to IC 22-3-3-16; IC 22-3-3-23(a); IC 22-3-3-24; IC 22-3-3-28; and IC 22-3-3-29. However, there are several differences, which are discussed below.

IC 22-3-7-16(a) and (e) provide for essentially the same compensation "on account of disablement from occupational disease" resulting in only temporary total or temporary partial disability to work as "on account of injuries," as set forth in IC 22-3-3-7(a) and (b), and IC 22-3-3-8. However, unlike IC 22-3-3-8, IC 22-3-7-16(e) contains no mention of "total permanent disability." Also, the payment of compensation, pursuant to IC 22-3-7-16(e), is premised upon the fact that the disabled employee is temporarily totally disabled from performing "any work."

IC 22-3-7-16(b), pertaining to the termination of TTD benefits, is essentially the same as IC 22-3-3-7(c). However, in IC 22-3-7-16(b)(1), it is provided that TTD benefits may be terminated if the employee has returned "to work." In IC 22-3-3-7(c)(1), TTD benefits may be terminated if the employee has returned "to any employment." That may be a distinction without a difference. IC 22-3-3-7(c)(3) allows for the termination of TTD benefits if the employee "has refused to accept suitable employment under . . . IC 22-3-3-11." No such provision appears in IC 22-3-7-16(b).

The current impairment schedules for disablements begin with IC 22-3-7-16(k). They essentially track the current impairment schedules contained in IC 22-3-3-10(i) of the Worker's Compensation Act, but subsection (2) is different. IC 22-3-3-10(i)(2) provides:

> Amputations: For the loss by separation of any of the body parts described in subdivision (1) on or after July 1, 1997, and for the loss by separation of any of the body parts described in subdivision (3) [phalange of thumb, finger, or toe], (5) [permanent and complete loss of vision by enucleation], or (8) [testicle(s)], on or after July 1, 1999, the dollar values per degree applying on the date of the injury as described in subsection (j) shall be multiplied by two (2). However, the doubling provision of this subdivision does not apply to a loss of use that is not a loss by separation.

IC 22-3-7-16(k)(2) provides:

> Amputations occurring on or after July 1, 1997: For the loss by separation of any of the body parts described in subdivision (1) on or after July 1, 1997, the dollar values per degree applying on the date of the injury as described in subsection (l) shall be multiplied by two (2). However, the doubling provision of this subdivision does not apply to a loss of use that is not a loss by separation.

As can be seen, the latter does not specifically refer to phalanges of the thumb, finger or toe, loss of vision by enucleation, or testicles. Since subdivision (1) of IC 22-3-7-16(k) does not mention these body parts either, it would appear that the doubling provision of (k)(2) has no application to a loss by separation of those particular parts of the body.

IC 22-3-7-16(o) to (r) deal with subsequent disabilities, disablements, permanent disabilities, and death, respectively. While the language of the subsections is somewhat different, the compensation scheme is essentially the same as contained in IC 22-3-3-12, IC 22-3-3-14, IC 22-3-3-15, and IC 22-3-3-16.

IC 22-3-7-16(v) is essentially the same provision as IC 22-3-3-28(b), however, with respect to the former, the Board has the authority to make payment to a minor directly.

IC 22-3-7-16(w) is more expansive than IC 22-3-3-29. The former provides that "[i]f an employee, or a dependent, is mentally incompetent, or a minor at the time when any right or privilege accrues to the employee under this chapter, the employee's guardian or trustee may, in the employee's behalf, claim and exercise such right and privilege." The latter provides that "if any injured employee or a dependent is under guardianship at the time when any right or privilege accrues to the employee or dependent . . . the employee or dependent's guardian shall claim and exercise the right or privilege of the employee or dependent." The worker's compensation provision allows a guardian, previously appointed, to protect the interests of an injured employee or dependent; the occupational disease provision seems to allow for the appointment of a guardian to protect the interests of either an employee or a dependent who is either mentally incompetent or a minor.

IC 22-3-7-16(x) reads, as follows: "All compensation payments named and provided for in this section, shall mean and be defined to be for only such occupational diseases and disabilities therefrom as are proved by competent evidence, of which there are or have been objective conditions or symptoms proven, not within the physical or mental control of the employee." No such extensive burden of proof requirement is to be found in the Worker's Compensation Act.

In *Walter Bledsoe & Co. v. Baker*,[1] an occupational disease claim was made based upon the employee's multi-year exposure to clay and coal dust. The expert medical witnesses who testified disagreed with respect to whether or not the claimant's lung condition and resulting disability were causally connected to his employment. The board awarded compensation, and the employer appealed. In affirming the board's award, the appellate court stated:

> The appellant insists the appellee failed to discharge his burden of proving there was an occupational disease health hazard in his employment, with resulting disabling occupational disease; that Dr. Sappington was the only competent witness on the question of the existence of an occupational health hazard; that he testified none such existed; and his testimony being uncontradicted we must reverse as a matter of law.
>
> We cannot agree. Those versed in the relevant sciences may disagree concerning the condition that would or could produce an occupational disease in a workman who has been exposed to such conditions. The testimony of such scientist is entitled to the careful consideration of the trier of the facts. Nevertheless, this court is committed to the doctrine that a workman does not have the burden of proving an exposure which meets the requirements of any particular scientific formula in order to recover. Neither is the workmen's

---

[Section 7:7]

[1]Walter Bledsoe & Co. v. Baker, 119 Ind. App. 147, 83 N.E.2d 620 (1949).

case destroyed, as a matter of law, by the opinion of an expert produced by the employer, that no occupational disease health hazard existed at the place of employment, even though such opinion may be based on tests conducted by such expert witness. We have held that when the evidence most favorable to the workman shows a long exposure to disease producing dust as a consequence of his employment, and further shows that he is afflicted with the disease, such evidence will support the inference that the disease producing dust was present in sufficient quantity and concentration to account for his affliction. *Inland Steel Co. v. Voutos*, 1948, Ind. App., 77 N.E.2d 126; *Harbison-Walker Refractories Co. v. Turks*, 1942, 110 Ind. App. 563, 39 N.E.2d 791; *Harbison-Walker Refractories Co. v. Harmon*, 1943, 114 Ind. App. 144, 51 N.E.2d 398.[2]

The definition of "average weekly wages" found in IC 22-3-7-19(u) is slightly different than the definition appearing in IC 22-3-6-1(d). The former states that "[f]or all disabilities occurring on and after July 1, 1985, 'average weekly wages' means the earnings of the injured employee during the period of fifty-two (52) weeks immediately preceding the disability divided by fifty-two (52)." The latter is more explicit and restrictive. It defines the term as "the earnings of the injured employee in the employment in which the employee was working at the time of the injury during the period of fifty-two (52) weeks immediately preceding the date of injury, divided by fifty-two (52), except as follows: . . . ." Four subsections follow which detail the manner in which an average weekly wage is to be computed. With one exception (calculating an average weekly wage for a student employee), those same subsections are also contained in IC 22-3-7-19(u).

Currently, computing compensation for TTD, TPD, and PTD based on one's average weekly wage is to be found in IC 22-3-7-19(j)(11)(A) and (B). That section is essentially the same as IC 22-3-3-22(j)(11)(A) and (B), and the dollar amounts specified therein are exactly the same.

Although the dollar values are the same, the wording of IC 22-3-7-19(t)(11) is different from that contained in IC 22-3-3-22(t)(11). The former states that "[t]he maximum compensation that shall be paid for occupational disease and the results of an occupational disease under this chapter or under any combination of the provisions of this chapter may not exceed the following amounts in any case . . . $347,000." The same provision in the Worker's Compensation Act states: "The maximum compensation, exclusive of medical benefits, that may be paid for an injury under any provision of this law or any combination of provisions may not exceed the following amounts in any case: . . . $347,000." Although it is not as clearly stated, it is likely that the legislature

---

[2]Walter Bledsoe & Co. v Baker, 119 Ind. App. 147, 83 N.E.2d 620, 621–22 (1949).

intended that, for occupational disease purposes, compensation and medical benefits are not one and the same, are to be treated separately and distinctly, and, therefore, there was no need to place the exclusionary language in IC 22-3-7-19(t)(11).

IC 22-3-7-19(v) sets a limit on the number of weeks (500) benefits can be paid (absent an application by one permanently totally disabled for admission to the Second Injury Fund) and a minimum total benefit for permanent total disability resulting from a disablement. The wording of this section is essentially the same as that contained in IC 22-3-3-32.

The lump sum payment provision contained in IC 22-3-7-18(a) is completely different than that contained in the Worker's Compensation Act (IC 22-3-3-25). The former states that:

> Any employer or employee or beneficiary who shall desire to have such compensation, or any unpaid part thereof, paid in a lump sum, may petition the . . . board, asking that such compensation be so paid, and if, upon proper notice to the interested parties, and a proper showing made before the . . . board, or any member thereof, it appears to the best interest of the parties that such compensation be so paid, the . . . board may order the commutation of the compensation to an equivalent lump sum, which commutation shall be an amount which will equal the total sum of the probable future payments capitalized at their present value upon the basis of interest calculated at three percent (3%) per year with annual rests. In cases indicating complete disability, no petition for a commutation to a lump sum basis shall be entertained by the board until after the expiration of six (6) months from the date of the disablement.

IC 22-3-3-25 pertains to "unusual cases." It requires the "agreement of the employer and the employee or his dependents, and the insurance carrier." There is contained therein a specific provision relating to minors. Finally, the commutation calculation is worded differently.

The trustee provision contained in IC 22-3-7-18(b) is essentially the same as that contained in IC 22-3-3-26.

In Bush v. Robinson Engineering and Oil Co.,[3] the employee suffered an injury he believed was to his low back. He received benefits and was paid TTD. At the end of his period of TTD he requested and received an independent medical examination which was performed by Dr. Sasso. Dr. Sasso noted that all of symptoms complained of were related to the work injury, and he ordered an MRI of the cervical and lumbar spines. The lumbar spine was negative; however, the cervical spine showed a need for further evaluation. The employer refused to provide the additional evaluation arguing there had been no mention of a neck injury in the record before the independent medical examination.

---

[3]Bush v. Robinson Engineering & Oil, Co., Inc., 54 N.E.3d 1073 (Ind. Ct. App. 2016).

The employee argued that Dr. Sasso was in the best position to determine whether a particular symptom is related to a work incident, and that the Board should defer to its duly appointed physician. The Board found that the employee was not entitled to the evaluation and treatment recommended by the Board IME.

At the Court of Appeals, the employee argued that an independent medical examination, when it is appointed pursuant to IC 22-3-3-7(c), creates a rebuttable presumption that the opinion of the independent medical examiner is correct. Further, the employer did not offer any post IME opinion rebutting Dr. Sasso's report. The Court, in affirming the Board, held that IC 22-3-3-7(c), (d) do not create rebuttable presumption in favor of the opinion of the independent medical examination because the plain language of the statute establishes the right of either party to disagree with the opinion and request a hearing.

§ 7:8 Occupational diseases—Medical services and examinations

IC 22-3-7-17, IC 22-3-7-17.1, IC 22-3-7-17.2, and IC 22-3-7-24(d), pertaining to the furnishing of medical services, contain essentially the same language as found in IC 22-3-3-4, IC 22-3-3-5, IC 22-3-3-5.1, and IC 22-3-3-5.2. However, in IC 22-3-3-5, the following language appears: "The pecuniary liability of the employer for medical, surgical, hospital and nurse service herein required shall be limited to such charges as prevail as provided under IC 22-3-6-1(j), in the same community (as defined in IC 22-3-6-1(h)) for a like service or product to injured persons." No such language appears in the occupational disease sections of the Act. In all likelihood, the General Assembly must have felt that such language was superfluous and unnecessary, since the definition of "pecuniary liability" contained in IC 22-3-7-9(m) is essentially the same as that contained in IC 22-3-6-1(k), the definitions of "community" contained in IC 22-3-7-9(j) and IC 22-3-6-1(h) are the same, and the definitions are broad enough to convey the essence of the omitted provision.

IC 22-3-3-5 is amended as follows: subsection (a) now reads:

(a) The pecuniary liability of the employer for a service or product herein required shall be limited to the following:

(1) This subdivision applies before July 1, 2014, to all medical service providers, and after June 30, 2014, to a medical service provider that is not a medical service facility. Such charges as prevail as provided under IC 22-3-6-1(k)(1), in the same community (as defined in IC 22-3-6-1(h)) for a like service or product to injured persons.

(2) This subdivision applies after June 30, 2014, to a medical service facility. The amount provided under IC 22-3-6-1(k)(2).

and subsection (c) and (d) now read:

(c) The right to order payment for all services or products provided under IC 22-3-2 through IC 22-3-6 is solely with the board.

(d) All claims by a medical service provider for payment for services or products are against the employer and the employer's insurance carrier, if any, and must be made with the board under IC 22-3-2 through IC 22-3-6. After June 30, 2011, a medical service provider must file an application for adjustment of a claim for a medical service provider's fee with the board not later than two (2) years after the receipt of an initial written communication from the employer, the employer's insurance carrier, if any, or an agent acting on behalf of the employer after the medical service provider submits a bill for services or products. To offset a part of the board's expenses related to the administration of medical service provider reimbursement disputes, a medical service facility shall pay a filing fee of sixty dollars ($60) in a balance billing case. The filing fee must accompany each application filed with the board. If an employer, an employer's insurance carrier, or an agent acting on behalf of the employer denies or fails to pay any amount on a claim submitted by a medical service facility, a filing fee is not required to accompany an application that is filed for the denied or unpaid claim. A medical service provider may combine up to ten (10) individual claims into one (1) application whenever:

(1) all individual claims involve the same employer, insurance carrier, or billing review service; and

(2) the amount of each individual claim does not exceed two hundred dollars ($200).

The opinion (upon rehearing) of the court of appeals in the case of *Bloomington Hosp. v. Stofko*,[1] provides some insight into the manner in which future medical expenses may be awarded. The court stated:

The interpretation urged by the Hospital is that sections 22-3-7-17 and 22-3-7-27 apply in every instance in which medical expenses are sought, regardless of the stage of the proceedings at which they are awarded. Moreover, the Hospital contends that the statutes limit the Board's jurisdiction to awarding the furnishing of medical treatment for one year from the first day for which compensation was paid for an employee's permanent partial impairment. Thus, the Board would have had the jurisdiction to order the Hospital to furnish medical treatment to Stofko only until August 24, 1994, which was one year from the first day for which he was paid permanent partial impairment compensation. However, Stofko's Applica-

_____

[Section 7:8]

[1]Bloomington Hosp. v. Stofko, 709 N.E.2d 1078 (Ind. Ct. App. 1999).

tion for Adjustment of Claim was not filed until August 10, 1995, which was within the statutory two year time limit for filing a claim, and the agreement between Stofko and the Hospital setting forth the impairment rating and compensation award and *specifically reserving the issue of future medical treatment* was not filed until March 31, 1997. Because worker's compensation is paid in arrears, relating back to the date of disablement, the Hospital's interpretation would have precluded Stofko from receiving medical expenses one year before he was even required to file his claim and nearly three years before he knew for what time frame he would ultimately be compensated. It is this result which we find incomprehensible.

In addition to requiring an impossible degree of foresight from applicants for worker's compensation benefits, the Hospital's interpretation ignores the language of Indiana Code section 22-3-7-17(b) which requires an employer to furnish medical services at least until the employee's occupational disease has been adjudicated by agreement or award. In this case, Stofko's occupational disease was not fully adjudicated until the Board's award on July 31, 1998. Only if the Board had not awarded future medical expenses to Stofko on that date would any time limitations contained in the statutes have become relevant.

The award of future medical expenses in favor of Stofko remains affirmed . . . .[2]

The language of IC 22-3-7-20, providing for medical examinations and autopsies, is essentially the same as that employed in IC 22-3-3-6.

§ 7:9 Occupational diseases—Bars to compensation

IC 22-3-7-21(a) provides that "[n]o compensation is allowed for any condition of physical or mental ill-being, disability, disablement, or death for which compensation is recoverable on account of accidental injury under chapters 2 through 6 of this article." No similar provision appears in the Worker's Compensation Act, and this simply appears to be a memorialization by the General Assembly that "injury by accident" and "disablement caused by occupational disease" are separate and distinct concepts.

IC 22-3-7-21(b) is essentially the same as IC 22-3-2-8; the misconduct which bars a claim for compensation under the worker's compensation sections will also bar a claim for compensation under the occupational disease sections.

§ 7:10 Occupational diseases—Administration

IC 22-3-7-22, which provides for the establishment of the

---

[2]Bloomington Hosp. v. Stofko, 709 N.E.2d 1078, 1079 (Ind. Ct. App. 1999). See also 705 N.E.2d 515 for the original opinion of the court of appeals.

Board's offices and the payment of its expenses, is essentially the same provisions as those contained in IC 22-3-1-1(h) and (i) and IC 22-3-4-1. However, in subsection (a), there is a requirement that travel expenses be sworn to by the person who incurs them, and, in subsection (b), the requirement that "[a]ll salaries . . . of the board" be audited has been deleted.

IC 22-3-7-23 provides:

> The worker's compensation board shall have jurisdiction over the operation and administration of the compensation provisions of this chapter, the board shall perform all of the duties imposed upon it by the provisions of this chapter, and such further duties as may be imposed by law and the rules of the board not inconsistent with this chapter.

The essence of the jurisdictional grant of authority to the board to administer the occupational disease sections of the worker's compensation law is similar to that expressed in IC 22-3-1-2 and IC 22-3-1-3, but the language employed is altogether different.

IC 22-3-7-24(a), which empowers the board to make its own rules and establish processes and procedures for carrying out its duties under the occupational disease sections of the law, outlines essentially the same provisions as found in IC 22-3-4-2(a), (b) and (c). Subsection (b) of IC 22-3-7-24, provides that the board has the authority to approve the fees of attorneys, physicians, nurses and hospitals. The "bad faith" language of IC 22-3-4-12 has been deleted from this subsection, but it is included in subsection (c) of IC 22-3-7-24, along with additional language which directs the board to impose a minimum attorney fee of $150 "on account of a lack of diligence or because of bad faith on the part of the employer." It should be noted here that the "lack of diligence . . . bad faith, (and) . . . independent tort" provisions contained in IC 22-3-4-12.1, and the potentially substantial pecuniary penalties which may be awarded for a violation of that section, are nowhere contained in the occupational disease sections of the worker's compensation law. Certainly, the omission had to have been an oversight, since it is inconceivable and incomprehensible that "bad faith" in adjusting or settling a worker's compensation claim could give rise to a substantial monetary penalty, including attorney fees, but that the same misconduct in adjusting or settling an occupational disease claim could not.

IC 22-3-7-25 regarding the board's forms and records in essentially the same provisions contained in IC 22-3-4-3(a).

IC 22-3-7-26 involving "disputes arising under this chapter" is essentially the same provision found in IC 22-3-4-5(c). Curiously, the General Assembly has excepted disputes arising under IC 22-3-7-3 regarding waivers of exemption and notice thereof. While such disputes may indeed be rare, if the board has no authority to resolve those disputes, who does?

IC 22-3-7-27(a), regarding disagreements and disputes between the parties, is similar to the language employed in IC 22-3-4-5(a). However, the concluding sentence of the subsection is newly added. It provides: "When compensation which is payable in accordance with an award or by agreement approved by the board is ordered paid in a lump sum by the board, no review shall be had as in this subsection mentioned." A similar provision is contained in subsection (i) of IC 22-3-7-27. It provides that "[w]hen compensation which is payable in accordance with an award *or settlement contract* approved by the board is ordered paid in a lump sum by the board, no review shall be had as in this subsection mentioned." (Emphasis added). This appears to be a rather radical departure from past practice and procedure. Perhaps cases involving disputes over lump sum payments are— and will in the future be—rare; however, it appears that, if a single hearing member orders a compensation payment made in a lump sum, the order is not reviewable by the full board. Could an argument then be made that, since other subsections refer to appeals from full board awards, no appeal is allowed with respect to an award of a single hearing member ordering payment in a lump sum? Do the parties have no right to have such an award reviewable by the full board or appealed to an appellate court? It could be argued that the language of this subsection supports the proposition that they have no such right of review or to an appeal.

Subsection (b) of IC 22-3-7-27 has no counterpart in the worker's compensation sections. It provides that an application making claim for compensation must state: (1) the approximate date of the last day of the last exposure and the approximate date of the disablement; (2) the general nature and character of the illness or disease claimed; (3) the name and address of the employer by whom employed on the last day of the last exposure, and, if employed by any other employer after such last exposure and before disablement, the name and address of such other employer or employers; and (4) in case of death, the date and place thereof. This subsection also authorizes the board, in its discretion, to permit amendments to applications and, in proper cases, to order a trial de novo. Any such proposed amendment must relate to the same disablement or disablement resulting in death originally claimed upon, and, if the amendment is permitted, it shall relate back to the date of the filing of the original application so amended.

IC 22-3-7-27(c) contains essentially the same language as IC 22-3-4-5(b); however, the notice of hearings is to be sent to "the parties" not "the employee, employer, and attorneys of record." Also, there is no mention in this subsection of "requests for continuances." The proper forum for a hearing upon an occupational disease claim is "in the county in which the last exposure occurred or in any adjoining county," unless the parties consent to a hearing elsewhere.

Subsection (d) of IC 22-3-7-27 is similar to IC 22-3-4-6, however, here, a copy of the award must be "sent by *registered* mail to each of the parties in dispute," (emphasis added) as opposed to "sent to each of the employee, employer, and attorney of record in the dispute."

IC 22-3-7-27(e) is essentially the same as IC 22-3-4-7, however, once again, copies of the award and the findings of facts are to be sent according to subsection (d) which is slightly different than the requirement contained in IC 22-3-4-6.

Subsection (f) of IC 22-3-7-27 is slightly different than IC 22-3-4-8. Much of the language of the two sections is similar, but the following sentence appears in IC 22-3-7-27(f): "An award by the full board shall be conclusive and binding unless either party to the dispute, within thirty (30) days after receiving a copy of such award, appeals to the court of appeals under the same terms and conditions as govern appeals in ordinary civil actions." IC 22-3-4-8(b) states, by contrast: "An award by the full board shall be conclusive and binding *as to all questions of the fact,* but either party to the dispute may, within thirty (30) days *from the date of such award,* appeal to the court of appeals *for errors of law* under the same terms and conditions as govern appeals in ordinary civil actions." (Emphasis added).

To reinforce the issue further, subsection (f) of IC 22-3-7-27 also provides that "[t]he court of appeals shall have jurisdiction to review all questions of law and of fact." It thus appears that judicial review of an occupational disease award may be more expansive and all-inclusive than that of an award pursuant to the worker's compensation sections. If that is indeed true, then does it follow that an occupational disease award by the full board is NOT conclusive and binding *as to all questions of fact* if an appeal is taken? And, if the answer to that question is in the affirmative, is the standard of judicial review applied by the appellate courts in any way altered, or the deference given by the appellate courts to the board's fact-finding abilities in any way diminished? In all fairness, it must be noted that both IC 22-3-7-27(f) and IC 22-3-4-8(d) continue to state that "[a]n assignment of errors that the award of the full board is contrary to law shall be sufficient to present both the sufficiency of the facts found to sustain the award and the sufficiency of the evidence to sustain the finding of facts."

In *Russell v. Auburn Central Mfg. Co.*,[1] an occupational disease case, the appellate court repeated the often espoused principle that

"[u]nder the statute the finding of the Industrial Board is conclusive and binding upon all questions of fact and where such a finding is sustained by any competent evidence this court will not reverse the board's award and substitute a finding by it for the board's finding. Before this court will reverse an award of the board upon the evidence it must be of such a conclusive character as to force a conclusion contrary to that of the board. See *Claypool Machine Company v. Cripe*, 104 Ind. App. 156, 10 N.E.2d 427."[2]

It could certainly be argued that, for occupational disease purposes, the statute simply does not say what the appellate courts have consistently stated that it says.

Subsections (g) and (h), regarding judgments of the circuit or superior courts and the taxing of costs, are essentially the same provisions as appear in IC 22-3-4-9(a) and (b) and IC 22-3-4-10, respectively.

IC 22-3-7-27(i), regarding modifications to or changes in awards, is essentially the same as the language contained in IC 22-3-3-27(a), (b) and (c), except for the nonreviewable nature of lump sum awards, previously discussed.

The provisions of IC 22-3-7-27(j), pertaining to independent medical examinations, is essentially the same as those contained in IC 22-3-4-11.

IC 22-3-7-27(k) contains a provision not found in the worker's compensation sections. It states:

The board or any member thereof may, upon the application of either party or upon its own motion, appoint a disinterested and duly qualified industrial hygienist, industrial engineer, industrial physician, or chemist to make any necessary investigation of the occupation in which the employee alleges that the employee was last exposed to the hazards of the occupational disease claimed upon, and testify with respect to the occupational disease health hazards found by such person or persons to exist in such occupation. Such person or persons shall be allowed traveling expenses and a reasonable fee, to be fixed by the board. The fees and expenses of such persons shall be paid by the state, only on special order of the board or a member thereof.

Although not, perhaps, true in every case, it would seem that

---

[Section 7:10]

[1]Russell v. Auburn Central Mfg. Co., 107 Ind. App. 17, 22 N.E.2d 889 (1939).

[2]Russell v. Auburn Central Mfg. Co., 107 Ind. App. 17, 22 N.E.2d 889 (1939). See also Durham Mfg. Co. v. Hutchins, 115 Ind. App. 479, 58 N.E.2d 444 (1945); Mills v. Princeton Min. Co., 133 Ind. App. 486, 183 N.E.2d 359 (1962); Collins v. Evansville State Hospital, 134 Ind. App. 471, 189 N.E.2d 106 (1963).

such investigations, and the testimony resulting therefrom, might be rather time consuming and expensive to obtain. This subsection does not definitively state who must pay for any such investigation and testimony, only that the state should not, in the absence of a special order to the contrary. In all likelihood, the party requesting the investigation will be the party paying for it.

IC 22-3-7-27(1), also, contains language not found in the worker's compensation sections. It reads:

> Whenever any claimant misconceives the claimant's remedy and files an application for adjustment of a claim under IC 22-3-2 to IC 22-3-6 and it is subsequently discovered, at any time before the final disposition of such cause, that the claim for injury or death which was the basis for such application should properly have been made under the provisions of this chapter, then the application so filed under I.C. 22-3-2 to I.C. 22-3-6 may be amended in form or substance or both to assert a claim for such disability or death under the provisions of this chapter, and it shall be deemed to have been so filed as amended on the date of the original filing thereof, and such compensation may be awarded as is warranted by the whole evidence pursuant to the provisions of this chapter. When such amendment is submitted, further or additional evidence may be heard by the worker's compensation board when deemed necessary. Nothing in this section contained shall be construed to be or permit a waiver of any of the provisions of this chapter with reference to notice or time for filing a claim, but notice of filing of a claim, if given or done, shall be deemed to be a notice or filing of a claim under the provisions of this chapter if given or done within the time required in this chapter.

In its opinion in the matter of *Mikel v. Ontario Corp.*,[3] the Indiana Court of Appeals stated: "We believe it to be more reasonable to assume that the legislature intended the words 'final disposition' to mean the conclusion of the evidentiary hearing before the hearing examiner, and his findings and judgment which he renders thereon."[4]

IC 22-3-7-28, regarding destruction of documents, is essentially the same provision as is contained in IC 22-3-4-3(b), except that "notices of election or rejection shall not be destroyed." Furthermore, "all records of insurance coverage shall be maintained for forty-five (45) years."

The provisions of IC 22-3-7-29, regarding the preference of rights to compensation against an employer's assets, the nonassignability of a claim for compensation, the exemption of a claim for compensation from all claims of creditors, and the fact that

---

[3]Mikel v. Ontario Corp., 142 Ind. App. 157, 233 N.E.2d 246 (1968).

[4]Mikel v. Ontario Corp., 142 Ind. App. 157, 233 N.E.2d 246, 248 (1968).

compensation awards are subject to child support income withholding, are essentially the same provisions contained in IC 22-3-2-16 and IC 22-3-2-17(a) and (b).

IC 22-3-7-30, relating to compensation agreements, contains essentially the same as provisions as those contained in IC 22-3-4-4.

IC 22-3-7-31(a) states that "[n]o employee, personal representative, or beneficiary shall have power to waive any of the provisions of this chapter in regard to the amount of compensation which may be payable to such employee, personal representative, or beneficiary except after approval by the worker's compensation board." This subsection, when read in conjunction with IC 22-3-7-35, conveys the essence of the requirements set forth in IC 22-3-2-15(a), even though the language employed is different. Note, also, that the word "regulation" appears in IC 22-3-7-35, but does not appear in the worker's compensation section. Subsections (b) and (c) of IC 22-3-7-31, regarding waivers, have no current application since they pertain specifically to waivers which had to have been filed by August 6, 1937.

The notice requirements contained in IC 22-3-7-32(a) and (b) are essentially the same requirements as those that appear in IC 22-3-3-1 and IC 22-3-3-2. The two-year limitation of actions provision contained in subsection (c), is essentially the same as that contained in IC 22-3-3-3. Subsection (d) is similar to IC 22-3-3-3, except that its application is restricted. It provides that "[n]o proceedings by dependents of a deceased employee for compensation for death under this chapter shall be maintained unless claim for compensation shall be filed by the dependents with the worker's compensation board within two (2) years after the date of death." Subsection (e) of IC 22-3-7-32 is essentially the same as IC 22-3-3-30, however it applies to a "minor dependent," instead of a "minor."

IC 22-3-7-33(a), to the extent that it seeks to prohibit a double recovery of compensation, is similar to IC 22-3-3-14. This subsection, however, provides much more than that, and reads:

> An employee shall be conclusively deemed to have been exposed to the hazards of an occupational disease when for any length of time, however short, he is employed in an occupation or process in which the hazard of the disease exists. The employer liable for the compensation provided for in this chapter shall be the employer in whose employment the employee was last exposed to the hazards of the occupational disease claimed upon regardless of the length of time of the last exposure. In cases involving silicosis or asbestos, the only employer liable shall be the last employer in whose employment the employee was last exposed during the period of sixty (60) days or more to the hazard of the occupational disease. In cases involving silicosis or asbestos, an exposure during a period of less than sixty (60) days shall not be considered a last exposure. The in-

surance carrier liable shall be the carrier whose policy was in effect covering the employer liable on the last day of the exposure rendering the employer liable, in accordance with the provisions of this chapter.

Subsection (b) of IC 22-3-7-33, regarding an employee in the joint service of two or more employers, is similar to the language contained in IC 22-3-3-31.

With respect to the liability of an insurance company to pay compensation to an employee for disablement resulting from an occupational disease, the opinion of the appellate court in the matter of *Durham Mfg. Co. v. Hutchins*,[5] is instructive. There, the court stated:

> Liability is not necessarily imposed upon the insurer whose policy is in effect on the last day the employee works for the employer, nor upon the insurer who carried the risk on the last day the employee was exposed to the disease causing disablement. It is imposed upon the insurer on the risk on the last day *of the exposure rendering the employer liable.* The question therefore is, what was the exposure rendering the employer liable in this case and what was the last day of that exposure? The question is one of fact for the board to determine, and its determination is conclusive if it is supported by any substantial evidence, including reasonable inferences that may be drawn therefrom. *Russell v. Johnson*, 1943, 220 Ind. 649, 46 N.E.2d 219.

> If the evidence is such as to force the conclusion that the employee's present disability resulted solely from the exposure prior to and causing the period of disablement commencing September 28, 1940, or, in other words, if the later disablement was a mere recurrence of the previous attack Bituminous Casualty cannot be liable regardless of the fact that her present disablement occurred while it was on the risk. Thus, had she continued to work for this employer after January 20, 1941, under such circumstances that she was not exposed to the disease, or, though exposed, was not so exposed as to render the employer liable as the result of that exposure under the terms of Section 6 of the Act, there could be no question of the correctness of the position taken by Bituminous Casualty. *Liberty Foundry Company v. Industrial Comm.*, 1940, 373 Ill. 146, 25 N.E.2d 790.

> The evidence in this case, however, presents a picture of continuous exposure throughout the period of active employment. After laying off on September 28, 1940, when her illness resulted in unconsciousness, she had sufficiently recovered on January 20, 1941, to return to work and thereafter continued to be exposed to the end. The evidence would therefore support the conclusion that the disablement commencing November 27, 1942, was not a mere recurrence of the first, but that the later exposure commencing on January 20, 1941, and terminating on November 27, 1942, a day when Bituminous Casualty carried the risk, bore a causal connec-

---

[5]Durham Mfg. Co. v. Hutchins, 115 Ind. App. 479, 58 N.E.2d 444 (1945).

tion with the present disability. The board in effect so found, and Bituminous Casualty must bear the loss.

We are not impressed by the contention that to hold Bituminous Casualty liable in this case achieves an absurd result and unduly penalizes an insurer who has carried a risk but a comparatively short time. The legislature intended that no employee should incur an uninsured risk. If the law of averages will not save an insurer harmless from disproportionate losses, they may of course refuse to write the business.[6]

IC 22-3-7-34.5, regarding certificates of exemption for independent contractors who do not make an election to be designated as an employee, is essentially the same provision as contained in IC 22-3-2-15, however, the former contains subsection (d) thereof which does not appear in the latter. It reads: "An independent contractor shall file with the department of state revenue, in the form prescribed by the department of state revenue, a statement containing the information required by IC 6-3-7-5."

IC 22-3-7-37, pertaining to an employer's records and reports concerning disablements, is similar to IC 22-3-4-13, but there are a few differences. In subsection (a), the words "or claimed to have been received by," which appear in the latter, have been omitted from the former. Also, an insurance carrier is permitted to mail reports to the board. Violations of this section of the worker's compensation law are Class C infractions only. The venue for all criminal actions arising under this section is in the county in which the employee was last exposed to the occupational disease causing disablement.

§ 7:11   Occupational diseases—Insurance

IC 22-3-7-34, pertaining to insurance requirements, is much the same as those insurance sections contained within the Worker's Compensation Act, but there are also a number of differences. For instance, subsections (a)(1) and (2) are essentially the same as the provisions contained in IC 22-3-2-14(a)(1) and (2), IC 22-3-2-2(d)(2), IC 22-3-6-1(a) and (b)(11), and IC 22-3-2-9(a)(4). Subsection (b) is essentially the same as IC 22-3-2-5(a), however, no mention is made of "banks, trust companies, and building and loan associations."

The provisions of subsection (c) are essentially the same as those contained in IC 22-3-5-1, however, the words "who, by elec-

---

[6]Durham Mfg. Co. v. Hutchins, 115 Ind. App. 479, 58 N.E.2d 444 (1945). See also Employers' Liability Assur. Corp. v. Merritt, 117 Ind. App. 697, 75 N.E.2d 803 (1947) ("Under the rule declared in [Dunham Mfg.] both insurance companies were carriers on the risk . . . on the last day the employee was exposed, rendering his employer liable for the payment of compensation herein, and, therefore, both insurance companies are liable under the statute."

tion, is bound by the compensation provisions of this chapter" has been added. The fees set forth in IC 22-3-5-1(b)(1), (2) and (3) have not been carried forward to this occupational disease section.

Subsection (d) is similar to the first sentence of IC 22-3-5-2, however, this section pertains to "every" employer, and the filing requirements and fees set forth in the latter have been excluded from this subsection. In addition, the second sentence of this subsection contains essentially the same language as that contained in IC 22-3-4-13(e), but the focus of the two sections is different.

Subsection (e) applies to note, as does IC 22-3-5-3(a), however, 30 days is allowed, not 10 days.

Subsection (f)(1) is similar to IC 22-3-5-4(a), however it is provided that a substitute system "may not be approved" unless the conditions noted are adhered to. The worker's compensation provision states that "no such substitute system shall be approved" unless the conditions are met. Subsection (f)(2) is essentially the same as that contained in IC 22-3-5-4(b).

Subsection (g)(1) has essentially the same provisions as does IC 22-3-5-5(a), except that the proposed form is to be submitted to and approved by the board, not the Department of Insurance. Furthermore, the following language has been added:

> The board shall not approve the policy form of any insurance company until the company shall file with it the certificate of the insurance commissioner showing that the company is authorized to transact the business of worker's compensation insurance in Indiana. The filing of a policy form by any insurance company or reciprocal insurance association with the board for approval constitutes on the part of the company or association a conclusive and unqualified acceptance of each of the compensation provisions of this chapter, and an agreement by it to be bound by the compensation provisions of this chapter.

Subsection (g)(2) is similar to IC 22-3-5-5(b), but the following language has been added to the end of the first sentence appearing in the latter: "under this chapter in all cases in which the last day of the exposure rendering the employer liable is within the effective period of such policy." The provision contained in subsection (g)(3) is essentially the same as that contained in the second sentence of IC 22-3-5-5(b).

There are some differences between subsection (g)(4) and IC 22-3-5-5(c). In subsection (g)(4)(a) the words "hospital services" is omitted. Subsection (g)(4)(b) is similar to IC 22-3-5-5(c)(2), however the words "and the liability of the insurer to pay the same are and shall be a part of this policy contract as fully and completely as if written in this policy" have been omitted. Subsections (g)(4)(c) and (g)(4)(d) are substantially the same provisions as those contained in IC 22-3-5-5(c)(3) and (4), respectively. The termination provisions contained in subsection (g)(4)(e) are essentially the same as those in IC 22-3-5-5(c)(5), however, 30 days notice is allowed, not 10 days. The expiration provisions of subsection (g)(4)(f) are similar to those in IC 22-3-5-5(c)(6), however the "continuous policy" provision contained in IC 22-3-5-5(c)(6)(B) and the "coverage of a period permitted in bureau rules" provision contained in IC 22-3-5-5(c)(6)(C) have been omitted.

The language contained in subsection (g)(5) is essentially the same as that contained in the first sentence of IC 22-3-5-5(d), however subsection (g)(6) is different than the second sentence of IC 22-3-5-5(d). The occupational disease section provides:

> If any insurer shall fail to pay any final award or judgment (except during the pendency of an appeal) rendered against it, or its insured, or, if it shall fail to comply with this chapter, the worker's compensation board shall revoke the approval of its policy forms, and shall not accept any further proofs of insurance from it until it shall have paid the award or judgment or complied with this chapter, and shall have resubmitted its policy form and received the approval of the policy by the worker's compensation board.

Subsection (h) contains language not found in the worker's compensation sections. It provides that:

> [n]o policy of insurance covering the liability of an employer for worker's compensation shall be construed to cover the liability of the employer under this chapter for any occupational disease unless the liability is expressly accepted by the insurance carrier issuing the policy and is endorsed in that policy. The insurance or security in force to cover compensation liability under this chapter shall be separate from the insurance or security under IC 22-3-2 to IC 22-3-6. Any insurance contract covering liability under either part of this article need not cover any liability under the other.

Subsection (i), regarding mutual insurance associations or reciprocal or interinsurance exchanges, is essentially the same provision as that contained in IC 22-3-6-2(a) and (c).

Subsection (j) is essentially the same as IC 22-3-6-2(b), however, the word "proved" has been substituted for the word "approved."

Subsections (k), (l), (m), and (n), regarding the failure to exact a certificate of compliance from a contractor, are similar to the provisions contained in IC 22-3-2-14(b) to (e), respectively. However, subsection (k) applies to "any person bound under the compensation provisions of this chapter," as opposed to the more expansive language contained in IC 22-3-2-14(b).

§ 7:12 Occupational diseases—Subrogation liens

IC 22-3-7-36(a), regarding third-party liability, is essentially the same as IC 22-3-2-13; however, the word "surgical" has been deleted, as well as the following language: "subject to its paying its pro rata share of the reasonable and necessary costs and expenses of asserting the third party claim."

Subsection (b) is worded essentially the same as the second paragraph of IC 22-3-2-13, however, the words "from the employer" have been deleted. The application of this section of the worker's compensation law was addressed by the court of appeals in the matter of *Roberts v. ACandS, Inc.*[1] There, Roberts, a union insulator, worked with asbestos-containing insulation products for more than 25 years while employed with ACandS. As a result, he developed terminal mesothelioma. He and his wife filed a civil action against a number of defendants whom they alleged contributed to Roberts's disease. Later, Roberts filed a claim against ACandS with the board. It did not appear from the record that Roberts ever sought or received benefits pursuant to his application. Prior to the civil jury trial, Roberts settled his case with some of the defendants. After trial, the jury returned a verdict for the Roberts's and against four defendants and a number of nonparties, including ACandS. An apportionment of fault was made by the jury, including 12% against Roberts and 36% against ACandS. The trial court entered judgment upon the jury's verdict, but the record did not indicate that the judgment, or any portion of it, was ever tendered, paid or accepted by the Robertses. ACandS, thereafter, moved to dismiss Roberts's application, and the board granted the motion. The single hearing member concluded that, since Roberts settled with one or more of the defendants in the civil action, ACandS had no further liability to compensate him for his occupational disease under IC 2-3-7-36(b). The full board adopted the single hearing member's decision. In reversing the board's order, the court of appeals stated:

> While the ODA permits employees to seek worker's compensation benefits as well as seek recovery from third parties, it also contains provisions to further the general policy prohibiting an employee from obtaining a 'double recovery' for his injury. *Cf. Waldridge v. Futurex Industries, Inc.,* 714 N.E.2d 783, 786 (Ind. Ct. App. 1999) (discussing the policy based upon nearly identical language under the WCA) *trans. denied.* Under the ODA, this policy is fostered in part by the subrogation provision found in I.C. § 22-3-7-36(a) and in the limitation on an employer's liability which is found in I.C. § 22-3-7-36(b) . . . .

Thus, under Roberts's interpretation of I.C. § 22-3-7-36(b), where there are multiple alleged tortfeasors, an injured employee would not be barred from seeking compensation benefits from his employer for an occupational disease unless he procures a judgment, which is

---

[Section 7:12]

[1]Roberts v. ACandS, Inc., 806 N.E.2d 1 (Ind. Ct. App. 2004).

paid, or settles with each of the alleged tortfeasors thereby fully concluding the third party action.

ACandS disagrees with such an interpretation of I.C. § 22-3-7-36(b) and directs our attention to *Waldridge v. Futurex Industries, Inc.*, 714 N.E.2d 783 (Ind. Ct. App. 1999), *trans. denied*. In *Waldridge*, another panel of this court interpreted an essentially identical provision under the WCA, i.e., I.C. § 22-3-2-13. In that case, Waldridge . . . filed with the worker's compensation board an application for adjustment of claim against Futurex, in addition to filing a third party action against 'various chemical manufacturers' in federal court . . . . Waldridge entered into a settlement agreement and release with one of the named defendants in the third party action. Thereafter, Futurex filed a motion to dismiss Waldridge's worker's compensation claim. The Board affirmed a single Hearing Member's decision to dismiss Waldridge's worker's compensation claim pursuant to I.C. § 22-3-2-13, concluding that Waldridge was barred from worker's compensation recovery after 'settlement of her third party claim in federal court.' *Id*.

Upon appeal to this court, ... (t)he court went on to conclude that pursuant to I.C. § 22-3-2-13, because Waldridge had entered into a settlement and release 'with a third party defendant,' she was barred from seeking worker's compensation benefits. *Id*. at 787 . . . .

ACandS thus argues that as soon as Roberts settled with any of the defendants in his civil action, as he did here prior to going to trial, Roberts was thereafter barred from recovering worker's compensation benefits from ACandS.

The policy of the law generally is to discourage litigation and encourage negotiation and settlement of disputes. *Mendenhall v. Skinner and Broadbent Co. Inc.*, 728 N.E.2d 140, 145 (Ind. 2000). To adopt ACandS's interpretation of I.C. § 22-3-7-36(b) would appear to do just the opposite—hinder negotiations and settlement and encourage litigation. Indeed, under circumstances where there are multiple alleged tortfeasors, injured employees would be discouraged from settling with even the least culpable tortfeasor for fear of terminating his employer's liability. Moreover, in such a situation, ACandS's interpretation does not foster the policy of prohibiting double recovery for which the provision was enacted.

Although the court in *Waldridge* concluded that the claimant was barred from seeking worker's compensation benefits because she had settled with 'a third party defendant,' the court so concluded in affirming the Board's decision to dismiss her application for benefits because of her 'settlement of her third party claim in federal court.' This language could be read to mean that Waldridge's third party claim was fully concluded. However, we note that the status of the other defendants initially named in Waldridge's action is unclear. If those other defendants still remained as part of the third party action, then Waldridge's action was not fully concluded. Thus, to the extent that the facts in *Waldridge* can be read to say that the third party action was fully concluded, we believe it was a correct application of the law. However, to the extent that *Waldridge* may be read as ACandS urges, we decline to follow it . . . .

Therefore, we hold that because there was no evidence before the Board as to whether Roberts's judgment has been paid, and thus, that his third party claim was fully concluded, we hold that the Board's dismissal of Roberts's Application for worker's compensation benefits pursuant to I.C. § 22-3-7-36(b) was premature.[2]

In a footnote, the court also stated the following:

Until such time as Roberts's third party action is fully concluded, Roberts may seek worker's compensation benefits. However, if Roberts receives worker's compensation benefits prior to the conclusion of his third party claim, Roberts will be subject to the subrogation provision found under I.C. § 22-3-7-36(a). Under such provision, Roberts will be required to reimburse his employer for any benefits paid out of his recovery in his third party action . . . .[3]

Subsequent to the issuance of the court's opinion, Roberts passed away and his estate was substituted as claimant. After the appeals in the third-party lawsuit had been exhausted and the verdict defendant had paid its portion of the civil judgment, ACandS, once again, moved to dismiss the application pursuant to IC 22-3-7-36(b). As before, the single hearing member granted the motion to dismiss and the full board affirmed. The court of appeals, in affirming further the full board's decision, stated:

As in the prior appeal, the Estate argues that the dismissal of the Application pursuant to Section 36(b) was premature. The Estate contends that it is not proper to dismiss the Application until all of the third-party actions are fully concluded. The Estate declares that it intends on seeking compensation from certain defendants that were originally named in the complaint but changed to the status of nonparty due to the companies filing for bankruptcy under Chapter 11 of the U.S. Bankruptcy Code . . . .

As stipulated by the parties, the third-party lawsuit is final, the verdict defendant paid its portion of the judgment in full, and the Estate received in excess of four million dollars as a result of the payment of the settlements and judgment. Also, the maximum allowable recovery under the ODA for the facts of this case is $274,000, making the recovery from third parties far in excess of what could have been obtained through the ODA. Here, the requirements of the release of liability statute are fulfilled: Roberts did not received any worker's compensation, the Estate procured a judgment against and settlements with third parties, and those sums have been paid in full. Furthermore, the amounts recovered are in excess of the potential amount recoverable under the ODA, and such a dismissal will not impair the Estate's pursuit of claims against the bankrupt defendants. The dismissal of the Application was proper.[4]

At first seemingly contradictory to ACandS, the appellate court

---

[2]Roberts v. ACandS, Inc., 806 N.E.2d 1, 3–6 (Ind. Ct. App. 2004).

[3]Roberts v. ACandS, Inc., 806 N.E.2d 1, 3–6 (Ind. Ct. App. 2004).

[4]Roberts v. ACandS, Inc., 873 N.E.2d 1055, 1059 (Ind. Ct. App. 2007). See

found in *Niegos v. ArcelorMittal Burns Harbor LLC,*[5] that Niegos' settlement with several, but not all, of 36 defendants in a third party case barred her recovery of occupational disease benefits. However, in this matter, Neigos failed to notify the defendant of any of the settlements with the third parties. The court concluded in doing so, she extinguished any claims the defendant might have had against those third parties, and as such, forfeited her right to proceed against the defendant under the Occupational Disease Act.[6]

Subsections (c) to (g), and (i) contain provisions almost identical to those contained in IC 22-3-2-13. Subsection (h), however, is markedly different. It provides as follows:

> If the employer does not join in the action within ninety (90) days after receipt of the notice, then out of any actual money reimbursement received by the employer or such employer's occupational disease insurance carrier pursuant to this section, they shall pay their pro rata share of all costs and reasonably necessary expenses in connection with such third party claim, action, or suit, and to the attorney at law selected by the employee or the employee's dependents, a fee of twenty-five percent (25%), if collected without trial, of the amount of benefits after the expenses and costs in connection with such third party claim have been deducted therefrom, and a fee of thirty-three and one-third percent (33 1/3%), if collected after trial, of the amount of such benefits after deduction of the costs and reasonable necessary expenses in connection with such third party claim, action, or suit. The employer may, within ninety (90) days after receipt of notice of suit from the employee or the employee's dependents, join in the action upon the employee's motion so that all orders of court after hearing and judgment shall be made for the employee's protection.

IC 22-3-7-36 is amended as follows: in subsection (a), "medical, hospital, and nurses' services and supplies" is replaced by "services and products"; and in subsection (b), "medical, surgical, hospital, or nurse's services and supplies" is replaced by "services and products."

---

also Casper v. L.E. Isley & Sons, Inc., 876 N.E.2d 776 (Ind. Ct. App. 2007).

[5]Niegos v. ArcelorMittal Burns Harbor LLC, 940 N.E.2d 323 (Ind. Ct. App. 2010), transfer denied, (May 13, 2011).

[6]Niegos v. ArcelorMittal Burns Harbor LLC, 940 N.E.2d 323, 328 (Ind. Ct. App. 2010), transfer denied, (May 13, 2011).

Chapter 8

Legal Representation

KeyCite®: Cases and other legal materials listed in KeyCite Scope can be researched through the KeyCite service on Westlaw®. Use KeyCite to check citations for form, parallel references, prior and later history, and comprehensive citator information, including citations to other decisions and secondary materials.

§ 8:1   Representation before Worker's Compensation Board

Chapter 8 of the Act governs those who are authorized to represent parties before the Worker's Compensation Board. IC 22-3-8-1 provides that, in order for a person to represent any claimant or defendant before the board, he or she must be admitted to practice law in the circuit or superior courts and before the Indiana Supreme Court.

Attorneys must also first register their names with the board, in a manner prescribed by the board, and take an oath in writing that he or she is qualified, as so provided in IC 22-3-8-1. The written oath is to be recorded in the permanent records of the board. The board or any member thereof must prohibit any person from representing a claimant or defendant until such person has complied with the requirements of this chapter.[1]

[Section 8:1]

[1]IC 22-3-8-2.

Chapter 9

The Residual Asbestos Injury Fund

§ 9:1   Residual asbestos injury fund
§ 9:2   —Eligibility

> **KeyCite®:** Cases and other legal materials listed in KeyCite Scope can be researched through the KeyCite service on Westlaw®. Use KeyCite to check citations for form, parallel references, prior and later history, and comprehensive citator information, including citations to other decisions and secondary materials.

§ 9:1   Residual asbestos injury fund

IC 22-3-11-1(a) provides for the creation of the Residual Asbestos Injury Fund. Its purpose is to provide compensation benefits to eligible employees who become permanently totally disabled from an exposure to asbestos while employed within Indiana and who are not eligible for benefits under the occupational disease sections of the worker's compensation law. The fund is administered by the Worker's Compensation Board.

This fund is not part of the general fund of the State of Indiana. It is to be used only for the payment of awards of compensation and the expense of medical examinations made and ordered by the board and chargeable against the fund. The Treasurer of the State of Indiana is to make payments from the fund upon an award or order of the board.[1]

IC 22-3-11-2 provides for the necessary funding of the fund. The initial balance for the fund was set at $200,000. If the balance of the fund on April 1 of any given year is less than $50,000, an assessment equal to 0.5% of the total amount of worker's compensation and occupational disease benefits paid to injured employees or their beneficiaries during the immediately preceding calendar year must be paid on or before April 10. The assessment is to be paid by each insurance carrier insuring employers who may be or who are liable to pay compensation, and each employer carrying its own risk to pay compensation under Indiana's worker's compensation laws.

[Section 9:1]
  [1]IC 22-3-11-1(b).

§ 9:2   Residual asbestos injury fund—Eligibility

Eligibility for fund benefits is governed by IC 22-3-11-3. Subsection (a) provides that an employee may be eligible for benefits from the fund if he or she is permanently totally disabled; is unable to be self-supporting in any gainful employment due to disability caused by asbestos exposure; is not eligible for benefits under the occupational disease sections of the law; and is not entitled to other available benefits from social security, disability, or other retirement benefits, or third-party settlements equal to or greater than 66 2/3% of his or her average weekly wage (as defined in IC 22-3-7-19) at the date of disablement. In addition, the employee must have become permanently totally disabled either: (1) on or after July 1, 1985, from an asbestos exposure in employment before July 1, 1988, *and* have filed a claim for benefits before July 1, 2006; or (2) before July 1, 1985, from an asbestos exposure in employment *and* have filed a claim prior to July 1, 1990.

IC 22-3-11-3(b) provides that if the employee has other available benefits but they are less than 66 2/3% of the average weekly wage at the date of disablement, the employee is still eligible to receive from the fund a weekly benefit amount not to exceed the difference between the other available benefits and 66 2/3% of the average weekly wage on the date of disablement for a period not to exceed 52 weeks.

IC 22-3-11-3(c) provides that if the employee dies before exhausting the remainder of the benefits to which he or she was entitled for the 52-week benefit period, his or her dependents are to be paid the greater of the remainder of the benefits or $4,000.

IC 22-3-11-3(d) provides that this section expired on August 1, 2007.

IC 22-3-11-4, which also expired on August 1, 2007, provided that, if the board made an award of additional compensation under this section prior to July 1, 2006, an employee who has exhausted the 52-week maximum may be awarded additional compensation by the board in periods of no more than 52 weeks upon a determination that the eligibility requirements are still met. The amount of the additional benefits determined for each subsequent award may not exceed the level of the initial determination.

IC 22-3-11-5 provides that the board may secure whatever expert medical testimony it considers necessary, at the expense of the fund, to protect the fund against questionable claims for benefits.

IC 22-3-11-6, which also expired on August 1, 2007, provides that the board shall adopt rules for the initial determination of an employee's eligibility for benefits, as well as his or her eligibility for additional benefits.

Chapter 10

Vocational Rehabilitation

§ 10:1   Vocational rehabilitation

An injured employee, who as a result of an injury or occupational disease is unable to perform work for which he or she has previous training or experience, is entitled to receive vocational rehabilitation services necessary to restore the employee to useful employment.[1]

When any compensable injury requires the filing of a first report of injury by an employer, its insurance carrier—or the self-insured employer—must forward a copy of the report to the central office of the Division of Disability and Rehabilitative Services, Rehabilitation Services Bureau, at the earlier of the following occurrences: when the compensable injury has resulted in temporary total disability of longer than 21 days, or when it appears that the compensable injury may be of such a nature as to permanently prevent the employee from returning to his or her previous employment.[2] Upon receipt of the report of injury, the Office of Vocational Rehabilitation must then immediately send a copy of the report to its local office nearest the employee's home.[3] Once the local office receives a copy of the report of injury, it must immediately notify the injured employee of the rehabilitation services that are available to the employee and the method by which he or she may make application for those services.[4]

The Office of Vocational Rehabilitation is charged with the responsibility of determining the injured employee's eligibility for

---

[Section 10:1]

[1]IC 22-3-12-1.
[2]IC 22-3-12-2.
[3]IC 22-3-12-3.
[4]IC 22-3-12-4(a)(1) and (2).

rehabilitation services and developing and implementing an individualized rehabilitation plan for the employee. After completion of the rehabilitation program, it must provide the injured employee job placement services.[5]

---

[5]IC 22-3-12-4(b) and (c).

Chapter 11

The Employers' Liability Act of 1911

> **KeyCite®:** Cases and other legal materials listed in KeyCite Scope can be researched through the KeyCite service on Westlaw®. Use KeyCite to check citations for form, parallel references, prior and later history, and comprehensive citator information, including citations to other decisions and secondary materials.

§ 11:1 Employers' Liability Act

The discussion which follows pertains to the Employers' Liability Act of 1911, now codified in IC 22-3-9-1 to IC 22-3-9-11. These provisions have absolutely nothing to do with the medical, compensation, and vocational rehabilitation benefit schemes set forth in the worker's compensation and occupational disease sections of the Indiana Worker's Compensation Act. The sections of the code which contain the Employers' Liability Act are not administered by the Worker's Compensation Board of Indiana, and its rules, practices, and procedures do not govern the prosecution of claims or the assertion of defenses under the Act in any manner. Therefore, this discussion of the Employers' Liability Act has intentionally been placed at the end of, and following the chapters on, worker's compensation and occupational diseases so as to highlight the fact that the latter are concepts wholly separate and distinct from those which follow.

It has been stated that:

> [O]ne of the purposes of the Employer's Liability Act of 1911 was to abolish the "unholy trinity" of common law defenses—contributory negligence, negligence, and assumption of risk and the fellow servant rule. These common law defenses had been formidable obstacles to any recovery for usual industrial accidents . . . . [T]he Employer's Liability Act was needed to eliminate these defenses in

actions brought by employees not covered by worker's compensation.[1]

As will be seen from the case opinions discussed below, that language, from the court's opinion in *Rossi*, appears to overstate the case for the elimination of the defenses under consideration. Other appellate decisions have taken a much more restrictive approach. For instance, it has been stated that:

> [W]hile the WCA [Worker's Compensation Act] eliminates the defenses altogether by allowing compensation to any employee whose injury arose out of and in the course of employment, . . . the ELA [Employers' Liability Act] merely restricts their use and provides for recovery upon a showing of negligence . . . . Unlike the Worker's Compensation Act which excludes all other remedies, the ELA does not purport to replace common law remedies but rather affords an alternative remedy for plaintiffs suing their employers for work-related injuries.[2]

At the outset, the Employers' Liability Act provides that any person, firm, limited liability company, or corporation, while engaged in business, trade, or commerce in Indiana, and employing therein five or more persons, shall be liable and respond in damages to any employee suffering injury, or, in the case of death, then to the employee's personal representative, for the benefit of the surviving spouse and children of the employee; and, if none, then to his or her parents; and, if none, then to the next of kin dependent upon the employee. Such injury or death must have resulted, in whole or in part, from the employer's negligence or the negligence of its agents, servants, employees, or officers, or by reason of any defect, mismanagement, or insufficiency, due to its or their carelessness, negligence, fault or omission of duty.[3]

It is interesting to note that the appellate courts of Indiana have permitted actions for damages arising from occupational diseases to be maintained under the Employers' Liability Act. The following excerpt from the opinion of the Indiana Supreme Court in *Illinois Steel Co. v. Fuller*[4] is instructive:

> The paramount purpose of the Employers' Liability Law seems to have been to restrict the use of the defenses of contributory negligence, assumption of risk, and negligence of a fellow servant. As to the duties imposed upon those coming within its terms, it has been said that the act is declaratory of the common law. Emerson Brantingham Co. v. Growe, 1922, 191 Ind. 564, 572, 133 N.E. 919.

[Section 11:1]

[1]City of Hammond v. Rossi, 540 N.E.2d 105, 108 (Ind. Ct. App. 1989).

[2]City of Hammond v. Biedron, 652 N.E.2d 110, 112 (Ind. Ct. App. 1995).

[3]IC 22-3-9-1.

[4]Illinois Steel Co. v. Fuller, 216 Ind. 180, 23 N.E.2d 259 (1939).

While it has been disputed, the weight of authority sustains the view that an action for negligence resulting in damages from an occupational disease was known to the common law . . . . To the extent that the Workmen's Occupational Diseases Act authorizes compensation for occupational diseases not caused by the employer's negligence, it is true that said act created new rights not theretofore existing under the common law or statutes of this state, and it does, of course, create distinctly new remedies. We do not recognize *In re Jeffries, supra,* as authority for the conclusion, however, that a common law action for the negligence of an employer, resulting in an occupational disease, could not have been maintained in this state prior to the compensation act of 1937.

As a corollary to what we have said, it must follow that the Employers' Liability Law embraces injuries from occupational diseases unless these are excluded by its terms. The title and body of the act purport to make it applicable to liability for *injuries,* rather than to accidental injuries. The word "injury" is a generic term of broad designation. As applied to the human body, it may result from other causes than trauma. Disability from an occupational disease may be no less an injury than one resulting from accident.[5]

§ 11:2   Employers' Liability Act—Burden of proof

In an action prosecuted under the Employers' Liability Act, the burden of proving that the employee did not use due care and diligence at the time he or she was injured or killed rests upon the defendant. But no such employee shall be held to have been guilty of contributory negligence by reason of the assumption of the risk thereof in any case where the violation by the employer, or its agents or employees, of any ordinance, statute, rule, regulation, or direction made by any public officer, bureau, or commission was the cause of the injury or death of the employee. Furthermore, it shall not be a defense to actions under the Act that the dangers or hazards inherent or apparent in the employment contributed to the employee's injury. Finally, no injured employee shall be held to have been guilty of contributory negligence where the injury complained of resulted from his or her obedience or conformity to any order or direction from the employer or of any employee to whose orders or directions he or she was under obligation to conform or obey, although such order or direction was a deviation from other rules, orders, or directions previously made by the employer.[1]

IC 22-3-9-3 is similar to IC 22-3-9-2, but pertains to the defense

---

[5]Illinois Steel Co. v. Fuller, 216 Ind. 180, 23 N.E.2d 259, 261 (1939). See also Dean v. Dalton Foundries, 109 Ind. App. 377, 34 N.E.2d 145 (1941).

[Section 11:2]

[1]IC 22-3-9-2.

of assumption of risk, rather than contributory negligence. It provides that an employee is not to be held to have assumed the risks of the employment in any case where the violation of the employer, or its agents or employees, of any ordinance, statute, rule, direction, or regulation made by any public officer or commission contributed to the employee's injury or death. An employee also is not held to have assumed the risk of the employment where his or her injury resulted from obedience to any order or direction of the employer or of any employee to whose orders or directions he or she was under an obligation to conform or obey, although such order or direction was a deviation from other orders, directions, or rules previously made by the employer. Finally, an employee is not to be held to have assumed the risk of any defect in the place of work or in the tool, implement, or appliance furnished him or her by the employer where such defect was, prior to the injury, known to the employer, or, by the exercise of ordinary care, might have been known to the employer in time to have repaired the same or to have discontinued the use of such defective workplace, tool, implement, or appliance. The burden of proof is upon the defendant.

A thorough examination of these sections of the Act was made by the Indiana Supreme Court in *J. Woolley Coal Co. v. Tevault.*[2] The Court stated:

> The statute does not purport to authorize a recovery for injuries sustained by a servant without negligence on the part of the master, or those for whose acts he is responsible, and such negligence still remains the essence of liability in all actions brought under its provisions . . . .
>
> Section 1 of the act . . . abrogates the common-law rule of assumed risks in so far as it applies to the particular risk of injury through the negligence of a fellow servant, and the failure of a fellow servant to exercise reasonable care for the safety of a coworker engaged in a common employment is now deemed to be a breach of duty on the part of the master, and is governed by the rules of law applicable thereto . . . .
>
> The above propositions are so firmly established as to render unnecessary their discussion at length in this opinion, and they are to be taken as a basis to be recognized throughout our inquiry into the questions raised in the present appeal . . . .
>
> Section 2 of the act . . . contains four separate provisions, of which the first is a restatement, in substance, of the rule relative to the burden of proof on the issue of the injured employee's want of due care and diligence which previously existed under earlier legislative enactment . . . . The second provision . . . finds a corollary in the first provision of section 3 of the act . . . . On comparison, it will be noted that the above correlative provisions are directed to

---

[2]J. Woolley Coal Co. v. Tevault, 187 Ind. 171, 118 N.E. 921 (1918).

the legal effect of substantially the same influence, and that their distinction rests largely in a transposition of terms . . . . Since contributory negligence on the part of an employee presupposes negligence on the part of his employer, it is apparent that each provision, in its legal effect, announces the same rule, *viz.*: That, where an employer fails to heed a legislative or administrative command to which he is bound to conform, he is negligent per se, and if his servant is injured as a result of such failure, however apparent, the latter's right to a recovery shall not be denied as a matter of law solely through a plea that he assumed the risk of injury or was negligent in continuing at his employment. Neither of these clauses, however, restricts the defense that the servant, under the circumstances in issue, failed to use due care for his own safety.

Passing, now, to the third provision of section 2, . . . we find again that section 3 contains a corresponding provision . . . . It is true that the two provisions just quoted contain greater differences in phraseology than those which we have heretofore considered, but, for the moment, we will treat those differences as superficial rather than vital and consider only the broad purpose of each provision. It is enough, now, to note generally that, under the above provision in section 3, the only "dangers or hazards inherent or apparent" into which the element of negligence on the part of an employer may enter, arise out of defects in "working place, tool, implement or appliance." Treating these phrases as synonymous in their practical interpretation, we are lead at once to the conclusion that the legislative purpose was to reach the same result through the language of either provision. In the one instance, the legal defense that apparent dangers contributed to the injury is removed, while in the other, the employee is held not to assume the risk of known defects as a matter of law, but the substantial aims of the two provisions are identical. Similarly, we may compare, without quoting, the last provision of section 2 and the corresponding clause in section 3. Each, in its legal effect, declares that no employee, injured through his obedience or conformity to any order or direction of his employer, etc., shall be denied a recovery as a matter of law solely because he obeyed such order, even though it involved apparent danger . . . .

In general, it was clearly the legislative intent greatly to restrict the defense of assumed risks in personal injury actions between employer and employee in all industries to which the act is applicable. This intent is apparent in section 1, which, as heretofore noted, abrogates the fellow-servant rule, and it is emphasized in sections 2 and 3, one of which expressly declares that no injured employee shall be held guilty of contributory negligence solely by reason of his assumption of certain risks of his employment, and the other destroys the legal effect of some risks which might otherwise be assumed. The similarity of these provisions suggests a purpose in their enactment in that form, and their phraseology indicates an intent to affect, in some manner, the rule of contributory negligence as well as the doctrine of assumed risks . . . .

Concisely stated, it is our conclusion: (1) That, in all actions to which it is applicable, the act of 1911 abrogates under all circumstances, and however, termed, the defense that an injured employee assumed the risk of the hazard or danger which caused his injury, provided such danger or hazard is a result of negligence on the part of the employer, or his agent, servant, officer, or other employee; (2) that the act does not restrict the defense that the conduct of the employee under the circumstances which resulted in his injury was not consistent with reasonable care for his own safety; (3) that the knowledge, or opportunity for knowledge, on the part of the employee of the hazard in question is of importance only as it affects the issue of his care and conduct under the circumstances; and (4) that, where the risk which results in injury contains no negligence on the part of the employer, such risk is assumed by the employee. Thus, if it appears that a defect in the place of work, or in the tool, implement, or appliance furnished to an employee by his employer, and which causes the former's injury, was unknown to such employer and could not have been known to him in the exercise of ordinary care in time to have remedied the condition, the employee must be held to have assumed the risk of injury therefrom. Similarly, if the injury complained of is the proximate result of a danger or hazard necessarily incident to a particular employment, and which may not be obviated by the employer in the exercise of ordinary care for the safety of his employee, the risk of injury from such danger or hazard is assumed by each of such employees as an element in his contract of employment.

From our conclusions above stated, it follows that in any action brought under the provisions of the act of 1911 to recover for personal injuries sustained by an employee during the course of his employment, the plaintiff is entitled to a judgment if the jury determines: (1) That negligence on the part of the employer, or of those for whose acts he is responsible, proximately contributed to the injury of the employee; and (2) that the employee's conduct in the face of the hazard which resulted from such negligence was characterized by the exercise of due care for his own safety.

On the other hand, the injured employee is not entitled to recover if the jury concludes either: (1) That his conduct under the circumstances was not characterized by due care for his own safety, in which case he was guilty of contributory negligence; or (2) that the danger or hazard which caused the injury was not known and could not have been known to the employer in time to have remedied the condition, or was necessarily incident to the employment, in which case the master was not negligent and the employee assumed the risk of injury from such danger or hazard by continuing at his work.

All questions of negligence, contributory negligence and assumption of risk are to be determined by the jury as issues of fact.[3]

---

[3]J. Wooley Coal Co. v. Tevault, 187 Ind. 171, 119 N.E. 485 (1918). See also Standard Steel Car Co. v. Martinecz, 66 Ind. App. 672, 113 N.E. 244 (1916); S.W. Little Coal Co. v. O'Brien, 63 Ind. App. 504, 113 N.E. 465, 469–70 (1916) ("Under some circumstances, contributory negligence is a defense in actions brought under the act of 1911 . . . . The burden of proof rests upon the defendant

The Seventh Circuit Court of Appeals weighed in on the subject in its opinion in *Rowe v. Galke Corporation*:[4]

Under the Employers' Liability Act, Burns' 1933, 40-1101 to 40-1114, a corporation employing five or more persons is liable to an employee injured by its negligence, and it provides further that in such cases contributory negligence shall be a defense and the burden of proving it is upon the employer; and where the injury is caused, among other things, by the violation of a statute enacted for the protection of the employee, the employee cannot be held guilty of contributory negligence by reason of the assumption of the risk. Thus it will be seen that the three causes of action stated in the complaint are founded respectively upon the alleged violation of a common law duty, the violation of the Factory Act and the Employers' Liability Act, and the violation of the Factory Act, the Employers' Liability Act, and the Occupational Diseases Act.

It would seem that under the common law of Indiana an action can be maintained for damages due to an injury received as a result of an occupational disease caused by the negligence of an employer. *Illinois Steel Co. v. Fuller*, 216 Ind. 180, 23 N.E.2d 259. Certainly the right has been widely recognized by other courts throughout the United States. See 105 *A.L.R.*, note p. 88. However, the plaintiff's right to recover is not based upon the common law alone. In Indiana it seems clear that where the employer has violated some statute enacted for the protection and safety of the employee and as a result thereof the employee contracts an occupational disease and is injured thereby, such employee has a cause of action. *Illinois Steel Co. v. Fuller, supra*; *Dean v. Dalton Foundries*, Ind. App., 34 N.E.2d 145; *General Printing Corp. v. Umback*, 100 Ind. App. 285, 195 N.E. 281 . . . .

Since the employer was guilty of a violation of the Factory Act, it was, under the Employers' Liability Act, deprived of the defense of an assumption of risk, and the burden of proving the plaintiff guilty of contributory negligence was placed upon the defendant. Burns' 1933, 40-1102 and 40-1103. The question of contributory negligence

---

. . . The plaintiff is not required either to allege or prove that the person for whose inquiry or death the action is brought was in the exercise of reasonable care. That he did not exercise such care is matter of defense, and may be proven under the general denial . . . [Plaintiff/employee] voluntarily and inexcusably assumed a position of danger. He was billed, not by reason of the use that he made of his place of work, or no conduct in such place. Knowing of the existence of the defect in place, as alleged, the fact that he continued in the employment, and thereby continued to be in touch with the defective place, presented a question of assumed risk, all defenses based on which are eliminated by the act of 1911. As to whether his conduct while in contact with such defective place was characterized by the exercise of reasonable care for his own safety presents a question of contributory negligence, a defense based on which, in a case such as this, remains available under the act of 1911 . . . [W]e are impressed that the complaint here discloses affirmatively that decedent's contributory negligence was the proximate cause of his death, and that the court therefore erred in overruling the demurrer.)"

[4]Rowe v. Gatke Corporation, 126 F.2d 61 (C.C.A. 7th Cir. 1942).

was one for the trial court. The trial court found the plaintiff free from contributory negligence and we think the evidence supports the court's finding.[5]

§ 11:3 Employers' Liability Act—Damages

The damages recoverable under the Employers' Liability Act are to be commensurate with the injuries sustained, and, in case death results from such injury, the action survives; provided that, where the injured person recovers a judgment and an appeal is taken and, pending such appeal the injured person dies and the judgment is thereafter reversed, or, where the injured person dies after the judgment is reversed and before trial, the right of action of such person survives to his or her personal representative, and the action may be continued in the name of the personal representative for the benefit of the person entitled to receive the same.[1]

Any contract, rule, regulation, bylaw, or device, the purpose, intent, or effect of which would be to enable any employer to exempt itself from any liability created by the Act shall, to that extent, be void; provided that, in any action brought against any such employer, it may set off any sum it has paid or contributed to any insurance, relief benefit, or indemnity for or on behalf of the injured employee that may have been paid to the employee or to the person entitled thereto on account of the injury or death for which said action is brought, but in no event shall the amount of the setoff exceed the amount paid to such employee or other person entitled thereto out of such insurance, relief benefit, or indemnity fund.[2]

Where any action is brought under the Act on account of the death of any person, the liability of the employer shall not exceed $10,000.[3]

---

[5]Rowe v. Gatke Corporation, 126 F.2d 61, 64–65 (C.C.A. 7th Cir. 1942).

[Section 11:3]

[1]IC 22-3-9-4.

[2]IC 22-3-9-5. See also IC 22-3-10-1, pertaining to contracts between an employer and an employee releasing the former from liability for damages; IC 22-3-10-2, pertaining to contracts between an employer and an employee releasing third parties from liability for their negligence; and IC 22-3-10-3, pertaining to contracts between an employee and a third party releasing the employer from liability for damages of such employee caused by the employer's negligence. All such contracts are also void as against public policy.

[3]IC 22-3-9-6. See also City of Hammond v. Rossi, 540 N.E.2d 105, 108 (Ind. Ct. App. 1989) ($10,000 maximum recovery set forth in this section, rather than the $300,000 maximum provided by the Tort Claims Act, applied to a suit brought by the widow of a firefighter electrocuted while on duty).

§ 11:4 Employers' Liability Act—Questions of fact

All questions of assumption of risk, negligence, or contributory negligence are questions of fact to be decided by the jury, unless the cause is being tried to the court without a jury, in which case such questions are questions for the court to decide.[1]

§ 11:5 Employers' Liability Act—Statute of limitations

No action shall be maintained under the Employers' Liability Act unless the action is commenced within two years from the date the cause of action accrued.[1]

§ 11:6 Employers' Liability Act—Definitions

For purposes of the Act, the terms "employer," "person," "firm," "limited liability company," and "corporation" include receivers or other persons charged with the duty of managing, conducting, or operating a business, trade, or commerce.[1]

§ 11:7 Employers' Liability Act—Benefits and detriments

Obviously, the Employers' Liability Act represents a trade-off: it provides an alternative form of relief for employees who, for one reason or another, cannot avail themselves of the benefits provided by the worker's compensation and occupational disease law of Indiana. While those employees are denied a swift, summary disposition of their claim, since they must pursue their action through the judicial system, they are relieved, in certain circumstances, of the harsh effects brought about by the defenses of contributory negligence, assumption of risk, and the fellow servant doctrine which might otherwise have been asserted against them. The Act, however, may have very limited appeal to dependents of a deceased employee, since the maximum amount recoverable under the Act is $10,000. A careful, thoughtful consideration of the beneficial and detrimental aspects of proceeding under the Act must be made before drafting and filing a complaint for damages with the court.

[Section 11:4]
  [1]IC 22-3-9-7.
[Section 11:5]
  [1]IC 22-3-9-8.
[Section 11:6]
  [1]IC 22-3-9-9.

Chapter 12

Forms

KeyCite®: Cases and other legal materials listed in KeyCite Scope can be researched through the KeyCite service on Westlaw®. Use KeyCite to check citations for form, parallel references, prior and later history, and comprehensive citator information, including citations to other decisions and secondary materials.

---

§ 12:1   First report of injury or illness

INDIANA WORKER'S COMPENSATION
FIRST REPORT OF EMPLOYEE INJURY, ILLNESS
State Form 34401 (R10 / 1-02)

FOR WORKER'S COMPENSATION BOARD USE ONLY		
Jurisdiction	Jurisdiction claim number	Process date

Please return completed form electronically by an approved EDI process.

PLEASE TYPE or PRINT IN INK

NOTE: Your Social Security number is being requested by this state agency in order to pursue its statutory responsibilities. Disclosure is voluntary and you will not be penalized for refusal.

EMPLOYEE INFORMATION

Social Security number	Date of birth	Sex ☐ Male ☐ Female ☐ Unknown		Occupation / Job title		NCCI class code
Name (last, first, middle)		Marital status ☐ Unmarried ☐ Married ☐ Separated ☐ Unknown	Date hired	State of hire	Employee status	
Address (number and street, city, state, ZIP code)			Hrs / Day	Days / Wk	Avg Wg / Wk	☐ Paid Day of Injury ☐ Salary Continued
			Wage Per			
Telephone number (include area		Number of dependents	$	☐ Hour ☐ Day ☐ Week ☐ Month ☐ Year ☐ Other		

EMPLOYER INFORMATION

Name of employer	Employer ID#	SIC code	Insured report number
Address of employer (number and street, city, state, ZIP code)	Location number	Employer's location address (if different)	
	Telephone number		
	Carrier / Administrator claim number	OSHA log number	Report purpose code
Actual location of accident / exposure (if not on employer's premises)			

CARRIER / CLAIMS ADMINISTRATOR INFORMATION

Name of claims administrator		Carrier federal ID number	Check if appropriate ☐ Self Insurance
Address of claims administrator (number and street, city, state, ZIP code)			Policy / Self-insured number
Telephone number		☐ Insurance Carrier ☐ Third Party Admin.	Policy period From To
Name of agent	Code number		

OCCURRENCE / TREATMENT INFORMATION

Date of Inj / Exp	Time of occurrence ☐ AM ☐ PM ☐ Cannot be determined	Date employer notified	Type of injury / exposure		Type code
Last work date	Time workday began	Date disability began	Part of body		Part code
RTW date	Date of death	Injury / Exposure occurred on employer's premises? ☐ Yes ☐ No	Name of contact	Telephone number	
Department or location where accident / exposure occurred			All equipment, materials, or chemicals involved in accident		
Specific activity engaged in during accident / exposure			Work process employee engaged in during accident / exposure		
How injury / exposure occurred. Describe the sequence of events and include any relevant objects or substances.				Cause of injury code	
Name of physician / health care provider					

Hospital or offsite treatment (name and address)				**INITIAL TREATMENT** ☐ No Medical Treatment ☐ Minor: By Employer
Name of witness		Telephone number	Date administrator notified	☐ Minor: Clinic / Hospital ☐ Emergency Care ☐ Hospitalized > 24 Hours
Date prepared	Name of preparer	Title	Telephone number	☐ Future Major Medical / Lost Time Anticipated

An employer's failure to report an occupational injury or illness may result in a $50 fine (IC 22-3-4-13).

§ 12:2 Report of attending physician

PHYSICIAN'S REPORT

State Form 2118 (R4 / 8-11)

INDIANA WORKER'S COMPENSATION BOARD
402 West Washington Street, Room W196
Indianapolis, IN 46204-2753
Telephone: (317) 232-3808

* This agency is requesting disclosure of your Social Security number in order to pursue its statutory responsibilities. Disclosure is voluntary and you will not be penalized for refusal.

INSTRUCTIONS: Page 1 of this form is for the examination; page 2 is for Permanent Partial Impairment (PPI).

PATIENT INFORMATION

Social Security number *

Name of injured employee

Age

Sex ☐ Male ☐ Female

Address *(number and street, city, state, and ZIP code)*

Name of employer

Date of this report *(month, day, year)*

Address *(number and street, city, state, and ZIP code)*

ACCIDENT INFORMATION

Date of injury *(month, day, year)*

Time of injury / illness / exposure

☐ AM
☐ PM

Briefly describe accident / exposure as reported by worker

PHYSICIAN'S FINDINGS - *Please attach causation.*

State objective findings of injury / illness / exposure

Ability to work
☐ Unable to work beginning _____ until _____. ☐ Able to work with restrictions beginning _____ until _____. ☐ Able to work full duty effective _____.

Is this the only cause of patient's condition? *(If No, state contributing causes)*
☐ Yes ☐ No

In your opinion, are the worker's current symptoms a result of the injury described above?
☐ Yes ☐ No

If no, did the injury aggravate, exacerbate, or accelerate a pre-existing condition?
☐ Yes ☐ No

Has normal recovery been delayed for any reason? *(If Yes, please explain)*
☐ Yes ☐ No

Medical status
☐ Maximum Medical Improvement (MMI) ☐ Disabled

If MMI, date achieved *(month, day, year)*

If disabled, type:
☐ Partial but temporary ☐ Totally but temporary ☐ Totally and permanent

ATTENDING PHYSICIAN TREATMENT

Date of your first treatment *(month, day, year)*

Who engaged your services?

Describe treatment given or ordered by you

Was patient treated by a previous physician? *(If Yes, by whom, give name)*
☐ Yes ☐ No

Date treated *(month, day, year)*

Was patient hospitalized?
☐ Yes ☐ No

Name of hospital

Date of admission *(month, day, year)*

Date of discharge *(month, day, year)*

Is further treatment needed? *(If Yes, please explain)*
☐ Yes ☐ No

Page 1 of 2

(Check one)

Patient ☐ was ☐ will be able to resume regular work on _____ *(month, day, year)*.

(Check one)

Patient ☐ was ☐ will be able to resume light duty work on _____ *(month, day, year)*. *Please explain any restrictions below.*

If there is permanent impairment as a result of this injury / illness / exposure, please give body part affected, degree of impairment and other pertinent information. *(If there is an amputation to the hand or the foot, please indicate the point of amputation on one of the diagrams below.)*

☐ Thumb _____%	☐ Toe, Great _____%	☐ Hand below elbow _____%	☐ Loss of vision to <1/10 normal _____%
☐ Finger 1 _____%	☐ Toe 2 _____%	☐ Arm above elbow _____%	☐ Loss of eye _____%
☐ Finger 2 _____%	☐ Toe 3 _____%	☐ Foot below knee _____%	☐ Hearing, left or right _____%
☐ Finger 3 _____%	☐ Toe 4 _____%	☐ Leg below knee _____%	☐ Hearing, both ears _____%
☐ Finger 4 _____%	☐ Toe 5 _____%	☐ Spine _____%	☐ Testicle loss, one _____%
			☐ Testicle loss, both _____%

To calculate the PPI amount, multiply the degree value by the percentage of loss. Multiply the result by the appropriate dollar amount for the date of injury. If an amputation, double the value.

Remarks: *(Use this section for an independent medical examination report or give any information of value not included above i.e. history, prognosis, or work restrictions of the patient.)*

_____

_____

_____

_____

_____

_____

_____

_____

Is this report submitted as an independent medical examination? ☐ Yes ☐ No	Is further treatment necessary? *(If necessary, please explain response in the remarks section above. Supplemental reports may be submitted with this form.)* ☐ Yes ☐ No
Signature of physician	Date *(month, day, year)*
Printed name of physician	Telephone number ( )
Address of physician *(number and street, city, state, and ZIP code)*	

PPI rating provided according to _____ Ed. AMA guidelines.

302

§ 12:3   Application for review by full board

APPLICATION FOR REVIEW BY FULL BOARD
State Form 1042 (R3 / 2-98)

| Workers Compensation Board |
| 402 W. Washington Street, Room W196 |
| Indianapolis, IN 46204-2753 |
| Application number |

INSTRUCTIONS: **This application must be filed within 30 days from the date of the award for which review is requested.**
The application should be filed in triplicate and captioned the same as the original claim for compensation. The application number assigned to the original cause should be shown on this application.

REVIEW BY THE FULL BOARD OF THE ORIGINAL AWARD

| Before the Worker's Compensation Board of Indiana: *(Name of plaintiff)* | **VS** | Name of defendant |
| Address of plaintiff *(number and street, city, state, ZIP code)* | | Address of defendant *(number and street, city, state, ZIP code)* |

The above named _____ respectfully makes application

for review by the Full Board of the award as to compensation made in the above captioned cause on the _____

day of _____, 19 _____, based upon, to wit:

   1.   that said award is not sustained by sufficient evidence; or

   2.   that said award is contrary to law.

☐ **I wish to order a transcript in this matter and ask that the court reporter contact me regarding said transcript. (***If you fail to indicate your desire for a transcript here, you must contact the court reporter immediately, as no continuance will be granted for this purpose after the hearing date is set.***)**

| Signature of plaintiff or defendant | Signature of attorney |

Address of attorney *(number and street, city, state, ZIP code)*

§ 12:4   Application for adjustment of claim for provider fee

**APPLICATION FOR ADJUSTMENT
OF CLAIM FOR PROVIDER FEE**
State Form 18487 (R7 / 1-15)
Approved by State Board of Accounts, 2015

WORKER'S COMPENSATION BOARD
402 West Washington Street, Room W196
Indianapolis, IN 46204-2753
Telephone: (317) 232-3808

INSTRUCTIONS:
1. The application must file an original and two (2) copies of this application for it to be processed.
2. Mail to the Worker's Compensation Board at the above address.
3. For detailed instructions, go to www.in.gov/wcb/files/Provider_Memo.pdf.

FOR STATE USE ONLY
Application number

PLAINTIFF vs DEFENDANT

Name of plaintiff (provider)		Name of defendant (employer)	
Address (number and street)		Address (number and street)	
City, state, and ZIP code		City, state, and ZIP code	
Telephone number ( )	National Provider Identification number (NPI)	Telephone number ( )	Federal identification number
Name of attorney (must complete)		Name of insurance carrier	Insurance claim number
Address (number and street)		Address (number and street)	
City, state, and ZIP code		City, state, and ZIP code	
Telephone number ( )	E-mail address	Name of adjuster	
Attorney number		Telephone number ( )	E-mail address
		Billing review company	

VS

Must check one: ☐ Total Billing (no payment received)
☐ Balance Billing (partial payment received)
☐ Single   ☐ Bundled
For Balance Billing (A $60.00 filing fee must accompany the application.):
Check number: _____

Name of reviewer

Telephone number ( )   E-mail address

THE PLAINTIFF RESPECTFULLY REPRESENTS TO THE BOARD AS FOLLOWS:

That the defendants, as employer and employer's compensation insurance carrier, owe and are indebted to the plaintiff on account in
the sum of _____ dollars for

provider's fee and supplies in the treatment of the injuries of _____
                                                                                    Name of patient

incurred as a result of an injury / illness arising out of and in the course of the employment with the defendant employer, on the _____

day of _____ , 20 _____ , in the county of _____ .

The patient's date of birth is (month, day, year): _____

The patient's address is (number and street, city, state, and ZIP code): _____

Latest date of service (month, day, year): _____

That said services were rendered as follows (check all that apply):
☐ In an emergency   ☐ The employee was in need of timely services provided
☐ The employer failed to provide such service   ☐ Employer or insurance carrier approved such services

Provider first requested payment for said services on (month, day, year): _____

The applicant certifies that required diligence has been accomplished and that the initial written response from the employer / representative
was received on (month, day, year): _____

Additional date(s) demands made (month, day, year): _____

Date(s) of follow-up (month, day, year): _____

Type of second request: ☐ Oral ☐ E-mail ☐ Written   Date(s) (month, day, year): _____

Wheretofore the plaintiff prays to the Board to find against the defendant on said account the sum of $ _____ .

Signature of plaintiff	Date signed (month, day, year)

§ 12:5 Application for adjustment of claim

APPLICATION FOR ADJUSTMENT
OF CLAIM

State Form 29109 (R5 / 6-05)

FOR STATE USE ONLY	INDIANA WORKER'S COMPENSATION BOARD
Application number	402 W. Washington St., Rm. W196 Indianapolis, IN 46204-2753

INSTRUCTIONS: *Please TYPE or PRINT.*
File ***ORIGINAL*** *and* ***4 COPIES.***

* The request for your Social Security number is VOLUNTARY and you will not be penalized for refusing to supply it.

Name of plaintiff / employee		Name of defendant / employer
Address (*number and street*)	**VS.**	Address (*number and street*)
City, state, ZIP code		City, state, ZIP code
Telephone number ( )	Social Security number *	Telephone number ( )

Employer's Worker's Compensation insurance company (*If known*)

The undersigned petitioner respectfully requests a hearing before a member of the Board for the following reasons. (*please check one*)

☐ Worker's Compensation Claim ☐ Occupational Disease Claim ☐ Change of Condition

ATTENTION: ONLY ONE INJURY DATE PER FORM

Date of injury / last exposure / death	Date employer notified of illness / injury / death	If not within 30 days explain

Actual location of incident (*number and street, city, state, ZIP code*)	County of incident

Average weekly earning of the employee at the time of illness / injury / death

$

Briefly describe how the accident / exposure occurred.

If an employee has died as a result of the injury / exposure, complete this section for all persons surviving as all and only dependents. (*attach extra information on dependedents if needed*)

NAME	AGE	RELATIONSHIP	WHOLLY OR PARTIALLY DEPENDENT	ADDRESS

Comments or additional information that you feel is pertinent to this claim.

Name of attorney	Attorney number	Signature of petitioner
Address (*number and street, city, state, ZIP code*)		SIGN HERE
Telephone number ( )		Date signed (*month, day, year*)

§ 12:6   Report of claim status

**REPORT OF TEMPORARY TOTAL DISABILITY (TTD) /
TEMPORARY PARTIAL DISABILITY (TPD) TERMINATION**
State Form 38911 (R8 / 1-14)

INDIANA WORKER'S COMPENSATION BOARD
402 West Washington Street, Room W196
Indianapolis, IN 46204
Telephone: (317) 232-3808
www.in.gov/wcb

* Your Social Security number is being requested by this state agency in accordance with IC 22-3-4-13; disclosure is voluntary, and you will not be penalized for refusal.

INSTRUCTIONS: 1.   You must report all compensation payments on this prescribed form. (IC 22-3-3-7)
                2.   Mail to the Worker's Compensation Board at the above address.

Date of injury *(month, day, year)*		Accident number

CLAIM INFORMATION

Name of employer	Federal identification number	Telephone number ( )
Address of employer *(number and street, city, state, and ZIP code)*		

Name of insurer		Insurer claim number
Address of insurer *(number and street, city, state, and ZIP code)*		

Name of adjuster / case manager	Telephone number ( )	E-mail address
Name of employee		Employee Social Security number *
Address of employee *(number and street, city, state, and ZIP code)*		
Telephone number ( )	E-mail address	

BENEFIT TERMINATION / REDUCTION *(check all that apply)*

☐ In accordance with IC 22-3-3-7 (c), TTD/TPD benefits have been terminated due to the following *(check all that apply)*:
　　☐ The employee has returned to **ANY** employment;
　　☐ The employee has died;
　　☐ The employee has refused to accept suitable employment under Section 11 (IC 22-3-3-11);
　　☐ The employee has refused to undergo a medical examination under Section 6 (IC 22-3-3-6);
　　☐ The employee has received five hundred (500) weeks of TTD benefits or has been paid the maximum compensation allowed under IC 22-3-3-22;
　　☐ The employee is unable or unavailable to work for reasons unrelated to the compensable injury.
☐ Other *(IF CHECKED, MEDICAL DOCUMENTATION MUST BE SERVED ON INJURED PARTY.)*
　　☐ TTD benefits shall be terminated and Temporary Partial Disability (TPD) begun because employee has been released to part time work
　　　suitable to employee's disability.
　　☐ Employer intends to terminate TTD/TPD benefits on _____ *(must be at least four (4) days after mailing or two (2) days after personal service)* because:
　　　　☐ Treating physician has released employee to full time light duty work and employer has appropriate light duty work available.
　　　　☐ Treating physician finds employee has reached MMI and/or employee is released to full time work *(check one)*:
　　　　　　☐ With restrictions   ☐ Without restrictions

Explanation

COMPENSATION PAYMENTS

Average weekly wage $	Number of weeks paid	Weekly rate $	Start date of payments *(month, day, year)*	End date *(month, day, year)*
Total amount paid $	Check one. ☐ Employee ☐ Dependent		Reason(s) for ending payments	

EMPLOYEE'S OBJECTION TO TERMINATION OF TTD BENEFITS

If the employee disagrees with the proposed benefit termination, the employee must complete, sign and return a copy of this notice to the **Worker's Compensation Board** and **the employer** within **seven (7) days** after receipt. This notice can also be filed via the Dispute Termination of Benefits link on the Board's website.

Please check all that apply.
☐ Employee disagrees with the termination / reduction of benefits.　　　☐ Employee requires further medical care.
☐ Employee believes an independent medical examination (IME) may be helpful to resolve this dispute.

Explanation

EMPLOYER CERTIFICATION / RECEIPT OF EMPLOYEE / DEPENDENT

Employer and employee must sign below to certify service or acknowledge receipt of this notice.
I certify that the foregoing is true and that a copy of the relevant medical documentation is attached.

Signature of employer	Date of service *(month, day, year)*
Printed name	By *(check one)*: ☐ US Mail ☐ Personal service
Signature of employee	Date received *(month, day, year)*
Printed name	By *(check one)*: ☐ US Mail ☐ Personal service

§ 12:7   Request for assistance

REQUEST FOR ASSISTANCE
State Form 45442 (R2 / 5-06)

INDIANA WORKER'S COMPENSATION BOARD
OMBUDSMAN DIVISION
402 West Washington Street, Room W196
Indianapolis, Indiana 46204
Telephone: (317) 232-3808
Toll free: (800) 824-COMP

INSTRUCTIONS: 1. Please print or type
2. Return completed request to the address listed at right.

EMPLOYEE INFORMATION	EMPLOYER INFORMATION
Name of employee	Name of employer
Address (number and street)	Address (number and street)
City, state, and ZIP code	City, state, and ZIP code
Telephone number ( )	Telephone number ( )
Social Security number *	County of employment
Date of birth (month, day, year)	**WORKER'S COMPENSATION INSURANCE COMPANY INFORMATION**
Date of accident (month, day, year)	Name of company
Nature of injury:	Address (number and street)
Have you hired an attorney? **	City, state, and ZIP code
If Yes, name and telephone number of attorney	Telephone number ( )
	Contact person(s)

Briefly describe your complaint / dispute (attach additional sheets if necessary):

I hereby request the Ombudsman Division of the Worker's Compensation Board to investigate my complaint. I understand that the Ombudsman Division is not a replacement for legal counsel, and that any specific legal questions should be addressed to my attorney.

Signature of employee	Date (month, day, year)

* PRIVACY NOTICE: This agency is requesting disclosure of your Social Security number in accordance with IC 22-3-4-13. This disclosure is not mandatory and you will not be penalized for refusing.
** You have no obligation to employ legal counsel under the Indiana Worker's Compensation and Occupational Diseases Acts.

§ 12:8   Notice of inability to determine liability/request for additional time

**NOTICE OF INABILITY TO DETERMINE LIABILITY/
REQUEST FOR ADDITIONAL TIME**
State Form 48557 (R2 / 7-12)

INSTRUCTIONS:
1. Please type or print in ink.
2. Complete appropriate sections of this document and sign in the space below.

Accident number

CLAIM INFORMATION		
Name of employer	Federal Identification number	Telephone number ( )
Address of employer *(number and street, city, state, and ZIP code)*		Insurer claim number
Name of Insurer / TPA	Date of injury *(month, day, year)*	Date employer notified of injury *(month, day, year)*
Name of adjuster	Date employer notified of work restriction or prohibition *(month, day, year)*	
E-mail address of adjuster		Telephone number of adjuster ( )
Name of employee		Social Security number *
Address of employee *(number and street, city, state, and ZIP code)*		Telephone number ( )

REQUEST FOR ADDITIONAL TIME

Notice of inability to determine liability must be made in writing and received by the Board and the employee not later than thirty (30) days after the employer's knowledge of the injury (IC 22-3-3-7). *(Check appropriate action below.)*

☐ Medical care only claim from _____ to _____

Nature of alleged injury: _____

☐ Initial request for additional sixty (60) days.
Reasons determination cannot be made within thirty (30) days:

_____

Facts or circumstances necessary to determine liability:

_____

☐ Request for additional time beyond sixty (60) days. *(Must include details of first request above.)*
Extraordinary circumstances which have precluded determination of liability:

_____

Status of investigation:

_____

Facts or circumstances necessary to determine liability:

_____

Timetable for completion of remaining investigation:

_____

EMPLOYER / CARRIER CERTIFICATION		FOR BOARD USE ONLY
Employer / Adjuster must sign below to certify service.	WORKERS COMPENSATION BOARD 402 W. Washington St., Rm. W196 Indianapolis, IN 46204-2753	
Signature of employer / adjuster		
Date issued *(month, day, year)* By: ☐ U.S. Mail ☐ Personal Service		

§12:9 Agreement to compensation of employee and employer

AGREEMENT TO COMPENSATION OF EMPLOYEE & EMPLOYER
State Form 1043 (R3 / 3-09)

INDIANA WORKER'S COMPENSATION BOARD
402 West Washington Street, Room W196
Indianapolis, IN 46204

* Your Social Security number is being requested by this state agency in accordance with IC 22-4-13; disclosure is voluntary, and you will not be penalized for refusal.

Please check appropriate box.	☐ Temporary Total Disability (TTD) ☐ Permanent Partial Impairment (PPI)	☐ Temporary Partial Disability (TPD) ☐ Permanent Total Disability (PTD)	File number
Name of employer		Employer's Federal identification number	Telephone number ( )
Address (number and street, city, state, and ZIP code)			
Name of employee		Employee's Social Security number *	Telephone number ( )
Address (number and street, city, state, and ZIP code)			

We (employee and employer) have reached an agreement in regards to compensation for the injury sustained by said employee and submit the following statement of facts relative thereto.

Date of injury / illness / exposure (month, day, year)	Date disability began (month, day, year)

Nature of injury / illness / exposure

Place of injury / illness / exposure

Cause of injury / illness / exposure

Probable length of disability

The terms of this agreement under the above facts are as follows:

That _____ shall receive compensation at the rate of $ _____ per

week based upon an average weekly wage of $ _____ and that said compensation shall be payable (i.e., weekly or

bi-weekly) _____ until terminated in accordance with the provisions of the Indiana Worker's Compensation / Occupational Disease Acts.

If PPI settlement, please provide impairment rating, number of weeks, and amount to be paid.

SIGNATURES		
Signature of employee		Date (month, day, year)
Signature of employer		Date (month, day, year)
Name of insurance carrier	Telephone number ( )	(FOR BOARD USE ONLY)
Address (number and street)		
City, state, and ZIP code		
Authorized signature	Date of agreement (month, day, year)	
Title		

309

§ 12:10   Agreement to compensation between deceased employee's dependents and employer

AGREEMENT TO COMPENSATION BETWEEN THE
DEPENDENTS OF DECEASED EMPLOYEE AND EMPLOYER
State Form 18875 (R2 / 5-10)

INDIANA WORKER'S COMPENSATION BOARD
402 West Washington Street, Room W196
Indianapolis, IN 46204-2753

Privacy Notice: This agency is requesting disclosure of employee's Social Security number in accordance with I.C. 22-3-4-13.

Federal Identification number	Name of Employer		Board number
Social Security number	Name of Employee	Date of injury / illness *(month, day, year)*	Date of death *(month, day, year)*

AGREEMENT STATEMENT

We, the undersigned being all the dependents of the deceased employee who are entitled to compensation under the provisions of the Indiana Worker's Compensation / Occupational Diseases Act due to the death of this employee resulting from an injury / illness arising out of a and in the course of their employment and said employer, have reached an agreement in regard to compensation.

The terms of this agreement are:

That the employer shall pay to the following dependents, in equal shares, a weekly compensation of
$_____, based on an average weekly wage of $_____,
beginning on the _____ day of _____, 20_____, and to continue
during the dependency of any one of them, not exceeding, in the aggregate, five hundred (500) weeks.
The employer shall also pay the reasonable and necessary medical expenses incurred as a result of the
injury / illness together with the statutory burial expenses of $_____ of said employee.

DEPENDENTS OF DECEASED EMPLOYEE

NAME	AGE	RELATIONSHIP	WHOLLY OR PARTIALLY DEPENDENT	ADDRESS *(number and street, city, state, and ZIP code)*

Remarks:

Signature of dependent	Date signed *(month, day, year)*	*(For board use only)*
Signature of parent / guardian for dependent	Date signed *(month, day, year)*	
Signature of employer	Date signed *(month, day, year)*	
Signature of insurance company adjustor / representative	Date signed *(month, day, year)*	
E-mail address of insurance company adjustor / representative	Telephone number of insurance company adjustor / representative ( )	
Name of insurance company		
Address of insurance company *(number and street, city, state, ZIP code)*		

§ 12:11 Subpoena

SUBPOENA
State Form 34877 (R3 / 5-10)

Cause number _____

INDIANA WORKER'S COMPENSATION BOARD
402 West Washington Street, Room W196
Indianapolis, IN 46204-2753

Name of Plaintiff	Name of Plaintiff's Attorney

VS

Name of Defendant	Name of Defendant's Attorney

STATEMENT AND SIGNATURE

State of Indiana
} SS:
County of _____   To the sheriff of _____ county, in the State of Indiana,

Greeting: You are hereby commanded to summon _____

to appear before the Worker's Compensation Board of Indiana at _____ , in the city-town

of _____ , in the county of _____ , in the state

of Indiana, on the _____ day of _____ , 20 _____ ,

at _____ o'clock _____ M, to give evidence in a certain proceeding pending before said Worker's Compensation Board of

Indiana, wherein _____ is the plaintiff, and _____

_____ is the defendant, on behalf of _____ .

Witness the hand of said Board this _____ day of _____ , 20 _____

_____
Signature of the Board Member / Secretary

Sheriff's return came to hand on the _____ day of _____ , 20 _____ ,

at _____ o'clock _____ M. and I served said subpoena by reading it to and within the hearing of the within

names, _____

or by leaving a true and correct certified copy thereof at the last usual place of residence of the within named _____

_____

Witness my hand this _____ day of _____ , at _____ o'clock _____ M

Signature of serving officer	County

FEES

Mileage	$
Service	$
Copy	$
Return	$
TOTAL	$

§ 12:12   Waiver of medical exam

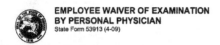

EMPLOYEE WAIVER OF EXAMINATION
BY PERSONAL PHYSICIAN
State Form 53913 (4-09)

INDIANA WORKER'S COMPENSATION BOARD
402 West Washington Street, Room W196
Indianapolis, IN 46204

INSTRUCTIONS: Please have claimant complete this form.
Submit together with Agreement to Compensation (Form 1043).

I have read the report of Dr. _____, dated the ____ day of _____,

20___, and understand that this medical opinion states that I have a _____% permanent partial impairment of

the _____ as a result of injuries sustained in the above mentioned accident.

I, _____, understand that, pursuant to the Workers Compensation Act of

Indiana, I have the right to have an examination by a qualified physician of my choice, at my own expense, for the

purpose of determining what degree of permanent partial impairment, if any, I may have as a result of injuries

suffered on the ____ day of _____, 20___, while in the employ of _____.

I understand that any impairment rating obtained from such an examination is not binding upon the employer or

insurance carrier, although it may be taken into consideration.

I do not wish to have an examination by a physician of my own choice and I hereby accept and agree with

the opinion of Dr. _____ concerning the extent of my permanent injuries as described in

the attached report. I understand that this waives only my right to an examination by a physician of my own

choosing regarding this particular settlement.

Signed and dated this ____ day of _____, 20___.

X_____
Signature of Employee

§ 12:13   Notice of denial of benefits

NOTICE OF DENIAL OF BENEFITS
State Form 53914 (R2 / 7-12)

WORKER'S COMPENSATION BOARD
402 West Washington Street, Room W196
Indianapolis, IN 46204-2753

* This agency is requesting disclosure of Social Security Number in accordance with IC 22-3-4-13; disclosure is voluntary and you will not be penalized for refusal.

INSTRUCTIONS: 1.   Notice of Denial of Benefits must be made in writing and received by the Workers Compensation Board not later than thirty (30) days after the employer's knowledge of the injury. (IC 22-3-3-7)
2.   Mail to the Worker's Compensation Board at the above address.

Date of injury (month, day, year)	Date employer notified of injury (month, day, year)	Date of employer notified of work restriction or prohibition (month, day, year)	Accident number

CLAIM INFORMATION

Name of employer	Federal identification number	Telephone number ( )

Address (number and street, city, state, and ZIP code)

Name of insurer	Insurer claim number

Address (number and street, city, state, and ZIP code)

Name of adjuster / case manager	Telephone number ( )	E-mail address

Name of employee	Social Security Number *

Address (number and street, city, state, and ZIP code)

Telephone number ( )	E-mail address

NOTICE OF DENIAL

☐ Claim deemed not compensable, no benefits paid.   ☐ Medical care only claim from _____, 20___ to _____, 20___; compensation denied.

Explanation: Explanation:

NOTICE TO EMPLOYEES

By filing this form, your employer or its insurance carrier has indicated to the Indiana Workers' Compensation Board that it has cause to deny workers compensation benefits for your reported injury. You may or may not agree with this denial of benefits.

If you disagree with the denial of benefits, you should discuss the reason for denial with your employer or your employer's insurance carrier. If, after having this discussion, you are not satisfied that benefits were properly denied, you may contact an attorney for legal advice, or contact an ombudsman at the Indiana Workers' Compensation Board for information at (317) 232-3808. Additional information can also be found at www.in.gov/wcb.

EMPLOYER CERTIFICATION

Employer must sign below to certify service of this notice.

Signature of employer	Date (month, day, year)

Printed name	By: ☐ US Mail ☐ Personal service

§ 12:14   Notice for worker's compensation and occupational diseases coverage

NOTICE FOR WORKER'S COMPENSATION AND OCCUPATIONAL DISEASES COVERAGE
State Form 36097 (R8 / 6-15)

Mail to: Worker's Compensation Board of Indiana, 402 W. Washington St., Room W196, Indianapolis, IN 46204-2753.

APPLICANT INFORMATION		
Name of employer		Federal Identification number
Address *(number and street, city, state, and ZIP code)*		
Name of insurer	Insurer policy number	Policy effective dates *(mm/dd/yy)* Start: End:
Name of applicant	Telephone number ( )	E-mail address

STATEMENT OF VOLUNTARY EXCLUSION (IC 22-3-6-1 (b)(1) / IC 22-3-7-9 (b)(9))

An officer of a corporation may not be considered to be excluded as an employee under IC 22-3-2 through IC 22-3-6 until the notice is received by the insurance carrier and the board.

☐ I am an officer with an ownership interest in the above named corporation, and I elect not to be an employee; hereby excluding myself from workers compensation coverage.

Signature of corporate officer	Date *(mm/dd/yyyy)*

STATEMENT OF VOLUNTARY ELECTION (IC 22-3-6-1 (b))

☐ (2) I am the executive officer in the above named municipal corporation or other governmental subdivision or of a charitable, religious, educational or other nonprofit corporation and am electing worker's compensation coverage.

☐ (4) I am the sole proprietor in the above named entity and am electing worker's compensation coverage.

☐ (5) I am a partner in the above named entity and am electing worker's compensation coverage.

☐ (8) I am an owner-operator that provides a motor vehicle and the services of a driver under a written contract that is subject to IC 8-2.1-24-23, 45 IAC 16-1-13, or 49 CFR 376 to a motor carrier and am electing worker's compensation coverage.

☐ (9) I am a member or manager in the above named limited liability company and am electing worker's compensation coverage.

STATEMENT OF VOLUNTARY ELECTION (IC 22-3-2-9)

The notice of acceptance referred to in subsection 22-3-2-9(b) shall be given thirty (30) days prior to any accident resulting in injury or death, provided that if any such injury occurred less than thirty (30) days after the date of employment, notice of acceptance given at the time of employment shall be sufficient notice thereof. A copy of the notice in prescribed form shall also be filed with the Worker's Compensation Board, within five (5) days after its service in such manner upon the employee or employer.

☐ (1) I am the employer of casual laborers and hereby elect to provide worker's compensation coverage.

☐ (2) I am the employer of farm or agricultural employees and hereby elect to provide worker's compensation coverage.

☐ (3) I am the employer of household employees and hereby elect to provide worker's compensation coverage.

☐ (4) I am the employer of part-time volunteer coaches for a nonprofit corporation and hereby elect to provide worker's compensation coverage.

STATEMENT OF VOLUNTARY ELECTION (IC 22-3-2-5)

☐ I am the owner or representative of a state, county, township, city, town, school city, school town, school township, other municipal corporation, state institution, state board, state commission, bank, trust company or building and loan association and am electing worker's compensation coverage.

STATEMENT OF VOLUNTARY ELECTION (IC 22-3-2-2)

☐ I am the employer of members of a fire department or police department of a municipal corporation, who are also members of a firefighters' pension fund or a police officers' pension fund; and hereby elect to purchase and procure worker's compensation insurance to insure said employees with respect to medical benefits.

☐ I am the employer of "rostered volunteers"; and hereby elect to cover said volunteers under the medical treatment provisions of the worker's compensation act.

Signature of employer or authorized agent	Date *(mm/dd/yyyy)*

§ 12:15   Second Injury Fund Report

WORKERS COMPENSATION BOARD OF INDIANA

**2016 SECOND INJURY FUND
CALCULATION OF FUNDING LEVEL**

December 23, 2015

Please note assessments greater than $1,000 may be paid in two installments.
The due dates are:
January 29, 2016
June 30, 2016

STATE OF INDIANA

MICHAEL R. PENCE, Governor

Linda Peterson Hamilton, Chairman

WORKERS COMPENSATION BOARD
402 West Washington Street, Room W196
Indianapolis, Indiana 46204-2753
Telephone: (317) 232-3808
http://www.in.gov/workcomp

SECOND INJURY FUND REPORT

By the Chair

AND ASSESSMENT FOR 2016

December 23, 2015

As we begin 2016, I am happy to report the Second Injury Fund will end
the year with $1,598,622 in the bank. Less than $10,000 was taken from the
Prudent Reserve in 2015. For the first time in my 10 year tenure, our
collections exceeded the assessment, if ever so slightly. This is a good sign
for the business climate in Indiana, as it means more businesses now exist
and are paying into the Fund than in 2013. Our assessment had been
$7,863,857 and we collected $7,880,341. $6,681,691 was paid out in benefits
and expenses.

The assessment for 2016 is significantly less than that of 2015. With direct
written premiums up, and losses paid by both self-insureds and carriers
down, all should be writing smaller (hopefully via e-checks) amounts this
year.

Included with this report are the Certification forms used to calculate
individual assessment obligations. These forms use numbers provided by
the ICRB as well as self-insured factors taken from new and renewal
applications for 2014. Historical data regarding Fund payouts can be
found on the last page.

2

We expect indemnity payments from the Fund to increase slightly in 2016 as new injured workers are added to the rolls at wages greater than those of the deceased recipients. Twenty-one recipients died in 2015 and eight were added. However, the cost of prosthetics in 2015 was once again the wild card. The variations in the years are not as pronounced as they used to be, with the increased cost of newer artificial members. As always, we continue to replace limbs with the "Chevy" not "Cadillac" model. With all of the uncertainty, our prudent reserve for prosthetics is a total of the three highest months in 2015.

A few years ago, the Board began tracking the quarterly time commitment of each staff member who works on SIF issues, as well as other factors such as IT expenses, postage and printing. The administrative expense assessed in 2016 will remain the same as in 2015.

Payments will be due on January 29th and June 30th, if you choose to use the installment option. This option is no longer available if your total assessment is less than $1,000. No reminder will be sent before the June due date. We also encourage you to take advantage of the State's new electronic payment system, which you can access at http://www.in.gov/wcb. This will be mandatory beginning in 2017.

Please call Mary Taivalkoski or me if you have questions or comments regarding the assessment, report, or the Fund.

Wishing you good health, happiness, peace, and prosperity in the 2016.

Yours very truly,

Linda Hamilton

Linda Peterson Hamilton

3

2nd INJURY FUND REPORT
December 23, 2015

Available Fund Balance 12/31/14	932,832
Revenue from 2015 Assessment	7,880,341
Total Available Monies 2015	8,813,173
Expenditures 2015:	
Indemnity (316 Recipients)	5,169,308
Prosthetics (76 Recipients)	1,402,237
Administrative Fees	107,926
SWCAP-Statewide Cost Allocation Plan	2,220
Total	6,681,691
Available Fund Balance 12/28/2015	**2,131,482**

2015 Assessment Factors

Indemnity (3 month expense)	1,380,510
Prosthetics (3 month expense)	793,246
Total Prudent Reserve	**2,173,756**
Estimated Expenditures	
Indemnity	5,376,080
Prosthetics	1,458,326
Administrative Fees	107,926
SWCAP-Statewide Cost Allocation Plan	1,549
Projected Expenditures	**6,943,881**
Estimated Need	**9,117,637**
12/31/2015 Available Fund Balance	-2,131,482
Final Assessment Amount	**6,986,155**

---

* 7.4.2.1 State-Wide Cost Allocation Plan (SWCAP)

4

Reported and Historical Data Utilized in Assessment of Fund

(Reported in dollars)

Reported by ICRB for 2014:

Total Losses Paid	416,215,000
Total Premiums Written	847,794,000

Reported by ICRB for 2013:

Total Losses Paid	457,915,000
Total Premiums Written	829,907,000

Reported by ICRB for 2012:

Total Losses Paid	445,461,000
Total Premiums Written	782,614,000

Reported by ICRB for 2011:

Total Losses Paid	436,329,000
Total Premiums Written	692,820,000

~~~~~~

Self-Insured Factors 2014:

Total Indemnity Paid	14,341,345
Total Medical Paid	50,020,132
Total Self Insured Factors	64,361,477

Self-Insured Factors 2013:

Total Indemnity Paid	14,779,695
Total Medical Paid	51,710,746
Total Self Insured Factors	66,490,441

Self-Insured Factors 2012:

Total Indemnity Paid	18,066,780
Total Medical Paid	43,575,323
Total Self Insured Factors	61,642,103

Self-Insured Factors 2011:

Total Indemnity Paid	21,016,610
Total Medical Paid	56,316,103
Total Self Insured Factors	77,332,713

5

Historical Second Injury Fund Data re.

Total Expenditures Reported By the WCB

(Reported in dollars)

Jan/Dec 2014
Prosthetics (79 Recipients)   1,298,573
Indemnity (325 Recipients)   5,143,074

Jan/Dec 2013
Prosthetics (65 Recipients)   780,300
Indemnity (312 Recipients)   4,794,848

Jan/Dec 2012
Prosthetics (68 Recipients)   1,019,258
Indemnity (302 Recipients)   4,735,990

Jan/Dec 2011
Prosthetics (67 Recipients)   585,801
Indemnity (293 Recipients)   4,375,287

Jan/Dec 2010
Prosthetics (62 Recipients)   561,247
Indemnity (291 Recipients)   4,227,113

Jan/Dec 2009
Prosthetics (63 Recipients)   624,711
Indemnity (289 Recipients)   4,099,537

Jan/Dec 2008
Prosthetics (50 Recipients)   527,506
Indemnity (281 Recipients)   3,413,452

Jan/Dec 2007
Prosthetics (53 Recipients)   539,340
Indemnity (271 Recipients)   3,539,032

6

§ 12:16 Application for Second Injury Fund benefits

**Indiana Worker's Compensation Board
Application for Second Injury Fund Benefits**
State Form 51247 (2-03)

Instructions: This form must be submitted in duplicate to: Indiana Workers Compensation Board
402 W. Washington, RM W196, Indianapolis, IN 46204-2753

PRIVACY NOTICE
*This agency is requesting disclosure of your Social Security number in accordance with IC 22-3-4-13. This disclosure is not mandatory and you will not be penalized for refusing.

Accident Number

CLAIMANT INFORMATION

Social Security Number *	Date of Birth	Last Name		First	Middle
Address			City		
State	Zip	Phone ( )			

INJURY INFORMATION

Date of Injury	Disputed Cause #	Date of Award	Type of Injury/Illness	Part of Body
Briefly describe the injury in your own words				

☐ Check here if you have received any second injury fund payments for this accident.

CLAIMANT'S AFFIDAVIT

As the injured party requesting benefits of the second injury fund administered by the Indiana Worker's Compensation fund, I do hereby

solemnly swear and affirm that the information given in this application is a true and accurate representation of the information regarding

my work-related injury, as witnessed on this _____ day of _____, two thousand and _____.

Notary Seal	Notary Signature	Applicant Signature
	Notary Printed Name	Applicant Printed Name
	Notary Commission Expiration Date	Date Prepared

APPLICATION CHECKLIST

In order to proceed in processing this application, The Board must receive from you the following items (Please Check):

☐ This completed application is signed and notarized   ☐ Form submitted in duplicate

☐ A current copy of the applicant's medical report.

§ 12:17   Certification for worker's compensation carriers

PLEASE TYPE OR PRINT LEGIBLY.   State Form 12386-b

CERTIFICATION FOR WORKER'S COMPENSATION CARRIERS

STATE OF _____

COUNTY OF _____

I, _____, hereby CERTIFY that I am _____
                                                                    (Official Title)

of _____ and that I have knowledge of the
            (Carrier)

workers' compensation records of Carrier. I further CERTIFY that the amount of **direct written premiums**
issued by Carrier for Indiana Worker's Compensation Insurance in the calendar year **2014** totaled $ _____.

I further CERTIFY that I have calculated Carrier's 2016 assessment for the Second Injury Fund by dividing the
above number representing Carrier's Direct Written Premiums by 847,794,000 (which, in dollars represents the total
direct written premiums for all worker's compensation carriers in Indiana in 2014), and then multiplying that figure
by 6,013,401 (which, in dollars represents the amount for all carriers portion of the 2016 assessment for the Second
Injury Fund).   This calculation gave me _____, which in dollars represents Carrier's total annual
assessment.

I further CERTIFY that the enclosed sum of $_____ represents one half of /entire
Company's calculated assessment, which is the first installment of the statutory assessment due by **January 29,
2016** and payable to the Worker's Compensation Board of Indiana for the Second Injury Fund. (This option is
available only if the assessment is greater than $1,00) I agree to pay $_____ as payment of the second half
of Company's assessment for 2016 *without notice* to the Board by **June 30, 2016.**

PLEASE PAY ELECTRONICALLY VIA http://www.in.gov/wcb.

I hereby verify, subject to penalties of perjury, that the facts contained herein are true.

_____   _____
Signature   Date

_____   _____
Carrier Name   Federal ID Number

_____   _____
Telephone Number   E-mail Address

_____   _____
Mailing Address   City, State, Zip

***Please note that IC§22-3-3-13(j) requires each company subject to this assessment to provide to the Board
the name, address, and E-mail address of a representative authorized to receive the notice of assessment.**

§ 12:18 Self-insured employer certification

PLEASE TYPE OR PRINT LEGIBLY.   State Form 12386

SELF-INSURED EMPLOYER CERTIFICATION

STATE OF _____

COUNTY OF _____

I, _____, hereby CERTIFY that I am _____
(Official Title)

of _____ and that I have knowledge of the
(Company)

workers' compensation records of (Company). I further CERTIFY that the amount of compensation, **including** medical, paid under the Indiana Worker's Compensation Act to injured employees, or their beneficiaries, during the calendar year **2014** was $_____.

I further CERTIFY that I have calculated this self-insured company's Second Injury Fund Assessment for 2016 by dividing the above number for total losses paid by 64,361,477 (which, in dollars represents the total amount of compensation paid by all self-insured employers), and then multiplying that figure by 930,480 (which, in dollars represents the amount for all self-insured employers' portion of the 2016 assessment for the Second Injury Fund). This calculation gave me _____, which in dollars, represents Company's annual assessment, payable in two equal installments.

I further CERTIFY that the enclosed sum of $_____ represents one half of/entire Company's calculated assessment, which is the first installment of the statutory assessment due on **January 29, 2016** and payable to the Worker's Compensation Board of Indiana for the Second Injury Fund. (This option is available only if the total assessment is greater than $1,000.) I agree to pay $_____ as payment of the second half of Company's assessment for 2013 *without notice* to the Board by **June 30, 2016.**

PLEASE PAY ELECTRONICALLY VIA: http://www.in.gov/wcb.

I hereby verify, subject to penalties of perjury, that the facts contained herein are true.

_____   _____
Signature   Date

_____   _____
Carrier Name   Federal ID Number

_____   _____
Telephone Number   E-mail Address

_____   _____
Mailing Address   City, State, Zip

***Please note that IC§22-3-3-13(j) requires each company subject to this assessment to provide to the Board the name, address, and E-mail address of a representative authorized to receive the notice of assessment.**

§ 12:19   Self-insurance guidelines

STATE OF INDIANA   - MICHAEL R. PENCE, Governor
WORKER'S COMPENSATION BOARD Linda Peterson Hamilton - Chairman
402 West Washington Street, Room W 196
Indianapolis, Indiana 46204-2753
Telephone: (317) 232-3808
www.in.gov/wcb

To: Indiana Self-Insured Employers

From: Linda Peterson Hamilton, Chairman

Re: 2016 Applications

Attached are the 2016 guidelines and renewal application for self-insuring in
the State of Indiana. Please keep in mind that it is extremely important that
you answer all of the questions on the application. All of the attachments and
additional information requested in item 7 must be provided. Incomplete
applications cannot be processed and will not be approved. The completed
application should be returned to our office no later than **July 31, 2016.** *Late
and incomplete applications are subject to a late fee as described below.*

Please note the following regarding the supplemental forms attached to the
application.

- Form SI-4 (Indemnity Agreement by the Parent Corporation for Wholly Owned or
  Majority Subsidiary) should be completed if you are adding or revising any
  subsidiaries.

- A valid surety bond or other approved security must be on file with the
  Board at all times. If we already have a bond (on the revised 2003 form) or
  other approved security, it is not necessary to include another with this
  application.

- A current SI-3 (Certificate of Excess Insurance) must be on file with the
  Board at all times. If we already have a current SI-3 on file for your
  company, it is not necessary to include another with this application.

- Only if you are specifically involved in the trucking industry, is it
  necessary to complete the Form SI-7 (Truckers Supplemental Application).

Pursuant to IC 22-3-5-1(b), renewal applications must be accompanied by a
payment of $250.00. The agency will not accept cash payments. Checks or money
orders must be payable to "Worker's Compensation Supplemental Administrative
Fund." **Incomplete applications and renewal applications received after July 31,
2016, will be charged an additional $250.00 late fee.** Filing extensions shall be
granted only under extraordinary circumstances and at the Chairman's
discretion.

All renewal applications and enclosures should be sent to the attention of Mary
Taivalkoski at the above address. If you have any questions, she can be
reached at (317) 232-3811 or via email at mtaivalkoski@wcb.in.gov.

(Revised 2016)

SELF-INSURANCE GUIDELINES
WORKER'S COMPENSATION BOARD OF INDIANA

Authority: Indiana Code 22-3-5-1 and 22-3-7-34

DEFINITIONS

As used in these guidelines, the following terms shall be construed as follows:

a. "Employer" includes any individual, firm, association or corporation, or the receiver or trustee of same, or the legal representatives of a deceased person, using the services of another for pay.

b. "Employee" includes every person, including a minor, in the service of another, under any contract of hire or apprenticeship, written or implied, except one whose employment is both casual and not in the usual course of the trade, business occupation or profession of the employer.

c. "Acts" includes the Worker's Compensation Act and the Occupational Diseases Act as found in IC 22-3.

d. "Rules" refers to the rules of the Worker's Compensation Board of Indiana as found in the Indiana Administrative Code (IAC) at Title 631.

e. "Board" refers to the Worker's Compensation Board of Indiana.

A. Applications

(1) An employer seeking waiver from insuring its risk under the Acts by receiving Board approval of becoming an individual self-insurer shall apply on the form prescribed by the Board.

(2) Initial and renewal applications shall contain answers to all questions and be executed by a qualified officer of the corporation, a partner or the sole proprietor.

B. Additional Requirements

As part of the application, compliance with all of the following shall be required:

(1) The applicant shall provide an audited financial statement disclosing the assets and liabilities of the business, prepared within the last six (6) months and signed by an officer, general partner or sole proprietor as is applicable to applicant's form of business. An annual report to the stockholders, if prepared within the last six (6) months and signed by an officer of the corporate applicant, is acceptable to fulfill this requirement. Such financial statement or annual report shall become part of the application. This information, upon receipt by the Board, shall be treated as confidential and shall not be released to any other entity.

(2) An employer shall have been in business for a period of not less than five continuous years and shall demonstrate sufficient financial strength and liquidity of the business to assure that all obligations concerning employees injured in the course and scope of their work for applicant shall be promptly met. An employer in business for less than five years may be considered if its liability is guaranteed by a parent corporation, provided such parent corporation has been in business for five continuous years or more, or upon other terms satisfactory to the Board.

(3) Specific and aggregate excess insurance, with acceptable policy limits and retention amounts, may be required in each self-insured program as a condition of approval.

(4) A surety bond shall be required as part of a self-insured program in a minimum amount of Five Hundred Thousand Dollars ($500,000.00).

   (a) No corporate surety shall be eligible to write self-insurance surety bonds unless authorized to transact such business in the State of Indiana by the Commissioner of Insurance.

   (b) Surety bonds shall be issued on a prescribed form and may be exchanged or replaced with another surety bond if 60 days notice of termination of liability is given and the replacement is approved by the Chairman.

   (c) Receipt by the Board of notice of cancellation of an employer's surety bond shall be grounds for termination of the employer's self-insured status unless a replacement surety bond acceptable to the Board is filed with the Board prior to the effective date of the cancellation.

(5) All parent companies must guarantee their subsidiary companies liability for payment of benefits. The form and substance of such guarantee shall be prescribed by the Board.

(6) Each individual self-insurer or its approved service company shall provide facilities and competent personnel to service its own program with respect to claims administration.

C. Compliance with Requirements, Notice, Additional Time, Certification and Renewal Application

(1) After considering the application and all supportive data, the Board will either grant approval or advise the employer in writing of the requirements to be met, and the time frame in which must be done, before approval will be granted. Self-insured status shall not become effective until all requirements for self-insured approval have been met and a certificate issued.

(2) The employer may be granted additional time to meet the requirements for the self-insured program provided it supplies security acceptable to the Board, at the sole discretion of the Board. A request for an extension of time shall be made in writing by the employer prior to the end of any period described in Section (C)(1). If the Board does not receive proof that all requirements for the self-insured program

have been met within the time prescribed, or any extension thereof, the application shall be denied.

(3) Upon meeting the requirements, an employer shall receive a certificate approving its status as a self-insured employer. The certificate shall expire on the 31st day of August of the following year. The employer shall submit a renewal application no less than thirty (30) days before expiration of its self-insured status, together with a current financial statement that meets the Board's requirements. Upon approval of a renewal application, the self-insured status shall be extended for one year.

D. Evaluating Employer- Factors for Approval, Notice of Denial or Termination

(1) In its sole discretion, the Board may decline to approve an application for self-insurance or terminate the self-insurance status if the employer is unable to demonstrate that it will be able to meet all obligations under the Acts, if it cannot supply security acceptable to the Board, or for failure to comply with the provisions of the Acts or Rules. The following factors may be used in determining if the employer can meet those obligations under the Acts.

    (a) Profit and loss history.
    (b) Organizational structure and management background.
    (c) Compensation loss history and proposed excess insurance coverage.
    (d) Source and reliability of financial information.
    (e) Number of employees.
    (f) Excess insurance.
    (g) Guarantee by parent company.
    (h) Surety bond.
    (i) Claims administration.
    (j) Dunn and Bradstreet rating, if any.

(2) Notice of denial or termination of self-insured status shall be given to the employer in writing. The notice will include the grounds for denial or termination.

E. Specific and Aggregate Excess Insurance

(1) No contract or policy of specific or aggregate excess insurance shall be recognized in considering the ability of an applicant to fulfill its financial obligations under the Acts unless such contract or policy complies with all of the following:

(a) Is issued by a casualty insurance company authorized to transact such business in this state.

(b) Is not subject to cancelation or nonrenewable unless written notice by registered or certified mail is given to the other party to the policy and to the Board at least thirty (30) days before termination is to occur.

(c) Regarding any type of commutation clause, shall provide that any commutation effected thereunder shall not relieve the underwriter or underwriters of further liability in respect to claims and expenses unknown at the initial commutation which is subsequently reopened by or through the Board or court. If the underwriter proposes to settle its liability for future payments payable as a lump sum to the employer, to be fixed as provided in the commutation, notice shall be given by the underwriter(s) or its (their) agent by registered or certified mail to the policy owner and the Board. If any commutation is effected, then the Board shall have the right to direct that such sum be placed in trust for the benefit of the injured employee(s) entitled to such future payments of compensation.

(d) Must state that, a self-insured employer becomes insolvent and is unable to make compensation payments, the excess carrier shall make, directly to claimants or their authorized representatives, such payments as would have been made by the excess carrier to the employer after it has been determined that the retention level has been reached on the excess contract.

(e) Shall contain language stating all of the following shall be applied toward achieving the retention level in the aggregate excess policy.

(f.) Payments made by the employer (ii.) Payments due and owing to claimants of the employees (iii.) Payments made on behalf of the employer by any surety required by the Board.

(g) Must contain certification that such policy fully complies with the policies of the Board and the directive of the Acts.

F. Third Party Administrators - Application, Requirements, Noncompliance

(1) Any individual, partnership, or corporation desiring to engage in the business of providing services through an approved compensation program for a self-insured employer shall, before entering into a contract with the employer, apply to the Board and satisfy the Board that it has adequate facilities and competent staff to administer the self-insurance program in such a manner as to fulfill the employer's obligations under the Acts and policies of the Board. Service may include, but is not limited to, claims adjusting, underwriting, and the capacity to provide required reporting, if any.

(2) Application for approval to act as a servicing company for self-insured employers shall be made on the required form. The application shall contain answers (under the penalties for perjury) to all questions propounded. Proof shall be furnisher that the applicant has within its organization, or has contracted on a full-time basis with, at least one person who has the knowledge and experience necessary to handle claims involving the Acts. The applicant must be approved before the third-party administrator (herein after TPA) service company enters into a contract with an approved self-insurer. Approvals shall be granted for an indefinite period, subject to revocation at the discretion of the Board Chairman.

(3) If the TPA seeks approval to provide underwriting services to self-insurers, proof shall be furnished that it has within its organization, or has contracted on a full-time basis with, at least one

person who has the knowledge and experience necessary to provide underwriting services for workers' compensation excess insurance coverage.

(4) TPA shall maintain adequate staff and the staff shall be authorized to act for the service company on all matters covered by the Acts and Rules.

(5) The TPA shall make available to the Board, upon demand, copies of all contracts entered into with Indiana self-insured employers. Such contracts, if requested, will be kept confidential by the Board. The TPA shall handle all claims with dates of injury or disease within the contract period until their conclusion, unless the TPA is relieved of the responsibility by subsequent agreement, an approved substitute TPA or administration by the self-insured entity is approved by the Board.

(6) Failure to comply with the provisions of the Acts or Rules shall be considered good cause for revocation of the approval to act as a TPA for Indiana self-insurers. Thirty (30) days notice of revocation shall be given and notice shall be served by certified or registered mail upon the employer and TPA.

(8) If incorporated, the service company must show proof that it is duly authorized to do business within the State of Indiana.

WORKERS COMPENSATION BOARD OF INDIANA

Date: 2/11/2016

Linda Peterson Hamilton, CHAIRPERSON

§ 12:20   Surety bond

WORKER'S COMPENSATION BOARD OF INDIANA   FORM SI-2
402 WEST WASHINGTON STREET, ROOM W196   (Revised 2003)
INDIANAPOLIS, IN 46204-2753
www.in.gov/workcomp

<u>SURETY BOND</u>

Bond Number _____

KNOW ALL MEN BE THESE PRESENTS THAT WE _____
_____, a/an _____Corporation
with principal place of business in the City of_____, State
of _____, as Principal, and_____, a/an
_____corporation, authorized to do business in Indiana, as Surety,
and held firmly bound unto the State of Indiana for the use and benefit of
all employees of the Principal and person who may be entitled to medical
treatment or compensation under the Worker's Compensation and Occupational
Diseases Acts ("the Acts") of the State of Indiana, in the sum of
_____dollars ($ _____),
lawful money of the United States, for the payment of which sum we bind
ourselves, our successors and assigns, jointly and severally firmly by these
presents.

WHEREAS, the principal has been granted the privilege of self-insuring its
workers' compensation liabilities under the Acts, as amended,

WHEREAS, the principal, by virtue of said self-insurer status, has undertaken
to pay employees all compensation, benefits and payments that are due, or
which may become due, then under the terms of the Acts, as amended, on
account of occupational disease, injury or death, with a personal injury date
that occurs while it is self-insured.

NOW, THEREFORE, the condition of this obligation is such that if the
principal, its heirs, executors, administrators (or its successors and
assigns in case of a corporation), shall well and truly discharge and pay all
compensation and all other benefits or payments for which it is liable, or
may become liable under the said Act on account of injury, disease or death
with a personal injury date that occurs during the effective period of this
bond, then this obligation shall be void, otherwise it shall remain in full
force and effect.

THE CONDITION OF THE FOREGOING OBLIGATION IS SUCH that the following
conditions shall also apply to this surety bond:

1) The Surety does, by these presents, undertake and agree that the
obligation of this bond shall cover and extend to all past, present, existing
and potential liability of said Principal, as a self-insurer, to the extent
of the penal sum herein named, without regard to specific injuries, date(s)
of injuries, happenings or events.

2)   This bond shall be continuous in form and shall remain in full force
and effect unless terminated in the manner hereinafter provided.

3) In the event said Principal shall fail to pay any award or awards which
shall be rendered against it by the Worker's Compensation Board of Indiana
("Board") with thirty (30) days after the same becomes, or became, final, the

Surety shall forthwith pay, to the extent of its liability under this bond, said award or awards, to the entitled thereto upon the order of the Board.

4) If the said Principal shall suspend payment or shall become insolvent or a receiver shall be appointed for its business, the undersigned Surety will pay said award(s), to the extent of its liability, under this bond, before the expiration of thirty (30) days after the same becomes, or became, final, without regard to any proceedings for liquidation of said Principal.

5) The undersigned are held and firmly bound for the payment of all legal costs, including reasonable attorney fees, litigation expenses and court costs incurred in all or any actions in proceedings taken to enforce payment of and all other provisions of this bond, or payments of any award or judgment rendered against the undersigned Surety, on account of the execution by it of this bond.

PROVIDED, the Surety herein, by and in the execution of this bond, does hereby recognize that said bond is a direct financial guarantee to and for the benefit of all unknown and unnamed employees of the Principal in connection with the Indiana Worker's Compensation and Occupational Disease Acts only.

IT IS FURTHER AGREED AND STIPULATED that the laws of the State of Indiana apply and any and all disputes that arise relating to this bond shall be within the jurisdiction of the State of Indiana.

IT IS FURTHER AGREED AND STIPULATED that this Bond may be cancelled at any time by the surety upon giving 60 days notice to the principal herein and to the Board, in which event the liabilities of the surety shall, at the expiration of said 60 days, cease and terminate, except as to such liabilities of the principal with a personal injury date or disablement that occurred during the effective period of the bond and prior to the expiration of said 60 days.

This Bond shall be effective until further order of the Board.

IN WITNESS WHEREOF, the said Principal has caused these presents to be executed by the signature of its_____ and attested by its_____ and said Surety has likewise caused these presents to be executed by the signature of its _____ and has caused its corporate name and seal to be attested by the signature of _____,its _____
     PROVIDED FURTHER, this Bond shall be effective as of the_____ day of _____20___ .

Signed, sealed and delivered this_____ day of _____ 20_____

FOR PRINCIPAL:

_____
(Signature)

_____

(Printed Name)

_____

Title

ATTEST:

_____
(Signature)

_____
(Printed Name)

_____
(Title)

FOR SURETY:

_____
(Signature)

_____
(Printed Name)

_____
(Title)

ATTEST:

_____
(Signature)

_____
(Printed Name)

_____
(Title)

§ 12:21 Certificate of excess insurance

WORKER'S COMPENSATION BOARD OF INDIANA   FORM SI-3
402 West Washington Street, Room W196   (Revised 2003)
Indianapolis, IN 46204
www.in.gov/workcomp

<u>WORKER'S COMPENSATION AND OCCUPATIONAL DISEASES ACTS</u>
<u>CERTIFICATE OF EXCESS INSURANCE</u>

This certifies that a Worker's Compensation and Occupational diseases Excess
Insurance Policy has been issued and delivered to the Employer named below,
and that by issuance and delivery of the said policy and the filing of this
certificate of insurance, it is admitted that said excess policy was
effective on the date stated below and that the coverage provided therein is
applicable to benefits under the Worker's Compensation Act and the
Occupational Diseases Act of the State of Indiana and that said policy shall
remain in full force and effect until thirty (30) days after receipt by the
Worker's Compensation Board of notice of its cancellation.

NAME OF INSURED EMPLOYER:_____

ADDRESS: _____

NAME OF INSURER: _____

ADDRESS: _____

NAME OF AUTHORIZED AGENT: _____

ADDRESS: _____

TELEPHONE NUMBER: _____

SIGNATURE OF AUTHORIZED AGENT: _____

POLICY NUMBER: _____

EFFECTIVE DATE: _____EXPIRATION DATE: _____

A copy of the policy is attached to this certificate.

FORM OF COVERAGE: Specific Excess_____ Aggregate Excess_____

     POLICY LIMITS: _____

     SELF-INSURED RETENTION: _____

It is specifically understood and agreed to by the excess insurance carrier
that this excess policy is issued for the purpose of inducing the Worker's
Compensation Board of Indiana to approve the Self-Insurance application of
the employer herein named and covered by this policy.

NOTE: This excess insurance coverage shall be for both worker's compensation
and occupational diseases unless otherwise specifically designated herein and
the express approval of the Board is specifically endorsed hereon.

§ 12:22   Trucker's supplemental application

WORKER'S COMPENSATION BOARD OF INDIANA   FORM SI-7
402 WEST WASHINGTON STREET, ROOM W196   (Revised 2003)
INDIANAPOLIS, IN 46204-2753
www.in.gov/workcomp

<u>TRUCKERS SUPPLEMENTAL APPLICATION</u>

1. Do you or your employees operate out of a base terminal? ___YES__ NO

A.   If YES, please give terminal address(es):

_____

_____

_____

  A list of drivers and their addresses assigned to each terminal must be
attached.

B.   If NO, do you or your employees spend a majority of driving time in any
one state?

_____YES - Give state of majority driving time for yourself and/or each
employee:

_____

_____

_____NO - Give your and/or your employees' state(s) of residence:

_____
_____

2. Do you lease employees to other firms? ___YES   ____NO

A.   If YES, list firm name(s) and street address(es) of locations where
leased employees are operating:

_____

_____

_____

AGREEMENT OF APPLICANT

The undersigned employer hereby certifies that the statements in this application have been read and understood. Furthermore, in consideration of the issuance of the approval to self-insure in the State of Indiana, the undersigned also certifies under the penalties of perjury, that the statements in this application are true and agrees:

A.____ To maintain a complete record of all payroll transactions in such a manner as the Worker's Compensation Board may reasonably require, and such record will be available to the Board at the designated address.

B.____ The applicant certifies that only those truckers/employees shall be assigned to this state in which the base terminal from which they truck on a regular basis is located.

For purposes of these procedures, the following definitions shall apply:

BASE TERMINAL: A permanent location with central loading docks and/or storage facilities where a trucker regularly goes to load, unload, store or transfer freight.

STATE OF RESIDENCE: The state in which the trucker resides as evidenced by the location used for the filing of federal income taxes.

REGULAR: A pattern of 40 hours per week or any other pattern that appears on a continuing basis.

STATE OF MAJORITY DRIVING TIME: State where trucker spends more time driving in or through than any others. Must be verifiable.

C.____ To comply substantially with all laws, orders, rules, guidelines, and regulations in force and effect made by the public authorities and with all reasonable recommendations made by the Worker's Compensation Board, relative to the welfare, health and safety of the employees.

_____	_____
BUSINESS NAME OF EMPLOYER	SIGNATURE OF COMPANY OFFICER
_____	_____
DATE OF APPLICATION	TITLE OF COMPANY OFFICER

§ 12:23 Employer's application for permission to carry risk without insurance

WORKER'S COMPENSATION BOARD OF INDIANA   STATE FORM 18488 9R13/3-990
402 WEST WASHINGTON STREET, ROOM W196   FORM SI-1 (Revised 2016)
INDIANAPOLIS, IN 46204-2753   Approved by State Board of Accounts
www.in.gov/wcb

WORKER'S COMPENSATION AND OCCUPATIONAL DISEASES ACTS
EMPLOYER'S APPLICATION FOR PERMISSION TO
CARRY RISK WITHOUT INSURANCE

The undersigned, an employer subject to the provisions of the "Indiana Worker's Compensation and Occupational Diseases Acts", hereby applies for a certificate to pay compensation directly, without insurance, to injured employees or to the dependents of employees who die in consequence of illness or injury for the period of September 1, 2016 to midnight, August 31, 2017; and, for the purpose of enabling the Worker's Compensation Board of Indiana to determine whether it possesses sufficient financial ability to render certain the payment of such compensation and medical expenses. This employer, under the penalties of perjury, hereby states the following facts:

1. EMPLOYER INFORMATION

_____New Applicant   _____Renewal Applicant

Applicant Name: _____

Address: _____

                      _____

                      _____

Nature of Business: _____

                      _____

Website Address: _____

FEIN: _____

If rated for credit standing by Dunn & Bradstreet, what is the rating?

_____

_____

If traded publicly, what is the stock symbol?   _____

2.   EMPLOYMENT INFORMATION/SUBSIDIARY INFORMATION

      Indiana Location(s)   Kind of Employment   # of Employees

          a. _____

          b. _____

          c. _____

          d. _____

          e. _____

      SUBSIDIARIES INCLUDED UNDER SELF-INSURANCE AUTHORITY

          FEIN #   TITLE NAME   CONTACT INFORMATION

          a. _____

          b. _____

          c. _____

          d. _____

          e. _____

3.   LOSS HISTORY

      Please find two alternative loss history charts. Only one chart
      is required to be filled out.

      Under Amount Paid, please provide the total paid for each
      category during the calendar year, regardless of the date of
      injury. Under # of Injuries, please provide the number of
      injuries which occurred during the calendar year that fell
      within, or resulted in payments in, each category(regardless of
      when paid). Some injuries will be counted in more than one
      category. The second alternative only requires you to breakdown
      number of injuries based on medical and indemnity.

      If this information is not provided on a calendar year basis, please
      specify the appropriate dates: _____ through _____ .

	2013		2014		2015	
	Amount Pd	# Injuries	Amount Pd	# Injuries	Amount Pd	# Injuries
Medical						
TTD						
TPD						
PTD						
PPI						
Death Benefits						
Burial Expenses						
Settlements						
First Report of Injury						
Amputation						
Prosthetic Device						
TOTAL	$		$		$	

4. BOND CALCULATION

(a) Determine three-year average of total medical/compensation paid per "Loss History"

        2013 Total Paid $_____
        2014 Total Paid   + $_____
        2015 Total Paid   + $_____
        Three-Year Total Paid $_____   divided by 3 = $_____
                                                            3yr average

(b) Multiply 3 year average by 2 $_____

(c) Enter total unpaid compensation liability for fatalities $_____

(d) Add lines (b) and (c) $_____

(e) Enter greater of $500,000 or line (d) $_____

(f) Increase/decrease in line (d) from prior year $_____

5. SECURITY

a. SURETY BOND
Amount of Bond $ _____   Cost of Bond $ _____ (Required)
                ($500,000.00 Minimum)   (Annual Premium)

Surety Name: _____ Telephone: _____

Address: _____

Bond # _____ **(Application cannot be processed if blank)**

b. EXCESS COVERAGE:

Specific $_____ Self-Insured Retention $ _____
Aggregate $_____ Cost of Excess $_____ (Required)
                                        (Annual Premium)

c. Does the employer have a system to establish a reserve to pay claims for medical treatment or compensation? _____

d. List other states, if any, in which the employer is self-insured

_____

6. SELF-INSURANCE ADMINISTRATION

It is the obligation of the employer to timely advise the Board of any
changes in the information provided below which occur during the
self-insured period. Please note that the Board now sends all notices
related to Self-Insurance via email.

(a) Identify the person within the employer's organization who is
    primarily responsible for the self-insurance program. This person
    will receive all notices as it relates to the self-insurance
    program, please list an alternative if you would like two
    individuals to receive notices:

Name: _____

E-Mail: _____

Address: _____

Telephone: _____

Fax: _____

Alternative:

Name: _____

E-Mail: _____

Address: _____

Telephone: _____

Fax: _____

(b) Identify the person who is primarily responsible for the adjustment
    of Indiana employee claims made pursuant of the self-insurance
    program (within your company or at your third-party administrator):

Name: _____

E-Mail: _____

Address: _____

Telephone: _____

Fax: _____

Number of years of experience in the adjustment of worker's
compensation and occupational disease claims: _____

(c) Identify the person who is primarily responsible to receive hearing notices and other official communications from the Worker's Compensation Board regarding Indiana disputed claims:

Name: _____

E-Mail: _____

Address: _____

Telephone: _____

Fax: _____

(d) All companies who carry risk without insurance must file first reports of injury electronically according to standards prescribed by the Board. Please indicate whether the applicant is able to comply with this mandate.
_____ Yes _____ No _____A copy of the approved plan is attached.

7. ATTACHMENTS

All applicants must attach the following items to this application:

_____ (a) An audited financial statement signed by an officer of the employer, such statement to become part of this application. A copy of the employer's last annual report to its stockholders may be accepted in lieu of a financial statement, if prepared within the last six (6) months. This information shall be treated as confidential by the Board and used only in evaluating this application. It will not be provided to any other entity.

_____ (b) Loss runs from the prior year to verify the information provided in the Loss History and Bond Calculation sections of the application. Detailed loss information is included, specifically claimants name and total payment amounts.

_____ (c) Information concerning involvement or membership in organizations or seminars specifically directed toward self-insured workers compensation issues.

_____ (d) Additional information concerning the knowledge of the Act, education and claims experience of the person responsible for receiving notices from injured employees, and the amount of time this person devotes to the workers compensation process (if self-administered).

_____ (e) Please provide information regarding training that those individuals responsible for the administration of self-insurance, have received in the past year regarding Indiana worker's compensation administration, laws, regulations, or other.

Additionally, new applicants must attach the following information:

_____ (i) Premium payments made the last three years and to what carrier(s).

_____ (ii) Loss runs from the prior three years to verify the information provided in the Loss History and Bond Calculation sections of the application.

_____ (iii) NCCI experience modification for the last three years.

_____ (iv) Audited financial statements, as described above, for the past three years.

_____ (v) Administrative costs anticipated in association with self-insuring, particularly if the applicant intends to utilize a third-party administrator.

8. CONDITIONS

The applicant hereby expressly understands and agrees as follows:

a. That this privilege may be revoked at any time at the discretion of the Worker's Compensation Board of Indiana ("Board").

b. That the applicant will fully discharge by immediately negotiable instrument payment of all installments of compensation for disability or impairment promptly when due, as well as liability for physician's fees, hospital services, hospital supplies, and burial.

c. That if the Board so requires, the applicant, within thirty (30) days after its continuing liability to pay compensation to an injured employee for a definite period for a permanent injury or to the dependents of a deceased employee has been determined, by agreement or award, will make a special deposit, with a bank or trust company within the State of Indiana approved by the Board, of the full amount of such definite continuing liability. Such special deposit to be made upon such terms as are prescribed by the Board.

d. That the applicant will promptly notify the Board of any change in condition which could ultimately affect its ability to pay medical expenses or compensation or administer its self-insurance program.

e. That the applicant will discharge all amounts due for statutory assessments under the Acts.

f. That the applicant will furnish and file with the Board any security agreement, surety bond, indemnity agreement, and/or excess insurance coverage, which may be required as a condition for approval of this application.

g. That the applicant, upon approval by the Board, recognizes, understands and agrees that in all cases the total assets of the applicant and its subsidiaries, if any, are pledged and available for the payment of any valid compensation or occupational disease claims made pursuant to Indiana law.

h. That the applicant understands that if its surety bond is canceled and no replacement bond is filed with the Board, its self-insured status shall terminate upon the effective date of the bond cancellation without further notice from the Board.

i. That the applicant understands and agrees that the surety posted will not be released until all possibility of additional losses has terminated and the Worker's Compensation Board has approved the bond's release, but in no event will the bond's release be granted prior to three years from the last date of self-insurance.

j. That the applicant understands and agrees that the surety bond posted will not be reduced until after two years from the last date of self-insurance and that the decision to reduce the bond will be based upon currently active claims and claims that have been closed within the two years prior to the date of the request for reduction of the bond.

The statements made herein are true and accurate to the best information and knowledge of the undersigned and are made for the express purpose of inducing the Worker's Compensation Board of Indiana to grant the applicant self-insured status as allowed by IC 22-3-5-1.

This application is executed at _____ this _____ day of

_____, _____.

FOR THE APPLICANT:

_____
Company)

BY: _____
(Signature)

_____
(Printed Name)

TITLE _____
(Must be an Officer of Applicant)

TELEPHONE NUMBER: _____

FOR BOARD USE ONLY:

_____APPROVED   _____DENIED

COMMENTS: _____

_____

_____

DATED: _____

WORKERS COMPENSATION BOARD OF INDIANA

_____

BY: Linda Peterson Hamilton, Chairman

Application Type	Amount Due	Payment Information
New application	$500.00	
Renewal Application	$250.00	
Late: filed after 7/31/16 or incomplete renewal application		

§ 12:24 Employer's request to include subsidiary within its self-insurance program

WORKER'S COMPENSATION BOARD OF INDIANA   FORM SI-5
402 WEST WASHINGTON STREET, ROOM W196   (Revised 2012)
INDIANAPOLIS, IN 46204-2753
www.in.gov/workcomp

WORKER'S COMPENSATION AND OCCUPATIONAL DISEASES ACTS
EMPLOYER'S REQUEST TO INCLUDE
A SUBSIDIARY WITHIN ITS SELF-INSURANCE PROGRAM

The undersigned, an employer subject to the provisions of the "Indiana
Worker's Compensation and Occupational Diseases Acts", hereby requests that a
subsidiary be added to its self-insurance program. This subsidiary will
remain within the self-insurance program until the parent company requests,
in writing, the subsidiary's withdrawal, and that request is approved by the
Worker's Compensation Board. This employer, under the penalties of perjury,
hereby states the following facts:

1. SELF-INSURED ENTITY   FEIN

    _____   _____

    SUBSIDIARY   FEIN

    _____   _____

2. EMPLOYMENT INFORMATION (For Subsidiary)

    Indiana Location(s)   Kind of Employment   # of Employees

        a. _____

        b. _____

        c. _____

        d. _____

        e. _____

3. LOSS HISTORY (Include Subsidiary to be added)

    Under Amount Paid, please provide the total paid for each category
during the calendar year, regardless of the date of the injury. Under #
Injuries, please provide the number of injuries which occurred during the
calendar year that fell within, or resulted in payments in, each category
(regardless of when paid.) Some injuries will be counted in more than one
category.

If this information is not provided on a calendar year basis, please specify the appropriate dates: _____ through_____.

	2009		2010		2011	
	Amount Pd	# Injuries	Amount Pd	# Injuries	Amount Pd	# Injuries
Medical						
TTD						
TPD						
PTD						
PPI						
Death Benefits						
Burial Expenses						
Settlements						
First Report of Injury						
Amputation						
Prosthetic Device						
TOTAL	$		$		$	

4. BOND CALCULATION

(a) Determine three-year average of total medical/compensation paid per "Loss History" (Be sure to include the subsidiary)

        2009 Total Paid $_____
        2010 Total Paid   + $_____
        2011 Total Paid   + $_____
        Three-Year Total Paid $_____   divided by 3 = $_____
                                                                      3yr average

(b) Multiply 3 year average by 2 $_____

(c) Enter total unpaid compensation liability for fatalities $_____

(d) Add lines (b) and (c) $_____

(e) Enter greater of $500,000 or line (d) $_____

WORKER'S COMPENSATION BOARD OF INDIANA
402 WEST WASHINGTON STREET, ROOM W196
INDIANAPOLIS, IN 46204-2753
www.in.gov/workcomp

FORM SI-4
(Revised 2012)

INDEMNITY AGREEMENT BY THE PARENT CORPORATION
FOR WHOLLY OWNED OR MAJORITY OWNED SUBSIDIARY

(Use a separate form for each subsidiary to be indemnified. Do not alter or modify.)

KNOW ALL MEN BY THESE PRESENTS, THAT _____
                                        (Name of Parent Company)
corporation, organized and existing under and by virtue of the laws of the State of _____
do hereby guarantee payment of the compensation, provided for under the compensation provisions of the Worker's Compensation and Occupational Diseases Acts of the State of Indiana, and in the event that said
_____ shall not pay or cause to be direct
      (Name of Subsidiary)
to its employees the compensation due or that may become due under said Acts, then the undersigned parent corporation covenants and agrees that it will pay to all such employees of the named subsidiary such compensation, including a reasonable attorney fee incurred by said employees in any action brought on this agreement, with the express agreement and understanding as a condition precedent to the execution and acceptance of this agreement, that it is, for the benefit of all unknown and unnamed employees of said named subsidiary, and that said employees are hereby empowered and authorized to maintain direct action on this agreement and that the parent corporation does recognize this agreement as a direct financial guarantee to said employees or the dependents of a deceased employee; that the parent corporation shall have a right to cancel and terminate this agreement at any time upon giving the named subsidiary and the Worker's Compensation Board of Indiana at least SIXTY (60) DAYS written notice of its intent to cancel. Such cancellation shall not affect its liability as to any compensation for injuries occurring prior to TEN (10) DAYS after the date of cancellation specified in such notice.

PROVIDED HOWEVER, that cancellation of this indemnity agreement shall be allowed only upon the presentation of proof of the financial ability of the subsidiary to pay compensation direct and upon the approval of the Worker's Compensation Board of Indiana. The liability of the parent corporation as a result of this Indemnity Agreement shall not terminate except-upon order of the Board.

This agreement shall be effective as of the_____day of_____20___.

Executed at_____ this_____day of_____ 20_____.

FOR PARENT CORPORATION: **ATTEST:**

_____   _____
Signature   Signature of Corporate Secretary

_____   _____
Printed Name   Printed Name

_____
Title

(SEAL)

§ 12:25 Indemnity agreement by parent corporation for wholly owned or majority owned subsidiary

WORKER'S COMPENSATION BOARD OF INDIANA   FORM SI-4
402 WEST WASHINGTON STREET, ROOM W196   (Revised 2003)
INDIANAPOLIS, IN 46204-2753
www.in.gov/workcomp

INDEMNITY AGREEMENT BY THE PARENT CORPORATION
FOR WHOLLY OWNED OR MAJORITY OWNED SUBSIDIARY

(Use a separate form for each subsidiary to be indemnified. Do not alter or modify.)

KNOW ALL MEN BY THESE PRESENTS, THAT _____
                                          (Name of Parent Company)
corporation, organized and existing under and by virtue of the laws of the
State of _____
do hereby guarantee payment of the compensation, provided for under the
compensation provisions of the Worker's Compensation and Occupational
Diseases Acts of the State of Indiana, and in the event that said
_____shall not pay or cause to be direct
       (Name of Subsidiary)
to its employees the compensation due or that may become due under said Acts,
then the undersigned parent corporation covenants and agrees that it will pay
to all such employees of the named subsidiary such compensation, including a
reasonable attorney fee incurred by said employees in any action brought on
this agreement, with the express agreement and understanding as a condition
precedent to the execution and acceptance of this agreement, that it is, for
the benefit of all unknown and unnamed employees of said named subsidiary,
and that said employees are hereby empowered and authorized to maintain
direct action on this agreement and that the parent corporation does
recognize this agreement as a direct financial guarantee to said employees or
the dependents of a deceased employee; that the parent corporation shall have
a right to cancel and terminate this agreement at any time upon giving the
named subsidiary and the Worker's Compensation Board of Indiana at least
SIXTY (60) DAYS written notice of its intent to cancel. Such cancellation
shall not affect its liability as to any compensation for injuries occurring
prior to TEN (10) DAYS after the date of cancellation specified in such
notice.

   PROVIDED HOWEVER, that cancellation of this indemnity agreement shall be
allowed only upon the presentation of proof of the financial ability of the
subsidiary to pay compensation direct and upon the approval of the Worker's
Compensation Board of Indiana. The liability of the parent corporation as a
result of this Indemnity Agreement shall not terminate except-upon order
of the Board.

   This agreement shall be effective as of the_____day of_____20___.

Executed at_____ this_____day of_____ 20_____.

FOR PARENT CORPORATION: **ATTEST:**

_____
Signature

_____
Signature of Corporate Secretary

_____
Printed Name

_____
Printed Name

_____
Title

(SEAL)

APPENDIX A

The Indiana Worker's Compensation Act

Article 3 WORKER'S COMPENSATION SYSTEM

Chapter 1. Worker's Compensation Board

22-3-1-1. Creation; members; terms of office; conflicts of interest; removal from office; compensation; executive administrator

Sec. 1. There is hereby created the worker's compensation board of Indiana, which shall consist of seven (7) members, not more than four (4) of whom shall belong to the same political party, appointed by the governor, one (1) of whom the governor shall designate as chairman. All members of the board shall be attorneys in good standing admitted to the practice of law in Indiana.

(b) Each member of said board shall hold office for four (4) years and until the member's successor is appointed and qualified.

(c) No member of the board shall hold any other position of trust or profit or engage in any occupation or business interfering with or inconsistent with the discharge of the member's duties.

(d) Any member of said board may be removed by the governor at any time for incompetency, neglect of duty, misconduct in office, or other good cause to be stated in writing in the order of removal. In case of a vacancy in the membership of the said board, the governor shall appoint for the unexpired term.

(e) The budget agency, with the approval of the governor, shall approve the salaries of the members of the board and the secretary.

(f) The board may appoint an executive administrator and may remove the executive administrator. The executive administrator shall have authority to administer oaths and issue subpoenas in connection with the administration of IC 22–3–2 through IC 22–3–7.

(g) The board, subject to the approval of the governor, may employ and fix the compensations of such clerical and other assistants as it may deem necessary.

(h) The members of the board and its assistants shall be entitled to receive from the state their actual and necessary expenses while traveling on the business of the board, but such expenses shall be approved by the chairman of the board before payment is made.

(i) All salaries and expenses of the board shall be audited and paid out of the state treasury in the manner prescribed for similar expenses in other departments or branches of the state service.

Amended by P.L.144–1986, SEC.21; P.L.28–1988, SEC.18; P.L.134–2006, SEC.1, eff. Mar. 22, 2006; P.L.168–2011, SEC.1.

22–3–1–2. Jurisdiction

Sec. 2. The worker's compensation board shall administer the worker's compensation law (IC 22–3–2 through IC 22–3–6).

Amended by P.L.37–1985, SEC.29; P.L.28–1988, SEC.19.

22–3–1–3. Rules; powers and duties

Sec. 3. The worker's compensation board may adopt rules under IC 4–22–2 to carry into effect the worker's compensation law (IC 22–3–2 through IC 22–3–6) and the worker's occupational diseases law (IC 22–3–7).

(b) The worker's compensation board is authorized:

(1) to hear, determine, and review all claims for compensation under IC 22–3–2 through IC 22–3–7;

(2) to require medical service for injured employees;

(3) to approve claims for medical service or attorney's fees and the charges for nurses and hospitals;

(4) to approve agreements;

(5) to modify or change awards;

(6) to make conclusions of facts and rulings of law;

(7) to certify questions of law to the court of appeals;

(8) to approve deductions in compensation made by employers for amounts paid in excess of the amount required by law;

(9) to approve agreements between an employer and an employee or the employee's dependents for the cash payment of compensation in a lump sum, or, in the case of a person under eighteen (18) years of age, to order cash payments;

(10) to establish and maintain a list of independent medical examiners and to order physical examinations;

(11) to subpoena witnesses;

(12) to administer oaths;

(13) to apply to the circuit or superior court to enforce the attendance and testimony of witnesses and the production and examination of books, papers, and records;

(14) to create and undertake a program designed to educate and provide assistance to employees and employers regarding the rights and remedies provided by IC 22–3–2 through IC 22–3–7, and to provide for informal resolution of disputes;

(15) to assess and collect, on the board's own initiative or on the motion of a party, the penalties provided for in IC 22–3–2 through IC 22–3–7; and

(16) to exercise all other powers and duties conferred upon the board by law.

Amended by P.L.37–1985, SEC.30; P.L.28–1988, SEC.20; P.L.170–1991, SEC.1.

22–3–1–4. Definitions

Sec. 4. As used in this section, "attorney's fees" means the fees requested for compensation for service provided by an attorney to a claimant under the worker's compensation law and the worker's occupational diseases law as provided under section 3(b)(3) of this chapter.

(b) As used in this section, "board" refers to the worker's compensation board of Indiana established by section 1 of this chapter.

(c) As used in this section, "claim" refers to a claim for compensation under IC 22–3–2 through IC 22–3–7 filed with the board.

(d) The following schedule of attorney's fees applies to an attorney who represents a claimant before the board when the claim for compensation results in a recovery:

(1) A minimum of two hundred dollars ($200).

(2) Twenty percent (20%) of the first fifty thousand dollars ($50,000) of recovery.

(3) Fifteen percent (15%) of the recovery in excess of fifty thousand dollars ($50,000).

(4) Ten percent (10%) of the value of:

(A) unpaid medical expenses;

(B) out–of–pocket medical expenses; or

(C) future medical expenses.

(e) The board maintains continuing jurisdiction over all attorney's fees in cases before the board and may order a different attorney's fee or allowance in a particular case.

As added by P.L.134–2006, SEC.2.

22–3–1–5. "Contractor" defined; improper classifications of contractors; disclosure of information

Sec. 5. This section applies after December 31, 2009.

(b) As used in this section, "contractor" means:

(1) a sole proprietor;

(2) a partnership;

(3) a firm;

(4) a corporation;

(5) a limited liability company;

(6) an association; or

(7) another legal entity;

that engages in construction and is authorized by law to do business in Indiana. The term includes a general contractor, a subcontractor, and a lower tiered contractor. The term does not include the state, the federal government, or a political subdivision.

(c) The worker's compensation board of Indiana shall cooperate with the:

(1) department of state revenue established by IC 6–8.1–2–1;

(2) department of labor created by IC 22–1–1–1; and

(3) department of workforce development established by IC 22–4.1–2–1;

by sharing information concerning any suspected improper classification by a contractor of an individual as an independent contractor (as defined in IC 22–3–6–1(b)(7) or IC 22–3–7–9(b)(5)).

(d) For purposes of IC 5–14–3–4, information shared under this section is confidential, may not be published, and is not open to public inspection.

(e) An officer or employee of the worker's compensation board of Indiana who knowingly or intentionally discloses information that is confidential under this section commits a Class A misdemeanor.

As added by P.L.164–2009, SEC.3.

Chapter 2. Worker's Compensation: Application, Rights, and Remedies

22–3–2–2. Mandatory compliance; exemptions

Sec. 2. Every employer and every employee, except as stated in IC 22–3–2 through IC 22–3–6, shall comply with the provisions of IC 22–3–2 through IC 22–3–6 respectively to pay and accept compensation for personal injury or death by accident arising out of and in the course of the employment, and shall be bound thereby. The burden of proof is on the employee. The proof by the employee of an element of a claim does not create a presumption in favor of the employee with regard to another element of the claim.

(b) IC 22–3–2 through IC 22–3–6 does not apply to railroad employees engaged in train service as:

(1) engineers;

(2) firemen;

(3) conductors;

(4) brakemen;

(5) flagmen;

(6) baggagemen; or

(7) foremen in charge of yard engines and helpers assigned thereto.

(c) IC 22–3–2 through IC 22–3–6 does not apply to employees of municipal corporations in Indiana who are members of:

(1) the fire department or police department of any such municipality; and

(2) a firefighters' pension fund or of a police officers' pension fund.

However, if the common council elects to purchase and procure worker's compensation insurance to insure said employees with respect to medical benefits under IC 22–3–2 through IC 22–3–6, the medical provisions of IC 22–3–2 through IC 22–3–6 apply to members of the fire department or police department of any such municipal corporation who are also members of a firefighters' pension fund or a police officers' pension fund.

(d) IC 22–3–2 through IC 22–3–6 do not apply to the following:

(1) A person who enters into an independent contractor agreement with a nonprofit corporation that is recognized as tax exempt under Section 501(c)(3) of the Internal Revenue Code[1] (as defined in IC 6–3–1–11(a)) to perform youth coaching services on a part-time basis.

(2) A nonprofit corporation that is recognized as tax exempt under Section 501(c)(3) of the Internal Revenue Code (as defined in IC 6–3–1–11(a)) to the extent the corporation enters into an independent contractor agreement with a person for the performance of youth coaching services on a part-time basis.

(e) When any municipal corporation purchases or procures worker's compensation insurance covering members of the fire department or police department who are also members of a

---

[1]26 U.S.C.A. § 501(c)(3).

firefighters' pension fund or a police officers' pension fund, and pays the premium or premiums for such insurance, the payment of such premiums is a legal and allowable expenditure of funds of any municipal corporation.

(f) Except as provided in subsection (g), where the common council has procured worker's compensation insurance under this section, any member of such fire department or police department employed in the city carrying such worker's compensation insurance under this section is limited to recovery of medical and surgical care, medicines, laboratory, curative and palliative agents and means, x-ray, diagnostic and therapeutic services to the extent that such services are provided for in the worker's compensation policy procured by such city, and shall not also recover in addition to that policy for such same benefits provided in IC 36–8–4.

(g) If the medical benefits provided under a worker's compensation policy procured by the common council terminate for any reason before the police officer or firefighter is fully recovered, the common council shall provide medical benefits that are necessary until the police officer or firefighter is no longer in need of medical care.

(h) The provisions of IC 22–3–2 through IC 22–3–6 apply to:

(1) members of the Indiana general assembly; and

(2) field examiners of the state board of accounts.

Amended by Acts 1981, P.L.11, SEC.125; P.L.28–1988, SEC.21; P.L.217–1989, SEC.1; P.L.201–2005, SEC.1; P.L.134–2006, SEC.3.

22–3–2–2.1. Coverage for rostered volunteers

Sec. 2.1.   As used in this section, "rostered volunteer" means a volunteer:

(1) whose name has been entered on a roster of volunteers for a volunteer program operated by a unit; and

(2) who has been approved by the proper authorities of the unit.

The term does not include a volunteer firefighter (as defined in IC 36–8–12–2) or an inmate assigned to a correctional facility operated by the state or a unit.

(b) As used in this section, "unit" means a county, a municipality, or a township.

(c) A rostered volunteer may be covered by the medical treatment provisions of the worker's compensation law (IC 22–3–2 through IC 22–3–6) and the worker's occupational disease law (IC 22–3–7). If compensability of an injury is an issue, the administrative procedures of IC 22–3–2 through IC 22–3–7 apply as appropriate.

(d) All expenses incurred for premiums of the insurance allowed or other charges or expenses under this section shall be paid out of the unit's general fund in the same manner as other expenses of the unit are paid.

As added by P.L.51–1993, SEC.2.

22–3–2–2.3. Volunteer workers; services; medical benefits

Sec. 2.3. As used in this section, "volunteer worker" means a person who:

(1) performs services:

(A) for a state institution (as defined in IC 12–7–2–184); and

(B) for which the person does not receive compensation of any nature; and

(2) has been approved and accepted as a volunteer worker by the director of:

(A) the division of disability and rehabilitative services; or

(B) the division of mental health and addiction.

(b) Services of any nature performed by a volunteer worker for a state institution (as defined in IC 12–7–2–184) are governmental services. A volunteer worker is subject to the medical benefits described under this chapter through IC 22–3–6. However, a volunteer worker is not under this chapter through IC 22–3–6.

As added by P.L.2–1992, SEC.739. Amended by P.L.4–1993, SEC.257; P.L.5–1993, SEC.270; P.L.24–1997, SEC.62; P.L.215–2001, SEC.98; P.L.141–2006, SEC.104.

22–3–2–2.5. School to work students

Sec. 2.5. As used in this section, "school to work student" refers to a student participating in on-the-job training under the federal School to Work Opportunities Act (20 U.S.C. 6101 et seq.).

(b) Except as provided in IC 22–3–7–2.5, a school to work student is entitled to the following compensation and benefits under this article:

(1) Medical benefits under IC 22–3–2 through IC 22–3–6.

(2) Permanent partial impairment compensation under IC 22–3–3–10. Permanent partial impairment compensation for a school to work student shall be paid in a lump sum upon agreement or final award.

(3) In the case that death results from the injury:

(A) death benefits in a lump sum amount of one hundred seventy-five thousand dollars ($175,000), payable upon agreement or final award to any dependents of the student under IC 22–3–3–18 through IC 22–3–3–20, or, if the student has no dependents, to the student's parents; and

(B) burial compensation under IC 22–3–3–21.

(c) For the sole purpose of modifying an award under IC 22–3–3–27, a school to work student's average weekly wage is presumed to be equal to the federal minimum wage.

(d) A school to work student is not entitled to the following compensation under this article:

(1) Temporary total disability compensation under IC 22–3–3–8.

(2) Temporary partial disability compensation under IC 22–3–3–9.

(e) Except for remedies available under IC 5–2–6.1, recovery under subsection (b) is the exclusive right and remedy for:

(1) a school to work student; and

(2) the personal representatives, dependents, or next of kin, at common law or otherwise, of a school to work student;

on account of personal injury or death by accident arising out of and in the course of school to work employment.

As added by P.L.235–1999, SEC.1.

22-3-2-4. Pre-existing contracts; continuance; minors

Sec. 4. Every contract of service between any employer and employee covered by IC 22–3–2 through IC 22–3–6, written or implied, in operation on May 21, 1929, or made or implied prior to May 21, 1929, shall, after May 21, 1929, be presumed to continue; and every such contract made subsequent to May 21, 1929, shall be presumed to have been made subject to the provisions of IC 22–3–2 through IC 22–3–6 unless either party, except as provided in section 15 of this chapter, shall give notice, as provided in section 9 of this chapter, to the other party to such contract that the provisions of IC 22–3–2 through IC 22–3–6 (other than IC 22–3–4–13) are not intended to apply.

(b) A like presumption shall exist equally in the case of all minors unless notice of the same character be given by or to the parent or guardian of the minor.

Amended by P.L.144–1986, SEC.23.

22-3-2-5. Insurance; certificates authorizing carrying of risk without insurance; state self-insurance program

Sec. 5.(a) Every employer who is bound by the compensation provisions of IC 22–3–2 through IC 22–3–6, except the state, counties, townships, cities, towns, school cities, school towns, other municipal corporations, state institutions, state boards, state commissions, banks, trust companies, and building and loan associations, shall insure the payment of compensation to the employer's employees and their dependents in the manner provided in IC 22-3-3, or procure from the worker's compensation board a certificate authorizing the employer to carry such risk without insurance. While such insurance or such certificate remains in force, the employer or those conducting the employer's business and the employer's worker's compensation insurance carrier shall be liable to any employee and the employee's dependents for personal injury or death by accident arising out of and in the course of employment only to the extent and in the manner specified in IC 22-3-2 through IC 22-3-6.

(b) The state may not purchase worker's compensation insurance. The state may establish a program of self-insurance to cover its liability under this article. The state may administer its program of self-insurance or may contract with any private agency, business firm, limited liability company, or corporation to administer any part of the program. The state department of insurance may, in the manner prescribed by IC 4-22-2, adopt the rules necessary to implement the state's program of self-insurance.

Amended by P.L.28-1983, SEC.56; P.L.28-1988, SEC.22; P.L.8-1993, SEC.279; P.L.233-2015, SEC.319, eff. July 1, 2015.

22–3–2–6. Exclusive remedies

Sec. 6. The rights and remedies granted to an employee subject to IC 22–3–2 through IC 22–3–6 on account of personal injury or death by accident shall exclude all other rights and remedies of such employee, the employee's personal representatives, dependents, or next of kin, at common law or otherwise, on account of such injury or death, except for remedies available under IC 5–2–6.1.

Amended by Acts 1982, P.L.21, SEC.50; P.L.2–1992, SEC.740; P.L.47–1993, SEC.11.

22–3–2–7. Performance of statutory duties; application of law

Sec. 7. Nothing in IC 22–3–2 through IC 22–3–6 shall be construed to relieve any employer or employee from penalty for failure or neglect to perform any statutory duty.

Amended by P.L.144–1986, SEC.24.

22–3–2–8. Qualifications; burden of proof

Sec. 8. No compensation is allowed for an injury or death due to the employee's knowingly self-inflicted injury, his intoxication, his commission of an offense, his knowing failure to use a safety appliance, his knowing failure to obey a reasonable written or printed rule of the employer which has been posted in a conspicuous position in the place of work, or his knowing failure to perform any statutory duty. The burden of proof is on the defendant.

Amended by Acts 1978, P.L.2, SEC.2209.

22–3–2–9.   Exempt employees; waiver of exemption; notice of acceptance

Sec. 9. IC 22–3–2 through IC 22–3–6 shall not apply to:

(1) casual laborers (as defined in IC 22–3–6–1);

(2) farm or agricultural employees;

(3) household employees; or

(4) a person who enters into an independent contractor agreement with a nonprofit corporation that is recognized as tax exempt under Section 501(c)(3) of the Internal Revenue Code[2] (as defined in IC 6–3–1–11(a)) to perform youth coaching services on a part-time basis.

IC 22–3–2 through IC 22–3–6 do not apply to the employers or contractors of the persons listed in this subsection.

(b) An employer who is exempt under this section from the operation of the compensation provisions of this chapter may at any time waive such exemption and thereby accept the provisions of this chapter by giving notice as provided in subsection (c).

(c) The notice of acceptance referred to in subsection (b) shall be given thirty (30) days prior to any accident resulting in injury or death, provided that if any such injury occurred less than thirty (30) days after the date of employment, notice of acceptance given at the time of employment shall be sufficient notice thereof. The notice shall be in writing or print in a substantial form prescribed by the worker's compensation board and shall be given by the employer by posting the same in a conspicuous place in the plant, shop, office, room, or place where the employee is employed, or by serving it personally upon the employee; and shall be given by the employee by sending the same in registered letter addressed to the employer at the employer's last known residence or place of business, or by giving it personally to the employer, or any of the employer's agents upon whom a summons in civil actions may be served under the laws of the state.

(d) A copy of the notice in prescribed form shall also be filed with the worker's compensation board, within five (5) days after its service in such manner upon the employee or employer.

Amended by P.L.28–1988, SEC.23; P.L.258–1997(ss), SEC.1; P.L.201–2005, SEC.2.

---

[2]26 U.S.C.A. § 501(c)(3).

22-3-2-13. Claims against third persons; subrogation; procedures

Sec. 13. Whenever an injury or death, for which compensation is payable under chapters 2 through 6 of this article shall have been sustained under circumstances creating in some other person than the employer and not in the same employ a legal liability to pay damages in respect thereto, the injured employee, or the injured employee's dependents, in case of death, may commence legal proceedings against the other person to recover damages notwithstanding the employer's or the employer's compensation insurance carrier's payment of or liability to pay compensation under chapters 2 through 6 of this article. In that case, however, if the action against the other person is brought by the injured employee or the injured employee's dependents and judgment is obtained and paid, and accepted or settlement is made with the other person, either with or without suit, then from the amount received by the employee or dependents there shall be paid to the employer or the employer's compensation insurance carrier, subject to its paying its pro-rata share of the reasonable and necessary costs and expenses of asserting the third party claim, the amount of compensation paid to the employee or dependents, plus the services and products and burial expenses paid by the employer or the employer's compensation insurance carrier and the liability of the employer or the employer's compensation insurance carrier to pay further compensation or other expenses shall thereupon terminate, whether or not one (1) or all of the dependents are entitled to share in the proceeds of the settlement or recovery and whether or not one (1) or all of the dependents could have maintained the action or claim for wrongful death.

In the event the injured employee or the employee's dependents, not having received compensation or services and products or death benefits from the employer or the employer's compensation insurance carrier, shall procure a judgment against the other party for injury or death, which judgment is paid, or if settlement is made with the other person either with or without suit, then the employer or the employer's compensation insurance carrier shall have no liability for payment of compensation or for payment of services and products or death benefits whatsoever, whether or not one (1) or all of the dependents are entitled to share in the proceeds of settlement or recovery and whether or not one (1) or all of the dependents could have maintained the action or claim for wrongful death.

In the event any injured employee, or in the event of the employee's death, the employee's dependents, shall procure a final judgment against the other person other than by agreement, and the judgment is for a lesser sum than the amount for which the employer or the employer's compensation insurance carrier is liable for compensation and for services and products, as of the date the judgment becomes final, then the employee, or in the event of the employee's death, the employee's dependents, shall have the option of either collecting the judgment and repaying the employer or the employer's compensation insurance carrier for compensation previously drawn, if any, and repaying the employer or the employer's compensation insurance carrier for services and products previously paid, if any, and of repaying the employer or the employer's compensation insurance carrier the burial benefits paid, if any, or of assigning all rights under the judgment to the employer or the employer's compensation insurance carrier and thereafter receiving all compensation and services and products, to which the employee or in the event of the employee's death, which the employee's dependents would be entitled if there had been no action brought against the other party.

If the injured employee or the employee's dependents shall agree to receive compensation from the employer or the employer's compensation insurance carrier or to accept from the employer or the employer's compensation insurance carrier, by loan or otherwise, any payment on account of the compensation, or institute proceedings to recover the same, the employer or the employer's compensation insurance carrier shall have a lien upon any settlement award, judgment or fund out of which the employee might be compensated from the third party.

The employee, or in the event of the employee's death, the employee's dependents, shall institute legal proceedings against the other person for damages, within two (2) years after the cause of action accrues. If, after the proceeding is commenced, it is dismissed, the employer or the employer's compensation insurance carrier, having paid compensation or having become liable therefor, may collect in their own name, or in the name of the injured employee, or, in case of death, in the name of the employee's dependents, from the other person in whom legal liability for damages exists, the compensation paid or payable to the injured employee, or the employee's dependents, plus services and products, and burial expenses paid by the employer or the employer's compensation insurance carrier or for which they have become liable. The employer or the employer's compensation insurance carrier may commence an action at law for collection against the other person in whom legal liability for damages exists, not later than one (1) year from the date the action so commenced has been dismissed, notwithstanding the provisions of any statute of limitations to the contrary.

If the employee, or, in the event of the employee's death, the employee's dependents, shall fail to institute legal proceedings against the other person for damages within two (2) years after the cause of action accrues, the employer or the employer's compensation insurance carrier, having paid compensation, or having been liable therefor, may collect in their own name or in the name of the injured employee, or in the case of the employee's death, in the name of the employee's dependents, from the other person in whom legal liability for damage exists, the compensation paid or payable to the injured employee, or to the employee's dependents, plus the services and products, and burial expenses, paid by them, or for which they have become liable, and the employer or the employer's compensation insurance carrier may commence an action at law for collection against the other person in whom legal liability exists, at any time within one (1) year from the date of the expiration of the two (2) years when the action accrued to the injured employee, or, in the event of the employee's death, to the employee's dependents, notwithstanding the provisions of any statute of limitations to the contrary.

In actions brought by the employee or the employee's dependents, the employee or the employee's dependents shall, within thirty (30) days after the action is filed, notify the employer or the employer's compensation insurance carrier by personal service or registered mail, of the action and the name of the court in which such suit is brought, filing proof thereof in the action.

The employer or the employer's compensation insurance carrier shall pay its pro rata share of all costs and reasonably necessary expenses in connection with asserting the third party claim, action or suit, including but not limited to cost of depositions and witness fees, and to the attorney at law selected by the employee or the employee's dependents, a fee of twenty-five percent (25%), if collected without suit, of the amount of benefits actually repaid after the expenses and costs in connection with the third party claim have been deducted therefrom, and a fee of thirty-three and one-third percent (33 1/3 %), if collected with suit, of the amount of benefits actually repaid after deduction of costs and reasonably necessary expenses in connection with the third party claim action or suit. The employer may, within ninety (90) days after receipt of notice of suit from the employee or the employee's dependents, join in the action upon the employee's motion so that all orders of court after hearing and judgment shall be made for the employee's protection. An employer or the employer's compensation insurance carrier may waive its right to reimbursement under this section and, as a result of the waiver, not have to pay the pro-rata share of costs and expenses.

No release or settlement of claim for damages by reason of injury or death, and no satisfaction of judgment in the proceedings, shall be valid without the written consent of both employer or the employer's compensation insurance carrier and employee or the employee's dependents, except in the case of the employer or the employer's compensation insurance carrier, consent shall not be required where the employer or the employer's compensation insurance carrier has been fully indemnified or protected by court order.

Amended by Acts 1977, P.L.260, SEC.1; P.L.31-2000, SEC.1; P.L.275-2013, SEC.1, eff. July 1, 2013.

22–3–2–14. Contractors; certificate of coverage; subrogation

Sec. 14. As used in this section, "person" does not include:

(1) an owner who contracts for performance of work on the owner's owner occupied residential property; or

(2) a nonprofit corporation that is recognized as tax exempt under Section 501(c)(3) of the Internal Revenue Code (as defined in IC 6–3–1–11(a)) to the extent the corporation enters into an independent contractor agreement with a person for the performance of youth coaching services on a part-time basis.

(b) The state, any political division thereof, any municipal corporation, any corporation, limited liability company, partnership, or person, contracting for the performance of any work exceeding one thousand dollars ($1,000) in value by a contractor subject to the compensation provisions of IC 22–3–2 through IC 22–3–6, without exacting from such contractor a certificate from the worker's compensation board showing that such contractor has complied with section 5 of this chapter, IC 22–3–5–1, and IC 22–3–5–2, shall be liable to the same extent as the contractor for compensation, physician's fees, hospital fees, nurse's charges, and burial expenses on account of the injury or death of any employee of such contractor, due to an accident arising out of and in the course of the performance of the work covered by such contract.

(c) Any contractor who shall sublet any contract for the performance of any work, to a subcontractor subject to the compensation provisions of IC 22–3–2 through IC 22–3–6, without obtaining a certificate from the worker's compensation board showing that such subcontractor has complied with section 5 of this chapter, IC 22–3–5–1, and IC 22–3–5–2, shall be liable to the same extent as such subcontractor for the payment of compensation, physician's fees, hospital fees, nurse's charges, and burial expenses on account of the injury or death of any employee of such subcontractor due to an accident arising out of and in the course of the performance of the work covered by such subcontract.

(d) The state, any political division thereof, any municipal corporation, any corporation, limited liability company, partnership, person, or contractor paying compensation, physician's fees, hospital fees, nurse's charges, or burial expenses under this section may recover the amount paid or to be paid from any person who, independently of such provisions, would have been liable for the payment thereof and may, in addition, recover the litigation expenses and attorney's fees incurred in the action before the worker's compensation board as well as the litigation expenses and attorney's fees incurred in an action to collect the compensation, medical expenses, and burial expenses.

(e) Every claim filed with the worker's compensation board under this section shall be instituted against all parties liable for payment. The worker's compensation board, in an award under subsection (b), shall fix the order in which said parties shall be exhausted, beginning with the immediate employer, and, in an award under subsection (c), shall determine whether the subcontractor has the financial ability to pay the compensation and medical expenses when due and, if not, shall order the contractor to pay the compensation and medical expenses.

Amended by P.L.28–1988, SEC.24; P.L.8–1993, SEC.280; P.L.258–1997(ss), SEC.2; P.L.202–2001, SEC.2; P.L.201–2005, SEC.3.

22–3–2–14.5. Independent contractor electing exemption from compensation provisions; filing of statement; certificate of exemption

Sec. 14.5.   As used in this section, "independent contractor" refers to a person described in IC 22–3–6–1(b)(7).

(b) As used in this section, "person" means an individual, a proprietorship, a partnership, a joint venture, a firm, an association, a corporation, or other legal entity.

(c) An independent contractor who does not make an election under IC 22–3–6–1(b)(4) or IC 22–3–6–1(b)(5) is not subject to the compensation provisions of IC 22–3–2 through IC 22–3–6 and must file a statement with the department of state revenue in accordance with IC 6–3–7–5 and obtain a certificate of exemption.

(d) Together with the statement required in subsection (c), an independent contractor shall file annually with the department documentation in support of independent contractor status before being granted a certificate of exemption. The independent contractor must obtain clearance from the department of state revenue before issuance of the certificate.

(e) An independent contractor shall pay a filing fee in the amount of fifteen dollars ($15) with the certificate filed under subsection (g). The fees collected under this subsection shall be deposited in the worker's compensation supplemental administrative fund and shall be used for all expenses the board incurs.

(f) The worker's compensation board shall maintain a data

base consisting of certificates received under this section and on request may verify that a certificate was filed.

(g) A certificate of exemption must be filed with the worker's compensation board. The board shall indicate that the certificate has been filed by stamping the certificate with the date of receipt and returning a stamped copy to the person filing the certificate. A certificate becomes effective as of midnight seven (7) business days after the date file stamped by the worker's compensation board. The board shall maintain a data base containing the information required in subsections (d) and (f).

(h) A person who contracts for services of another person not covered by IC 22–3–2 through IC 22–3–6 to perform work must secure a copy of a stamped certificate of exemption filed under this section from the person hired. A person may not require a person who has provided a stamped certificate to have worker's compensation coverage. The worker's compensation insurance carrier of a person who contracts with an independent contractor shall accept a stamped certificate in the same manner as a certificate of insurance.

(i) A stamped certificate filed under this section is binding on and holds harmless from all claims:

(1) a person who contracts with an independent contractor after receiving a copy of the stamped certificate; and

(2) the worker's compensation insurance carrier of the person who contracts with the independent contractor.

The independent contractor may not collect compensation under IC 22–3–2 through IC 22–3–6 for an injury from a person or the person's worker's compensation carrier to whom the independent contractor has furnished a stamped certificate.

As added by P.L.75–1993, SEC.2. Amended by P.L.202–2001, SEC.3.

22–3–2–15. Contracts, rules, etc., relieving employers of obligations; voluntary settlement agreements; minors; approval; effect

Sec. 15. No contract, agreement (written or implied), rule, or other device shall, in any manner, operate to relieve any employer in whole or in part of any obligation created by IC 22–3–2 through IC 22–3–6. However, nothing in IC 22–3–2 through IC 22–3–6 shall be construed as preventing the parties to claims under IC 22–3–2 through IC 22–3–6 from entering into voluntary agreements in settlement thereof, but no agreement by an employee or his dependents to waive his rights under IC 22–3–2 through IC 22–3–6 shall be valid nor shall any agreement of settlement or compromise of any dispute or claim for compensation under IC 22–3–2 through IC 22–3–6 be valid until approved by a member of the board, nor shall a member of the worker's compensation board approve any settlement which is not in accordance with the rights of the parties as given in IC 22–3–2 through IC 22–3–6. No such agreement shall be valid unless made after seven (7) days from the date of the injury or death.

(b) A compromise settlement approved by a member of the worker's compensation board during the employee's lifetime shall extinguish and bar all claims for compensation for the employee's death if the settlement compromises a dispute on any question or issue other than the extent of disability or the rate of compensation.

(c) A minor dependent, by parent or legal guardian, may compromise disputes and may enter into a compromise settlement agreement, and upon approval by a member of the worker's compensation board, the settlement agreement shall have the same force and effect as though the minor had been an adult. The payment of compensation by the employer in accordance with the settlement agreement shall discharge the employer from all further obligation.

Amended by P.L.28–1988, SEC.25; P.L.1–1991, SEC.148.

22–3–2–16. Claims for compensation; priorities

Sec. 16. All rights of compensation granted by IC 22–3–2 through IC 22–3–6 shall have the same preference or priority for the whole thereof against the assets of the employer as is allowed by law for any unpaid wages for labor.

Amended by P.L.144–1986, SEC.25.

22–3–2–17. Claims for compensation; assignment; creditor claims; child support income withholding

Sec. 17. Except as provided in subsection (b), no claims for compensation under IC 22–3–2 through IC 22–3–6 shall be assignable, and all compensation and claims therefor shall be exempt from all claims of creditors.

(b) Compensation awards under IC IC 22–3–2 through IC 22–3–6 are subject to child support income withholding under IC 31–16–15 and other remedies available for the enforcement of a child support order. The maximum amount that may be withheld under this subsection is one-half ($1/2$) of the compensation award.

Amended by P.L.144–1986, SEC.26; P.L.95–1988, SEC.2; P.L.1–1997, SEC.106; P.L.213–1999, SEC.7.

22–3–2–18. Coal mining; application of law

Sec. 18. The provisions of IC 22–3–2 through IC 22–3–6 shall apply to the state, to all political divisions thereof, to all municipal corporations within the state, to persons, partnerships, limited liability companies, and corporations engaged in mining coal, and to the employees thereof, without any right of exemption from the compensation provisions of IC 22–3–2 through IC 22–3–6, except as provided in section 15 of this chapter.

Amended by P.L.144–1986, SEC.27; P.L.8–1993, SEC.281.

22–3–2–19. Interstate or foreign commerce; exemptions

Sec. 19. IC 22–3–2 through IC 22–3–6 shall not apply to employees and employers engaged in interstate or foreign commerce wherein the laws of the United States provide for compensation or for liability for injury or death by accident to such employees.

Amended by P.L.144–1986, SEC.28.

22–3–2–20. Place of accident

Sec. 20. Every employer and employee under IC 22–3–2 through IC 22–3–6 shall be bound by the provisions of IC 22–3–2 through IC 22–3–6 whether injury by accident or death resulting from such injury occurs within the state or in some other state or in a foreign country.

Amended by P.L.144–1986, SEC.29.

22–3–2–21. Prior injuries; application of law

Sec. 21. The provisions of IC 22–3–2 through IC 22–3–6 shall not apply to injuries or death nor to accident which occurred prior to May 21, 1929.

Amended by P.L.144–1986, SEC.30.

22–3–2–22. Notice; worker's compensation coverage

Sec. 22. Each employer subject to IC 22–3–2 through IC 22–3–6 shall post a notice in the employer's place of business to inform the employees that their employment is covered by worker's compensation. The notice must also contain the name, address, and telephone number of the employer's insurance carrier or the person responsible for administering the employer's worker's compensation claims if the employer is self insured.

(b) The notice required under this section must be in a form approved by the board and shall be posted at a conspicuous location at the employer's place of business to provide reasonable notice to all employees. If the employer is required by federal law or regulation to post a notice for the employer's employees, the notice required under this section must be posted in the same location or locations where the notice required by federal law or regulation is posted.

(c) An employer who fails to comply with this section is subject to a civil penalty under IC 22–3–4–15.

As added by P.L.170–1991, SEC.2. Amended by P.L.168–2011, SEC.2.

Chapter 3. Worker's Compensation: Notice of Injury; Treatment; Compensation Schedule; Payments

22–3–3–1. Notice of injury; time

Sec. 1. Unless the employer or his representative shall have actual knowledge of the occurrence of an injury or death at the time thereof or shall acquire such knowledge afterward, the injured employee or his dependents, as soon as practicable after the injury or death resulting therefrom, shall give written notice to the employer of such injury or death.

Unless such notice is given or knowledge acquired within thirty (30) days from the date of the injury or death, no compensation shall be paid until and from the date such notice is given or knowledge obtained. No lack of knowledge by the employer or his representative, and no want, failure, defect or inaccuracy of the notice shall bar compensation, unless the employer shall show that he is prejudiced by such lack of knowledge or by such want, failure, defect or inaccuracy of the notice, and then only to the extent of such prejudices.

22–3–3–2. Notice of injury; contents; signature

Sec. 2. The notice provided for in the preceding section shall state the name and address of the employee, the time, place, nature and cause of the injury or death, and shall be signed by the injured employee or by some one in his behalf or by one (1) or more of the dependents, in case of death, or by some person in their behalf. Said notice may be served personally upon the employer, or upon any foreman, superintendent or manager of the employer to whose orders the injured or deceased employee was required to conform or upon any agent of the employer upon whom a summons in a civil action may be served under the laws of the state, or may be sent to the employer by registered letter, addressed to his last known residence or place of business.

22–3–3–3. Limitation of actions; radiation

Sec. 3. The right to compensation under IC 22–3–2 through IC 22–3–6 shall be forever barred unless within two (2) years after the occurrence of the accident, or if death results therefrom, within two (2) years after such death, a claim for compensation thereunder shall be filed with the worker's compensation board. However, in all cases wherein an accident or death results from the exposure to radiation, a claim for compensation shall be filed with the board within two (2) years from the date on which the employee had knowledge of his injury or by exercise of reasonable diligence should have known of the existence of such injury and its causal relationship to his employment.

Amended by P.L.144–1986, SEC.31; P.L.28–1988, SEC.26.

22-3-3-4. Medical treatment pending adjudication of impairment

Sec. 4.(a) After an injury and prior to an adjudication of permanent impairment, the employer shall furnish or cause to be furnished, free of charge to the employee, an attending physician for the treatment of the employee's injuries, and in addition thereto such services and products as the attending physician or the worker's compensation board may deem necessary. If the employee is requested or required by the employer to submit to treatment outside the county of employment, the employer shall also pay the reasonable expense of travel, food, and lodging necessary during the travel, but not to exceed the amount paid at the time of the travel by the state to its employees under the state travel policies and procedures established by the department of administration and approved by the state budget agency. If the treatment or travel to or from the place of treatment causes a loss of working time to the employee, the employer shall reimburse the employee for the loss of wages using the basis of the employee's average daily wage.

(b) During the period of temporary total disability resulting from the injury, the employer shall furnish the physician, services and products, and the worker's compensation board may, on proper application of either party, require that treatment by the physician and services and products be furnished by or on behalf of the employer as the worker's compensation board may deem reasonably necessary.

(c) After an employee's injury has been adjudicated by agreement or award on the basis of permanent partial impairment and within the statutory period for review in such case as provided in section 27 of this chapter, the employer may continue to furnish a physician or surgeon and other medical services and products, and the worker's compensation board may within the statutory period for review as provided in section 27 of this chapter, on a proper application of either party, require that treatment by that physician and other services and products be furnished by and on behalf of the employer as the worker's compensation board may deem necessary to limit or reduce the amount and extent of the employee's impairment. The refusal of the employee to accept such services and products, when provided by or on behalf of the employer, shall bar the employee from all compensation otherwise payable during the period of the refusal, and the employee's right to prosecute any proceeding under IC 22-3-2 through IC 22-3-6 shall be suspended and abated until the employee's refusal ceases. The employee must be served with a notice setting forth the consequences of the refusal under this section. The notice must be in a form prescribed by the worker's compensation board. No compensation for permanent total impairment, permanent partial impairment, permanent disfigurement, or death shall be paid or payable for that part or portion of the impairment, disfigurement, or death which is the result of the failure of the employee to accept the services and products required under this section. However, an employer may at any time permit an employee to have treatment for the employee's injuries by spiritual means or prayer in lieu of the physician or surgeon and other services and products required under this section.

(d) If, because of an emergency, or because of the employer's failure to provide an attending physician or services and products, or treatment by spiritual means or prayer, as required by this section, or because of any other good reason, a physician other than that provided by the employer treats the injured employee during the period of the employee's temporary total disability, or necessary and proper services and products are procured within the period, the reasonable cost of those services and products shall, subject to the approval of the worker's compensation board, be paid by the employer.

(e) An employer or employer's insurance carrier may not delay the provision of emergency medical care whenever emergency medical care is considered necessary in the professional judgment of the attending health care facility physician.

(f) Regardless of when it occurs, where a compensable injury results in the amputation of a body part, the enucleation of an eye, or the loss of natural teeth, the employer shall furnish an appropriate artificial member, braces, and prosthodontics. The cost of repairs to or replacements for the artificial members, braces, or prosthodontics that result from a compensable injury pursuant to a prior award and are required due to either medical necessity or normal wear and tear, determined according to the employee's individual use, but not abuse, of the artificial member, braces, or prosthodontics, shall be paid from the second injury fund upon order or award of the worker's compensation board. The employee is not required to meet any other requirement for admission to the second injury fund.

(g) If an accident arising out of and in the course of employment after June 30, 1997, results in the loss of or damage to an artificial member, a brace, an implant, eyeglasses, prosthodontics, or other medically prescribed device, the employer shall repair the artificial member, brace, implant, eyeglasses, prosthodontics, or other medically prescribed device or furnish an identical or a reasonably equivalent replacement.

(h) This section may not be construed to prohibit an agreement between an employer and the employer's employees that has the approval of the board and that binds the parties to:

(1) medical care furnished by medical service providers selected by agreement before or after injury; or

(2) the findings of a medical service provider who was chosen by agreement.

Amended by Acts 1979, P.L.227, SEC.1; P.L.95-1988, SEC.3; P.L.170-1991, SEC.3; P.L.258-1997(ss), SEC.3; P.L.31-2000, SEC.2; P.L.67-2010, SEC.1; P.L.275-2013, SEC.2, eff. July 1, 2013.

22-3-3-4.5. Maximum reimbursement amount for repackaged legend drugs

Sec. 4.5.(a) As used in this section, "legend drug" has the meaning set forth in IC 25-26-14-7.

(b) As used in this section, "repackage" has the meaning set forth in IC 25-26-14-9.3.

(c) This subsection does not apply to a retail or mail order pharmacy. Except as provided in subsection (d), whenever a prescription covered by IC 22-3-2 through IC 22-3-6 is filled using a repackaged legend drug:

(1) the maximum reimbursement amount for the repackaged legend drug must be computed using the average wholesale price set by the original manufacturer for the legend drug;

(2) the medical service provider may not be reimbursed for more than one (1) office visit for each repackaged legend drug prescribed; and

(3) the maximum period during which a medical service provider may receive reimbursement for a repackaged legend drug begins on the date of the injury and ends at the beginning of the eighth day after the date of the injury.

(d) If the National Drug Code (established under Section 510 of the federal Food, Drug, and Cosmetic Act, 21 U.S.C. 360) for a legend drug cannot be determined from the medical service provider's billing or statement, the maximum reimbursement amount for the repackaged legend drug under subsection (c) is the lowest cost generic for that legend drug.

As added by P.L.275-2013, SEC.3, eff. July 1, 2013. Amended by P.L.99-2014, SEC.1, eff. July 1, 2014.

22-3-3-5. Limitation on employer, employee or estate liability for certain services or products; claims for payment; withholding approval of certain fees

Sec. 5.(a) The pecuniary liability of the employer for a service or product herein required shall be limited to the following:

(1) This subdivision applies before July 1, 2014, to all medical service providers, and after June 30, 2014, to a

medical service provider that is not a medical service facility. Such charges as prevail as provided under IC 22-3-6-1(k)(1), in the same community (as defined in IC 22-3-6-1(h)) for a like service or product to injured persons.

(2) This subdivision applies after June 30, 2014, to a medical service facility. The amount provided under IC 22-3-6-1(k)(2).

(b) The employee and the employee's estate do not have liability to a health care provider for payment for services obtained under IC 22-3-3-4.

(c) The right to order payment for all services or products provided under IC 22-3-2 through IC 22-3-6 is solely with the board.

(d) All claims by a medical service provider for payment for services or products are against the employer and the employer's insurance carrier, if any, and must be made with the board under IC 22-3-2 through IC 22-3-6. After June 30, 2011, a medical service provider must file an application for adjustment of a claim for a medical service provider's fee with the board not later than two (2) years after the receipt of an initial written communication from the employer, the employer's insurance carrier, if any, or an agent acting on behalf of the employer after the medical service provider submits a bill for services or products. To offset a part of the board's expenses related to the administration of medical service provider reimbursement disputes, a medical service facility shall pay a filing fee of sixty dollars ($60) in a balance billing case. The filing fee must accompany each application filed with the board. If an employer, an employer's insurance carrier, or an agent acting on behalf of the employer denies or fails to pay any amount on a claim submitted by a medical service facility, a filing fee is not required to accompany an application that is filed for the denied or unpaid claim. A medical service provider may combine up to ten (10) individual claims into one (1) application whenever:

(1) all individual claims involve the same employer, insurance carrier, or billing review service; and

(2) the amount of each individual claim does not exceed two hundred dollars ($200).

(e) The worker's compensation board may withhold the approval of the fees of the attending physician in a case until the attending physician files a report with the worker's compensation board on the form prescribed by the board.

Amended by P.L.170-1991, SEC.4; P.L.216-1995, SEC.1; P.L.258-1997(ss), SEC.4; P.L.168-2011, SEC.3; P.L.275-2013, SEC.4, eff. July 1, 2013.

22-3-3-5.1. Collection of medical expense payments; civil penalties; good faith errors

Sec. 5.1. A medical service provider or a medical service provider's agent, servant, employee, assignee, employer, or independent contractor on behalf of the medical service provider may not knowingly collect or attempt to collect the payment of a charge for medical services or products covered under IC 22 from an employee or the employee's estate or family members.

(b) If after a hearing, the worker's compensation board finds that a medical service provider has violated this section, the worker's compensation board may assess a civil penalty against the medical service provider in an amount that is at least one hundred dollars ($100) but less than one thousand dollars ($1,000) for each violation.

(c) The worker's compensation board may not assess a civil penalty against a medical service provider for a violation of this section that is the result of a good faith error.

As added by P.L.216–1995, SEC.2.

22-3-3-5.2. Billing review service standards

Sec. 5.2.(a) A billing review service shall adhere to the following requirements to determine the pecuniary liability of an employer or an employer's insurance carrier for a specific service or product covered under worker's compensation provided before July 1, 2014, by all medical service providers, and after June 30, 2014, by a medical service provider that is not a medical service facility:

(1) The formation of a billing review standard, and any subsequent analysis or revision of the standard, must use data that is based on the medical service provider billing charges as submitted to the employer and the employer's insurance carrier from the same community. This subdivision does not apply when a unique or specialized service or product does not have sufficient comparative data to allow for a reasonable comparison.

(2) Data used to determine pecuniary liability must be compiled on or before June 30 and December 31 of each year.

(3) Billing review standards must be revised for prospective future payments of medical service provider bills to provide for payment of the charges at a rate not more than the charges made by eighty percent (80%) of the medical service providers during the prior six (6) months within the same community. The data used to perform the analysis and revision of the billing review standards may not be more than two (2) years old and must be periodically updated by a representative inflationary or deflationary factor. Reimbursement for these charges may not exceed the actual charge invoiced by the medical service provider.

(b) This subsection applies after June 30, 2014, to a medical service facility. The pecuniary liability of an employer or an employer's insurance carrier for a specific service or product covered under worker's compensation and provided by a medical service facility is equal to a reasonable amount, which is established by payment of one (1) of the following:

(1) The amount negotiated at any time between the medical service facility and any of the following:

(A) The employer.

(B) The employer's insurance carrier.

(C) A billing review service on behalf of a person described in clause (A) or (B).

(D) A direct provider network that has contracted with a person described in clause (A) or (B).

(2) Two hundred percent (200%) of the amount that would be paid to the medical service facility on the same date for the same service or product under the medical service facility's Medicare reimbursement rate, if an amount has not been negotiated as described in subdivision (1).

(c) A medical service provider may request an explanation from a billing review service if the medical service provider's bill has been reduced as a result of application of the eightieth percentile or of a Current Procedural Terminology (CPT) or Medicare coding change. The request must be made not later than sixty (60) days after receipt of the notice of the reduction. If a request is made, the billing review service must provide:

(1) the name of the billing review service used to make the reduction;

(2) the dollar amount of the reduction;

(3) the dollar amount of the service or product at the eightieth percentile; and

(4) in the case of a CPT or Medicare coding change, the basis upon which the change was made;
not later than thirty (30) days after the date of the request.

(d) If, after a hearing, the worker's compensation board finds that a billing review service used a billing review standard that did not comply with subsection (a)(1) through (a)(3), as applicable, in determining the pecuniary liability of an employer or an employer's insurance carrier for a medical service provider's charge for services or products covered under worker's compensation, the worker's compensation board may assess a civil penalty against the billing review service in an amount not less than one hundred dollars ($100) and not more than one thousand dollars ($1,000).

As added by P.L.216-1995, SEC.3. Amended by P.L.202-2001, SEC.4; P.L.275-2013, SEC.5, eff. July 1, 2013; P.L.99-2014, SEC.2, eff. July 1, 2014.

22-3-3-6. Physical examination; physician's statement; autopsy

Sec. 6. After an injury and during the period of claimed resulting disability or impairment, the employee, if so requested by the employee's employer or ordered by the worker's compensation board, shall submit to an examination at reasonable times and places by a duly qualified physician or surgeon designated and paid by the employer or by order of the worker's compensation board. The employee shall have the right to have present at any such examination any duly qualified physician or surgeon provided and paid for by the employee. No fact communicated to, or otherwise learned by, any physician or surgeon who may have attended or examined the employee, or who may have been present at any examination, shall be privileged, either in the hearings provided for in IC 22-3-2 through IC 22-3-6, or in any action at law brought to recover damages against any employer who is subject to the compensation provisions of IC 22-3-2 through IC 22-3-6. If the employee refuses to submit to or in any way obstructs such examinations, the employee's right to compensation and his right to take or prosecute any proceedings under IC 22-3-2 through IC 22-3-6 shall be suspended until such refusal or obstruction ceases. No compensation shall at any time be payable for the period of suspension unless in the opinion of the worker's compensation board the circumstances justified the refusal or obstruction. The employee must be served with a notice setting forth the consequences of the refusal under this subsection. The notice must be in a form prescribed by the board.

(b) Any employer requesting an examination of any employee residing within Indiana shall pay, in advance of the time fixed for the examination, sufficient money to defray the necessary expenses of travel by the most convenient means to and from the place of examination, and the cost of meals and lodging necessary during the travel. If the method of travel is by automobile, the mileage rate to be paid by the employer shall be the rate currently being paid by the state to its employees under the state travel policies and procedures established by the department of administration and approved by the budget agency. If such examination or travel to or from the place of examination causes any loss of working time on the part of the employee, the employer shall reimburse the employee for such loss of wages upon the basis of the employee's average daily wage. When any employee injured in Indiana moves outside Indiana, the travel expense and the cost of meals and lodging necessary during the travel payable under this section shall be paid from the point in Indiana nearest to the employee's then residence to the place of examination. No travel and other expense shall be paid for any travel and other expense required outside Indiana.

(c) A duly qualified physician or surgeon provided and paid for by the employee may be present at an examination if the employee so desires. In all cases where the examination is made by a physician or surgeon engaged by the employer and the injured employee has no physician or surgeon present at such examination, it shall be the duty of the physician or surgeon making the examination to deliver to the injured employee, or the employee's representative, a statement in writing of the conditions evidenced by such examination. The statement shall disclose all facts that are reported by such physician or surgeon to the employer. Such statement shall be furnished to the employee or the employee's representative, as soon as practicable, but not later than thirty (30) days before the time the case is set for hearing. The statement may be submitted by either party as evidence by that physician or surgeon at a hearing before the worker's compensation board if the statement meets the requirements of subsection (e). If such physician or surgeon fails or refuses to furnish the employee or the employee's representative with such statement thirty (30) days before the hearing, then the statement may not be submitted as evidence, and such physician or surgeon shall not be permitted to testify before the worker's compensation board as to any facts learned in such examination. All of the requirements of this subsection apply to all subsequent examinations requested by the employer.

(d) In all cases where an examination of an employee is made by a physician or surgeon engaged by the employee, and the employer has no physician or surgeon present at such examination, it shall be the duty of the physician or surgeon making the examination to deliver to the employer or the employer's representative a statement in writing of the conditions evidenced by such examination. The statement shall disclose all facts that are reported by such physician or surgeon to the employee. Such statement shall be furnished to the employer or the employer's representative as soon as practicable, but not later than thirty (30) days before the time the case is set for hearing. The statement may be submitted by either party as evidence by that physician or surgeon at a hearing before the worker's compensation board if the statement meets the requirements of subsection (e). If such physician or surgeon fails or refuses to furnish the employer, or the employer's representative, with such statement thirty (30) days before the hearing, then the statement may not be submitted as evidence, and such physician or surgeon shall not be permitted to testify before the worker's compensation board as to any facts learned in such examination. All of the requirements of this subsection apply to all subsequent examinations made by a physician or surgeon engaged by the employee.

(e) All statements of physicians or surgeons required by this section, whether those engaged by employee or employer, shall contain the following information:

(1) The history of the injury, or claimed injury, as given by the patient.

(2) The diagnosis of the physician or surgeon concerning the patient's physical or mental condition.

(3) The opinion of the physician or surgeon concerning the causal relationship, if any, between the injury and the patient's physical or mental condition, including the physician's or surgeon's reasons for the opinion.

(4) The opinion of the physician or surgeon concerning whether the injury or claimed injury resulted in a disability or impairment and, if so, the opinion of the physician or surgeon concerning the extent of the disability or impairment and the reasons for the opinion.

(5) The original signature of the physician or surgeon.

Notwithstanding any hearsay objection, the worker's compensation board shall admit into evidence a statement that meets the requirements of this subsection unless the statement is ruled inadmissible on other grounds.

(f) Delivery of any statement required by this section may be made to the attorney or agent of the employer or employee and such action shall be construed as delivery to the employer or employee.

(g) Any party may object to a statement on the basis that the statement does not meet the requirements of subsection (e). The objecting party must give written notice to the party providing the statement and specify the basis for the objection. Notice of the objection must be given no later than twenty (20) days before the hearing. Failure to object as provided in this subsection precludes any further objection as to the adequacy of the statement under subsection (e).

(h) The employer upon proper application, or the worker's compensation board, shall have the right in any case of death to require an autopsy at the expense of the party requesting the same. If, after a hearing, the worker's compensation board orders an autopsy and such autopsy is refused by the surviving spouse or next of kin, then any claim for compensation on account of such death shall be suspended and abated during such refusal. The surviving spouse or dependent must be served with a notice setting forth the consequences of the refusal under this subsection. The notice must be in a form prescribed by the worker's compensation board. No autopsy, except one performed by or on the authority or order of the coroner in the discharge of the coroner's duties, shall be held in any case by any person, without notice first being given to the surviving spouse or next of kin, if they reside in Indiana or their whereabouts can reasonably be ascertained, of the time and place thereof, and reasonable time and opportunity given such surviving spouse or next of kin to have a representative or representatives present to witness same. However, if such notice is not given, all evidence obtained by such autopsy shall be suppressed on motion duly made to the worker's compensation board.

Amended by P.L.28–1988, SEC.27; P.L.95–1988, SEC.4; P.L.109–1992, SEC.1; P.L.1–2006, SEC.337, eff. Mar. 24, 2006.

22–3–3–7. Temporary disability benefits; installment payments; termination; overpayment

Sec. 7. Compensation shall be allowed on account of injuries producing only temporary total disability to work or temporary partial disability to work beginning with the eighth day of such disability except for medical benefits provided in section 4 of the chapter. Compensation shall be allowed for the first seven (7) calendar days only if the disability continues for longer than twenty-one (21) days.

(b) The first weekly installment of compensation for temporary disability is due fourteen (14) days after the disability begins. Not later than fifteen (15) days from the date that the first installment of compensation is due, the employer or the employer's insurance carrier shall tender to the employee or to the employee's dependents, with all compensation due, a properly prepared compensation agreement in a form prescribed by the board. Whenever an employer or the employer's insurance carrier denies or is not able to determine liability to pay compensation or benefits, the employer or the employer's insurance carrier shall notify the worker's compensation board and the employee in writing on a form prescribed by the worker's compensation board not later than thirty (30) days after the employer's knowledge of the claimed injury. If a determination of liability cannot be made within thirty (30) days, the worker's compensation board may approve an additional thirty (30) days upon a written request of the employer or the employer's insurance carrier that sets forth the reasons that the determination could not be made within thirty (30) days and states the facts or circumstances that are necessary to determine liability within the additional thirty (30) days. More than thirty (30) days of additional time may be approved by the worker's compensation board upon the filing of a petition by the employer or the employer's insurance carrier that sets forth:

(1) the extraordinary circumstances that have precluded a determination of liability within the initial sixty (60) days;

(2) the status of the investigation on the date the petition is filed;

(3) the facts or circumstances that are necessary to make a determination; and

(4) a timetable for the completion of the remaining investigation.

An employer who fails to comply with this section is subject to a civil penalty, under IC 22–3–4–15.

(c) Once begun, temporary total disability benefits may not be terminated by the employer unless:

(1) the employee has returned to any employment;

(2) the employee has died;

(3) the employee has refused to undergo a medical examination under section 6 of this chapter or has refused to accept suitable employment under section 11 of this chapter;

(4) the employee has received five hundred (500) weeks of temporary total disability benefits or has been paid the maximum compensation allowed under section 22 of this chapter; or

(5) the employee is unable or unavailable to work for reasons unrelated to the compensable injury.

In all other cases the employer must notify the employee in writing of the employer's intent to terminate the payment of temporary total disability benefits and of the availability of employment, if any, on a form approved by the board. If the employee disagrees with the proposed termination, the employee must give written notice of disagreement to the board and the employer within seven (7) days after receipt of the notice of intent to terminate benefits. If the board and employer do not receive a notice of disagreement under this section, the employee's temporary total disability benefits shall be terminated. Upon receipt of the notice of disagreement, the board shall immediately contact the parties, which may be by telephone or other means, and attempt to resolve the disagreement. If the board is unable to resolve the disagreement within ten (10) days of receipt of the notice of disagreement, the board shall immediately arrange for an evaluation of the employee by an independent medical examiner. The independent medical examiner shall be selected by mutual agreement of the parties or, if the parties are unable to agree, appointed by the board under IC 22–3–4–11. If the independent medical examiner determines that the employee is no longer temporarily disabled or is still temporarily disabled but can return to employment that the employer has made available to the employee, or if the employee fails or refuses to appear for examination by the independent medical examiner, temporary total disability benefits may be terminated. If either party disagrees with the opinion of the independent medical examiner, the party shall apply to the board for a hearing under IC 22–3–4–5.

(d) An employer is not required to continue the payment of temporary total disability benefits for more than fourteen (14) days after the employer's proposed termination date unless the independent medical examiner determines that the employee is temporarily disabled and unable to return to any employment that the employer has made available to the employee.

(e) If it is determined that as a result of this section temporary total disability benefits were overpaid, the overpayment shall be deducted from any benefits due the employee under section 10 of this chapter and, if there are no benefits due the employee or the benefits due the employee do not equal the amount of the overpayment, the employee shall be responsible for paying any overpayment which cannot be deducted from benefits due the employee.

Amended by P.L.170–1991, SEC.5; P.L.258–1997(ss), SEC.5; P.L.168–2011, SEC.4.

22–3–3–7.5. Average weekly wages of public employee; determination

Sec. 7.5. For purposes of this chapter, the average weekly wages of a public employee shall be determined without regard to any salary reduction agreement under Section 125 of the Internal Revenue Code.[3]

As added by P.L.5–1992, SEC.8.

22–3–3–8. Temporary total disability or total permanent disability; awards

Sec. 8. With respect to injuries occurring prior to April 1, 1951, causing temporary total disability for work there shall be paid to the injured employee during such total disability for work a weekly compensation equal to fifty-five percent (55%) of his average weekly wages for a period not to exceed five hundred (500) weeks. With respect to injuries occurring on and after April 1, 1951, and prior to July 1, 1971, causing temporary total disability for work there shall be paid to the injured employee during such total disability a weekly compensation equal to sixty per cent (60%) of his average weekly wages for a period not to exceed five hundred (500) weeks. With respect to injuries occurring on and after July 1, 1971, and prior to July 1, 1974, causing temporary total disability for work there shall be paid to the injured employee during such total disability a weekly compensation equal to sixty per cent (60%)

---

[3] 26 U.S.C.A. § 125.

of his average weekly wages, as defined in IC 22–3–3–22 a period not to exceed five hundred (500) weeks. With respect to injuries occurring on and after July 1, 1974, and before July 1, 1976, causing temporary total disability or total permanent disability for work there shall be paid to the injured employee during such total disability a weekly compensation equal to sixty-six and two-thirds percent (66 2/3%) of his average weekly wages up to one hundred and thirty-five dollars ($135.00) average weekly wages, as defined in section 22 of this chapter, for a period not to exceed five hundred (500) weeks. With respect to injuries occurring on and after July 1, 1976, causing temporary total disability or total permanent disability for work, there shall be paid to the injured employee during the total disability a weekly compensation equal to sixty-six and two-thirds percent (66 2/3%) of his average weekly wages, as defined in IC 22–3–3–22, for a period not to exceed five hundred (500) weeks.

Compensation shall be allowed for the first seven (7) calendar days only if the disability continues for longer than twenty-one (21) days.

Amended by Acts 1976, P.L.112, SEC.1.

22–3–3–9. Temporary partial disability; awards

Sec. 9. With respect to injuries occurring prior to April 1, 1951 causing temporary partial disability for work, compensation shall be paid to the injured employee during such disability, as prescribed in section 7 of this chapter, a weekly compensation equal to fifty-five per cent (55%) of the difference between his average weekly wages and the weekly wages at which he is actually employed after the injury, for a period not to exceed three hundred (300) weeks. With respect to injuries occurring on and after April 1, 1951 and prior to July 1, 1974 causing temporary partial disability for work, compensation shall be paid to the injured employee during such disability, as prescribed in section 7 of this chapter, a weekly compensation equal to sixty per cent (60%) of the difference between his average weekly wages and the weekly wages at which he is actually employed after the injury, for a period not to exceed three hundred (300) weeks. With respect to injuries occurring on and after July 1, 1974 causing temporary partial disability for work, compensation shall be paid to the injured employee during such disability as prescribed in section 7 of this chapter, a weekly compensation equal to sixty-six and two-thirds per cent (66 2/3%) of the difference between his average weekly wages and the weekly wages at which he is actually employed after the injury, for a period not to exceed three hundred (300) weeks.

In case the partial disability begins after the period of temporary total disability, the latter period shall be included as a part of the maximum period allowed for partial disability.

22–3–3–10. Scheduled injuries

Sec. 10. With respect to injuries in the schedule set forth in subsection (d) occurring on and after July 1, 1979, and before July 1, 1988, the employee shall receive, in addition to temporary total disability benefits not to exceed fifty-two (52) weeks on account of the injury, a weekly compensation of sixty percent (60%) of the employee's average weekly wages, not to exceed one hundred twenty-five dollars ($125) average weekly wages, for the period stated for the injury.

(b) With respect to injuries in the schedule set forth in subsection (d) occurring on and after July 1, 1988, and before July 1, 1989, the employee shall receive, in addition to temporary total disability benefits not exceeding seventy-eight (78) weeks on account of the injury, a weekly compensation of sixty percent (60%) of the employee's average weekly wages, not to exceed one hundred sixty-six dollars ($166) average weekly wages, for the period stated for the injury.

(c) With respect to injuries in the schedule set forth in subsection (d) occurring on and after July 1, 1989, and before July 1, 1990, the employee shall receive, in addition to temporary total disability benefits not exceeding seventy-eight (78) weeks on account of the injury, a weekly compensation of sixty percent (60%) of the employee's average weekly wages, not to exceed one hundred eighty-three dollars ($183) average weekly wages, for the period stated for the injury.

(d) With respect to injuries in the following schedule occurring on and after July 1, 1990, and before July 1, 1991, the employee shall receive, in addition to temporary total disability benefits not exceeding seventy-eight (78) weeks on account of the injury, a weekly compensation of sixty percent (60%) of the employee's average weekly wages, not to exceed two hundred dollars ($200) average weekly wages, for the period stated for the injury.

(1) Amputation: For the loss by separation of the thumb, sixty (60) weeks, of the index finger forty (40) weeks, of the second finger thirty-five (35) weeks, of the third or ring finger thirty (30) weeks, of the fourth or little finger twenty (20) weeks, of the hand by separation below the elbow joint two hundred (200) weeks, or the arm above the elbow two hundred fifty (250) weeks, of the big toe sixty (60) weeks, of the second toe thirty (30) weeks, of the third toe twenty (20) weeks, of the fourth toe fifteen (15) weeks, of the fifth or little toe ten (10) weeks, for loss occurring on and after April 1, 1959, by separation of the foot below the knee joint, one hundred seventy-five (175) weeks and of the leg above the knee joint two hundred twenty-five (225) weeks. The loss of more than one (1) phalange of a thumb or toes shall be

considered as the loss of the entire thumb or toe. The loss of more than two (2) phalanges of a finger shall be considered as the loss of the entire finger. The loss of not more than one (1) phalange of a thumb or toe shall be considered as the loss of one-half (1/2) of the thumb or toe and compensation shall be paid for one-half (1/2) of the period for the loss of the entire thumb or toe. The loss of not more than one (1) phalange of a finger shall be considered as the loss of one-third (1/3) of the finger and compensation shall be paid for one-third (1/3) the period for the loss of the entire finger.

The loss of more than one (1) phalange of the finger but not more than two (2) phalanges of the finger, shall be considered as the loss of one-half (1/2) of the finger and compensation shall be paid for one-half (1/2) of the period for the loss of the entire finger.

(2) For the loss by separation of both hands or both feet or the total sight of both eyes, or any two (2) such losses in the same accident, five hundred (500) weeks.

(3) For the permanent and complete loss of vision by enucleation or its reduction to one-tenth (1/10) of normal vision with glasses, one hundred seventy-five (175) weeks.

(4) For the permanent and complete loss of hearing in one (1) ear, seventy-five (75) weeks, and in both ears, two hundred (200) weeks.

(5) For the loss of one (1) testicle, fifty (50) weeks; for the loss of both testicles, one hundred fifty (150) weeks.

(e) With respect to injuries in the schedule set forth in subsection (h) occurring on and after July 1, 1979, and before July 1, 1988, the employee shall receive, in addition to temporary total disability benefits not exceeding fifty-two (52) weeks on account of the injury, a weekly compensation of sixty percent (60%) of the employee's average weekly wages not to exceed one hundred twenty-five dollars ($125) average weekly wages for the period stated for the injury.

(f) With respect to injuries in the schedule set forth in subsection (h) occurring on and after July 1, 1988, and before July 1, 1989, the employee shall receive, in addition to temporary total disability benefits not exceeding seventy-eight (78) weeks on account of the injury, a weekly compensation of sixty percent (60%) of the employee's average weekly wages, not to exceed one hundred sixty-six dollars ($166) average weekly wages, for the period stated for the injury.

(g) With respect to injuries in the schedule set forth in subsection (h) occurring on and after July 1, 1989, and before July 1, 1990, the employee shall receive, in addition to temporary total disability benefits not exceeding seventy-eight

(78) weeks on account of the injury, a weekly compensation of sixty percent (60%) of the employee's average weekly wages, not to exceed one hundred eighty-three dollars ($183) average weekly wages, for the period stated for the injury.

(h) With respect to injuries in the following schedule occurring on and after July 1, 1990, and before July 1, 1991, the employee shall receive, in addition to temporary total disability benefits not exceeding seventy-eight (78) weeks on account of the injury, a weekly compensation of sixty percent (60%) of the employee's average weekly wages, not to exceed two hundred dollars ($200) average weekly wages, for the period stated for the injury.

(1) Loss of use: The total permanent loss of the use of an arm, hand, thumb, finger, leg, foot, toe, or phalange shall be considered as the equivalent of the loss by separation of the arm, hand, thumb, finger, leg, foot, toe, or phalange, and compensation shall be paid for the same period as for the loss thereof by separation.

(2) Partial loss of use: For the permanent partial loss of the use of an arm, hand, thumb, finger, leg, foot, toe, or phalange, compensation shall be paid for the proportionate loss of the use of such arm, hand, thumb, finger, leg, foot, toe, or phalange.

(3) For injuries resulting in total permanent disability, five hundred (500) weeks.

(4) For any permanent reduction of the sight of an eye less than a total loss as specified in subsection (d)(3), compensation shall be paid for a period proportionate to the degree of such permanent reduction without correction or glasses.

However, when such permanent reduction without correction or glasses would result in one hundred percent (100%) loss of vision, but correction or glasses would result in restoration of vision, then in such event compensation shall be paid for fifty percent (50%) of such total loss of vision without glasses, plus an additional amount equal to the proportionate amount of such reduction with glasses, not to exceed an additional fifty percent (50%).

(5) For any permanent reduction of the hearing of one (1) or both ears, less than the total loss as specified in subsection (d)(4), compensation shall be paid for a period proportional to the degree of such permanent reduction.

(6) In all other cases of permanent partial impairment, compensation proportionate to the degree of such permanent partial impairment, in the discretion of the worker's compensation board, not exceeding five hundred (500) weeks.

(7) In all cases of permanent disfigurement which may

impair the future usefulness or opportunities of the employee, compensation, in the discretion of the worker's compensation board, not exceeding two hundred (200) weeks, except that no compensation shall be payable under this subdivision where compensation is payable elsewhere in this section.

(i) With respect to injuries in the following schedule occurring on and after July 1, 1991, the employee shall receive in addition to temporary total disability benefits, not exceeding one hundred twenty-five (125) weeks on account of the injury, compensation in an amount determined under the following schedule to be paid weekly at a rate of sixty-six and two-thirds percent (66 2/3%) of the employee's average weekly wages during the fifty-two (52) weeks immediately preceding the week in which the injury occurred.

(1) Amputation: For the loss by separation of the thumb, twelve (12) degrees of permanent impairment; of the index finger, eight (8) degrees of permanent impairment; of the second finger, seven (7) degrees of permanent impairment; of the third or ring finger, six (6) degrees of permanent impairment; of the fourth or little finger, four (4) degrees of permanent impairment; of the hand by separation below the elbow joint, forty (40) degrees of permanent impairment; of the arm above the elbow, fifty (50) degrees of permanent impairment; of the big toe, twelve (12) degrees of permanent impairment; of the second toe, six (6) degrees of permanent impairment; of the third toe, four (4) degrees of permanent impairment; of the fourth toe, three (3) degrees of permanent impairment; of the fifth or little toe, two (2) degrees of permanent impairment; by separation of the foot below the knee joint, thirty-five (35) degrees of permanent impairment; and of the leg above the knee joint, forty-five (45) degrees of permanent impairment.

(2) Amputations: For the loss by separation of any of the body parts described in subdivision (1) on or after July 1, 1997, and for the loss by separation of any of the body parts described in subdivision (3), (5), or (8), on or after July 1, 1999, the dollar values per degree applying on the date of the injury as described in subsection (j) shall be multiplied by two (2). However, the doubling provision of this subdivision does not apply to a loss of use that is not a loss by separation.

(3) The loss of more than one (1) phalange of a thumb or toe shall be considered as the loss of the entire thumb or toe. The loss of more than two (2) phalanges of a finger shall be considered as the loss of the entire finger. The loss of not more than one (1) phalange of a thumb or toe shall be considered as the loss of one-half (1/2) of the degrees of permanent impairment for the loss of the entire thumb or toe.

The loss of not more than one (1) phalange of a finger shall be considered as the loss of one-third (¹/₃) of the finger and compensation shall be paid for one-third (¹/₃) of the degrees payable for the loss of the entire finger. The loss of more than one (1) phalange of the finger but not more than two (2) phalanges of the finger shall be considered as the loss of one-half (¹/₂) of the finger and compensation shall be paid for one-half (¹/₂) of the degrees payable for the loss of the entire finger.

(4) For the loss by separation of both hands or both feet or the total sight of both eyes or any two (2) such losses in the same accident, one hundred (100) degrees of permanent impairment.

(5) For the permanent and complete loss of vision by enucleation, thirty-five (35) degrees of permanent impairment.

(6) For the reduction of vision to one-tenth (¹/₁₀) of normal vision with glasses, thirty-five (35) degrees of permanent impairment.

(7) For the permanent and complete loss of hearing in one (1) ear, fifteen (15) degrees of permanent impairment, and in both ears, forty (40) degrees of permanent impairment.

(8) For the loss of one (1) testicle, ten (10) degrees of permanent impairment; for the loss of both testicles, thirty (30) degrees of permanent impairment.

(9) Loss of use: The total permanent loss of the use of an arm, a hand, a thumb, a finger, a leg, a foot, a toe, or a phalange shall be considered as the equivalent of the loss by separation of the arm, hand, thumb, finger, leg, foot, toe, or phalange, and compensation shall be paid in the same amount as for the loss by separation. However, the doubling provision of subdivision (2) does not apply to a loss of use that is not a loss by separation.

(10) Partial loss of use: For the permanent partial loss of the use of an arm, a hand, a thumb, a finger, a leg, a foot, a toe, or a phalange, compensation shall be paid for the proportionate loss of the use of the arm, hand, thumb, finger, leg, foot, toe, or phalange.

(11) For injuries resulting in total permanent disability, the amount payable for impairment or five hundred (500) weeks of compensation, whichever is greater.

(12) For any permanent reduction of the sight of an eye less than a total loss as specified in subsection (h)(4), the compensation shall be paid in an amount proportionate to the degree of a permanent reduction without correction or

387

glasses. However, when a permanent reduction without correction or glasses would result in one hundred percent (100%) loss of vision, then compensation shall be paid for fifty percent (50%) of the total loss of vision without glasses, plus an additional amount equal to the proportionate amount of the reduction with glasses, not to exceed an additional fifty percent (50%).

(13) For any permanent reduction of the hearing of one (1) or both ears, less than the total loss as specified in subsection (h)(5), compensation shall be paid in an amount proportionate to the degree of a permanent reduction.

(14) In all other cases of permanent partial impairment, compensation proportionate to the degree of a permanent partial impairment, in the discretion of the worker's compensation board, not exceeding one hundred (100) degrees of permanent impairment.

(15) In all cases of permanent disfigurement which may impair the future usefulness or opportunities of the employee, compensation, in the discretion of the worker's compensation board, not exceeding forty (40) degrees of permanent impairment except that no compensation shall be payable under this subdivision where compensation is payable elsewhere in this section.

(j) Compensation for permanent partial impairment shall be paid according to the degree of permanent impairment for the injury determined under subsection (i) and the following:

(1) With respect to injuries occurring on and after July 1, 1991, and before July 1, 1992, for each degree of permanent impairment from one (1) to thirty-five (35), five hundred dollars ($500) per degree; for each degree of permanent impairment from thirty-six (36) to fifty (50), nine hundred dollars ($900) per degree; for each degree of permanent impairment above fifty (50), one thousand five hundred dollars ($1,500) per degree.

(2) With respect to injuries occurring on and after July 1, 1992, and before July 1, 1993, for each degree of permanent impairment from one (1) to twenty (20), five hundred dollars ($500) per degree; for each degree of permanent impairment from twenty-one (21) to thirty-five (35), eight hundred dollars ($800) per degree; for each degree of permanent impairment from thirty-six (36) to fifty (50), one thousand three hundred dollars ($1,300) per degree; for each degree of permanent impairment above fifty (50), one thousand seven hundred dollars ($1,700) per degree.

(3) With respect to injuries occurring on and after July 1,

1993, and before July 1, 1997, for each degree of permanent impairment from one (1) to ten (10), five hundred dollars ($500) per degree; for each degree of permanent impairment from eleven (11) to twenty (20), seven hundred dollars ($700) per degree; for each degree of permanent impairment from twenty-one (21) to thirty-five (35), one thousand dollars ($1,000) per degree; for each degree of permanent impairment from thirty-six (36) to fifty (50), one thousand four hundred dollars ($1,400) per degree; for each degree of permanent impairment above fifty (50), one thousand seven hundred dollars ($1,700) per degree.

(4) With respect to injuries occurring on and after July 1, 1997, and before July 1, 1998, for each degree of permanent impairment from one (1) to ten (10), seven hundred fifty dollars ($750) per degree; for each degree of permanent impairment from eleven (11) to thirty-five (35), one thousand dollars ($1,000) per degree; for each degree of permanent impairment from thirty-six (36) to fifty (50), one thousand four hundred dollars ($1,400) per degree; for each degree of permanent impairment above fifty (50), one thousand seven hundred dollars ($1,700) per degree.

(5) With respect to injuries occurring on and after July 1, 1998, and before July 1, 1999, for each degree of permanent impairment from one (1) to ten (10), seven hundred fifty dollars ($750) per degree; for each degree of permanent impairment from eleven (11) to thirty-five (35), one thousand dollars ($1,000) per degree; for each degree of permanent impairment from thirty-six (36) to fifty (50), one thousand four hundred dollars ($1,400) per degree; for each degree of permanent impairment above fifty (50), one thousand seven hundred dollars ($1,700) per degree.

(6) With respect to injuries occurring on and after July 1, 1999, and before July 1, 2000, for each degree of permanent impairment from one (1) to ten (10), nine hundred dollars ($900) per degree; for each degree of permanent impairment from eleven (11) to thirty-five (35), one thousand one hundred dollars ($1,100) per degree; for each degree of permanent impairment from thirty-six (36) to fifty (50), one thousand six hundred dollars ($1,600) per degree; for each degree of permanent impairment above fifty (50), two thousand dollars ($2,000) per degree.

(7) With respect to injuries occurring on and after July 1, 2000, and before July 1, 2001, for each degree of permanent impairment from one (1) to ten (10), one thousand one hundred dollars ($1,100) per degree; for each degree of permanent impairment from eleven (11) to thirty-five (35), one

thousand three hundred dollars ($1,300) per degree; for each degree of permanent impairment from thirty-six (36) to fifty (50), two thousand dollars ($2,000) per degree; for each degree of permanent impairment above fifty (50), two thousand five hundred fifty dollars ($2,500) per degree.

(8) With respect to injuries occurring on and after July 1, 2001, and before July 1, 2007, for each degree of permanent impairment from one (1) to ten (10), one thousand three hundred dollars ($1,300) per degree; for each degree of permanent impairment from eleven (11) to thirty-five (35), one thousand five hundred dollars ($1,500) per degree; for each degree of permanent impairment from thirty-six (36) to fifty (50), two thousand four hundred dollars ($2,400) per degree; for each degree of permanent impairment above fifty (50), three thousand dollars ($3,000) per degree.

(9) With respect to injuries occurring on and after July 1, 2007, and before July 1, 2008, for each degree of permanent impairment from one (1) to ten (10), one thousand three hundred forty dollars ($1,340) per degree; for each degree of permanent impairment from eleven (11) to thirty-five (35), one thousand five hundred forty-five dollars ($1,545) per degree; for each degree of permanent impairment from thirty-six (36) to fifty (50), two thousand four hundred seventy-five dollars ($2,475) per degree; for each degree of permanent impairment above fifty (50), three thousand one hundred fifty dollars ($3,150) per degree.

(10) With respect to injuries occurring on and after July 1, 2008, and before July 1, 2009, for each degree of permanent impairment from one (1) to ten (10), one thousand three hundred sixty-five dollars ($1,365) per degree; for each degree of permanent impairment from eleven (11) to thirty-five (35), one thousand five hundred seventy dollars ($1,570) per degree; for each degree of permanent impairment from thirty-six (36) to fifty (50), two thousand five hundred twenty-five dollars ($2,525) per degree; for each degree of permanent impairment above fifty (50), three thousand two hundred dollars ($3,200) per degree.

(11) With respect to injuries occurring on and after July 1, 2009, and before July 1, 2010, for each degree of permanent impairment from one (1) to ten (10), one thousand three hundred eighty dollars ($1,380) per degree; for each degree of permanent impairment from eleven (11) to thirty-five (35), one thousand five hundred eighty-five dollars ($1,585) per degree; for each degree of permanent impairment from thirty-six (36) to fifty (50), two thousand six hundred dollars ($2,600) per degree; for each degree of permanent impair-

ment above fifty (50), three thousand three hundred dollars ($3,300) per degree.

(12) With respect to injuries occurring on and after July 1, 2010, and before July 1, 2014, for each degree of permanent impairment from one (1) to ten (10), one thousand four hundred dollars ($1,400) per degree; for each degree of permanent impairment from eleven (11) to thirty-five (35), one thousand six hundred dollars ($1,600) per degree; for each degree of permanent impairment from thirty-six (36) to fifty (50), two thousand seven hundred dollars ($2,700) per degree; for each degree of permanent impairment above fifty (50), three thousand five hundred dollars ($3,500) per degree.

(13) With respect to injuries occurring on and after July 1, 2014, and before July 1, 2015, for each degree of permanent impairment from one (1) to ten (10), one thousand five hundred seventeen dollars ($1,517) per degree; for each degree of permanent impairment from eleven (11) to thirty-five (35), one thousand seven hundred seventeen dollars ($1,717) per degree; for each degree of permanent impairment from thirty-six (36) to fifty (50), two thousand eight hundred sixty-two dollars ($2,862) per degree; for each degree of permanent impairment above fifty (50), three thousand six hundred eighty-seven dollars ($3,687) per degree.

(14) With respect to injuries occurring on and after July 1, 2015, and before July 1, 2016, for each degree of permanent impairment from one (1) to ten (10), one thousand six hundred thirty-three dollars ($1,633) per degree; for each degree of permanent impairment from eleven (11) to thirty-five (35), one thousand eight hundred thirty-five dollars ($1,835) per degree; for each degree of permanent impairment from thirty-six (36) to fifty (50), three thousand twenty-four dollars ($3,024) per degree; for each degree of permanent impairment above fifty (50), three thousand eight hundred seventy-three dollars ($3,873) per degree.

(15) With respect to injuries occurring on and after July 1, 2016, for each degree of permanent impairment from one (1) to ten (10), one thousand seven hundred fifty dollars ($1,750) per degree; for each degree of permanent impairment from eleven (11) to thirty-five (35), one thousand nine hundred fifty-two dollars ($1,952) per degree; for each degree of permanent impairment from thirty-six (36) to fifty (50), three thousand one hundred eighty-six dollars ($3,186) per degree; for each degree of permanent impairment above fifty (50), four thousand sixty dollars ($4,060) per degree.

(k) The average weekly wages used in the determination of compensation for permanent partial impairment under subsections (i) and (j) shall not exceed the following:

(1) With respect to injuries occurring on or after July 1, 1991, and before July 1, 1992, four hundred ninety-two dollars ($492).

(2) With respect to injuries occurring on or after July 1, 1992, and before July 1, 1993, five hundred forty dollars ($540).

(3) With respect to injuries occurring on or after July 1, 1993, and before July 1, 1994, five hundred ninety-one dollars ($591).

(4) With respect to injuries occurring on or after July 1, 1994, and before July 1, 1997, six hundred forty-two dollars ($642).

(5) With respect to injuries occurring on or after July 1, 1997, and before July 1, 1998, six hundred seventy-two dollars ($672).

(6) With respect to injuries occurring on or after July 1, 1998, and before July 1, 1999, seven hundred two dollars ($702).

(7) With respect to injuries occurring on or after July 1, 1999, and before July 1, 2000, seven hundred thirty-two dollars ($732).

(8) With respect to injuries occurring on or after July 1, 2000, and before July 1, 2001, seven hundred sixty-two dollars ($762).

(9) With respect to injuries occurring on or after July 1, 2001, and before July 1, 2002, eight hundred twenty-two dollars ($822).

(10) With respect to injuries occurring on or after July 1, 2002, and before July 1, 2006, eight hundred eighty-two dollars ($882).

(11) With respect to injuries occurring on or after July 1, 2006, and before July 1, 2007, nine hundred dollars ($900).

(12) With respect to injuries occurring on or after July 1, 2007, and before July 1, 2008, nine hundred thirty dollars ($930).

(13) With respect to injuries occurring on or after July 1, 2008, and before July 1, 2009, nine hundred fifty-four dollars ($954).

(14) With respect to injuries occurring on or after July 1, 2009, and before July 1, 2014, nine hundred seventy-five dollars ($975).

(15) With respect to injuries occurring on or after July 1, 2014, and before July 1, 2015, one thousand forty dollars ($1,040).

(16) With respect to injuries occurring on or after July 1, 2015, and before July 1, 2016, one thousand one hundred five dollars ($1,105).

(17) With respect to injuries occurring on or after July 1, 2016, one thousand one hundred seventy dollars ($1,170).

Amended by Acts 1977, P.L.261, SEC.1; Acts 1979, P.L.227, SEC.2; P.L.223-1985, SEC.1; P.L.95-1988, SEC.5; P.L.3-1989, SEC.132; P.L.170-1991, SEC.6; P.L.258-1997(ss), SEC.6; P.L.235-1999, SEC.2; P.L.31-2000, SEC.3; P.L.134-2006, SEC.4; P.L.3-2008, SEC.156, eff. March 13, 2008; P.L.275-2013, SEC.6, eff. July 1, 2013.

22–3–3–11. Partial disability; refusing employment; notice

Sec. 11. If an injured employee, only partially disabled, refuses employment suitable to his capacity procured for him, he shall not be entitled to any compensation at any time during the continuance of such refusal unless in the opinion of the worker's compensation board such refusal was justifiable.

(b) Before compensation can be denied under this section the employee must be served with a notice setting forth the consequences of the refusal of employment under this section. The notice must be in a form prescribed by the worker's compensation board.

Amended by P.L.95–1988, SEC.6.

22–3–3–12. Subsequent permanent injuries; aggravation; awards

Sec. 12. If an employee has sustained a permanent injury either in another employment, or from other cause or causes than the employment in which he received a subsequent permanent injury by accident, such as specified in section 31,[4] he shall be entitled to compensation for the subsequent permanent injury in the same amount as if the previous injury had not occurred: Provided, however, That if the permanent injury for which compensation is claimed, results only in the aggravation or increase of a previously sustained permanent injury or physical condition, regardless of the source or cause of such previously sustained injury or physical condition, the board shall determine the extent of the previously sustained permanent injury or physical condition, as well as the extent of the aggravation or increase resulting from the subsequent permanent injury, and shall award compensation only for that part of such injury, or physical condition resulting from the subsequent permanent injury. Provided further, however, That amputation of any part of the body or loss of any or all of the vision of one or both eyes shall be considered as a permanent injury or physical condition.

---

[4]Section 22–3–3–10.

22-3-3-13. Second injuries

Sec. 13. As used in this section, "board" refers to the worker's compensation board created under IC 22-3-1-1.

(b) If an employee who from any cause, had lost, or lost the use of, one (1) hand, one (1) arm, one (1) foot, one (1) leg, or one (1) eye, and in a subsequent industrial accident becomes permanently and totally disabled by reason of the loss, or loss of use of, another such member or eye, the employer shall be liable only for the compensation payable for such second injury. However, in addition to such compensation and after the completion of the payment therefor, the employee shall be paid the remainder of the compensation that would be due for such total permanent disability out of a special fund known as the second injury fund, and created in the manner described in subsection (c).

(c) Whenever the board determines under the procedures set forth in subsection (d) that an assessment is necessary to ensure that fund beneficiaries, including applicants under section 4(f) of this chapter, continue to receive compensation in a timely manner for a reasonable prospective period, the board shall send notice not later than November 1 in any year to:

(1) all insurance carriers and other entities insuring or providing coverage to employers who are or may be liable under this article to pay compensation for personal injuries to or the death of their employees under this article; and

(2) each employer carrying the employer's own risk;

stating that an assessment is necessary. Not later than January 31 of the following year, each entity identified in subdivisions (1) and (2) shall send to the board a statement of total paid losses and premiums (as defined in subsection (d)(4)) paid by employers during the previous calendar year. The board may conduct an assessment under this subsection not more than one (1) time annually. The total amount of the assessment may not exceed two and one-half percent (2.5%) of the total amount of all worker's compensation paid to injured employees or their beneficiaries under IC 22-3-2 through IC 22-3-6 for the calendar year next preceding the due date of such payment. The board shall assess a penalty in the amount of ten percent (10%) of the amount owed if payment is not made under this section within thirty (30) days from the date set by the board. If the amount to the credit of the second injury fund on or before November 1 of any year exceeds one hundred thirty-five percent (135%) of the previous year's disbursements, the assessment allowed under this subsection shall not be assessed or collected during the ensuing year. But when on or before November 1 of any year the amount to the credit of the fund is less than one hundred thirty-five percent (135%) of the previous year's disbursements, the payments of not more than two and one-half percent (2.5%) of the total amount of all worker's compensation paid to injured employees or their beneficiaries under IC 22–3–2 through IC 22–3–6 for the calendar year next preceding that date shall be resumed and paid into the fund. The board may not use an assessment rate greater than twenty-five hundredths of one percent (0.25%) above the amount recommended by the study performed before the assessment.

(d) The board shall assess all employers for the liabilities, including administrative expenses, of the second injury fund. The assessment also must provide for the repayment of all loans made to the second injury fund for the purpose of paying valid claims. The following applies to assessments under this subsection:

(1) The portion of the total amount that must be collected from self-insured employers equals:

(A) the total amount of the assessment as determined by the board; multiplied by

(B) the quotient of:

(i) the total paid losses on behalf of all self-insured employers during the preceding calendar year; divided by

(ii) the total paid losses on behalf of all self-insured employers and insured employers during the preceding calendar year.

(2) The portion of the total amount that must be collected from insured employers equals:

(A) the total amount of the assessment as determined by the board; multiplied by

(B) the quotient of:

(i) the total paid losses on behalf of all insured employers during the preceding calendar year; divided by

(ii) the total paid losses on behalf of all self-insured employers and insured employers during the preceding calendar year.

(3) The total amount of insured employer assessments under subdivision (2) must be collected by the insured employers' worker's compensation insurers. The amount of employer assessments each insurer shall collect equals:

(A) the total amount of assessments allocated to insured employers under subdivision (2); multiplied by

(B) the quotient of:

(i) the worker's compensation premiums paid by employers to the carrier during the preceding calendar year; divided by

(ii) the worker's compensation premiums paid by employers to all carriers during the preceding calendar year.

(4) For purposes of the computation made under subdivision (3), "premium" means the direct written premium.

(5) The amount of the assessment for each self-insured employer equals:

(A) the total amount of assessments allocated to self-insured employers under subdivision (1); multiplied by

(B) the quotient of:

(i) the paid losses attributable to the self-insured employer during the preceding calendar year; divided by

(ii) paid losses attributable to all self-insured employers during the preceding calendar year.

An employer that has ceased to be a self-insurer continues to be liable for prorated assessments based on paid losses made by the employer in the preceding calendar year during the period that the employer was self-insured.

(e) The board may employ a qualified employee or enter into a contract with an actuary or another qualified firm that has experience in calculating worker's compensation liabilities. Not later than December 1 of each year, the actuary or other qualified firm shall calculate the recommended funding level of the fund and inform the board of the results of the calculation. If the amount to the credit of the fund is less than the amount required under subsection (c), the board may conduct an assessment under subsection (c). The board shall pay the costs of the contract under this subsection with money in the fund.

(f) An assessment collected under subsection (c) on an employer who is not self-insured must be assessed through a surcharge based on the employer's premium. An assessment collected under subsection (c) does not constitute an element of loss, but for the purpose of collection shall be treated as a separate cost imposed upon insured employers. A premium surcharge under this subsection must be collected at the same time and in the same manner in which the premium for coverage is collected, and must be shown as a separate amount on a premium statement. A premium surcharge under this subsection must be excluded from the definition of premium for all purposes, including the computation of insurance producer commissions or premium taxes. However, an insurer may cancel a worker's compensation policy for nonpayment of the premium surcharge. A cancellation under this subsection must be carried out under the statutes applicable to the nonpayment of premiums.

(g) The sums shall be paid by the board to the treasurer of state, to be deposited in a special account known as the second injury fund. The funds are not a part of the general fund of the state. Any balance remaining in the account at the end of any fiscal year shall not revert to the general fund. The funds shall be used only for the payment of fund liabilities described in subsection (d) and awards of compensation ordered by the board and chargeable against the fund pursuant to this section, and shall be paid for that purpose by the treasurer of state upon award or order of the board.

(h) If an employee who is entitled to compensation under IC 22–3–2 through IC 22–3–6 either:

(1) exhausts the maximum benefits under section 22 of this chapter without having received the full amount of award granted to the employee under section 10 of this chapter; or

(2) exhausts the employee's benefits under section 10 of this chapter;

then such employee may apply to the board, who may award the employee compensation from the second injury fund established by this section, as follows under subsection (i).

(i) An employee who has exhausted the employee's maximum benefits under section 10 of this chapter may be awarded additional compensation equal to sixty-six and two-thirds percent (66 2/3%) of the employee's average weekly wage at the time of the employee's injury, not to exceed the maximum then applicable under section 22 of this chapter, for a period of not to exceed one hundred fifty (150) weeks upon competent evidence sufficient to establish:

(1) that the employee is totally and permanently disabled from causes and conditions of which there are or have been objective conditions and symptoms proven that are not within the physical or mental control of the employee; and

(2) that the employee is unable to support the employee in any gainful employment, not associated with rehabilitative or vocational therapy.

(j) The additional award may be renewed during the employee's total and permanent disability after appropriate hearings by the board for successive periods not to exceed one hundred fifty (150) weeks each. The provisions of this section apply only to injuries occurring subsequent to April 1, 1950, for which awards have been or are in the future made by the board under section 10 of this chapter. Section 16 of this chapter does not apply to compensation awarded from the second injury fund under this section.

(k) All insurance carriers subject to an assessment under this section are required to provide to the board:

(1) not later than January 31 each calendar year; and

(2) not later than thirty (30) days after a change occurs;

the name, address, and electronic mail address of a representative authorized to receive the notice of an assessment.

Amended by Acts 1979, P.L.227, SEC.3; Acts 1980, P.L.22, SEC.14; P.L.28–1988, SEC.28; P.L.170–1991, SEC.7; P.L.235–1999, SEC.3; P.L.202–2001, SEC.5; P.L.178–2003, SEC.9; P.L.134–2006, SEC.5; P.L.1–2007, SEC.158, eff. Mar. 30, 2007; P.L.173–2007, SEC.5, eff. May 4, 2007; P.L.67–2010, SEC.2; P.L.168–2011, SEC.5, eff. May 10, 2011.

22–3–3–14. Subsequent injuries; two awards

Sec. 14. If an employee receives an injury for which compensation is payable while he is still receiving or entitled to compensation for a previous injury in the same employment, he shall not at the same time be entitled to compensation for both injuries, unless it be for a permanent injury, such as specified in section 10 of this chapter; but he shall be entitled to compensation for that injury and from the time of that injury which will cover the longest period and the largest amount payable under IC 22–3–2 through IC 22–3–6.

Amended by P.L.144–1986, SEC.32.

22–3–3–15. Subsequent injuries; awards; extending period of payment

Sec. 15. If an employee receives a permanent injury such as specified in section 10 of this chapter after having sustained another permanent injury in the same employment, he shall be entitled to compensation for both injuries, but the total compensation shall be paid by extending the period and not by increasing the amount of weekly compensation, and when such previous and subsequent permanent injuries in combination result in total permanent disability or permanent total impairment, compensation shall be payable for such permanent total disability or permanent total impairment, but payments made for the previous injury shall be deducted from the total payment of compensation due.

Amended by P.L.144–1986, SEC.33.

22–3–3–16. Death while receiving awards; dependents; payment

Sec. 16. When an employee has been awarded or is entitled to an award of compensation for a definite period under IC 22–3–2 through IC 22–3–6 for an injury occurring prior to April 1, 1945, and dies from any other cause than such injury, payment of the unpaid balance of such compensation, not exceeding three hundred (300) weeks, shall be made to his dependents as defined in section 18 of this chapter; provided that where the compensable injury occurred on and after April 1, 1945, and prior to April 1, 1951, the maximum shall not exceed three hundred fifty (350) weeks. With respect to any such injury occurring on and after April 1, 1951, the maximum shall not exceed three hundred fifty (350) weeks for dependents of the second or third class and the maximum shall not exceed five hundred (500) weeks for dependents of the first class.

Amended by P.L.144–1986, SEC.34.

22–3–3–17. Death benefits

Sec. 17. On and after April 1, 1965, and prior to April 1, 1969, when death results from an injury within four hundred fifty (450) weeks, there shall be paid to total dependent[5] of said deceased, as determined by IC 22–3–3–18, 19 and 20, a weekly compensation amounting to sixty percent (60%) of the deceased's average weekly wage, until compensation so paid, when added to any compensation paid to deceased employee, shall equal four hundred fifty (450) weeks, and to partial dependents as hereinafter provided.

On and after April 1, 1969, and prior to July 1, 1971, when death results from an injury within five hundred (500) weeks, there shall be paid to the total dependents of said deceased, as determined by the provisions of IC 22–3–3–18, 19 and 20, weekly compensation amounting to sixty percent (60%) of the deceased's average weekly wage, until the compensation so paid, when added to any compensation paid to the deceased employee, shall equal five hundred (500) weeks, and to partial dependents as hereinafter provided.

On and after July 1, 1971, and prior to July 1, 1974, when death results from an injury within five hundred (500) weeks, there shall be paid to the total dependents of said deceased, as determined by the provisions of IC 22–3–3–18, 19 and 20, weekly compensation amounting to sixty percent (60%) of the deceased's average weekly wage, not to exceed one hundred dollars ($100) average weekly wages, until the compensation so paid, when added to any compensation paid to the deceased employee, shall equal five hundred (500) weeks, and to partial dependents as hereinafter provided.

On and after July 1, 1974, and before July 1, 1976, when death results from an injury within five hundred (500) weeks, there shall be paid the total dependents of the deceased, as determined by the provisions of sections 18, 19 and 20 of this chapter, weekly compensation amounting to sixty-six and two-thirds percent (66²/₃%) of the deceased's average weekly wage, not to exceed a maximum of one hundred thirty-five dollars ($135) average weekly wages, until the compensation so paid, when added to any compensation paid to the deceased em-

---

[5]So in enrolled Indiana Code. Probably should read "dependents."

ployee, shall equal five hundred (500) weeks, and to partial dependents as hereinafter provided. On and after July 1, 1976, when death results from an injury within five hundred (500) weeks, there shall be paid the total dependents of the deceased as determined by sections 18, 19 and 20 of this chapter, weekly compensation amounting to sixty-six and two-thirds percent (66²/₃%) of the deceased's average weekly wage, as defined by IC 22–3–3–22, until the compensation paid, when added to the compensation paid to the deceased employee, equals five hundred (500) weeks, and to partial dependents, as provided in sections 18 and 20 of this chapter.
Amended by Acts 1976, P.L.112, SEC.2.

22–3–3–18. Death resulting from injuries; award; payment to dependents

Sec. 18. Dependents under IC 22–3–2 through IC 22–3–6 shall consist of the following three (3) classes:

(1) Presumptive dependents.

(2) Total dependents in fact.

(3) Partial dependents in fact.

(b) Presumptive dependents shall be entitled to compensation to the complete exclusion of total dependents in fact and partial dependents in fact and shall be entitled to such compensation in equal shares.

(c) Total dependents in fact shall be entitled to compensation to the complete exclusion of partial dependents in fact and shall be entitled to such compensation, if more than one (1) such dependent exists, in equal shares. The question of total dependency shall be determined as of the time of death.

(d) Partial dependents in fact shall not be entitled to any compensation if any other class of dependents exist. The weekly compensation to persons partially dependent in fact shall be in the same proportion to the weekly compensation of persons wholly dependent as the average amount contributed weekly by the deceased to such partial dependent in fact bears to his average weekly wages at the time of the occurrence of the accident. The question of partial dependency in fact shall be determined as of the time of the occurrence of the accident.
Amended by P.L.144–1986, SEC.35.

22–3–3–19. Presumptive dependents; termination of dependency

Sec. 19. The following persons are conclusively presumed to be wholly dependent for support upon a deceased employee and shall constitute the class known as presumptive dependents in section 18 of this chapter:

(1) A wife upon a husband with whom she is living at the time of his death, or upon whom the laws of the state impose

the obligation of her support at such time. The term "wife", as used in this subdivision, shall exclude a common law wife unless such common law relationship was entered into before January 1, 1958, and, in addition, existed openly and notoriously for a period of not less than five (5) years immediately preceding the death.

(2) A husband upon his wife with whom he is living at the time of her death. The term "husband", as used in this subdivision, shall exclude a common law husband unless such common law relationship was entered into before January 1, 1958, and, in addition, existed openly and notoriously for a period of not less than five (5) years immediately preceding the death.

(3) An unmarried child under the age of twenty-one (21) years upon the parent with whom the child is living at the time of the death of such parent.

(4) An unmarried child under twenty-one (21) years upon the parent with whom the child may not be living at the time of the death of such parent, but upon whom, at such time, the laws of the state impose the obligation to support such child.

(5) A child over the age of twenty-one (21) years who has never been married and who is either physically or mentally incapacitated from earning the child's own support, upon a parent upon whom the laws of the state impose the obligation of the support of such unmarried child.

(6) A child over the age of twenty-one (21) years who has never been married and who at the time of the death of the parent is keeping house for and living with such parent and is not otherwise gainfully employed.

(b) As used in this section, the term "child" includes stepchildren, legally adopted children, posthumous children, and acknowledged children born out of wedlock. The term "parent" includes stepparents and parents by adoption.

(c) The dependency of a child under subsections (a)(3) and (a)(4) shall terminate when the child attains the age of twenty-one (21).

(d) The dependency of any person as a presumptive dependent shall terminate upon the marriage of such dependent subsequent to the death of the employee, and such dependency shall not be reinstated by divorce. However, for deaths from injuries occurring on and after July 1, 1977, a surviving spouse who is a presumptive dependent and who is the only surviving dependent of the deceased employee is entitled to receive, upon remarriage before the expiration of the maximum statutory compensation period, a lump sum settlement equal to the smaller of one hundred four (104) weeks of compensation or the compensation for the remainder of the maximum statutory compensation period.

(e) The dependency of any child under subsection (a)(6) shall be terminated at such time as such dependent becomes gainfully employed or marries.

Amended by Acts 1977, P.L.261, SEC.2; P.L.152–1987, SEC.6; P.L.134–1990, SEC.1.

22–3–3–20. Total or partial dependents; eligibility; termination

Sec. 20. Total or partial dependents in fact shall include only those persons related to the deceased employee by blood or by marriage, except an unmarried child under the age of eighteen (18) years. Any such person who is actually totally or partially dependent upon the deceased employee is entitled to compensation as such dependent in fact. The right to compensation of any person totally or partially dependent in fact shall be terminated by the marriage of such dependent subsequent to the death of the employee and such dependency shall not be reinstated by divorce.

22–3–3–21. Burial expenses

Sec. 21. In cases of the death of an employee from an injury by an accident arising out of and in the course of the employee's employment under circumstances that the employee would have been entitled to compensation if death had not resulted, the employer shall pay the burial expenses of such employee, not exceeding seven thousand five hundred dollars ($7,500).

Amended by P.L.225–1983, SEC.1; P.L.16–1984, SEC.15; P.L.95–1988, SEC.7; P.L.170–1991, SEC.8; P.L.201–2005, SEC.4.

22–3–3–22. Awards; computation

Sec. 22. In computing compensation for temporary total disability, temporary partial disability, and total permanent disability, with respect to injuries occurring on and after July 1, 1985, and before July 1, 1986, the average weekly wages are considered to be:

(1) not more than two hundred sixty-seven dollars ($267); and

(2) not less than seventy-five dollars ($75).

However, the weekly compensation payable shall not exceed the average weekly wages of the employee at the time of the injury.

(b) In computing compensation for temporary total disability, temporary partial disability, and total permanent disability, with respect to injuries occurring on and after July 1, 1986, and before July 1, 1988, the average weekly wages are considered to be:

(1) not more than two hundred eighty-five dollars ($285); and

(2) not less than seventy-five dollars ($75).

However, the weekly compensation payable shall not exceed the average weekly wages of the employee at the time of the injury.

(c) In computing compensation for temporary total disability, temporary partial disability, and total permanent disability, with respect to injuries occurring on and after July 1, 1988, and before July 1, 1989, the average weekly wages are considered to be:

(1) not more than three hundred eighty-four dollars ($384); and

(2) not less than seventy-five dollars ($75).

However, the weekly compensation payable shall not exceed the average weekly wages of the employee at the time of the injury.

(d) In computing compensation for temporary total disability, temporary partial disability, and total permanent disability, with respect to injuries occurring on and after July 1, 1989, and before July 1, 1990, the average weekly wages are considered to be:

(1) not more than four hundred eleven dollars ($411); and

(2) not less than seventy-five dollars ($75).

However, the weekly compensation payable shall not exceed the average weekly wages of the employee at the time of the injury.

(e) In computing compensation for temporary total disability, temporary partial disability, and total permanent disability, with respect to injuries occurring on and after July 1, 1990, and before July 1, 1991, the average weekly wages are considered to be:

(1) not more than four hundred forty-one dollars ($441); and

(2) not less than seventy-five dollars ($75).

However, the weekly compensation payable shall not exceed the average weekly wages of the employee at the time of the injury.

(f) In computing compensation for temporary total disability, temporary partial disability, and total permanent disability, with respect to injuries occurring on and after July 1, 1991, and before July 1, 1992, the average weekly wages are considered to be:

(1) not more than four hundred ninety-two dollars ($492); and

(2) not less than seventy-five dollars ($75).

However, the weekly compensation payable shall not exceed the average weekly wages of the employee at the time of the injury.

(g) In computing compensation for temporary total disability, temporary partial disability, and total permanent disability, with respect to injuries occurring on and after July 1, 1992, and before July 1, 1993, the average weekly wages are considered to be:

(1) not more than five hundred forty dollars ($540); and

(2) not less than seventy-five dollars ($75).

However, the weekly compensation payable shall not exceed the average weekly wages of the employee at the time of the injury.

(h) In computing compensation for temporary total disability, temporary partial disability, and total permanent disability, with respect to injuries occurring on and after July 1, 1993, and before July 1, 1994, the average weekly wages are considered to be:

(1) not more than five hundred ninety-one dollars ($591); and

(2) not less than seventy-five dollars ($75).

However, the weekly compensation payable shall not exceed the average weekly wages of the employee at the time of the injury.

(i) In computing compensation for temporary total disability, temporary partial disability, and total permanent disability, with respect to injuries occurring on and after July 1, 1994, and before July 1, 1997, the average weekly wages are considered to be:

(1) not more than six hundred forty-two dollars ($642); and

(2) not less than seventy-five dollars ($75).

However, the weekly compensation payable shall not exceed the average weekly wages of the employee at the time of the injury.

(j) In computing compensation for temporary total disability, temporary partial disability, and total permanent disability, the average weekly wages are considered to be:

(1) with respect to injuries occurring on and after July 1, 1997, and before July 1, 1998:

(A) not more than six hundred seventy-two dollars ($672); and

(B) not less than seventy-five dollars ($75);

(2) with respect to injuries occurring on and after July 1, 1998, and before July 1, 1999:

(A) not more than seven hundred two dollars ($702); and

(B) not less than seventy-five dollars ($75);

(3) with respect to injuries occurring on and after July 1, 1999, and before July 1, 2000:

(A) not more than seven hundred thirty-two dollars ($732); and

(B) not less than seventy-five dollars ($75);

(4) with respect to injuries occurring on and after July 1, 2000, and before July 1, 2001:

(A) not more than seven hundred sixty-two dollars ($762); and

(B) not less than seventy-five dollars ($75);

(5) with respect to injuries occurring on and after July 1, 2001, and before July 1, 2002:

(A) not more than eight hundred twenty-two dollars ($822); and

(B) not less than seventy-five dollars ($75);

(6) with respect to injuries occurring on and after July 1, 2002, and before July 1, 2006:

(A) not more than eight hundred eighty-two dollars ($882); and

(B) not less than seventy-five dollars ($75);

(7) with respect to injuries occurring on and after July 1, 2006, and before July 1, 2007:

(A) not more than nine hundred dollars ($900); and

(B) not less than seventy-five dollars ($75);

(8) with respect to injuries occurring on and after July 1, 2007, and before July 1, 2008:

(A) not more than nine hundred thirty dollars ($930); and

(B) not less than seventy-five dollars ($75);

(9) with respect to injuries occurring on and after July 1, 2008, and before July 1, 2009:

(A) not more than nine hundred fifty-four dollars ($954); and

(B) not less than seventy-five dollars ($75); and

(10) with respect to injuries occurring on and after July 1, 2009, and before July 1, 2014:

(A) not more than nine hundred seventy-five dollars ($975); and

(B) not less than seventy-five dollars ($75);

(11) with respect to injuries occurring on and after July 1, 2014, and before July 1, 2015:

(A) not more than one thousand forty dollars ($1,040); and

(B) not less than seventy-five dollars ($75);

(12) with respect to injuries occurring on and after July 1, 2015, and before July 1, 2016:

(A) not more than one thousand one hundred five dollars ($1,105); and

(B) not less than seventy-five dollars ($75); and

(13) with respect to injuries occurring on and after July 1, 2016:

(A) not more than one thousand one hundred seventy dollars ($1,170); and

(B) not less than seventy-five dollars ($75).

However, the weekly compensation payable shall not exceed the average weekly wages of the employee at the time of the injury.

(k) With respect to any injury occurring on and after July 1, 1985, and before July 1, 1986, the maximum compensation, exclusive of medical benefits, which may be paid for an injury under any provisions of this law or any combination of provisions may not exceed eighty-nine thousand dollars ($89,000) in any case.

(l) With respect to any injury occurring on and after July 1, 1986, and before July 1, 1988, the maximum compensation, exclusive of medical benefits, which may be paid for an injury under any provisions of this law or any combination of provisions may not exceed ninety-five thousand dollars ($95,000) in any case.

(m) With respect to any injury occurring on and after July 1, 1988, and before July 1, 1989, the maximum compensation, exclusive of medical benefits, which may be paid for an injury under any provisions of this law or any combination of provisions may not exceed one hundred twenty-eight thousand dollars ($128,000) in any case.

(n) With respect to any injury occurring on and after July 1, 1989, and before July 1, 1990, the maximum compensation, exclusive of medical benefits, which may be paid for an injury under any provisions of this law or any combination of provisions may not exceed one hundred thirty-seven thousand dollars ($137,000) in any case.

(o) With respect to any injury occurring on and after July 1, 1990, and before July 1, 1991, the maximum compensation, exclusive of medical benefits, which may be paid for an injury under any provisions of this law or any combination of provisions may not exceed one hundred forty-seven thousand dollars ($147,000) in any case.

(p) With respect to any injury occurring on and after July 1, 1991, and before July 1, 1992, the maximum compensation, exclusive of medical benefits, that may be paid for an injury under any provisions of this law or any combination of provisions may not exceed one hundred sixty-four thousand dollars ($164,000) in any case.

(q) With respect to any injury occurring on and after July 1, 1992, and before July 1, 1993, the maximum compensation, exclusive of medical benefits, that may be paid for an injury under any provisions of this law or any combination of provisions may not exceed one hundred eighty thousand dollars ($180,000) in any case.

(r) With respect to any injury occurring on and after July 1, 1993, and before July 1, 1994, the maximum compensation, exclusive of medical benefits, that may be paid for an injury under any provisions of this law or any combination of provisions may not exceed one hundred ninety-seven thousand dollars ($197,000) in any case.

(s) With respect to any injury occurring on and after July 1, 1994, and before July 1, 1997, the maximum compensation, exclusive of medical benefits, which may be paid for an injury under any provisions of this law or any combination of provisions may not exceed two hundred fourteen thousand dollars ($214,000) in any case.

(t) The maximum compensation, exclusive of medical benefits, that may be paid for an injury under any provision of this law or any combination of provisions may not exceed the following amounts in any case:

(1) With respect to an injury occurring on and after July 1, 1997, and before July 1, 1998, two hundred twenty-four thousand dollars ($224,000).

(2) With respect to an injury occurring on and after July 1, 1998, and before July 1, 1999, two hundred thirty-four thousand dollars ($234,000).

(3) With respect to an injury occurring on and after July 1, 1999, and before July 1, 2000, two hundred forty-four thousand dollars ($244,000).

(4) With respect to an injury occurring on and after July 1, 2000, and before July 1, 2001, two hundred fifty-four thousand dollars ($254,000).

(5) With respect to an injury occurring on and after July 1, 2001, and before July 1, 2002, two hundred seventy-four thousand dollars ($274,000).

(6) With respect to an injury occurring on and after July 1, 2002, and before July 1, 2006, two hundred ninety-four thousand dollars ($294,000).

(7) With respect to an injury occurring on and after July 1, 2006, and before July 1, 2007, three hundred thousand dollars ($300,000).

(8) With respect to an injury occurring on and after July 1, 2007, and before July 1, 2008, three hundred ten thousand dollars ($310,000).

(9) With respect to an injury occurring on and after July 1, 2008, and before July 1, 2009, three hundred eighteen thousand dollars ($318,000).

(10) With respect to an injury occurring on and after July 1, 2009, and before July 1, 2014, three hundred twenty-five thousand dollars ($325,000).

(11) With respect to an injury occurring on and after July 1, 2014, and before July 1, 2015, three hundred forty-seven thousand dollars ($347,000).

(12) With respect to an injury occurring on and after July 1, 2015, and before July 1, 2016, three hundred sixty-eight thousand dollars ($368,000).

(13) With respect to an injury occurring on and after July 1, 2016, three hundred ninety thousand dollars ($390,000).

Amended by Acts 1976, P.L.112, SEC.3; Acts 1977, P.L.261, SEC.3; Acts 1979, P.L.227, SEC.4; Acts 1980, P.L.22, SEC.15; P.L.225-1983, SEC.2; P.L.223-1985, SEC.2; P.L.95-1988, SEC.8; P.L.170-1991, SEC.9; P.L.258-1997(ss), SEC.7; P.L.31-2000, SEC.4; P.L.134-2006, SEC.6; P.L.275-2013, SEC.7, eff. July 1, 2013.

22-3-3-23. Mistake in payments; deductions; payments to state employees

Sec. 23. Any payments made by the employer to the injured employee during the period of his disability, or to his dependents, which by the terms of IC 22-3-2 through IC 22-3-6 were not due and payable when made, may, subject to the approval of the worker's compensation board, be deducted from the amount to be paid as compensation. However, the deduction shall be made from the distal end of the period during which compensation must be paid, except in cases of temporary disability.

(b) Payments to state employees under the terms of IC 5-10-8-7(d)(5) shall be taken as a credit by the state against payments of compensation for temporary total disability during the time period in which the employee is eligible for compensation under both IC 5–10–8–7(d)(5) and section 8 of this chapter.

After a state employee is ineligible for payments under IC 5–10–8–7(d)(5) and if he is still eligible for payments for temporary total disability under section 8 of this chapter, any payments for temporary total disability shall be deducted from the amount of compensation payable under section 10 of this chapter. Payments to state employees under the terms of IC 5–10–8–7(d)(5) may not be deducted from compensation payable under section 10 of this chapter.

Amended by Acts 1976, P.L.113, SEC.1; P.L.28–1988, SEC.29; P.L.1–1994, SEC.107.

22–3–3–24. Payments; time of payment

Sec. 24. When so provided in the compensation agreement or in the award of the worker's compensation board, compensation may be paid semimonthly, or monthly, instead of weekly.

Amended by P.L.28–1988, SEC.30.

22–3–3–25. Lump sum payments; minors; interest rate

Sec. 25. In unusual cases, upon the agreement of the employer and the employee or his dependents, and the insurance carrier, and the approval of the worker's compensation board, compensation may be redeemed, in whole or in part, by the cash payment, in a lump sum, of the commutable value of the installments to be redeemed.

(b) The board may, at any time, in the case of permanently disabling injuries of a minor, require that he be compensated by the cash payment in a lump sum of the commutable value of the unredeemed installments of the compensation to which he is entitled.

(c) In all such cases, the commutable value of the future unpaid installments of compensation shall be the present value thereof, at the rate of three percent (3%) interest, compounded annually.

Amended by P.L.28–1988, SEC.31.

22–3–3–26. Lump sum payments; trustees

Sec. 26. Whenever the worker's compensation board deems it expedient, any lump sum under section 25 of this chapter shall be paid by the employer to some suitable person or corporation appointed by the circuit or superior court, as trustee, to administer the same for the benefit of the person entitled thereto, in the manner authorized by the court appointing such trustee. The receipt of such trustee for the amount so paid shall discharge the employer or anyone else who is liable therefor.

Amended by P.L.144–1986, SEC.36; P.L.28–1988, SEC.32.

22–3–3–27. Jurisdiction; modification of award

Sec. 27. The power and jurisdiction of the worker's compensation board over each case shall be continuing and from time to time it may, upon its own motion or upon the application of either party, on account of a change in conditions, make such modification or change in the award ending, lessening, continuing, or extending the payments previously awarded, either by agreement or upon hearing, as it may deem just, subject to the maximum and minimum provided for in IC 22–3–2 through IC 22–3–6.

(b) Upon making any such change, the board shall immediately send to each of the parties a copy of the modified award. No such modification shall affect the previous award as to any money paid thereunder.

(c) The board shall not make any such modification upon its own motion nor shall any application therefor be filed by either party after the expiration of two (2) years from the last day for which compensation was paid. The board may at any time correct any clerical error in any finding or award.

Amended by P.L.144–1986, SEC.37; P.L.28–1988, SEC.33; P.L.134–2006, SEC.7.

22–3–3–28. Children and minors; direct payments

Sec. 28. When the aggregate payments of compensation, awarded by agreement or upon hearing to an employee or dependent under eighteen (18) years of age, do not exceed one hundred dollars ($100), the payment thereof may be made directly to such employee or dependent, except when the worker's compensation board shall order otherwise.

(b) Whenever the aggregate payments of compensation, due to any person under eighteen (18) years of age, exceed one hundred dollars ($100), the payment thereof shall be made to a trustee, appointed by the circuit or superior court, or to a duly qualified guardian, or to a parent upon the order of the worker's compensation board. The payment of compensation, due to any person eighteen (18) years of age or over, may be made directly to such person.

Amended by P.L.28–1988, SEC.34.

22–3–3–29. Injured employee or dependent under guardianship

Sec. 29. If any injured employee or a dependent is under guardianship at the time when any right or privilege accrues to the employee or dependent under IC 22–3–2, IC 22–3–3, IC 22–3–4, IC 22–3–5, or IC 22–3–6, the employee or dependent's guardian shall claim and exercise the right or privilege of the employee or dependent.

Amended by P.L.144–1986, SEC.38; P.L.33–1989, SEC.19.

22–3–3–30. Incompetent persons; limitation of actions

Sec. 30. No limitation of time provided in IC 22–3–2 through IC 22–3–6 shall run against any person who is mentally incompetent or a minor so long as he has no guardian or trustee.

Amended by P.L.144–1986, SEC.39.

22–3–3–31. Joint service of two or more employers; apportionment of award

Sec. 31. Whenever any employee for whose injury or death compensation is payable under IC 22–3–2 through IC 22–3–6 shall at the time of the injury be in the joint service of two (2) or more employers subject to IC 22–3–2 through IC 22–3–6, such employers shall contribute to the payment of such compensation in proportion to their wage liability to such employees; provided, however, that nothing in this section shall prevent any reasonable arrangements between such employers for a different distribution as between themselves of the ultimate burden of compensation.

Amended by P.L.144–1986, SEC.40.

22–3–3–32. Construction of article

Sec. 32. The provisions of this article may not be construed to result in an award of benefits in which the number of weeks paid and to be paid for temporary total disability, temporary partial disability, or permanent total disability combined exceeds five hundred (500) weeks. This section shall not be construed to prevent a person who is permanently totally disabled from applying for an award under IC 22–3–3–13.

However, in case of permanent total disability resulting from an injury occurring on or after January 1, 1998, the minimum total benefit shall not be less than seventy-five thousand dollars ($75,000).

As added by P.L.258–1997(ss), SEC.8.

Chapter 4. Worker's Compensation: Administration and Procedures

22–3–4–1. Industrial board; office space; furniture and supplies; meetings

Sec. 1. The board shall be provided with adequate offices in the capitol or some other suitable building in the city of Indianapolis in which the records shall be kept and its official business be transacted during regular business hours; it shall also be provided with necessary office furniture, stationery and other supplies.

The board or any member thereof may hold sessions at any place within the state as may be deemed necessary.

22–3–4–2. Rules and regulations; subpoenas; service; hearings

Sec. 2. The worker's compensation board may make rules not inconsistent with IC 22–3–2 through IC 22–3–6 for carrying out the provisions of IC 22–3–2 through IC 22–3–6.

Processes and procedures under IC 22–3–2 through IC 22–

3–6 shall be as summary and simple as reasonably may be.

The board or any member of the board shall have the power for the purpose of IC 22–3–2 through IC 22–3–6 to subpoena witnesses, administer or cause to have administered oaths, and to examine or cause to have examined such parts of the books and records of the parties to a proceeding as relate to questions in dispute.

(b) The county sheriff shall serve all subpoenas of the board and shall receive the same fees as provided by law for like service in civil actions. Each witness who appears in obedience to such subpoenas of the board shall receive for attendance the fees and mileage for witnesses in civil cases in the courts.

(c) The circuit or superior court shall, on application of the board or any member of the board, enforce by proper proceedings the attendance and testimony of witnesses and the production and examination of books, papers, and records.

Amended by P.L.144–1986, SEC.41; P.L.28–1988, SEC.35.

22–3–4–3. Inspection of records; confidential information; destruction of records

Sec. 3. The board shall prepare and cause to be printed, and upon request furnish free of charge to any employer or employee, such blank forms and literature as it shall deem requisite to facilitate or promote the efficient administration of this chapter, IC 22–3–2 through IC 22–3–3, and IC 22–3–5 through IC 22–3–6. The accident reports and reports of attending physicians shall be the private records of the board, which shall be open to the inspection of the employer, the employee and their legal representatives, but not the public unless, in the opinion of the board, the public interest shall so require.

(b) In order to prevent the accumulation of unnecessary and useless files of papers, the board may destroy or otherwise dispose of under IC 5–15–5.1–14 all papers that have been on file for more than two (2) years, when there is no claim for compensation pending, or, when compensation has been awarded either by agreement or upon hearing, and more than one (1) year has elapsed since the termination of the compensation period as fixed by such board.

Amended by Acts 1979, P.L.17, SEC.33; P.L.121–1995, SEC.2.

22–3–4–4. Awards; private agreements; approval

Sec. 4. If after seven (7) days from the date of the injury or at any time in case of death, the employer and the injured employee or his dependents reach an agreement in regard to compensation under IC 22–3–2 through IC 22–3–6, a memorandum of the agreement in the form prescribed by the worker's compensation board shall be filed with the board; otherwise such agreement shall be voidable by the employee or his dependent. If approved by the board, thereupon the memorandum shall for all purposes be enforceable by court decree as specified in section 9 of this chapter. Such agreement shall be approved by said board only when the terms conform to the provisions of IC 22–3–2 through IC 22–3–6.

Amended by P.L.144–1986, SEC.42; P.L.28–1988, SEC.36.

22–3–4–4.5. Mediation of claim

Sec. 4.5. In addition to any other method available to the board to resolve a claim for compensation under IC 22–3–2 through IC 22–3–7, the board may, with the consent of all parties, mediate the claim using a mediator certified by the Indiana Continuing Legal Education Forum. The board may not order the mediation of a claim without the consent of all parties.

(b) The board shall establish by rule a schedule of fees and charges for a mediation conducted to resolve a claim for compensation under IC 22–3–2 through IC 22–3–7.

As added by P.L.168–2011, SEC.6.

22–3–4–5. Disputes; hearings

Sec. 5. If the employer and the injured employee or the injured employee's dependents disagree in regard to the compensation payable under IC 22–3–2 through IC 22–3–6 or, if they have reached such an agreement, which has been signed by them, filed with and approved by the worker's compensation board, and afterward disagree as to the continuance of payments under such agreement, or as to the period for which payments shall be made, or to the amount to be paid, because of a change in conditions since the making of such agreement, either party may then make an application to the board for the determination of the matters in dispute.

(b) Upon the filing of such application, the board shall set the date of hearing, which shall be as early as practicable, and shall notify the employee, employer, and attorneys of record in the manner prescribed by the board of the time and place of all hearings and requests for continuances. The hearing of all claims for compensation, on account of injuries occurring within the state, shall be held in the county in which the injury occurred, in any adjoining county, except when the parties consent to a hearing elsewhere. Claims assigned to an individual board member that are considered to be of an emergency nature by that board member, may be heard in any county within the board member's jurisdiction.

(c) All disputes arising under IC 22–3–2 through IC 22–3–6, if not settled by the agreement of the parties interested therein, with the approval of the board, shall be determined by the board.

Amended by P.L.144–1986, SEC.43; P.L.28–1988, SEC.37; P.L.95–1988, SEC.9; P.L.170–1991, SEC.10.

22–3–4–6. Disputes; summary proceedings

Sec. 6. The board by any or all of its members shall hear the parties at issue, their representatives and witnesses, and shall determine the dispute in a summary manner. The award shall be filed with the record of proceedings, and a copy thereof shall immediately be sent to each of the employee, employer, and attorney of record in the dispute.
Amended by P.L.95–1988, SEC.10.

22–3–4–7. Disputes; administrative review

Sec. 7. If an application for review is made to the board within thirty (30) days from the date of the award made by less than all the members, the full board, if the first hearing was not held before the full board, shall review the evidence, or, if deemed advisable, hear the parties at issue, their representatives, and witnesses as soon as practicable and shall make an award and file the same with the finding of the facts on which it is based and send a copy thereof to each of the parties in dispute, in like manner as specified in section 6 of this chapter.
Amended by P.L.144–1986, SEC.44; P.L.258–1997(ss), SEC.9.

22–3–4–8. Disputes; awards; appeals

Sec. 8. An award of the board by less than all of the members as provided in section 6 of this chapter, if not reviewed as provided in section 7 of this chapter, shall be final and conclusive.

(b) An award by the full board shall be conclusive and binding as to all questions of the fact, but either party to the dispute may, within thirty (30) days from the date of such award, appeal to the court of appeals for errors of law under the same terms and conditions as govern appeals in ordinary civil actions.

(c) The board of its own motion may certify questions of law to said court of appeals for its decision and determination.

(d) An assignment of errors that the award of the full board is contrary to law shall be sufficient to present both the sufficiency of the facts found to sustain the award and the sufficiency of the evidence to sustain the finding of facts.

(e) All such appeals and certified questions of law shall be submitted upon the date filed in the court of appeals, shall be advanced upon the docket of said court, and shall be determined at the earliest practicable date, without any extensions of time for filing briefs.

(f) An award of the full board affirmed on appeal, by the employer, shall be increased thereby five percent (5%), and by order of the court may be increased ten percent (10%).
Amended by P.L.144–1986, SEC.45.

22–3–4–9. Contracts; private agreements; appeals

Sec. 9. Upon order of the worker's compensation board made after five (5) days notice is given to the opposite party, any party in interest may file in the circuit or superior court of the county in which the injury occurred a certified copy of the memorandum of agreement approved by the board, or of an order or decision of the board, or of an award of the full board unappealed from, or of an award of the full board affirmed upon an appeal, whereupon said court shall render judgment in accordance therewith and notify the parties. Such judgment shall have the same effect and all proceedings in relation thereto shall thereafter be the same as though said judgment had been rendered in a suit duly heard and determined by said court.

(b) Any such judgment of said circuit or superior court unappealed from or affirmed on appeal or modified in obedience to the mandate of the court of appeals shall be modified to conform to any decision of the worker's compensation board ending, diminishing, or increasing any weekly payment under the provisions of IC 22–3–3–27 upon the presentation to it of a certified copy of such decision.

Amended by P.L.144–1986, SEC.46; P.L.28–1988, SEC.38.

22–3–4–10. Actions and proceedings; costs

Sec. 10. In all proceedings before the worker's compensation board or in a court under IC 22–3–2 through IC 22–3–6, the costs shall be awarded and taxed as provided by law in ordinary civil actions in the circuit court.

Amended by P.L.144–1986, SEC.47; P.L.28–1988, SEC.39.

22–3–4–11. Medical examination; physician or surgeon

Sec. 11. The board or any member thereof may, upon the application of either party or upon its own motion, appoint a disinterested and duly qualified physician or surgeon to make any necessary medical examination of the employee and to testify in respect thereto. Said physician or surgeon shall be allowed traveling expenses and a reasonable fee to be fixed by the board.

The fees and expenses of such physician or surgeon shall be paid by the state only on special order of the board or a member thereof.

22–3–4–12. Rates and charges; attorney's fees; payment

Sec. 12. Except as provided in section 12.1 of this chapter, the fees of attorneys and physicians and charges of nurses and hospitals for services under IC 22–3–2 through IC 22–3–6 shall be subject to the approval of the worker's compensation board.

When any claimant for compensation is represented by an attorney in the prosecution of his claim, the worker's compensation board shall fix and state in the award, if compensation be awarded, the amount of the claimant's attorney's fees. The fee so fixed shall be binding upon both the claimant and his attorney, and the employer shall pay to the attorney out of the award the fee so fixed, and the receipt of the attorney therefor shall fully acquit the employer for an equal portion of the award; provided, that whenever the worker's compensation board shall determine upon hearing of a claim that the employer has acted in bad faith in adjusting and settling said award, or whenever the worker's compensation board shall determine upon hearing of a claim that the employer has not pursued the settlement of said claim with diligence, then the board shall, if compensation be awarded, fix the amount of the claimant's attorney's fees and such attorney fees shall be paid to the attorney and shall not be charged against the award to the claimant.

Amended by P.L.144–1986, SEC.48; P.L.258–1997(ss), SEC.10; P.L.1–2006, SEC.338, eff. Mar. 24, 2006.

22–3–4–12.1. Bad faith in adjusting or settling claim for compensation; awards; attorney fees

Sec. 12.1.   The worker's compensation board, upon hearing a claim for benefits, has the exclusive jurisdiction to determine whether the employer, the employer's worker's compensation administrator, or the worker's compensation insurance carrier has acted with a lack of diligence, in bad faith, or has committed an independent tort in adjusting or settling the claim for compensation.

(b) If lack of diligence, bad faith, or an independent tort is proven under subsection (a), the award to the claimant shall be at least five hundred dollars ($500), but not more than twenty thousand dollars ($20,000), depending upon the degree of culpability and the actual damages sustained.

(c) An award under this section shall be paid by the employer, worker's compensation administrator, or worker's compensation insurance carrier responsible to the claimant for the lack of diligence, bad faith, or independent tort.

(d) The worker's compensation board shall fix in addition to any award under this section the amount of attorney's fees payable with respect to an award made under this section. The attorney's fees may not exceed thirty-three and one-third percent (33 1/3%) of the amount of the award.

(e) If the worker's compensation board makes an award under this section, it shall reduce the award to writing and forward a copy to the department of insurance for review under IC 27–4–1–4.5.

(f) An award or awards to a claimant pursuant to subsection (b) shall not total more than twenty thousand dollars ($20,000) during the life of the claim for benefits arising from an accidental injury.

As added by P.L.258–1997(ss), SEC.11.   Amended by P.L.31–2000, SEC.5.

22–3–4–13. Reports of injuries and deaths; violations of article

Sec. 13. Every employer shall keep a record of all injuries, fatal or otherwise, received by or claimed to have been received by the employer's employees in the course of their employment and shall provide a copy of the record to the board upon request.

Within seven (7) days after the first day of a disability that arises from a workplace injury and the employer's knowledge of the disability, as provided in IC 22–3–3–1, and that causes an employee's death or absence from work for more than one (1) day, a report thereof shall be made in writing and mailed to the employer's insurance carrier or, if the employer is self insured, delivered to the worker's compensation board in the manner provided in subsections (b) and (c). The insurance carrier shall deliver the report to the worker's compensation board in the manner provided in subsections (b) and (c) not later than seven (7) days after receipt of the report or fourteen (14) days after the employer's knowledge of the injury, whichever is later. An employer or insurance carrier that fails to comply with this subsection is subject to a civil penalty under section 15 of this chapter.

(b) All insurance carriers, companies who carry risk without insurance, and third party administrators reporting accident information to the board in compliance with subsection (a) shall report the information using electronic data interchange standards prescribed by the board.

(c) The report shall contain the name, nature, and location of the business of the employer, the name, age, sex, wages, occupation of the injured employee, the date and hour of the accident causing the alleged injury, the nature and cause of the injury, and such other information as may be required by the board.

(d) A person who violates any provision of this article, except IC 22–3–5–1, IC 22–3–7–34(b), or IC 22–3–7–34(c), commits a Class C misdemeanor. A person who violates IC 22–3–5–1, IC 22–3–7–34(b), or IC 22–3–7–34(c) commits a Class A misdemeanor. The worker's compensation board in the name of the state may seek relief from any court of competent jurisdiction to enjoin any violation of this article.

(e) The venue of all actions under this section lies in the county in which the employee was injured. The prosecuting attorney of the county shall prosecute all such violations upon written request of the worker's compensation board. Such violations shall be prosecuted in the name of the state.

(f) In an action before the board against an employer who at the time of the injury to or occupational disease of an employee had failed to comply with IC 22–3–5–1, IC 22–3–7–34(b), or IC 22–3–7–34(c), the board may award to the employee or the dependents of a deceased employee:

(1) compensation not to exceed double the compensation provided by this article;

(2) medical expenses; and

(3) reasonable attorney fees in addition to the compensation and medical expenses.

(g) In an action under subsection (d), the court may:

(1) require the employer to obtain coverage and furnish proof of insurance as required by IC 22–3–5–1 and IC 22–3–7–34(b) or IC 22–3–7–34(c) every six (6) months for a period not to exceed three (3) years;

(2) require satisfactory proof of the employer's financial ability to pay any compensation or medical expenses in the amount and manner, and when due, as provided for in IC 22–3, for all injuries which occurred during any period of noncompliance; and

(3) require the employer to deposit with the worker's compensation board an acceptable security, indemnity, or bond to secure the payment of such compensation and medical expense liabilities.

(h) The penalty provision of subsection (d) shall apply only to the employer and shall not apply for a failure to exact a certificate of insurance under IC 22–3–2–14 or IC 22–3–7–34(i) or IC 22–3–7–34(j).

(i) In an action under subsection (d), if a compensable worker's compensation or occupational disease claim has been filed and the employer fails or refuses to pay benefits when due, a court may order the employer to temporarily cease doing business in Indiana until the employer:

(1) furnishes proof of insurance as required by IC 22–3–5–1 and IC 22–3–7–34(b) or IC 22–3–7–34(c); and

(2) provides any other assurances required by the board to establish that the employer has the ability to meet all worker's compensation liabilities incurred during the employer's period of noncompliance.

(j) An appeal of the court's decision under subsection (i) to enjoin the employer from doing business in Indiana automatically stays the court's order.

Amended by Acts 1978, P.L.2, SEC.2210; Acts 1982, P.L.135, SEC.1; P.L.145–1986, SEC.1; P.L.28–1988, SEC.40; P.L.170–1991, SEC.11; P.L.75–1993, SEC.3; P.L.1–1994, SEC.108; P.L.235–1999, SEC.4; P.L.1–2007, SEC.159, eff. Mar. 30, 2007; P.L.1–2010, SEC.85, eff. March 12, 2010; P.L.168–2011, SEC.7.

22–3–4–14. Awards; termination; reports

Sec. 14. Every employer paying compensation directly without insurance and every insurance carrier paying compensation in behalf of an employer shall, within ten (10) days from the termination of the compensation period fixed in any award against him or its insured, for an injury or death, either by the approval of an agreement or upon hearing, and within ten (10) days from the full redemption of any such award by the cash payment thereof in a lump sum as provided in IC 22–3–2 through IC 22–3–6, make such report or reports as the worker's compensation board may require.

Amended by P.L.144–1986, SEC.49; P.L.28–1988, SEC.41.

22–3–4–15. Civil penalties

Sec. 15. In addition to any other remedy available to the board under this article or at law, the board may, after notice and a hearing, assess a civil penalty under this section for any of the following:

(1) Failure to post a notice required by IC 22–3–2–22.

(2) Failure to comply with IC 22–3–3–7 or IC 22–3–7–16.

(3) Failure to file an injury record with the board as required by section 13 of this chapter or to file a report of a disablement by occupational disease as required by IC 22–3–7–37.

(b) For the first violation of an offense listed in subsection (a), the board may assess a civil penalty not to exceed fifty dollars ($50).

(c) For the second unrelated violation of the same offense listed in subsection (a), the board may assess a civil penalty not to exceed one hundred fifty dollars ($150).

(d) For the third or subsequent unrelated violation of the same offense listed in subsection (a), the board may assess a civil penalty not to exceed three hundred dollars ($300).

(e) Civil penalties collected under this section shall be deposited in the worker's compensation supplemental administrative fund established by IC 22–3–5–6.

As added by P.L.168–2011, SEC.8.

Chapter 5. Worker's Compensation: Insurance Requirements

22–3–5–1. Requirements; self-insurance; security; fees

Sec. 1. Every employer under IC 22–3–2 through IC 22–3–6, except those exempted by IC 22–3–2–5, shall:

(1) insure and keep insured the employer's liability under IC 22–3–2 through IC 22–3–6 in some corporation, association, or organization authorized to transact the business of worker's compensation insurance in this state; or

(2) furnish to the worker's compensation board satisfactory proof of the employer's financial ability to pay direct the compensation in the amount and manner and when due as provided in IC 22–3–2 through IC 22–3–6.

(b) Under subsection (a)(2) the board may require the deposit of an acceptable security, indemnity, or bond to secure the payment of compensation liabilities as they are incurred. The board shall charge the following:

(1) An initial application fee of five hundred dollars ($500) to be paid along with the proof of financial ability required under this section.

(2) A renewal fee of two hundred fifty dollars ($250) if the employer holds a certificate of self insurance.

(3) A late filing fee of two hundred fifty dollars ($250).

Amended by P.L.144–1986, SEC.50; P.L.28–1988, SEC.42; P.L.170–1991, SEC.12.

22-3-5-2. Termination of insurance; filing fees; evidence of compliance

Sec. 2. An employer required to carry insurance under IC 22-3-2-5 and section 1 of this chapter shall file with the worker's compensation board, in the form prescribed by the board, within ten (10) days after the termination of the employer's insurance by expiration or cancellation, evidence of the employer's compliance with section 1 of this chapter and other provisions relating to the insurance under IC 22-3-2 through IC 22-3-6 and shall pay a filing fee in the amount of:

(1) ten dollars ($10) before July 1, 1992;

(2) five dollars ($5) on and after July 1, 1992, and before July 1, 1995; and

(3) two dollars ($2), after July 1, 2013.

This filing fee shall be deposited in the worker's compensation supplemental administrative fund established by section 6 of this chapter and used to offset a part of the board's expenses related to the administration of health care provider reimbursement disputes. Proof of renewal of an existing insurance policy may be filed every three (3) years, but the filing fee for the policy shall be paid annually. An employer coming under the compensation provisions of IC 22-3-2 through IC 22-3-6 shall in a like manner file like evidence of compliance on the employer's part.

Amended by Acts 1978, P.L.2, SEC.2211; P.L.28-1988, SEC.43; P.L.170-1991, SEC.13; P.L.275-2013, SEC.8, eff. July 1, 2013.

22–3–5–2.5. Provision of proof of compliance by employer

Sec. 2.5. The worker's compensation board is entitled to request that an employer provide the board with current proof of compliance with section 2 of this chapter.

(b) If an employer fails or refuses to provide current proof of compliance by the tenth day after the employer receives the board's request under subsection (a), the board:

(1) shall send the employer a written notice that the employer is in violation of section 2 of this chapter; and

(2) may assess a civil penalty against the employer of fifty dollars ($50) per employee per day.

(c) An employer may challenge the board's assessment of a civil penalty under subsection (b)(2) by requesting a hearing in accordance with procedures established by the board.

(d) The board shall waive a civil penalty assessed under subsection (b)(2) if the employer provides the board current proof of compliance by the twentieth day after the date the employer receives the board's notice under subsection (b)(1).

(e) If an employer fails or refuses to:

(1) provide current proof of compliance by the twentieth day after the date the employer receives the board's notice under subsection (b)(1); or

(2) pay a civil penalty assessed under subsection (b)(2);

the board may, after notice to the employer and a hearing, order that the noncompliant employer's name be listed on the board's Internet web site.

(f) A noncompliant employer's name may be removed from the board's Internet web site only after the employer does the following:

(1) Provides current proof of compliance with section 2 of this chapter.

(2) Pays all civil penalties assessed under subsection (b)(2).

(g) The civil penalties provided for in this section are cumulative.

(h) Civil penalties collected under this section shall be deposited in the worker's compensation supplemental administrative fund established by section 6 of this chapter.
As added by P.L.168–2011, SEC.9.

22–3–5–3. Self-insurance; certificates; revocation

Sec. 3. Whenever an employer has complied with the provisions of section 1 of this chapter relating to self-insurance, the worker's compensation board shall issue to such employer a certificate which shall remain in force for a period fixed by the board, but the board may upon at least ten (10) days notice and a hearing to the employer revoke the certificate upon satisfactory evidence for such revocation having been presented. At any time after such revocation the board may grant a new certificate to the employer upon the employer's petition and satisfactory proof of financial ability.

(b) All such certificates issued by the industrial board before May 21, 1929, shall remain in force for the period for which they were issued unless revoked as in this section provided.
Amended by P.L.144–1986, SEC.51; P.L.28–1988, SEC.44.

22–3–5–4. Substitute system of insurance

Sec. 4. Subject to the approval of the worker's compensation board, any employer may enter into or continue any agree-

WORKER'S COMPENSATION LAW

ment with the employer's employees to provide a system of compensation, benefit, or insurance in lieu of the compensation and insurance provided by IC 22–3–2 through IC 22–3–6. No such substitute system shall be approved unless it confers benefits upon injured employees and their dependents at least equivalent to the benefits provided by IC 22–3–2 through IC 22–3–6, nor if it requires contributions from the employees unless it confers benefits in addition to those provided under IC 22–3–2 through IC 22–3–6 at least commensurate with such contributions.

(b) Such substitute system may be terminated by the worker's compensation board on reasonable notice and hearing to the interested parties if it appears that the same is not fairly administered, its operation discloses latent defects threatening its solvency, or if for any substantial reason it fails to accomplish the purpose of IC 22–3–2 through IC 22–3–6. In this case the board shall determine upon the proper distribution of all remaining assets, if any, subject to the right of any party in interest to take an appeal to the court of appeals.

Amended by P.L.144–1986, SEC.52; P.L.28–1988, SEC.45.

22–3–5–5. Policy provisions; failure to pay claims

Sec. 5.   No insurer shall enter into or issue any policy of insurance under IC 22–3–2 through IC 22–3–6 until its policy form shall have been submitted to and approved by the department of insurance.

(b) All policies of insurance companies and of reciprocal insurance associations insuring the payment of compensation under IC 22–3–2 through IC 22–3–6 are conclusively presumed to cover all the employees and the entire compensation liability of the insured. Any provision in any policy attempting to limit or modify the liability of the company or association issuing the same shall be wholly void.

(c) Every policy of any such company or association is deemed to include the following provisions and any change in the policy which may be required by any statute enacted after May 21, 1929, as fully as if they were written in the policy:

(1) Except as provided in section 5.5 of this chapter, the insurer hereby assumes in full all the obligations to pay physician's fees, nurse's charges, hospital services, hospital supplies, burial expenses, compensation, or death benefits imposed upon or accepted by the insured under the provisions of IC 22–3–2 through IC 22–3–6.

(2) This policy is made subject to IC 22–3–2 through IC 22–3–6 relative to the liability of the insured to pay physician's fees, nurse's charges, hospital services, hospital supplies, burial expenses, compensation, or death benefits to and for the employees, the acceptance of such liability by the

insured, the adjustment, trial, and adjudication of claims for such physician's fees, nurse's charges, hospital services, hospital supplies, burial expenses, compensation, or death benefits, and the liability of the insurer to pay the same are and shall be a part of this policy contract as fully and completely as if written in this policy.

(3) As between this insurer and the employee, notice to or knowledge of the occurrence of the injury on the part of the insured (the employer) shall be notice or knowledge thereof, on the part of the insurer. The jurisdiction of the insured (the employer) for the purpose of IC 22–3–2 through IC 22–3–6 shall be the jurisdiction of this insurer. This insurer shall in all things be bound by and shall be subject to the awards, judgments, and decrees rendered against the insured (the employer) under IC 22–3–2 through IC 22–3–6.

(4) This insurer will promptly pay to the person entitled to the same all benefits conferred by IC 22–3–2 through IC 22–3–6, including physician's fees, nurse's charges, hospital services, hospital supplies, burial expenses, and all installments of compensation or death benefits that may be awarded or agreed upon under IC 22–3–2 through IC 22–3–6. The obligation of this insurer shall not be affected by any default of the insured (the employer) after the injury or by any default in giving of any notice required by this policy, or otherwise. This policy is a direct promise by this insurer to the person entitled to physician's fees, nurse's charges, fees for hospital services, charges for hospital supplies, charges for burial compensation, or death benefits, and shall be enforceable in the name of the person.

(5) Any termination of this policy by cancellation shall not be effective as to employees of the insured covered hereby unless at least ten (10) days prior to the taking effect of such cancellation, a written notice giving the date upon which such termination is to become effective has been received by the worker's compensation board of Indiana at its office in Indianapolis, Indiana.

(6) This policy shall automatically expire one (1) year from the effective date of the policy unless:

(A) the policy covers a period of three (3) years, in which event, it shall automatically expire three (3) years from the effective date of the policy; or

(B) the policy is issued as a continuous policy, in which event it shall not expire until terminated by the insured or the insurer in accord with applicable state law and applicable policy provisions; or

(D) the policy covers a period permitted in bureau rules under IC 27-7-2-20.

The termination of a policy, as provided in this subdivision, shall be effective as to the employees of the insured covered by the policy.

(d) All claims for compensation, nurse's charges, hospital services, hospital supplies, physician's fees, or burial expenses may be made directly against either the employer or the insurer or both, and the award of the worker's compensation board may be made against either the employer or the insurer or both. If any insurer shall fail or refuse to pay final award or judgment (except during the pendency of an appeal) rendered against it, or its insured, or, if it shall fail or refuse to comply with any provision of IC 22–3–2 through IC 22–3–6, the board shall not accept any further proofs of insurance from it until it shall have paid the award or judgment or complied with the violated provision of IC 22–3–2 through IC 22–3–6.

Amended by P.L.144-1986, SEC.53; P.L.28-1988, SEC.46; P.L.3-1989, SEC.133; P.L.249-1989, SEC.18; P.L.170-1991, SEC.14; P.L.1-1994, SEC.109; P.L.116-1994, SEC.2; P.L.2-1995, SEC.83; P.L.217-1995, SEC.1; P.L.275-2013, SEC.9, eff. July 1, 2013.

22–3–5–5.5. Deductibles and co-insurance

Sec. 5.5.   Each insurer entering into or issuing an insurance policy under IC 22–3–2 through IC 22–3–7 may, as a part of the policy or as an optional endorsement to the policy, offer deductibles or co-insurance, or both, that are optional to the insured for benefits under IC 22–3–2 through IC 22–3–7.   Each insurer may do the following:

(1) Offer deductibles in multiples of five hundred dollars ($500), up to a maximum of five thousand dollars ($5,000) per compensable claim.

(2) Offer co-insurance for each compensable claim.   The following apply to co-insurance provided under this subdivision:

(A) The co-insurance must require the insurer to pay eighty percent (80%) and the insured to pay twenty percent (20%) of the amount of benefits due to an employee for an injury compensable under IC 22–3–2 through IC 22–3–7.

(B) An insured employer may not be required to pay more than four thousand two hundred dollars ($4,200) in co-insurance under this subdivision for each compensable claim.

(b) An insurer shall fully disclose in writing to prospective policyholders the deductibles and co-insurance offered under subsection (a).   An insured employer who chooses a deductible under subsection (a):

(1) may choose only one (1) deductible amount; and

(2) is liable for the amount of the deductible for benefits

paid for each compensable claim of an employee under IC 22–3–2 through IC 22–3–7.

(c) An insurer shall do the following:

(1) Where a policy provides for a deductible, the insurer shall:

(A) pay all or a part of the deductible amount, whichever is applicable to a compensable claim, to the person or medical service provider entitled to the benefits under IC 22–3–2 through IC 22–3–7; and

(B) seek reimbursement from the employer from the applicable deductible.

(2) Where a policy provides a deductible or co-insurance, the insurance company shall pay the full cost of the claim. The insurance company shall seek reimbursement from the insured employer for its portion of the liability following closing of the claim or when twenty percent (20%) of the benefits paid exceed four thousand two hundred dollars ($4,200).

(d) The payment or nonpayment of a deductible or co-insurance amount by an insured employer to the insurer shall be treated under the policy insuring the liability for worker's compensation in the same manner as payment or nonpayment of premiums is treated.

(e) The premium reduction for deductibles or for co-insurance shall be determined before the application of any experience modifications, premium surcharges, or premium discounts. The applicable premium reduction percentage is the percentage corresponding to the appropriate deductible or co-insurance amount. The premium reduction is obtained by the application of the appropriate reduction percentage, shown under miscellaneous values in the rate pages, to the premium determined before application of any experience or schedule modification, premium discounts, or any retrospective rating plan.

(f) This section does not apply to the following:

(1) An employer that is authorized to self-insure against liability for claims under IC 22–3–2 through IC 22–3–6.

(2) Group self-insurance funds for claims under IC 22–3–2 through IC 22–3–6.

(g) A deductible or co-insurance provided under this section applies against the total of all benefits paid for a compensable claim, including benefits paid under the following:

(1) IC 22–3–3–4.

(2) IC 22–3–3–8 through IC 22–3–3–10.

(3) IC 22–3–3–17.

(4) IC 22–3–3–22.

(h) An employer may not use the employer's election of a deductible or co-insurance under this section or the payment of a deductible or co-insurance under this section in negotiating with the employer's employees on any terms of employment.

An employee of an employer that knowingly violates this subsection may file a complaint with the department of labor.

The department of labor may impose a civil penalty of not more than one thousand dollars ($1,000) against an employer that knowingly violates this subsection.

(i) This subsection applies to an employee of an employer that has paid a deductible or co-insurance under this section and to the employee's dependents. If an employee or a dependent recovers damages against a third party under IC 22–3–2–13, the insurer shall provide reimbursement to the insured equal to a pro-rata share of the net recovery by the insurer.

As added by P.L.170-1991, SEC.15. Amended by P.L.275-2013, SEC.10, eff. July 1, 2013.

22-3-5-6. Supplemental administrative fund

Sec. 6. The worker's compensation supplemental administrative fund is established for the purpose of carrying out the administrative purposes and functions of the worker's compensation board.

(b) The fund consists of:

(1) fees collected from employers under sections 1 through 2 of this chapter;

(2) fees collected under IC 22–3–2–14.5, IC 22–3–3–5(d), IC 22–3–7–17(g), and IC 22–3–7–34.5; and

(3) civil penalties assessed under IC 22–3–4–15, section 2.5 of this chapter, and IC 22–3–7–34.3.

(c) The fund shall be administered by the worker's compensation board. Money in the fund is annually appropriated to the worker's compensation board and shall be used for all expenses incurred by the worker's compensation board.

(d) The money in the fund is not to be used to replace funds otherwise appropriated to the board. Money in the fund at the end of the state fiscal year does not revert to the state general fund.

As added by P.L.170–1991, SEC.16. Amended by P.L.75–1993, SEC.4; P.L.202–2001, SEC.6; P.L.168–2011, SEC.10.

Chapter 6. Worker's Compensation: Miscellaneous Provisions

22-3-6-1. Definitions

Sec. 1. In IC 22-3-2 through IC 22-3-6, unless the context otherwise requires:

(a) "Employer" includes the state and any political subdivision, any municipal corporation within the state, any individual or the legal representative of a deceased individual, firm, association, limited liability company, or corporation or the receiver or trustee of the same, using the services of another for pay. A parent corporation and its subsidiaries shall each be considered joint employers of the corporation's, the parent's, or the subsidiaries' employees for purposes of IC 22-3-2-6 and IC 22-3-3-31. Both a lessor and a lessee of employees shall each be considered joint employers of the employees provided by the lessor to the lessee for purposes of IC 22-3-2-6 and IC 22-3-3-31. If the employer is insured, the term includes the employer's insurer so far as applicable. However, the inclusion of an employer's insurer within this definition does not allow an employer's insurer to avoid payment for services rendered to an employee with the approval of the employer. The term also includes an employer that provides on-the-job training under the federal School to Work Opportunities Act (20 U.S.C. 6101 et seq.) to the extent set forth in IC 22-3-2-2.5. The term does not include a nonprofit corporation that is recognized as tax exempt under Section 501(c)(3) of the Internal Revenue Code (as defined in IC 6-3-1-11(a)) to the extent the corporation enters into an independent contractor agreement with a person for the performance of youth coaching services on a part-time basis.

(b) "Employee" means every person, including a minor, in the service of another, under any contract of hire or apprenticeship, written or implied, except one whose employment is both casual and not in the usual course of the trade, business, occupation, or profession of the employer.

(1) An executive officer elected or appointed and empowered in accordance with the charter and bylaws of a corporation, other than a municipal corporation or governmental subdivision or a charitable, religious, educational, or other nonprofit corporation, is an employee of the corporation under IC 22-3-2 through IC 22-3-6. An officer of a corporation who is an employee of the corporation under IC 22-3-2 through IC 22-3-6 may elect not to be an employee of the corporation under IC 22-3-2 through IC 22-3-6. An officer of a corporation who is also an owner of any interest in the corporation may elect not to be an employee of the corporation under IC 22-3-2 through IC 22-3-6. If an officer makes this election, the officer must serve written notice of the election on the corporation's insurance carrier and the board. An officer of a corporation may not be considered to be excluded as an employee under IC 22-3-2 through IC 22-3-6 until the notice is received by the insurance carrier and the board.

(2) An executive officer of a municipal corporation or other governmental subdivision or of a charitable, religious, educational, or other nonprofit corporation may, notwithstanding any other provision of IC 22-3-2 through IC 22-3-6, be brought within the coverage of its insurance contract by the corporation by specifically including the executive officer in the contract of insurance. The election to bring the executive officer within the coverage shall continue for the period the contract of insurance is in effect, and during this period, the executive officers thus brought within the coverage of the insurance contract are employees of the corporation under IC 22-3-2 through IC 22-3-6.

(3) Any reference to an employee who has been injured, when the employee is dead, also includes the employee's legal representatives, dependents, and other persons to whom compensation may be payable.

(4) An owner of a sole proprietorship may elect to include the owner as an employee under IC 22-3-2 through IC 22-3-6 if the owner is actually engaged in the proprietorship business. If the owner makes this election, the owner must serve upon the owner's insurance carrier and upon the board written notice of the election. No owner of a sole proprietorship may be considered an employee under IC 22-3-2 through IC 22-3-6 until the notice has been received. If the owner of a sole proprietorship:

(A) is an independent contractor in the construction trades and does not make the election provided under this subdivision, the owner must obtain a certificate of exemption under IC 22-3-2-14.5; or

(B) is an independent contractor and does not make the election provided under this subdivision, the owner may obtain a certificate of exemption under IC 22-3-2-14.5.

(5) A partner in a partnership may elect to include the partner as an employee under IC 22-3-2 through IC 22-3-6 if the partner is actually engaged in the partnership business. If a partner makes this election, the partner must serve upon the partner's insurance carrier and upon the board written notice of the election. No partner may be considered an employee under IC 22-3-2 through IC 22-3-6 until the notice has been received. If a partner in a partnership:

(A) is an independent contractor in the construction trades and does not make the election provided under this subdivision, the partner must obtain a certificate of exemption under IC 22-3-2-14.5; or

(B) is an independent contractor and does not make the election provided under this subdivision, the partner may obtain a certificate of exemption under IC 22-3-2-14.5.

(6) Real estate professionals are not employees under IC 22-3-2 through IC 22-3-6 if:

(A) they are licensed real estate agents;

(B) substantially all their remuneration is directly related to sales volume and not the number of hours worked; and

(C) they have written agreements with real estate brokers stating that they are not to be treated as employees for tax purposes.

(7) A person is an independent contractor and not an employee under IC 22-3-2 through IC 22-3-6 if the person is an independent contractor under the guidelines of the United States Internal Revenue Service.

(8) An owner-operator that provides a motor vehicle and the services of a driver under a written contract that is subject to IC 8-2.1-24-23, 45 IAC 16-1-13, or 49 CFR 376 to a motor carrier is not an employee of the motor carrier for purposes of IC 22-3-2 through IC 22-3-6. The owner-operator may elect to be covered and have the owner-operator's drivers covered under a worker's compensation insurance policy or authorized self-insurance that insures the motor carrier if the owner-operator pays the premiums as requested by the motor carrier. An election by an owner-operator under this subdivision does not terminate the independent contractor status of the owner-operator for any purpose other than the purpose of this subdivision.

(9) A member or manager in a limited liability company may elect to include the member or manager as an employee under IC 22-3-2 through IC 22-3-6 if the member or manager is actually engaged in the limited liability company business. If a member or manager makes this election, the member or manager must serve upon the member's or manager's insurance carrier and upon the board written notice of the election. A member or manager may not be considered an employee under IC 22-3-2 through IC 22-3-6 until the notice has been received.

(10) An unpaid participant under the federal School to Work Opportunities Act (20 U.S.C. 6101 et seq.) is an employee to the extent set forth in IC 22-3-2-2.5.

(11) A person who enters into an independent contractor agreement with a nonprofit corporation that is recog-

nized as tax exempt under Section 501(c)(3) of the Internal Revenue Code (as defined in IC 6-3-1-11(a)) to perform youth coaching services on a part-time basis is not an employee for purposes of IC 22-3-2 through IC 22-3-6.

(12) An individual who is not an employee of the state or a political subdivision is considered to be a temporary employee of the state for purposes of IC 22-3-2 through IC 22-3-6 while serving as a member of a mobile support unit on duty for training, an exercise, or a response, as set forth in IC 10-14-3-19(c)(2)(B).

(c) "Minor" means an individual who has not reached seventeen (17) years of age.

(1) Unless otherwise provided in this subsection, a minor employee shall be considered as being of full age for all purposes of IC 22-3-2 through IC 22-3-6.

(2) If the employee is a minor who, at the time of the accident, is employed, required, suffered, or permitted to work in violation of IC 20-33-3-35, the amount of compensation and death benefits, as provided in IC 22-3-2 through IC 22-3-6, shall be double the amount which would otherwise be recoverable. The insurance carrier shall be liable on its policy for one-half ($1/2$) of the compensation or benefits that may be payable on account of the injury or death of the minor, and the employer shall be liable for the other one-half ($1/2$) of the compensation or benefits. If the employee is a minor who is not less than sixteen (16) years of age and who has not reached seventeen (17) years of age and who at the time of the accident is employed, suffered, or permitted to work at any occupation which is not prohibited by law, this subdivision does not apply.

(3) A minor employee who, at the time of the accident, is a student performing services for an employer as part of an approved program under IC 20-37-2-7 shall be considered a full-time employee for the purpose of computing compensation for permanent impairment under IC 22-3-3-10. The average weekly wages for such a student shall be calculated as provided in subsection (d)(4).

(4) The rights and remedies granted in this subsection to a minor under IC 22-3-2 through IC 22-3-6 on account of personal injury or death by accident shall exclude all rights and remedies of the minor, the minor's parents, or the minor's personal representatives, dependents, or next of kin at common law, statutory or otherwise, on account of the injury or death. This subsection does not apply to minors who have reached seventeen (17) years of age.

(d) "Average weekly wages" means the earnings of the

injured employee in the employment in which the employee was working at the time of the injury during the period of fifty-two (52) weeks immediately preceding the date of injury, divided by fifty-two (52), except as follows:

(1) If the injured employee lost seven (7) or more calendar days during this period, although not in the same week, then the earnings for the remainder of the fifty-two (52) weeks shall be divided by the number of weeks and parts thereof remaining after the time lost has been deducted.

(2) Where the employment prior to the injury extended over a period of less than fifty-two (52) weeks, the method of dividing the earnings during that period by the number of weeks and parts thereof during which the employee earned wages shall be followed, if results just and fair to both parties will be obtained. Where by reason of the shortness of the time during which the employee has been in the employment of the employee's employer or of the casual nature or terms of the employment it is impracticable to compute the average weekly wages, as defined in this subsection, regard shall be had to the average weekly amount which during the fifty-two (52) weeks previous to the injury was being earned by a person in the same grade employed at the same work by the same employer or, if there is no person so employed, by a person in the same grade employed in the same class of employment in the same district.

(3) Wherever allowances of any character made to an employee in lieu of wages are a specified part of the wage contract, they shall be deemed a part of the employee's earnings.

(4) In computing the average weekly wages to be used in calculating an award for permanent impairment under IC 22-3-3-10 for a student employee in an approved training program under IC 20-37-2-7, the following formula shall be used. Calculate the product of:

(A) the student employee's hourly wage rate; multiplied by

(B) forty (40) hours.

The result obtained is the amount of the average weekly wages for the student employee.

(e) "Injury" and "personal injury" mean only injury by accident arising out of and in the course of the employment and do not include a disease in any form except as it results from the injury.

(f) "Billing review service" refers to a person or an entity that reviews a medical service provider's bills or statements for the purpose of determining pecuniary liability. The term includes an employer's worker's compensation insurance carrier if the insurance carrier performs such a review.

(g) "Billing review standard" means the data used by a billing review service to determine pecuniary liability.

(h) "Community" means a geographic service area based on ZIP code districts defined by the United States Postal Service according to the following groupings:

(1) The geographic service area served by ZIP codes with the first three (3) digits 463 and 464.

(2) The geographic service area served by ZIP codes with the first three (3) digits 465 and 466.

(3) The geographic service area served by ZIP codes with the first three (3) digits 467 and 468.

(4) The geographic service area served by ZIP codes with the first three (3) digits 469 and 479.

(5) The geographic service area served by ZIP codes with the first three (3) digits 460, 461 (except 46107), and 473.

(6) The geographic service area served by the 46107 ZIP code and ZIP codes with the first three (3) digits 462.

(7) The geographic service area served by ZIP codes with the first three (3) digits 470, 471, 472, 474, and 478.

(8) The geographic service area served by ZIP codes with the first three (3) digits 475, 476, and 477.

(i) "Medical service provider" refers to a person or an entity that provides services or products to an employee under IC 22-3-2 through IC 22-3-6. Except as otherwise provided in IC 22-3-2 through IC 22-3-6, the term includes a medical service facility.

(j) "Medical service facility" means any of the following that provides a service or product under IC 22-3-2 through IC 22-3-6 and uses the CMS 1450 (UB-04) form for Medicare reimbursement:

(1) A hospital (as defined in IC 16-18-2-179).

(2) A hospital based health facility (as defined in IC 16-18-2-180).

(3) A medical center (as defined in IC 16-18-2-223.4).

The term does not include a professional corporation (as defined in IC 23-1.5-1-10) comprised of health care professionals (as defined in IC 23-1.5-1-8) formed to render professional services as set forth in IC 23-1.5-2-3(a)(4) or a health care professional (as defined in IC 23-1.5-1-8) who bills for a service or product provided under IC 22-3-2 through IC 22-3-6 as an individual or a member of a group practice or another medical service provider that uses the CMS 1500 form for Medicare reimbursement.

(k) "Pecuniary liability" means the responsibility of an employer or the employer's insurance carrier for the payment of the charges for each specific service or product for human medical treatment provided under IC 22-3-2 through IC 22-3-6, as follows:

(1) This subdivision applies before July 1, 2014, to all medical service providers, and after June 30, 2014, to a medical service provider that is not a medical service facility. Payment of the charges in a defined community, equal to or less than the charges made by medical service providers at the eightieth percentile in the same community for like services or products.

(2) Payment of the charges in a reasonable amount, which is established by payment of one (1) of the following:

(A) The amount negotiated at any time between the medical service facility and any of the following, if an amount has been negotiated:

(i) The employer.

(ii) The employer's insurance carrier.

(iii) A billing review service on behalf of a person described in item (i) or (ii).

(iv) A direct provider network that has contracted with a person described in item (i) or (ii).

(B) Two hundred percent (200%) of the amount that would be paid to the medical service facility on the same date for the same service or product under the medical service facility's Medicare reimbursement rate, if an amount has not been negotiated as described in clause (A).

(l) "Service or product" or "services and products" refers to medical, hospital, surgical, or nursing service, treatment, and supplies provided under IC 22-3-2 through IC 22-3-6.

Amended by Acts 1979, P.L.228, SEC.1; Acts 1981, P.L.199, SEC.2; P.L.37-1985, SEC.31; P.L.28-1988, SEC.47; P.L.95-1988, SEC.11; P.L.106-1992, SEC.11; P.L.8-1993, SEC.282; P.L.75-1993, SEC.5; P.L.1-1994, SEC.110; P.L.110-1995, SEC.33; P.L.216-1995, SEC.4; P.L.2-1996, SEC.265; P.L.258-1997(ss), SEC.12; P.L.235-1999, SEC.5; P.L.31-2000, SEC.6; P.L.202-2001, SEC.7; P.L.1-2005, SEC.182; P.L.201-2005, SEC.5; P.L.1-2006, SEC.339, eff. Mar. 24, 2006; P.L.180-2009, SEC.1, eff. May 13, 2009; P.L.168-2011, SEC.11; P.L.71-2013, SEC.10, eff. July 1, 2013; P.L.275-2013, SEC.11, eff. July 1, 2013; P.L.99-2014, SEC.3, eff. July 1, 2014; P.L.225-2015, SEC.1, eff. July 1, 2015.

22–3–6–2. Mutual insurance associations and reciprocal or interinsurance exchanges

Sec. 2.   For the purpose of complying with IC 22–3–5–1, groups of employers are hereby authorized to form mutual insurance associations or reciprocal or interinsurance exchanges subject to such reasonable conditions and restrictions as may be fixed by the department of insurance.

(b) Membership in such mutual insurance associations or reciprocal or interinsurance exchanges so approved, together with evidence of the payment of premiums due, shall be evidence of compliance with IC 22–3–5–1.

(c) Subsection (a) does not apply to mutual insurance associations and reciprocal or interinsurance exchanges formed and operating on or before January 1, 1991, which shall continue to operate subject to the provisions of IC 22–3–2 through IC 22–3–6 and to such reasonable conditions and restrictions as may be fixed by the worker's compensation board.

Amended by P.L.144–1986, SEC.54; P.L.28–1988, SEC.48; P.L.170–1991, SEC.17.

22–3–6–3.   Compliance with former law

Sec. 3. Every employer who has complied with the requirements of the provisions of Acts 1915, c.106, or the industrial board or worker's compensation board under that act, which compliance is effective as of May 21, 1929, shall to the same extent be deemed to have complied with the requirements of IC 22–3–2 through IC 22–3–6.

Amended by P.L.144–1986, SEC.55; P.L.1–2006, SEC.340, eff. Mar. 24, 2006.

Chapter 7. Worker's Occupational Diseases Compensation

22–3–7–2.   Acceptance of provisions; certain youth coaches; police and firefighters; coverage

Sec. 2. Every employer and every employee, except as stated in this chapter, shall comply with this chapter, requiring the employer and employee to pay and accept compensation for disablement or death by occupational disease arising out of and in the course of the employment, and shall be bound thereby.

The burden of proof is on the employee. The proof by the employee of an element of a claim does not create a presumption in favor of the employee with regard to another element of the claim.

(b) This chapter does not apply to the following:

(1) A person who enters into an independent contractor agreement with a nonprofit corporation that is recognized as tax exempt under Section 501(c)(3) of the Internal Revenue

Code[6] (as defined in IC 6–3–1–11(a)) to perform youth coaching services on a part-time basis.

(2) A nonprofit corporation that is recognized as tax exempt under Section 501(c)(3) of the Internal Revenue Code (as defined in IC 6–3–1–11(a)) to the extent the corporation enters into an independent contractor agreement with a person for the performance of youth coaching services on a part-time basis.

(c) This chapter does not apply to employees of municipal corporations in Indiana who are members of:

(1) the fire department or police department of any such municipality; and

(2) a firefighters' pension fund or a police officers' pension fund.

However, if the common council elects to purchase and procure worker's occupational disease insurance to insure said employees with respect to medical benefits under this chapter, the medical provisions apply to members of the fire department or police department of any such municipal corporation who are also members of a firefighters' pension fund or a police officers' pension fund.

(d) When any municipal corporation purchases or procures worker's occupational disease insurance covering members of the fire department or police department who are also members of a firefighters' pension fund or a police officers' pension fund and pays the premium or premiums for the insurance, the payment of the premiums is a legal and allowable expenditure of funds of any municipal corporation.

(e) Except as provided in subsection (f), where the common council has procured worker's occupational disease insurance as provided under this section, any member of the fire department or police department employed in the city carrying the worker's occupational disease insurance under this section is limited to recovery of medical and surgical care, medicines, laboratory, curative and palliative agents and means, x-ray, diagnostic and therapeutic services to the extent that the services are provided for in the worker's occupational disease policy so procured by the city, and may not also recover in addition to that policy for the same benefits provided in IC 36–8–4.

(f) If the medical benefits provided under a worker's occupational disease policy procured by the common council terminate for any reason before the police officer or firefighter is fully recovered, the common council shall provide medical benefits that are necessary until the police officer or firefighter is no longer in need of medical care.

---

[6]26 U.S.C.A. § 501(c)(3).

(g) Nothing in this section affects the rights and liabilities of employees and employers had by them prior to April 1, 1963, under this chapter.

Amended by Acts 1981, P.L.11, SEC.126; P.L.28–1988, SEC.49; P.L.217–1989, SEC.2; P.L.201–2005, SEC.6; P.L.134–2006, SEC.8.

22–3–7–2.5. School to work students

Sec. 2.5.   As used in this section, "school to work student" refers to a student participating in on-the-job training under the federal School to Work Opportunities Act (20 U.S.C. 6101 et seq.).

(b) A school to work student is entitled to the following compensation and benefits under this chapter:

(1) Medical benefits.

(2) Permanent partial impairment compensation under section 16 of this chapter. Permanent partial impairment compensation for a school to work student shall be paid in a lump sum upon agreement or final award.

(3) In the case that death results from the injury:

(A)   death benefits in a lump sum amount of one hundred seventy-five thousand dollars ($175,000), payable upon agreement or final award to any dependents of the student under sections 11 through 14 of this chapter, or, if the student has no dependents, to the student's parents; and

(B)   burial compensation under section 15 of this chapter.

(c) For the sole purpose of modifying an award under section 27 of this chapter, a school to work student's average weekly wage is presumed to be equal to the federal minimum wage.

(d) A school to work student is not entitled to the following compensation under this chapter:

(1) Temporary total disability compensation under section 16 of this chapter.

(2) Temporary partial disability compensation under section 19 of this chapter.

(e) Except for remedies available under IC 5–2–6.1, recovery under subsection (b) is the exclusive right and remedy for:

(1) a school to work student; and

(2) the personal representatives, dependents, or next of kin, at common law or otherwise, of a school to work student;

on account of disablement or death by occupational disease arising out of and in the course of school to work employment.

As added by P.L.235–1999, SEC.6.

22–3–7–3.   Waiver of exemption from act by employer; notice of acceptance; filing

Sec. 3.   An employer who is exempt under this section from the operation of the compensation provisions of this chapter may at any time waive such exemption and thereby accept the provisions of this chapter by giving notice as provided in subsection (b).

(b) The notice of acceptance referred to in subsection (a) shall be given thirty (30) days prior to any accident resulting in injury or death, provided that if any such injury occurred less than thirty (30) days after the date of employment, notice of acceptance given at the time of employment shall be sufficient notice thereof. The notice shall be in writing or print in a substantial form prescribed by the worker's compensation board and shall be given by the employer by posting the same in a conspicuous place in the plant, shop, office, room, or place where the employee is employed, or by serving it personally upon the employee. The notice shall be given by the employee by sending the same in registered letter addressed to the employer at his last known residence or place of business, or by giving it personally to the employer, or any of his agents upon whom a summons in civil actions may be served under the laws of the state.

(c) A copy of the notice in prescribed form shall also be filed with the worker's compensation board, within five (5) days after its service in such manner upon the employee or employer.

Amended by P.L.28–1988, SEC.50.

22–3–7–5. Coal mining; application of law

Sec. 5. On and after April 1, 1963, the provisions of this chapter shall apply to the state, to all political divisions thereof, to all municipal corporations within the state, to persons, partnerships, limited liability companies, and corporations engaged in mining coal, and to employees thereof, without any right of exemption from the compensation provisions of this chapter, except as provided in section 34(i) of this chapter.

Amended by P.L.144–1986, SEC.57; P.L.8–1993, SEC.283.

22–3–7–6. Exclusive remedies

Sec. 6. The rights and remedies granted under this chapter to an employee subject to this chapter on account of disablement or death by occupational disease arising out of and in the course of the employment shall exclude all other rights and remedies of such employee, his personal representatives, dependents, or next of kin, at common law or otherwise, on account of such disablement or death.

Amended by P.L.144–1986, SEC.58.

22–3–7–7. Statutory duties; application of law

Sec. 7. Nothing in this chapter shall be construed to relieve any employer or employee from penalty for failure or neglect to perform any statutory duty.

Amended by P.L.144–1986, SEC.59.

22–3–7–8. Place of exposure; foreign states or foreign countries

Sec. 8. Every employer and employee under this chapter shall be bound by the provisions of this chapter whether exposure and disablement therefrom or death resulting from an occupational disease occurs within the state or in some other state or in a foreign country.

Amended by P.L.144–1986, SEC.60.

22–3–7–9. Definitions; applicability of chapter; prerequisites for payment of compensation

Sec. 9.(a) As used in this chapter, "employer" includes the state and any political subdivision, any municipal corporation within the state, any individual or the legal representative of a deceased individual, firm, association, limited liability company, or corporation or the receiver or trustee of the same, using the services of another for pay. A parent corporation and its subsidiaries shall each be considered joint employers of the corporation's, the parent's, or the subsidiaries' employees for purposes of sections 6 and 33 of this chapter. Both a lessor and a lessee of employees shall each be considered joint employers of the employees provided by the lessor to the lessee for purposes of sections 6 and 33 of this chapter. The term also includes an employer that provides on-the-job training under the federal School to Work Opportunities Act (20 U.S.C. 6101 et seq.) to the extent set forth under section 2.5 of this chapter. If the employer is insured, the term includes the employer's insurer so far as applicable. However, the inclusion of an employer's insurer within this definition does not allow an employer's insurer to avoid payment for services rendered to an employee with the approval of the employer. The term does not include a non-profit corporation that is recognized as tax exempt under Section 501(c)(3) of the Internal Revenue Code (as defined in IC 6-3-1-11(a)) to the extent the corporation enters into an independent contractor agreement with a person for the performance of youth coaching services on a part-time basis.

(b) As used in this chapter, "employee" means every person, including a minor, in the service of another, under any contract of hire or apprenticeship written or implied, except one whose employment is both casual and not in the usual course of the trade, business, occupation, or profession of the employer. For purposes of this chapter the following apply:

(1) Any reference to an employee who has suffered disablement, when the employee is dead, also includes the employee's legal representative, dependents, and other persons to whom compensation may be payable.

(2) An owner of a sole proprietorship may elect to include the owner as an employee under this chapter if the owner is actually engaged in the proprietorship business. If the owner makes this election, the owner must serve upon the owner's insurance carrier and upon the board written notice of the election. No owner of a sole proprietorship may be considered an employee under this chapter unless the notice has been received. If the owner of a sole proprietorship:

(A) is an independent contractor in the construction trades and does not make the election provided under this subdivision, the owner must obtain a certificate of exemption under section 34.5 of this chapter; or

(B) is an independent contractor and does not make the election provided under this subdivision, the owner may obtain a certificate of exemption under section 34.5 of this chapter.

(3) A partner in a partnership may elect to include the partner as an employee under this chapter if the partner is actually engaged in the partnership business. If a partner makes this election, the partner must serve upon the partner's insurance carrier and upon the board written notice of the election. No partner may be considered an employee under this chapter until the notice has been received. If a partner in a partnership:

(A) is an independent contractor in the construction trades and does not make the election provided under this subdivision, the partner must obtain a certificate of exemption under section 34.5 of this chapter; or

(B) is an independent contractor and does not make the election provided under this subdivision, the partner may obtain a certificate of exemption under section 34.5 of this chapter.

(4) Real estate professionals are not employees under this chapter if:

(A) they are licensed real estate agents;

(B) substantially all their remuneration is directly related to sales volume and not the number of hours worked; and

(C) they have written agreements with real estate brokers stating that they are not to be treated as employees for tax purposes.

(5) A person is an independent contractor in the construction trades and not an employee under this chapter if the person is an independent contractor under the guidelines of the United States Internal Revenue Service.

(6) An owner-operator that provides a motor vehicle and the services of a driver under a written contract that is subject to IC 8-2.1-24-23, 45 IAC 16-1-13, or 49 CFR 376, to a motor carrier is not an employee of the motor carrier for purposes of this chapter. The owner-operator may elect to be covered and have the owner-operator's drivers covered under a worker's compensation insurance policy or authorized self-insurance that insures the motor carrier if the owner-operator pays the premiums as requested by the motor carrier. An election by an owner-operator under this subdivision does not terminate the independent contractor status of the owner-operator for any purpose other than the purpose of this subdivision.

(7) An unpaid participant under the federal School to Work Opportunities Act (20 U.S.C. 6101 et seq.) is an employee to the extent set forth under section 2.5 of this chapter.

(8) A person who enters into an independent contractor agreement with a nonprofit corporation that is recognized as tax exempt under Section 501(c)(3) of the Internal Revenue Code (as defined in IC 6-3-1-11(a)) to perform youth coaching services on a part-time basis is not an employee for purposes of this chapter.

(9) An officer of a corporation who is an employee of the corporation under this chapter may elect not to be an employee of the corporation under this chapter. An officer of a corporation who is also an owner of any interest in the corporation may elect not to be an employee of the corporation under this chapter. If an officer makes this election, the officer must serve written notice of the election on the corporation's insurance carrier and the board. An officer of a corporation may not be considered to be excluded as an employee under this chapter until the notice is received by the insurance carrier and the board.

(10) An individual who is not an employee of the state or a political subdivision is considered to be a temporary employee of the state for purposes of this chapter while serving as a member of a mobile support unit on duty for training, an exercise, or a response, as set forth in IC 10-14-3-19(c)(2)(B).

(c) As used in this chapter, "minor" means an individual who has not reached seventeen (17) years of age. A minor employee shall be considered as being of full age for all purposes of this chapter. However, if the employee is a minor who, at the time of the last exposure, is employed, required, suffered, or permitted to work in violation of the child labor laws of this state, the amount of compensation and death benefits, as provided in this chapter, shall be double the amount which would otherwise be recoverable. The insurance carrier shall be liable on its policy for one-half ($1/2$) of the compensation or benefits that may be payable on account of the disability or death of the minor, and the employer shall be wholly liable for the other one-half ($1/2$) of the compensation or benefits. If the employee is a minor who is not less than sixteen (16) years of age and who has not reached seventeen (17) years of age, and who at the time of the last exposure is employed, suffered, or permitted to work at any occupation which is not prohibited by law, the provisions of this subsection prescribing double the amount otherwise recoverable do not apply. The rights and remedies granted to a minor under this chapter on account of disease shall exclude all rights and remedies of the minor, the minor's parents, the minor's personal representatives, dependents, or next of kin at common law, statutory or otherwise, on account of any disease.

(d) This chapter does not apply to casual laborers as defined in subsection (b), nor to farm or agricultural employees, nor to household employees, nor to railroad employees engaged in train service as engineers, firemen, conductors, brakemen, flagmen, baggagemen, or foremen in charge of yard engines and helpers assigned thereto, nor to their employers with respect to these employees. Also, this chapter does not apply to employees or their employers with respect to employments in which the laws of the United States provide for compensation or liability for injury to the health, disability, or death by reason of diseases suffered by these employees.

(e) As used in this chapter, "disablement" means the event of becoming disabled from earning full wages at the work in which the employee was engaged when last exposed to the hazards of the occupational disease by the employer from whom the employee claims compensation or equal wages in other suitable employment, and "disability" means the state of being so incapacitated.

(f) For the purposes of this chapter, no compensation shall be payable for or on account of any occupational diseases unless disablement, as defined in subsection (e), occurs within two (2) years after the last day of the last exposure to the hazards of the disease except for the following:

(1) In all cases of occupational diseases caused by the inhalation of silica dust or coal dust, no compensation shall be payable unless disablement, as defined in subsection (e), occurs within three (3) years after the last day of the last exposure to the hazards of the disease.

(2) In all cases of occupational disease caused by the exposure to radiation, no compensation shall be payable unless disablement, as defined in subsection (e), occurs within two (2) years from the date on which the employee had knowledge of the nature of the employee's occupational disease or, by exercise of reasonable diligence, should have known of the existence of such disease and its causal relationship to the employee's employment.

(3) In all cases of occupational diseases caused by the inhalation of asbestos dust, no compensation shall be payable unless disablement, as defined in subsection (e), occurs within three (3) years after the last day of the last exposure to the hazards of the disease if the last day of the last exposure was before July 1, 1985.

(4) In all cases of occupational disease caused by the inhalation of asbestos dust in which the last date of the last exposure occurs on or after July 1, 1985, and before July 1, 1988, no compensation shall be payable unless disablement, as defined in subsection (e), occurs within twenty (20) years after the last day of the last exposure.

(5) In all cases of occupational disease caused by the inhalation of asbestos dust in which the last date of the last exposure occurs on or after July 1, 1988, no compensation shall be payable unless disablement (as defined in subsection (e)) occurs within thirty-five (35) years after the last day of the last exposure.

(g) For the purposes of this chapter, no compensation shall be payable for or on account of death resulting from any occupational disease unless death occurs within two (2) years after the date of disablement. However, this subsection does not bar compensation for death:

(1) where death occurs during the pendency of a claim filed by an employee within two (2) years after the date of disablement and which claim has not resulted in a decision or has resulted in a decision which is in process of review or appeal; or

(2) where, by agreement filed or decision rendered, a compensable period of disability has been fixed and death occurs within two (2) years after the end of such fixed period, but in no event later than three hundred (300) weeks after the date of disablement.

(h) As used in this chapter, "billing review service" refers to a person or an entity that reviews a medical service provider's bills or statements for the purpose of determining pecuniary liability. The term includes an employer's worker's compensation insurance carrier if the insurance carrier performs such a review.

(i) As used in this chapter, "billing review standard" means the data used by a billing review service to determine pecuniary liability.

(j) As used in this chapter, "community" means a geographic service area based on ZIP code districts defined by the United States Postal Service according to the following groupings:

(1) The geographic service area served by ZIP codes with the first three (3) digits 463 and 464.

(2) The geographic service area served by ZIP codes with the first three (3) digits 465 and 466.

(3) The geographic service area served by ZIP codes with the first three (3) digits 467 and 468.

(4) The geographic service area served by ZIP codes with the first three (3) digits 469 and 479.

(5) The geographic service area served by ZIP codes with the first three (3) digits 460, 461 (except 46107), and 473.

(6) The geographic service area served by the 46107 ZIP code and ZIP codes with the first three (3) digits 462.

(7) The geographic service area served by ZIP codes with the first three (3) digits 470, 471, 472, 474, and 478.

(8) The geographic service area served by ZIP codes with the first three (3) digits 475, 476, and 477.

(k) As used in this chapter, "medical service provider" refers to a person or an entity that provides services or products to an employee under this chapter. Except as otherwise provided in this chapter, the term includes a medical service facility.

(l) As used in this chapter, "medical service facility" means any of the following that provides a service or product under this chapter and uses the CMS 1450 (UB-04) form for Medicare reimbursement:

(1) A hospital (as defined in IC 16-18-2-179).

(2) A hospital based health facility (as defined in IC 16-18-2-180).

(3) A medical center (as defined in IC 16-18-2-223.4).

The term does not include a professional corporation (as defined in IC 23-1.5-1-10) comprised of health care professionals (as defined in IC 23-1.5-1-8) formed to render professional services as set forth in IC 23-1.5-2-3(a)(4) or a health care professional (as defined in IC 23-1.5-1-8) who bills for a service or product provided under this chapter as an individual or a member of a group practice or another medical service provider that uses the CMS 1500 form for Medicare reimbursement.

(m) As used in this chapter, "pecuniary liability" means the responsibility of an employer or the employer's insurance carrier for the payment of the charges for each specific service or product for human medical treatment provided under this chapter as follows:

(1) This subdivision applies before July 1, 2014, to all medical service providers, and after June 30, 2014, to a medical service provider that is not a medical service facility. Payment of the charges in a defined community, equal to or less than the charges made by medical service providers at the eightieth percentile in the same community for like services or products.

(2) Payment of the charges in a reasonable amount, which is established by payment of one (1) of the following:

(A) The amount negotiated at any time between the medical service facility and any of the following, if an amount has been negotiated:

(i) The employer.

(ii) The employer's insurance carrier.

(iii) A billing review service on behalf of a person described in item (i) or (ii).

(iv) A direct provider network that has contracted with a person described in item (i) or (ii).

(B) Two hundred percent (200%) of the amount that would be paid to the medical service facility on the same date for the same service or product under the medical service facility's Medicare reimbursement rate, if an amount has not been negotiated as described in clause (A).

(n) "Service or product" or "services and products" refers to medical, hospital, surgical, or nursing service, treatment, and supplies provided under this chapter.

Amended by Acts 1979, P.L.228, SEC.2; P.L.224-1985, SEC.1; P.L.95-1988, SEC.12; P.L.75-1993, SEC.5; P.L.8-1993, SEC.284; P.L.1-1994, SEC.111; P.L.110-1995, SEC.34; P.L.216-1995, SEC.5; P.L.2-1996, SEC.266; P.L.258-1997(ss), SEC.13; P.L.235-1999, SEC.7; P.L.31-2000, SEC.7; P.L.202-2001, SEC.8; P.L.201-2005, SEC.7; P.L.1-2009, SEC.127, eff. April 30, 2009; P.L.180-2009, SEC.2, eff. May 13, 2009; P.L.42-2011, SEC.38, eff. April 20, 2011; P.L.168-2011, SEC.12; P.L.6-2012, SEC.150, eff. Feb. 22, 2012; P.L.71-2013, SEC.11, eff. July 1, 2013; P.L.275-2013, SEC.12, eff. July 1, 2013; P.L.99-2014, SEC.4, eff. July 1, 2014; P.L.225-2015, SEC.2, eff. July 1, 2015.

22-3-7-9.2. "Violation of the child labor laws of this state" defined

Sec. 9.2. As used in section 9(c) of this chapter, the term "violation of the child labor laws of this state" means a violation of IC 20–33–3–35. The term does not include a violation of any other provision of IC 20–33–3.

As added by P.L.37–1985, SEC.32. Amended by P.L.106–1992, SEC.12; P.L.1–2005, SEC.183.

22–3–7–10. Definitions; course of employment

Sec. 10. As used in this chapter, "occupational disease" means a disease arising out of and in the course of the employment. Ordinary diseases of life to which the general public is exposed outside of the employment shall not be compensable, except where such diseases follow as an incident of an occupational disease as defined in this section.

(b) A disease arises out of the employment only if there is apparent to the rational mind, upon consideration of all of the circumstances, a direct causal connection between the conditions under which the work is performed and the occupational disease, and which can be seen to have followed as a natural incident of the work as a result of the exposure occasioned by the nature of the employment, and which can be fairly traced to the employment as the proximate cause, and which does not come from a hazard to which workers would have been equally exposed outside of the employment. The disease must be incidental to the character of the business and not independent of the relation of employer and employee. The disease need not have been foreseen or expected but after its contraction it must appear to have had its origin in a risk connected with the employment and to have flowed from that source as a rational consequence.

Amended by P.L.144–1986, SEC.61; P.L.28–1988, SEC.51.

22–3–7–10.5. Average weekly wages of public employee; determination

Sec. 10.5. For purposes of this chapter, the average weekly wages of a public employee shall be determined without regard to any salary reduction agreement under Section 125 of the Internal Revenue Code.[7]

As added by P.L.5–1992, SEC.9.

22–3–7–11. Death benefits; payment

Sec. 11. On and after April 1, 1957, and prior to April 1, 1967, when death results from an occupational disease within four hundred (400) weeks, there shall be paid to total dependents of said deceased, as determined by the provisions of IC 22–3–7–12, IC 22–3–7–13, IC 22–3–7–14, IC 22–3–7–15, a weekly compensation amounting to sixty (60) per centum of the deceased's average weekly wage until the compensation so paid when added to any compensation paid to the deceased employee shall equal four hundred (400) weeks, and to partial dependents as hereinafter provided.

---

[7] 26 U.S.C.A. § 125.

On and after April 1, 1967, and prior to April 1, 1969, when death results from an occupational disease within four hundred fifty (450) weeks, there shall be paid to total dependents of said deceased, as determined by the provisions of IC 22–3–7–12, IC 22–3–7–13, IC 22–3–7–14, IC 22–3–7–15, a weekly compensation amounting to sixty (60) per centum of the deceased's average weekly wage, until the compensation so paid when added to any compensation paid to the deceased employee shall equal four hundred fifty (450) weeks, and to partial dependents as hereinafter provided.

On and after April 1, 1969, and prior to July 1, 1974, when death results from occupational disease within five hundred (500) weeks, there shall be paid to total dependents of said deceased, as determined by the provisions of IC 22–3–7–12, IC 22–3–7–13, IC 22–3–7–14, IC 22–3–7–15, a weekly compensation amounting to sixty (60) per centum of the deceased's average weekly wage, until the compensation so paid when added to any compensation paid to the deceased employee shall equal five hundred (500) weeks, and to partial dependents as hereinafter provided.

On and after July 1, 1974, and before July 1, 1976, when death results from occupational disease within five hundred (500) weeks, there shall be paid to total dependents of said deceased as determined by the provisions of IC 22–3–7–12, IC 22–3–7–13, IC 22–3–7–14, IC 22–3–7–15, a weekly compensation amounting to sixty-six and two-thirds (66 $\frac{2}{3}$) per centum of the deceased's average weekly wage, up to one hundred thirty-five dollars ($135.00) average weekly wages, until the compensation so paid when added to any compensation paid to the deceased employee shall equal five hundred (500) weeks, and to partial dependents as hereinafter provided.

On and after July 1, 1976, when death results from occupational disease within five hundred (500) weeks, there shall be paid to total dependents of the deceased, as determined by the provisions of IC 22–3–7–12 through IC 22–3–7–15, a weekly compensation amounting to sixty-six and two-thirds percent (66 $\frac{2}{3}$%) of the deceased's average weekly wage, as defined in IC 22–3–7–19, until the compensation paid, when added to compensation paid to the deceased employee, equals five hundred (500) weeks, and to partial dependents as provided in this chapter.

Amended by Acts 1976, P.L.112, SEC.4.

22–3–7–12. Dependents; classification

Sec. 12. Dependents under this chapter shall consist of the following three (3) classes:

(1) Presumptive dependents.

(2) Total dependents in fact.

(3) Partial dependents in fact.

(b) Presumptive dependents shall be entitled to compensation to the complete exclusion of total dependents in fact and partial dependents in fact and shall be entitled to such compensation in equal shares.

(c) Total dependents in fact shall be entitled to compensation to the complete exclusion of partial dependents in fact and shall be entitled to such compensation, if more than one (1) such dependent exists, in equal shares. The question of total dependency shall be determined as of the time of death.

(d) Partial dependents in fact shall not be entitled to any compensation if any other class of dependents exist. The weekly compensation to persons partially dependent in fact shall be in the same proportion to the weekly compensation of persons wholly dependent as the average amount contributed weekly by the deceased to such partial dependent in fact bears to his average weekly wages at the time of the disablement.

The question of partial dependency in fact shall be determined as of the time of the disablement.

Amended by P.L.144–1986, SEC.62.

22–3–7–13. Presumptive dependents; termination of dependency

Sec. 13. The following persons are conclusively presumed to be wholly dependent for support upon a deceased employee and shall constitute the class known as presumptive dependents in section 12 of this chapter:

(1) A wife upon a husband with whom she is living at the time of his death, or upon whom the laws of the state impose the obligation of her support at such time. The term "wife", as used in this subdivision, shall exclude a common law wife unless such common law relationship was entered into before January 1, 1958, and, in addition, existed openly and notoriously for a period of not less than five (5) years immediately preceding the death.

(2) A husband upon his wife with whom he is living at the time of her death. The term "husband", as used in this subdivision, shall exclude a common law husband unless such common law relationship was entered into before January 1, 1958, and, in addition existed openly and notoriously for a period of not less than five (5) years immediately preceding the death.

(3) An unmarried child under the age of twenty-one (21) years upon the parent with whom the child is living at the time of the death of such parent.

(4) An unmarried child under twenty-one (21) years upon the parent with whom the child may not be living at the time

of the death of such parent, but upon whom at such time, the laws of the state impose the obligation to support such child.

(5) A child over the age of twenty-one (21) years who has never been married and who is either physically or mentally incapacitated from earning the child's own support, upon a parent upon whom the laws of the state impose the obligation of the support of such unmarried child.

(6) A child over the age of twenty-one (21) years who has never been married and who at the time of the death of the parent is keeping house for and living with such parent and is not otherwise gainfully employed.

(b) As used in this section, the term "child" includes stepchildren, legally adopted children, posthumous children, and acknowledged children born out of wedlock. The term "parent" includes stepparents and parents by adoption.

(c) The dependency of a child under subsections (a)(3) and (a)(4) shall terminate when the child attains the age of twenty-one (21).

(d) The dependency of any person as a presumptive dependent shall terminate upon the marriage of such dependent subsequent to the death of the employee, and such dependency shall not be reinstated by divorce. However, for deaths from injuries occurring on and after July 1, 1977, a surviving spouse who is a presumptive dependent and who is the only surviving dependent of the deceased is entitled to receive, upon remarriage before the expiration of the maximum statutory compensation period, a lump sum settlement equal to the smaller of one hundred four (104) weeks of compensation or the compensation for the remainder of the maximum statutory period.

(e) The dependency of any child under subsection (a)(6) shall be terminated at such time as such dependent becomes gainfully employed or marries.

Amended by Acts 1977, P.L.261, SEC.4; P.L.152–1987, SEC.7; P.L.134–1990, SEC.2.

22–3–7–14. Dependents; total or partial dependents; relatives; termination of dependency

Sec. 14. Total or partial dependents in fact shall include only those persons related to the deceased employee by blood or by marriage, except an unmarried child under eighteen (18) years of age. Any such person who is actually totally or partially dependent upon the deceased employee is entitled to compensation as such dependent in fact. The right to compensation of any person totally or partially dependent in fact shall be terminated by the marriage of such dependent subsequent to the death of the employee and such dependency shall not be reinstated by divorce.

22–3–7–15. Death benefits; burial expenses

Sec. 15. In cases of the death of an employee from an occupational disease arising out of and in the course of the employee's employment under circumstances that the employee would have been entitled to compensation if death had not resulted, the employer shall pay the burial expenses of such employee, not exceeding seven thousand five hundred dollars ($7,500).

Amended by P.L.225–1983, SEC.3; P.L.95–1988, SEC.13; P.L.170–1991, SEC.18; P.L.201–2005, SEC.8.

22–3–7–16. Disablements; awards

Sec. 16. Compensation shall be allowed on account of disablement from occupational disease resulting in only temporary total disability to work or temporary partial disability to work beginning with the eighth day of such disability except for the medical benefits provided for in section 17 of this chapter.

Compensation shall be allowed for the first seven (7) calendar days only as provided in this section. The first weekly installment of compensation for temporary disability is due fourteen (14) days after the disability begins. Not later than fifteen (15) days from the date that the first installment of compensation is due, the employer or the employer's insurance carrier shall tender to the employee or to the employee's dependents, with all compensation due, a properly prepared compensation agreement in a form prescribed by the board. Whenever an employer or the employer's insurance carrier denies or is not able to determine liability to pay compensation or benefits, the employer or the employer's insurance carrier shall notify the worker's compensation board and the employee in writing on a form prescribed by the worker's compensation board not later than thirty (30) days after the employer's knowledge of the claimed disablement. If a determination of liability cannot be made within thirty (30) days, the worker's compensation board may approve an additional thirty (30) days upon a written request of the employer or the employer's insurance carrier that sets forth the reasons that the determination could not be made within thirty (30) days and states the facts or circumstances that are necessary to determine liability within the additional thirty (30) days. More than thirty (30) days of additional time may be approved by the worker's compensation board upon the filing of a petition by the employer or the employer's insurance carrier that sets forth:

(1) the extraordinary circumstances that have precluded a determination of liability within the initial sixty (60) days;

(2) the status of the investigation on the date the petition is filed;

(3) the facts or circumstances that are necessary to make a determination; and

(4) a timetable for the completion of the remaining investigation.

An employer who fails to comply with this section is subject to a civil penalty under IC 22–3–4–15.

(b) Once begun, temporary total disability benefits may not be terminated by the employer unless:

(1) the employee has returned to work;

(2) the employee has died;

(3) the employee has refused to undergo a medical examination under section 20 of this chapter;

(4) the employee has received five hundred (500) weeks of temporary total disability benefits or has been paid the maximum compensation allowable under section 19 of this chapter; or

(5) the employee is unable or unavailable to work for reasons unrelated to the compensable disease.

In all other cases the employer must notify the employee in writing of the employer's intent to terminate the payment of temporary total disability benefits, and of the availability of employment, if any, on a form approved by the board. If the employee disagrees with the proposed termination, the employee must give written notice of disagreement to the board and the employer within seven (7) days after receipt of the notice of intent to terminate benefits. If the board and employer do not receive a notice of disagreement under this section, the employee's temporary total disability benefits shall be terminated. Upon receipt of the notice of disagreement, the board shall immediately contact the parties, which may be by telephone or other means and attempt to resolve the disagreement. If the board is unable to resolve the disagreement within ten (10) days of receipt of the notice of disagreement, the board shall immediately arrange for an evaluation of the employee by an independent medical examiner. The independent medical examiner shall be selected by mutual agreement of the parties or, if the parties are unable to agree, appointed by the board under IC 22–3–4–11. If the independent medical examiner determines that the employee is no longer temporarily disabled or is still temporarily disabled but can return to employment that the employer has made available to the employee, or if the employee fails or refuses to appear for examination by the independent medical examiner, temporary total disability benefits may be terminated. If either party disagrees with the opinion of the independent medical examiner, the party shall apply to the board for a hearing under section 27 of this chapter.

(c) An employer is not required to continue the payment of temporary total disability benefits for more than fourteen (14) days after the employer's proposed termination date unless the independent medical examiner determines that the employee is temporarily disabled and unable to return to any employment that the employer has made available to the employee.

(d) If it is determined that as a result of this section temporary total disability benefits were overpaid, the overpayment shall be deducted from any benefits due the employee under this section and, if there are no benefits due the employee or the benefits due the employee do not equal the amount of the overpayment, the employee shall be responsible for paying any overpayment which cannot be deducted from benefits due the employee.

(e) For disablements occurring on and after July 1, 1976, from occupational disease resulting in temporary total disability for any work there shall be paid to the disabled employee during the temporary total disability weekly compensation equal to sixty-six and two-thirds percent (66 2/3%) of the employee's average weekly wages, as defined in section 19 of this chapter, for a period not to exceed five hundred (500) weeks. Compensation shall be allowed for the first seven (7) calendar days only if the disability continues for longer than twenty-one (21) days.

(f) For disablements occurring on and after July 1, 1974, from occupational disease resulting in temporary partial disability for work there shall be paid to the disabled employee during such disability a weekly compensation equal to sixty-six and two-thirds percent (66 2/3%) of the difference between the employee's average weekly wages, as defined in section 19 of this chapter, and the weekly wages at which the employee is actually employed after the disablement, for a period not to exceed three hundred (300) weeks. Compensation shall be allowed for the first seven (7) calendar days only if the disability continues for longer than twenty-one (21) days. In case of partial disability after the period of temporary total disability, the latter period shall be included as a part of the maximum period allowed for partial disability.

(g) For disabilities occurring on and after July 1, 1979, and before July 1, 1988, from occupational disease in the schedule set forth in subsection (j), the employee shall receive in addition to disability benefits, not exceeding fifty-two (52) weeks on account of the occupational disease, a weekly compensation of sixty percent (60%) of the employee's average weekly wages, not to exceed one hundred twenty-five dollars ($125) average weekly wages, for the period stated for the disabilities.

(h) For disabilities occurring on and after July 1, 1988, and before July 1, 1989, from occupational disease in the schedule set forth in subsection (j), the employee shall receive in addition to disability benefits, not exceeding seventy-eight (78) weeks on account of the occupational disease, a weekly compensation of sixty percent (60%) of the employee's average weekly wages, not to exceed one hundred sixty-six dollars ($166) average weekly wages, for the period stated for the disabilities.

(i) For disabilities occurring on and after July 1, 1989, and before July 1, 1990, from occupational disease in the schedule set forth in subsection (j), the employee shall receive in addition to disability benefits, not exceeding seventy-eight (78) weeks on account of the occupational disease, a weekly compensation of sixty percent (60%) of the employee's average weekly wages, not to exceed one hundred eighty-three dollars ($183) average weekly wages, for the period stated for the disabilities.

(j) For disabilities occurring on and after July 1, 1990, and before July 1, 1991, from occupational disease in the following schedule, the employee shall receive in addition to disability benefits, not exceeding seventy-eight (78) weeks on account of the occupational disease, a weekly compensation of sixty percent (60%) of the employee's average weekly wages, not to exceed two hundred dollars ($200) average weekly wages, for the period stated for the disabilities.

(1) Amputations: For the loss by separation, of the thumb, sixty (60) weeks; of the index finger, forty (40) weeks; of the second finger, thirty-five (35) weeks; of the third or ring finger, thirty (30) weeks; of the fourth or little finger, twenty (20) weeks; of the hand by separation below the elbow, two hundred (200) weeks; of the arm above the elbow joint, two hundred fifty (250) weeks; of the big toe, sixty (60) weeks; of the second toe, thirty (30) weeks; of the third toe, twenty (20) weeks; of the fourth toe, fifteen (15) weeks; of the fifth or little toe, ten (10) weeks; of the foot below the knee joint, one hundred fifty (150) weeks; and of the leg above the knee joint, two hundred (200) weeks. The loss of more than one (1) phalange of a thumb or toe shall be considered as the loss of the entire thumb or toe. The loss of more than two (2) phalanges of a finger shall be considered as the loss of the entire finger. The loss of not more than one (1) phalange of a thumb or toe shall be considered as the loss of one-half (1/2) of the thumb or toe and compensation shall be paid for one-half (1/2) of the period for the loss of the entire thumb or toe.

The loss of not more than two (2) phalanges of a finger shall be considered as the loss of one-half (1/2) the finger and compensation shall be paid for one-half (1/2) of the period for the loss of the entire finger.

(2) Loss of Use: The total permanent loss of the use of an

arm, hand, thumb, finger, leg, foot, toe, or phalange shall be considered as the equivalent of the loss by separation of the arm, hand, thumb, finger, leg, foot, toe, or phalange and the compensation shall be paid for the same period as for the loss thereof by separation.

(3) Partial Loss of Use: For the permanent partial loss of the use of an arm, hand, thumb, finger, leg, foot, toe, or phalange, compensation shall be paid for the proportionate loss of the use of such arm, hand, thumb, finger, leg, foot, toe, or phalange.

(4) For disablements for occupational disease resulting in total permanent disability, five hundred (500) weeks.

(5) For the loss of both hands, or both feet, or the total sight of both eyes, or any two (2) of such losses resulting from the same disablement by occupational disease, five hundred (500) weeks.

(6) For the permanent and complete loss of vision by enucleation of an eye or its reduction to one-tenth ($^{1}/_{10}$) of normal vision with glasses, one hundred fifty (150) weeks, and for any other permanent reduction of the sight of an eye, compensation shall be paid for a period proportionate to the degree of such permanent reduction without correction or glasses. However, when such permanent reduction without correction or glasses would result in one hundred percent (100%) loss of vision, but correction or glasses would result in restoration of vision, then compensation shall be paid for fifty percent (50%) of such total loss of vision without glasses plus an additional amount equal to the proportionate amount of such reduction with glasses, not to exceed an additional fifty percent (50%).

(7) For the permanent and complete loss of hearing, two hundred (200) weeks.

(8) In all other cases of permanent partial impairment, compensation proportionate to the degree of such permanent partial impairment, in the discretion of the worker's compensation board, not exceeding five hundred (500) weeks.

(9) In all cases of permanent disfigurement, which may impair the future usefulness or opportunities of the employee, compensation in the discretion of the worker's compensation board, not exceeding two hundred (200) weeks, except that no compensation shall be payable under this paragraph where compensation shall be payable under subdivisions (1) through (8). Where compensation for temporary total disability has been paid, this amount of compensation shall be deducted from any compensation due for permanent disfigurement.

(k) With respect to disablements in the following schedule occurring on and after July 1, 1991, the employee shall receive in addition to temporary total disability benefits, not exceeding one hundred twenty-five (125) weeks on account of the disablement, compensation in an amount determined under the following schedule to be paid weekly at a rate of sixty-six and two-thirds percent (66 2/3%) of the employee's average weekly wages during the fifty-two (52) weeks immediately preceding the week in which the disablement occurred:

(1) Amputation: For the loss by separation of the thumb, twelve (12) degrees of permanent impairment; of the index finger, eight (8) degrees of permanent impairment; of the second finger, seven (7) degrees of permanent impairment; of the third or ring finger, six (6) degrees of permanent impairment; of the fourth or little finger, four (4) degrees of permanent impairment; of the hand by separation below the elbow joint, forty (40) degrees of permanent impairment; of the arm above the elbow, fifty (50) degrees of permanent impairment; of the big toe, twelve (12) degrees of permanent impairment; of the second toe, six (6) degrees of permanent impairment; of the third toe, four (4) degrees of permanent impairment; of the fourth toe, three (3) degrees of permanent impairment; of the fifth or little toe, two (2) degrees of permanent impairment; of separation of the foot below the knee joint, thirty-five (35) degrees of permanent impairment; and of the leg above the knee joint, forty-five (45) degrees of permanent impairment.

(2) Amputations occurring on or after July 1, 1997: For the loss by separation of any of the body parts described in subdivision (1) on or after July 1, 1997, the dollar values per degree applying on the date of the injury as described in subsection (l) shall be multiplied by two (2). However, the doubling provision of this subdivision does not apply to a loss of use that is not a loss by separation.

(3) The loss of more than one (1) phalange of a thumb or toe shall be considered as the loss of the entire thumb or toe. The loss of more than two (2) phalanges of a finger shall be considered as the loss of the entire finger. The loss of not more than one (1) phalange of a thumb or toe shall be considered as the loss of one-half (1/2) of the degrees of permanent impairment for the loss of the entire thumb or toe. The loss of not more than one (1) phalange of a finger shall be considered as the loss of one-third (1/3) of the finger and compensation shall be paid for one-third (1/3) of the degrees payable for the loss of the entire finger. The loss of more than one (1) phalange of the finger but not more than two (2) phalanges of the finger shall be considered as the loss of one-

half (¹/₂) of the finger and compensation shall be paid for one-half (¹/₂) of the degrees payable for the loss of the entire finger.

(4) For the loss by separation of both hands or both feet or the total sight of both eyes or any two (2) such losses in the same accident, one hundred (100) degrees of permanent impairment.

(5) For the permanent and complete loss of vision by enucleation or its reduction to one-tenth (¹/₁₀) of normal vision with glasses, thirty-five (35) degrees of permanent impairment.

(6) For the permanent and complete loss of hearing in one (1) ear, fifteen (15) degrees of permanent impairment, and in both ears, forty (40) degrees of permanent impairment.

(7) For the loss of one (1) testicle, ten (10) degrees of permanent impairment; for the loss of both testicles, thirty (30) degrees of permanent impairment.

(8) Loss of use: The total permanent loss of the use of an arm, a hand, a thumb, a finger, a leg, a foot, a toe, or a phalange shall be considered as the equivalent of the loss by separation of the arm, hand, thumb, finger, leg, foot, toe, or phalange, and compensation shall be paid in the same amount as for the loss by separation. However, the doubling provision of subdivision (2) does not apply to a loss of use that is not a loss by separation.

(9) Partial loss of use: For the permanent partial loss of the use of an arm, a hand, a thumb, a finger, a leg, a foot, a toe, or a phalange, compensation shall be paid for the proportionate loss of the use of the arm, hand, thumb, finger, leg, foot, toe, or phalange.

(10) For disablements resulting in total permanent disability, the amount payable for impairment or five hundred (500) weeks of compensation, whichever is greater.

(11) For any permanent reduction of the sight of an eye less than a total loss as specified in subdivision (5), the compensation shall be paid in an amount proportionate to the degree of a permanent reduction without correction or glasses. However, when a permanent reduction without correction or glasses would result in one hundred percent (100%) loss of vision, then compensation shall be paid for fifty percent (50%) of the total loss of vision without glasses, plus an additional amount equal to the proportionate amount of the reduction with glasses, not to exceed an additional fifty percent (50%).

(12) For any permanent reduction of the hearing of one (1)

or both ears, less than the total loss as specified in subdivision (6), compensation shall be paid in an amount proportionate to the degree of a permanent reduction.

(13) In all other cases of permanent partial impairment, compensation proportionate to the degree of a permanent partial impairment, in the discretion of the worker's compensation board, not exceeding one hundred (100) degrees of permanent impairment.

(14) In all cases of permanent disfigurement which may impair the future usefulness or opportunities of the employee, compensation, in the discretion of the worker's compensation board, not exceeding forty (40) degrees of permanent impairment except that no compensation shall be payable under this subdivision where compensation is payable elsewhere in this section.

(l) With respect to disablements occurring on and after July 1, 1991, compensation for permanent partial impairment shall be paid according to the degree of permanent impairment for the disablement determined under subsection (k) and the following:

(1) With respect to disablements occurring on and after July 1, 1991, and before July 1, 1992, for each degree of permanent impairment from one (1) to thirty-five (35), five hundred dollars ($500) per degree; for each degree of permanent impairment from thirty-six (36) to fifty (50), nine hundred dollars ($900) per degree; for each degree of permanent impairment above fifty (50), one thousand five hundred dollars ($1,500) per degree.

(2) With respect to disablements occurring on and after July 1, 1992, and before July 1, 1993, for each degree of permanent impairment from one (1) to twenty (20), five hundred dollars ($500) per degree; for each degree of permanent impairment from twenty-one (21) to thirty-five (35), eight hundred dollars ($800) per degree; for each degree of permanent impairment from thirty-six (36) to fifty (50), one thousand three hundred dollars ($1,300) per degree; for each degree of permanent impairment above fifty (50), one thousand seven hundred dollars ($1,700) per degree.

(3) With respect to disablements occurring on and after July 1, 1993, and before July 1, 1997, for each degree of permanent impairment from one (1) to ten (10), five hundred dollars ($500) per degree; for each degree of permanent impairment from eleven (11) to twenty (20), seven hundred dollars ($700) per degree; for each degree of permanent impairment from twenty-one (21) to thirty-five (35), one thousand dollars ($1,000) per degree; for each degree of per-

manent impairment from thirty-six (36) to fifty (50), one thousand four hundred dollars ($1,400) per degree; for each degree of permanent impairment above fifty (50), one thousand seven hundred dollars ($1,700) per degree.

(4) With respect to disablements occurring on and after July 1, 1997, and before July 1, 1998, for each degree of permanent impairment from one (1) to ten (10), seven hundred fifty dollars ($750) per degree; for each degree of permanent impairment from eleven (11) to thirty-five (35), one thousand dollars ($1,000) per degree; for each degree of permanent impairment from thirty-six (36) to fifty (50), one thousand four hundred dollars ($1,400) per degree; for each degree of permanent impairment above fifty (50), one thousand seven hundred dollars ($1,700) per degree.

(5) With respect to disablements occurring on and after July 1, 1998, and before July 1, 1999, for each degree of permanent impairment from one (1) to ten (10), seven hundred fifty dollars ($750) per degree; for each degree of permanent impairment from eleven (11) to thirty-five (35), one thousand dollars ($1,000) per degree; for each degree of permanent impairment from thirty-six (36) to fifty (50), one thousand four hundred dollars ($1,400) per degree; for each degree of permanent impairment above fifty (50), one thousand seven hundred dollars ($1,700) per degree.

(6) With respect to disablements occurring on and after July 1, 1999, and before July 1, 2000, for each degree of permanent impairment from one (1) to ten (10), nine hundred dollars ($900) per degree; for each degree of permanent impairment from eleven (11) to thirty-five (35), one thousand one hundred dollars ($1,100) per degree; for each degree of permanent impairment from thirty-six (36) to fifty (50), one thousand six hundred dollars ($1,600) per degree; for each degree of permanent impairment above fifty (50), two thousand dollars ($2,000) per degree.

(7) With respect to disablements occurring on and after July 1, 2000, and before July 1, 2001, for each degree of permanent impairment from one (1) to ten (10), one thousand one hundred dollars ($1,100) per degree; for each degree of permanent impairment from eleven (11) to thirty-five (35), one thousand three hundred dollars ($1,300) per degree; for each degree of permanent impairment from thirty-six (36) to fifty (50), two thousand dollars ($2,000) per degree; for each degree of permanent impairment above fifty (50), two thousand five hundred fifty dollars ($2,500) per degree.

(8) With respect to disablements occurring on and after July 1, 2001, and before July 1, 2007, for each degree of per-

manent impairment from one (1) to ten (10), one thousand three hundred dollars ($1,300) per degree; for each degree of permanent impairment from eleven (11) to thirty-five (35), one thousand five hundred dollars ($1,500) per degree; for each degree of permanent impairment from thirty-six (36) to fifty (50), two thousand four hundred dollars ($2,400) per degree; for each degree of permanent impairment above fifty (50), three thousand dollars ($3,000) per degree.

(9) With respect to disablements occurring on and after July 1, 2007, and before July 1, 2008, for each degree of permanent impairment from one (1) to ten (10), one thousand three hundred forty dollars ($1,340) per degree; for each degree of permanent impairment from eleven (11) to thirty-five (35), one thousand five hundred forty-five dollars ($1,545) per degree; for each degree of permanent impairment from thirty-six (36) to fifty (50), two thousand four hundred seventy-five dollars ($2,475) per degree; for each degree of permanent impairment above fifty (50), three thousand one hundred fifty dollars ($3,150) per degree.

(10) With respect to disablements occurring on and after July 1, 2008, and before July 1, 2009, for each degree of permanent impairment from one (1) to ten (10), one thousand three hundred sixty-five dollars ($1,365) per degree; for each degree of permanent impairment from eleven (11) to thirty-five (35), one thousand five hundred seventy dollars ($1,570) per degree; for each degree of permanent impairment from thirty-six (36) to fifty (50), two thousand five hundred twenty-five dollars ($2,525) per degree; for each degree of permanent impairment above fifty (50), three thousand two hundred dollars ($3,200) per degree.

(11) With respect to disablements occurring on and after July 1, 2009, and before July 1, 2010, for each degree of permanent impairment from one (1) to ten (10), one thousand three hundred eighty dollars ($1,380) per degree; for each degree of permanent impairment from eleven (11) to thirty-five (35), one thousand five hundred eighty-five dollars ($1,585) per degree; for each degree of permanent impairment from thirty-six (36) to fifty (50), two thousand six hundred dollars ($2,600) per degree; for each degree of permanent impairment above fifty (50), three thousand three hundred dollars ($3,300) per degree.

(12) With respect to disablements occurring on and after July 1, 2010, and before July 1, 2014, for each degree of permanent impairment from one (1) to ten (10), one thousand four hundred dollars ($1,400) per degree; for each degree of permanent impairment from eleven (11) to thirty-five (35),

one thousand six hundred dollars ($1,600) per degree; for each degree of permanent impairment from thirty-six (36) to fifty (50), two thousand seven hundred dollars ($2,700) per degree; for each degree of permanent impairment above fifty (50), three thousand five hundred dollars ($3,500) per degree.

(13) With respect to disablements occurring on and after July 1, 2014, and before July 1, 2015, for each degree of permanent impairment from one (1) to ten (10), one thousand five hundred seventeen dollars ($1,517) per degree; for each degree of permanent impairment from eleven (11) to thirty-five (35), one thousand seven hundred seventeen dollars ($1,717) per degree; for each degree of permanent impairment from thirty-six (36) to fifty (50), two thousand eight hundred sixty-two dollars ($2,862) per degree; for each degree of permanent impairment above fifty (50), three thousand six hundred eighty-seven dollars ($3,687) per degree.

(14) With respect to disablements occurring on and after July 1, 2015, and before July 1, 2016, for each degree of permanent impairment from one (1) to ten (10), one thousand six hundred thirty-three dollars ($1,633) per degree; for each degree of permanent impairment from eleven (11) to thirty-five (35), one thousand eight hundred thirty-five dollars ($1,835) per degree; for each degree of permanent impairment from thirty-six (36) to fifty (50), three thousand twenty-four dollars ($3,024) per degree; for each degree of permanent impairment above fifty (50), three thousand eight hundred seventy-three dollars ($3,873) per degree.

(15) With respect to disablements occurring on and after July 1, 2016, for each degree of permanent impairment from one (1) to ten (10), one thousand seven hundred fifty dollars ($1,750) per degree; for each degree of permanent impairment from eleven (11) to thirty-five (35), one thousand nine hundred fifty-two dollars ($1,952) per degree; for each degree of permanent impairment from thirty-six (36) to fifty (50), three thousand one hundred eighty-six dollars ($3,186) per degree; for each degree of permanent impairment above fifty (50), four thousand sixty dollars ($4,060) per degree.

(m) The average weekly wages used in the determination of compensation for permanent partial impairment under subsections (k) and (l) shall not exceed the following:

(1) With respect to disablements occurring on or after July 1, 1991, and before July 1, 1992, four hundred ninety-two dollars ($492).

(2) With respect to disablements occurring on or after July 1, 1992, and before July 1, 1993, five hundred forty dollars ($540).

(3) With respect to disablements occurring on or after July 1, 1993, and before July 1, 1994, five hundred ninety-one dollars ($591).

(4) With respect to disablements occurring on or after July 1, 1994, and before July 1, 1997, six hundred forty-two dollars ($642).

(5) With respect to disablements occurring on or after July 1, 1997, and before July 1, 1998, six hundred seventy-two dollars ($672).

(6) With respect to disablements occurring on or after July 1, 1998, and before July 1, 1999, seven hundred two dollars ($702).

(7) With respect to disablements occurring on or after July 1, 1999, and before July 1, 2000, seven hundred thirty-two dollars ($732).

(8) With respect to disablements occurring on or after July 1, 2000, and before July 1, 2001, seven hundred sixty-two dollars ($762).

(9) With respect to disablements occurring on or after July 1, 2001, and before July 1, 2002, eight hundred twenty-two dollars ($822).

(10) With respect to disablements occurring on or after July 1, 2002, and before July 1, 2006, eight hundred eighty-two dollars ($882).

(11) With respect to disablements occurring on or after July 1, 2006, and before July 1, 2007, nine hundred dollars ($900).

(12) With respect to disablements occurring on or after July 1, 2007, and before July 1, 2008, nine hundred thirty dollars ($930).

(13) With respect to disablements occurring on or after July 1, 2008, and before July 1, 2009, nine hundred fifty-four dollars ($954).

(14) With respect to disablements occurring on or after July 1, 2009, and before July 1, 2014, nine hundred seventy-five dollars ($975).

(15) With respect to disablements occurring on or after July 1, 2014, and before July 1, 2015, one thousand forty dollars ($1,040).

(16) With respect to disablements occurring on or after July 1, 2015, and before July 1, 2016, one thousand one hundred five dollars ($1,105).

(17) With respect to disablements occurring on or after

July 1, 2016, one thousand one hundred seventy dollars ($1,170).

(n) If any employee, only partially disabled, refuses employment suitable to the employee's capacity procured for the employee, the employee shall not be entitled to any compensation at any time during the continuance of such refusal unless, in the opinion of the worker's compensation board, such refusal was justifiable. The employee must be served with a notice setting forth the consequences of the refusal under this subsection. The notice must be in a form prescribed by the worker's compensation board.

(o) If an employee has sustained a permanent impairment or disability from an accidental injury other than an occupational disease in another employment than that in which the employee suffered a subsequent disability from an occupational disease, such as herein specified, the employee shall be entitled to compensation for the subsequent disability in the same amount as if the previous impairment or disability had not occurred. However, if the permanent impairment or disability resulting from an occupational disease for which compensation is claimed results only in the aggravation or increase of a previously sustained permanent impairment from an occupational disease or physical condition regardless of the source or cause of such previously sustained impairment from an occupational disease or physical condition, the board shall determine the extent of the previously sustained permanent impairment from an occupational disease or physical condition as well as the extent of the aggravation or increase resulting from the subsequent permanent impairment or disability, and shall award compensation only for that part of said occupational disease or physical condition resulting from the subsequent permanent impairment. An amputation of any part of the body or loss of any or all of the vision of one (1) or both eyes caused by an occupational disease shall be considered as a permanent impairment or physical condition.

(p) If an employee suffers a disablement from an occupational disease for which compensation is payable while the employee is still receiving or entitled to compensation for a previous injury by accident or disability by occupational disease in the same employment, the employee shall not at the same time be entitled to compensation for both, unless it be for a permanent injury, such as specified in subsection (k)(1), (k)(4), (k)(5), (k)(8), or (k)(9), but the employee shall be entitled to compensation for that disability and from the time of that disability which will cover the longest period and the largest amount payable under this chapter.

(q) If an employee receives a permanent disability from an occupational disease such as specified in subsection (k)(1), (k)(4), (k)(5), (k)(8), or (k)(9) after having sustained another such permanent disability in the same employment the employee shall be entitled to compensation for both such disabilities, but the total compensation shall be paid by extending the period and not by increasing the amount of weekly compensation and, when such previous and subsequent permanent disabilities, in combination result in total permanent disability or permanent total impairment, compensation shall be payable for such permanent total disability or impairment, but payments made for the previous disability or impairment shall be deducted from the total payment of compensation due.

(r) When an employee has been awarded or is entitled to an award of compensation for a definite period from an occupational disease wherein disablement occurs on and after April 1, 1963, and such employee dies from other causes than such occupational disease, payment of the unpaid balance of such compensation not exceeding three hundred fifty (350) weeks shall be paid to the employee's dependents of the second and third class as defined in sections 11 through 14 of this chapter and compensation, not exceeding five hundred (500) weeks shall be made to the employee's dependents of the first class as defined in sections 11 through 14 of this chapter.

(s) Any payment made by the employer to the employee during the period of the employee's disability, or to the employee's dependents, which, by the terms of this chapter, was not due and payable when made, may, subject to the approval of the worker's compensation board, be deducted from the amount to be paid as compensation, but such deduction shall be made from the distal end of the period during which compensation must be paid, except in cases of temporary disability.

(t) When so provided in the compensation agreement or in the award of the worker's compensation board, compensation may be paid semimonthly, or monthly, instead of weekly.

(u) When the aggregate payments of compensation awarded by agreement or upon hearing to an employee or dependent under eighteen (18) years of age do not exceed one hundred dollars ($100), the payment thereof may be made directly to such employee or dependent, except when the worker's compensation board shall order otherwise.

(v) Whenever the aggregate payments of compensation, due to any person under eighteen (18) years of age, exceed one hundred dollars ($100), the payment thereof shall be made to a trustee, appointed by the circuit or superior court, or to a duly qualified guardian, or, upon the order of the worker's compensation board, to a parent or to such minor person. The payment of compensation, due to any person eighteen (18) years of age or over, may be made directly to such person.

(w) If an employee, or a dependent, is mentally incompetent, or a minor at the time when any right or privilege accrues to the employee under this chapter, the employee's guardian or trustee may, in the employee's behalf, claim and exercise such right and privilege.

(x) All compensation payments named and provided for in this section, shall mean and be defined to be for only such occupational diseases and disabilities therefrom as are proved by competent evidence, of which there are or have been objective conditions or symptoms proven, not within the physical or mental control of the employee.

Amended by Acts 1976, P.L.112, SEC.5; Acts 1977, P.L.261, SEC.5; Acts 1979, P.L.227, SEC.5; P.L.95-1988, SEC.14; P.L.170-1991, SEC.19; P.L.258-1997(ss), SEC.14; P.L.31-2000, SEC.8; P.L.1-2001, SEC.28; P.L.134-2006, SEC.9; P.L.168-2011, SEC.13; P.L.275-2013, SEC.13, eff. July 1, 2013.

22-3-7-17. Medical attendance and treatment; prosthetic devices; emergency treatment; liability to providers

Sec. 17.(a) During the period of disablement, the employer shall furnish or cause to be furnished, free of charge to the employee, an attending physician for the treatment of the employee's occupational disease, and in addition thereto such services and products as the attending physician or the worker's compensation board may deem necessary. If the employee is requested or required by the employer to submit to treatment outside the county of employment, the employer shall also pay the reasonable expense of travel, food, and lodging necessary during the travel, but not to exceed the amount paid at the time of the travel by the state of Indiana to its employees. If the treatment or travel to or from the place of treatment causes a loss of working time to the employee, the employer shall reimburse the employee for the loss of wages using the basis of the employee's average daily wage.

(b) During the period of disablement resulting from the occupational disease, the employer shall furnish such physician, services and products, and the worker's compensation board may, on proper application of either party, require that treatment by such physician and such services and products be furnished by or on behalf of the employer as the board may deem reasonably necessary. After an employee's occupational disease has been adjudicated by agreement or award on the basis of permanent partial impairment and within the statutory period for review in such case as provided in section 27(i) of this chapter, the employer may continue to furnish a physician or a surgeon and other services and products, and the board may, within such statutory period for review as provided in section 27(i) of this chapter, on a proper application of either party, require that treatment by such physician or surgeon and such services and products be furnished by and on behalf of the employer as the board may deem necessary to limit or reduce the amount and extent of such impairment. The refusal of the employee to accept such services and products when so provided by or on behalf of the employer, shall bar the employee from all compensation otherwise payable during the period of such refusal and the employee's right to prosecute any proceeding under this chapter shall be suspended and abated until such refusal ceases. The employee must be served with a notice setting forth the consequences of the refusal under this section. The notice must be in a form prescribed by the worker's compensation board. No compensation for permanent total impairment, permanent partial impairment, permanent disfigurement, or death shall be paid or payable for that part or portion of such impairment, disfigurement, or death which is the result of the failure of such employee to accept such services and products, provided that an employer may at any time permit an employee to have treatment for the employee's disease or injury by spiritual means or prayer in lieu of such physician, services and products.

(c) Regardless of when it occurs, where a compensable occupational disease results in the amputation of a body part, the enucleation of an eye, or the loss of natural teeth, the employer shall furnish an appropriate artificial member, braces, and prosthodontics. The cost of repairs to or replacements for the artificial members, braces, or prosthodontics that result from a compensable occupational disease pursuant to a prior award and are required due to either medical necessity or normal wear and tear, determined according to the employee's individual use, but not abuse, of the artificial member, braces, or prosthodontics, shall be paid from the second injury fund upon order or award of the worker's compensation board. The employee is not required to meet any other requirement for admission to the second injury fund.

(d) If an emergency or because of the employer's failure to provide such attending physician or such services and products or such treatment by spiritual means or prayer as specified in this section, or for other good reason, a physician other than that provided by the employer treats the diseased employee within the period of disability, or necessary and proper services and products are procured within the period, the reasonable cost of such services and products shall, subject to approval of the worker's compensation board, be paid by the employer.

(e) An employer or employer's insurance carrier may not

delay the provision of emergency medical care whenever emergency medical care is considered necessary in the professional judgment of the attending health care facility physician.

(f) This section may not be construed to prohibit an agreement between an employer and employees that has the approval of the board and that:

(1) binds the parties to medical care furnished by medical service providers selected by agreement before or after disablement; or

(2) makes the findings of a medical service provider chosen in this manner binding upon the parties.

(g) The employee and the employee's estate do not have liability to a medical service provider for payment for services obtained under this section. The right to order payment for all services provided under this chapter is solely with the board. All claims by a medical service provider for payment for services are against the employer and the employer's insurance carrier, if any, and must be made with the board under this chapter. After June 30, 2011, a medical service provider must file an application for adjustment of a claim for a medical service provider's fee with the board not later than two (2) years after the receipt of an initial written communication from the employer, the employer's insurance carrier, if any, or an agent acting on behalf of the employer after the medical service provider submits a bill for services. To offset a part of the board's expenses related to the administration of medical service provider reimbursement disputes, a medical service facility shall pay a filing fee of sixty dollars ($60) in a balance billing case. The filing fee must accompany each application filed with the board. If an employer, employer's insurance carrier, or an agent acting on behalf of the employer denies or fails to pay any amount on a claim submitted by a medical service facility, a filing fee is not required to accompany an application that is filed for the denied or unpaid claim. A medical service provider may combine up to ten (10) individual claims into one (1) application whenever:

(1) all individual claims involve the same employer, insurance carrier, or billing review service; and

(2) the amount of each individual claim does not exceed two hundred dollars ($200).

Amended by P.L.144-1986, SEC.63; P.L.28-1988, SEC.52; P.L.95-1988, SEC.15; P.L.170-1991, SEC.20; P.L.258-1997(ss), SEC.15; P.L.31-2000, SEC.9; P.L.67-2010, SEC.3; P.L.168-2011, SEC.14; P.L.275-2013, SEC.14, eff. July 1, 2013.

22-3-7-17.1. Collection of medical expense payments; civil penalties; good faith errors

Sec. 17.1.   A medical service provider or a medical service provider's agent, servant, employee, assignee, employer, or independent contractor on behalf of the medical service provider may not knowingly collect or attempt to collect the payment of a charge for medical services or products covered under IC 22 from an employee or the employee's estate or family members.

(b) If after a hearing, the worker's compensation board finds that a medical service provider has violated this section, the worker's compensation board may assess a civil penalty against the medical service provider in an amount that is at least one hundred dollars ($100) but less than one thousand dollars ($1,000) for each violation.

(c) The worker's compensation board may not assess a civil penalty against a medical service provider for a violation of this section that is the result of a good faith error.

As added by P.L.216–1995, SEC.6.

22-3-7-17.2.   Billing review service standards

Sec. 17.2.(a) A billing review service shall adhere to the following requirements to determine the pecuniary liability of an employer or an employer's insurance carrier for a specific service or product covered under this chapter provided before July 1, 2014, by all medical service providers, and after June 30, 2014, by a medical service provider that is not a medical service facility:

(1)   The formation of a billing review standard, and any subsequent analysis or revision of the standard, must use data that is based on the medical service provider billing charges as submitted to the employer and the employer's insurance carrier from the same community. This subdivision does not apply when a unique or specialized service or product does not have sufficient comparative data to allow for a reasonable comparison.

(2)   Data used to determine pecuniary liability must be compiled on or before June 30 and December 31 of each year.

(3)   Billing review standards must be revised for prospective future payments of medical service provider bills to provide for payment of the charges at a rate not more than the charges made by eighty percent (80%) of the medical service providers during the prior six (6) months within the same community. The data used to perform the analysis and revision of the billing review standards may not be more than two (2) years old and must be periodically updated by a representative inflationary or deflationary factor. Reimbursement for these charges may not exceed the actual charge invoiced by the medical service provider.

(b) This subsection applies after June 30, 2014, to a medical service facility. The pecuniary liability of an employer or an employer's insurance carrier for a specific service or product covered under this chapter and provided by a medical service facility is equal to a reasonable amount, which is established by payment of one (1) of the following:

(1) The amount negotiated at any time between the medical service facility and any of the following:

(A) The employer.

(B) The employer's insurance carrier.

(C) A billing review service on behalf of a person described in clause (A) or (B).

(D) A direct provider network that has contracted with a person described in clause (A) or (B).

(2) Two hundred percent (200%) of the amount that would be paid to the medical service facility on the same date for the same service or product under the medical service facility's Medicare reimbursement rate, if an amount has not been negotiated as described in subdivision (1).

(c) A medical service provider may request an explanation from a billing review service if the medical service provider's bill has been reduced as a result of application of the eightieth percentile or of a Current Procedural Terminology (CPT) or Medicare coding change. The request must be made not later than sixty (60) days after receipt of the notice of the reduction. If a request is made, the billing review service must provide:

(1) the name of the billing review service used to make the reduction;

(2) the dollar amount of the reduction;

(3) the dollar amount of the medical service at the eightieth percentile; and

(4) in the case of a CPT or Medicare coding change, the basis upon which the change was made;
not later than thirty (30) days after the date of the request.

(d) If, after a hearing, the worker's compensation board finds that a billing review service used a billing review standard that did not comply with subsection (a)(1) through (a)(3), as applicable, in determining the pecuniary liability of an employer or an employer's insurance carrier for a medical service provider's charge for services or products covered under occupational disease compensation, the worker's compensation board may assess a civil penalty against the billing review service in an amount not less than one hundred dollars ($100) and not more than one thousand dollars ($1,000).

As added by P.L.216-1995, SEC.7. Amended by P.L.202-2001, SEC.9; P.L.275-2013, SEC.15, eff. July 1, 2013; P.L.2-2014, SEC.100, eff. March 13, 2014; P.L.99-2014, SEC.5, eff. July 1, 2014.

22-3-7-17.4. Maximum reimbursement amount for repackaged legend drugs

Sec. 17.4.(a) As used in this section, "legend drug" has the meaning set forth in IC 25-26-14-7.

(b) As used in this section, "repackage" has the meaning set forth in IC 25-26-14-9.3.

(c) This subsection does not apply to a retail or mail order pharmacy. Except as provided in subsection (d), whenever a prescription covered by this chapter is filled using a repackaged legend drug:

(1) the maximum reimbursement amount for the repackaged legend drug must be computed using the average wholesale price set by the original manufacturer for the legend drug;

(2) the medical service provider may not be reimbursed for more than one (1) office visit for each repackaged legend drug prescribed; and

(3) the maximum period during which a medical service provider may receive reimbursement for a repackaged legend drug begins on the date of the disablement and ends at the beginning of the eighth day after the date of the disablement.

(d) If the National Drug Code (established under Section 510 of the Federal Food, Drug, and Cosmetic Act, 21 U.S.C. 360) for a legend drug cannot be determined from the medical service provider's billing or statement, the maximum reimbursement amount for the repackaged legend drug under subsection (c) is the lowest cost generic for that legend drug.

As added by P.L.275-2013, SEC.16, eff. July 1, 2013. Amended by P.L.99-2014, SEC.6, eff. July 1, 2014.

22-3-7-18. Awards; lump sum payments

Sec. 18. Any employer or employee or beneficiary who shall desire to have such compensation, or any unpaid part thereof, paid in a lump sum, may petition the worker's compensation board, asking that such compensation be so paid, and if, upon proper notice to the interested parties, and a proper showing made before the worker's compensation board, or any member thereof, it appears to the best interest of the parties that such compensation be so paid, the worker's compensation board may order the commutation of the compensation to an equivalent lump sum, which commutation shall be an amount which will equal the total sum of the probable future payments capitalized at their present value upon the basis of interest calculated at three percent (3%) per year with annual rests. In cases indicating complete disability, no petition for a commutation to a lump sum basis shall be entertained by the board until after the expiration of six (6) months from the date of the disablement.

(b) Whenever the worker's compensation board deems it expedient, any lump sum under this section shall be paid by the employer to some suitable person or corporation appointed by the circuit or superior court, as trustee, to administer the same for the benefit of the person entitled thereto, in the manner authorized by the court appointing such trustee. The receipt of such trustee for the amount so paid shall discharge the employer or anyone else who is liable therefor.

Amended by P.L.28–1988, SEC.53; P.L.1–2006, SEC.341, eff. Mar. 24, 2006.

22–3–7–19. Awards; computation; average weekly wages

Sec. 19.

(a) In computing compensation for temporary total disability, temporary partial disability, and total permanent disability, with respect to occupational diseases occurring on and after July 1, 1985, and before July 1, 1986, the average weekly wages are considered to be:

(1) not more than two hundred sixty-seven dollars ($267); and

(2) not less than seventy-five dollars ($75).

(b) In computing compensation for temporary total disability, temporary partial disability, and total permanent disability, with respect to occupational diseases occurring on and after July 1, 1986, and before July 1, 1988, the average weekly wages are considered to be:

(1) not more than two hundred eighty-five dollars ($285); and

(2) not less than seventy-five dollars ($75).

(c) In computing compensation for temporary total disability, temporary partial disability, and total permanent disability, with respect to occupational diseases occurring on and after July 1, 1988, and before July 1, 1989, the average weekly wages are considered to be:

(1) not more than three hundred eighty-four dollars ($384); and

(2) not less than seventy-five dollars ($75).

(d) In computing compensation for temporary total disability, temporary partial disability, and total permanent disability, with respect to occupational diseases occurring on and after July 1, 1989, and before July 1, 1990, the average weekly wages are considered to be:

(1) not more than four hundred eleven dollars ($411); and

(2) not less than seventy-five dollars ($75).

(e) In computing compensation for temporary total disability, temporary partial disability, and total permanent disability, with respect to occupational diseases occurring on and after July 1, 1990, and before July 1, 1991, the average weekly wages are considered to be:

(1) not more than four hundred forty-one dollars ($441); and

(2) not less than seventy-five dollars ($75).

(f) In computing compensation for temporary total disability, temporary partial disability, and total permanent disability, with respect to occupational diseases occurring on and after July 1, 1991, and before July 1, 1992, the average weekly wages are considered to be:

(1) not more than four hundred ninety-two dollars ($492); and

(2) not less than seventy-five dollars ($75).

(g) In computing compensation for temporary total disability, temporary partial disability, and total permanent disability, with respect to occupational diseases occurring on and after July 1, 1992, and before July 1, 1993, the average weekly wages are considered to be:

(1) not more than five hundred forty dollars ($540); and

(2) not less than seventy-five dollars ($75).

(h) In computing compensation for temporary total disability, temporary partial disability, and total permanent disability, with respect to occupational diseases occurring on and after July 1, 1993, and before July 1, 1994, the average weekly wages are considered to be:

(1) not more than five hundred ninety-one dollars ($591); and

(2) not less than seventy-five dollars ($75).

(i) In computing compensation for temporary total disability, temporary partial disability and total permanent disability, with respect to occupational diseases occurring on and after July 1, 1994, and before July 1, 1997, the average weekly wages are considered to be:

(1) not more than six hundred forty-two dollars ($642); and

(2) not less than seventy-five dollars ($75).

(j) In computing compensation for temporary total disability, temporary partial disability, and total permanent disability, the average weekly wages are considered to be:

(1) with respect to occupational diseases occurring on and after July 1, 1997, and before July 1, 1998:

(A) not more than six hundred seventy-two dollars ($672); and

(B) not less than seventy-five dollars ($75);

(2) with respect to occupational diseases occurring on and after July 1, 1998, and before July 1, 1999:

(A) not more than seven hundred two dollars ($702); and

(B) not less than seventy-five dollars ($75);

(3) with respect to occupational diseases occurring on and after July 1, 1999, and before July 1, 2000:

(A) not more than seven hundred thirty-two dollars ($732); and

(B) not less than seventy-five dollars ($75);

(4) with respect to occupational diseases occurring on and after July 1, 2000, and before July 1, 2001:

(A) not more than seven hundred sixty-two dollars ($762); and

(B) not less than seventy-five dollars ($75);

(5) with respect to disablements occurring on and after July 1, 2001, and before July 1, 2002:

(A) not more than eight hundred twenty-two dollars ($822); and

(B) not less than seventy-five dollars ($75);

(6) with respect to disablements occurring on and after July 1, 2002, and before July 1, 2006:

(A) not more than eight hundred eighty-two dollars ($882); and

(B) not less than seventy-five dollars ($75);

(7) with respect to disablements occurring on and after July 1, 2006, and before July 1, 2007:

(A) not more than nine hundred dollars ($900); and

(B) not less than seventy-five dollars ($75);

(8) with respect to disablements occurring on and after July 1, 2007, and before July 1, 2008:

(A) not more than nine hundred thirty dollars ($930); and

(B) not less than seventy-five dollars. ($75);

(9) with respect to disablements occurring on and after July 1, 2008, and before July 1, 2009:

(A) not more than nine hundred fifty-four dollars ($954); and

(B) not less than seventy-five dollars. ($75);

(10) with respect to disablements occurring on and after July 1, 2009, and before July 1, 2014:

(A) not more than nine hundred seventy-five dollars ($975); and

(B) not less than seventy-five dollars ($75);

(11) with respect to disablements occurring on and after July 1, 2014, and before July 1, 2015:

(A) not more than one thousand forty dollars ($1,040); and

(B) not less than seventy-five dollars ($75);

(12) with respect to disablements occurring on and after July 1, 2015, and before July 1, 2016:

(A) not more than one thousand one hundred five dollars ($1,105); and

(B) not less than seventy-five dollars ($75); and

(13) with respect to disablements occurring on and after July 1, 2016:

(A) not more than one thousand one hundred seventy dollars ($1,170); and

(B) not less than seventy-five dollars ($75).

(k) The maximum compensation with respect to disability or death occurring on and after July 1, 1985, and before July 1, 1986, which shall be paid for occupational disease and the results thereof under the provisions of this chapter or under any combination of its provisions may not exceed eighty-nine thousand dollars ($89,000) in any case.

(l) The maximum compensation with respect to disability or death occurring on and after July 1, 1986, and before July 1, 1988, which shall be paid for occupational disease and the results thereof under the provisions of this chapter or under any combination of its provisions may not exceed ninety-five thousand dollars ($95,000) in any case.

(m) The maximum compensation with respect to disability or death occurring on and after July 1, 1988, and before July 1, 1989, that shall be paid for occupational disease and the results thereof under this chapter or under any combination of its provisions may not exceed one hundred twenty-eight thousand dollars ($128,000) in any case.

(n) The maximum compensation with respect to disability or death occurring on and after July 1, 1989, and before July 1, 1990, that shall be paid for occupational disease and the results thereof under this chapter or under any combination of its provisions may not exceed one hundred thirty-seven thousand dollars ($137,000) in any case.

(o) The maximum compensation with respect to disability or death occurring on and after July 1, 1990, and before July 1, 1991, that shall be paid for occupational disease and the results thereof under this chapter or under any combination of its provisions may not exceed one hundred forty-seven thousand dollars ($147,000) in any case.

(p) The maximum compensation with respect to disability or death occurring on and after July 1, 1991, and before July 1, 1992, that shall be paid for occupational disease and the results thereof under this chapter or under any combination of the provisions of this chapter may not exceed one hundred sixty-four thousand dollars ($164,000) in any case.

(q) The maximum compensation with respect to disability or death occurring on and after July 1, 1992, and before July 1, 1993, that shall be paid for occupational disease and the results thereof under this chapter or under any combination of the provisions of this chapter may not exceed one hundred eighty thousand dollars ($180,000) in any case.

(r) The maximum compensation with respect to disability or death occurring on and after July 1, 1993, and before July 1, 1994, that shall be paid for occupational disease and the results thereof under this chapter or under any combination of the provisions of this chapter may not exceed one hundred ninety-seven thousand dollars ($197,000) in any case.

(s) The maximum compensation with respect to disability or death occurring on and after July 1, 1994, and before July 1, 1997, that shall be paid for occupational disease and the results thereof under this chapter or under any combination of the provisions of this chapter may not exceed two hundred fourteen thousand dollars ($214,000) in any case.

(t) The maximum compensation that shall be paid for occupational disease and the results of an occupational disease under this chapter or under any combination of the provisions of this chapter may not exceed the following amounts in any case:

(1) With respect to disability or death occurring on and after July 1, 1997, and before July 1, 1998, two hundred twenty-four thousand dollars ($224,000).

(2) With respect to disability or death occurring on and after July 1, 1998, and before July 1, 1999, two hundred thirty-four thousand dollars ($234,000).

(3) With respect to disability or death occurring on and after July 1, 1999, and before July 1, 2000, two hundred forty-four thousand dollars ($244,000).

(4) With respect to disability or death occurring on and after July 1, 2000, and before July 1, 2001, two hundred fifty-four thousand dollars ($254,000).

(5) With respect to disability or death occurring on and after July 1, 2001, and before July 1, 2002, two hundred seventy-four thousand dollars ($274,000).

(6) With respect to disability or death occurring on and after July 1, 2002, and before July 1, 2006, two hundred ninety-four thousand dollars ($294,000).

(7) With respect to disability or death occurring on and after July 1, 2006, and before July 1, 2007, three hundred thousand dollars ($300,000).

(8) With respect to disability or death occurring on and after July 1, 2007, and before July 1, 2008, three hundred ten thousand dollars ($310,000).

(9) With respect to disability or death occurring on and after July 1, 2008, and before July 1, 2009, three hundred eighteen thousand dollars ($318,000).

(10) With respect to disability or death occurring on or and after July 1, 2009, and before July 1, 2014, three hundred twenty-five thousand dollars ($325,000).

(11) With respect to disability or death occurring on and after July 1, 2014, and before July 1, 2015, three hundred forty-seven thousand dollars ($347,000).

(12) With respect to disability or death occurring on and after July 1, 2015, and before July 1, 2016, three hundred sixty-eight thousand dollars ($368,000).

(13) With respect to disability or death occurring on and after July 1, 2016, three hundred ninety thousand dollars ($390,000).

(u) For all disabilities occurring on and after July 1, 1985, "average weekly wages" means the earnings of the injured employee during the period of fifty-two (52) weeks immediately preceding the disability divided by fifty-two (52). If the employee lost seven (7) or more calendar days during the period, although not in the same week, then the earnings for the remainder of the fifty-two (52) weeks shall be divided by the number of weeks and parts of weeks remaining after the time lost has been deducted. If employment before the date of disability extended over a period of less than fifty-two (52) weeks, the method of dividing the earnings during that period by the number of weeks and parts of weeks during which the employee earned wages shall be followed if results just and fair to both parties will be obtained. If by reason of the shortness of the time during which the employee has been in the employment of the employer or of the casual nature or terms of the employment it is impracticable to compute the average weekly wages for the employee, the employee's average weekly wages shall be considered to be the average weekly amount that, during the fifty-two (52) weeks before the date of disability, was being earned by a person in the same grade employed at the same work by the same employer or, if there is no person so employed, by a person in the same grade employed in that same class of employment in the same district. Whenever allowances of any character are made to an employee instead of wages or a specified part of the wage contract, they shall be considered a part of the employee's earnings.

(v) The provisions of this article may not be construed to result in an award of benefits in which the number of weeks paid or to be paid for temporary total disability, temporary partial disability, or permanent total disability benefits combined exceeds five hundred (500) weeks. This section shall not be construed to prevent a person from applying for an award under IC 22–3–3–13. However, in case of permanent total disability resulting from a disablement occurring on or after January 1, 1998, the minimum total benefit shall not be less than seventy-five thousand dollars ($75,000).

Amended by Acts 1976, P.L.112, SEC.6; Acts 1977, P.L.261, SEC.6; Acts 1979, P.L.227, SEC.6; P.L.225-1983, SEC.4; P.L.223-1985, SEC.3; P.L.224-1985, SEC.2; P.L.95-1988, SEC.16; P.L.170-1991, SEC.21; P.L.258-1997(ss), SEC.16; P.L.31-2000, SEC.10; P.L.134-2006, SEC.10; P.L.275-2013, SEC.17, eff. July 1, 2013.

22–3–7–20. Physical examinations; board and lodging; traveling expenses; reports; autopsy

Sec. 20. After disablement and during the period of claimed resulting disability or impairment, the employee, if so requested by the employee's employer or ordered by the worker's compensation board, shall submit to an examination at reasonable times and places by a duly qualified physician or surgeon designated and paid by the employer or by order of the board.

The employee shall have the right to have present at any such examination any duly qualified physician or surgeon provided and paid for by the employee. No fact communicated to or otherwise learned by any physician or surgeon who may have attended or examined the employee, or who may have been present at any examination, shall be privileged either in the hearings provided for in this chapter, or in any action at law brought to recover damages against any employer who is subject to the compensation provisions of this chapter. If the employee refuses to submit to, or in any way obstructs the examinations, the employee's right to compensation and right to take or prosecute any proceedings under this chapter shall be suspended until the refusal or obstruction ceases. No compensation shall at any time be payable for the period of suspension unless in the opinion of the board, the circumstances justified the refusal or obstruction. The employee must be served with a notice setting forth the consequences of the refusal under this subsection. The notice must be in a form prescribed by the worker's compensation board.

(b) Any employer requesting an examination of any employee residing within Indiana shall pay, in advance of the time fixed for the examination, sufficient money to defray the necessary expenses of travel by the most convenient means to and from the place of examination, and the cost of meals and lodging necessary during the travel. If the method of travel is by automobile, the mileage rate to be paid by the employer shall be the rate as is then currently being paid by the state to its employees under the state travel policies and procedures established by the department of administration and approved by the state budget agency. If the examination or travel to or from the place of examination causes any loss of working time on the part of the employee, the employer shall reimburse the employee for the loss of wages upon the basis of such employee's average daily wage.

(c) When any employee injured in Indiana moves outside Indiana, the travel expense and the cost of meals and lodging necessary during the travel, payable under this section, shall be paid from the point in Indiana nearest to the employee's then residence to the place of examination. No travel and other expense shall be paid for any travel and other expense required outside Indiana.

(d) A duly qualified physician or surgeon provided and paid for by the employee may be present at an examination, if the employee so desires. In all cases, where the examination is made by a physician or surgeon engaged by the employer and the employee who has a disability or is injured has no physician or surgeon present at the examination, it shall be the duty of the physician or surgeon making the examination to deliver to the injured employee, or the employee's representative, a statement in writing of the conditions evidenced by such examination. The statement shall disclose all facts that are reported by the physician or surgeon to the employer. This statement shall be furnished to the employee or the employee's representative as soon as practicable, but not later than thirty (30) days before the time the case is set for hearing. The statement may be submitted by either party as evidence by that physician or surgeon at a hearing before the worker's compensation board if the statement meets the requirements of subsection (f). If the physician or surgeon fails or refuses to furnish the employee or the employee's representative with such statement thirty (30) days before the hearing, then the statement may not be submitted as evidence, and the physician shall not be permitted to testify before the worker's compensation board as to any facts learned in the examination. All of the requirements of this subsection apply to all subsequent examinations requested by the employer.

(e) In all cases where an examination of an employee is made by a physician or surgeon engaged by the employee, and the employer has no physician or surgeon present at such examination, it shall be the duty of the physician or surgeon making the examination to deliver to the employer or the employer's representative a statement in writing of the conditions evidenced by such examination. The statement shall disclose all the facts that are reported by such physician or surgeon to the employee. The statement shall be furnished to the employer or the employer's representative as soon as practicable, but not later than thirty (30) days before the time the case is set for hearing. The statement may be submitted by either party as evidence by that physician or surgeon at a hearing before the worker's compensation board if the statement meets the requirements of subsection (f). If the physician or surgeon fails or refuses to furnish the employer or the employer's representative with such statement thirty (30) days before the hearing, then the statement may not be submitted as evidence, and the physician or surgeon shall not be permitted to testify before the worker's compensation board as to any facts learned in such examination. All of the requirements of this subsection apply to all subsequent examinations made by a physician or surgeon engaged by the employee.

(f) All statements of physicians or surgeons required by this section, whether those engaged by employee or employer, shall contain the following information:

(1) The history of the injury, or claimed injury, as given by the patient.

(2) The diagnosis of the physician or surgeon concerning the patient's physical or mental condition.

(3) The opinion of the physician or surgeon concerning the causal relationship, if any, between the injury and the patient's physical or mental condition, including the physician's or surgeon's reasons for the opinion.

(4) The opinion of the physician or surgeon concerning whether the injury or claimed injury resulted in a disability or impairment and, if so, the opinion of the physician or surgeon concerning the extent of the disability or impairment and the reasons for the opinion.

(5) The original signature of the physician or surgeon.

Notwithstanding any hearsay objection, the worker's compensation board shall admit into evidence a statement that meets the requirements of this subsection unless the statement is ruled inadmissible on other grounds.

(g) Delivery of any statement required by this section may be made to the attorney or agent of the employer or employee and such an action shall be construed as delivery to the employer or employee.

(h) Any party may object to a statement on the basis that the statement does not meet the requirements of subsection (e).

The objecting party must give written notice to the party providing the statement and specify the basis for the objection.

Notice of the objection must be given no later than twenty (20) days before the hearing. Failure to object as provided in this subsection precludes any further objection as to the adequacy of the statement under subsection (f).

(i) The employer upon proper application, or the worker's compensation board, shall have the right in any case of death to require an autopsy at the expense of the party requesting the same. If, after a hearing, the board orders an autopsy and the autopsy is refused by the surviving spouse or next of kin, in this event any claim for compensation on account of the death shall be suspended and abated during the refusal. The surviving spouse or dependent must be served with a notice setting forth the consequences of the refusal under this subsection.

The notice must be in a form prescribed by the worker's compensation board. No autopsy, except one performed by or on the authority or order of the coroner in discharge of the coroner's duties, shall be held in any case by any person without notice first being given to the surviving spouse or next of kin, if they reside in Indiana or their whereabouts can reasonably be ascertained, of the time and place thereof, and reasonable time and opportunity shall be given such surviving spouse or next of kin to have a representative or representatives present to witness same. However, if such notice is not given, all evidence obtained by the autopsy shall be suspended on motion duly made to the board.

Amended by P.L.28–1988, SEC.54; P.L.95–1988, SEC.17; P.L.109–1992, SEC.2; P.L.99–2007, SEC.183, eff. May 2, 2007.

22–3–7–21. Awards; disqualification

Sec. 21. No compensation is allowed for any condition of physical or mental ill-being, disability, disablement, or death for which compensation is recoverable on account of accidental injury under chapters 2 through 6 of this article.

(b) No compensation is allowed for any disease or death knowingly self-inflicted by the employee, or due to his intoxication, his commission of an offense, his knowing failure to use a safety appliance, his knowing failure to obey a reasonable written or printed rule of the employer which has been posted in a conspicuous position in the place of work, or his knowing failure to perform any statutory duty. The burden of proof is on the defendant.

Amended by Acts 1978, P.L.2, SEC.2212.

22–3–7–22. Industrial board; expenses; office space; meetings

Sec. 22. The members of the board and its assistants shall be entitled to receive from the state their actual and necessary expenses while traveling on the business of the board, but such expenses shall be sworn to by the person who incurred the same, and shall be approved by the chairman of the board before payment is made. All expenses of the board in connection with this chapter shall be audited and paid out of the state treasury in the manner prescribed for similar expenses in other departments or branches of the state service.

(b) The board shall be provided with adequate offices in the capitol or some other suitable building in the city of Indianapolis in which the records shall be kept and its official business be transacted during regular business hours. It shall also be provided with necessary office furniture, stationery, and other supplies. The board or any member thereof may hold sessions at any place within the state as may be deemed necessary.

Amended by P.L.144–1986, SEC.64.

22–3–7–23. Jurisdiction; administration

Sec. 23. The worker's compensation board shall have jurisdiction over the operation and administration of the compensation provisions of this chapter, the board shall perform all of the duties imposed upon it by the provisions of this chapter, and such further duties as may be imposed by law and the rules of the board not inconsistent with this chapter.

Amended by P.L.144–1986, SEC.65; P.L.28–1988, SEC.55.

22–3–7–24. Rules and regulations; hearings; subpoenas; production of books and papers; attorney's fees

Sec. 24. The worker's compensation board may make rules not inconsistent with this chapter for carrying out the provisions of this chapter. Processes and procedures under this chapter shall be as summary and simple as reasonably may be.

The board, or any member thereof, shall have the power, for the purpose of this chapter, to subpoena witnesses, administer or cause to have administered oaths, and to examine or cause to have examined such parts of the books and records of the parties to a proceeding as relate to questions in dispute. The county sheriff shall serve all subpoenas of the board and shall receive the same fees as provided by law for like service in civil actions. Each witness who appears in obedience to such subpoena of the board shall receive for attendance the fees and mileage for witnesses in civil cases in the courts. The circuit or superior court shall, on application of the board or any member thereof, enforce by proper proceedings the attendance and testimony of witnesses and the production and examination of books, papers, and records.

(b) The fees of attorneys and physicians and charges of nurses and hospitals for services under this chapter shall be subject to the approval of the worker's compensation board. When any claimant for compensation is represented by an attorney in the prosecution of his claim, the board shall fix and state in the award, if compensation be awarded, the amount of the claimant's attorney's fees. The fee so fixed shall be binding upon both the claimant and his attorney, and the employer shall pay to the attorney, out of the award, the fee so fixed, and the receipt of the attorney therefor shall fully acquit the employer for an equal portion of the award.

(c) Whenever the worker's compensation board shall determine upon hearing of a claim that the employer has acted in bad faith in adjusting and settling said award, or whenever the board shall determine upon hearing of a claim that the employer has not pursued the settlement of said claim with diligence, then the board shall, if compensation be awarded, fix the amount of the claimant's attorney's fees and such attorney's fees shall be paid to the attorney and shall not be charged against the award to the claimant. Such fees as are fixed and awarded on account of a lack of diligence or because of bad faith on the part of the employer shall not be less than one hundred fifty dollars ($150).

(d) The worker's compensation board may withhold the approval of the fees of the attending physician in any case until he shall file a report with the board on the form prescribed by such board.

Amended by P.L.144–1986, SEC.66; P.L.28–1988, SEC.56.

22–3–7–25. Forms and literature; reports; confidential information

Sec. 25. The board shall prepare and cause to be printed, and upon request furnish free of charge to any employer or employee, such blank forms and literature as it shall deem requisite to facilitate or promote the efficient administration of this chapter. The reports of occupational diseases and reports of attending physicians shall be the private records of the board, which shall be open to the inspection of the employer, the employee, and their legal representatives, but not to the public unless, in the opinion of the board, the public interest shall so require.

Amended by P.L.144–1986, SEC.67.

22–3–7–26. Disputes; settlement

Sec. 26. All disputes arising under this chapter, except section 3 of this chapter, if not settled by the agreement of the parties interested therein, with the approval of the board, shall be determined by the board.

Amended by P.L.144–1986, SEC.68.

22–3–7–27. Awards; modification; hearings; appeals; investigations

Sec. 27. If the employer and the employee or the employee's dependents disagree in regard to the compensation payable under this chapter, or, if they have reached such an agreement, which has been signed by them, filed with and approved by the worker's compensation board, and afterward disagree as to the continuance of payments under such agreement, or as to the period for which payments shall be made, or as to the amount to be paid, because of a change in conditions since the making of such agreement, either party may then make an application to the board for the determination of the matters in dispute.

When compensation which is payable in accordance with an award or by agreement approved by the board is ordered paid in a lump sum by the board, no review shall be had as in this subsection mentioned.

(b) The application making claim for compensation filed with the worker's compensation board shall state the following:

(1) The approximate date of the last day of the last exposure and the approximate date of the disablement.

(2) The general nature and character of the illness or disease claimed.

(3) The name and address of the employer by whom employed on the last day of the last exposure, and if employed by any other employer after such last exposure and before disablement, the name and address of such other employer or employers.

(4) In case of death, the date and place of death.

(5) Amendments to applications making claim for compensation which relate to the same disablement or disablement resulting in death originally claimed upon may be allowed by the board in its discretion, and, in the exercise of such discretion, it may, in proper cases, order a trial de novo. Such amendment shall relate back to the date of the filing of the original application so amended.

(c) Upon the filing of such application, the board shall set the date of hearing, which shall be as early as practicable, and shall notify the parties, in the manner prescribed by the board, of the time and place of hearing. The hearing of all claims for compensation on account of occupational disease shall be held in the county in which the last exposure occurred or in any adjoining county, except when the parties consent to a hearing elsewhere. Claims assigned to an individual board member that are considered to be of an emergency nature by that board member, may be heard in any county within the board member's jurisdiction.

(d) The board by any or all of its members shall hear the parties at issue, their representatives, and witnesses, and shall determine the dispute in a summary manner. The award shall be filed with the record of proceedings, and a copy thereof shall immediately be sent by registered mail to each of the parties in dispute.

(e) If an application for review is made to the board within thirty (30) days from the date of the award made by less than all the members, the full board, if the first hearing was not held before the full board, shall review the evidence, or, if deemed advisable, hear the parties at issue, their representatives, and witnesses as soon as practicable, and shall make an award and file the same with the finding of the facts on which it is based and send a copy thereof to each of the parties in dispute, in like manner as specified in subsection (d).

(f) An award of the board by less than all of the members as provided in this section, if not reviewed as provided in this section, shall be final and conclusive. An award by the full board shall be conclusive and binding unless either party to the dispute, within thirty (30) days after receiving a copy of such award, appeals to the court of appeals under the same terms and conditions as govern appeals in ordinary civil actions. The court of appeals shall have jurisdiction to review all questions of law and of fact. The board, of its own motion, may certify questions of law to the court of appeals for its decision and determination. An assignment of errors that the award of the full board is contrary to law shall be sufficient to present both the sufficiency of the facts found to sustain the award and the sufficiency of the evidence to sustain the finding of facts. All such appeals and certified questions of law shall be submitted upon the date filed in the court of appeals, shall be advanced upon the docket of the court, and shall be determined at the earliest practicable date, without any extensions of time for filing briefs. An award of the full board affirmed on appeal, by the employer, shall be increased thereby five percent (5%), and by order of the court may be increased ten percent (10%).

(g) Upon order of the worker's compensation board made after five (5) days notice is given to the opposite party, any party in interest may file in the circuit or superior court of the county in which the disablement occurred a certified copy of the memorandum of agreement, approved by the board, or of an order or decision of the board, or of an award of the full board unappealed from, or of an award of the full board affirmed upon an appeal, whereupon the court shall render judgment in accordance therewith and notify the parties. Such judgment shall have the same effect and all proceedings in relation thereto shall thereafter be the same as though such judgment has been rendered in a suit duly heard and determined by the court. Any such judgment of such circuit or superior court, unappealed from or affirmed on appeal or modified in obedience to the mandate of the court of appeals, shall be modified to conform to any decision of the worker's compensation board ending, diminishing, or increasing any weekly payment under the provisions of subsection (i) upon the presentation to it of a certified copy of such decision.

(h) In all proceedings before the worker's compensation board or in a court under the compensation provisions of this chapter, the costs shall be awarded and taxed as provided by law in ordinary civil actions in the circuit court.

(i) The power and jurisdiction of the worker's compensation board over each case shall be continuing, and, from time to time, it may, upon its own motion or upon the application of either party on account of a change in conditions, make such modification or change in the award ending, lessening, continuing, or extending the payments previously awarded, either by agreement or upon hearing, as it may deem just, subject to the maximum and minimum provided for in this chapter. When compensation which is payable in accordance with an award or settlement contract approved by the board is ordered paid in a lump sum by the board, no review shall be had as in this subsection mentioned. Upon making any such change, the board shall immediately send to each of the parties a copy of the modified award. No such modification shall affect the previous award as to any money paid thereunder. The board shall not make any such modification upon its own motion, nor shall any application therefor be filed by either party after the expiration of two (2) years from the last day for which compensation was paid. The board may at any time correct any clerical error in any finding or award.

(j) The board or any member thereof may, upon the application of either party or upon its own motion, appoint a disinterested and duly qualified physician or surgeon to make any necessary medical examination of the employee and to testify in respect thereto. Such physician or surgeon shall be allowed traveling expenses and a reasonable fee, to be fixed by the board. The fees and expenses of such physician or surgeon shall be paid by the state only on special order of the board or a member thereof.

(k) The board or any member thereof may, upon the application of either party or upon its own motion, appoint a disinterested and duly qualified industrial hygienist, industrial engineer, industrial physician, or chemist to make any necessary investigation of the occupation in which the employee alleges that the employee was last exposed to the hazards of the occupational disease claimed upon, and testify with respect to the occupational disease health hazards found by such person or persons to exist in such occupation. Such person or persons shall be allowed traveling expenses and a reasonable fee, to be fixed by the board. The fees and expenses of such persons shall be paid by the state, only on special order of the board or a member thereof.

(l) Whenever any claimant misconceives the claimant's remedy and files an application for adjustment of a claim under IC 22–3–2 through IC 22–3–6 and it is subsequently discovered, at any time before the final disposition of such cause, that the claim for injury or death which was the basis for such application should properly have been made under the provisions of this chapter, then the application so filed under IC 22–3–2 through IC 22–3–6 may be amended in form or substance or both to assert a claim for such disability or death under the provisions of this chapter, and it shall be deemed to have been so filed as amended on the date of the original filing thereof, and such compensation may be awarded as is warranted by the whole evidence pursuant to the provisions of this chapter.

When such amendment is submitted, further or additional evidence may be heard by the worker's compensation board when deemed necessary. Nothing in this section contained shall be construed to be or permit a waiver of any of the provisions of this chapter with reference to notice or time for filing a claim, but notice of filing of a claim, if given or done, shall be deemed to be a notice or filing of a claim under the provisions of this chapter if given or done within the time required in this chapter.

Amended by P.L.144–1986, SEC.69; P.L.28–1988, SEC.57; P.L.170–1991, SEC.22; P.L.235–1999, SEC.8; P.L.1–2006, SEC.342, eff. Mar. 24, 2006; P.L.134–2006, SEC.11.

22–3–7–28. Destruction of records

Sec. 28. In order to prevent the accumulation of unnecessary and useless files of papers, the board, in its discretion, may destroy all papers which have been on file for more than two (2) years when there is no claim for compensation pending, or, when compensation has been awarded either by agreement or upon hearing, and more than one (1) year has elapsed since the termination of the compensation period as fixed by the board, but notices of election or rejection shall not be destroyed.

However, all records of insurance coverage shall be maintained for forty-five (45) years.

Amended by Acts 1979, P.L.17, SEC.34; P.L.224–1985, SEC.3; P.L.95–1988, SEC.18.

22–3–7–29. Priorities and preferences; assignment; claims of creditors; child support income withholding

Sec. 29. All rights of compensation granted by this chapter shall have the same preference or priority for the whole thereof against the assets of the employer as is allowed by law for any unpaid wages for labor.

(b) Except as provided in subsection (c), no claims for compensation under this chapter shall be assignable, and all compensation and claims therefor shall be exempt from all claims of creditors.

(c) Compensation awards under section 16 of this chapter are subject to child support income withholding under IC 31–16–15 and other remedies available for the enforcement of a child support order. The maximum amount that may be withheld under this subsection is one-half (½) of the compensation award.

Amended by P.L.144–1986, SEC.70; P.L.95–1988, SEC.19; P.L.1–1997, SEC.107.

22–3–7–30. Awards; private agreements; filing

Sec. 30. If, after seven (7) days from the date of disablement or any time, in case of death, the employer and the employee or his dependents reach an agreement in regard to compensation under this chapter, a memorandum of the agreement in the form prescribed by the worker's compensation board shall be filed with the board; otherwise such agreement shall be voidable by the employee or his dependent.

(b) If approved by the board, the memorandum shall for all purposes be enforceable by the court decree as specified in this chapter.

(c) An agreement under this section shall be approved by the board only when the terms conform to this chapter.

Amended by P.L.144–1986, SEC.71; P.L.28–1988, SEC.58.

22–3–7–31. Waiver of compensation; approval; silicosis or asbestosis

Sec. 31. No employee, personal representative, or beneficiary shall have power to waive any of the provisions of this chapter in regard to the amount of compensation which may be payable to such employee, personal representative, or beneficiary except after approval by the worker's compensation board.

(b) Any employee who, prior to June 7, 1937, has contracted silicosis or asbestosis but is not disabled therefrom may, by August 6, 1937, file with the industrial board a request for permission to waive full compensation on account of disability or death resulting from silicosis or asbestosis, or any direct result thereof, supported by medical evidence satisfactory to the industrial board that he has actually contracted silicosis or asbestosis but is not disabled therefrom.

(c) If the industrial board shall approve a waiver filed under subsection (b), the compensation payable for such resulting disability or death of such employee, after further exposure in the employment of any employer shall be fifty percent (50%) of the compensation which but for such waiver would have been payable by any such employer.

Amended by P.L.144–1986, SEC.72; P.L.28–1988, SEC.59.

22-3-7-32. Actions and proceedings; notice; limitation of actions

Sec. 32. No proceedings for compensation under this chapter shall be maintained unless notice has been given to the employer of disablement arising from an occupational disease as soon as practicable after the date of disablement. No defect or inaccuracy of such notices shall be a bar to compensation unless the employer proves that he is unduly prejudiced in such proceedings by such defect or inaccuracy.

(b) The notice provided for in subsection (a) shall state the name and address of the employee and the nature and cause of the occupational disease and disablement or death therefrom, and shall be signed by the employee with a disability or by someone in the employee's behalf, or by one (1) or more of the dependents, in case of death, or by some person in their behalf. Such notice may be served personally upon the employer or upon any foreman, superintendent, or manager of the employer to whose orders the employee with a disability or deceased employee was required to conform or upon any agent of the employer upon whom a summons in a civil action may be served under the laws of the state or may be sent to the employer by registered letter, addressed to the employer's last known residence or place of business.

(c) No proceedings by an employee for compensation under this chapter shall be maintained unless claim for compensation shall be filed by the employee with the worker's compensation board within two (2) years after the date of the disablement.

(d) No proceedings by dependents of a deceased employee for compensation for death under this chapter shall be maintained unless claim for compensation shall be filed by the dependents with the worker's compensation board within two (2) years after the date of death.

(e) No limitation of time provided in this chapter shall run against any person who is mentally incompetent or a minor dependent, so long as the person has no guardian or trustee.

Amended by P.L.144–1986, SEC.73; P.L.28–1988, SEC.60; P.L.99–2007, SEC.184, eff. May 2, 2007.

22-3-7-33. Exposure; presumptions; joint employers

Sec. 33. An employee shall be conclusively deemed to have been exposed to the hazards of an occupational disease when for any length of time, however short, he is employed in an occupation or process in which the hazard of the disease exists.

The employer liable for the compensation provided for in this chapter shall be the employer in whose employment the employee was last exposed to the hazards of the occupational disease claimed upon regardless of the length of time of the last exposure. In cases involving silicosis or asbestos, the only employer liable shall be the last employer in whose employment the employee was last exposed during the period of sixty (60) days or more to the hazard of the occupational disease. In cases involving silicosis or asbestos, an exposure during a period of less than sixty (60) days shall not be considered a last exposure. The insurance carrier liable shall be the carrier whose policy was in effect covering the employer liable on the last day of the exposure rendering the employer liable, in accordance with the provisions of this chapter.

(b) Whenever any employee for whose disability or death compensation is payable under this chapter shall, at the time of the last exposure, be exposed in the joint service of two (2) or more employers subject to the compensation provisions of this chapter, the employers shall contribute to the payment of the compensation in proportion to their wage liability to the employees. Nothing in this section shall prevent any reasonable arrangements between employers for a different distribution between themselves of the ultimate burden of compensation.

Amended by P.L.224–1985, SEC.4.

22–3–7–34. Insurance; self-insurance; exemptions

Sec. 34. As used in this section, "person" does not include:

(1) an owner who contracts for performance of work on the owner's owner occupied residential property; or

(2) a nonprofit corporation that is recognized as tax exempt under Section 501(c)(3)[8] of the Internal Revenue Code (as defined in IC 6–3–1–11(a)) to the extent the corporation enters into an independent contractor agreement with a person for the performance of youth coaching services on a part-time basis.

(b) Every employer bound by the compensation provisions of this chapter, except the state, counties, townships, cities, towns, school cities, school towns, other municipal corporations, state institutions, state boards, and state commissions, shall insure the payment of compensation to the employer's employees and their dependents in the manner provided in this chapter, or procure from the worker's compensation board a certificate authorizing the employer to carry such risk without insurance.

While that insurance or certificate remains in force, the employer, or those conducting the employer's business, and the employer's occupational disease insurance carrier shall be liable to any employee and the employee's dependents for disablement or death from occupational disease arising out of and in the course of employment only to the extent and in the manner specified in this chapter.

---

[8]26 U.S.C.A. § 501(c)(3).

(c) Every employer who, by election, is bound by the compensation provisions of this chapter, except those exempted from the provisions by subsection (b), shall:

(1) insure and keep insured the employer's liability under this chapter in some corporation, association, or organization authorized to transact the business of worker's compensation insurance in this state; or

(2) furnish to the worker's compensation board satisfactory proof of the employer's financial ability to pay the compensation in the amount and manner and when due as provided for in this chapter.

In the latter case the board may require the deposit of an acceptable security, indemnity, or bond to secure the payment of compensation liabilities as they are incurred.

(d) Every employer required to carry insurance under this section shall file with the worker's compensation board in the form prescribed by it, within ten (10) days after the termination of the employer's insurance by expiration or cancellation, evidence of the employer's compliance with subsection (c) and other provisions relating to the insurance under this chapter.

The venue of all criminal actions under this section lies in the county in which the employee was last exposed to the occupational disease causing disablement. The prosecuting attorney of the county shall prosecute all violations upon written request of the board. The violations shall be prosecuted in the name of the state.

(e) Whenever an employer has complied with subsection (c) relating to self-insurance, the worker's compensation board shall issue to the employer a certificate which shall remain in force for a period fixed by the board, but the board may, upon at least thirty (30) days notice, and a hearing to the employer, revoke the certificate, upon presentation of satisfactory evidence for the revocation. After the revocation, the board may grant a new certificate to the employer upon the employer's petition, and satisfactory proof of the employer's financial ability.

Subject to the approval of the worker's compensation board, any employer may enter into or continue any agreement with the employer's employees to provide a system of compensation, benefit, or insurance in lieu of the compensation and insurance provided by this chapter. A substitute system may not be approved unless it confers benefits upon employees and their dependents at least equivalent to the benefits provided by this chapter. It may not be approved if it requires contributions from the employees unless it confers benefits in addition to those provided under this chapter, which are at least commensurate with such contributions.

The substitute system may be terminated by the worker's

compensation board on reasonable notice and hearing to the interested parties, if it appears that the same is not fairly administered or if its operation shall disclose latent defects threatening its solvency, or if for any substantial reason it fails to accomplish the purpose of this chapter. On termination, the board shall determine the proper distribution of all remaining assets, if any, subject to the right of any party in interest to take an appeal to the court of appeals.

No insurer shall enter into or issue any policy of insurance under this chapter until its policy form has been submitted to and approved by the worker's compensation board. The board shall not approve the policy form of any insurance company until the company shall file with it the certificate of the insurance commissioner showing that the company is authorized to transact the business of worker's compensation insurance in Indiana. The filing of a policy form by any insurance company or reciprocal insurance association with the board for approval constitutes on the part of the company or association a conclusive and unqualified acceptance of each of the compensation provisions of this chapter, and an agreement by it to be bound by the compensation provisions of this chapter.

All policies of insurance companies and of reciprocal insurance associations, insuring the payment of compensation under this chapter, shall be conclusively presumed to cover all the employees and the entire compensation liability of the insured under this chapter in all cases in which the last day of the exposure rendering the employer liable is within the effective period of such policy.

Any provision in any such policy attempting to limit or modify the liability of the company or association insuring the same shall be wholly void.

Every policy of any company or association shall be deemed to include the following provisions:

"The insurer assumes in full all the obligations to pay physician's fees, nurse's charges, hospital supplies, burial expenses, compensation or death benefits imposed upon or accepted by the insured under this chapter.

This policy is subject to the provisions of this chapter relative to the liability of the insured to pay physician's fees, nurse's charges, hospital services, hospital supplies, burial expenses, compensation or death benefits to and for such employees, the acceptance of such liability by the insured, the adjustment, trial and adjudication of claims for such physician's fees, nurse's charges, hospital services, hospital supplies, burial expenses, compensation, or death benefits.

Between this insurer and the employee, notice to or knowledge of the occurrence of the disablement on the part of the insured (the employer) shall be notice or knowledge thereof, on the part of the insurer. The jurisdiction of the insured (the employer) for the purpose of this chapter is the jurisdiction of this insurer, and this insurer shall in all things be bound by and shall be subject to the awards, judgments and decrees rendered against the insured (the employer) under this chapter.

This insurer will promptly pay to the person entitled to the same all benefits conferred by this chapter, including all physician's fees, nurse's charges, hospital services, hospital supplies, burial expenses, and all installments of compensation or death benefits that may be awarded or agreed upon under this chapter. The obligation of this insurer shall not be affected by any default of the insured (the employer) after disablement or by any default in giving of any notice required by this policy, or otherwise. This policy is a direct promise by this insurer to the person entitled to physician's fees, nurse's charges, fees for hospital services, charges for hospital services, charges for hospital supplies, charges for burial, compensation, or death benefits, and shall be enforceable in the name of the person.

Any termination of this policy by cancellation shall not be effective as to employees of the insured covered hereby unless at least thirty (30) days prior to the taking effect of such cancellation, a written notice giving the date upon which such termination is to become effective has been received by the worker's compensation board of Indiana at its office in Indianapolis, Indiana.

This policy shall automatically expire one (1) year from the effective date of the policy, unless the policy covers a period of three (3) years, in which event, it shall automatically expire three (3) years from the effective date of the policy. The termination either of a one (1) year or a three (3) year policy, is effective as to the employees of the insured covered by the policy."

All claims for compensation, nurse's charges, hospital services, hospital supplies, physician's fees, or burial expenses may be made directly against either the employer or the insurer or both, and the award of the worker's compensation board may be made against either the employer or the insurer or both.

If any insurer shall fail to pay any final award or judgment (except during the pendency of an appeal) rendered against it, or its insured, or, if it shall fail to comply with this chapter, the worker's compensation board shall revoke the approval of its policy forms, and shall not accept any further proofs of insurance from it until it shall have paid the award or judgment or complied with this chapter, and shall have resubmitted its policy form and received the approval of the policy by the worker's compensation board.

(h) No policy of insurance covering the liability of an employer for worker's compensation shall be construed to cover the liability of the employer under this chapter for any occupational disease unless the liability is expressly accepted by the insurance carrier issuing the policy and is endorsed in that policy. The insurance or security in force to cover compensation liability under this chapter shall be separate from the insurance or security under IC 22–3–2 through IC 22–3–6. Any insurance contract covering liability under either part of this article need not cover any liability under the other.

(i) For the purpose of complying with subsection (c), groups of employers are authorized to form mutual insurance associations or reciprocal or interinsurance exchanges subject to any reasonable conditions and restrictions fixed by the department of insurance. This subsection does not apply to mutual insurance associations and reciprocal or interinsurance exchanges formed and operating on or before January 1, 1991, which shall continue to operate subject to the provisions of this chapter and to such reasonable conditions and restrictions as may be fixed by the worker's compensation board.

(j) Membership in a mutual insurance association or a reciprocal or interinsurance exchange so proved, together with evidence of the payment of premiums due, is evidence of compliance with subsection (c).

(k) Any person bound under the compensation provisions of this chapter, contracting for the performance of any work exceeding one thousand dollars ($1,000) in value, in which the hazard of an occupational disease exists, by a contractor subject to the compensation provisions of this chapter without exacting from the contractor a certificate from the worker's compensation board showing that the contractor has complied with subsections (b), (c), and (d), shall be liable to the same extent as the contractor for compensation, physician's fees, hospital fees, nurse's charges, and burial expenses on account of the injury or death of any employee of such contractor, due to occupational disease arising out of and in the course of the performance of the work covered by such contract.

(l) Any contractor who sublets any contract for the performance of any work to a subcontractor subject to the compensation provisions of this chapter, without obtaining a certificate from the worker's compensation board showing that the subcontractor has complied with subsections (b), (c), and (d), is liable to the same extent as the subcontractor for the payment of compensation, physician's fees, hospital fees, nurse's charges, and burial expense on account of the injury or death of any employee of the subcontractor due to occupational disease arising out of and in the course of the performance of the work covered by the subcontract.

(m) A person paying compensation, physician's fees, hospital fees, nurse's charges, or burial expenses, under subsection (k) or (l), may recover the amount paid or to be paid from any person who would otherwise have been liable for the payment thereof and may, in addition, recover the litigation expenses and attorney's fees incurred in the action before the worker's compensation board as well as the litigation expenses and attorney's fees incurred in an action to collect the compensation, medical expenses, and burial expenses.

(n) Every claim filed with the worker's compensation board under this section shall be instituted against all parties liable for payment. The worker's compensation board, in an award under subsection (k), shall fix the order in which such parties shall be exhausted, beginning with the immediate employer and, in an award under subsection (l), shall determine whether the subcontractor has the financial ability to pay the compensation and medical expenses when due and, if not, shall order the contractor to pay the compensation and medical expenses.

Amended by Acts 1978, P.L.2, SEC.2213; Acts 1982, P.L.135, SEC.2; P.L.28-1988, SEC.61; P.L.170-1991, SEC.23; P.L.258-1997(ss), SEC.17; P.L.202-2001, SEC.10; P.L.201-2005, SEC.9; P.L.1-2006, SEC.343, eff. Mar. 24, 2006; P.L.233-2015, SEC.320, eff. July 1, 2015.

22–3–7–34.3. Provision of proof of compliance by employer

Sec. 34.3. The worker's compensation board is entitled to request that an employer provide the board with current proof of compliance with section 34 of this chapter.

(b) If an employer fails or refuses to provide current proof of compliance by the tenth day after the employer receives the board's request under subsection (a), the board:

(1) shall send the employer a written notice that the employer is in violation of section 34 of this chapter; and

(2) may assess a civil penalty against the employer of fifty dollars ($50) per employee per day.

(c) An employer may challenge the board's assessment of a civil penalty under subsection (b)(2) by requesting a hearing in accordance with procedures established by the board.

(d) The board shall waive a civil penalty assessed under subsection (b)(2) if the employer provides the board current proof of compliance by the twentieth day after the date the employer receives the board's notice under subsection (b)(1).

(e) If an employer fails or refuses to:

(1) provide current proof of compliance by the twentieth day after the date the employer receives the board's notice under subsection (b)(1); or

(2) pay a civil penalty assessed under subsection (b)(2);

the board may, after notice to the employer and a hearing, order that the noncompliant employer's name be listed on the board's Internet web site.

(f) A noncompliant employer's name may be removed from the board's Internet web site only after the employer does the following:

(1) Provides current proof of compliance with section 34 of this chapter.

(2) Pays all civil penalties assessed under subsection (b)(2).

(g) The civil penalties provided for in this section are cumulative.

(h) Civil penalties collected under this section shall be deposited in the worker's compensation supplemental administrative fund established by IC 22–3–5–6.

As added by P.L.168–2011, SEC.15.

22–3–7–34.5. Independent contractors seeking exemption from chapter; filing of statement and fees; certificate of exemption

Sec. 34.5.   As used in this section, "independent contractor" refers to a person described in section 9(b)(5) of this chapter.

(b) As used in this section, "person" means an individual, a proprietorship, a partnership, a joint venture, a firm, an association, a corporation, or other legal entity.

(c) An independent contractor who does not make an election under section 9(b)(2) of this chapter or section 9(b)(3) of this chapter is not subject to the compensation provisions of this chapter and must file a statement with the department of state revenue and obtain a certificate of exemption.

(d) An independent contractor shall file with the department of state revenue, in the form prescribed by the department of state revenue, a statement containing the information required by IC 6–3–7–5.

(e) Together with the statement required in subsection (d), an independent contractor shall file annually with the department documentation in support of independent contractor status before being granted a certificate of exemption.   The independent contractor must obtain clearance from the department of state revenue before issuance of the certificate.

(f) An independent contractor shall pay a filing fee in the amount of fifteen dollars ($15) with the certificate filed under subsection (h).   The fees collected under this subsection shall be deposited in the worker's compensation supplemental administrative fund and shall be used for all expenses the board incurs.

(g) The worker's compensation board shall maintain a data base consisting of certificates received under this section and on request may verify that a certificate was filed.

(h) A certificate of exemption must be filed with the worker's compensation board. The board shall indicate that the certificate has been filed by stamping the certificate with the date of receipt and returning a stamped copy to the person filing the certificate. A certificate becomes effective as of midnight seven (7) business days after the date file stamped by the worker's compensation board. The board shall maintain a data base containing information required in subsections (e) and (g).

(i) A person who contracts for services of another person not covered by this chapter to perform work must secure a copy of a stamped certificate of exemption filed under this section from the person hired. A person may not require a person who has provided a stamped certificate to have worker's compensation coverage. The worker's compensation insurance carrier of a person who contracts with an independent contractor shall accept a stamped certificate in the same manner as a certificate of insurance.

The independent contractor may not collect compensation under this chapter for an injury from a person or the person's worker's compensation carrier to whom the independent contractor has furnished a stamped certificate.

(j) A stamped certificate filed under this section is binding on and holds harmless for all claims:

(1) a person who contracts with an independent contractor after receiving a copy of the stamped certificate; and

(2) the worker's compensation insurance carrier of the person who contracts with the independent contractor.

As added by P.L.75–1993, SEC.6. Amended by P.L.202–2001, SEC.11.

22–3–7–35. Contract relieving employer of obligations

Sec. 35. No contract or agreement, written or implied, rule, regulation, or other device shall in any manner operate to relieve any employer, in whole or in part, of any obligation created by this chapter, except as provided in this chapter.

Amended by P.L.144–1986, SEC.74.

22-3-7-36. Third parties; actions to recover damages; subrogation; limitation of actions

Sec. 36.(a) Whenever disablement or death from an occupational disease arising out of and in the course of the employment for which compensation is payable under this chapter, shall have been sustained under circumstances creating in some other person than the employer and not in the same employ a legal liability to pay damages in respect thereto, the injured employee, or the employee's dependents, in case of death, may commence legal proceedings against such other person to recover damages notwithstanding such employer's or such employer's occupational disease insurance carrier's payment of, or liability to pay, compensation under this chapter. In such case, however, if the action against such other person is brought by the injured employee or the employee's dependents and judgment is obtained and paid and accepted and settlement is made with such other person, either with or without suit, then from the amount received by such employee or dependents there shall be paid to the employer, or such employer's occupational disease insurance carrier, the amount of compensation paid to such employee or dependents, plus the services and products and burial expense paid by the employer or such employer's occupational disease insurance carrier, and the liability of the employer or such employer's occupational disease insurance carrier to pay further compensation or other expenses shall thereupon terminate, whether or not one (1) or all of the dependents are entitled to share in the proceeds of the settlement or recovery and whether or not one (1) or all of the dependents could have maintained the action or claim for wrongful death.

(b) In the event such employee or the employee's dependents, not having received compensation or services and products or death benefits, or such employer's occupational disease insurance carrier, shall procure a judgment against such other party for disablement or death from an occupational disease arising out of and in the course of the employment, which judgment is paid, or if settlement is made with such other person, either with or without suit, then the employer or such employer's occupational disease insurance carrier shall have no liability for payment of compensation or for payment of medical, surgical, hospital, or nurse's services and supplies or death benefits whatsoever, whether or not one (1) or all of the dependents are entitled to share in the proceeds of settlement or recovery and whether or not one (1) or all of the dependents could have maintained the action or claim for wrongful death.

(c) In the event an employee, or in the event of the employee's death, the employee's dependents, shall procure a final judgment against such other person other than by agreement, for disablement or death from an occupational disease arising out of and in the course of the employment and such judgment is for a lesser sum than the amount for which the employer or such employer's occupational disease insurance carrier is liable for compensation and for services and products, as of the date the judgment becomes final, then the employee, or in the event of the employee's death, the employee's dependents, shall have the option of either collecting such judgment and repaying the employer or such employer's occupational disease insurance carrier for compensation previously drawn, if any, and repaying the employer or such employer's occupational disease insurance carrier for services and products previously paid, if any, and of repaying the employer or such employer's occupational disease insurance carrier, the burial benefits paid, if any, or of assigning all rights under said judgment to the employer or such employer's occupational disease insurance carrier and thereafter receiving all compensation and services and products to which the employee, or in the event of the employee's death, to which the employee's dependents would be entitled if there had been no action brought against such other party.

(d) If the employee or the employee's dependents agree to receive compensation, because of an occupational disease arising out of and in the course of the employment, from the employer or such employer's occupational disease insurance carrier, or to accept from the employer or such employer's occupational disease insurance carrier by loan or otherwise, any payment on account of such compensation or institute proceedings to recover the same, the said employer or such employer's occupational disease insurance carrier shall have a lien upon any settlement award, judgment, or fund out of which such employee might be compensated from the third party.

(e) The employee, or in the event of the employee's death, the employee's dependents, shall institute legal proceedings against such other person for damages within two (2) years after said cause of action accrues. If, after said proceeding is commenced, the same is dismissed, the employer or such employer's occupational disease insurance carrier, having paid compensation or having become liable therefor, may collect in their own name or in the name of the employee with a disability, or in the case of death, in the name of the employee's dependents, from the other person in whom legal liability for damages exists, the compensation paid or payable to the employee with a disability, or the employee's dependents, plus such services and products and burial expense paid by the employer or such employer's occupational disease insurance carrier for which they have become liable. The employer or such employer's occupational disease insurance carrier may commence such action at law for such collection against the other person in whom legal liability for damages exists, not later than one (1) year from the date said action so commenced, has been dismissed, notwithstanding the provisions of any statute of limitations to the contrary.

(f) If said employee, or in the event of the employee's death, the employee's dependents, shall fail to institute legal proceedings, against such other person for damages within two (2) years after said cause of action accrues, the employer or such employer's occupational disease insurance carrier, having paid compensation or having been liable therefor, may collect in their own name or in the name of the employee with a disability, or in the case of the employee's death, in the name of the employee's dependents, from the other person in whom legal liability for damage exists, the compensation paid or payable to the employee with a disability or to the employee's dependents, plus the services and products and burial expenses, paid by them or for which they have become liable, and the employer or such employer's occupational disease insurance carrier may commence such action at law for such collection against such other person in whom legal liability exists at any time within one (1) year from the date of the expiration of the two (2) years when the action accrued to the employee with a disability or, in the event of the employee's death, to the employee's dependents, notwithstanding the provisions of any statute of limitations to the contrary.

(g) In such actions brought as provided in this section by the employee or the employee's dependents, the employee or the employee's dependents shall, within thirty (30) days after such action is filed, notify the employer or such employer's occupational disease insurance carrier, by personal service or registered or certified mail, of such fact and the name of the court in which suit is brought, filing proof thereof in such action.

(h) If the employer does not join in the action within ninety (90) days after receipt of the notice, then out of any actual money reimbursement received by the employer or such employer's occupational disease insurance carrier pursuant to this section, they shall pay their pro rata share of all costs and reasonably necessary expenses in connection with such third party claim, action, or suit, and to the attorney at law selected by the employee or the employee's dependents, a fee of twenty-five percent (25%), if collected without trial, of the amount of benefits after the expenses and costs in connection with such third party claim have been deducted therefrom, and a fee of thirty-three and one-third percent (33 1/3%), if collected after trial, of the amount of such benefits after deduction of the costs and reasonably necessary expenses in connection with such third party claim, action, or suit. The employer may, within ninety (90) days after receipt of notice of suit from the employee or the employee's dependents, join in the action upon the employee's motion so that all orders of court after hearing and judgment shall be made for the employee's protection.

(i) No release or settlement of claim for damages by reason of such injury or death, and no satisfaction of judgment in such proceedings shall be valid without the written consent of both employer or such employer's occupational disease insurance carrier, and employee, or the employee's dependents. However, in the case of the employer or such employer's occupational disease insurance carrier, such consent shall not be required where the employer or such employer's occupational disease insurance carrier has been fully indemnified or protected by court order.

Amended by P.L.28-1988, SEC.62; P.L.99-2007, SEC.185, eff. May 2, 2007; P.L.275-2013, SEC.18, eff. July 1, 2013.

22-3-7-37. Reports of disablements; penalties; venue

Sec. 37. Every employer operating under the compensation provisions of this chapter shall keep a record of all disablements by occupational disease, fatal or otherwise, received by the employer's employees in the course of their employment and shall provide a copy of the record to the board upon request.

Within seven (7) days after the first day of a disablement by occupational disease and the employer's knowledge of the disablement, as provided in section 32 of this chapter, that causes the employee's death or absence from work for more than one (1) day, a report thereof shall be made in writing and mailed to the employer's insurance carrier or, if the employer is self insured, to the worker's compensation board on blanks to be procured from the board for the purpose. The insurance carrier shall mail the report to the worker's compensation board not later than seven (7) days after receipt or fourteen (14) days after the employer's knowledge of the occurrence, whichever is later. An employer or insurance carrier that fails to comply with this subsection is subject to a civil penalty under IC 22-3-4-15.

(b) The report shall contain the name, nature and location of the business of the employer, the name, age, sex, wages, occupation of the employee, the approximate dates between which exposure occurred, the nature and cause of the occupational disease, and such other information as may be required by the board.

(c) A person who violates this section commits a Class C misdemeanor.

(d) The venue of all criminal actions for the violation of this section lies in the county in which the employee was last exposed to the occupational disease causing disablement. The prosecuting attorney of the county shall prosecute these violations upon written request of the worker's compensation board.

These shall be prosecuted in the name of the state.

Amended by Acts 1978, P.L.2, SEC.2214; P.L.28–1988, SEC.63; P.L.170–1991, SEC.24; P.L.168–2011, SEC.16.

22-3-7-38. Application of law

Sec. 38. Acts 1937, c.69, s.31 does not extinguish or in any way affect any right of action existing on June 7, 1937, and no employer shall be liable for compensation or damages under the provisions of this chapter in any case in which the disablement on which claim is predicated shall have occurred prior to June 7, 1937; but nothing contained in this section shall affect any case in which exposure as defined in this chapter shall have taken place after June 7, 1937.

Amended by P.L.144–1986, SEC.75.

Chapter 8. Representation Before Worker's Compensation Board

22-3-8-1. Attorneys; qualifications

Sec. 1. Any person representing any plaintiff or defendant in the prosecution or defense of any claim or claims before the worker's compensation board must be admitted to practice law in the circuit or superior courts and supreme court of Indiana.

Amended by P.L.28–1988, SEC.64.

22-3-8-2. Attorneys; registration; oath; records

Sec. 2. All persons so representing plaintiffs or defendants as provided by section 1 of this chapter shall first register their names with the worker's compensation board in a manner prescribed by the board and shall, before proceeding to represent either plaintiffs or defendants before the board, be required to take oath in writing either before the board or a member thereof that the person is qualified as provided by section 1 of this chapter.

(b) The written oath shall be recorded in the permanent records of the worker's compensation board, and the board or any member thereof shall prohibit any person from so representing plaintiffs or defendants until the person has complied with this chapter.

Amended by P.L.144–1986, SEC.76; P.L.28–1988, SEC.65.

Chapter 9. Employer Liability

22-3-9-1. Personal injuries or death; damages

Sec. 1. Any person, firm, limited liability company, or corporation while engaged in business, trade or commerce within this state, and employing in such business, trade or commerce five (5) or more persons shall be liable and respond in damages to any person suffering injury while in the employ of such person, firm, limited liability company, or corporation, or in case of the death of such employee, then to his or her personal representative, for the benefit of the surviving widow or husband and children of such employee; and if none, then to such employee's parents; and if none, then to the next of kin dependent upon such employee, where such injury or death resulted in whole or in part from the negligence of such employer or his, its or their agents, servants, employees or officers, or by reason of any defect, mismanagement or insufficiency, due to his, its or their carelessness, negligence, fault or omission of duty.

Amended by P.L.8–1993, SEC.285.

22–3–9–2. Personal injuries or death; contributory negligence; burden of proof

Sec. 2. In any action prosecuted under the provisions of this chapter the burden of proving that such injured or killed employee did not use due care and diligence at the time of such injury or death shall be upon the defendant, but the same may be proved under the general denial. No such employee who may have been injured or killed shall be held to have been guilty of negligence or contributory negligence by reason of the assumption of the risk thereof in any case where the violation by the employer or his, its, or their agents or employees of any ordinance or statute enacted, or of any rule, regulation, or direction made by any public officer, bureau, or commission, was the cause of the injury or death of such employee. In actions brought against any employer under the provisions of this chapter for the injury or death of any employee, it shall not be a defense that the dangers or hazards inherent or apparent in the employment in which such injured employee was engaged contributed to such injury. No such injured employee shall be held to have been guilty of negligence or contributory negligence where the injury complained of resulted from such employee's obedience or conformity to any order or direction of the employer or of any employee to whose orders or directions he was under obligation to conform or obey, although such order or direction was a deviation from other rules, orders, or directions previously made by such employer.

Amended by P.L.144–1986, SEC.77.

22–3–9–3. Personal injuries or death; assumption of risk; safe place to work; defective tools

Sec. 3. In any action brought against any employer under or by virtue of this chapter to recover damages for injuries or the death of any of his, its, or their employees, such employee shall not be held to have assumed the risks of the employment in any case where the violation of such employer or his, its, or their agents or employees of any ordinance or statute enacted, or of any rule, direction, or regulation made by any public officer or commission, contributed to the injury or death of such employee; nor shall such injured employee be held to have assumed the risk of the employment where the injury complained of resulted from his obedience to any order or direction of the employer or of any employee to whose orders or directions he was under obligations to conform or obey although such order or direction was a deviation from other orders or directions or rules previously made by such employer. In any action brought against any employer under the provisions of this chapter to recover damages for injury to or the death of any of his, its, or their employees, such employee shall not be held to have assumed the risk of any defect in the place of work furnished to such employee, or in the tool, implement, or appliance furnished him by such employer, where such defect was, prior to such injury, known to such employer, or by the exercise of ordinary care might have been known to him in time to have repaired the same or to have discontinued the use of such defective working place, tool, implement, or appliance. The burden of proving that such employer did not know of such defect or that he was not chargeable with knowledge thereof in time to have repaired the same or to have discontinued the use of such working place, tool, implement, or appliance shall be on the defendant, but the same may be proved under the general denial.

Amended by P.L.144–1986, SEC.78.

22–3–9–4. Personal injuries or death; survival of actions

Sec. 4. The damages recoverable under this chapter shall be commensurate with the injuries sustained, and in case death results from such injury the action shall survive; provided, that where any such injured person recovers a judgment under the provisions of this chapter and an appeal is taken from such judgment, and pending such appeal the injured person dies and said judgment be thereafter reversed, or where such injured person dies after said judgment is reversed and before trial, the right of action of such person shall survive to his or her personal representative, and such action may be continued in the name of such personal representative for the benefit of the person entitled under this chapter to receive the same.

Amended by P.L.144–1986, SEC.79.

22–3–9–5. Contracts; rules and regulations; exemption from liability; set-off

Sec. 5. Any contract, rule, regulation, bylaw, or device whatsoever, the purpose, intent, or effect of which would be to enable any employer to exempt himself or itself from any liability created by this chapter, shall to that extent be void; provided, that in any action brought against any such employer under or by virtue of any of the provisions of this chapter, such employer may set off therein by special plea any sum such employer has contributed or paid to any insurance, relief benefit, or indemnity for and on behalf of such injured employee that may have been paid to him or to the person entitled thereto on account of the injury or death for which said action is brought, but in no event shall the amount of such setoff exceed the amount paid to such employee or other person entitled thereto out of such insurance, relief benefit, or indemnity fund.

Amended by P.L.144–1986, SEC.80.

22–3–9–6. Wrongful death damages; amount

Sec. 6. Where any action is brought on account of the death of any person under this chapter, the liability of any such employer shall not exceed ten thousand dollars ($10,000), and the provisions of the law in force as to parties plaintiff shall apply.

Amended by P.L.144–1986, SEC.81.

22–3–9–7. Assumption of risk; negligence; contributory negligence; questions of fact

Sec. 7. All questions of assumption of risk, negligence or contributory negligence shall be questions of fact for the jury to decide, unless the cause is being tried without a jury, in which case, such questions shall be questions of fact for the court.

22–3–9–8. Limitation of actions

Sec. 8. No action shall be maintained under this chapter unless the same is commenced within two (2) years from the date the cause of action accrued.

Amended by P.L.144–1986, SEC.82.

22–3–9–9. Definitions

Sec. 9. The term "employer", "persons", "firm", "limited liability company", and "corporation" shall include receivers or other persons charged with the duty of managing, conducting or operating business, trade or commerce.

Amended by P.L.8–1993, SEC.286.

22–3–9–10. Application of law

Sec. 10. This chapter shall not apply to injuries received by any employee before March 2, 1911, nor affect any suit or legal proceedings pending in any court on March 2, 1911.

Amended by P.L.144–1986, SEC.83.

22–3–9–11. Supplemental remedies; common law rights

Sec. 11. This chapter shall be construed as supplemental to all statutes in force on March 2, 1911, concerning employers and employees and shall repeal only such statutes as are in direct conflict with the provisions of this chapter. Nothing in this chapter shall be held to limit the duty or liability of employers or to impair the rights of their employees under the common law or any other statute existing on March 2, 1911, or to affect the prosecution of any proceeding or right of action pending on March 2, 1911.

Amended by P.L.144–1986, SEC.84.

Chapter 10. Ban on Employer Waiver of Liability

22–3–10–1. Negligence; employer; liability for damages

Sec. 1. All contracts between employer and employee releasing the employer from liability for damages arising out of the negligence of the employer by which the employee is injured, or, in case of the employee's death, to his representative, are against public policy, and hereby declared null and void.

22–3–10–2. Negligence; third persons; liability for damages

Sec. 2. All contracts between employer and employee releasing third persons, copartnerships or corporations from liability for damages arising out of the negligence of such third persons, copartnerships or corporations by which the employee of such employer is injured, or in case of the death of such employee, to his representative, are against public policy and are hereby declared null and void.

22–3–10–3. Negligence; employer; liability for damages; contract between employee and third person

Sec. 3. All contracts between an employee and a third person, copartnership, or corporation in which it is agreed that the employer of such employee shall be released from liability for damages of such employee arising out of the negligence of the employer, or in case of the death of such employee to his representative, are against public policy and are hereby declared null and void; provided, that nothing in this chapter shall apply to voluntary relief departments or associations organized for the purpose of insuring employees. Nothing in this chapter shall be construed to revert back to contracts made prior to March 11, 1901. Nor shall this chapter affect litigation pending on March 11, 1901; provided, that nothing in any section of this chapter shall be so construed as to affect or apply to any contract or agreement that may be made between the employer and employee, or in case of death his next of kin or his representative after an injury to the employee has occurred, but the provisions of this chapter shall apply solely to contracts made prior to any injury.
Amended by P.L.144–1986, SEC.85.

Chapter 11. Residual Asbestos Injury Fund

22–3–11–1. Creation; administration; use of fund

Sec. 1. There is created a special fund known as the residual asbestos injury fund (referred to as "the fund" in this chapter) for the purpose of providing compensation to employees who become totally and permanently disabled from an exposure to asbestos while in employment within Indiana and who are eligible for benefits under section 3 of this chapter (expired August 1, 2007, and repealed) and not eligible for benefits under IC 22–3–7. The fund shall be administered by the worker's compensation board (referred to as "the board" in this chapter).

(b) The fund is not a part of the general fund. Money in the fund at the end of a particular fiscal year and interest accruing from the investment of the money does not revert to the state general fund. The fund shall be used only for the payment of awards of compensation and expense of medical examinations made and ordered by the board and chargeable against the fund under this section and shall be paid for that purpose by the treasurer of state upon award or order of the board.

As added by P.L.224–1985, SEC.5. Amended by P.L.28–1988, SEC.66; P.L.3–2008, SEC.157, eff. March 13, 2008.

22–3–11–2. Assessments; deposit in fund

Sec. 2. This section applies to:

(1) each insurance carrier insuring employers who may be or who are liable under IC 22–3–2 through IC 22–3–7 to pay compensation; and

(2) each employer carrying its own risk to pay compensation under IC 22–3–2 through IC 22–3–7.

(b) Before August 1, 1985, and April 10 in all subsequent years, each insurance carrier described in subsection (a)(1) and each employer described in subsection (a)(2) shall pay to the board for deposit in the fund the assessment specified in subsection (c):

(1) until the initial balance in the fund is equal to or greater than two hundred thousand dollars ($200,000); and

(2) after the initial balance in the fund satisfies subdivision (1), only if the balance in the fund on April 1 of the year of the assessment is less than fifty thousand dollars ($50,000).

(c) An assessment required under subsection (b) equals one-half of one percent (0.5%) of the total amount of worker's compensation and occupational diseases benefits paid to injured employees or their beneficiaries during the calendar year immediately preceding the due date of the assessment.

As added by P.L.224–1985, SEC.5. Amended by P.L.28–1988, SEC.67.

22–3–11–5. Expert medical testimony

Sec. 5. The board may secure expert medical testimony as it considers necessary at the expense of the fund to protect the fund against questionable claims for benefits.

As added by P.L.224–1985, SEC.5.

Chapter 12. Vocational Rehabilitation

22–3–12–1. Entitlement to vocational rehabilitation services

Sec. 1. An injured employee, who as a result of an injury or occupational disease is unable to perform work for which the employee has previous training or experience, is entitled to vocational rehabilitation services necessary to restore the employee to useful employment.

As added by P.L.218–1989, SEC.1.

22–3–12–2. Report of injury; copy to central office

Sec. 2. When any compensable injury requires the filing of a first report of injury by an employer, the employer's worker's compensation insurance carrier or the self-insured employer shall forward a copy of the report to the central office of the division of disability and rehabilitative services, rehabilitation services bureau at the earlier of the following occurrences:

(1) When the compensable injury has resulted in temporary total disability of longer than twenty-one (21) days.

(2) When it appears that the compensable injury may be of such a nature as to permanently prevent the injured employee from returning to the injured employee's previous employment.

As added by P.L.218–1989, SEC.1. Amended by P.L.2–1992, SEC.741; P.L.4–1993, SEC.258; P.L.5–1993, SEC.271; P.L.2–2005, SEC.60, eff. April 25, 2005; P.L.141–2006, SEC.105.

22–3–12–3. Report of injury; copy to local office

Sec. 3. Upon receipt of a report of injury under section 2 of this chapter, the office of vocational rehabilitation shall immediately send a copy of the report to the local office of vocational rehabilitation located nearest to the injured employee's home.

As added by P.L.218–1989, SEC.1.

22–3–12–4. Explanation of services; eligibility determination; plan implementation

Sec. 4. The local office of vocational rehabilitation shall, upon receipt of the report of injury, immediately provide the injured employee with a written explanation of:

(1) the rehabilitation services that are available to the injured employee; and

(2) the method by which the injured employee may make application for those services.

(b) The office of vocational rehabilitation shall determine the eligibility of the injured employee for rehabilitation services and, where appropriate, develop an individualized rehabilitation plan for the employee.

(c) The office of vocational rehabilitation shall implement the rehabilitation plan. After completion of the rehabilitation program, the office of vocational rehabilitation shall provide job placement services to the rehabilitated employee.

As added by P.L.218–1989, SEC.1.

22–3–12–5. Construction of chapter; employee's benefits

Sec. 5. Nothing contained in this chapter shall be construed to affect an injured employee's status regarding any benefit provided under IC 22–3–2 through IC 22–3–7.

As added by P.L.218–1989, SEC.1.

Table of Laws and Rules

INDIANA CODE—Continued

INDIANA CODE—Continued

INDIANA CODE—Continued

INDIANA CODE—Continued

INDIANA ACTS

INDIANA PUBLIC LAWS

INDIANA ADMINISTRATIVE CODE

INDIANA ATTORNEY GENERAL OPINIONS

Table of Cases

N

Index